Talking With God

The Radioactive Ark Of The Testimony

Communication Through It
Protection From It

An Etymological Study

Roger D. Isaacs

Edited by
Janice Williams Miller

Sacred
Closet
Books

CHICAGO

A Division of The Publishing Institute, Inc.
Chicago, Illinois USA

Published by Sacred Closet Books,
a division of the Publishing Institute, Inc. Chicago, Illinois.

Cover image courtesy of Tim Ivanic.

Permission for reprints has been granted courtesy of the Oriental Institute of the University of Chicago; Caroll Boltin. © The Trustees of the British Museum. All rights reserved. PRITCHARD, JAMES; THE ANCIENT NEAR EAST. © 1958 Princeton University Press, 1986 renewed PUP Reprinted by permission of Princeton University Press. Mendenhall, George E. The Tenth Generation: The Origins of the Biblical Tradition. pp. 35, 42, 19. © 1973 The Johns Hopkins University Press. Reprinted with permission of The Johns Hopkins University Press. Reprinted by permissions of Eisenbrauns.

Library of Congress Control Number: 2010930313

Isaacs, Roger D.

Talking with God: the radioactive ark of the testimony—communication through it, protection from it, an etymological study / by Roger D. Isaacs.

Includes bibliographical references and indices.

ISBN 978-1-4125-4997-4

Manufactured in the United States of America.

Dedication

To my wife, Joyce Isaacs, and my father,
the late Dr. Raphael Isaacs

Contents

Acknowledgements

Over the many years I have been working on this project, most of my time has been spent in research, pouring over materials in libraries and, quite importantly, talking to many people for advice and counsel. Without exception, all of them have been gracious and helpful, even though most had no idea what my subject was.

Research is really another word for learning, and these wonderful scientists, scholars, and students have taught me so much. In the area of science, physicist David Rossin, then at Argonne National Laboratory, answered my questions and demonstrated the effects of radioactive bombardment on various materials. He also made available many publications on the subject.

Scholars Martha Roth, Professor of Assyriology and Editor in charge of The Chicago Assyrian Dictionary Project, Emily Teeter, Research Associate and Director of Special Projects, and Geoff Emberling, Research Associate and Museum Director, all at the Oriental Institute, University of Chicago, cannot possibly know how their answers to my questions and exposure to their lectures have clarified many ancient areas for me. Also, at the Oriental Institute I want to thank Professor Norman Golb, Ludwig Rosenberger Professor in Jewish History and Civilization, for introducing me to Dennis Pardee, Professor of Northwest Semitic Philology. Professor Pardee listened to my needs and solved an important problem by putting me in touch with Robert Hawley, who at the time was working on his PhD dissertation. In a 115-page critique, Bob focused razor sharply on my linguistics, and held my feet to the fire every time I strayed. Any judgment errors that remain are strictly my responsibility. I wouldn't have been able to navigate the Oriental Institute archives without the always patient help of Charles Jones, then research archivist.

I also want to make special note of the kind comments by Jacob Milgrom, Rabbi, Biblical Scholar, and U. C. Berkeley Professor Emeritus of Near Eastern Studies. His reputation is unmatched for the enormous contributions he has made to the study of Leviticus. Sadly, Jacob Milgrom died this year, but his works will live forever.

Another librarian who provided me with book and article suggestions was Dan Sharon, the recently retired Senior Reference Librarian of Spertus

Institute of Jewish Studies. I also wish to thank Peggy Barber for her advice and vast knowledge on the subject of libraries.

Two people who played major roles in the direction of the book were Professor and Rabbi Byron Sherwin of Spertus and writer and publisher Robert Wolf. They read my original manuscript and their suggestions radically altered where I was aiming my writing relative to the audience I had planned for it. In fact, were it not for their agreement that my first writing was "too dense," there never would have been a book in its present form.

The person most responsible for "dedensifying" this book was my editor and publisher, Janice Miller. I can honestly say that not one sentence was allowed to stand unless it was crystal clear to her. I dreaded seeing the one word "clarify" written opposite a paragraph, but learned quickly that she was always right. Janice was assisted by Donna Marie Williams in the reader and editorial capacity, and the extremely important task of proofreading fell to Hyacinth A. Williams. I must also note most importantly that Janice was introduced to me by David Brent, Executive Editor of the University of Chicago Press. Also, for his constant encouragement and patient work at the copy machine whenever he visited us, honorable mention goes to grandson Adam Raphael Hemmings.

Finally, this book is dedicated to two wonderful people: my wife, Joyce Isaacs, and my father, the late Dr. Raphael Isaacs. Many years ago Joyce first transferred my "horrorglyphic" handwriting to a primitive, non-electric machine called a typewriter. Subsequently, her willingness and courage to accompany me in this 40-odd year trek through the wilderness are simply unparalleled. I will explain my father's role in this project later, but for now I will only say that it was his early thinking on the subject that lit the flame that has burned through what has become my lifework.

List of Charts

List of Pictures and Illustrations

Tree of Life Images

Abbreviations

adj.	adjective		Heb.	Hebrew
BCE	before the common era —relates to BC		Hos.	Hosea
			Isa.	Isaiah
BDB	*The New Brown-Driver-Briggs Gesenius Hebrew and English Lexicon*		J	Yahwist Source
			Jer.	Jeremiah
			Jon.	Jonah
ca.	circa		Josh.	Joshua
CAD	*The Chicago Assyrian Dictionary of the Oriental Institute*		JPS	*The JPS Torah Commentary*
			Judg.	Judges
			Kgs.	Kings
CDA	*A Concise Dictionary of Akkadian*		Lam.	Lamentations
			Lev.	Leviticus
CE	common era		lit.	iterally
cf.	compare		Mal.	Malachi
Chr.	Chronicles		Mic.	Micah
D	Deuteronomist Source		N	north
Dan.	Daniel		n.	noun
Deut.	Deuteronomy		Nah.	Nahum
DLU	*Diccionario de la Lengua Ugaritica*		Neh.	Nehemiah
			Num.	Numbers
Dtr	Deuteronomist		Obad.	Obadiah
DtrH	Deuteronomist History		OT	Old Testament
E	Elohist Source, east		P	Priestly Source
e.g.	*exempli gratia* – for example		p., pp.	page, pages
Eccl.	Ecclesiastes		pl.	plural
esp.	especially		Prov.	Proverbs
Est.	Esther		Ps.	Psalms
Exod.	Exodus		RS	Ras Shamra
Ezek.	Ezekiel		Sam.	Samuel
fem.	feminine		Targums	Aramaic translations of the Hebrew Bible
fig.	figure			
Gen.	Genesis		vb.	verb
H	Holiness Code		vol.	volume
Hab.	Habakkuk		Zech.	Zechariah
Hag.	Haggai		Zeph.	Zephaniah
HAL	*The Hebrew and Aramaic Lexicon of the Old Testament*			

Dating

(BCE except where noted)

Old Akkadian. 2334–2154
Old Babylonian 1850–1650
Middle Babylonian. 1600–1160
Standard Babylonian 930–612
Neo-Babylonian. 625–539
Old Assyrian 1900–1650
Middle Assyrian. 1360–1075
Neo-Assyrian 930–612

Egyptian Dynasties

Old Egyptian 3000–2155
Middle Egyptian 2155–1350
Neo-Egyptian. 930–612

Hittite

Old Kingdom. 2000–1500
New Kingdom 1500–1000
Neo-Hittite States 1000–500

Sumer*

Prehistory (earliest inhabitants) . . . . ca. 4000–3300
History (coming of Sumerians). . . . . ca. 3300–3000
Early dynastic period . . . . ca. 3000–2300
Conquest by Akkadians and Guti . . . . ca. 2300–2100
Sumerian revival. . . . . ca. 2100–1720

The Amarna Tablets . . . . .Latter half, second millennium
Letters mostly from Syria and Palestine to Egyptian rulers Amenhotep III and Amenhotep IV. They are mostly in Old Babylonian, which was used at the time as the diplomatic language of the Near East, regardless of the languages or dialects spoken by the senders.

Ras Shamra Texts. . . . . .14th–13th centuries BCE
Ras Shamra is the name of the mound in northern Syria where Ugarit is located. The tablets are written in cuneiform. Ugaritic is a West Semitic language.

Ebla Tablets . . . . .24th–23rd century BCE
Ebla is located at Tell Mardikh in northwest Syria. The tablets are written in Sumerian and Eblaite, a Semitic language.

* See Kramer, "Sumer," *The Interpreter's Dictionary of the Bible*, volume 4.

Hebrew Chronology

(Early dates open to debate)

"And I will meet with you there and will speak to you from above the ark cover, from between the two cherubim, which are on the ark of the testimony." (Exodus 25:22)

Introduction

Read This First!

From the time man first turned his eyes upward and looked beyond himself to the leaves on the trees or the stars in the sky, he was probably overcome with one powerful sensation, perhaps an ageless instinct: curiosity. To the degree that a man is curious, so is he civilized. We judge a child to be bright if he asks many questions. If he still questions later in life, he is probably a scientist or philosopher.

A former public relations man by trade, I'm perhaps the most unlikely sort of scientist or philosopher to ponder the great mysteries of the universe, but ever since I was a young child, I was full of curiosity and wonder. I listened with rapt attention to the Hebrew Bible stories my father told me on our regular Saturday walks. Then, years later, one particular part of the Bible caught my father's attention and subsequently so intrigued me that I've made researching and pondering it my life's avocation.

The story is well known. According to the Hebrew Bible, around 3,300 years ago, a group of Hebrew men, women, and children were dramatically emancipated from Egyptian enslavement. Moses, former favorite of Pharaoh's court turned revolutionary, led this people on an historic exodus out of Egypt. They set up camp in the wilderness of the Sinai Peninsula at the base of Mount Sinai (exact location is open to debate). The ultimate destination was Canaan, The Promised Land. The plan was to dwell in this area that God had promised their forefathers Abraham, his son Isaac, and grandson Jacob. They didn't know that it would take 40 plus years to get there.

In the meantime, Moses, their leader, had a tough job on his hands. He had to maintain order and begin the grueling, thankless task of building a community, a nation out of a people who had never known freedom. Although now free, these former slaves no doubt still suffered the psychological trauma of their long ordeal. They were unruly, unlettered, disobedient, and afraid.

Moses' challenge was to raise the consciousness of the people as he shaped them into a strong nation.

I Will Speak With You

The task would have been impossible had it not been for the Lord's constant intervention into the affairs of His people. In one highly significant intervention, Moses climbed the lonely heights of Mount Sinai. It was there that, in addition to receiving the laws directly from God, he was given two stone tablets.[1]

> [12]And the Lord said to Moses, "Come up to Me to the mountain, and be there; and I will give you the tablets of stone, and the law and the commandment, which I have written, to teach them." (Exod. 24:12)

Then the Lord commanded Moses to make a box, the ark, to contain the tablets. He gave him specific instructions as to its design. Technicians were able to make all parts of the apparatus except the tablets, which were given to Moses on the mountain. "Make [them] according to their pattern that you have been shown on the mountain."[a] Centuries later, when the ark was installed in King Solomon's temple, Solomon was able to replace most of the parts of the apparatus, but had to use the original ark with its "two tablets of stone."[b]

a. Exod. 25:40

b. 1 Kgs. 8:6, 9, 6:19, 2 Chr. 5:7

A gold cover for the ark was made with gold *cherubim* on each end.[c] God said,

c. Exod. 25:18

> [22]"I will meet with you there and I will speak with you from above the covering, from between the two *cherubim* that are on the ark of the testimony, all that I command you for the Israelites." (Exod. 25:22)

God also provided instructions for the construction of a tent that would house the ark. The ark was placed in the inner area of the tent called the sanctuary or the holy place. This portable facility always accompanied the Israelites on their journey through the wilderness.

Aaron, Moses' brother, was the high priest in charge of the ark. When standing in this official capacity, Aaron was instructed to wear a device called an *ephod*, which included a breastpiece and two items called *Urim* and *Thummin*. He was also instructed to make a number of very specific sacrifices. After that, it was Moses' duty to actually communicate with God.

> [89]And when Moses went into the tent of meeting to speak with Him, then he heard the voice speaking to him from above the covering, which [is] on the ark of the testimony from between two *cherubim*, and [thus] He spoke to him. (Num. 7:89)

That's the bare bones of the story of the ark, the *ephod*, the *Urim* and *Thummim*, and the *cherubim*. Over the years, theologians, historians, and even scientists have wrestled with the mystery of these items and the puzzling laws surrounding them. My father, Dr. Raphael Isaacs, was among them.

Dr. Isaacs was a distinguished hematologist who gained an international reputation for his research and discoveries relative to diseases of the blood, particularly pernicious anemia and leukemia. He also spent much of his life studying and thinking about the Bible, and incidentally imparted a good bit of his prodigious knowledge to me. As a scientist, he couldn't help but wonder about the actual purpose of the ark. As he wondered, a theory took shape. My father and I would spend countless hours discussing it and its ramifications.

In 1953, we described the tentative theory in a preliminary, unpublished essay. Finally, we wrote a monograph titled *Puzzling Biblical Laws*, published by Bloch in 1965. In it we suggested that many of the phenomena surrounding the ark could be explained in terms of the laws of contemporary physics. It seemed to us that the mechanism could best be understood when compared to a radio. That is, the ark with its tablets was an instrument that received and transmitted waves and converted them into sound between the *cherubim*. The biblical description of the *ephod* startlingly resembled a portable version of the same.

In the same year the monograph was published, my father suddenly died. I didn't look at it for some time after that, but from the intense effort we had intermittently put into it, there seemed no doubt that a little more work was needed to crystallize a few thoughts rattling around in my head.

For example, we had only touched on the cloud that accompanied the Israelites on their 40-year trek through the wilderness. Two things have become clear to me about that cloud. First, whenever communication ensued between God and man, the distinctive cloud would settle on the ark. The same cloud was present when the ark was installed in Solomon's temple some 300 years later. Second, the cloud was extremely dangerous because it was radioactive.

Exposure to it involved high risk, indeed possible radiation burn or even death.

> [2]And the Lord said to Moses, "Speak to your brother Aaron and he shall not come in at all times to the sanctuary within the veil before the mercy seat, which is on the ark, so that he will not die, for in the cloud I appear on the mercy seat." (Lev. 16:2)

Even when the cloud wasn't actually present, there was still residual danger from the items it touched. The assistants who carried the tent's equipment through the wilderness were not to touch the "holy things and they die."[d] The residual danger lasted hundreds of years, e.g., during the reigns of Kings Uzziah and Hezekiah, even though there is no mention of its actually being used as a communication device after the time of King David.

d. Num. 4:15

Another observation: There are specific descriptions of the cloud's effect on Moses, his sister Miriam, King Uzziah, and possibly King Hezekiah. The symptoms are carefully detailed. They are exactly the same as those suffered by victims of radiation burn today. Although the effect wrought by the cloud is commonly translated "plague of leprosy," the two Hebrew words used to describe it indicate a sudden strike and stinging or burning.

And more: In order to protect the priests working in the tent area as well as anyone or thing indiscriminately touched by the cloud when it drifted, a number of safeguards were painstakingly spelled out. They included incense, alcohol, wine, water, salt, fat, oil, blood, periodic rest, protective clothing and equipment worn by the priests, and certain sacrifices including meal and meat offerings.

It was becoming clear to me that the Bible was indicating that the laws prescribing all of these precautions were for one purpose only—to effectuate safe communication between God and man. In other words, the sacrifices were made, not as acts of expiation, but to chemically protect against the danger radiated by the cloud. These and countless other bits and pieces of what were looking more and more like an unfinished jigsaw puzzle intrigued me. Eventually I went back to the subject with the idea that a year or so of weekend and late night work would satisfactorily finish the job. That was over 40 years ago, and I've been at it ever since.

What I have found is that there is a logical, unvarying flow throughout the Bible when it comes to the description of the phenomena surrounding the ark. I presume observers orally transmitted their descriptions as accurately as possible and scribes wrote them down. However, the phenomena and events were of a highly technical nature. (I use the word "technical" in its dictionary definition: "peculiar to or used only in a particular trade, profession, science, art ... highly specialized ... as, technical words."[1]) Without seeing the events or having a complete technical, scientific understanding of them, the scribes would have had a virtually impossible job of relating the observers' words accurately.

This problem created a time warp and weakened the historicity of the stories. Exactly when the stories were written, scholars struggle to guess. Because of sometimes contradictory entries in the Bible, scholars have vigorously debated who the transcribers, writers, and editors were, what their motivations were, and during what time frame their contributions were made. Over the last couple of centuries, many theories have been developed to establish a framework within which various texts may be studied—Textual, Historical, Documentary, Literary, Form, and Redaction Criticisms. The more prevalent are those known by the designations J, E, P, and D. (For a full explanation of the Documentary Hypothesis in the context of the ark, see Appendix C.)

Armed with their various forms of biblical analysis, scholars today feel that the general lack of archaeological corroboration (with some notable exceptions) does not bode well for putting the Bible in a truly historical setting. The common view is that almost all of the stories in the Five Books were fabricated by priestly groups living either just before or just after the Babylonian exile in 587 CE. They believe the stories were then cast back in time to form a history, which included the patriarchs, Moses, the Exodus, etc. Thus, scholars say neither the events nor the people really existed. There is great disagreement as to the who, what, where, when, and why of the storytellers. Essentially, one would be hard-pressed to find any but the most diehard fundamentalist who still believes that "Joshua fit the battle of Jericho," much less that Moses, guided by the Lord, led the Israelites on a quest for The Promised Land.

My contribution to the argument is this: The important point is not when or by whom the events were written, but when they were observed. Contrary to scholarly opinion, the words in the Hebrew Bible are trying to convey instructions relative to the care and feeding of a unique communication system. My goal in this book has been to bring clarity to those puzzling ancient Hebrew words and ideas not previously understood by studying the ark within a totally new, technological context. (If you are reading from the Hebrew, you will notice slight differences in verse numberings from time to time.) Eventually this effort stimulated additional conjecture, which led to my humble attempt to think like a scientist and to take my curiosity to the outreach of my imagination. In the final chapter, I wonder, "What is God?"

Methodology

A few words now about my approach. In the beginning of my research, I was faced with that giant jigsaw puzzle, and words were my only pieces. I fit them together, piece by piece, until finally a total picture emerged.

I conducted an etymological study of some of the Hebrew words that the Bible uses to describe ark-related events and phenomena. I noticed that their translations often differed before and after the last recorded use of the ark during the reign of King David. For that reason, I scrutinized their translations as they were found in the Five Books (Genesis, Exodus, Leviticus, Numbers, and Deuteronomy—the books of Moses, the Pentateuch) versus the following books.[2] I also carefully considered derivations for clues of early meanings.

Finally, I made comparisons of many ark-related Hebrew words with their counterparts in Sumerian, Assyrian, Babylonian, Egyptian, Ugaritic, Eblaite, Hittite, and Greek. I used the well-attested assumption that these neighboring cultures shared words from their languages with Hebrew. I carefully noted those that were older or contemporary with Hebrew because they would have been especially instrumental in developing the ark-related terminology. The comparison yielded a fascinating fact: Hebrew words whose common translations have shaped our lives over the centuries—words such as holy, glory, sin, iniquity, clean, unclean, and even soul—had other possible translations and meanings within the context of the events recorded in Exodus, Leviticus, and Numbers. (This was not necessarily true in the other biblical books.) Without exception, they were all related in one way or another to the ark's communication system. It was fascinating to see so many related foreign words neatly fitting the system. For example, the *cherubim* structures on the ark have been related to the Akkadian word *karabu,* which has two primary meanings, one of which is "prayer." Prayer is a mode of communication with God, and the ark with its *cherubim* was a communication device.

Through this study, I was able to reinterpret certain phenomena in a scientific framework, specifically, modern physics and chemistry. The general theory that *Talking With God* propounds, conceived so many years ago by my father, now has solid, logical, etymological, corroborative support.

The Oriental Institute at the University of Chicago became my second home. I used many sources in my study that are listed in the bibliography if readers care to further their own study of this fascinating topic. For my transliterations of the Hebrew, I used the accepted non-technical, phonetic spelling. I did this to make it easier for those who are not familiar with the signs used by scholars. However, when I quote other authors, using either Hebrew or any other language, the transliterations are in their scholarly form. The numbers related to the Hebrew words refer to those used in *Strong's Exhaustive Concordance of the Bible* (Strong's). As to the Hebrew translations, I use works such as the *Soncino Chumash* (Soncino), *The Pentateuch and Haftorahs* (Hertz), the *JPS Torah Commentary* (JPS), *Analytical Key to the Old Testament* (Owens), *The Hebrew & Chaldee Lexicon to the Old Testament* (Fuerst), the *Hebrew & Aramaic Lexicon of the Old Testament* (HAL), interlinear versions such as *Magil's Linear School Bible* (Magil's), *The Interlinear Hebrew-Aramaic Old Testament* (Green), and *The NIV Interlinear Hebrew-English Old Testament* (Kohlenberger), or my own.[5]

Curiosity or Heresy?

The tyrant shuts off all debates and draws the veil of ignorance around his people. He shuns curiosity as a dangerous tendency and regards the curious as oddballs. The curious go on—in quest of the top of the mountain, the bottom of the sea, the moon, the universe, the smallest particle of matter, the origin and meaning of life—for no other real reason than that they are curious. And that is reason enough.

The curious man has history as a guide for the present and future, but history is like the fishing guide. It can only lead one to a likely spot. It's then up to the fisherman himself to cast and hope he gets a strike.

Historians, theologians, politicians, and simply the curious have been fishing in the waters of the Five Books of Moses for hundreds of years. They have all come up with catches of one sort or another, mostly to suit their fancies or the fads and fashions of their times. Several great, organized religions have been built around these Books. Their words have been twisted, turned, pressed, expanded, diluted, seasoned, carved, shouted, whispered, revered, and reviled. Miraculously, in spite of it all, the Hebrew words have remained pretty much intact as they have been passed along from generation to generation. They are still there for anyone to look at, wonder about, and question.

So I'll cast my line, along with all the others, into these fascinating waters and try to catch some of those evasive, shadowy fish that have so far eluded anglers in the past. Some will feel that I have hooked the Loch Ness monster with no hope of landing it. Others will agree that this is a substantial catch, and that with some skill and patience I can bring it to net.

Science is really a mechanism for learning how things work, which, to us, means trying to find out the laws by which God develops the universe. To those who look on science as antagonistic or non–relevant to theology, there must be two systems, one as observed by scientists, which describes how observation and experiment seems to indicate the laws of matter, and a second set of laws which govern observations recorded in the Bible. Thus, while we assume that an invisible energy–substance carries radio waves from the transmitter to the receiver, it is considered sacrilegious by some to assume that the same mechanism is used in the communication of God with people, (i.e. God uses two sets of laws.) What is the mechanism for carrying the words? Nothing, they would say. It is a miracle.

Each generation tries to explain this miracle in terms of its current education and line of thought. The wave length theory is the current concept; in the future it may be something else. The older explanations, under the general heading of miracles seem inadequate today. The mechanism of study today is observation and experiment; in the ancient literature it was rationalization (i.e., a system of opinions deduced from reasoning).

Raphael Isaacs, M.A., M.D.

This note was probably written sometime in the late 1950's or early 1960's.

Chapter 1

Learning to Communicate

When the first men strolled on the surface of the moon on July 20, 1969, I, along with millions of viewers around the globe watched in amazement at the televised unfolding of this great scientific achievement. Every step of the journey was impressive—from the launch of the rocket ship into space, to the astronauts' walk on the moon, to the return journey and splashdown into the Pacific Ocean. Given my interest in the communication function of the ark, what really struck me about the mission was the relative ease with which the astronauts and NASA scientists, who were separated by some 238,700 miles of space, were able to talk to one another.

Today, telephones, televisions, radios, and communication satellites are taken for granted, but during biblical times there were no such devices. To communicate over vast distances, they had to beat a drum, make a smoke signal, send a messenger, blow a horn, or shout very loudly.

As the Israelites' leader, Moses felt the heavy burden of communicating with God to receive His laws and thereby establish order among a nation in its formative years. Because of their newly won freedom and the harsh realities of nomadic life in the wilderness, the Israelites required guidance and constant attention to mediate their disputes. They had not yet learned how to coexist peacefully and responsibly.

Jethro, Moses' father-in-law, saw the toll governance was taking on Moses and advised him to appoint capable men to serve as

²¹"... rulers of thousands, rulers of hundreds, rulers of fifties, and rulers of tens.

²²And they will judge the people ... and it will be every great matter they will bring to you, but every small matter they will judge themselves." (Exod.18:21–22)

Then Jethro further implored Moses:

> [19]"Listen to my voice. I will advise you, and may God be with you. Be you for the people before God [a mediator with God], and bring you the matters to God.

> [20]And you warn [or teach] them the statutes and laws and make known to them the way in which they should walk and the work they should do.

> [23]... and also all this people will come to its place in peace." (Exod. 18:19–20, 23)

Moses followed Jethro's advice and from then on used his time and energy primarily to communicate with God. However, the development of a system of communication was not easy. The steps to its eventual appearance evolved out of uncertainty, fear, confusion, and extreme danger. What happened is outlined in Exodus 19–20.

Moses' Ups and Downs

In the third month following the exodus from Egypt, the Israelites set up camp at Mount Sinai. Moses went up the mountain to meet with God. God told him that if the people would keep His covenant, they would become "a kingdom of priests and a holy nation."[a] Then Moses came down and laid God's charge before them.[b] The people said they would do the Lord's bidding, and Moses went up to tell Him they had agreed.[c] Then the Lord told Moses He would appear in a thick cloud. He commanded him to go down to sanctify the people, have them wash their clothes, and be ready for His appearance in three days.[d]

So Moses went down, sanctified the people, and brought them to the base of the mountain.[e] However, when the Lord came down onto the mountain, it smoked and quaked so much that the people became afraid (trembled).[f] God called Moses back up the mountain. He then told him to go down and warn the people not to come up the mountain on pain of death. So Moses went down and told them to keep away from the base of the

a. Exod. 19:3–6

b. Exod. 19:7

c. Exod. 19:8

d. Exod. 19:10–11

e. Exod. 19:14

f. Exod. 19:18

mountain. At that point, the Lord began dictating a version of the Ten Commandments.[g]

g. Exod. 20:1–14

The continuing thunder, lightning, quaking, and smoking of the mountain so frightened the people that they begged Moses to be their intermediary with the Lord.[h] So, instead of the original plan for God to speak directly to the people, there was a change: "And the people stood far off."[i] With this new arrangement, Moses went back up and God transmitted laws called the "Covenant Code" directly to him.[j] Moses in turn related them to the people.[1]

h. Exod. 20:18–19

i. Exod. 20:21

j. Exod. 20:23–23:33

Then a remarkable series of events ensued. I believe they have not been properly analyzed. After giving all the laws, the Lord suddenly called Moses, Aaron, Nadab, Abihu, and 70 elders: "Come up to the Lord ... and prostrate yourselves from a distance. And Moses alone will approach to the Lord; but they will not come near; neither will the people go up with him."[k] Moses went about relating the laws as if nothing had happened:

k. Exod. 24:1–2

> [3] And Moses came and communicated to the people ALL the words of the Lord, and ALL the ordinances; and ALL the people answered [with] one voice, and they said, "ALL the words that the Lord has spoken we will do." (Exod. 24:3)

No reason is given for this re-ascent, but it couldn't have been to get any more laws since all the words and all the laws had been given. The next verses leave no doubt that the body of laws was complete.

> [4] And Moses wrote ALL the words of the Lord. And he rose early in the morning and he built an altar below the mountain, and 12 memorial pillars for the 12 tribes of Israel.

> [5] And he sent the young men of the Israelites, and they offered burnt offerings, and they sacrificed peace offerings of oxen to the Lord.

> [6] And Moses took half the blood and he put [it] in basins and half the blood he sprinkled on the altar.

> [7] And he took the book of the covenant, and he read in the ears of the people; and they said [again!], "All the Lord has spoken we will do and obey [literally, "hear"]."

[8]And Moses took the blood and he sprinkled [it] on the people. (Exod. 24:4–8)

Moses, Aaron, Nadab, Abihu, and the 70 elders were probably the group sprinkled since it would have been impossible to sprinkle the thousands of Israelites with one basin of blood. Then the group came part way up the mountain for the meeting with the Lord.[1]

l. Exod. 24:9

[10]And they saw the God of Israel; and under His feet like the work of a pavement of sapphire and as the heaven for clearness.

[11]And to the nobles of the Israelites He stretched not out His hand; and they beheld God, and they ate and they drank. (Exod. 24:10–11)

What happened? Why was this ascent no longer deadly? The answer is found in the order to sanctify the people. The process of sanctification was to protect the people during communication with God and is spelled out in the Covenant Code's beginning instructions to build "an altar of earth … and you will sacrifice the burnt offerings on it and the peace offerings."[m] Other sanctification processes included sprinkling with blood. That's exactly what Moses did. Before this re-ascent, they built an altar and sacrificed on it and used the blood to sprinkle the group, thereby chemically abating the radioactive danger of the cloud. Thus, the statement seemingly out of nowhere that the Lord "stretched not out His hand." I'll prove later that this meant that His presence didn't harm them due to the sacrifices.

m. Exod. 20:24

Only after the feast did Moses finally get a hint as to why he was summoned once again to climb to the top of the mountain.

[12]And the Lord said to Moses, "Come to Me to the mountain and be there; and I will give you the tables of stone and the law and the commandment that I have written to teach them." (Exod. 24:12)

Still in the dark as to exactly what this meant …

[15]Moses went [back] up to the mountain, and the cloud covered the mountain.

¹⁶And the glory of the Lord dwelt on Mount Sinai, and the cloud covered it six days; and He called to Moses on the seventh day from the midst of the cloud.

¹⁷And the appearance of the glory of the Lord [was] like a consuming fire on top of the mountain to the eyes of the Israelites.

¹⁸And Moses came into the midst of the cloud, and he went up into the mountain, and Moses was in the mountain forty day[s] and forty night[s]. (Exod. 24:15–18)

I believe that both the Lord and Moses saw that direct communication to the people through the cloud just would not work. The people were too frightened by the whole process, which is why they told Moses to communicate for them. It was just too dangerous. The constant changing of plans probably sapped their faith in both Moses and the Lord. It was becoming apparent that a simple altar with limited sacrifices wouldn't be enough to protect the entire congregation.

What to do? Go back up again and work out a system in which the cloud would settle on a designated safe place for communication: the tabernacle.[2] This is exactly what happened in Exodus 25–31. Moses may have been puzzled at first, but the reason he went up again was to receive instructions for constructing the tabernacle.[n] The purpose for this structure was to house the main communication apparatus, the ark. The tabernacle would also have two specially constructed altars—one overlaid with gold for burning incense, the other with copper for performing a large number of various sacrifices—a table, a candlestick (menorah), and the other instruments. A professional cadre (priests) had to be trained to carry out the plan.[o]

The general assumption has been that this was the plan from the very start, but I don't think so. There was no previous mention of a tabernacle with highly complex safety mechanisms. The instructions for using the ark to safely communicate with God evolved out of necessity. Moses spent 40 days and nights receiving them from (collaborating with?) the Lord. Actually, that still didn't solve the problems. Moses spent another 40 days and nights on the mountain receiving new tables (because he broke the first in anger when he learned the people had given him up and rebelled) and more laws to meet exigencies theretofore unknown.[p]

n. Exod. 25–28

o. Exod. 29–31

p. Exod. 32:1

Chapter 2

Puzzling Laws

It is easy to make two erroneous assumptions about Moses' descent from fiery Mount Sinai: (1) Moses was the first to receive God's laws. False. It's well known that the Israelites weren't the first to utilize sophisticated legal codes. (2) These laws were only moral or civil in nature. False. Some of them did address man's relation to man, but others were a formal codification of certain systems and phenomena that had been taken for granted by the first group of men God put on earth—Cain and Abel, Noah and the patriarchs, Abraham, Isaac, and Jacob. These men had at least a nodding acquaintance with these laws and the process of sacrifice that was central to them and to the thesis of this book. God was telling the Israelites through Moses that if they closely adhered to these laws and to the sacrificial process, their safety would be assured. If they didn't, they'd be flying in the face of nature itself, and you can't tamper with the laws of nature and expect to exist for very long. The people of that time had no idea what God was talking about, so they either obeyed because He told them to, or they disobeyed and took the consequences. They were like two-year-old children who are warned by Mother not to go near the flame. They don't know what the flame is, so they either obey because Mommy says so, or they disobey and get burned.

I don't know whether there was ever a group of people prior to the Israelites who really understood why they should follow these natural laws of God, but as far as I know, no group from Moses' time to the present has had any inkling of how or why they worked. It's no wonder. Take a look at most of the Leviticus 2–14 translations and you will find a strange wilderness of words and concepts. Many skip over them on their first reading of the Bible because they seem to have no earthly application to our complicated world of bombs, ROMS, and taxes. For example, take the admonitions to eat only clean animals that have a cloven hoof and chew their cud, to tear down your house if it has plague of leprosy, or to stay out of the sanctuary of the tent

a. Lev. 11:3; Lev.
14:44–45; Lev. 16:2

when the cloud is on the ark, lest you die.[a] These and many other related, puzzling regulations have been lumped together with the civil laws when, in fact, they constitute a separate set of natural laws having little or nothing to do with civil law. The problem is that language evolves, and over the years the Hebrew words pertaining to these natural laws have been translated according to modern perception rather than according to the original meaning of the observers' statements. This skew, along with the tendency to assign them moral relevance like the adjoining laws, has led to some strange and wondrous interpretations. It has also led modern day scholars to bury entire sections of biblical law in a grave of obsolescence.

Whether it's wise to consign portions of the Bible to legend and myth, only time will tell. However, if we are to do so, at least we should understand what we are discarding. The natural laws are a small part of the Covenant Code that Moses received from God on Mount Sinai and relayed to the Israelites probably sometime around the middle of the 13th century BCE. They tend to be quite boring unless suddenly you realize the tantalizing mystery of why they are there in the first place. Most of these natural laws, detailed in Exodus, Leviticus, and Numbers, revolve around the words "clean" and "unclean" and the process of sacrifice.

Clean and Unclean

When translating these natural law concepts from the Hebrew, the words "clean" and "unclean" are probably the most confusing of all the word choices. When used in a moral context, they immediately set up a characterization of good, bad, or evil, which opens the door to the concepts of wrongdoing, sin, and atonement. In a natural context, and quite apart from the traditional translation of "clean," Webster gives the following definition: "producing little or no radioactive fallout or contamination."[1] This is an example of modern terminology fitting the ancient scene. This is exactly the technical sense in which I'm using the word throughout this book. Many other words in the Bible have technical meanings, which are relevant to my theory. Thus, my intense scrutiny.

The original meanings of the words "clean," "unclean," "sin," and "atonement" have been mistranslated and misunderstood. This has caused problems from both religious and academic perspectives because certain meanings work within certain frames of reference and not in others. Take "unclean" for example. According to traditional translations, eating or touching an "unclean" animal makes me a "sinner," but I can expiate that "sin" by taking a bath and washing my clothes in the evening.[b] Also, how can an animal be "unclean" when alive but "clean" when dead?[c] And something is definitely amiss when a mother must offer a sacrifice to "atone" for the "sin of uncleanness" caused by having a baby. Imagine using words like "sin" and "atone" in connection with giving birth to a child![d] But that's the way these terms are translated today in most versions of the Bible.

b. Lev. 5:2,5; 11:25

c. e.g., Lev. 11:6–8,24

d. Lev. 12:6,7

The dietary laws are all based on the concepts of clean and unclean. Certain animals were not to be eaten because they were considered unclean when dead. The rest fell into the category of clean and could be eaten without a problem. For the most part, instead of specifying which animals are prohibited, the Bible defines broad groupings with examples.[e]

e. Lev. 11:1–2

The first of four dietary categories permits eating any animal that has a split hoof and chews its cud. Then follow some examples of forbidden animals one might think fall into this category but which really do not. The camel does not, because while it chews its cud, it does not have a split hoof. The hare does not for the same reason. The pig, on the other hand, has a split hoof but does not chew its cud. No bacon with those eggs.

The second dietary stipulation prohibits eating sea animals that don't have fins and scales. That cuts out lobster thermidor, shrimp cocktail, and turtle soup.

The third grouping involves birds, which were not so easily categorized. They are specified by name.

Finally, insects are categorized, the only edible kind being those that leap. Perhaps this means grasshoppers and the like, but no one knows for sure, and, unlike the case of sizzling bacon, few seem to care.

Now these are the creatures and categories that the Israelites were repeatedly exhorted not to eat or touch when dead. Well, what happened if they did? Did they shrivel up and die? Were they tried in a court and sentenced to prison? No. This is what the Lord commanded:

> ²⁴"And by these you will become unclean; whoever touches their carcass will be unclean until evening.

> ²⁵And whoever carries their carcass will wash his clothes, and he will be unclean until evening." (Lev. 11:24–25)

It was true that a citizen who deliberately and repeatedly broke these rules would find himself in trouble with the authorities. However, the person who accidentally touched one of the proscribed animals had to carry out a simple antidote. That's a little suspicious. Maybe by washing himself and his clothes he was getting rid of something that was on him, something that came off of the unclean animal.

The Lord continues:

> ³²"And everything on which it falls, any of them [unclean animals], when they are dead, will be unclean; whether it be a vessel of wood, or a garment, or skin, or sack, any vessel in which work is done, will be brought into water, and it will be unclean until the evening, then it will be clean.

> ³³And every earthen vessel into which any of them fall, whatever is in it will be unclean and you will break it [the vessel].

> ³⁴All food therein which may be eaten, that on which water comes, will be unclean; and all drink that may be drunk in all [such] vessels will be unclean.

> ³⁵And everything on which [any] of their carcass falls will be unclean; an oven or a range for pots will be destroyed; they are unclean and unclean they will be to you." (Lev. 11:32–35)

An interesting exception was in the case of a carcass of an unclean animal falling into a spring, "or a pit of a collection of water," i.e., a cistern.ᶠ The water in the cistern did not become

f. Lev. 11:36

unclean, but anyone who took the carcass out was unclean. The flowing water of a fountain or a stream or rainwater feeding a cistern simply dissipated and was not affected.

If a carcass fell on sowing seed before it was sown, it was alright, but if water was put on the seed and a carcass fell on it, then it would be unclean. Something also happened to a clean animal that died by itself or was killed [torn] by wild beasts. It became unclean, and anyone who touched or ate it would wash his clothes and be unclean until evening. Then he was clean. In this case, there does not seem to be any objection to anyone other than the priests eating the animal as long as one followed the prescribed formula afterwards.[g] With these examples in mind, the question must be asked, what is the true meaning of the words "clean" and "unclean"?

g. Lev. 17:15

Laws of Sacrifice

The laws of sacrifice also raise questions as to their true meaning. It is easy to equate the purpose of the Hebrew sacrifices with that of the other ancient civilizations, i.e., to propitiate their gods. A careful study shows this just isn't correct.

Many chapters in Exodus, Leviticus, and Numbers are devoted to the laws of sacrifice. For example, chapters 13 and 14 of Leviticus are concerned with sacrifice as it pertained to the plague of leprosy and the priest's obligation to observe and quarantine sufferers outside the camp. The point here is that after the priest declared the person well, there were several sacrifices that had to be offered. Among these was a sin offering:

> [19]"And the priest will make a sin offering, and will make atonement for him that is to be cleansed of his uncleanness …

> [20]And the priest will offer the burnt offering on the altar; and the priest will make atonement for him and he will be clean." (Lev. 14:19–20)

Once again the concepts of sin and atonement arise, this time in connection with the uncleanness brought about by disease.

The plague of leprosy could also affect clothing and houses, rendering them unclean. If it affected cloth, one either had to wash it or cut off the affected portion, provided the plague didn't spread. If it spread, the material had to be completely burned. If the plague was in a house, then one removed the areas that were affected. If it spread, one had to tear down the whole house, being careful to take the unclean material to an unclean place outside the camp.[h] In those cases when the plague didn't spread, once the affected areas were washed or removed, the priest pronounced the house clean. However, it was still necessary for him to use the blood of a bird, among other items, to completely decontaminate the house. Included in this process (sacrifice) was a living bird, which afterward was let go "outside of the city into an open field; thus, he will make atonement for the house, and it will be clean."[i] In these cases and the case of the leper, sacrifice seemed to have the purpose of somehow mitigating or neutralizing plague. Now, following the generally accepted translation, an utterly impossible use of the word "atonement" pops up, unless one is to conclude that houses sin! There must be something wrong with using the English word "atone" in these cases.

So, one by one, the meanings of these words hit a wall. Many other words will experience the same fate as this book progresses.

h. Lev. 14:40

i. Lev. 14:53

Chapter 3

Holy isn't Holy

So ingrained in Jewish and Christian thought are the translations "sanctify" and "holy" that they have literally shaped these religions. They have taken on rather mystical meanings of sacredness and reverence for God, but they were never meant to signify these concepts. These terms have everything to do with talking with God.

Sanctify/Condition

Though commonly read "sanctify," I have translated *qawdash* as "to condition or process." It signifies "the conditioning of people and things so they are safe to communicate with the Lord through the radioactive cloud above the ark." Effective conditioning (*qawdash*) led to being holy (*qodesh*), which I define as "conditioned."

The Sabbath

The first mention of *qawdash* is in Genesis 2:3, which states, "And God blessed the seventh day and conditioned it, because in it He rested from all His work that God had created and made." So rest was the first conditioning method and was literally established "in the beginning."[1] It was one of the protective measures necessary when dealing with the drifting cloud. As related to the Sabbath days, conditioning is mentioned in Exodus 20:8, 11 and Exodus 31:13. In Leviticus 19:30 and 26:2, a strange juxtaposition is made between keeping the Sabbaths (resting) and fearing the sanctuary: "My Sabbaths you will keep and My sanctuary you will *yawray*."[a] For some reason, only here do Magil, Kohlenberger, Green, Hertz,

a. *yawray*, 3372

Owens, and Soncino translate the word *yawray* as "revere" or "reverence." JPS translates it "venerate." However, *yawray* means *fear* and is so translated everywhere else. Considering that the dangerous cloud descended onto the sanctuary, fear seems to be an appropriate translation.

Firstborn Man and Beast

Exodus 13:2 states, "And the Lord said to Moses, saying, 'Condition to Me every firstborn … both of man and beast; it belongs to me.'" This concept relates to when blood was used to protect the people from "the destroyer."[b] This is further explained in Numbers 3:12–13:

b. Exod. 12:3–7, 12–13, 21–23, 29

> [12]"I have taken the Levites from the midst of the Israelites instead of every firstborn … and the Levites shall be Mine.

> [13]For Mine is every firstborn. In the day when I struck every firstborn in the land of Egypt I conditioned to Me every firstborn in Israel, both man and beast."

The rule regarding animals is repeated in Deuteronomy 15:19. This is one of the few times Deuteronomy refers to "condition."

The People

When Moses came down from Mt. Sinai "he conditioned the people and they washed their garments."[c] No mention is made at this point of how conditioning was done, but the reason for conditioning was that the Lord was coming down *to speak with the* people.[d] The verses simply say,

c. Exod. 19:14

d. Exod. 19:9

> [10]And the Lord said to Moses, "Go to the people, and condition them today and tomorrow, and let them wash their garments.

> [11]And let them be prepared for the third day; for on the third day the Lord will come down before the eyes of all the people on Mt. Sinai." (Exod. 19:10–11)

The Priests

"And also the priests who come near to the Lord shall condition themselves lest the Lord break forth among them."[e] This, too, was at Mt. Sinai.

e. Exod. 19:14

Mt. Sinai

Mt. Sinai itself was conditioned. "And Moses said to the Lord ... 'You have warned us, saying *set bounds* [to] the mount, and condition it.'"[f]

f. Exod. 19:23

The Conditioned Things

The conditioned things were the sanctuary and the items pertaining to it.[g] They were conditioned by 'the conditioning gifts' from the people, which were items used for sacrifice.

g. Exod. 28:38

Aaron, His Sons, and the Ram

Exodus 25–27 covers the manufacture of the tabernacle and related items. Exodus 28 explains how and why Aaron and his sons—the ones tasked with managing everything in this dangerous environment—were to be conditioned: so they could serve in the sanctuary safely.[h] Leviticus 8:8 shows them actually being conditioned.

h. Exod. 28:41–43

Exodus 29 has the complete description of the conditioning process, including use of the sacrifices, oil, blood, and protective clothing.[i] Parts of the sacrifices were to be eaten for internal conditioning or protection: "And they will eat those [things] by which atonement was made ... to condition them and a stranger will not eat for they are *conditioned*."[j] Before eating the ram's breast and shoulder, these pieces had to be conditioned, too.

i. Exod. 29:1–43

j. Exod. 29:33

> 27"And you will condition the breast ... and the shoulder ... of the ram of consecration [filling] of that which is for Aaron and of that which is for his sons." (Exod. 29:27)

There is no mention as to how or why these parts were conditioned, but since they were to be eaten, they may have been covered with oil as an additional protection.

The Altars

The priest used a sacrificed bullock's blood and oil to anoint and condition the brass (main) altar.[k] The reason is underscored in Exod. 29:37: "Seven days you will make atonement on the altar and you shall condition it, *and the altar will become super-*

k. Exod. 29:36–37, 40:9–11, 30:27; Lev. 8:14–15

l. Exod. 30:27

conditioned (qodesh qawdawsheem, holy of holies)" (my emphasis). The incense altar was also anointed with blood to condition it.[1]

The Tent

m. Exod. 30:26, 40:9; Lev. 8:10

The tent and everything in it was conditioned by oil.[m]

> [43]"And I will meet there with the Israelites, and it [the tent] will be conditioned to receive My communication safely against My glory.
>
> [44]And I will condition the tent of meeting and the altar, and Aaron and his sons I will condition that they may be priests to Me." (Exod. 29:43–44)

The Fiftieth Year

Leviticus 25:1–13 summarizes the law regarding the Sabbaths, or resting of the land. Every seven years the land was to lay fallow. After seven cycles, the 50th jubilee year was to be conditioned. This law connects the land's rest (every seventh year for forty-nine years) with conditioning (the fiftieth jubilee year, which also was a rest year for the land).

House

Leviticus 27:14–15 refer to a man giving his house "to the Lord." In actuality, the property would go to the priests for their use or be converted into money. Conditioning the house could be accomplished by cleansing it according to the sacrificial laws.

Field

> [16]And if a man shall condition to the Lord some part of a field of his possession ...
>
> [24]The field, when it goes out in the jubilee, will be conditioned to the Lord as a field devoted (*cherem*). (Lev. 27:16 ... 24)

Because of the large space a field occupies, conditioning it would require many sacrifices. (The effectiveness of a sacrifice is directly related to the area it covers.) Rather than "condition," the likely signification is "devoted." Milgrom says it is considered "the ultimate in dedication. It is 'most sacred to the Lord' in that it may never be redeemed."[2] The word *cherem* was also used for man or animals, but in the case of "man" (slaves) who had to be super-conditioned, it probably simply meant that they should be properly cleansed and possibly circumcised before being turned over to the priests.[n]

n. Lev. 27:21, 26

The Nazirite

The nazirite was a man or woman who vowed to be "separated to the Lord" for a specified period of time.[o] It was probably for service to the Lord in the tent, although in what capacity I do not know. Numbers 6:8 says, "All the days of his separation he is conditioned (*qodesh*) to the Lord."

o. Num. 6:2

Note how purely physical the idea of separation is in the phenomenon of the nazirite. Numbers 6:9–12 explains how the nazirite had to be re-conditioned if someone died next to him during the time of his vow. He had to shave his head, bring sacrifices,

> [11]"And the priest … shall atone for him for what he has sinned through the [dead] person, and he shall condition his head …
>
> [12]And he shall separate [himself] to the Lord the days of his separation … but the former days shall be void because his separation has been unclean." (Num. 6:11–12)

He had to condition himself again so that exposure to the cloud wouldn't put him in danger.

The Lord

There are several references to conditioning of the Lord. I believe this actually means that the priests were to protect the people from the danger inherent in the Lord's (the cloud's) appearance. This is made quite clear in the following examples.

Leviticus 10:3 shows the conditioning of the Lord by incense after the deaths of Aaron's sons: "This is what the Lord spoke … 'By those that are near Me I will be conditioned, and before all the people I will be glorified .'" Other related verses further serve to clarify Leviticus 10:3. For example, at the end of Leviticus 22, which generally discusses the priests' handling of the sacrifices, verses 31–32 say the following:

³¹"I am the Lord. And you shall keep My commandments, and you will do them; I am the Lord.

³²And you will not profane My conditioned name; and I will be conditioned in the midst of the Israelites: I am the Lord who conditions you."

As to the Lord conditioning the people, I think this simply meant that He had given them the knowledge and means to do it. Looking back again to Exodus 20:8, the Lord admonished the people to condition the Sabbath, and yet verse 11 says He conditioned it.

Another reference to conditioning the Lord (in this case *not* conditioning Him) is seen in Numbers 20:1–13. There was no water. The people complained. Note the important sequence of events: Moses and Aaron came to the door of the tent. They fell on their faces as the glory of the Lord *appeared*. The Lord commanded them to take the staff *from before the Lord*, speak to the rock, and it would give forth water. Moses struck the rock, water came out, and the people and cattle drank. Then the Lord said,

¹²"Because you have not believed in Me to condition Me before the eyes of the Israelites, therefore you will not bring this assembly into the land …

¹³They are the waters of Meribah where the Israelites quarreled with the Lord and he was conditioned by them." (Num. 20:12–13)

p. Num. 27:14;
Deut. 32:51

This passage and its other references have long been puzzling.ᴾ The prevalent theory has been that the Lord was angry with Moses because he didn't give Him credit for the miracle of the waters. The rabbis have used it in sermons to demonstrate that for a man of Moses' stature and direct relationship with God, even the smallest mistake was enough to merit severe punishment. However, if in light of what I propose is the translation of *qawdash*, failing to condition Him was a *giant* mistake! God had come to the Meribah through His dangerous cloud, but Moses and Aaron forgot or neglected to protect the people. This was a very significant oversight. In this case it seems that the Lord had to do the conditioning by means of the water. That is, if "conditioned by them" means "conditioned by the waters," then somehow the water itself protected the people and cattle that drank it. The conditioning was not done by Moses and Aaron, nor by the people, who had nothing to do with the process here.

That this is the proper reading seems to be indicated in Numbers 27:14: "Because you rebelled against My order ... to condition Me through ('by means of') the waters." Taking a closer look at Numbers 20:13, it is possible to translate it, "These are the waters of Meribah, where the Israelites quarreled with the Lord, and He conditioned *Himself* (*y'eeqawdaysh*) by them [*the waters*]." Condition is *y'eeqawdaysh* in the Hebrew, niphal tense, which *can* be reflexive.[3] In other words, by the protective nature of the water the Lord was able to (had to) do the job Himself without using Moses and Aaron as intermediaries.

Following Books

In the Uzzah story, he accidentally touched the ark and died. Afterward, the priests and Levites had to condition themselves in order to work with it. The meaning of *qawdash* is consistent.[q]   q. 2 Sam. 6:6–7, 1 Chr. 13: 9 10, 15:11 13

The same holds true in the Joshua/Achan story. The Lord told Joshua, after a failed attempt to attack Ai with a few men, "Up! Condition yourselves ... Take all the people of war and arise. Go up to Ai. See I have given into your hand the King of Ai and his people and his city and his land."[r] King Hezekiah   r. Josh. 7:14–8:1
instituted reforms that carefully followed the biblical precepts, including celebration of Passover.[s] To do this properly, the   s. 2 Chr. 30
priests and the Levites had to condition themselves.[t] Since they   t. 2 Chr. 30:13–15
had not conditioned themselves in time to celebrate it in the first month, they did so in the second month according to law. They attempted to condition everyone else:

> [17]For there were many in the congregation who had not conditioned themselves. Therefore the Levites had the charge of killing the Passover lambs for everyone who was not clean to condition them to the Lord. (2 Chr. 30:17)

So many people flocked in from everywhere to observe this first reinstituted Passover that they couldn't condition them all, try though they did:

> [18]For many in the congregation … had not cleansed themselves, yet they did eat the Passover otherwise than was written, for Hezekiah had prayed for them saying, "The good Lord atone for everyone
>
> [19]Who has set his heart to seek God, but not as the cleanness of the sanctuary."
>
> [20]And the Lord listened to Hezekiah and *healed* the people. (2 Chr. 30:18–20)

If the people had to be *healed* (and that *is* the correct translation), then they must have been sick from coming too near the conditioned place unprepared, unconditioned.

It is interesting that at the same time Hezekiah was bringing about his fundamental reforms, the prophet Isaiah was continuing the humanistic approach to the Hebrew "religion" that was being adopted by men such as Amos and Hosea. Isaiah also followed the prior prophets' altered attitude toward sacrifice.[u] In fact, Isaiah's rather puzzling omission of Hezekiah's return to fundamentals and very significant Passover ceremony is justified by his radically different beliefs.[4] Isaiah's approach would completely change the Hebrew paradigm throughout history up to and including the present time. Of *qodesh* Isaiah says, "But the Lord of hosts is exalted through justice, and God the *qodesh* One is *qodesh through righteousness*" (my emphasis).[v] Isaiah did not accept the chemical nature of people's relationship to God, so he changed the physical operation of conditioning to a humanistic one.

Joel had a completely different understanding of *qawdash*. He exhorted, "Set apart (*qawdash*) a fast."[w] Then he said, "Condition the congregation."[x] Then he called to the people, "Condition war," a phrase also used in Jeremiah and Micah.[y] This is said to refer to sacrifices offered before a war.

u. Isa. 1:11–14, 17; cf., Amos 5:21–24

v. Isa. 5:16

w. Joel 1:14, 2:15

x. Joel 2:16

y. Joel 3:9 (Heb: 4:9)

~~~~~~

OTHER LANGUAGES

As blurry as the meaning of the word becomes later on in the Hebrew, this doesn't seem to be the case in the Akkadian and Babylonian. The word *qadayshu* means,

> 1. ... to be free of claims (?) (RS only): [The question mark means that this is a questionable translation and one wonders if, in the quote given, it might mean "purified."] ... the *kunahi* building belongs to Ištar and is free of claims [purified?] for [Ištar?] and is transferred to Ištar ... 2. ... to clean ... 3. ... to make ritually clean, to purify a) persons ... b) buildings and divine images ... c) appurtenances for a rit.[ual] ... you purify the golden ax ... 4. ... to consecrate, dedicate ... 5. ... to purify oneself: he purifies himself with cedar, juniper, and sulphur.[5]

There are also the words *qashaydu*(m), "to be(come) pure," and *qushshudu*, "very holy, sanctified."[6] Then the adjective *quddushu* is simply translated "holy" in Standard Babylonian. It is

> a) said of temples: ... to the holy temple, the sacred dwelling of Anu (and) Ištar ... b) said of offerings and ritual appurtenances: "... bulls were slaughtered, lambs slain, holy *armannu* wood was scattered on the censer."[7]

Then the Ugaritic has *qdsh*, "dedicate, consecrate."[8] From this it is seen that the processes described above are purely physical in nature.

~~~~~~

Holy/Conditioned

"Holy" is the common translation of the Hebrew word *qodesh*.[7] I translate *qodesh* as "conditioned." It signifies the condition or state of people or things necessary for safety from the hazardous effects of the cloud during communication with the Lord through the ark and other equipment. *s. qodesh, 6944; qawdash, 6942*

In spite of its common usage in other languages, the derivation of the word *qodesh* is uncertain.[9] HAL says it "can only with difficulty be traced back to a root [*qd*] 'to cut'; if this is the case the basic meaning of [*qdsh*] would be 'to set apart.'"[10] Klein agrees that the original meaning probably was "to separate."[11] Milgrom says, "Holiness means not only 'separation from' but 'separation to.'"[12] Along these lines J. Muilenberg, in his article entitled "Holiness," says there are two major theories regarding the etymology of *qodesh*. The first associates the root ... [*qdsh*], with a hypothetical primitive root ... [*qd*], whence ... [*qdqd*], "crown of head," "hairy crown," (cf., Ugaritic *qdqd*) inferentially "cutting." According to this view, the root ... [*qdsh*] is related to ... [*chdsh*], "to be new" ("cut off," cf., ... [*qtsv*] and ... [*chtsv*] ... [*qtsf*] and ... [*chtsf*], ... [*qtsr*] and ... [*chtsr*]). In all these cases the meaning of "separation" is paramount.[13]

(The second theory may be dismissed because it relies on a translation of an Akkadian word that is no longer accepted.)

In relation to *qodesh*, *The New Brown-Driver-Briggs Gesenius Hebrew and English Lexicon* (BDB) also mentions *qdqd*, pronounced *qawdqode*.[14] It means the crown of the head.[aa] They derive *qawdqode* from *qawdad*, which means *bow*.[ab] According to Strong's, *qdqd* means the crown of the head because it is the top of the head that is seen when one bows down.[15] For example, Genesis 24:26 says that Abraham's servant "bowed (*vayeeqode*) and prostrated himself before the Lord." Exodus 4:31 says that when Aaron showed the people the signs of the Lord in Egypt, "the people believed; and [when] they heard that the Lord had visited the Israelites and that He had seen their affliction, then they bowed (*vayeeqdoo*) and prostrated themselves."[16]

In the Five Books, *qawdqode* is only found in Genesis 49:26 (in the prophecy of Jacob), Deuteronomy 33:16, 20 (in Moses' final blessing, which is related in many ways to that prophecy), and Deuteronomy 28:35 (in the curses). In the following books, *qawdqode* is found in Jeremiah 26:1, 48:45, Isaiah 3:17, 2 Samuel 14:25, and Job 2:7.

In the Five Books, except for the Joseph story in Genesis 43:28, all references to the word *qawdad* relate to bowing before the Lord.[ac] (None are found in Leviticus or Deuteronomy.) In the following books, in 1 and 2 Chronicles and Nehemiah, *qawdad* is used only relative to the Lord.[ad] Only 1 Kings 1:16 (in the David-Bathsheba stories) and 1 Samuel 24:8 (in the David-Saul stories) do not relate to the Lord.

Qawdad is always used with *shawchaw*, which means to "prostrate" oneself, and in combination they are always in connection with the Lord.[ae] However, *shawchaw* alone is also used in many scenarios that do not include the Lord. This seems

aa. *qawdqode*, 6936

ab. *qawdad*, 6915

ac. See Gen. 24:26, 48; Exod. 4:31, 12:27, 34:8; Num. 22:31.

ad. 1 Chr. 29:20, 2 Chr. 20:18, 29:30; Neh. 8:6

ae. *shawchaw*, 7812

to strongly indicate that *qawdad* was a technical word used to mean what one did when coming in contact with the Lord.

Bowing to or before the Lord is traditionally understood to be a reverent gesture, but I think it was a protective move. Consider how dangerous the environment became when the Lord descended on Mount Sinai in the cloud. Exodus 34:5–8 shows Moses there: "The Lord descended in the cloud … Moses *hastened* and bowed [*qawdad shawchaw*] *to the earth* and he prostrated himself." I think that when *qawdad* is used in this way, it means to "separate" oneself from the danger inherent in facing the Lord. Prostration, or covering the face, is a practical act that protects and shields one from the effects of the cloud.

So the words *qd, qdqd,* and *qdsh* are all evidently related. They all indicate separation and seem to fit into my definition of *qodesh* as being in a conditioned, and thus, protected state.

Chapter 4

Tables of Stone

¹⁸And He gave to Moses when He had finished speaking with him on Mount Sinai, two tables ... of stone (*edut*) written with the finger of God. (Exod. 31:18)

O f primary importance to the communication system were the stones that God gave Moses on Mount Sinai. In fact, they were the key components for the entire operation. They were the heart of the communication device that would allow the Israelites to literally, audibly hear the voice of God.

The first mention of the stones is in Exodus 24:12. This was when the Lord commanded Moses to go to the mountain to get the "tables of stone." Here, the actual word for stone, *eben*, is used.[a]

a. *eben*, 68

After that, in Exodus, Leviticus, and Numbers, the Hebrew word *edut* (pronounced *aydut*) is used for the stones.[b] *Edut* is traditionally translated "witness" or "testimony," but these translations actually refer to their use in the following books.[1] The word *edut* is the feminine of *ayd*, also translated "witness." *Ayd*'s denominative is *ood*.[c] *Ood* is translated "admonish, charge, warning, bear witness."[2] Notice the communication implication in warn, admonish, and charge. Any one of them could have been used when the Lord spoke to Moses at Mount Sinai:

b. *edut*, 5715

c. *ayd*, 5707; *ood*, 5749

> ²¹And the Lord said to Moses, "Go down and warn [admonish, charge—*ood*] the people lest they break through to gaze at the Lord and many of them fall." (Exod. 19:21)

> ²³And Moses said to the Lord, "The people are not able to come up to Mount Sinai for You warned (admonished, charged—*ha-aydotaw*) us saying, 'Set limits to the mountain and condition it.'" (Exod. 19:23)

The first *edut* reference in chronological order is in Exodus 25:16.[3] It follows the rules for construction of the ark and simply states, "You will put into the ark the *edut* that I will give you." This is repeated in Exodus 25:21. Then in Exodus 25:22, the Lord makes the all-important statement: "And I will meet with you there, and I will speak with you from above (or on) the covering from between the two *cherubim*, which are on the *arone ha edut*." This is the first time the apparatus is called *arone ha*

d. *arone*, 727

edut, traditionally translated "ark of the *testimony*."[d] But a look at the related words above shows that *edut*, when used with the ark, has the sense of communication, rather than testimony. So the true translation of *arone ha edut* is the ark of *communication*. This nomenclature underscores the essential role of the stones in the operation of the ark. So the stones themselves could be called the "stones of communication." However, a look at Chart A on page 29 shows that the use of *edut*, when related to the ark, is confined to Exodus, Leviticus, and Numbers. (See Appendix A for two exceptions.) In the following books there is an astounding shift from a technological device to theological concept of *edut* when describing the ark. In these books, *edut* is no longer connected to the ark but changes completely to the sense of "testimony" or "witness," e.g., "Because you ... have not obeyed the voice of the Lord in His law, in His statutes and

e. Jer. 44:23

did not walk in His testimonies."[e] This meaning doesn't exist in Exodus, Leviticus, and Numbers! (See Section 3 of Chart A.)

Then an equally amazing shift takes place. The concept of the ark containing stones, *arone ha edut*, is replaced by ark of the

f. *b'rith*, 1285

covenant, *arone b'rith*.[f] (See Appendix B for two exceptions.) This new usage is only found in Deuteronomy and the following books! It is true that covenant, *b'rith*, is a commonly used word found in all Five Books as well as most of the following ones. For instance, God commanded Moses to write the words of the

g. Exod. 34:27–28

covenant, the ten words, on the tables.[g] But now there is the specific reference to "ark of *b'rith*" instead of "ark of *edut*," as well as other "ark of ..." designations seen in Chart A.

All of the Deuteronomy references to the ark of the covenant, *b'rith*, pertain to an historical review of the sojourn experience in the wilderness. Each verse refers to the Levites as the bearers of the ark. References to tables of the covenant in Deuteronomy are also Moses' historical recounts of the wilderness period and of his receiving "the tables of stone, tables of the covenant of the Lord."[h] Significantly, there is no incidence of *edut* meaning stones anywhere in Deuteronomy. However, for the first time the meaning "testimony" is closely related to *edut*: "These are the testimonies (*hawaydote*) and the statutes and the ordinances, which Moses spoke to the Israelites."[i] This verse also shows a pattern of *edut* being coupled with "commandments" and similar words. For example, 1 Kings 2:3 says,

[3]"Keep the charge of the Lord your God, to walk in His ways, to keep His statutes and His commandments, and His ordinances, and His testimonies (*aydotav*) [plural of *edut*] according to that which is written in the law of Moses."[4]

From Deuteronomy on, *edut* and its close relatives are no longer connected with the ark. This shift is seen in 1 and 2 Kings, 1 and 2 Chronicles, Nehemiah, Psalms, and Jeremiah.

There have been two significant changes: (1) *Edut* no longer pertains to the stones that go into the ark but takes on the traditional meaning of testimony or witness. (2) Ark of the *edut* changed to ark of the *b'rith*.

So what is happening here? I believe the eventual substitution of *b'rith* for *edut* (stones) signifies the end of the ark's use as a communication device by the Israelites. Comprehending this shift is a good first step toward clarifying this most significant biblical concept.

My explanation here is far from the only one. Quite contrary to mine are the critics' who use the Documentary Hypothesis among others I mentioned in the Introduction. Put in simplest terms, the Documentary Hypothesis suggests there are four basic strands or documents running through the Five Books. It is claimed that each of these documents was written by a different person or persons at different times and then brought together,

h. Deut. 9:9, 11, 15

i. Deut. 4:45; *aydaw,* 5713; see also Deut. 6:17, 20

redacted, still later. This theory evolved because the books are said to contain repetitions, contradictions and stylistic differences. The various writers took older material and developed their documents with their own specific agendas in mind. The documents are termed J for Yahwist (German pronunciation of J), E for Elohist, P for Priest or Priestly, and D for Deuteronomist.

For a detailed explanation of how the Documentary Hypothesis relates to this discussion of the ark, please refer to Appendix C. I can't agree with the critics. I believe that the more deeply one studies the ark's function, the more logical the descriptions become.

Chart A shows the shift in name and meaning regarding the stones God gave to Moses on Mount Sinai. Notice the clustering of references to the ark containing stones (*arone edut*) in the early books versus the ark of the covenant (*arone b'rith*) in the following books. This indicates the ark's disappearance as a communication device over time.

Chart A Tables of Stone	3300 BCE ← → 450–350 BCE														
	Exodus	Leviticus	Numbers	Deuteronomy	Joshua	Judges	1 Samuel	2 Samuel	1 Kings	2 Kings	1 Chronicles	2 Chronicles	Jeremiah	Psalms	Nehemiah
1. TABLES without *edut* or *b'rith*															
Tables (*loach**)	7			6											
Tables of stone (*eben*)	5			7											
2. *EDUT*—stones placed in the ark															
Tables of *edut*	3														
Edut	7	1	2												
Tables of *ha edut*	1														
Ark of *ha edut*	10		2		1†										
Tabernacle of *ha edut*	1		4												
Tent of *edut*			4									1‡			
Veil of *ha edut*		1													
3. *EDUT*—translated testimony															
Non-stone testimonies (*edut*)				1					1	2	1	1	1	14	1
4. *B'RITH*															
Ark of *b'rith*					6										
Ark of *b'rith* of the Lord (*YWH§*)			2**	4	8		3		5		9	3			1
Ark of *ha b'rith* of God (*Elohim††*)						1‡‡	1	2			1				
Tables of *ha b'rith*				3					1		1				
5. ARK without *edut* or *b'rith*															
Ark of Lord (*YWH*)					12		15		2§§		4	1			
Ark of God (*Elohim*)							31				15	1			
Ark of Your strength (*oze****)											1			1	
Conditioned ark											1				
Ark					5		2	3	6		8	8			

* *looach*, 3871
† See Appendix A.
‡ See Appendix A.
§ *YWH*, 3068
** See Appendix B.
†† *Elohim*, 430
‡‡ *Ephod* with *Urim* and *Thummim* is probably meant here, <u>not</u> ark.
§§ 1 Kings 2:26 is "The ark of the Lord God" in the first of the two 1 Kings references.
*** *oze*, 5797

Chapter 5

Communication Station

While upon Mount Sinai, God commanded Moses to instruct the Israelites,

"And let them make for Me a conditioned place, and I will dwell in their midst according to all that I will show you, the model of the tabernacle and the model of all its instruments. And so will you make it." (Exod. 25:8-9)

The purpose of this construction project was to house the *edut*, the tables of stone, in what would be the headquarters for communication with the Lord. It was vitally necessary to have an isolated area where the priests and the high priest could conduct safe and effective communication with God without constantly endangering the people during the process.

The tabernacle, tent, ark of communication, ark cover, and *cherubim* were the major components of the communication process. The etymology of these key items reveals their functions and some of the intricacies of the master plan.

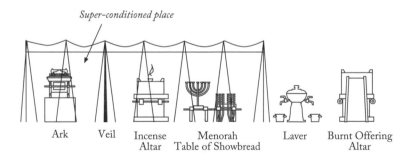

Super-conditioned place

| Ark | Veil | Incense Altar | Menorah Table of Showbread | Laver | Burnt Offering Altar |

Fig. 1

The Hebrew word for "tabernacle" is *mishkawn*. The word for "tent" is *ohel*. The tent was made to cover the tabernacle, creating a structure where they were inextricably linked in function.[a]

a. Exod. 26:7, 27:21, 36:14, Lev. 16:33

Moade was often used with *ohel* to mean "tent of meeting" or "congregation."[b]

b. *ohel*, 168; *moade*, 4150; *mishkawn*, 4908

In the Ugaritic, *mskn* means "tabernacle" and *ahl* means "tent." In the Akkadian, *maskanu* is "tabernacle."

Some scholars say the structure never really existed. They say postexilic priests (those after the Babylonian captivity of the Jewish people, 587–539 BCE) made up the tent story (along with the rest of the exodus) and based its design on Solomon's Temple. Others claim it refers to the tabernacle at Shiloh during Eli's time. Still, others say the original wilderness tent was a simple structure, not the elegant one described in the Exodus chapters. It has also been suggested that the tent was an idea borrowed from the Hittites or Canaanites or more likely from the Egyptians.

All well and good. My intent is not to indulge the debate but simply to describe the general architecture and, more importantly, what it contained. Instructions for its construction are in Exodus 25:1–31:11 and 35:5–40:38.

The tent was made of curtains of goats' hair fastened with bronze clasps. It was covered with rams' skins and *tachash* (animal unknown) skins.

The tabernacle was divided into three areas: the outer court, the conditioned place, and the super-conditioned place. The outer court was framed by 10 linen curtains fastened with 50 gold clasps. The construction of the curtains also included blue, purple, and scarlet material and *cherubim*. The entrance was a screen or gate. The tabernacle's supporting boards were made of acacia wood. Silver sockets, or foundations, were under the boards, and crossbars of gold-covered acacia linked the boards together.

The tabernacle contained an altar made of acacia wood covered with bronze for burnt offerings. Accompanying utensils were made of bronze. The priests carried the altar using bronze-covered acacia poles running through bronze rings at its four ends. A bronze laver or basin was also placed in the outer court for the priests to wash themselves.

In the conditioned place, there was a table made of gold-covered acacia for the "showbread" or "bread of presence."c On it were gold bowls, ladles, pitchers, and jugs. A candelabrum or *menorah* was set next to the table.d It was made of pure gold, as were its snuffers and fire pans. An incense altar of gold-covered acacia was placed near the entrance to the super-conditioned place.

A veil divided the conditioned place from the super-conditioned place.e It was made of blue, purple, and scarlet material and linen. It was hung on four gold-covered acacia pillars attached with gold hooks on silver sockets.

c. Exod. 25:30

d. Exod. 25:31

e. Exod. 26:36

> [32]"And you will hang up the veil under the hooks and bring in there within [or behind] the veil the ark of communication, and the veil will divide to you between the conditioned place and between the super-conditioned place." (Exod. 26:32)

The super-conditioned place contained only the ark of communication.

Fig. 2

Egypt. "The small golden shrine is in the form of the sanctuary of the vulture goddess Nekhbet."[1]

Fig. 3

Egypt. The interior of the golden shrine, with a pedestal that probably once supported a golden statuette of Tutankhamun.[2]

Ark

f. *arone*, 727

The ark, *arone*, was a container.[f] Its sole purpose was to hold the tables of stone, *edut*. *Arone* is also the common word

g. e.g., 2 Kgs. 12:10; 2 Chr. 24:8; Gen. 50:26

for chest, coffin, or mummy case.[g] (See Appendix C for how Documentary Hypothesis calls coffin or mummy case "E.") In Exodus, Leviticus, Numbers, Deuteronomy, Joshua, 1, 2 Samuel, 1 Kings, 1, 2 Chronicles, Psalms, and Jeremiah, *arone* appears as the ark.

In Standard and Neo-Babylonian, *aranu* means "chest, coffer, cashbox, coffin."[3] In Ugaritic, *arn* means "box, chest."[4]

Ark Cover

h. *caporet*, 3727

Caporet means "cover," nothing more or less.[h] It is a highly specific technical word used *only* in its role as a cover for the ark. *Caporet* is found only in Exodus, Leviticus, and Numbers in the directions for making and using it. Later, it is found once in 1 Chronicles 28:11 in David's fatherly pep talk with Solomon, who would soon embark on the construction of the temple.[5]

The word *caporet* does not seem to have cognates in the early languages. It has been translated as "mercy seat" because of its perceived affinity to the idea of atoning and its real connection to

i. *kawfar*, 3722

the word *kawfar*.[i] *Kawfar* has many meanings, including "cover."

While the *caporet's* use as a covering is clear, the strange creations called *cherubim* that were affixed to the top of it are difficult to understand.

Cherubim

No matter how much has been written about the *cherubim*, and there has been a surfeit, no one knows what they looked like

j. *cherubim*, 3742

or how they were used on the ark and in the tent.[j] As to their appearance, speculations run from the ridiculous to the sublime. Some say they were well-nourished angelic babies hovering in space, blithely, if precariously, defying the laws of gravity with totally inadequate wings. One legend says they had the faces of young boys; another says they were similar to a curious being Moses saw in heaven. Some suggest a resemblance to the winged animal-man found in the art of the Assyrians, Phoenicians, and Egyptians.

In 1 Kings and 1 and 2 Chronicles, when speaking of the *cherubim* in Solomon's temple, there is no further description. To Ezekiel, they were living beings or pictures of living beings.[6] They moved, flew, and in his temple depiction, had the faces of man and lion, but since there is no mention of the ark in the book of Ezekiel, that doesn't help us understand their original function.[k] k. Ezek. 41:19 To describe them as images of something living violates one of the commandments given at the same time as the directions for making the ark: "You will not make for yourself an image of any likeness that is in the heavens above or that is in the earth below or that is in the waters under the earth."[l] Nevertheless, the l. Exod. 20:4 notion of an image comes from the following two verses:

> [20]"And the *cherubim* will be spreading out wings above the covering with their wings on the *caporet* and their faces (*p'nayhem*) each to his brother (*ach*); toward the *caporet* will be the faces (*p'nay*) of the *cherubim*." (Exod. 25:20)[m]   m. *p'nay*, 6440

> [9]And the *cherubim* were spreading out their wings above the covering with their wings on the *caporet* and their faces (*p'nayhem*) each toward his brother (*ach*); toward the *caporet* were the faces (*p'nay*) of the *cherubim*. (Exod. 37:9)

"Faces," *p'nayhem*, has many meanings, all of which depend on how the word is used within the sentence. In the Bible, it is often translated "before." Exodus 26:9 talks of making the curtains for the tent: "And you will double the six curtains at the front before (*p'nay*) the tent." Leviticus 24:4 says, "The lamps of the *menorah* will be arranged before (*leep'nay*) the Lord continually." 2 Kings 16:14 has both *leep'nay Yaweh*, "before the Lord," and *p'nay habayeet*, "the front of the house." Thus, the faces of the *cherubim* may simply be the fronts of the objects rather than images with eyes, ears, nose, and mouth.

Indeed, *p'nay* can be interpreted metaphorically as well as literally. For example, the face of a mountain or, in biblical stories, the face or front of a temple, the face of the deep, the face of the waters, or the face of the earth.[n] In my opinion, its n. Ezek. 41:14; Gen. 1:2; Exod. 32:12 use with *cherubim* is also metaphorical.

Personification is another figure of speech used in these two verses. The term *ach*, though translated "brother," is used with inanimate objects.[o] *Ach*, found in all Five Books, has several meanings including "other" and "another."[p] Thus, "You will join each [curtain of the tabernacle] to its sister (*eeshaw al achosaw*) by the hooks."[q] So it would be accurate to translate the two verses, "And their fronts one toward the other." Interpreting it this way removes the human attributes, leaving simply "wings" as the description of the *cherubim*.

o. *ach*, 251

p. Gen. 13:11

q. Exod. 26:6

A possible description of the *cherubim's* purpose is in their enigmatic mention way back in Genesis when Adam and Eve were being expelled from the Garden of Eden: "And He drove out the man and He placed at the east of the Garden of Eden the *cherubim* and the flaming, revolving sword to guard the way of the tree of life" (Gen. 3:24).[7] Here the *cherubim* seem to be part of some kind of security or warning system.

Cherubim are included in the manufacture of the 10 curtains and the veil of the tabernacle.

> 1"And the tabernacle you will make [with] ten curtains; linen twined and blue and purple and scarlet [with] *cherubim* the work of a skilled workman will you make them." (Exod. 26:1)
>
> 31"And you will make a veil blue and purple and scarlet and linen twined by the work of a skilled workman will it be made [with] *cherubim*." (Exod. 26:31)

At this point, the look or use of the *cherubim* is no clearer than at the start. So it is time to investigate possible derivations to see if they help.

A popular thought is that *cherubim* relate to foreign depictions of animal-men. Nahum Sarna notes,

> Biblical references, in assuming prior familiarity with the cherubim, suggest a connection with an existing tradition. Closest is the Akkadian term *kuribu*, a protective genius fashioned for the entrances of temples and palaces in Mesopotamia. These creatures are composites of human, animal, and avian features. Hybrids of this kind have turned up over a wide area of the Ancient Near East and the Mediterranean lands, including Canaan.[8]

Sarna then makes a leap and compares them to Ezekiel's description: "As bearers of the celestial throne, they evoke the belief in divine, transcendent sovereignty."[9] I have two objections to this theory. First is the aforementioned prohibition against graven images. Second is the fact that, according to the Chicago Assyrian Dictionary (CAD), *kuribu* is a Standard Babylonian, Neo-Assyrian word.[10] Since these periods spanned the 900s to the 600s BCE, the word appeared at least 200 years after its use in the biblical report.

Another theory that's more compelling supports my theory that *cherubim* are part of the communication device. *The Hebrew and Aramaic Lexicon of The Old Testament* (HAL) agrees that the Akkadian *karibu/btu* is a participle of *karabu* meaning "to pray, to consecrate, bless."[11] CAD indicates that it means much more. Seven pages are devoted to *karabu* to give examples of two primary meanings: "1. prayer 2. blessings."[12] Over and over, the examples include the idea of praying—communicating—to the gods. Also evident is the idea of dedicating an offering "by pronouncing relevant formulas."[13] Just one example is enough to give one pause: "If a man prays to (his) god and a chance utterance keeps answering him promptly …"[14] Thus, *cherub* is identified with communication.

In the realm of pure conjecture, consider this connection: There is a Hebrew word *qawrav* (spelled with a *koof* rather than a *kaf*), which has a meaning of "to draw near, approach."[r] It has other relatives, among which are *qawrban* and *qoorban*, meaning "an offering" or "sacrifice," and *qerev*, "midst."[s] HAL discusses these extensively.[15] The same word is in Ugaritic, namely *qrb*, "to draw near" or "to offer (a sacrifice)" and *qrb* or *bqrb*, "in the midst (of)."[16] In the Egyptian, there are the words *hr-ib* and *hr(y)-ib*, meaning "in the middle of, midst of," e.g., "who dwells in, of god or king."[17]

The Hebrew letter *kaf* starting *cherub* is different from the letter *koof* starting these related Ugaritic and Egyptian words. I think, though, that it is worth considering the possibility of a relationship since a) the sound is so similar, and b) the various meanings are used directly in connection with the subject at hand.[18] For example, Exodus 12:48 says, "And when a stranger

r. *qawrav*, 7126

s. *qoorban*, 7133; *qerev*, 7130

will sojourn with you and will prepare a Passover to the Lord, let all his males be circumcised and then he may come near (*yeeq'rab*) to prepare it." Leviticus 10:1 says, "And Aaron and his sons ... took each man his firepan ... and they offered (*vayaq'reeboo*) before the Lord." Exodus 40:30–32 is very specific in its description of the construction and consecration of the tent:

> And he set the laver between the tent of meeting and the altar ... and out of it washed Moses and Aaron ... when they went into the tent of meeting and when they came near (*oob'qawrbawtawm*) to the altar.

In a negative statement in Exodus 33:2–3 the Lord said, "And I will send before you a messenger ... to a land flowing [with] milk and honey, for I will not go up in the midst of you (*b'qeerb'chaw*)." With these examples in mind, one might wonder about a connection between the *cherubim* of the communication device and the activities involved in working with that device, even though the connection between the words might have been distant.

Regardless of the distant possibilities, the chance that *karabu* is the ancestor of *cherub* seems quite good. The important point here is the prayer idea, talking with, which is a far cry from imaginary beings and has nothing to do with a seat, a throne, or as later mentioned, a footstool.

If they were not human and/or animal figures, then what did they look like? There is only one descriptive hint: WINGS. Was there a term or concept suggesting the wings of an inanimate object that was commonly known to the peoples of the time? The answer is yes—the WINGED DISK.

Winged Disk

The winged disk is found in the sculpture of many ancient cultures including Egyptian, Assyrian, Hittite, Ugaritic, Eblaite, and Phoenician. (See illustrations below.) Othamar Keel, in *The Symbolism of the Biblical World*, points out that originally in Egypt, wings probably represented the sky. Later, "the wings of the sky came to be understood as a winged sun. In that form the image spread from Egypt throughout the whole of Asia Minor."[19] He continues, "As a rule, wings appear in Egyptian iconography as means of shelter rather than instruments of flight." And, "the winged sun over the temple gate frequently represents the sheltering sky."[20]

After the New Kingdom (1570–1090 BCE), the winged disk came to represent the guarding of the temples over whose doors it was incised. It was used for the same purpose on stelae.[21]

Fig. 4

Judaea. Royal stamp-seal impressions on jar handles. Stamp seals were found "on the handles of large storage jars mostly during the reign of King Hezekiah (c. 700 BC)."[22]

Fig. 5

Neo-Hittite. Composite creature supporting a winged sun-disk, from Karatepe. Neo-Hittite city ninth to eighth centuries BCE in what is Turkey today.[23]

Fig. 6

Hittite. Seal impression of Tudhaliyas, King of the Hittites.[24]

Fig. 7

Egypt. Ramses II before Amon-Re, on a 13th century stela found at Beth-shan. [25]

Fig. 8

Phoenicia. King Yehowmilk presents a libation to his goddess, the "Lady of Byblos." Byblos is the Greek name for Gebel, city in Phoenicia. Fifth century limestone stela. [26]

Fig. 9

Ugarit. Presentation of offering to god El on a 13th century stela from Ras Sharma in what is Syria today. [27]

Fig. 10

Hittite. Stone relief. 1250–1230 BCE. [28]

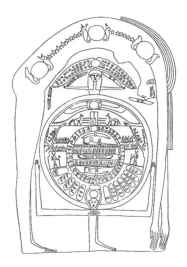

Fig. 11

*Egypt. Relief of sarcophagus cover,
Necropolis of Sakkarah, 30th dynasty,
378–341 BCE.*[29]

Fig. 12

*Assyria: Bronze tablet, "beginning of the
first millenium B.C."*[30]

Fig. 13

*Egypt. "Limestone relif, Abydos, Temple
of Seti I (1317–1301 B.C.)"*[31]

A. Side View   B. Front View

Fig. 14

Phoenicia. "White limestone NAOS (inner portion
of a temple) 5th century B.C."[32]

Fig. 15

Phoenicia. Limestone NAOS. "First half
of the fifth century BC."[33]

Fig. 16

Ugarit. "Stele, serpentine
(mineral used as a decorative
stone) … 14th century BC."
"Wings touching both heads."[34]

Fig. 17

Ebla. "Seal impression, ceramic ... Tell Mardik ca. 1725 B.C."[35]

Fig. 18

*Megiddo. "Ivory carving ... Megiddo 1350–1150 B.C."
Megiddo is a tell in Israel consisting of 26 layers
of ancient cities.[36]*

Fig. 19

*Kurkh (Southeastern Turkey). Limestone stele of
Shalmaneser III. The text includes a description of
Shalmaneser's defeat of a coalition of Asiatic rulers
at Qarqar on the Orontes in 853 BCE. The coalition
included King Ahab of Israel.[37]*

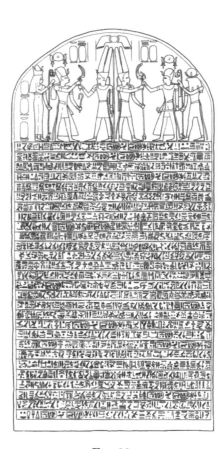

Fig. 20

*Egypt. Israel Stela of Merneptah, 1211–1202
BCE, from Thebes. Granite.*[38]

Fig. 21

*Lachish. Royal stamped jar handles from Tell
ed-Duweir. Late eighth century BCE.*[39]

Fig. 22

Persia. Cylinder seal of Parshandata, Achaemenia.
Achaemenian dynasty, 559–330 BCE.[40]

Fig. 23

Hittite. "Rock cut relief at Yazilikaya, near the Hititte capitol of Hattusas
at Boghazkale, Turkey. Probably a goddess holding the king whose name,
Tudhalias, supports a winged sun disk
~13th century B.C."[41]

Fig. 24

*Assur. "One of the capitals of ancient Assyria." "The god Assur in a
fiery winged sun disk surrounded by heavy rain clouds flies above the
king in his chariot. From the reign of Tukulti–Ninurta II or Assur–
Bel–Kala, and thus either early ninth or mid tenth century B.C."[42]*

Fig. 25

*Egypt. "Naos stela of Tuthmosis IV. Winged sun disk
over the 'false door.'"[43]*

Fig. 26

*Alahan (southern Turkey). "Head of Christ in winged sun disk over
the gateway to the Byzantine monastery."[44]*

Fig. 27

*Assyria. "Detail of the 'Black Obelisk' of Shalmaneser III, showing King Jehu of
Israel, or as he is called here, 'son of Omri,' submitting to the Assyrian king.
Mid–ninth century B.C." The melammu of the god Assur is over the vassal.[45]*

Fig. 28

Palestine. Megiddo: Stratum VII A; photo and restoration drawing of a Hittite carved ivory plaque in five registers; carvings show a sun god, demi-gods, monsters, and bulls; from the treasury in the palace of the princes of Megiddo; Late Bronze 1350–1150 BCE.[46]

Tree of Life

There are Assyrian cylinder seals from the 10th and 9th centuries BCE showing the winged disk above the tree of life. Note the similarity of these to the concept of the *cherubim* guarding the tree of life in Genesis 3:24. The fact that the same image is used over temples, stelae, and the tree of life indicates that, however the winged disk was regarded, its function was the same—to guard or protect.

Fig. 29

Assyria. Ninth century BCE cylinder seal. "Sun disc is primarily representative of the sky god ... in highly stylized tree of life."47

Fig. 30

Assyria. 10th century BCE limestone cylinder seal.48

Fig. 31

Mesopotamia. Cylinder seal. The god of the ground waters was a god of magic and healing. Here his priests are shown at the tree of life. Ninth–eighth century BCE.49

Fig. 32

*Assyria. "Ivory inlay of Syrian origin
found in Assyrian palace at Nimrud."
Ninth century BCE in
what is now Iraq.[50]*

Fig. 33

*Neo–Assyria. Seal of winged sun disk
over fruit bearing tree of life.[51]*

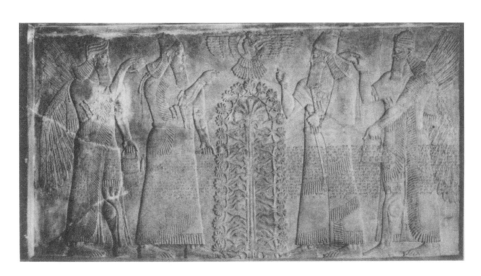

Fig. 34

*Assyria. "Relief of Assur-nasir-pal, showing winged sun disk over tree of life.
Early 9th century B.C."[52]*

What am I saying? I have indicated that the *arone ha edut* was the ark of communication, a communication device. The Lord used this transmitter/receiver to advise, warn, and admonish the Israelites—protecting them from impending trouble. The *cherubim* played a role in this function. They were made in the shape of a protective symbol that was absolutely universal, therefore well-known to the master craftsmen Oholiab and Bezalel when they manufactured the ark and related items.[t]   t. Exod. 35:30–35, 38:23

As a matter of fact, in her fascinating article "The God Salmu and the Winged Disk," Stephanie Dalley postulates that the word *edut* was borrowed and used for winged disk in the Akkadian!

Hebrew *edut* and Phoenician *'dt(?)*

There is already evidence from the Levant that a Hebrew and Phoenician cognate of *adē* in a slightly different form was used for the winged disk, although the two passages in which it is thought to occur are open to question.

Yeivin has pointed out that, during the coronation of Joash in Jerusalem in the 9th century, *'edūt* was "put over" him (2 Kings 11:42) [sic 11:12] and that the same word almost certainly occurs (the middle letter is damaged) in the Byblos stela of Yehaumilk in the 5th century BC. In the latter case scholars agree that the winged disk is almost certainly meant, but in the former, 400 years earlier, there is the possibility that the word had not developed that specific meaning. In any case, the word was established in use in the Levant during the early first millennium, and it is thought to be a late loanword in the form *'dy*, as found in the Sefiré treaty, from Aramaic to Akkadian, both as a common noun in neo-Assyrian, and much later as a deity in Seleucid Babylonian names. The form *adēšu* in Akkadian may represent a secondary development rather than a direct transfer of the form of *edut*, but the root is cognate. According to the function of the winged disk as extracted below from cuneiform sources, the traditional translation of *edut* as "testimony" is compatible with its suggested meaning as "winged disk."[53]

Dalley's concept is one more indication that *cherubim*, relative to the *edut*, were never considered to have human or animal attributes. It also indicates that from early times on, *edut* and winged disk were considered as being in combination. Although her explanation would result in the later groups equating the *edut* with the winged disk, rather than only the *cherubim* on top of the ark, the similarities in our theories are quite interesting.

But does the actual command in the Bible agree with this theory? Exodus 25:17–20 says this:

[17]"And you will make a *caporet* of pure gold...

[18]And you will make two *cherubim* of gold...on the two ends of the covering.

[19]And make one *cherub* from one end and one *cherub* from one [the other] end, from the covering [of one piece] will you make the *cherubim* on its two ends.

[20]And the *cherubim* will be spreading out their wings above, covering with their wings over the *caporet*, with their fronts one toward the other; toward the *caporet* will be the fronts of the *cherubim*."

Thus, there must have been two winged disks that looked like this:

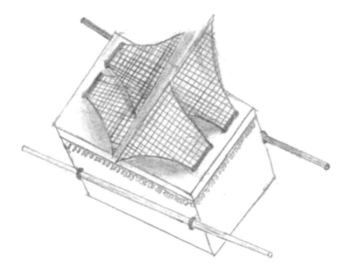

Fig. 39
Ark of communication.

Fig. 40
Television antennae—wings.

If the *edut* was the transmitter/receiver part of the device, what then was the specific function of the *cherubim*? I believe they served as antennae to attract sound waves to the *edut*. Thus, they were similar to the television antennae shown here, aptly called "video wings."

The *cherubim* in both the veil and curtains may have served the same function, enhancing reception, while the ark apparatus was in the super-conditioned place. When it was used separately from the tabernacle, the ark would have been completely dependent on the ark cover's *cherubim*. However, the veils of the tent and the court contained no *cherubim*. Since they were flexible entrances, their use as antennae would be questionable as antennae need to be stationary. In addition, since the *cherubim* and flaming (heat producing, laser-like?), revolving sword in the Garden of Eden suggest some sort of electronic device, the antennae function (radar-like?) would also apply there. The biblical scribes were doing their best to detail a system they could not possibly have understood.

There are a few hints regarding the *cherubim*'s function. Exodus 25:20 says, "And the *cherubim* will be spreading out wings above, covering (*soch'cheem*) with their wings on the covering."

The word for covering, *sawchach*, connotes screening.[u] It is related to the Babylonian word *sakaku*, "to block."[54] It and the word derived from it, *mawsawch*, are *only* used elsewhere in the Five Books relative to the following:[v]

* the "veil of the covering (*pawrochet ha mawsawch*) before the ark," where both *mawsawch* and *sawchach* are used;[w]
* "You will cover the ark with the veil *sakosaw al haawrone et hapawrochet*;"[x]
* where the *pawrochet* is used along with other materials, to cover the ark in transit;[y]
* the screens or gates of the tabernacle and court; and
* the word used for God's covering Moses with His palm.

Thus, the wings of the *cherubim* were also used to screen the ark cover. So the *cherubim*, and for that matter the veil, which was also used to cover the ark when the people were traveling, had dual uses—protection and communication.

Finally, one might ask how, electronically, could stones with antennae act as a receiving device? Consider the crystal sets used in the early days of radio. The first ones consisted of a mineral such as galena, a wire called a cat's whisker, a wire for an antenna, another wire attached to a water pipe for a ground, and a pair

u. *sawchach*, 5526

v. *mawsawch*, 4539

w. Exod. 35:12, 39:34, 40:21

x. Exod. 40:3

y. Num. 4:5

of earphones. One touched various places on the surface of the galena rock with the tip of the cat's whisker until it detected electromagnetic waves from a transmitter. The only electricity needed was generated by the waves flowing across the antenna. Whether this was similar in any way to the ark device with its stones I don't know, but the principle of a mineral being able to detect sound waves puts it within the realm of possibility.

The *edut*, with its *cherubim* as antennae, wasn't the only communication device. God commanded Moses to develop another instrument—a portable walkie talkie.

Fig. 41
Crystal set.

Chapter 6

Walkie Talkie

Another part of the communication system was the *ephod*, a walkie talkie of sorts that allowed direct communication with God.[a] The *ephod* was used both in the communication station— a. *ephod*, 646 the super-conditioned place housing the tables of stone—and in remote locations. The apparatus was incorporated into the high priest's garment.

The Bible provides tremendous detail about the manufacture of this walkie talkie, but says little or nothing directly about its purpose. I encourage you to explore Exodus 28:4–30 in order to appreciate the emphasis and space devoted to the subject.

God says,

> [4]"And these are the garments that they will make: a breastpiece and *ephod* and robe and a tunic woven and a miter and a girdle: and they will make conditioning garments for Aaron your brother and his sons that he may be a priest to Me.
>
> [6]And they will make the *ephod* [of] gold, blue, and purple [and] scarlet, and twined linen, the work of a skillful workman.
>
> [7]It will have two shoulder-pieces joined to the two ends; that it may be joined together.
>
> [8]And the band of the *ephod* that [is] on it, like its work will be of the same piece; gold, blue, and purple, and scarlet and twined linen.
>
> [13]And you will make settings of gold:
>
> [14]And two chains of pure gold; [like] cords will you make them, of wreathen work: and you will put the wreathen chains on the settings." (Exod. 28:4, 6–8, 13–14)

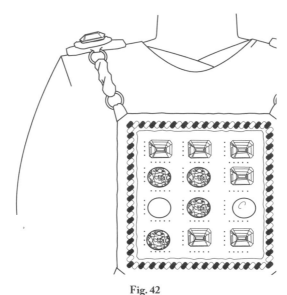

Fig. 42

Representation of breastpiece.

It's hard to tell if there was knowledge of the *ephod* before the Israelites received instructions for its manufacture. The first mention speaks of "onyx stones ... for **the** *ephod*" in relation to the materials that were to be supplied for it.[b] Calling it **the** *ephod* here seems out of place because it is directly followed by directions to make **a** super-conditioned place and **an** ark, etc., according to the model that God was showing Moses.[c] The second mention says, "These are the garments that they will make, **a** breastpiece and **an** *ephod*," possibly indicating they were unknown up to that time.[d] Then, giving greater detail, "And they will make **the** *ephod* gold, blue, and purple."[e] Every mention after that (29 more times in Exodus and twice in Leviticus) assumes an understanding of its use.

The Hebrew word *awphod* is related to *ephod* and is translated "bind, fasten, or gird": "And you will gird (*awphod'taw*) him with the band of the *ephod*."[f] The *ephod*, then, was something that could be bound onto someone or something.

The next references, which describe the use of the communication *ephod* of Exodus and Leviticus, are in 1 Samuel:

b. Exod. 25:7

c. Exod. 25:8–21

d. Exod. 28:4

e. Exod. 28:6

f. *awphod*, 640;
Exod. 29:5

Eli

[27]And there came a man of God to Eli, and said to him, "Thus said the Lord …

[28]'Did I choose him [Aaron] out of all the tribes … to be My priest, to go up to My altar, to burn incense, to wear [an] *ephod* before Me?'" (1 Sam. 2:27–28)

While He did not say "**the** (*ha*) *ephod*," the Lord did refer to the high priest's garment.

Ahijah

1 Samuel 14:3 is a reference to Ahijah, the great grandson of "Eli, the priest of the Lord in Shiloh, wearing an *ephod*." Shiloh was the first home of the tent, and it was there that Ahijah had responsibility for the ark, etc., and wore the communication *ephod*.

David and Ahimelech

[8]And David said to Ahimelech the priest, "And is there perhaps here under your hand a spear or sword?" …

[9]And the priest said, "The sword of Goliath … is here wrapped in a cloth behind the *ephod*." (1 Sam. 21:8 9)

This scene relates David's ongoing difficulties with King Saul. It occurred in the super-conditioned place in the city of priests, Nob, where the tent was thought to dwell after the destruction of Shiloh. Since this *ephod* was located in there, it was probably the communication *ephod*, and judging from the 1 Samuel 22:10, 13, and 15 references, it was actually used to contact the Lord.[1]

David and Saul

1 Samuel 23 leaves no doubt as to the purpose of the communication *ephod*. King Saul was in one of his irrational moods, and he was chasing after the young hero, David, to do him in. David used the *ephod* to seek the advice of the Lord.

[5]And David and his men went to Keilah, and he fought with the Philistines, and he brought away their cattle, and he slew them with a great slaughter; and David saved the inhabitants of Keilah.

⁶And it came to pass, when Abiathar the son of Ahimelech fled to David to Keilah that he *brought down an ephod in his hand*.

⁷And it was told Saul that David had come to Keilah. And Saul said, "God has delivered him into my hand; for he is shut in, by coming into a town [that has] gates and bar[s]."

⁸And Saul summoned all the people to war, to go down [to] Keilah to besiege David and his men.

⁹And David knew that it was against him Saul devised the evil; and he said to Abiathar the priest, *"Bring the ephod!"*

¹⁰*Then David said, "O Lord, God of Israel*, Your servant heard that Saul seeks to come to Keilah to destroy the city for my sake.

¹¹Will the men of Keilah deliver me up into his hand? Will Saul come down as Your servant has heard? O Lord, God of Israel, I beseech You. Tell Your servant." And the Lord said, "He will come down."

¹²Then said David, "Will the men of Keilah deliver me and my men into the hand of Saul?" And the Lord said, "They will deliver [you]." (1 Sam. 23:5–12, my emphasis)

At that point David and his men got out as fast as they could.

David at Ziklag

David (this time having fled to the protection of Acish, the King of Gath) returned to Ziklag, the city that Acish had given to him and his men. They found Ziklag burned by the Amalekites, and the men, women, and children, including David's two wives, taken captive.

⁶And David was greatly distressed; for the people said to stone him, because the soul of all the people was embittered, every man for his sons and for his daughters; but David strengthened himself in the Lord his God.

⁷And David said to Abiathar the priest, the son of Ahimelech: *"I pray you bring me the ephod."* And Abiathar brought the *ephod* to David.

⁸*And David inquired of the Lord* saying: "Will I pursue after this troop? Will I overtake them?" And He said to him, "Pursue, for you will surely overtake (them), and you will certainly recover (all)." (1 Sam. 30:6–8, my emphasis)[2]

Here again David used the *ephod*, as the priests did, to communicate with the Lord.

OTHER LANGUAGES

A look at related words in other languages shows that the Israelites described the *ephod* with a very ancient, well-known word. G. R. Driver, in *Canaanite Myths and Legends*, says that in Ugaritic *epd* means "garment, robe" and relates it to *eppatu* in Assyrian, meaning "wrapper," as well as to *ephod* in Hebrew.[3] Cyrus Gordon, in *Ugaritic Textbook Glossary*, calls it *ipd* with the same translation.[4] DLU says it is a type of garment and also relates it to *ephod*.[5]

Perhaps most revealing is the Egyptian word *ifd* (pronounced *i* as in *filled* or *aw—fd*). With the determinative ▭ it means "rectangular" (⟨image⟩). (A determinative is a sign or signs at the end of an Egyptian word that helps to define its meaning.) The same word with the additional determinative means "cloth."[6] It means "quadruple" with the determinative ⟨image⟩. The whole idea seems to relate to the concept of a four-cornered cloth and probably gives a hint about the shape and material of the *ephod*.

Now about the material used to make the *ephod*. It's conjecture, but I believe that the name of the material provides a clue to the material's protective nature.

Twined Linen

[2]"And he made the *ephod* of gold and blue and purple [and] scarlet and twined linen (*shaysh mawsh'zawr*).[8]

g. *shaysh*, 8336; *sh'zawr*, 7806

[3]And they beat the plates of gold, and cut wires to work in the midst of the blue and in the midst of the purple and in the midst of the scarlet and in the midst of the linen (*shaysh*), the work of a skillful workman." (Exod. 39:2–3)

The words "twined linen" (most frequently translated "fine twined linen") are *shaysh*, "linen," and *sh'zawr*, "twined." *Shaysh* is found once in Genesis 41:42 where Pharaoh honored Joseph with, among other items, "garments of linen (*shaysh*)." Exodus, the only other book in the Five Books where *shaysh* is found, only uses it in connection with the materials for the tent, the clothing that Aaron and his sons wore to minister there, and the *ephod*.

Ezekiel and Proverbs are the only two following books that mention *shaysh*. Proverbs is the only following book that refers to *shaysh* as cloth. Ezekiel talks of the impending doom of the kingdom of Judah. He likens Judah to a newborn infant, which God has found abandoned (Israel in Egypt) and which He

h. Ezek. 16:10

saves and nurtures. Judah then became unfaithful, as did the Israelites, and God said, "I clothed you with richly woven work ... and clothed you in linen (*shaysh*)."[h] Soncino points out that the Targums (the Aramaic translation of the Hebrew Bible), which are the Aramaic translations of the Hebrew Bible, say of *shaysh*, "The allusion is to the costly garments that the Israelites obtained from the Egyptians at the time of the exodus."[7] Ezekiel 27 finds the prophet lamenting the destruction of Tyre by Nebuchadnezzar, king of Babylon. This time he likens Tyre to a ship that has been wrecked, losing all. Ezekiel says, "Of

i. Ezek. 27:7

linen (*shaysh*) with woven work from Egypt was your sail."[i] In Proverbs 31:32 the ideal wife "makes for herself fine coverlets; her clothing is linen (*shaysh*) and purple."[8]

DERIVATION

As to the derivation of *shaysh*, HAL calls both the linen and alabaster translations "loan words from the Egyptian *shs* (with the clothing-determinative) ... limestone alabaster and pure linen share the same property in that they are both dazzling white; ... the word probably also means brilliant white."[9] Sarna says, "Hebrew *shesh* is a very early term, borrowed from Egyptian *shs,* used for cloth of exceptional quality."[10]

Just to emphasize, if the Targum assumption is correct, with the exception of Proverbs, the Bible either relates *shaysh* directly to Egypt or to the tent and priests in the wilderness. Like the word *ephod* itself, *shaysh* is extremely old.

Now *sh'zawr*, the word that goes with *shaysh*, is even more rare than *shaysh*. Translated "twined" or "twisted," *sh'zawr* is only used in Exodus and only in relation to the veil, the curtains for the door of the tent and the gate of the court, the *ephod*, its band and robe, and the breastpiece.

OTHER LANGUAGES

While *sh'zawr* is not found in related Semitic languages of the time, there is an Arabic word, *shazara*, meaning "to spin threads together, twist."[11] It has been accepted as meaning "interweave" in Middle and New Hebrew. There are plenty of derivatives in New Hebrew.[12] Strong's says it is a primitive root meaning, "to twist (a thread of straw):—twine."[13] Fuerst uses the idea of "spin" or "twist."[14] *Sh'zawr* may be an exclusively Hebrew word used hand-in-hand with *shaysh* (an Egyptian related word) to describe how something that had been known for centuries, Egyptian linen, was made.

Another possible root of *sh'zawr* is an Egyptian word *djesar*, roughly pronounced *djesar*.[15] Depending on the document and the exact word represented, *djesar* is spelled 𓊨𓏤 or 𓊨.[16] There are other variations, depending on the grammar, but basically, the rough pronunciation is *djesar* or *djezar*.[17] The closely related meanings are reported as follows:

djesar	set apart, be private, holy[18]
	holy, sacred (adjective), separate (verb)[19]
djeseru	seclusion, privacy, holy place (with different determinative)[20]
djesar djeseru	Holy of Holies[21]
tcheser	to put in good order, to be or make holy[22]
djesar	holy, sacred, consecrated, set apart[23]

If *djesar* or *djezar* (or *tssr* or *tszr*) are the equivalent of *sh'zawr*, then it is possible that both *shaysh* and *sh'zawr* were from the Egyptian language. Thus, the translation could be "linen (*shaysh*) being holy/separate (*sh'zawr*)."[24] Possibly, the writer went to a lot of trouble to construct a phrase showing the linen's definite purpose: to be, in my terminology, a conditioner or separator.

There is one place where *sh'zawr* stands without *shaysh* regarding the robe of the *ephod*: "And they made the lower hems of the robe [of the *ephod*] pomegranates of blue and purple and scarlet *mawsh'zawr*."[j]   j. Exod. 39:24
According to my thesis, what this verse says is that the pomegranates were to be conditioning/protectors, *mawsh'zawr*. (It should be noted that the Septuagint does use *shaysh* and *sh'zawr*.)[25]

<hr />

Unknown Substances

In addition to the basic material, *shaysh*, Exodus 28:6 shows that the *ephod* was made of other materials collected from the Israelites:

> [1]And the Lord spoke to Moses saying,
>
> [2]"Speak to the Israelites that they take for Me a heave offering
>
> …
>
> [3]And this is the heave offering that you will take of them: gold and silver and copper
>
> [4]And *blue* and *purple* and *scarlet* and *shaysh* and goat's [hair]."
> (Exod. 25:1–4)

Exodus 3:22 hints that these materials were supplied by the Egyptians when each Hebrew woman, as she fled Egypt, was to "ask of her neighbor and of the sojourner in her house for articles of silver and articles of gold and garments." In Exodus 12:35 all the Israelites made this request for the articles. Several chapters later the heave offering was rendered:

²¹Then came every man whose heart was lifted up and all whose spirit made him willing brought the heave offering of the Lord for the work of the tent of meeting and for all its service and for the conditioning garments.

²²And the men came with the women … brought bracelets [?] and nose rings and rings and armlets [?] every article of gold …

²³And every man [with] whom was found blue and purple and scarlet and *shaysh* and goat's [hair], and skins of rams being red and skins of *tachasheem* [meaning unknown] they brought.ᵏ

k. *tachash*, 8476

²⁴Everyone heaving a heave offering of silver and gold and copper … brought the heave offering of the Lord. And every one [with] whom was found acacia wood for any work of the service brought [it].

²⁵And every wise-hearted woman spun with her hands and they brought what they spun the blue and the purple and the scarlet and the *shaysh*.

²⁶And all the women whose hearts lifted them up in wisdom spun the goats' [hair]. (Exod. 35:21–26)

All the materials supplied by the Israelites are commonly known today, except three: blue, purple, and scarlet. When the Bible uses them as colors, it is explicit about the item that is colored:

³¹"And you will make the robe of the *ephod* all of blue." (Exod. 28:31)

⁶"And they will put upon it a covering of *tachash* and they will spread a cloth of blue from above." (Num. 4:6)

Also, Numbers 4:8 talks of a cloth of scarlet and Numbers 4:13 a cloth of purple.

However, blue, purple, and scarlet were also used independently. They were evidently well-known to the workmen at the time, just as were silver, gold, and copper.

⁷"Now send me a man wise to work in gold, and in silver, and in brass, and in iron, and in purple, and crimson (*charmeel*), and blue (*t'chaylet*)." (2 Chr. 2:7)ˡ

l. *charmeel*, 3758

¹⁴And his father was a man of Tyre who knew how to work in gold, and in silver, in brass, in iron, in stone, and in timber, in purple, in blue, and in *shaysh* in crimson. (2 Chr. 2:14)

They were specified in the making of the *ephod* and in the other parts of the tabernacle. They appear to have been weavable, dyed substances.

Blue, *t'chaylet*, purple, *argawmawn*, and scarlet, *toela'at shawnee*, are said to relate to dyes from natural sources.[m] Blue and purple were obtained from mollusks; scarlet came from "the eggs of scale insects of the Coccidae family."[26] The materials they colored could have been anything including yarn, but in the case of the *ephod* and the tabernacle items, the material is unspecified.

T'chaylet is found in the Akkadian as *takiltu*.[27] *Argawmawn* is found in the Akkadian as *argamannu* as well as the Ugaritic *argmn*, which also means "tribute."

Why on earth is any of this detail important? The colors are critical in the function of the *ephod* with its breastpiece.[n] The three significant elements of the *ephod* were the wires, the stones, and the *Urim* and *Thummim*.

Wires

Gold plates were beaten thin and cut into wires (*p'teeleem*) and then worked "in the midst of the blue and in the midst of the purple and in the midst of the scarlet and in the midst of the *shaysh* [of the *ephod*]."[o] The *ephod* is usually depicted as a piece of cloth that is made of *shaysh* with blue, purple, and scarlet yarns running through it with gold threads running between the colored yarns. In other words, there would be a pattern of blue, purple, scarlet, gold, and white (the linen). But reading this literally, it seems to be saying that gold wires are running *through* the unidentified material, which is dyed in three colors.

It seems to me that if the writer(s) wanted to describe the *ephod*'s construction as having gold threads running *between* the colored yarns, he (they) would have used the word *bane*.[p] Sometimes *bane* is translated as "interval," but mostly as "between."[28] For example,

> [16]"And it will be for a sign on your hand, and for frontlets between (*bane*) your eyes." (Exod. 13:16)

m. *t'chaylet*, 8504; *argawmawn*, 713; *toela'at*, 8438; *shawnee*, 8144

n. Exod. 39:2–3

o. *p'teeleem*, 6616; Exod. 39:3

p. *bane*, 996

> [22]"And I will speak with you from above the covering from between (*meebane*) the two *cherubim* that are on the ark." (Exod. 25:22)

> [33]"And the veil will separate to you between (*bane*) the conditioned place and between (*oobane*) the super-conditioned place." (Exod. 26:33)

> [33]The flesh was yet between (*bane*) their teeth ... when the anger of the Lord glowed against the people. (Num. 11:33)

While *bane* is translated variously, the English "between" represents the best nuance of the word. So, if "between" was meant to be used, the verse would have read, "And they beat the plates of gold and cut wires to work *between* the blue and *between* the purple and *between* the scarlet and *between* the shaysh."[q]

q. Exod. 39:3

The words for "in the midst of" the blue, etc., are *b'toch*: *b'* is translated "in" and *toch* (*tawvech*), "midst."[r] Take, for example, the tabernacle construction:

r. *tawvech*, 8432

> [28]"And the middle bar in the midst (*b'toch*) of the boards will pass through from end to end." (Exod. 26:28)

In the Israelites fleeing Egypt,

> [16]"And the Israelites will go on dry ground in the midst (*b'toch*) of the sea." (Exod. 14:16)

HAL calls the derivation uncertain, but quotes several authors as saying that *btk* is "in, within" in Ugaritic. Gordon asserts that *tk* is "(in the) midst."[29]

Depending on how *b'* and *toch* are used, they can also mean "between," "among," or "through," and the different translations can appear in the same chapter. For example, Exodus 39:25 speaks of pomegranates and bells on the hem of the robe of the *ephod*: "They put the bells in the midst (*b'toch*) of the pomegranates on the lower hems of the robe among (*b'toch*) the pomegranates."

Important to the discussion of the communication *ephod* is the translation of *b'toch* as "through." The fact that such care was taken to use the very specific *b'toch* to explain what was done with the gold wires makes the point, I think, that the wires were to be enclosed in and threaded through the material. The different colored wires seem similar to the insulation covering modern wires or cables. They are colored variously for identification purposes.

Whatever the material was, it was weavable: "And every wise-hearted woman spun with her hands and they brought what was spun, the blue and the purple and the scarlet and the *shaysh*."[s] It must have been special material, or at least specifically worked, as evidenced by the fact that the women did not carry their task any further.

s. Exod. 35:25–26

Specialists vs. Skilled Workers

The construction of the *ephod* was assigned to men who were skilled at specialized work, *chawshab*.[t] They worked under the supervision of the master craftsmen Bezalel and Oholiab. These two men knew how to do all of the various operations.[u]

t. *chawshab*, 2803; Exod. 39:3, etc.

u. Exod. 35:30–35, 38:23

> [30]And Moses said to the Israelites, "See, the Lord has called by name Bezalel the son of Uri ...
>
> [31]And He has filled him [with] the spirit of God, in wisdom ... in all workmanship,
>
> [32]And to devise designs, to work in gold and in silver and in copper,
>
> [33]And in cutting of stone for setting and in carving of wood, to work in all skillful workmanship,
>
> [34]And to teach, He put in his heart, he and Oholiab ...
>
> [35]He has filled them [with] wisdom of heart to do all work of a craftsman (*chawrawsh*) and a skillful workman (*choshayb*) and an embroiderer (*rawqam*) in blue and in purple, in scarlet and in *shaysh*, and a weaver (*oreg*), doers of all work and devisors of designs."[v] (Exod. 35:30–35)[30]

v. *chawrawsh*, 2796; *choshayb*, qal active participle of *chawshab*, 2803; *rawqam*, 7551; *oreg*, 707

DERIVATION

Chawshab, from which *choshayb* derives, is an interesting word with its many meanings. The general idea is to "think, count, account, reckon." From this sense comes the idea of "to devise designs" or invent, i.e., to do something by thinking.[w] Finally, there is the so-called skillful or "cunning man, work, workman."[31] Only Exodus uses *chawshab* relative to working skillfully with materials!

w. Exod. 31:4, 35:32, 35 and many following books

x. Exod. 35:35

HAL says the original meaning of *chawshab* was "to weave."[32] The Septuagint uses "weaver."[x] There is no hint of this use in any book other than Exodus.

The following Hebrew words are related to *chawshab*:

y. *chaysheb*, 2805

chaysheb (only in Exodus and Leviticus)[y]
- the band or strap
- curious girdle of the *ephod*
- of the same piece as the *ephod*

z. *cheshbown*, 2808

cheshbown (only in the following books)[z]
- account, device, reason

aa. *cheeshawbown*, 2810

cheeshawbown (only in the following books)[aa]
- device
- engine
- invention

OTHER LANGUAGES

Chesbown is found in Ugaritic as *hthbn* meaning "settlement, balance, balance sheet, bookkeeping." The Ugaritic *hthb* is translated "invoice, make account, computation, bill."[33] In the Egyptian, specifically Middle Egyptian, *chesef* is roughly pronounced *chesef*, which Alan Gardiner translates as "spin."[34] The determinative is a spindle ⌇. Raymond O. Faulkner, in *A Concise Dictionary of Middle Egyptian*, agrees and says spin "yarn."[35] The word *hsb* has a softer *ch*, but nevertheless a *ch* pronounced roughly *cheseb*.[36] Faulkner gives another *hsb* starting with the determinative ◌ (also included in the first *hsb*). This *hsb* is followed by an ideogram of a seated man 𓀀. While the pronunciation remains the same, *hsb* now means workman! In fact, in the *Ramesside Inscription*, it is used as "workmen," written ◌𓂝𓏼 (*hsbw*) or "to count," written as 𓂝 𓎡 (*hsb*).[37] From *Hieratic Papyri*, the word 𓏼𓀀 (*hsb*) appears in a line that is translated, "Behold, also, 5 *labourers* dragging stone continue in the quarry" (my emphasis).[38] The Petrie Papyri, from which this text was taken, is primarily from the Middle Kingdom, 9th–13th Dynasties (2240–1740 BCE), and also proves the extreme age of the word.

Thus, there is one word *chesef*, meaning "spin (yarn)," and another, *hsb*, meaning "count, reckon" or "workman" depending on the determinative. *Hsb* has the elements of *chawshab*, "count, reckon," and [skilful] "work, workman," etc. *Chesef* describes one of the operations done in the manufacture of the *ephod*. The Egyptian *hsb* has a consonantal structure similar to the Hebrew.

All indications are that the Egyptian is a more complete description of the total, highly specific meaning of *chawshab* as used in Exodus. So it is possible that the word was borrowed from Egypt when the Israelites lived there.

One other point should be made. I have said that Hebrew emphasizes the specialized knowledge *chawshab* involved in constructing the *ephod*. The other items that necessitated *chawshab* were the tabernacle curtains, the veil, the band of the *ephod*, and the breastpiece of judgment. Each of these items had one of two features: (1) the curtains and the veil had *cherubim*/antennae, and (2) the band and the breastpiece had gold wires like the *ephod*.[ab] These features are not found in any other part of the tabernacle or items relating to it. In other words, the items that were a part of the communication apparatus had to be specially devised, *chawshab*.

ab. Exod. 36:8, 36:35, 28:8, 28:15

On the other hand, the screen for the door of the tent, probably the hanging for the court, the screen for the gate of the court, the miter and girdle for Aaron, and the girdles and turbans for his sons were made by embroidering, *rawqam*. The coats for Aaron and his sons and the robe of the *ephod* were made by weaving, *oreg*. None of these items had gold wires or *cherubim* and so they could have been wrought by more ordinary methods.

Stones of Communication

Another element that appeared to have been involved in communication was the set of stones. They were the exception to the *chawshab* rule because they were not constructed. A skilled craftsman, *charawsh*, engraved them.

These stones have for so long been the choice topic of folklore. They are referenced in Exodus:

> [9]"And you will take two onyx stones, and grave on them the names of the sons of Israel:

> [10]Six of their names on one stone, and the names of the six that remain on the other stone, according to their birth.

> [11]With the work of an engraver in stone, the engravings of a signet, will you engrave the two stones, according to the names of the sons of Israel: you will make them enclosed [in] settings of gold.

> [12]And you will put the two stones upon the shoulder-pieces of the *ephod*, stones of memorial for the sons of Israel: and

Aaron will bear their names before the Lord upon his two shoulders for a memorial.

[17]And you will set in it the setting of stones, four rows of stones: a row of ruby, topaz, and emerald will be the first row;

[18]And the second row a carbuncle, a sapphire, and a diamond;

[19]And the third row a jacinth, and agate, and an amethyst;

[20]And the fourth row a beryl, and an onyx, and a jasper: they will be enclosed in gold in their settings.

[21]And the stones will be according to the names of the sons of Israel, twelve, according to their names; [like] the engravings of a signet every one according to his name, they will be for the twelve tribes …

[29]Aaron will bear the names of the sons of Israel in the breastpiece of judgment on his heart when he goes to the holy place for a memorial before the Lord continually." (Exod. 28:9–12, 17–21, 29)

The shoulder-pieces of the *ephod* contained two stones, each with the engraved names of the 12 tribes of Israel, six on one stone and six on the other. In addition, the breastpiece contained 12 stones, each of which was engraved with a name of one of the twelve tribes.

Several of the stones have distinctly Egyptian derivations.

Chart B—Breastpiece stones		
ENGLISH	HEBREW	EGYPTIAN
amethyst red jasper[40]	*achalomaw*[ac]	*chenm.t*[39]
amber, opal, jacinth green feldspar, white-blue feldspar, orange colored zircon[42]	*leshem*[ad]	*nsh'mt*[41]
carbuncle, emerald, turquoise, malachite[43]	*nofek*[ae]	*mefkat*
agate	*ah'boo*[af]	*abu*
necklace[44]	*shboo*	*subu*

Marginal notes:

ac. *achalomaw*, 306, Exod. 28:19

ad. *leshem*, 3958, Exod.28:19

ae. *nofek*, Exod. 28:18

af. *ah'boo*, 7619, Exod. 28:19

The derivations are not nearly as important as the *chawrawsh*, *chawshab*, etc. These precious stones were common to all cultures. The Israelites took the stones from Egypt during the exodus and still later imported them. Notable still, some of the items in the *ephod* were named in the much older Egyptian. The stones were considered oracular in nature and later became connected with the Zodiac. Folk legend suggests that letters on the breastpiece would become luminous, allowing answers to questions to be worked out much as a telegraph signal is interpreted.[45]

Josephus

The Jewish historian-soldier Flavius Josephus (38–100 CE) wrote about the shoulder and breastpiece stones:

> For as to those stones ... the high priest bare them on his shoulders, which were sardonyxes, (and I think it needless to describe their nature, they being known to everybody,) the one of them shined out when God was present at their sacrifices; I mean that which was in the nature of a button on his right shoulder, bright rays darting out thence, and being seen even by those that were most remote; which splendor yet was not before natural to the stone ... Yet I will mention what is still more wonderful than this: for God declared beforehand, by those twelve stones which the high priest bare on his breast, and which were inserted into his breastplate, when they should be victorious in battle; for so great a splendour shone forth from them before the army began to march, that all the people were sensible of God's being present for their assistance. Whence it came to pass that those Greeks, who had a veneration for our laws, because they could not possibly contradict this, called that breastplate *The Oracle*. Now this breastplate, and this sardonyx, left off shining two hundred years before I composed this book, God having been displeased at transgressions of his laws.[46]

I cannot base a theory explaining the function of the stones on Rabbinic legends or the rationalization of an historian who says he lived at least 200 years after its final use. (Actually, there's no indication that the device was used after David's reign, which would put his writing more like 1,000 years afterward.) The Bible itself rarely mentions the stones. In fact, they are *only* mentioned in Exodus, and then only relative to the instructions for making the shoulder-pieces and breastpiece. Of the two stones on the shoulder-pieces, it says only,

> [12]"And you will put the two stones on the shoulder-pieces of the *ephod* (as) stones of memorial for the sons of Israel; and Aaron will bear their names before the Lord on his two shoulders for a memorial." (Exod. 28:12)

The purpose of the twelve stones was also sparsely described:

²⁹"And Aaron will bear the names of the sons of Israel in the breastpiece of judgment upon his heart when he goes into the conditioned place, for a memorial before the Lord continually." (Exod. 28:29)

Cryptic it is, but nevertheless the Bible does tell the purpose of the two stones and the twelve stones. The two stones were called

ag. *zeekawrone*, 2146; Exod. 28:12

"stones of memorial (*abnay zeekawrone*) for the Israelites."^{ag} The twelve stones were to serve the same purpose. The name of a tribe was engraved on each stone for a memorial. Now the purpose of all 14 stones is clear. They were for a memorial before the Lord.

For a what?!

I am not as confident as Josephus that "their [the stones'] nature is known to everyone." I looked closely at the word that Strong's says means "memorial" and that describes the stones' purpose, *zeekawrone*.

<<<<<<<<<<<<<<<<<<<<<<<<<<<<<<<<<<<<<<<<<<<<<<<<<<<<<<<<<<<<<<<<<<<<<<<<<<<>

DERIVATION

ah. *zawchar*, 2142

Zeekawrone comes from the verb *zawchar.*^{ah} *Zawchar* means "to remember," and significantly, "to mention."[47] Genesis 40:14 uses both meanings in Joseph's statement to Pharaoh's chief cupbearer: "If you remember (*z'chartanee*) me ... mention (*v'heez'kartanee*) me ... to Pharaoh."[48] The Lord commanded in Exodus 23:13, "The name of other gods you will not mention (*tazkeerroo*); it will not be heard out of your mouth." The same translation of *zawchar*, "mention" is also found in Psalms 20:7, Isaiah 49:1, and Amos 6:10. Thus, the purpose of the stones may have been communication.

ai. *zecher*, 2143

The noun form of *zawchar* is *zaycher* or *zecher*, meaning "memorial."^{ai} "Memorial," in one or another of these forms, is found in Exodus, Leviticus, and Numbers.[49] In following books *zeekawrone* is translated "memory." Once, in Hosea 14:7, it is translated "scent."

Another Hebrew word related to *zawchar* is *azkawraw*, which is only

aj. *azkawraw*, 234

translated "memorial," "memorial portion," or "memorial part."^{aj} For example, Leviticus 2:2 says of the meal offering,

> ²"And he will bring it (the meal offering) to Aaron's sons, the priests; and he will take there from his handful of its fine flour, and of its oil, [with] all of its frankincense; and the priests will burn its memorial on the altar; a fire offering of a sweet savor to the Lord."

Or in Leviticus 2:9, "And the priest will take up from the meal offering its memorial and he will burn it on the altar; a fire offering of sweet savor to

ak. cf., Lev. 2:16

the Lord."^{ak} I believe the idea is that one attribute of flour, when turned to smoke, was that it could stimulate memory.

<<<<<<<<<<<<<<<<<<<<<<<<<<<<<<<<<<<<<<<<<<<<<<<<<<<<<<<<<<<<<<<<<<<<<<<<<<<>

OTHER LANGUAGES

In both Assyrian and Babylonian, the primary meaning of the word *zakaru* (long noted as a relative of Hebrew) rests in the idea of communication. In CAD, there are six basic meanings under its A classification:[50]

1. "to declare," as in "to declare under oath," "to make mention"

2. "to invoke," as in to invoke "the name of a deity" or "to name, as king"

3. "to speak"

4. "to name, proclaim"

5. "to *mention*, to invoke, to name"

6. "to take an oath"

Under CAD's B classification, *zakaru* means "to remember." Interestingly, *zakaru* is a West Semitic word, which is only found in cuneiform and Akkadian tablets at Tel el-Amarna.[51]

In the Ugaritic, the word for "remember" is *ches's*. The Ugaritic word *zg* translates as "to make a sound" and "lowed."[52] Driver likens it to the Arabic *zagzaga*, which translates "spoke faintly." The *g* is roughly pronounced *cha*. The point is that *zawchar* was well known in the Semitic world and used in the definition of "communication," particularly as it related to communication with a deity.[53] Turning now to the Egyptian, *secha* means "remember" and "mention."[54] Amazingly, similar to the two meanings in the Genesis story of Joseph in Egypt, in the *Papyrus of Ani* dated the second half of the 18th dynasty is the following from Ani's soliloquy: "My tongue is of Ptah, my throat is of Hathor. I make mention [*secha-a*] of the words of Tmu, my father, with my mouth."[55] As to "remember," Ani says in the same papyrus, "May I remember [*secha-a*] my name in the House of Fire."[56] In the same document, "I rest. I have remembered him [*sechai-f*]."[57] As a noun *shw* means "remembrance, mention, memorial."[58] Though the relationship of *zawchar* and *zaycher* to *secha* is conjecture, they all share the same meanings.

The fact that the prevalent meaning of very similar sounding words in the Amarna tablets had to do with communication persuades me that *zawchar* is a very ancient concept. Normally translated "remember," it can just as readily be tied in with "speak" or "communicate." Therefore, instead of *abnay zeekawrone* meaning "stones of memorial," perhaps it means "stones of communication," literally "of mention."[59] The persistent legends and ancient histories regarding the stones' oracular nature suddenly take on a more logical meaning. The modern translation, "stones of memorial," has made the purpose of the stones cryptic though it was clear when they were in use. I think the stones were for communication.

Are there any other uses of *zawchar* in its communication mode other than the Joseph story and the Lord's commandment not to mention the names of other gods?[al] There are several. They have mostly translated in the remembrance sense and as such their actual meanings have been rather clouded.

al. Gen. 40:14, 41:9; Exod. 23:13

Zawchar is found where Moses, having initially met the Lord, asks what he is to call Him.

¹⁴And God said to Moses, "I Will Be Who I Will Be." And He said, "This you will say to the Israelites: I Will Be has sent me to you."

¹⁵And God said moreover to Moses, "Thus will you say to the Israelites: The Lord God of your fathers ... has sent me to you ... This is My name forever and this is My *memorial* (*zeech'ree*) to all generations [literally, for generation [and] generation]." (Exod. 3:14–15)

It is almost a strain to use "memorial" here in the sense of reminding. If a communicative word such as "declare" is used instead, a more sensible reading results: "Say to the Israelites ... this is My name forever ... and this is My declaration to all generations," meaning *the name I am telling you is My name forever and I am declaring this fact to you and all future generations.*

Zawchar is in Moses' instruction concerning the feast of unleavened bread:

⁸"And you will tell it to your son in that day, saying it is because of that [which] the Lord did for me when I went out from Egypt.

⁹ And it will be for a sign on your hand and for a *zeekawrone* between your eyes in order that the law of the Lord may be in your mouth; for with a strong hand has the Lord brought you out of Egypt." (Exod. 13:8–9)

This verse is also found in Exodus 13:16, Deuteronomy 6:8, and Deuteronomy 11:18. However, instead of *zeekawrone* they use *totawfote*, which is translated "frontlets": "a sign on your hand and frontlets between your eyes." *Totawfote* is seen in the familiar passages, which have become part of the Jewish morning prayers, "Hear, oh Israel (*Sh'ma Yisroel*) ... there will be these words, which I command you today ... and you will bind them for a sign on your hand and they will be for frontlets (*totawfote*) between your eyes."[am] Apparently, frontlets were actual objects of some kind. They evolved into the symbolic phylacteries (*tefillin* in Hebrew), which had small boxes containing references to Exodus 13:8–9. They were worn on straps on the forehead and left arm during morning prayers. Even though *zeekawrone* in Exodus 13:8–9 is rightly translated in the remembering sense, the statement still has a declarative emphasis: "a reminder between your eyes in order that the law of the Lord may **be in your mouth**." In other words, *so that you can speak about the law.*

Zawchar is found in Exodus 17:14 after the victory over Amalek. It is used here in both contexts:

¹⁴And the Lord said, "Write this *zeekawrone* in a book and **put it in the ears** of Joshua that I will utterly wipe the remembrance (*zaycher*) of Amalek from under the heavens." (Exod. 17:14)

It is more logical to write a "declaration" than a "memorial," especially if the purpose was to wipe off the remembrance.[60]

The next set of *zawchar*/communication references are in Exodus 28 and 39. They refer to the stones in the *ephod*.[an]

Then *zawchar* shows up in the use of trumpets for communication. Trumpets were used to declare the start of *Rosh Hashana*. Today, one might use trucks with loudspeakers, radio, television, or the Internet.

am. Deut. 6: 4–8

an. Exod. 28:12, 29, 39:7

[24]"Speak to the Israelites, saying in the seventh month on the first [day] of the month [there] will be to you a solemn rest, a memorial (*zeekawrone*) of blowing [of trumpets], a conditioning convocation." (Lev. 23:24)[61]

The order was given in Numbers 10:2 to make two silver trumpets for "calling the congregation." Later, one or two were used for various other signaling purposes:

[9] "And when you go [to] war in your land against the adversary ... Then you will sound an alarm with the trumpets and you will be remembered (*v'neez'kartam*) before the Lord your God and you will be saved from your enemies.

[10]And on the day of your gladness and your set feasts, and on the beginning of your months, then you will blow with your trumpets over your burnt offerings and over your sacrifices of your peace offerings, and they will be for a signal (*l'zekroi*) before the Lord. I am the Lord your God." (Num. 10:9–10)

In verse 9, the trumpets were blown to remind (*v'neez'kartum*) the Lord of the necessity to save Israel. In verse 10, the trumpets were blown over the burnt and peace offerings at the various holidays to signal (*zekroi*) the Lord. (Verse 10 is sometimes misinterpreted to read that the offerings were the signal, but only the meal offerings were ever used for a memorial.) These verses strengthen the notion that there was a dual usage of *zeekawrone*, "remembrance" and "declaration." Correctly translated, they also help to clarify portions of the communication process.

The last example is the most interesting. It comes unexpectedly from 1 Chronicles and not the Pentateuch. David (an active user of the *ephod*), his army, and the elders of Israel are bringing the ark to the city of David:

[1]And they brought in the ark of God and set it in the midst of the tent that David had pitched for it, and they offered burnt offerings and peace offerings before God.

[2]And when David had made an end of offering ... he blessed the people in the name of the Lord.

[4]And he appointed certain of the Levites to minister *before the ark of the Lord*, and to *v'l'haz'keer* and praise the Lord, the God of Israel. (1 Chr. 16:1–2, 4)

Z'keer is the infinitive of *zawchar*. The question at hand is whether it should be translated as "to remember ... the Lord" or "to mention ... the Lord." The list below shows some translations of the root *z'keer*:

- invoke[62]
- petition[63]
- celebrate[64]
- speak of
- to celebrate[65]
- make mention
- call to mind
- commemorate
- profess, praise[66]
- record[67]
- lift up the voice[68]
- commemorate, praise[69]

With the exception of BDB, all translations of *z'keer* include the communicative sense. It is most significant that *z'keer* was used in connection with the handling of the ark (rightly or wrongly) and communicating with and/or at least speaking to God in David's time. Both the ark and the *ephod* were communication devices.

∞∞

The Craft

Before leaving the stones, there is one more interesting point. Remember the word *charawsh* referring to the engraver who fashioned the stones for the shoulder and breastpieces? *Charawsh* is only used in connection with the stones. Both *charawsh* and the stones are found only in Exodus.

In the following books, *charawsh* is translated mason, worker, smith, craftsman, and carpenter. A related word, *choresh*, is used as forger or artificer in Genesis 4:22 and nowhere else: "Tubal-cain, forger of every cutting [tool] of copper and iron."[ao] Relative to the work assigned, Bazalel was filled with "the spirit of God ... in cutting (*charoshet*) of stone for setting and in carving (*charoshet*) of wood."[ap] Interestingly, the appearance of *charawsh* in the Ugaritic suggests that this was a common Semitic term.[70] By most, it is simply translated "craftsman."[71]

ao. *choresh*, 2794

ap. *charoshet*, 2799; Exod. 31:5, 35:33

Urim and *Thummim*

Now to the third set of elements located in the breastpiece, the *Urim* and *Thummim*.[aq]

aq. *Urim*, 224; *Thummim*, 8550

> [30]"And you will put in the breastpiece of judgment the *Urim* and *Thummim*, and they will be on Aaron's breast when he goes in before the Lord; and Aaron will carry the judgment of the Israelites on his heart before the Lord continually." (Exod. 28:30)

The *Urim* are mentioned a grand total of four times in the Five Books and only three more times elsewhere. The *Thummim* are found three times in the Five Books, twice elsewhere. The first two mentions in the Five Books, Exodus 28:30 and Leviticus 8:8, are simply directions to put the two objects into the breastpiece. The third reference suggests that the *Urim* were a part of the communication system. When the Lord told Moses to appoint Joshua as his successor, He said, "And before Eleazer the priest he [Joshua] will stand and he will ask of him after the judgment

of *Urim* before the Lord."ar Finally, when Moses blessed each
of the tribes before he died, he said of the tribe of Levi, "Your
Thummim and your *Urim* (be) with your pious one."as While the
passage can be interpreted several ways, the sense is simply the
hope that the *Urim* and *Thummim* should remain in responsible
hands.

ar. Num. 27:21

as. Deut. 33:8

That's it for the *Urim* and *Thummim* in the Five books. Not
until 1 Samuel 28:6 are they mentioned again. There Saul,
the first king of Israel, tried to communicate with Him after
disobeying the Lord. "And Saul inquired of the Lord, but the
Lord did not answer him, neither by dreams, nor by *Urim*, nor
by the prophets." The only other references are identical ones in
Ezra 2:63 and Nehemiah 7:65, which shed no light on their use
or characteristics.

DERIVATION

Due to the sparseness of these scriptural references, it is difficult to get
at the derivation of *Urim* and *Thummim*. There have, however, been many
attempts. For example, *The Jewish Encyclopedia* says that they are probably
adaptations of the words *urtu* meaning "command, order, decision" and
tamitu meaning "oracle" found in the Babylonian Tablets of Destiny. These
items were said to rest on the breast of a god.[72]

Another popular translation of *Urim and Thummim* is "lights and
perfections." The concept of light is from the Hebrew word *oor*, meaning
"fire" or "light," *oorim* simply being the plural.at In Ugaritic, *ar* means "light"
and *ur* means "heat." *Urru* is the same word in Assyrian and perhaps even
ra, meaning both "sun" and the sun god of Egypt. *Thummim* is related to a
group of words, including *tawm*, *tome*, and *tawmim*, all of which are said to
derive from the root *tmm*.au The general meaning of these words is "finish,
make an end, perfect" or "to complete something." Similarly, the Ugaritic
tm means "entire, whole, completion," and the same *tm* in the Egyptian
means "complete, entire."[73]

at. *oor*, 215

au. *tawm*, 8535; *tome*, 8537; *tawmim*, 8549

I would take a guess that *Urim* and *Thummim* derive from the idea of *light*
and *completion*. The trick is to find out what they were not, relative to the
communication device, before trying to discover what they were.

One of the most prevalent theories is that the *Urim* and *Thummim*
were lots, items to decide a question by chance. This is gathered from one
reference only:

> 41And Saul said to the Lord God of Israel, "Give *tawmim*." And Jonathan
> and Saul were taken and the people went away.

> 42And Saul said, "Let fall, between me and Jonathan my son." And Jonathan
> was taken. (1 Sam. 14:41–42)

The word *tawmim* has the same Hebrew letters as *Thummim* but with different vowel signs, and "give *tawmim*" is supposed to mean "cast lots." This is because the "let fall" is sometimes used with lots to mean "cast lots" and "taken" can mean "chosen by lot."[av]

av. e.g., 1 Chr. 24:31

The real complication comes from the fact that additional words are in the Septuagint. A common translation is,

> [41]And Saul said to Lord God of Israel, "Why have You not answered Your servant this day? If this iniquity be in me or in Jonathan my son, Lord, God of Israel, give *Urim*, but if it be in Your people Israel, give *tawmim*." (1Sam. 14:41)[74]

These additional words would seem to settle the question of lots. The problem here is that, while this is the accepted translation of the Septuagint version, I can see no real reason for it. In the Septuagint, the word here for *Urim* is *dilos*, translated "clear, manifest," or *dilosis*, translated "manifestation, indication."[75] However, in the Ezra and Nehemiah references, the Septuagint uses the word *photezo*, "to give light," instead of *Urim*. In the above Samuel reference, instead of *tawmim*, the Septuagint uses *osios/osioteta*, translated "holy." Hastings translates *osioteta* as "innocence," but instead of *tawmim*, he uses *aletheia*, translated "truth" in Exodus, Leviticus, and Deuteronomy, and *teleios*, translated "perfect" in Ezra.[76]

In the unique Samuel verse, the fact is that, while Greek translations use all sorts of words for *Urim* and *Thummim*, none indicates lots. After revisiting the Septuagint's usage as carefully as I know how, this is the translation I have come up with: "If this impurity be in me or in Jonathan my son, give an *indication* if indeed it be so. Give to Your people Israel conditioning [clear of any impurity]." Whether or not lots were incidentally used to determine Jonathan's guilt or innocence is beside the point. The fact is that the words prior to verse 43, the "let fall" verse, simply do not indicate that *Urim* and *Thummim* were the lots themselves. I believe additional support for this argument is in what actually happened.

<<<<<<<<<<<<<<<<<<<<<<<<<<<<<<<<<<<<<<<<<<<<<<<<<<<<<<<<<<<<<<<<<

Saul, Jonathan, and the Philistines

In 1 Samuel 14, the Philistines and Saul's beleaguered group faced off, ready to do battle. Saul had 600 men plus Ahijah, "the priest of the Lord in Shiloh wearing an *ephod*."[aw] Unbeknownst to Saul, his son Jonathan and Jonathan's armor-bearer sneaked out of the Israelite camp, attacked the Philistine garrison, and killed about 20 men. The Philistines panicked. Saul, who was waiting at the border of Gibeah, saw his chance. He called to Ahijah, "Bring the ark of God here, for the ark of God was [there] on that day with [actually "and"] the Israelites."[ax]With the increased confusion in the Philistines' camp, Saul, not

aw. 1 Sam. 14:3

ax. 1 Sam. 14:18

wanting to wait, said to the priest, "Withdraw your hand."[ay] ay. 1 Sam. 14:19
Saul then made his men swear not to eat any food until evening.
Jonathan, who was away battling the Philistines, did not hear
the order and ate some honey. Meanwhile, the battle was over;
the Israelites had won. Famished, they hurriedly devoured the
spoil, sheep, oxen, and calves, along with the animals' blood. This
was a breach of an important law. It was absolutely forbidden for
the Israelites to eat blood.[az] az. Lev. 3:17

When Saul heard what they had done, he was greatly
distressed. He said, "You've acted treacherously; roll a great
stone to me today."[ba] His idea was to build an altar so that the ba. 1 Sam. 14:33
people could sacrifice and eat any additional food in the proper
way. Saul said,

> [34]"Disperse yourselves among the people and say to them,
> bring to me every man his ox and every man his sheep, and
> slay them here, and eat and do not sin against the Lord in
> eating with the blood." And all the people brought every man
> his ox with him that night and slew them there …
>
> [35]And Saul **began** to build an altar to the Lord. (1 Sam. 14:34–
> 35, my emphasis)

There is no evidence, however, that Saul ever finished the altar
or actually sacrificed. Instead, he suddenly changed the subject
and said, "Let's go down after the Philistines by night, and let
us take spoil among them until the morning light, and let us not
leave of them a man."[bb] bb. 1 Sam. 14:36

One Way Communication

At that point his priest said, "Let's approach here to God,"
meaning, *Let's see what God says about this.*[bc] "And Saul asked bc. 1 Sam. 14:36
God, 'Will I go down after the Philistines? Will You deliver
them into the hand of Israel?' But He did not answer him in
that day."[bd] bd. 1 Sam. 14:37

When Saul's men ate the blood, they made the area unclean.
If the Lord had communicated in this defiled environment, He
(His cloud) would have endangered the people. So there was
no answer when Saul attempted to use the ark—to approach

God—but Saul had no idea why the ark didn't work. In his haste to go after the Philistines, he evidently forgot that he hadn't completed the altar, and therefore hadn't sacrificed. Without the proper sacrifice, the area wasn't conditioned. (I will detail in the Danger Danger chapter how sacrifice was a key method for conditioning an unclean environment.) Saul didn't understand the reason he got no response from the Lord. He imputed the contamination to a person or persons:

> 38"Draw near all chiefs of the people and know and see how this contamination has happened today,

> 39For as the Lord lives who saves Israel, though it is in Jonathan my son he will surely die." But none answered him of all the people.

> 40Then he said to all Israel, "You be on one side and I and Jonathan my son will be on one side." (1Sam. 14:38–40)

Saul's request of the Lord to "give an *indication* (*tawmim*)" is in the next verse (41). Since the ark wasn't working that day, Saul turned to magic to troubleshoot the problem of the contamination. Here he may well have used lots. The story ends by saying, "Jonathan was taken." So Saul, having sworn to punish whoever caused the contamination, wanted to kill him, but the people refused to let him.

The use of magic for this or any other purpose was absolutely prohibited.^{be} Nevertheless, magic was being surreptitiously used in those times. Saul himself, who enforced the prohibition, sought the witch of En-Dor (another time when the *Urim*, etc., wouldn't work) because she could bring up the dead. He wanted to consult the ghost of Samuel.^{bf} Here the writer(s) of Samuel veers between the completely logical, technical mechanisms and the mystical, which was still very much a part of everyday life. The story alternates between the concepts, meaning the *people* alternated between the concepts. So to them, lots may have been perfectly usable items in lieu of the proper instruments that had been operating in a natural manner for many years. But to confuse the lots with the instruments is, I think, an error.

be. Lev. 19:31

bf. 1 Sam. 28:6–7, 9

Incidentally, regarding the instruments, the Septuagint uses *ephod* instead of ark in 1 Samuel 14:18: "Bring the *ephod* near." Actually this seems a more likely happening. Ahijah wore the *ephod*.[bg] It would have been much more likely that in the midst of all the tumult, rather than going to the ark, Saul would have asked the priest to bring this portable device to him. And, if the *ephod* was being used, there would have been no need for him to put his hand out to the ark, which was a lethal thing to do anyway.[bh] There is no record anywhere else of Saul ever having anything to do with the ark.[77]

bg. 1 Sam. 14:3

bh. cf., 2 Sam. 6:6–7

Getting to the Root

Whether or not the Septuagint's use of *ephod* instead of ark is correct, I believe the real purpose of the *Urim* and *Thummim* was to switch the *ephod*, or more precisely the stones in the breastpiece of the *ephod*, *on* and *off*. Thus the derivation of *Urim* as "lights" would mean that it had the function of turning on the stones so, as the legend said, they would light up and be capable of communicating by signal. Remember, the purpose of the stones was communication.

The derivation of *Thummim* as "complete" or "finished" meant, in effect, that it was an "off" switch. Therefore, if *ephod* was meant, it would explain Saul's retraction of his original order, "Withdraw your hand," i.e., "Take your hand off the switch. We don't have time to ask questions!"

What else supports this statement? Of the very few times the *Urim* and *Thummim* are mentioned, there are only two that actually spell out their use. Remember one reference was, "And before Eleazer the priest he will stand, and he will ask of him after the judgment of *Urim* before the Lord."[bi] The other is seen in the instance of Saul getting no answer: "And Saul inquired of the Lord, but the Lord answered him not, neither by dreams, nor by *Urim*, nor by prophets."[bj] So why does it not read *Urim* **and** *Thummim*? I do not believe this to be merely a scribal error, nor do I believe that *Thummim* was taken for granted. I believe *Thummim* was not mentioned because it simply had nothing to

bi. Num. 27:21

bj. 1 Sam. 28:6

do with "asking after the judgment," or getting or not getting an answer. The *Urim* activated the machine so that with it the user could communicate. The only function of the *Thummim* was to turn it off.

Back to the device itself. As noted, the breastpiece was attached to the *ephod*. The breastpiece held both the stones of communication and the *Urim* and *Thummim*, that is to say the on-off switches. It was called the *choshen*, or sometimes *choshen meeshpawt* from *shawfat*, meaning "to judge" or *choshen hameeshpawt*, meaning "breastpiece" or "*the* breastpiece of judgment."[bk] It is only mentioned in Exodus and Leviticus. Nowhere else. The derivation has always been a mystery, and it is said there is nothing in Hebrew or related languages to give a hint.[78]

bk. *choshen*, 2833, Exod. 25:7; *meeshpawt*, 4941; *shawfat*, 8199

It is interesting to note that words like *thnt, ifd, ss, djesar, chesef, hsb, sh3, chenm.t, nshmt, mefkat, sbnu* are all Egyptian and conceivably relate to the *ephod* mechanism. This certainly won't be the last of these relationships.

After substantial digging and unearthing the most probable meanings of each word, filtering through the mire of misunderstandings and improper translations, my interpretation of the *ephod* with the breastpiece, the wires, the stones of communication, and the *Urim* and *Thummim* switches is that it was a portable communication device.

Chapter 7

Danger, Danger!

The system for talking with God included the ark of communication with the tables of stone, *cherubim*, veil, *ephod* with its breastpiece of wires, stones of communication, and *Urim* and *Thummim* switches. The final, most critical element that fueled the whole process was the radioactive cloud.[1]

> [21]And the Lord went before them by day in a pillar of cloud to guide them [in] the way and by night in a pillar of fire to give light to them to go by day and by night. (Exod. 13:21)

The Cloud and the Lord

The cloud was the vehicle by which the Lord guided the people through the wilderness. (Note: a radioactive cloud would look like fire at night.) It also acted as a screen to protect them against the Egyptian army at the Sea of Reeds.[a] Most importantly, it a. Exod. 14:19–25 was the material through which the Lord communicated with the people. Look at the relationship between the Lord and the cloud:

> [9]And the Lord said to Moses, "Behold I come to you in a thick cloud in order that the people may hear when I speak with you." (Exod. 19:9)

> [15]And Moses went up to the mountain and the cloud covered the mountain.

> [16]And the glory of the Lord dwelt on Mount Sinai ... and He called to Moses on the seventh day out of the midst of the cloud. (Exod. 24:15–16)

> [9]It was when Moses entered the tent, the pillar of cloud would come down and it stood at the door of the tent and He spoke with Moses. (Exod. 33:9)

⁵And the Lord came down in a cloud, and stood with him there and he proclaimed [or "called in"] the name of the Lord. (Exod. 34:5)

³⁴Then the cloud covered the tent of meeting, and the glory of the Lord filled the tabernacle.

³⁵And Moses was not able to come into the tent of meeting because the cloud dwelt upon it. (Exod. 40:34–35)

This also occurred when Solomon's temple was completed.[b]

b. 1 Kgs. 8:10–11; 2 Chr. 5:13–14

²And the Lord said to Moses, "Speak to Aaron your brother, that he come not at all times to the conditioned place within the veil before the covering that is on the ark, that he die not for in a cloud I will appear on the covering." (Lev. 16:2)

²⁵And the Lord came down in a cloud and He spoke to him. (Num. 11:25)

⁵And the Lord came down in a pillar of cloud and stood at the door of the tent. (Num. 12:5)

²²These words the Lord spoke to all your assembly on the mountain out of the midst of the fire, the cloud, and the darkness. (Deut. 5:22)

¹⁵And the Lord appeared in the tent in a pillar of cloud …

¹⁶And the Lord said to Moses. (Deut. 31:15–16)

The cloud-connected communication system caused no end of trouble. Recall how frightening and difficult the development process was in Exodus 19.² Apparently, when God was there in the dense cloud, a deadly condition could be contracted and transmitted by touch, making it too dangerous to come near. To protect the people, He told Moses to condition them and have them wash their garments, but warned them to stay away from the mountain on pain of death. Death here cannot be construed as punishment because both people and animals had to be stoned or shot (with bow and arrow) from a distance if they got too near to the mountain, and animals surely could not know they were doing wrong. The Lord later warned Moses, "Also the flocks and herds will not feed before that mountain."[c] Something they would have ingested was deadly in this setting!

c. Exod. 34:3

Two clues point to the indiscriminate nature of the danger: (1) Exodus 19:18 explains that the cloud came all the way down to the people in the fire. (2) The Lord was terribly concerned about the people's safety because He told Moses to go back down the mountain and warn the people "lest they break through ... and many of them fall." God's concern was that an uncontrollable, natural catastrophe would occur; He was not meting out punishment as most translations imply. The danger was so serious that when Moses protested to God that he had already told the people to stay away, God ordered him to go back down anyway and then added that the priests, too, should stay down. (Remember He had at first said it was alright for the priests to come up as long as they conditioned themselves.) Moses was the only one to go "to the thick darkness" to talk to God.[d]   d. Exod. 20:21

The Cloud and the Ark

Once the communication process was established, the Israelites used it reasonably safely in the wilderness and later during the reigns of Kings Saul and David. It worked just as one would expect of any complex machine—with hazards and risk. The danger lay in the radioactive cloud coming in contact with the ark and making it highly radioactive. It was arguably the most dangerous technology in ancient times and would have no rival until the discovery of nuclear power. It could kill its users if they didn't exactly follow the plan God gave Moses on Mt. Sinai. In fact, the priests who first used it did not understand this, and the results were disastrous.

> [1]And the sons of Aaron, Nadab and Abihu, took strange fire before the Lord, which He had not commanded,
>
> [2]And the fire went out from before the Lord and consumed them, and they died before the Lord. (Lev. 10: 1–2)

Later, when King Solomon built a fancy temple to replace the mobile tabernacle, he could reconstruct all its instruments, but he had to use the original ark:

> [51]All the work that King Solomon made in the house of the Lord was finished ...

¹Then Solomon assembled the elders of Israel … to bring up the ark of the covenant of the Lord …

⁴And the tent of meeting, and all the conditioning vessels that were in the tent …

⁶And the priests brought in the ark of the covenant of the Lord to its place, into the super-conditioned place of the house, to the super-conditioned place under the wings of the *cherubim* …

⁹There was nothing in the ark except the two tables of stone, which Moses put there at Horeb …

¹⁰And it came to pass, when the priests were come out of the conditioned place that the cloud filled the house of the Lord,

¹¹So that the priests could not stand to minister by reason of the cloud; for the glory of the Lord filled the house of the Lord. (1 Kgs. 7:51–8:11)

Note the interworking of the ark and the cloud.

Moses

Moses had a reaction to the cloud induced radioactivity to which he was exposed on the mountain. When he came back down the mountain the second time with the new tables, his face "had become luminous."

²⁹And it came to pass when Moses came down from Mount Sinai with two tables of the communication in Moses' hand, when he came down from the mountain that Moses did not know that the skin of his face had become luminous while he talked with Him.

³⁰And when Aaron and all the Israelites saw Moses, behold the skin of his face had become luminous. And they were afraid to come near to him. (Exod. 34:29–30)

The luminosity was not something he could turn off and on at will. The people feared because they had no way of knowing what had happened. However, their fear lessened when Moses put on the veil and explained the situation.

Miriam

Another dramatic example of the cloud's effect is seen in the story of the short-lived rebellion of Moses' brother and sister, Aaron and Miriam, against Moses:

¹And Miriam and Aaron spoke against Moses on account of the Cushite [Ethiopian] woman whom he married; for he married a Cushite woman.

2And they said, "Has the Lord indeed only spoken by Moses? Has he not spoken also with us?" And the Lord heard.

3Now the man Moses [was] very meek above all the men that [were] on the face of the earth.

4And the Lord spoke suddenly to Moses and to Aaron and to Miriam: "Come out you three to the tent of meeting." And they three came out.

5And the Lord came down in a *pillar of cloud*, and He stood [at] the door of the tent, and He called Aaron and Miriam, and both of them came out.

6And He said, "Hear now My words: if there is a prophet among you, [I] the Lord, in vision I make Myself known to him; in dreams I speak with him.

7Not so is My servant Moses. In all My house he is faithful.

8Mouth to mouth I speak to him, even evidently, and not in dark speeches; and the form of the Lord does he behold. Why then were you not afraid to speak against My servant, against Moses?"

9And the *anger of the Lord glowed* against them, and He went away.

10And *the cloud* departed from above the tent, and behold Miriam [was] leprous (*m'tsora-at*) as snow.e And Aaron turned to Miriam, and behold, [she was] leprous (*m'tsoraw-at*).

e. *m'tsora-at*, 6879

11 And Aaron said to Moses, "Oh my lord, I beg you, do not lay sin on *us* by which *we* have done foolishly and by which *we* have sinned."

13And Moses in turn cried to the Lord saying, "O God, heal her, I pray You."

14And the Lord spoke to Moses: "If her father had but spit in her face, would she not be ashamed seven days? Let her be shut up seven days outside of the camp, and after that she will be brought in [again]." (Num. 12:1–14)

It is easy to conclude that God punished Miriam because she and Aaron spoke against Moses, but what happened to her was incidental to God speaking to them. God's purpose seemed merely to give them a good tongue-lashing. However, since in addition to the scolding Miriam had been exposed to the cloud, she suffered what was the typical reaction to it. That reaction was not leprosy as it is usually translated. It has long been recognized that there is no relation between the various forms of Hansen's Disease and the symptoms that Miriam suffered, or those described in detail in Leviticus 13 and 14 as making the victim unclean for that matter. So, if it wasn't leprosy that afflicted Miriam, then what was it? And why weren't Moses and Aaron also affected?

Leprosy

To answer the first question, let's look at the words contemporary observers used to describe Miriam's problem. The Hebrew verb for being struck with leprosy is *tsawrah*.[f] The technical term for a person declared by the priest to be leprous is *m'tsoraw*.[3] The noun for leprosy is *tsawra-at*.[g] *Tsawra-at* has always been considered some sort of disease, but a look at the word and its relatives implies something else.

f. *tsawrah*, 6879

g. *tsawra-at*, 6883

Leviticus 13–14 uses the words translated leper(s), leprosy, or leprous a total of 34 times. This passage refers to the laws pertaining to the handling of leprosy and the leper. Outside of Leviticus the three words appear rarely:

- leper(s): once in Numbers, once in 2 Samuel, five times in 2 Kings, three times in 2 Chronicles
- leprosy: once in Deuteronomy, four times in 2 Kings
- leprous: once in Exodus, twice in Numbers, once in 2 Kings, once in 2 Chronicles

Slow Burn

Tsawra-at has nothing to do with a disease. It actually denotes "burn." Note how the following words also have the Hebrew letters *tsawday-resh* as their first two letters and have burn as their basic meaning.

(1) The noun *tsawrebet*, while usually translated "scar," actually means "burn."[h] In Leviticus 13:23 *tsawrebet* means "burn" or

h. *tsawrebet*, 6867

"scorch." In the following books, the verb form *tsawrab*, meaning
to burn or scorch is shown only once; the adjective *tsawrawb*,
meaning burning or scorching, is shown once.[i]

i. *tsawrab*, 6866; Ezek. 20:47; *tsawrawb*, 6867 (fem. of *tsarawbet*); Prov. 16:27

(2) *Tseeraw* is translated "hornet."[j] Its three references are to
the Lord sending hornets to drive out the inhabitants of Canaan
before the arrival of the Israelites, but the actual verses strongly
contradict the concept of hornets having the capability to do
this task.[k]

j. *tseeraw*, 6880

k. Exod. 23:28; Deut. 7:20; Josh. 24:12

> [28]"And I will send the hornet before you and it will drive out the Hivite, the Canaanite, and the Hittite from before you.
>
> [29]I will not drive him out from before you in one year lest the land become a desolation and [there] multiply against you the beast of the field.
>
> [30]Little by little I will drive him out from before you, until you be increased, and you will possess the land." (Exod. 23:28–30)

Certainly hornets would not be able to drive out whole
populations "little by little" so that the Israelites could possess
the land over a period of time. Also, logically, the hornets would
have affected the Israelites as well. In fact, while there are
different explanations, very few commentators seemed to think
hornets were literally meant:

- Abraham Ibn Ezra, born in Spain in 1092, says, "The word connotes a disease which weakens the body." Regarding Deuteronomy 7:20, he said *tseeraw* is "a form of leprosy."[4]
- Physician Jonah Ibn Janah, born in Spain around 990, said *tseeraw* means "pestilence."[5]
- *The JPS Torah Commentary: Exodus* (*JPS Exodus*) translates *tseeraw* "plague." It describes *tseeraw* as a campaign brought on Canaan by a succession of Pharaohs.[6]
- Strong's says *tseeraw* is from *tsawraw*.[l] *Tsawraw* means leper, leprous.[7]

l. *tsawraw*, 6869

Whatever *tseeraw* is in actuality isn't the important point.
What is important is that the result, described by a *tsawday-resh* word, relates to burning or stinging and was a Lord-related

phenomenon. Possibly, "hornets" was the best observers could do at the time.

(3) *Tsawday-resh* is seen in *tsor*, knife, in Exodus 4:25 and following books.[m] It is a knife made of flint and is therefore related to "rock," *tesoor*.[n] The pain inflicted by sharp flint would certainly relate to burning.

(4) The burning idea is found in following books in the word *tsawraf*.[o] Fuerst says *tsawraf* means "to glow, to burn ... to smelt."[8] BDB says it is used as "smelt, refine," the operation to produce silver or gold by melting away the impurities over an intensely hot fire.[9]

m. *tsor*, 6864

n. *tesoor*, 6697

o. *tsawraf*, 6884

OTHER LANGUAGES

The study of similar words in other languages proves interesting, as usual. It seems the ancients were at home with the concept of *tsawday-resh* type words connoting burning or hurting. In the Assyrian and Babylonian, I find the following s (pronounced *ts*) words:

Word & Usage	Definition
sarahu A[10] "On the surface his flesh is cool, (while) underneath his bones are burning."	1. to heat, to scorch 2. to be hot, feverish, excitable, angry 3. *surruhu* to keep warm (Middle Assyrian only) 4. to become feverish … angry … hot (Middle Assyrian, Standard Babylonian)
sarahu C[11] "It (the *samanu*-disease) twinkles like a star."	1. to flare up, to display a sudden luminosity, to twinkle (said of stars) (Old Assyrian, Old Babylonian, Mari) 2. to cause to flare up (Standard Babylonian)
sarapu A[12] "A god—I do not know exactly which one—makes my (body) burn." "They (the demons, etc.) make the people living in the cities sick, they make their bodies burn." In literature, "oath and curse burned his body." In the discussion of the word *surrupu*, the point is made that "there seems to be no reason to assume a [meaning] 'to press' or the like … on the basis of an Arabic etymology. All the [references] are shown to belong to *sarapu*, 'to burn,' by the [*Sumerian*] correspondences attested in vocabulary and bilingual passages" (my emphasis). This reference to the Sumerian indicates the extreme age of the original word.	1. to refine (metals by firing), to fire (bricks) cf., Gen. 11:3 (Old Assyrian, Old Babylonian, Mari) 2. to burn 3. *surrupu* to burn … to cause a burning sensation, to groan loudly (?), to melt glass (?) In medical, "if the *dugānu*-disease has taken hold of a man, his epigastrium burns."
saraput[13] HAL relates *saraput* to *tsawraf* and refers to von Soden's translation, "to dye fiery red."[14]	to dye fiery red
sararu B[15]	1. to flash (said mainly of shooting stars) 2. to flit (said of demons) (Standard Babylonian, Neo-Babylonian)
sarhu A[16] *sarhu* can refer to fever.	1. fiery hot 2. a hot dish (Standard Babylonian, Neo-Assyrian)
sarhu C[17] Refers to stars.	glittering (Standard Babylonian)

Word & Usage	Definition
sarpu A[18]	refined (said of silver) (From Old Babylonian on)
sarrisu[19] "May Lady Gula cause a proliferating disease to appear on him."	spreading, proliferating, of rank growth (Middle Babylonian)
sirihtu A[20] cf., *sarahu* A	1. anger 2. inflammation (Standard Babylonian)
siriptu[21] cf., *sarapu* A "If his (the sick person's) throat is spotted with *s*." "While the [Sumerian] equivalents connect *siriptu* with *sarapu* A 'to burn' in the [medical reference] *siriptu* may refer to a red spot and be connected [with] *sarapu* B," which means to dye red, etc.	a burn (a disease) (Middle Babylonian, Standard Babylonian)
sirpu B[22] cf., *sarapu* A	1. fired (clay) object; 2. refining (process) (Old Babylonian Qatna, Neo-Babylonian)
sirsu[23] cf., *surrusu* "If the fungus is speckled with protuberances ..."	protuberance (Standard Babylonian)
surbu[24] cf., *sarahu* A	attack of fever (Middle Assyrian, Neo-Assyrian)
surru A[25]	1. obsidian, flint 2. flint blade (Middle Assyrian, Middle Babylonian, Tel El Amarna tablets, Nuzi, Standard Babylonian, Neo-Babylonian)
surrupu[26] cf., *sarapu* A	refined (said of silver only) (Old Assyrian, Standard Babylonian)

In the Ugaritic, Gordon develops *srp* to equal the Hebrew *tsrf*, meaning "'to purify by fire' ... & *sarpu* 'purified silver.'"[27] DLU translates it "dye red" and refers to *sarapu A*, comparing it to the Hebrew, and translates it "silver ... kind of aromatic gum ... silversmith."[28]

From Old Babylonian on, *sahar* is the Sumerian equivalent of *eperu* and it means "dust, earth, loose earth, debris, *scales*, ore;" *subbu* means "covered" and is equated with the Sumerian *sub. ba*.[29] This seems to be an observer's description of a condition that looked like dust or scales. From Middle Babylonian on, *saharsubbu* (thought to be pronounced *saharshubbu*), a loanword from the Sumerian sachar.sub.ba, means leprosy. *The Chicago Assyrian Dictionary of the Oriental Institute of the University of Chicago* (CAD) lists the following quotes:[30]

- "If leprosy appears on a man's body."
- "He must not eat roast meat (or) he will be covered with leprosy."
- "May Sin clothe his whole body in leprosy which will never lift."
- "You put (wool from a sheep's forehead) either on an unclean man or on a leper." (Standard Babylonian ritual)
- "One who had leprosy has been cleansed and may reenter his house."

Since eating roast meat does not cause Hansen's disease and cleansing a person would not heal him from leprosy, one can surmise that these quotes do not refer to leprosy.

These Hebrew and foreign words are related and have one overriding meaning: "burn." *Tsawra-at* does not mean leprosy, and, moreover, is not even a disease in the accepted sense of the word. Especially in relation to houses and clothing, it is simply not logical to translate it as "disease." *Tsawra-at* is a symptom of a phenomenon being described as well as possible. That phenomenon was the dangerous, radioactive cloud coming into contact with and burning the skin.

Plague of Leprosy

p. *negah*, 5061

Negah tsawra-at, the so-called "plague of leprosy," was the phrase used to describe what affected Miriam.[p] In a later warning to the Israelites, Moses said,

> [8]"Watch out with the *negah tsawra-at* that you watch closely and do all the priests, the Levites, will teach you …

> [9]Remember that which the Lord your God did to Miriam in the way as you came out of Egypt." (Deut. 24: 8–9)

Leviticus 13–14 gives instructions for the handling of a person with *negah tsawra-at*. The laws do not treat *negah tsawra-at* in the sense of a disease, but simply as one of the many things that contributed to the condition of being unclean. Thus, differing from other things that could contribute to uncleanness, there is no category where it is stated, "These are the diseases that will make one unclean and prohibit him from entry into the super-conditioned place."

q. *nawgah*, 5060

The noun *negah* is derived from the verb *nawgah*.[q] *Nawgah* can mean "smite" or "beat," but it primarily means "to touch" in all the Five Books as well as in many of the following ones. Importantly, every use of *nawgah* in Exodus, Leviticus, and Numbers relates to (a) prohibitions against touching radioactive, dangerous/unclean things, or (b) being properly protected when working with sacrificial items.[r] *Nawgah* is translated as "plagued" once in Genesis, where it could just as well be translated as "struck," and twice in Psalms in a non-literal, poetic fashion.[s] Both Psalms references could also be translated "smitten" or among other things, "reach."[t] *Nawgah* is translated "strike" in reference to striking the lintels of the Israelites' doors with blood.[u] It is seen as "smitten" or "struck" in connection with the Lord striking King Uzziah with leprosy.[v]

r. Exod. 19:12, 13, Num. 4:15, 19:11, 13, 16, 21, 22; Lev. 6:11, 6:18

s. Gen. 12:17; Ps. 73:5, 73:14

t. cf., Isa. 53:4, Gen. 28:12

u. Exod. 12:22

v. 2 Kgs. 15:5; 2 Chr. 26:20

Negah is the derivative of great importance; Strong's translates *negah* as follows:

w. Gen. 12:17; Exod. 11:1; Deut. 24:8

x. Lev. 13:42–43; Ps. 38:11; 2 Chr. 6:28–29

y. Isa. 53:8

- plague[w]
- sore[x]
- stricken[y]

- stripe[z]
- stroke[aa]
- wound[ab]

z. 2 Sam. 7:14;
Ps. 89:32
aa. Deut. 17:8, 21:5
ab. Prov. 6:33

All the "sore" references could just as well be translated "plague." Of all the verses where *negah* is found, Psalms 38:11 is the only one that might refer to leprosy: "My friends ... stand aloof from my plague; and my kinsmen stand afar off."

The importance of *negah* is proved by the fact that it shows up 62 times in Leviticus 13 and 14. These chapters describe the rules for dealing with the *negah tsawra-at*. No matter where it is used, *negah tsawra-at* is a phenomenon that is always, intentionally or unintentionally, caused by the Lord. Within the context of the laws, the word *negah* relates over and over to a physical affliction.

Thus, I must conclude that *negah tsawra-at* resulted from proximity to the radioactive cloud. From here forward I replace the traditional "plague of leprosy" translation with what it actually was, "radiation burn."

Four other nouns have been translated "plague:" (1) *negef*, (2) *magayfaw*, (3) *mukaw*, and (4) *deber*.[ac]

ac. *negef*. 5063;
magayfaw, 4046;
makaw, 4347; d
eber, 1698

The first noun, *negef*, is a derivative of *nawgaf*.[ad] In Exodus 32:35, *nawgaf*, in its verb form, is translated "plague:" "And the Lord plagued the people because they made the calf." *Negef* is in Joshua 24:5, which recounts the Lord's plaguing of Egypt. The usual translation, though, is "strike" or "smite," which is the preponderant meaning of the word. All uses of the word refer to a Lord-inflicted phenomenon.[ae] Strong's other meanings are "beat, dash, hurt, slay" and even "stumble" as seen in Jeremiah 13:16. Except in Isaiah 8:14 where it is translated "stumbling" (*nawgaf*), *negef* is translated "blow, striking, plague, pestilence" and "affliction."[31] It is found in Exodus 12:13, 30:12, Numbers 8:19, 16:46–47, 17:11–12, Joshua 22:17 and nowhere else!

ad. *nawgaf*, 5062

ae. Exod. 8:2; Lev. 26:17; Num. 14:42; Deut. 28:25

The second noun, *magayfaw*, is found in the story of the Philistines' capture of the ark.[af] *Magayfaw* also relates to *nawgaf*. In the Five Books, *magayfaw* is only found in 10

af. 1 Sam 6:3–5

ag. Exod. 9:14; Num. 14:37, 17:13, 14, 15, 25:8, 9, 18, 26:1, 31:16

places.[ag] It is translated, "blow, slaughter, plague, pestilence."[32] HAL specifically terms it "plague brought on by God" in reference to Exodus 9:14 where it is plural.[33] HAL also says it is "wound," and again, all references are connected with the Lord. In following books it can also mean "slaughter, stroke."

The third noun, *makaw,* is translated "blow, wound, slaughter," as well as "plague." *Makaw* is derived from *nawchaw,* a common verb found in all Five Books and many following ones meaning "smite, wound, kill."[ah]

ah. *nawchaw,* 5221

The fourth noun, *deber,* is translated "pestilence." HAL relates *deber* to I *dbr,* which has the general meanings of "turn aside, drive away, pursue."[34] II *dbr* comprises the various forms of "speak."[35] With its many shades of meanings, Strong's and BDB relate *deber* to the verb *dabar,* essentially, "to speak."[ai] Directly related to *deber* is the noun *dawbawr,* which also has countless variations.[aj] Basically, *dawbawr* means "word, matter, thing."[36] In fact, where there are negative connotations and translations that might connect them more closely to "pestilence" ("destroyed, disease, hurt"), there either seems to be "a scribal error" or the word "thing" would do just as well.[37] There is no doubt that "word" and "speak" are the major meanings. Most important, to quote BDB, is "word of God, as a divine communication in the form of commandments, prophecy, and words of help to his people, used 394 times."[38] So, if it is true that *deber* is derived from words primarily connoting communication, how did it come to mean "pestilence"? The word appears in Exodus, Leviticus, Numbers, and Deuteronomy a total of only five times. It occurs fairly frequently in the following books as early as 2 Samuel, but especially in Jeremiah and Ezekiel.

ai. *dabar,* 1696

aj. *dawbawr,* 1697

In the following books, *deber* is always mentioned with at least one other punishment, usually sword and famine. In Five Books, it is mostly used alone, e.g., Exodus 9:3, 9:15, and Numbers 14:12. Exceptions are in Exodus 5:3 and Leviticus 26:25 where it is mentioned with a sword. Exodus 5:3 is part of Moses' request to Pharaoh to let the people go to the wilderness to sacrifice to the Lord "lest He strike us with pestilence or with sword."

However, protection from the cloud's effect was the actual reason the Israelites had to sacrifice, which Pharaoh couldn't have understood. Moses probably added "sword" to emphasize the danger of not obeying the Lord.

As to the use of "sword" with *deber* in Leviticus 26:25, both are part of an escalating, sevenfold series of punishments inflicted if the people walked contrary to the Lord.[ak] The punishments include burning fever, crops destroyed by enemies, drought, and attacks by wild beasts.

ak. Lev. 26:14–33

> [25]"And I will bring on you a sword avenging the vengeance of the covenant, and you will be gathered to your cities, and I will send pestilence (*deber*) in the midst of you, and you will be delivered into the hand of the enemy." (Lev. 26:25)

While sword is mentioned in the series of punishments, it is not connected in a literary fashion to pestilence as in the listings in the following books. In this Leviticus verse, the enemy would attack the Israelites with swords and drive them into confined areas. Then, in a completely separate operation, the Lord would send His *deber*. The idea here is that the *deber* would so weaken the people that the enemy would prevail. So this reference to *deber* is quite different from the simple listings of sword, famine, and pestilence usually found in the following books. This same treatment is found in Deuteronomy 28:21. While the passage has a long list of calamities that would befall the Israelites if they didn't obey the Lord, verse 21 isolates "pestilence" but contains no list. In fact, the whole section is similar to the Leviticus 26 wording with one important exception. Both Leviticus 26 and Deuteronomy 28 discuss "pestilence" (*deber*) and "plague" (*makaw*), but in Leviticus 26:21 *makaw* is singular as it should be if speaking of a specific phenomenon. In Deuteronomy 28:59 and 29:21, it is plural, making plagues a general word referring to different kinds of scourges. Thus, Deuteronomy at this point no longer uses plague as a special situation.[al] As to Numbers 14:12, *deber is* isolated, but I will show that it relates directly to a plague (*magayfaw*) that came a little later.

al. cf., Deut. 24:8

As to foreign words that might be helpful, the pickings are slim. There is a very late Babylonian word, *dibiru*, which Von Soden relates directly to *deber* and translates "calamity, distress," "harm, ruin, disaster, mischief," and "evil."[39] CAD says there is no relation.[40] Driver says the root *dbr* means "decease."[41] DLU has the usual translations and does call *dbr* (II) "pestilence, plague."[42] Referring to the Hebrew, however, DLU uses the same passage as Driver for attribution.

None of this explains what *deber* means, and nowhere is there an explanation of its meaning. There are a few hints: *deber* is related to the communication words "to speak" and "word"; *deber* is always Lord-related; and originally, in the early books, *deber* is related directly or indirectly to one of the words for plague. Possibly, *deber* stood completely alone to describe a complex phenomenon that in no way was comprehended by the local peoples.

Given all of this information, "pestilence" must be a mistranslation of *deber*. I believe that *deber* really refers to radiation sickness caused by contact with the cloud. *Deber* must have been such a powerful description at the outset that it was never tampered with later. It is one of the few words describing the dangerous situation surrounding the communication system about which one can make this claim.[43]

Back to Miriam. The reporters described her condition exactly as it was. When exposed to the cloud, she was burned (*m'tsora-at*) and her appearance was as white "as snow."[am] This was a normal reaction, not a miracle.

am. Num. 12:10

God's rather offhanded remark to Moses now makes sense. When Moses pleaded with Him to cure her, the Lord said in effect, "If her father had spit in her face, she would have been banished in shame for a week. So do you think a seven-day quarantine is that big a deal seeing that she was contaminated by My cloud? She'll be fine and able to rejoin the community after the effects have subsided."[an] And that's what happened.

an. Num. 12:14

My rationale for thinking that only a verbal punishment was meant is strengthened by the fact that Aaron was equally guilty and duly scolded, but he did not become exposed. "And Aaron said to Moses, 'Oh my lord, I beg you, do not lay sin on *us* by which *we* have done foolishly and by which *we* have sinned'" (my emphasis).[ao] Aaron, being a priest, was doubtless properly protected against the effects of the cloud.

ao. Num. 12:11

Contamination by Cause

Several times I have alluded to seemingly strange translations of the words *chawtaw*, *chayt*, *chatwaw*, and *chatawt* as "sin" throughout the Bible.[ap] While in the Five Books these words may have meant "to do wrong," I believe that they also had the following, technical meanings: to become contaminated with the dangerous materials in the cloud; to contaminate, that is to trigger a situation on purpose or in error that could lead to contamination or at least to susceptibility to the cloud's effects. From this point forward I will refer to the traditionally translated words for sin as contamination and sin offering as decontamination offering.

ap. *chawtaw*, 2398; *chayt*, 2399; *chatwaw*, 2401, *chatawt*, 2403

Thus, in the Miriam story, Aaron begged Moses not to "lay on *contamination* (*chatawt*)."[aq] He was using the newly adopted technical meaning and evidently was convinced, after the Lord's appearance in the cloud, that Moses had direct influence and could alter the situation. He was afraid he would be affected like Miriam was, thus the "we" and "us." While he probably did not understand the specific cause-effect for Miriam turning white, he knew her problem happened suddenly as a result of something being put on her. Thus, the use of the word *sheet*, which definitely means "to lay" or "put on."[ar] It can also mean "set" (which is the same idea), "show," and in following books, "make" and "stayed."[as] Mostly, it is the idea of putting something on something, e.g., "put" or "lay a hand on," "put ornaments on," "lay a penalty on."[at] So while Aaron was using the technical meaning of *chatawt* to describe a physical change, he felt it resulted from wrongdoing. Thus, he finished the sentence by using the word *chawtaw* in its more commonly understood meaning of "sinning."

aq. Num. 12:11

ar. *sheet*, 7896

as. Exod. 7:23, 23:31; Num. 24:1; Exod. 10:1; Jer. 22:6; Ps. 21:7; Job 38:11

at. Gen. 46:40; Exod. 33:4; Exod. 21:22

So why didn't Aaron turn white? He and Moses must have been properly protected from the effects of the cloud (to be discussed in the Protections chapter).

Uzziah

For another cause-effect example, let's jump all the way to Uzziah (or Azariah), the 10th king of Judah (790–739 BCE), who appears in 2 Chronicles. Uzziah became a mighty king with a fearsome, well-equipped army, but as he became powerful he also became inordinately proud:

> [16]He trespassed against the Lord his God, for he went into the temple of the Lord to burn incense on the altar of incense.
>
> [17]And Azariah the high priest went in after him and eighty priests of the Lord, valiant men.
>
> [18]And they stood up against Uzziah the king, and they said to him, "[It is] not for you Uzziah to burn incense to the Lord, but for the priests of Aaron, who are conditioned to burn incense. Go out of the super-conditioned place for you have trespassed …"
>
> [19]Then Uzziah was angry, and in his hand was a censer to burn incense and he was angry with the priests, and the radiation burn (*hatsawra-at*) rose in his forehead before the priests in the house of the Lord beside the altar of incense.
>
> [20]And Azariah the chief priest and all the priests turned toward him and behold he was burned in his forehead. And they hurried him from there, and he also hurried himself, for the Lord had smitten him.
>
> [21]And Uzziah the king was a burned one (*m'tsoraw*) to the day of his death, and lived in a house set apart, a burned one, for he was cut off from the house of the Lord. (2 Chr. 26:16–21)

Whether the writer of this story understood what was happening or was just reporting, there is a definite cause-effect situation. Uzziah was not protected (conditioned) and he may well have used "strange" incense, i.e., the wrong kind. So what happened was perfectly predictable. When he went into the ark area, which was always dangerous, regardless of whether or not the ark was in use, he was immediately stricken.

Hezekiah

While not specifically mentioning the cloud and the ark, another intrusion into the dangerous ark area was made by the reformer Hezekiah, the thirteenth king of Judah (715–687 BCE). The events in Isaiah 37 and 38 are possibly another example of this cause-effect. During a period of trouble with Assyria, a messenger delivered a threatening letter to the king.

> [14]And Hezekiah went up to the house of the Lord and spread it before the Lord.
>
> [15]And Hezekiah prayed to the Lord saying,
>
> [16]"O Lord of hosts that *sits on the cherubim*." (Isa. 37:14–16)[au]

au. cf., 2 Kgs. 19:14–15

In other words, he went directly into the conditioned place, evidently with no protection. A non-priest should never visit there. Actually, he had done this at least once before, so there is no reason to doubt this was a common practice for him.[av] Then, in a seemingly unrelated event, Isaiah 38:1 says, "In those days Hezekiah was sick unto death." Two separate things happened.[aw] One was supernatural. Isaiah told Hezekiah he was to die. He prayed to the Lord and received a 15-year reprieve. The next was natural. Verse 21 says, "And Isaiah said, 'Let them take a cake of figs and lay it for a plaster upon the inflammation (*sh'cheen*) and he will recover.'"[ax]

av. Isa. 37:1

aw. Isa. 38:2–5

ax. *sh'cheen*, 7822; 2 Kgs. 20:7

Sh'cheen is a common word found in many languages, which generally denotes "heat." In the Ugaritic, *shn* means "feverish" and *sahanu* means "to become warm," "to heat," etc.[45] In the Egyptian, a possibly related word is *shn* meaning "swelling."[46] Thus, while the word is not burn (*tsawra-at*), in this passage the meaning of *sh'cheen* is similar. (There is no mention of *tsawra-at* anywhere in Isaiah, although it is mentioned in 2 Kings.)

So, removing the supernatural and leaving the realistic, it is possible that a writer was unwittingly pointing out that Hezekiah had gone into the danger area and had become almost fatally contaminated. In this case he might have been using *sh'cheen* in a general way to mean burn. This certainly is not the case when speaking of the specific law in Leviticus 13:18–28 where a primary inflammation could have been contaminated with radioactive substance. There is the possibility that Hezekiah might have been likewise contaminated.

The 2 Kings 20:7–8 version of the same story,

> [7]Then Isaiah said, "Take a cake of figs." And they took it and laid it on the inflammation, *and he recovered.*

> [8]And Hezekiah said to Isaiah, "What *will be* the sign that the Lord *will* heal me?"

In this version, the indication may be that the figs cured the local inflammation, but that the total healing of the entire body from contamination lay in the future. One must strip away the magic to try to determine the actual meaning.[ay]

ay. 2 Kgs. 20:9–11

Inside the Philistine Camp

One of the most dramatic episodes relating to the danger of the ark takes place when the Philistines captured the ark. The story illustrates how the people approached a phenomenon they did not understand. It sheds light on the difficulty of translating words or thoughts in the strict context of when the story was set. The whole story, 1 Samuel 4:1–6:21, is well worth a careful read, but the relevant part begins with 1 Samuel 4. The setting is concurrent with the establishment of Samuel as a prophet, prior to the installation of the monarchy. The Israelites had gone out to fight one of their innumerable battles with the Philistines, perennial rivals who were "a sea people who migrated from the Aegean region ... about the first quarter of the 12th century B.C."[47] This time things looked very dark for Israel, so dark that they decided to call for the ark, which had been located at Shiloh, a sanctuary town in the hill country of Ephraim. When the Philistines heard that the ark was on the battlefield, they were terribly frightened because they knew all about it. They knew that where the ark was, that's where God was, and they cried,

> [8]"Woe to us! Who will deliver us from the hand of these mighty gods? These are the gods that struck the Egyptians with all plague(s) in the wilderness." (1 Sam. 4:8)

But they overcame their fright and not only whipped the Israelites but captured the ark. They moved the ark to their temple in Ashdod, "But the hand of the Lord was heavy on the people of Ashdod and He destroyed them and struck them with hemorrhoids (*afoleem*) even Ashdod and the borders."[az] Those who were left got a result of the "plague," which might have been hemorrhoids caused by extreme diarrhea.[48] *Afoleem* is the plural of *ohfel*.[ba] *Ohfel* is translated hemorrhoids, emerods, boils, or tumors.[49] *Apholeem* is the *k'ri* (spoken) word of *t'chor*.[bb] *T'chor* is the *k'tib* (written) word.[50] *T'chor* is only used in the plural, *t'chorim*, meaning ulcers, hemorrhoids.

> [8]And they sent and they gathered all the lords of the Philistines to them, and they said, "What will we do with the ark of the God of Israel?" And they answered, "[To] Gath let be carried about the ark of the God of Israel." (1 Sam. 5:8)

This move did no good. The people of Gath "both small and great" were smitten with *t'chorim*.[bc] So, they sent the ark to Ekron and the same thing happened. The Ekronites were, of course, terrified. They pleaded with the Philistine lords to send the ark back to Israel. "And the men that did not die were smitten with *afoleem*, and the cry of the city went up to heaven."[bd] The desperate Philistines now called on their priests and diviners to help them get rid of the terrible machine. Their advice was to send it back to Israel, but ...

> [3]"If you send away the ark of the God of Israel, send it not empty, but certainly you will return to Him a guilt offering. Then *you will be healed* ..."
>
> [4]Then they said, "What [will be] the guilt offering ...?" And they said, "According to the number of the lords of the Philistines five golden images of the sores[!] (*afolaychem*) and five golden mice for one *plague* (*magayfaw*) was on you all, and on your lords.
>
> [5]And you will make images of your sores and images of your mice that destroy the land." (1 Sam. 6:3–5)

What is becoming clear is that there were two events affecting the Philistines. The first was the plague (*magayfaw*). The second

az. 1 Sam. 5:6

ba. *ohfel*, 6076

bb. 1 Sam. 5:6, 9:12, 6:4, 5

bc. *t'chor*, 2914; 1 Sam. 6:11, 17

bd. 1 Sam. 5:12

was the *afoleem/t'chorim*, understood to be some sort of tumor or hemorrhoids. Making it clearer still are the Septuagint and Vulgate.[51] Referring to the use of *afoleem* in Deuteronomy 28:27, "the interpretation hemorrhoids is supported by the paraphrases in the [Septuagint] and Vulgate here ("in the seat," "in the part of your body from which excrement is cast out") and Arabic *afl/afal*, which refers to swellings and other symptoms in the genital-anal area."[52]

The people were stricken by plague because of their close proximity to the ark, and many died right away. The survivors may have gotten the hemorrhoids because of the extreme diarrhea. Soon it will be clear how important this result is.

While the sores' relation to plague seems to make sense, why the mice? Traditionally, mice were thought to be carriers of the plague, and one explanation is that the mice carried bubonic plague.[53] This is perfectly logical. But following my contention that the ark's massive doses of radiation were responsible for the plague, why were mice involved? Fortunately, this is quite simple. 1 Samuel 6 reads, "And the ark of the Lord was in the field ["pasture" or "territory"] of the Philistines seven months."[54] It is interesting that the Septuagint introduces the mice right here, continuing the verse with, "and their land brought forth swarms of mice."

After the ark had been bounced from city to city, wreaking havoc in its path, the panic-stricken Philistines had simply dumped it in a place outside the populous urban areas, where it stayed for seven months. What populates fields or open areas? Mice! And now the mice, having been exposed to the ark, were contaminated. When they made their way to more populated areas, these radioactive rodents spread the plague far and wide. "For one plague was on you all."[be]

be. 1 Sam. 6:4

The Ark Returns

Remember the conditions at Mount Sinai when God descended? People or animals that came too near the mountain had to be shot or stoned because touching them would have transmitted the radioactivity, which would have resulted in death.^{bf} The Philistines, realizing that just leaving the ark in the bf. Exod. 19:13 open would not solve their problem, finally decided to get rid of it altogether by returning it to Israel. So they put the ark and the images on a cart and sent them over the border to Beth-Shemesh in Israel. If the ark was a miraculous magic maker for the Israelites as one would expect in a proper legend, then the story would end here with the Israelites ecstatically returning it to its rightful place. But what actually happened? The ark was pulled to the field (*sawdeh*) of Joshua the Beth-Shemite where men were working. They were overjoyed to see it and called some Levites, the priest tribe, who took it down from the cart on which it was being hauled. They offered sacrifices, which was nice but not the correct thing to do.

> ¹⁹And He struck among the men of Beth-Shemesh, because they looked into the ark of the Lord, and He struck among the people seventy men, [and] fifty thousand men; and the people mourned because the Lord had smitten among the people [with] a great plague.*

> ²⁰Then said the men of Beth-Shemesh, "Who is able to stand before the Lord, this conditioned God?" (1 Sam. 6:19–20)

* Astonishingly, the word is *makaw*, which can be translated plague and as such would make perfect sense here. I have changed the usual translation "great slaughter" to "great plague" to clarify that these people were not killed as in war, but because they came too near to the ark.

They solved the problem by sending messengers to the inhabitants of Kiriath-Jearim, who came and took the ark "into the house of Abinadab on the hill, and they conditioned Eleazar his son, to keep the ark of the Lord."^{bg} There it stayed under the bg. 1 Sam. 7:1 care of Eleazar for 20 years.

This little end to the story is loaded with significance. Instead of being a nice, friendly magic maker, safe only for God's people, the ark functioned predictably as the dangerous machine it was. It continued to indiscriminately kill anyone who came near it. The Hebrew sentence describing this isn't very clear. Instead of "and He struck among the people seventy men, [and] fifty thousand men," it should probably read something like "and

He struck of the 50,000 men of Beth-Shemesh, 70 men of the people." It would seem inconceivable that 50,000 people came close enough to die from the great plague, but much more possible for 70.

Interestingly, Josephus makes no mention of the 50,000, only the 70.[55] When handling the ark, the rules had to be remembered and respected. Numbers says:

> [18]"Do not cut off the tribe of the families of the Kehothites from the midst of the Levites.
>
> [19]But this do to them that they may live and not die when they approach the super-conditioned place. Aaron and his sons will go in and they will appoint them each man to his service and to his burden.
>
> [20]But they *will not go in to see* for a moment (*bawlah*) the super-conditioned place lest they die."[bh] (Num. 4:18–20)

bh. *bawlah,* 1104

Among *bawlah*'s many meanings, it literally means "swallow." From this comes the saying "until I swallow my spit," implying that even going into the super-conditioned place "for a moment" was mortally dangerous.

It is easy to read that the Lord killed the Beth-Shemites "because they looked into the ark" as though it were a punishment. But it should be clear by now that it was strictly cause and effect. The men had done nothing morally wrong. They had simply violated a natural law. On the other hand, when the ark was finally given into the care of people who knew how to handle it, and they had properly prepared (conditioned) Eleazar, everything was once again under control.

Uzzah's Story

Still another experience with the inevitable danger of the ark is the story of Uzzah, during the reign of King David. David, after beating our old friends the Philistines in yet another battle, made preparations to bring the ark from the house of Abinadab to the new city of Jerusalem. Uzzah and Ahio, sons of Abinadab, were put in charge of driving the cart and oxen, which carried the ark. But…

⁶When they came to the threshing floor of Nacon, then Uzzah reached to the ark of God and he took hold of it; for the oxen stumbled.

⁷And the anger of the Lord was kindled against Uzzah; and God struck him there for his error; and he died there by the ark of God. (2 Sam. 6:6–7)

David was afraid to move the ark any further, so he "carried it aside to the house of Obed-edom the Gittite."[bi] This man was a Levite who later became a doorkeeper for the ark, so he must have known how to handle it.[bj] Finally, after he saw that all was well with Obed-edom, David removed the ark to Jerusalem with great celebration, singing, dancing, and sacrificing. He evidently thought this would protect him or appease God.

bi. 2 Sam. 6:10

bj. 1 Chr. 15:16–24

The word for what Uzzah did is *shal*, generally translated "error."[bk] In this story, 1 Chronicles 13:10 says that the Lord struck Uzzah "because he put forth his hand on the ark." And 1 Chronicles 15 indicates a complete understanding by David of the error he and the priests made, which led to Uzzah's death.[56]

bk. *shal*, 7944

¹¹And David called for Zadok and Abiathar the priests, and for the Levites …

¹²And said to them, "… condition yourselves … that you may bring up the ark of the Lord …

¹³Because you did not [condition yourselves] at first, the Lord God broke through on us because we did not seek Him according to the ordinance." (1 Chr. 15:11–13)

Uzzah had not done anything wrong. If something as important as the ark started to fall, the reflex would be to grab it. Still, the natural law of the ark was in effect. If you touched the machine, it could kill you.[57] Numbers 4:15 spelled it out clearly:

¹⁵"And when Aaron and his sons have finished the conditioning furniture and all the conditioning vessels, as the camp is set forward, after that the sons of Kohath will come to bear them; but they will not *touch* the conditioning things, lest they die." (Num. 4:15)

It was perfectly logical that if you couldn't touch the ark and things that had come in contact with it at the time of Moses and Aaron, it could also be dangerous at a later time.

Joshua even made clear to the people just how near they could get. When the Israelites were to make their momentous crossing of the Jordan River into the promised land, the officers went through the camp:

> ³And they commanded the people saying, "When you see the ark of the covenant of the Lord your God, and the priests the Levites bearing it, then you will remove from your place and go after it.

> ⁴Let there be a space between you and it, about two thousand cubits by measure; come not near to it that you may know the way by which you must go, for you have not passed this way before." (Josh. 3:3–4)

Strange Fire

Remember Moses descending from Mt. Sinai during that period of intense exposure to the cloud and the stones? Here and repeatedly thereafter, the ark with its stones became saturated with radioactivity when the cloud lit on the tent. So the ark was always dangerous to handle.

> ¹²"And he [Aaron] will take a firepan [censer] full of coals of fire from off the altar before the Lord, and his hands full of incense of spices [pounded] fine, and he will bring [it] within the veil. And he will put the incense on the fire before the Lord that the cloud of the incense may cover the covering, which is on the stones, that he die not." (Lev. 16:12)

This precaution was taken after the deaths of Aaron's sons Nadab and Abihu. During the original consecration of the tabernacle, when all of the preparations were finished, "the glory of the Lord appeared to all the people."[bl] Then fire came from before the Lord and consumed the burnt offering made during the consecration process:

bl. Lev. 9:23

> ¹And [there] took Aaron's sons, Nadab and Abihu each man his firepan and they put in them fire, and they put on it incense, and they offered before the Lord strange fire, which He had not commanded them.

²And [there] came forth fire from before the Lord and it
· devoured them and they died before the Lord. (Lev. 10:1–2)

Just as I posited that King Uzziah may have used strange
incense when he went into the Temple, Aaron's sons used the
wrong materials specifically forbidden in Exodus 30:9. So the
environment remained dangerous—"defiled"—especially to
them because they were nearest to the cloud-covered stones.

Incidentally, a remarkable thing happened that strengthens
the argument for the radioactive nature of the cloud. Moses
instructed Mishael and Elzaphan, Aaron's cousins, to carry
Aaron's dead sons outside the camp, "And they came near and
carried them in their coats outside of the camp."[bm] They were   bm. Lev. 10:5
burned to death with their clothes still intact. This suggests
the type of reaction one would expect from a massive dose of
radiation.

Mechanism vs. Misconception

In these examples of the ark's dangerous aspects so clearly
described in the various biblical texts from the time of Moses
to the kings David, Solomon, Uzziah, and possibly Hezekiah,
there is unvarying uniformity. When the cloud transmitted the
dangerous condition first on Mt. Sinai, then on the tent and ark,
the ark soaked up the radiation from the cloud. Thus, it became
highly radioactive and dangerous, and it remained so.

The important point is that as the ark of communication's
use faded in later periods, so did the danger of getting radiation
sickness. The ark itself might still have been very dangerous
because at one time it had been repeatedly covered by the cloud,
but the possibility of the cloud appearing for communication
later on was next to nil. Thus, only those who went unprotected
into the super-conditioned area or who touched the ark would
get burned.

Understandably, there was complete ignorance at the time
about why the ark was dangerous. This is why there is an overlay
of mysticism, which up to now has blurred the fact that it was
a mechanism of some sort, and therefore, like any mechanism,

it had to behave in a uniform manner. It would be much like a television set somehow getting into the hands of some primitive people who had no contact with the civilized world. It would be considered a most awesome thing around which all sorts of customs would grow. Those who touched its insides would receive a terrific shock each time they touched it, and conceivably some would be killed. From the histories of the Israelites, it might be pretty hard to realize that what they were describing was a mechanical device following natural laws in its operation. Fortunately for us today, there is enough detail in the Bible concerning the ark that makes it possible to see through the blur of misunderstanding to the very clear implications behind it.

Chapter 8

Radioactive Fallout
From Moses to the Marshall Islands

Whenever the cloud settled on the ark, the natural laws of protection had to be scrupulously followed or ... BEWARE OF RADIOACTIVE FALLOUT!! Radiation burn ranged in severity from pain to death, so the Lord gave Moses and Aaron detailed instructions for observing and managing it. Anything the radiation touched, living or inert, could be rendered "unclean." It was the cloud-unclean relationship that was of paramount importance in the life and death of the community. All regulation of daily activities vis-à-vis the Lord centered on making certain there was proper balance between them.

Clean and Unclean

Clean and unclean, pure and impure, cleanse and defile— these are the traditional translations. Remember, though, from "Puzzling Laws" that one definition of clean is "producing little or no radioactive fallout or contamination." This technical sense is the one intended in these instructions.

The adjective *tawmay* (unclean) is found in Leviticus, Numbers, Deuteronomy, and following books.[a] It has always been understood in traditional terms, even if it was sometimes used metaphorically, e.g., "the unclean spirit."[b] The verb *tawmay*, translated "defile," is found in Genesis, Leviticus, Numbers, Deuteronomy, and following books.[c] Most of the following translations refer to the defiling of the super-conditioned place, the land, or a woman.[1] There is no question that the people of the time did understand the technical definition of *tawmay*. Sometimes, however, they seemed to disagree with it:

a. *tawmay*, 2931

b. Zech. 13:2

c. *tawmay*, 2930

> [2]All things come alike to all; there is one event to the righteous and to the wicked; to the good and to the clean and the unclean; to him that sacrifices and to him that does not sacrifice; as is the good, so is the sinner, and he that swears, as he that fears an oath. (Ecc. 9:2)

There doesn't seem to be a cognate in the contemporary or more ancient languages. *Tawmay* is used later in Jewish Aramaic and Syriac with traditional meanings. Interestingly, the Samaritan Pentateuch translates *tawmay* as "to be weak, diseased." In later Arabic there is *tammay*, mud, as in "mud of the Nile."[2] In its narrow, technical sense and in light of radiation burn, I believe the adjective *tawmay* means "unclean due to any of several conditions or substances that could attract radiation from the cloud." These could include bodily emissions, certain infections, burns, certain sexual activities, certain dead animals, dead humans, or the blood of a murdered person. Also, under certain conditions, materials such as cloth, leather, brick, mortar, and so on could attract radiation. Thus, the verb *tawmay* is "to make something susceptible to radiation poisoning by creating a condition that could attract radiation from the cloud, thereby preventing the Lord from dwelling safely in the midst of the people because of the danger."

Amazingly, the Five Books only use *tawhor* (clean) in its technical sense.[d] Exodus 24:10 uses the related word *tohar* as "clearness" regarding the stone under the feet of the Lord: "like the body of the heavens for clearness."[e] However, *tohar* is used in the technical sense regarding the chemical cleansing process for woman after childbirth and after menstruation.[f] Following books have no problem with a metaphorical use like clean hearts, hands, eyes, etc.

d. *tawhor*, 2889

e. *tohar*, 2892

f. Lev. 12:4, 6, 15:28

OTHER LANGUAGES

Among *tawhor*'s neighbors is the word *thr* in Ugaritic, meaning a "gem." Gordon says, "(pure) gem."[3] Driver says *thr* and *zhr* mean "gem, jewel," and compares it to *tohar*, "lustre."[4] So the Ugaritic word also emphasizes the clearness, brightness aspect.

The Egyptian is directly comparable. Faulkner says the word *twr* (roughly pronounced *toor*) is "be clean" or "cleanse."[5] Gardiner translates *tw(r)i*, as "be pure."[6] It is probable that, again, an ancient word was borrowed for technical use. That *twr is* very old is shown by the use of the determinant 𓅯 in Faulkner's example. As far as the Egyptians were concerned, with 𓅯 as the determinant, this word for clean was meant to carry the idea of actively doing something to cleanse oneself, which would then lead to Gardiner's word denoting the condition of being pure.

There is another *twr* but with the determinant 𓀃, signifying "praise." It means, "show respect to."[7] Still another word, *tr*, 𓂝𓏏𓀗, also means "respect" and "worship" god.[8] If it is possible to link the two concepts in the Egyptian, "cleanse, be pure" with "respect, worship," it may show why the Hebrews might have borrowed it for their *tawhor* concept. *Tawhor*, then, can be defined as "a condition wherein the danger of the cloud's radiation is either a) minimized because the person or thing is properly protected, or b) removed by washing, sacrifice, etc." Someone or something could also be *tawhor* simply because there was no radiation around. I should note that two references use *tawhor* in relation to incense, and three use it in relation to the menorah.[g] All the rest refer to the gold that is used for the articles in the tabernacle, including that for the menorah. The important point is that *tawhor* related to radiation danger and nothing else.

g. Exod. 30:35, 37:29; Exod. 31:8, 39:37, Lev. 24:4,6

With *tawhor* and *tawmay* clarified, look at Leviticus 13:1–46, which describes in detail the symptoms of radiation burn, *negah tsawra-at*. The comparison to the effects of ionizing radiation is striking!

∞∞

Radiation Burn

[1]And the Lord spoke to Moses and to Aaron, saying,

[2]"When a man will have in the skin of his flesh a rising or a patch or a bright spot, and it turns in the skin of his flesh to radiation burn (*negah tsawra-at*), then he will be brought to Aaron the priest, or to one of his sons the priests.

³And the priest will see the plague (*negah*) in the skin of the flesh; and [if] the hair in the plague is turned white, and the appearance of the plague [is] deeper than the skin of his flesh, it is the radiation burn (*negah tsawra-at*); when the priest sees him, then he will pronounce him unclean (*tawmay*).

⁴But if the bright spot is white in the skin of his flesh, and its appearance is not deeper than the skin, and its hair is not turned white, then the priest will shut up the plague seven days.

⁵And the priest will see him on the seventh day: and if the plague is at a stay in his eyes, the plague is not spread in the skin; then the priest will shut him up seven days a second [time].

⁶And the priest will see him on the seventh day a second time; and if the plague is dim, and the plague is not spread in the skin, then the priest will pronounce him clean (*tawhor*); it is a patch; and he will wash his clothes, and he will be *tawhor*.

⁷But if the patch spread abroad in the skin after he has shown himself to the priest for his *tawhor*ing, then he will show himself a second [time] to the priest,

⁸And the priest will see [him]; and if the patch is spread in the skin, then the priest will pronounce him *tawmay*; it is a burning (*tsawra-at*).

⁹When radiation burn is in a man, then he will be brought to the priest.

¹⁰And the priest will see [him]; and if [there is] a white rising in the skin, and it has turned the hair white, and [there is] quick raw flesh in the rising,

¹¹It is an old burning in the skin of his flesh, and the priest will pronounce him *tawmay*; he will not shut him up, for he is *tawmay*.

¹²And if the burning breaks out greatly in the skin, and the burning covers all the skin of the plagued [one] from his head to his feet as far as it appears to the priest,

¹³Then the priest will see [him]; and if the burning has covered all his flesh, then he will pronounce the plague *tawhor*; it is all turned white; he is *tawhor*.

¹⁴But in the day when it appears in it raw flesh, he will be *tawmay*.

¹⁵And the priest will see the raw flesh, and he will pronounce him *tawmay*; the raw flesh is *tawmay*; it is burning.

¹⁶Or when the raw flesh turns, and it changes to white, then he will come to the priest.

¹⁷And the priest will see him; and if the plague turned to white, then the priest will pronounce *tawhor* the burning; he is *tawhor*.

¹⁸And flesh, when [there] is in its skin an inflammation and it is healed,

¹⁹And [there] is in the place of the inflammation a white rising, or a bright spot, reddish-white, then it will be shown to the priest.

[20]And the priest will see [it]; and if its appearance is lower than the skin and its hair is turned white, then the priest will pronounce him *tawmay*; it is radiation burn; it has broken out in the inflammation.

[21]But if the priest sees it and, behold, [there] is no white hair therein and it is not lower than the skin and it is dim, then the priest will shut him up seven days.

[22]And if it spread abroad in the skin, then the priest will pronounce him *tawmay*; it is radioactive.

[23]But if in its place stay the bright spot, it is not spread, it is the scar of the inflammation and the priest will pronounce him *tawhor*.

[24]Or flesh, when [there] is in its skin a burning by fire, and the quick [flesh] of the burning become a bright spot, reddish-white, or white,

[25]Then the priest will see it; and if the hair is turned white in the spot and its appearance is deeper than the skin, it is [radiation] burning; it has broken out in the [fire] burning and the priest will pronounce him *tawmay*; it is radiation burn.

[26]But if the priest sees it, and, behold, [there] is no white hair in the bright spot, and it is not lower than the skin and it is dim, then the priest will shut him up seven days.

[27]And the priest will see him on the seventh day, if it spread abroad in the skin. Then the priest will pronounce him *tawmay*; it is radiation burn.

[28]And if the bright spot stays in place, it is not spread in the skin, and it is dim, it is the rising of the [fire] burning and the priest will pronounce him *tawhor*; for it is the scar of the [fire] burning.

[29]And a man or a woman, when [there] is in him plague on the head or on the beard,

[30]Then the priest will see the plague; and if its appearance is deeper than the skin, and [there] is in it yellow, thin hair, then the priest will pronounce him *tawmay*; it is a scall; it is a burn of the head or of the beard.

[31]And when the priest sees the radiation of the scall and, behold, its appearance is not deeper than the skin and there is no black hair in it, then the priest will shut up the radiation of the scall seven days.

[32]And the priest will see the radiation on the seventh day; and if the scall is not spread and [there] is not in it yellow hair and the appearance of the scall is not deeper than the skin,

[33]Then he will be shaved, but the scall he will not shave; and the priest will shut up the scall seven days a second [time].

[34]And the priest will see the scall on the seventh day; and if the scall is not spread in the skin and its appearance is not deeper than the skin, then the priest will pronounce him *tawhor*; and he will wash his clothes, and he will be *tawhor*.

³⁵But if the scall spread abroad in the skin after his *tawho*ring,

³⁶Then the priest will see him; and if the scall is spread abroad in the skin, the priest will not seek for the yellow hair. He is *tawmay*.

³⁷But if in his eyes the scall is at a stay, and black hair is grown up therein, the scall is healed. He is *tawmay*.

³⁸And the priest will pronounce him *tawhor*. And a man or a woman, when there is in the skin of their flesh bright spots, white bright spots,

³⁹Then the priest will see [it]; and if in the skin of their flesh are bright spots of a dull white, it is a tetter. It has broken out in the skin. He is *tawhor*.

⁴⁰And a man, when [the hair] is fallen off his head, he is bald. He is *tawhor*.

⁴¹And if from the side of his face [the hair] is fallen off his head, he is forehead bald. He is *tawhor*.

⁴²But when there is in the bald head or in the bald forehead, a reddish-white radiation, it is burning breaking out in his bald head or in his bald forehead.

⁴³And the priest will see him, and if the rising of the radiation is reddish white in his bald head or in his bald forehead, as the appearance of burning of the skin of flesh,

⁴⁴He is a burned man. He is *tawmay*. The priest will surely pronounce him *tawmay*; his radiation is in his head.

⁴⁵And the burned one in whom the radiation is [or, who is radioactive], his clothes will be torn, and [the hair of] his head will go loose, and (upon) his upper lip he will cover, and, '*Tawmay, tawmay,*' he will cry.

⁴⁶All the days that the radiation is in him he will be *tawmay*; alone he will dwell; outside the camp [will be] his habitation." (Lev. 13:1–46)

Visible changes in a person's skin or hair indicated a possibility of radiation burn. If the flesh was raw and broken open, the victim was *tawmay* (unclean). If it then changed to white, he was *tawhor* (clean). If the hair turned yellow and thin, then the victim was *tawmay*. When black hair grew in again, he was *tawhor*. The radiation could hit anywhere on the body or cover it completely.[h] It could stay on the surface or dig deeper into the skin.

h. Lev. 13:12

Is there anything in contemporary literature that can offer us an analogous situation as to these symptoms in humans? Perhaps. A 106-page study entitled *Some Effects of Ionizing Radiation on Human Beings* begins thus:

> On March 1, 1954, an experimental thermonuclear device was exploded at the U. S. Atomic Energy Commission's Eniwetok Proving Grounds in the Marshall Islands. Following the detonation, unexpected changes in the wind structure deposited radioactive materials on inhabited atolls.[9] The radioactive material that floated over the various atolls, Rongelap, Ailinginae, Rongerik, and Utirik, contaminated the residents in varying degrees of intensity. Rongelap received the highest doses of radiation. About two-thirds of the people there "were nauseated during the first 2 days and one-tenth vomited and had diarrhea."[10] Remember, in describing the results of the plague on the Philistines, one was probably hemorrhoids. This could have been caused by extreme diarrhea.

> On the most heavily contaminated island, Rongelap, the fallout was described as a powdery material, "snowlike," which fell over a period of several hours and *whitened* the hair and adhered to the skin. Less striking fallout described as "mist-like" was observed on Ailinginae and Rongerik. (my emphasis)[11]

Remember the discussion of Miriam's appearance in "Danger, Danger"? Her skin became like "snow" when the Lord came down in the cloud.[i] The description of the "less striking fallout" i. Num. 12:10 on two atolls as "mist-like" brings to mind the cloud.

During the first 24–48 hours after exposure, about 25 percent of the Marshallese in the two higher exposure groups experienced itching and a *burning sensation* of the skin ... These symptoms were present to a lesser extent in the Americans on Rongerik Atoll who were aware of the danger, took shelter in aluminum buildings, *bathed* and *changed clothes*. These precautions greatly reduced the subsequent development of skin lesions in this group. (my emphasis)[12]

Leviticus 16:23–24 carefully spells out how the priest had to wash himself when he exited the super-conditioned place where he was exposed to the cloud. Aaron put on his linen garments, made atonement in the super-conditioned place, took off the garments when he was through, bathed, and finally put on his regular garments to finish his work outside the super-conditioned place.

While the monograph on the Marshall Islands incident is a thorough study of the physiological aspects of radiation poisoning, I am most interested in the gross appearance of the skin lesions. As expected, the lesions varied in intensity depending on the amount of fallout. They developed mostly on "exposed parts of the body not covered by clothing during the fallout. The majority of individuals developed multiple lesions … most of which were superficial."[13] As to appearance,

> In the early stages all lesions were characterized by hyperpigmented macules [discolored spots], papules [small elevations in the skin], or raised plaques [patches].[14]

In the Rongelap group, 20 percent developed ulcerative lesions, which was more than on the other atolls. The lesions frequently started out small, one to two millimeters, and then within a few days "tended to coalesce" into larger lesions, with a dry, leathery texture.

> The pigmented stage of the superficial lesions within several days was followed by dry, scaly desquamation [shedding, peeling] which proceeded from the center part of the lesion outward, leaving a *pink* to *white* thinned epithelium [tissue composed of contiguous cells that forms the epidermis or outer layer of skin]. As the desquamation proceeded outward, a characteristic appearance of a central depigmented [in this case whitened] area fringed with an irregular hyperpigmented zone was seen. *Repigmentation* began in the central area and spread outward over the next few weeks leaving the skin of *relatively normal* appearance. (my emphasis)[15]

In the actual pictures of the patients (seen below), areas that were touched by fallout rise up from the rest of the skin, even break into open sores. A few days later, the outer skin peels off, leaving white areas that heal. Eventually, the white areas repigment except if they were deeply affected, in which case they simply remain white, but otherwise are normal. Epilation (removal of hair) was caused primarily by "radiation from the fallout material on the skin."[16] "It was of a spotty nature and was confined almost entirely to the head region."[17] The following photos show hair loss and, near the bald spot, thinning and lighter colored hair. "Regrowth of hair in all individuals commenced some time during the third month after exposure. At the 6 months' examination, complete regrowth of hair, normal in color, texture, and abundance had taken place."[18]

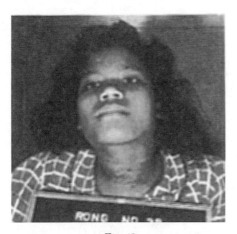

Fig. 43

Plate 1. Early hyperpigmented maculopapular neck lesions at 15 days. Case 39, age 15, F.

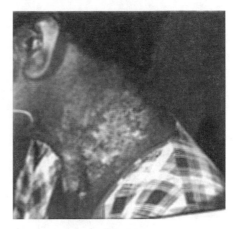

Fig. 44

Plate 2. Neck lesions at 28 days. Wet desquamation. White color is calamine lotion. Case 78, age 37, F.

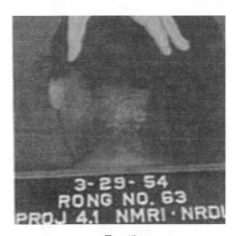

Fig. 45

Plate 3. Neck lesions 28 days post-exposure. Note pigmented and desquamated, depigmented areas. Case 63, age 33, F.

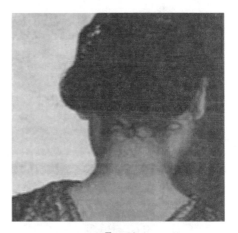

Fig. 46

Plate 4. Same case as in Plate 3, six months after exposure. Neck has healed completely.

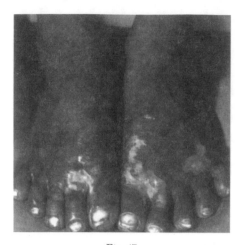

Fig. 47

Plate 5. Hyperpigmented raised plaques and bullae on dorsum of feet and toes at 28 days. One lesion on left foot shows deeper involvement. Feet were painful at this time.

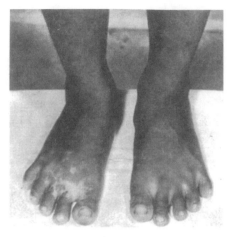

Fig. 48

Plate 6. Lesions 10 days later. Bullae have broken, desquamation is essentially complete, and lesions have healed. Feet no longer painful.

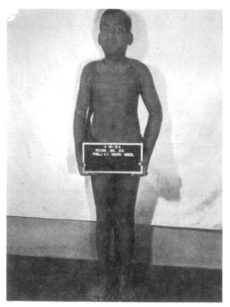

Fig. 49

Plate 7. Lesions 6 days later showing repigmentation except for small scar on dorsum of left foot at site of deepest lesion.

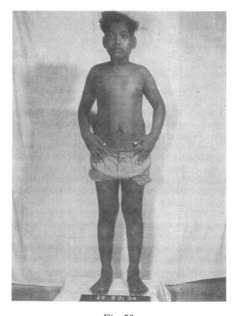

Fig. 50

Plate 8. Same case as in Plate 5, six months later. Foot lesions have healed with repigmentation, except depigmented spots persist in small areas where deeper lesions were.

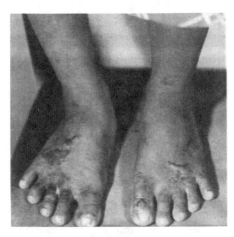

Fig. 51

Plate 9. Foot lesions at 29 days showing deeper involvemenet between 1st and 2nd toes, right foot. Case 26, age 13, M.

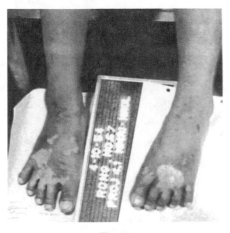

Fig. 52

Plate 10. Same case as in Plage 9, six months after exposure. Note persisting depigmented areas where worst lesions were.

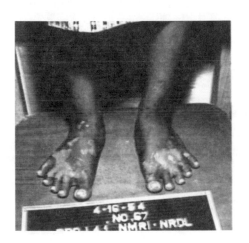

Fig. 53

Plate 11. Extensive lesions in 13 year old boy at 45 days post-exposure. Case 26.

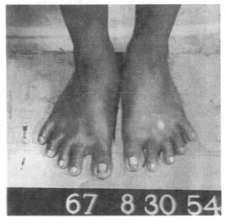

Fig. 54

Plate 12. Same boy as in Plate 11 six months after exposure showing healed lesions and regrowth of hair.

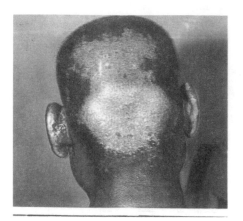

Fig. 55

Plate 13. Desquamation of back of scalp at 28 days. Epilation occurred earlier in desquamated area. Note ulceration of left ear.

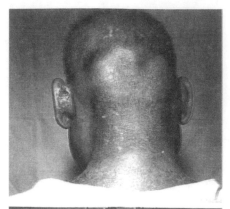

Fig. 56

Plate 14. Same case. Epilation back of head at 46 days. Note persistent ulceration of left ear. Case 79, age 41, M.

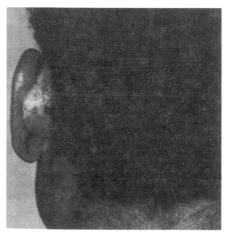

Fig. 57

Plate 15. Same case as in Plate 14 showing complete regrowth of hair of normal color and texture at six months after exposure. Ear lesion has healed with considerable scarring. See Plate 16.

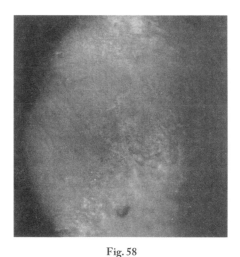

Fig. 58

Plate 16. Ear lesion shown in Plate 15 magnified 20 times. Note atrophy and scaling of scar tissue. Telangiectatic vessels can be seen in the upper part of the picture.

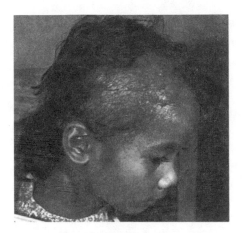

Fig. 59

*Plate 17. Epilation in 7 yr. old girl at 28 days.
Case 72.*

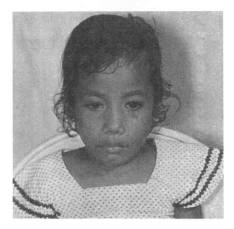

Fig. 60

*Plate 18. Same case as in Plate 17, six months
after exposure showing complete regrowth
of normal hair.*

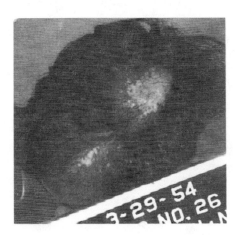

Fig. 61

*Plate 19. Spotty epilation in boy, age 13, at
28 days. Case 26. Note scalp lesions in areas of
epilation. (Same case as in Plates 9–12).*

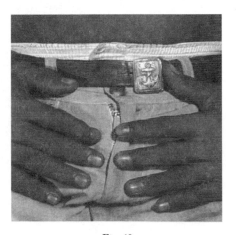

Fig. 62

*Plate 20. Pigmented bands in semilunar area of
fingernails at 77 days.*

There is remarkable similarity between the symptoms described in Leviticus 13:1–29 and those resulting from fallout.

> [2]"When a man will have in the skin of his flesh a *rising* or a patch (*safachat*) or a bright spot, and it will become in the skin of his flesh the radiation burn, then he will be brought to Aaron the priest or to one of his sons the priests." (Lev. 13:2)[j]

j. *safachat*, 5597

Compare these symptoms to the Marshallese elevations and patches. Then compare the spots in the Marshallese that followed the risings and patches by a few days.

Incidentally, I have translated *safachat* here as "patch." The usual translation is "scab," but that is probably incorrect. A meaning more like the Marshallese patches (plaques) is more applicable. Leviticus 13:8 states, "If the *safachat* be spread in the skin … it is a burning." A scab would not spread, but a patch of some sort could. Some Bibles translate the word as "rash." Whether the Egyptian *sfhw*, "excretion," is related is conjectural.[19] *Sapahu*, whose third meaning is "to spread," would seem to fit the bill.[20] Then there is the possibility of ulceration. Leviticus 13:12–13, among other places, points out that as long as the plague is white, even if the body is covered from head to foot, the victim is *tawhor*.

> [14]"But in the day when it is seen in him raw flesh, he will be *tawmay*.
>
> [15]And the priest will see the raw flesh and he will pronounce him *tawmay* …
>
> [16]Or when the raw flesh turns, *and it changes to white* …
>
> [17]And the priest will see him; and if the plague is turned to white, then the priest will pronounce *tawhor* the burning; he is *tawhor*." (Lev. 13:14–17, my emphasis)

The biblical description parallels the Marshallese situation perfectly, because when their skin turned white, the islanders were well on their way back to normalcy.

As to radiation burn on the head, note that "if its appearance is deeper than the skin, and [there] be in it yellow, thin hair, then the priest will pronounce him *tawmay*; it is a scall; it is a burn of the head or the beard."[k] The priest must quarantine him if it

k. Lev. 13:30

is not readily obvious that it is more than skin deep and might spread. Leviticus 13:37 says, "if in his [the priest's] eyes the scall be at a stay and *black hair be grown up* therein, the scall is *healed. He is tawhor.*"[21] This is exactly how the healing of the Marshall Islanders was described.

Yellow

Now I'm going to take a close look at "yellow," *tsawhov*, as it refers to the burned person's "yellow (*tsawhov*), thin (*dawq*) hair."[l] It is only found three times and only in Leviticus 13.[m] No one knows exactly what it means, but the phrase *tsawhov dawq* signifies a change from the normal condition and color, which is black.

For once there is no hint in other early languages. *Tsawhov* is seen in later languages, e.g., the Arabic *sahba,* "to be gleaming like gold."[22] Milgrom opts for "yellow."[23] There is also the word *tsawhav*, which means "fine" according to Strong's and is only used in Ezra 8:28 regarding bowls.[n] Strong's says that it's from a primitive "root meaning 'to glitter,' i.e., to be golden in color," and that the *tsawhov* in question comes from it. BDB says the adjective *tsawhav* means "gleaming, yellow."[24] It says the verb *tsawhav* means "gleam."[o] Relating them, the fact that the similar word *zawhawv* means "gold" might reinforce the idea of both "gleaming" and "yellow."[p] Also, many words beginning with *tsaday-hay, tsaday-chet* have the meaning of "brightness, glowing, parched," etc., but they are mostly in following books.

The most logical reason I can think of for describing the changed appearance of the hair with such a rarely used word is that it was never seen before. The word *tsawhov*, possibly having the combined meaning of yellow and gleam, gives a hint that both phenomena were being described. If, indeed, radiation burn caused hair to shine, its effect on Moses' face on Mount Sinai would be in perfect harmony! Incidentally, did Moses wear a veil at the time so as not to frighten the people and so that they would not become contaminated by the beams that shone from his face? It would seem perfectly possible.

l. *tsawhov*, 6669; *dawq*, 1850
m. Lev. 13:30, 32, 36

n. *tsawhav*, 6668

o. *tsawhav*, 6669

p. *zawhawv*, 2091

The Culprit

Leviticus 13:18–28 shows *tawmay*ness to be the result of radiation burn, not skin problems. Inflammation or burning by fire are in themselves not the cause of becoming *tawmay*.^q In fact, one explicitly remained *tawhor* with these problems. However, if the plague settled in the inflammation and "spread abroad in the skin," then the victim became *tawmay*.^r

q. Lev 13:24–25

r. Lev. 13:22, 27

Another major commonality shared by those with radiation burn and the Marshall Islanders is genetic consequences. Several verses in the Bible refer to the Lord "visiting the iniquity (*avone*) of the fathers on the children down to the third and fourth generation."^s The Hebrew word *avone* is always translated "iniquity" with the connotation of wrongdoing, but a more accurate translation is "impurity," specifically resulting from being contaminated by the radioactive cloud. (See Appendix G for more discussion on *avone*.) The point here is that when one was exposed to the cloud, the effects of its hazardous radioactivity could reach down to the third or fourth generation descendants.

s. *avone*, 5771; Exod. 20:5, 34:5–9, Num. 14:18, Deut. 5:9

In a December 27, 2006 paper titled "Understanding Radiation," the U.S. Environmental Protection Agency says about ionizing radiation,

> Genetic effects are those that can be passed from parent to child. Health physicists estimate that about fifty severe hereditary effects will occur in a group of one million live-born children whose parents were both exposed to one rem [of radiation]. About one hundred twenty severe hereditary effects would occur in all descendants.

The Washington State Department of Health's Hanford Health Information Network published "An Overview of Hanford and Radiation Health Effects" on July 16, 2004. Hanford was a former nuclear weapons site in Washington. It "released radioactive material into the air, water and soil." Releases were made partly from operations, partly accidentally, and partly intentionally. "Many of those who lived in areas downwind from Hanford or who used the Columbia River downstream from Hanford received doses of radiation. Those doses may have caused health problems or might cause them in the future." The report explains: "If the damage is passed on when new cells are formed there may be a delayed health, such as cancer or genetic effects." A sidebar says, "Radiation exposure may be internal or external. Internal exposure comes from eating or drinking contaminated food or water, or from breathing contaminated air ... Both internal and external radiation can directly harm cell."

Specifically referring to the radiation effects on the Marshallese, a paper by Drs. Nussbaum and Köhnlein reports the following:

> Medical examination of 297 children and 147 adults from Rongelap atoll – 34 years after the inhabitants had been affected by the fallout and environmental contamination caused by the explosion – were combined with data from earlier medical testing and a radiological survey sponsored by U.S. governmental agencies. The health survey showed dose-related increases in miscarriages, stillbirths, neonatal and infant deaths, *congenital defects,* thyroid cancer, and leukemia, together with a general deterioration of health. (my emphasis)[25]

Probably the most horrendous description of the genetic effects of radioactive fallout is by Matthew Chance in a CNN report dated August 31, 2007. In his report titled "Inside the Nuclear Underworld: Deformity and Fear," he describes what happened to the inhabitants of the Soviet city of Semipalatinsk, now Semey, Kazakhstan.

> Decades of Soviet nuclear testing unleashed a plague of birth defects ... Almost every family ... is affected—from cancers to impotency to birth defects and other deformities ... The problem of defects is so big, there's even a museum of mutations ... It's a small room filled with jars containing deformed fetuses and human organs preserved in formaldehyde.

The most amazing testimony was in the video that accompanied the story. It was by a woman whose face was horribly deformed by the testing. She was born two years after the tests ceased. She said that her daughter was also born with a deformity, meaning that the results had extended to the third generation.[26]

The explosion of a nuclear reactor in Chernobyl, Russia affected everything from buildings to clothes. It was so dangerous that the entire area had to be avoided. To a lesser extent, the same phenomena occurred in the Bible. Leviticus 13:47–59 describes what happened to garments, and Leviticus 14:33–53 speaks of when God "put radiation burn in a house in the land of your possession."

Radiation Burn in Garments

⁴⁷"And the garment, when [there] is in it radiation burn, in a woolen garment or in a linen garment

⁴⁸Or in warp or in woof of linen or of wool or in a skin or in anything made of skin,

⁴⁹And the plague is greenish or reddish in the garment or in the skin or in the warp or in the woof or in any article of skin, it is the radiation burn; and it will be shown [to] the priest.

⁵⁰And the priest will see the plague, and he will shut up the plague seven days.

⁵¹And when he sees the plague on the seventh day that the plague has spread in the garment or in the warp or in the woof or in the skin, for whatever skin is used in service, the plague is an erupting burning. It is *tawmay*.

⁵²And he will burn the garment or the warp or the woof in the wool or in the linen or any article of skin wherein the plague is, for it is an erupting burning; with fire it will be burned.

⁵³And if the priest sees and, behold, the plague has not spread in the garment or in the warp or in the woof or in any article of skin,

⁵⁴Then the priest will command that they wash [the thing] wherein the plague is, and he will shut it up seven days a second time.

⁵⁵And the priest will see after the plague has been washed, and if the plague has not changed its appearance and the plague has not spread. It is *tawmay*; you will burn it with fire; it is a fret in its inside or in its outside.

⁵⁶And if the priest sees, and behold, the plague is dim after its being washed, then he will tear it out of the garment or out of the skin or out of the warp or out of the woof,

⁵⁷And if it appears again in the garment or in the warp or in the woof or in any article of skin, it is a spreading [plague]; you will burn with fire that where the plague is.

⁵⁸And the garment or the warp or the woof or any article of skin that you will wash, and [if] the plague depart from them, then it will be washed a second time and it will be *tawhor*.

⁵⁹This is the law of the radiation burn of a woolen or of linen or of the warp or of the woof or of any article of skin, to pronounce it *tawhor*, or to pronounce it *tawmay*." (Lev. 13:47–59)

Radiation Burn in Houses

³³And the Lord spoke to Moses and to Aaron, saying,

³⁴"When you are come into the land of Canaan, which I give to you for a possession, and I put the radiation burn in a house of the land of your possession,

³⁵Then will come he to whom the house belongs. And he will tell (to) the priest, saying, '[Something] like a plague has appeared to me in the house.'

³⁶And the priest will command that they will empty the house before the priest goes in to see the plague, that it will not become *tawmay* all that is in the house.

³⁷And afterward the priest will go in to see the house. And he will see the plague; and if the plague [is] in the walls of the house [with] cavities, greenish or reddish, and their appearance is lower than the wall,

³⁸And the priest will go out of the house to the door of the house, and he will shut up the house seven days.

³⁹And the priest will return on the seventh day, and he will see [it]; and if the plague is spread in the walls of the house,

⁴⁰Then the priest will command that they take out the stones in which the plague is, and they will cast them outside of the city into a *tawmay* place.

⁴¹And the house he will cause to be scraped within round about and they will pour out the mortar, which they scraped off, outside of the city into a *tawmay* place.

⁴²And they will take other stones, and they will put [them] into the place of those stones; and other mortar he will take, and he will plaster the house.

⁴³And if the plague come again, and it break out in the house, after he has taken out the stones and after he has scraped the house and after it has been plastered,

⁴⁴Then the priest will come and see [it]; and if the plague is spread in the house, it is an erupting burn in the house. It is *tawmay*.

⁴⁵And he will break down the house, its stones, and its timber and all the mortar of the house, and he will bring [them] out outside of the city into a *tawmay* place.

⁴⁶And he that goes into the house all the days that it is shut up will be *tawmay* unto the evening.

⁴⁷And he that lies in the house will wash his clothes; and he that eats in the house will wash his clothes.

⁴⁸But if the priest will come in and see [it] and, behold, the plague has not spread in the house after the house was plastered, then the priest will pronounce *tawhor* the house, because the plague is healed.

⁴⁹And he will take to *tawhor* the house two birds and cedar wood and scarlet yarn and hyssop.

[50]And he will slaughter one of the birds in an earthen vessel over running water.

[51]And he will take the cedar wood and the hyssop and the scarlet yarn and the living bird, and he will dip them in the blood of the slaughtered bird and in the running water. He will sprinkle upon the house seven times.

[52]And he will *tawhor* the house with the blood of the bird and with the running water and with the living bird and with the cedar wood and with the hyssop and with the scarlet yarn.

[53]But he will let go the living bird outside of the city to the open field; thus will he make atonement for the house; and it will be *tawhor*.

[54]"This is the law for any radiation burn and for a scall

[55]And for the burn of a garment and for a house

[56]And for a rising and for a scab and for a bright spot,

[57]To teach when it is *tawmay* and when it is *tawhor*. This is the law of [radiation] burn." (Lev. 14:33–57)

The symptoms that manifested in both houses and garments were described in the same way. The radiation produced a reddish or greenish color in the walls of the house and in the fibers of the garments.[27]

The garments had to be observed by the priest over a period of days. If the plague persisted or spread, the cloth or skin had to be burned. If it was possible to cut the plague out of the material, then washing was all that was necessary to restore it to usefulness.

If the plague spread in a house, the house had to be dismantled and taken to a *tawmay* place (waste dump?) outside the city. If the stones that contained the plague could be removed and if the plague did not reappear, then a conditioning process had to be executed. Interestingly, it was the same conditioning process that was performed when a person recovered from radiation burn.

[3]"And the priest will go to the outside of the camp, and the priest will look and … if the radiation burn is healed in the burned one,

[4]Then the priest will command and he will take from him who is to be *tawhor*ed two *tawhor* living birds and cedar wood and scarlet and hyssop;

[5]And the priest will command and he will kill the one bird on an earthen vessel over running water,

[6]And he will take the living bird and the cedar wood and the scarlet and the hyssop and will dip them and the living bird in the blood of the killed bird over the running water.

⁷And he will sprinkle on him who is to be *tawhor*ed seven times and will pronounce him *tawhor*. And he will send the living bird to the open field." (Leviticus 14:3–7)

Finally, a most important point to be deduced from this section is that Leviticus 14:34 says quite literally it is God who will put the plague in a house. Why He would do this is never stated. Thus, it can be concluded that the phenomenon was an accidental concomitant to the communication process. That is, as the cloud traveled to or from the ark, sometimes the radioactivity from the cloud would fall indiscriminately. The precautions the homeowner had to take and the operations needed to repair the contaminated garments were typical of what one does today to decontaminate an area afflicted with a harmful substance, especially a substance that could spread. That it could spread is clear, because when a house was suspected of having plague, the first thing the priest did was to command that all belongings be removed "that it will not become *tawmay*, all that is in the house."ᵗ So much of what we know about the effects of ionizing radiation today seem to coincide with the description of *negah tsawra-at* several thousand years ago.

t. Lev. 14:36

Chart C—Radioactive Fallout	
BIBLE	**MARSHALL ISLANDS**
General Appearance	
The cloud came down and the anger of the Lord "glowed." The result was that Miriam's skin became white "as snow." (Num. 12:10)	Fallout described as "snow like." It whitened hair and adhered to skin. The fallout was "mistlike" on more distant atolls. This was reminiscent of the Bible's radioactive cloud.
Effect on Skin	
Unclean: rising, scab, patch, bright spot—reddish-white, inflammation, flesh raw, broken open. Clean: skin eventually changed to white. (Lev. 13)	Lesions appeared in discolored spots, elevations in the skin, and ulcerations in highly exposed people. Skin turned to white and eventually became normal.
Hair	
Unclean: turned "yellow" and thin from plague (scall). Person *tawmay*. Clean: if plague stopped and black hair returns. (Lev. 13)	Fallout caused hair loss. Remaining hair thinner, lighter color. After 6 months normal color hair returned.
Washing	
Garments were washed after exposure to plague. (Lev. 13)	Americans washed clothes and bathed to get rid of contamination.
Diarrhea	
Diarrhea could have been the cause of the Philistines' hemorrhoids. (1 Sam. 5:6)	Diarrhea was one of the symptoms caused by fallout.

Chapter 9

Priestly Protections

The ever present danger of radiation burn required the priests to take scrupulous precautions when working around the ark in the super-conditioned place, especially when the cloud settled over the ark cover. In fact, there was a long list of protective measures the priests had to use, including washing with water, wearing special clothing, and using a variety of materials such as blood, fat, and meat from animals, oil, bread, meal, alcohol, and specially prepared incense.

Most of these protections were effective because they covered people and/or things. Covering was the crucial concept of the protective process. (I explain this fully in the Congregation Covers chapter.) The Five Books use several words for "cover," including *chawfaf, kawsaw, kawsaw* (with a sin), *nawsach, sawchach, mawsawch,* and *keeper,* the most important in this context.[a] Though usually translated "atone," *keeper* and words related to it do mean "cover," and I will use them as such from this point forward.

a. *chawfaf,* 2653 (Deut. only); *kawsaw,* 3680; *kawsaw,* 3780 (Deut. only); *nawsach,* 5258; *nesech,* 5262; *kofer,* 3724; *keeper* (piel of *kawfar*), 3722

The laws for using the protections reveal that, rather than offerings to propitiate the Lord as is traditionally thought, they were indeed protections. Some were used in the communication process and others were necessary because of the peoples' proximity to the dangerous cloud.

Water

Washing with water was a simple precaution the priest had to take to be sure that any contamination was removed before entering the dangerous area. "With this will Aaron come into the super-conditioned place … and he will bathe his flesh in water."[b]

b. Lev. 16:3–4

Also, upon exiting the super-conditioned place, the priest used water as it is used today to wash away radioactive particles. "And Aaron will come into the tent of meeting [from the super-conditioned place], and he will take off the protective garments, which he put on when he went into the super-conditioned place ... And he will bathe his flesh in water."[c]

c. Lev. 16:23–24

If the priests failed to wash before or after working in the dangerous area, death would ensue.

> [18]"Then you will also make a laver of copper and its base of copper for washing; and you will put it between the tent of meeting and the altar, and you will put water there.

> [19]And Aaron and his sons will wash from it their hands and their feet.

> [20]When they go into the tent of meeting, they will wash [with] water *that they die not;* or when they come near the altar to minister, to burn a fire offering to the Lord.

> [21]And they will wash their hands and their feet that *they die not*; and it will be a perpetual statute to him and to his seed for their generations." (Exod. 30:18–21, my emphasis)

Clothing and Devices

Once washed, the priests put on their uniforms. Much of what the high priest wore was part of the communication mechanism.[d] However, Exodus 28:31–43 also details other articles of clothing and various devices that had to be worn when entering the tent of meeting in order to prevent death. This passage is a treasure trove of difficult, mistranslated, and important words. Grappling and finally making sense of them was a challenge, but doing so opened a view to the mechanism with which these people were endowed and the enormous influence it had over their daily lives.

d. Exod. 28:4–30

The Robe of the Ephod

> [31]"And you will make the robe of the *ephod* all blue.

> [32]And its head-opening will be in its middle; its opening will have a binding round about, the work of the weaver;

it will have an opening like a coat of mail so that it will not be torn."
(Exod. 28:31–32)

It was very important to make the binding around the neck of the robe tear-proof. This spot was most vulnerable to wear and tear, and a rip in a weakened area would expose the skin to radiation.

Bells and Pomegranates

> [33]"And you will make on its hems pomegranates of blue and purple and scarlet on its hems round about, and bells of gold between them round about,
>
> [34]A golden bell and a pomegranate on the hems of the robe round about.
>
> [35]And it will be on Aaron to minister. And its sound will be heard when he goes into the conditioned place before the Lord and when he comes out, *that he die not.*" (Exod. 28:33–35, my emphasis)

The high priest used the bells as some sort of protective or warning device. He utilized their ringing when going in or out of the super-conditioned place to avoid grave consequence, "that he die not." Nothing else is said about the use of the bells in the Five Books.

The painstaking descriptions of the ancient historian Josephus add nothing to our knowledge. Comments by Jeshua Ben-Sirach, the Hebrew sage who lived around 180 BCE, are of little help, except possibly to show that he was leaning on the description in the Five Books with no more supplementary aid than is available today.

> God encompassed Aaron with pomegranates and with many golden bells round about, that as he went there might be a sound and a noise made that might be heard in the temple for a memorial to the children of his people.[1]

It may be that the famous Biblical and Talmudic commentator R. Samuel ben Meir (known as Rashbam, ca. 1090–1174) was unwittingly on the right track in explaining that when those around the temple heard the bells, they would immediately evacuate the area:

> [17]"And no man will be in the tent of meeting when he goes in to cover in the conditioned [place] until he comes out; and he will cover for himself and for his household and for all the assembly of Israel." (Lev. 16:17)

The pomegranates were made of blue, purple, and scarlet *mawsh'zawr* . As I have shown in the Walkie Talkie chapter, *mawsh'zawr* could mean conditioner or protector when used with blue, purple, and scarlet. It is probable that bells and pomegranates together constituted some type of protective device. After all, they were part of the conditioning garments, but how it worked is still unclear.

The Plate of Pure Gold

> [36]"And you will make a plate of pure gold, and you will engrave on it … CONDITIONED TO THE LORD.
>
> [37]And you will put it on a wire of blue, and it will be on the miter; on the front of the miter it will be.
>
> [38]And it will be on Aaron's forehead and Aaron will bear the iniquity of the conditioned things, which the Israelites will condition in all their conditioning gifts; and it will be on his forehead continually for acceptance for them before the Lord." (Exod. 28:36–38)

e. *tsitz*, 6731

f. *tsootz*, 6692

g. Num. 17:33

h. Exod. 28:36, 39:30, Lev. 8:9

The word used for "plate" is the noun *tsitz*.[e] It is interesting that it is said to derive from *tsootz*, a verb that means "to bloom, blossom, flourish, shine, gaze."[f] Thus, *tsitz* is said to mean "blossom, flower, plate, wing, shining thing."

A "blossom" or "bud" is what appeared on Aaron's staff, but not the rebels' when exposed to the ark.[g] "Flower" is seen in Job, Isaiah, 1 Kings, Psalms, but not the Five Books. "Wings" is used once in Jeremiah 48:9: "Give wings (*tsitz*) to Moab, for it will fly away and its cities shall be a dessert without an inhabitant in them." It's fascinating that the equivalent verse in the Septuagint, Jeremiah 31:9, uses a completely different translation, "Set marks upon Moab, for she shall *touch* with a plague-spot [or "kindled with a carbuncle"], and her cities shall become desolate; whence shall there be an inhabitant for her?"[2] This "touch" is the equivalent of the verb *nawgah*, from which *negah*, "plague," is derived.[3] However, *tsitz* is only used three times as "plate" and then always in connection with *the* plate of the high priest.[h]

OTHER LANGUAGES

What can other languages tell us about the *tsitz*? In the Old Babylonian, *sissatu* is "an ornament." (In the Babylonian and Ugaritic, the s is pronounced ts.) The quote used in CAD is a "necklace (having) on it one golden s ornament with a lapis lazuli (and) *dušû*-stone inlay." The comment following says, "to be connected with Heb. *sis* (pl. *sissim*) denoting golden floral ornamentation."[4] The CDA calls it a "floral ornament" and says it is West Semitic spoken at Qatna or Tel Mishrifreh.[5] Milgrom says *sissatu* is a "'flower ornament' passed into the Egyptian *didi* 'flower' (as a form of ornamentation)."[6] HAL refers to the Egyptian (*dd*) and translated *tsitz* "flowers, blossoms," "rosette, medallion."[7] Driver translates the Ugaritic word *ss* as "forelock."[8] Pritchard translates it as "frontlet."[9] Pritchard puts the phrase containing the word in italics, designating a doubtful translation. In his footnote 11, he says that the Ugaritic *ss* may equate with the Hebrew *sîs*, and references Exodus 28:36, the commandment to make the plate. Driver equates it with the Hebrew *sis*, "diadem," and *sisit*, "hanging forlock" or "tassel."[10] HAL gives another translation of *tsitz*, "salt," and Gordon and DLU translate the Ugaritic *ss* as "salt mine."[11]

There is a remarkable similarity between a passage in the famous Ugaritic Baal epic and Ezekiel 8:2–5. After Baal's victory over an enemy, his sister Anat loyally finished the job by smashing the remaining foes to pieces. She recounts her grizzly deed:

> I have smitten ... El's bitch the *fire*, made an end of El's daughter the blazing *flame*. I have fought and become possessed of the gold of him who drove Baal forth from the *heights of the north* (*spn*), dragged (him) by the *forelock* (*ss*) and slit his ears, banished him from the throne of his kingship. How many foes will rise up against Baal, enemies against the rider on the clouds? (my emphasis)[12]

The Ezekiel passage reads as follows:

> [2]Then I beheld, and lo a likeness as the *appearance of fire*: from the appearance of his loins and downward, *fire*; and from his loins and upward, as the appearance of brightness, as the color of electrum.

> [3]And the form of a hand was put forth, and I was taken by a *lock* (*tsitzit*) of my head; and a spirit lifted me up between the earth and the heaven and brought me in the visions of God (*Elohim*) to Jerusalem, to the door of the gate of the inner court that faces *north where was the seat of the image* of jealousy, which provokes to jealousy.

> [4]And behold, the glory of the God (*Elohim*) of Israel was there ...

> [5]Then said He to me, "Son of man, lift up your eyes ... *toward the north*." So I lifted up my eyes ... toward the *north, and beheld northward* of the gate of the altar this *image* of jealousy in the entry. (Ezek. 8:2–5, my emphasis)

In the Baal story, the chief god El's daughter is described as *fire*, *est* (pronounced *aysht*). In Ezekiel, God (*Elohim*) is described as the appearance of *fire* (*aysh*).[i] In the Baal verses, Baal's throne resides in the "heights of the *north* (*tspn*)." In Ezekiel, "toward the *north* (*tsawfone*)" is the "image of jealousy."[j] It seems that the "image of jealousy" was Baal. In fact, in C. G. Howies' outline, he calls Ezekiel 8:1–6 the "Baal Image."[13] If that is correct, this is a first-hand view of the Canaanites' and Hebrews' opposing attitudes toward Baal. What is interesting is that Ezekiel used the word *tsitzit* to mean forelock just as *ss* means forelock in Ugaritic, and this is the only time *tsitzit* is used as such in all the books of the Bible.[k] So it is conceivable that Ezekiel picked up *tsitzit* and the elements of the Baal epic from these writings

i. *aysh,* 784

j. *tsawfone,* 6828

k. *tsitzit,* 6734

somewhere along the line. It has often been noted that there are many similarities between Ugaritic and biblical writings. However, Ezekiel could have gotten his general images from writings such as Exodus 24:17 and Numbers 9:15–16. In any case, the meaning "forelock" or even "frontlet" is extremely ancient, regardless where or how Ezekiel learned of it.

So tsitzit (f.)-tsitz (m.) is something worn in front. Early forms of the words indicate direction or position more than anything else. The high priest wore a tsitz made of gold on the forehead. This meaning, rather than that of something gleaming or shining, seems to be the more accurate one, though being gold may have contributed to its "shining" meaning. Even when used as "fringe" in its only other mention in Numbers, the tsitz was worn in front.[l] Otherwise, it would not have been seen. If the description of the Old Babylonian sissatu as a golden ornament worn on a necklace is a guide, then even though the flower idea dominated, this too is an indication of something carried in the front. In this case, the sissatu and the plate were both gold.

l. Num. 15:38, 39

~~~~~~

The Miter

Now comes a puzzling problem. Exodus 28:36 is a clear command to fasten the tsitz to the miter.[14] The miter was probably a turban because the word means "to wind about." Exodus 29:6 however reads, "And you will set the miter on his head and you will put the conditioning crown on the miter." Then Exodus 39:30 says, "And they made the tsitz, the conditioning crown, pure gold, and they wrote on it ... 'CONDITIONER TO THE LORD.'" Leviticus 8:9 says, "And he set the miter on his head, and he set on the miter on its forefront the golden tsitz, the conditioning crown, as the Lord commanded Moses."

What conditioning crown? The Hebrew for crown is nezer.[m] The commentaries say the conditioning crown refers to the plate of gold (tsitz). For instance, Sarna says, "tsits is ... either identical with or associated with the nezer."[15] Hertz and HAL say that the gold plate is a crown or diadem.[16] However, there has been no previous reference to a crown, and there seems to be no reason to use two different words for the same thing. So, if tsitz described the object worn on the high priest's forehead, what does nezer really mean?

m. nezer, 5145

The word nezer is derived from nawzar, which means "to separate, consecrate, dedicate," the idea of separation being paramount.[n] From *nawzar* also comes the nazirite, *nawzir*, or the person who makes a vow and is then separated for a specified period of time from *tawmay* things and alcohol.[o]

In the following books, *nawzar* as "separation" is found only three times and once as "hair."[p] *Nezer*, in the sense of a royal head-covering, is found in seven references.[q] So *nezer* seems to have changed its meaning from a technical word to a royal headdress, although it is used both ways in Zechariah 9:16.

n. *nawzar*, 5144; Gen 49:26, Lev. 15:31, 22:16, Num. 6:2–21, Deut. 33:16

o. *nawzir*, 5139; Num. 6:1–9

p. Ezek. 14:7, Zech. 7:3, Hos. 9:10; Jer. 7:29

q. 2 Sam. 1:10, 2 Kgs. 11:12, 2 Chr. 23:11, Ps. 89:40, 132:18, Prov. 27:24, Zech. 9:16

◇◇◇

OTHER LANGUAGES

In the Egyptian, there is *nsr*. One meaning of *nsr* is "anoint" as in anointing an injury with oil to protect it.[17]

From the Old Akkadian era on is *nasaru*, which could also be pronounced *nazeru*. *Nasaru* has many meanings, all with the general idea of keeping somebody or something under guard and, more specifically, "to protect," "to keep safe ... said of protection granted by gods."[18]

So the *tsitz* is not a crown at all, but a conditioning separator, *nezer hakodesh*! But conditioning separator from what? The answer, the purpose of the plate, is in this loaded verse:

> [38]"And it will be on Aaron's forehead, and Aaron will *bear* the *iniquity* of *the conditioning things*, which the Israelites will condition *in all* their conditioning *gifts*, and it will be on his head continually for acceptance for them before the Lord." (Exod. 28:38, my emphasis)

This translation has Aaron bearing the wickedness of the sacrifices, "which the Israelites will condition in all the conditioning gifts." The first part of the verse becomes almost unintelligible by the time you get to the end of it. There are so many mystery words here that it's hard to know where to begin. I'm going to start at "bear."

◇◇◇

1. Bear

Bear, *nawsaw*, has almost as many meanings as there are words in the dictionary, but it basically denotes "to carry," "to take away," or "to lift up."[r] It is used all through the Five Books and onward in many different ways.

r. *nawsaw*, 5375

2. Iniquity

Traditionally translated "iniquity," *awvone* is another word that is used repeatedly throughout the Five Books.[s] Oftentimes it refers to wrongdoing but, as in this verse, sometimes that translation presents a problem. How can the conditioning things

s. *awvone*, 5771; Exod. 20:5, 34:5–9; Num. 14:18; Deut. 5:9

be iniquitous? I believe that *awvone* conveys the idea of *impurity* or contamination from the radioactive cloud.

3. The Conditioning Things

Understanding the word *haqawdawsheem* will help unravel the mystery of this verse. *Haqawdawsheem* is traditionally translated "the holy things." Translators add "things" to refer to the materials for sacrifices, and this is accurate in many places.

> ⁶The soul that touches any such shall be *tawmay* until the evening, and he shall not eat of the conditioned *things* (*min haqawdawsheem*) unless he has bathed his flesh in water. (Lev. 22:6)

It is also true that the word *haqawdawsheem*, when paired with *qodesh*, is traditionally translated "holy of holies," referring to the super-conditioned place that housed the ark.

> ³³And you shall hang the veil under the hooks, and you shall bring in to the veil the ark of communication, and the veil shall divide to you between the conditioned place (*haqodesh*) and between the super-conditioned place (*qodesh haqawdawsheem*).

> ³⁴And you shall put the covering on the ark of communication in the super-conditioned place (*qodesh haqawdawsheem*). (Exod. 26:33–34)

Finally, *qodesh haqawdawsheem* could also refer specifically to the condition of the burnt offerings altar, the incense altar, the tent, the ark, the table and associated instruments, the laver, the *menorah* and associated instruments, the incense, the meal offering, the decontamination offering, the guilt offering, the bread (under certain circumstances), the 12 cakes on the table in the tent, and "every devoted thing."[t]

I believe *haqawdawsheem* in verse 33 refers to the super-conditioned place, the instruments, and the altars that had to be conditioned, not the sacrifices. This would be easier to see if the shortened version *haqodesheem* hadn't been used, but the closely related words *qawdosh*, *qodesh*, *qodesh qawdawsheem*, and *qawdash* are interchangeable (sometimes even in terms of singular versus plural) because of their common root, *qdsh*, *qoof-*

t. Exod. 29:37, 30:26–29, 36; Lev. 2:3, 6:18, 7:1, 21:22, 24:9, 27:28

daleth-shin. For example, in Exodus 29:30, Leviticus 6:23, and Leviticus 16:2–3, *qodesh* means the super-conditioned place, but in Leviticus 22:10 it means the sacrifice. That the plural was unquestionably used for the super-conditioned place is seen in Leviticus 21:23. There the plural word *meeq'dawshai* appears in the prohibition of a man with a blemish who was "of the seed of Aaron" coming to offer "the bread of his God."[u] Leviticus 21:22 says,

> [22]The bread of his God of the super-conditioned (*meeqawd'shay haqawdawsheem*) and of the conditioned (*oomeen haqawdawsheem*) he shall eat.

Here the references are to sacrifices, but verse 23 warns,

> [23]"Only into the veil he shall not go in, and to the altar he shall not come near, because a blemish is in him, that he not profane My conditioned place(s) (*meeq'dawshai*) for I am the Lord who conditions them (*m'qad'shawm*)."

Since there was only one super-conditioned place (whether or not the plural was used here), verse 23 clearly refers to that area.[19] In this case the shortened version, *meeq'dawshai*, was used instead of something like *qodesh meeq'dawshai*. The Septuagint also uses the Greek shortened plural version, *αγιων*, for the super-conditioned place, but for some reason in Leviticus 21:23 it uses the singular form, *αγιον*, as differing from the Hebrew. Both the Hebrew and the Greek use the plural, "conditions *them* [the super-conditioned place and its instruments]" at the end of the sentence. It makes me wonder if dropping the *qodesh* from *qodesh haqawdawsheem* in the Exodus passage was a simple scribal error that got frozen in time.

4. In All

Simple words such as by, to, for, etc., can create huge changes in meaning. "In all (*l'chal*) their conditioning gifts" uses an important letter *lamed*, *l*, for "in." The *Compendious Hebrew English Dictionary* says *lamed* can be translated as "to, into, at, near, for, with reference to, in regard to, after, by, towards, against, during." It can also be translated as "with" but not "in."[v] "In" is the letter *bet* and is so used throughout Exodus 28:31–43. For example, Exodus 28:32 says, "And an opening will be in its midst (*b'tocho*)." In fact, the words "in all" are used 33 times in Exodus. In 32 of those, it is *b'chal* with a *bet*. Only in the verse I am dissecting is "in all" translated from *l'chal* with a *lamed!* Exodus' use of *lamed* as "in" in any sense is so rare that it is practically non-existent. The only place where it could be said to mean "in" is Exodus 4:18: "Go in peace (*laych l'shawlome*)." All other uses are acceptably translated as "to" or "for."

Even Exodus 28:38, the very verse being discussed, uses *lamed* as "for" twice, "for acceptance (*l'rawtson*) for them (*lawchem*)." Why Oxford, Soncino, Strong's, and Magil suddenly turn "*l'chal*" into "in all" is a mystery.

While "in" is a mistranslation of *lamed*, "by" as in "by means of" or "through the offices of" is an acceptable translation. For example, in the Judah-Tamar story Genesis 38:24 says, "She is pregnant by prostitution (*leez'nooneem*)." It is interesting that the very same verse goes on to say, "And it was after three months it was told to Judah *(leeyahooda)*." The former *lamed* could only mean "by" and the latter could only mean "to."

The next verse is peppered with *lamed*s:

> [25]She sent *to* (*el*) [separate but related preposition] her father-in-law to say (*laymore*) by the man (*l'eesh*) whose these [are] to him (*low*) [that is, that these tokens belong to him], "I [am] pregnant." And she said, "Notice here to whom (*l'mee*) the seal and the belts and the staff are." (Gen. 38:25)

"To" and "by" could be the only meanings. Incidentally, all translations I've checked agree.

So, in Exodus 28:38 it is perfectly possible to translate the phrase, "*by* all their conditioning gifts." The list of such examples is extensive. I'll note one more that appears in this same passage. "CONDITIONER TO THE LORD" was engraved on the plate.[w] This time *lamed* is with the *petah*, the vowel sign for the sound *ah*, pronounced *la*.[20] *La* is traditionally translated as "to," but it can also be translated "for." The engraving on the plate then could be, "CONDITIONER *FOR* THE LORD," or in my new terminology, "CONDITIONER FOR THE

w. Exod. 28:36

LORD'S APPEARANCE." It served as a written explanation of the plate's purpose, a permanent reminder of the conditioning, protective measures that had to be taken in anticipation of the cloud's appearance.

Note an interesting parallel between the *tsitz* and the *tsitzit*: the *tsitz*, the plate, had a written reminder to the priest of its purpose and the need to protect himself properly; the *tsitzit*, fringe, had its blue wires to remind and warn the people of the Lord's commandments.

5. Gifts

The final mystery word, gift, *matawnaw*, is simply a metaphor for sacrifice.[x] Sacrifice was the system for clearing the area of contamination through the use of the materials such as incense, water, blood, fat, etc.

x. *matawnaw*, 4979

Now substituting the possible, more plausible translations, the passage reads this way:

> [36]"And you will make a plate of pure gold, and you will engrave on it ... CONDITIONER FOR THE LORD'S APPEARANCE.

> [37]And you will put it on a wire of blue, and it will be on the miter; on the front of the miter it will be.

> [38]And it [the plate] will be on Aaron's forehead, and Aaron will take away the impurity [radioactive contamination] of the super-conditioned place [the whole area and items pertaining to it], which the Israelites will condition [or decontaminate for safe communication] by all their conditioning sacrifices; and it will be on his forehead continually for acceptance for them [the super-conditioned place and the accompanying instruments] before the Lord." (Exod. 28:36–38)

In short, in addition to its function as a reminder, the plate was another protector from the area's radioactivity. The Hebrew word *nezer*, the Egyptian *nsr*, and the Old Akkadian *nasaru*, all illustrate this meaning. The plate was used as a protection for Aaron, specifically for his forehead, a most vulnerable area. When Moses came down from Sinai with his face shining, he had to wear a veil, ostensibly to protect those near him from the radioactivity he received while on the mountain. When Uzziah went unprotected into the temple, burning broke out "in his forehead." The anointing oil, when used on the high priest's head, was called *nezer*. Numbers speaks of the need to condition the nazirite's head, or specifically, "the head of his *nezer*."[y] Thus, the plate seemed to be a personal protection for Aaron.

y. Num. 6:7, 9, 11, 18, 19

Breeches

Linen breeches are yet another protective garment that the priests wore when they went into the tent.

> [39]"And you will make the checkered coat of linen, and you will make a miter of linen and a girdle will you make, the work of an embroiderer.
>
> [40]And for the sons of Aaron you will make coats and you will make for them girdles, and head-tires you will make for them for glory and for beauty.
>
> [41]And you will clothe [with] them Aaron your brother and his sons with him; and you will anoint them, and you will fill their hands and you will condition them that they may be priests to Me.
>
> [42]And make for them breeches of linen to cover the flesh of [their] nakedness; from the loins to the thighs they will be.
>
> [43]And they will be on Aaron and on his sons when they go into the tent of meeting or when they come near to the altar to minister in the super-conditioned place and not carry impurity and die, a statute forever for him and his seed after him." (Exod. 28:39–43)

The word "breeches," *meech'nawss*, is used four times in the Five Books, once in Ezekiel, and nowhere else![z] Breeches were to be worn only by the priests and only when working in the dangerous area.

z. *meech'nawss*, 4370; Exod. 28:42, 39:28; Lev. 6:3, 16:4; Ezek. 44:18

In the following books, Ezekiel 44:18 alone refers to priests wearing the linen breeches when coming into the super-conditioned place, albeit Ezekiel's particular concept of that area.

> [18]"Turbans of linen will be on their heads and breeches (*meechnawsay*) of linen will be on their loins and they will

not gird with sweat." [They shouldn't wear wool, which would cause sweat.]

Strong's says *meech'nawss* is related to the *kawnas*, meaning "to gather (together), heap up, wrap oneself."[aa] Fuerst says the same, stating *kawnas* means "cover."[21] BDB says the connection is "obscure."[22] These translations of *kawnas*, though, are only in following books.

aa. *kawnas*, 3664

OTHER LANGUAGES

There are some interesting possible foreign equivalents in Egyptian. Way back in the Middle Egyptian is a word *kns*, which Faulkner and Gardiner say means "pubic region."[23] Gardiner explains that the determinative ꕯ used with *kns* is a piece of flesh. So he says ▭ꕯ, *kns*, is "vagina." He also notes that it has been proposed to derive the phonetic sign ꕯ, from *ỉsw*, meaning "testicle."[24] Whatever the exact usage, the word pertains to the genitals.

Both the Bible and historians agree that the garment was used to cover the area from the loins to the thighs. Josephus says it "is put about the privy parts ... and it ends at the thighs and is there tied fast."[25] Milgrom explains that the Leviticus 6:3 reference to his flesh being covered is "a euphemism for genitals."[26] So while later Hebrew meanings seen in the word *kawnas* only vaguely relate to the idea of covering, it is possible that the *meech'nawss*, a unique garment that only covered the privy parts, was described using a then common word learned during the Egyptian sojourn.

Linen

In each reference, the breeches are described as being made of linen. There are four Hebrew words for linen:[27]

- *shaysh* (explored in the Walkie Talkie chapter)
- *bootz* (nowhere in the Five Books)[ab]
- *peeshteh*[ac]
- *bad*.[ad]

Peeshteh is translated "flax, linen." It and a related word, *peeshtaw*, refer directly to the flax plant from which linen is made.[ae]

ab. *bootz*, 948

ac. *peeshteh*, 6593

ad. *bad*, 906

ae. *peeshtaw*, 6594; Exod. 9:31; as flax, Josh. 2:6, Judg. 15:14, Prov. 31:13, Isa. 14:4, 42:3, Ezek. 40:3, Hos. 2:7

In the Ugaritic, Gordon translates *ptt* as "flax," DLU as "linen," "flax," and "linen cloth."[28] According to HAL and BDB, *ptt* relates to the Hebrew *payshet*.[af] *Payshet* means "flax, linen."[29]

af. *payshet*, 6593

Bad requires study in order to understand its role with the breeches. In the first reference, Exodus 28:42, the breeches of *bad* were used "to cover the flesh of nakedness" of Aaron and his sons "from the loins to the thighs" so that when they came into the tent of meeting or near the altar to minister in the conditioned place "they carry not impurity and die." It is interesting that they do not appear in the first listing of garments in Exodus 28:4, but are first mentioned here. It seems almost like an afterthought following the discussion of the protective warning of the plate. No source theorist I have read has claimed that this is a later addition.

The second reference in Exodus 39 explains that the commandments to make the garments have been executed.

> [28]And [they made] the miter of linen (*shaysh*) and the headbands [or caps or headdresses] of the turbans linen (*shaysh*) and the linen (*bad*) breeches linen separators (*shaysh mawsh'zawr*). (Exod. 39:28)

Repeating two different words for linen, *shaysh* and *bad*, seems somewhat strange. It is the only place two words are translated "linen" for the same item. Something is amiss here.

The third reference is to the law of the burnt offering:

> [10]"And the fire of the altar will be kept burning on it. And the priest will put on his *bad* garment and *bad* breeches he will put on his flesh: and he will take up the ashes, which the fire has consumed, the burnt offering on the altar, and he will put them beside the altar.

> [11]And he will take off his garments, and he will put on other garments, and he will bring out the ashes outside the camp to a clean place." (Lev. 6:10–11; Heb. 3–4)[30]

ag. *mad* or *med*, 4055

The term translated garment is *mad/med*.[ag] It is used once in the Five Books when actually ministering in the dangerous place. Note that when simply removing the relatively harmless ashes, they were not necessary. In other words, the regular garments were protection enough when dealing with the residue. *Mad/ med* has several meanings in following books, but as a garment it is most often used as military dress for protection in combat or metaphorically in connection with beligerancy.[ah]

ah. e.g., 1 Sam. 4:12, 17:38, 39, 18:4; 2 Sam. 20:8; Ps. 109:18, Jdg. 3:16

The fourth *bad* reference comes after the deaths of Aaron's sons and the warning forbidding entry into the super-conditioned place at certain times. Aaron was instructed what to wear when he did enter:

> 4"A conditioning *bad* coat he will put on, and *bad* breeches will be on his flesh, and with a *bad* girdle ... and a *bad* miter he will attire; they are conditioning garments." (Lev. 16:4)

Here is an astonishing word change if one is to believe that *bad* means "linen," because Exodus 39:28 says all these items, including the *bad* breeches, were made of *shaysh*![31]

More clues show up in other non-breeches references to *bad*. For example, Leviticus 16:32–33 says that the priest "who will be anointed in place of his father will put on the *bad* garments, the conditioning garments. And he will cover the super-conditioned place." In following books, there are few mentions of *bad*. 1 Samuel 2:18–19 talks of Samuel as a child wearing a *bad ephod* when his mother gave him to the Lord. His task was to aid Eli the priest in "the house of the Lord at Shiloh." He "ministered before the Lord, a child girded with a *bad ephod*."[32] 1 Samuel 22:18 mentions the Edomite Doeg's killing of "four score and five [priests] who wore the *bad ephod*."[33] 2 Samuel 6:14 tells the story of David bringing up the ark and dancing while wearing a *bad ephod*. 1 Chronicles 15:27 is the same story, but details the fact that David had on a robe of linen (*bootz*) and the *bad ephod*. Ezekiel talks of his vision wherein he saw "the man clothed in *badeem*."[ai] This personage was probably thought of as an angel and is so identified in the Talmud as Gabriel.[34] Ezekiel speaks of *shaysh*, *bootz*, and *peeshteem*, but he does not seem to understand the purpose of *bad* breeches. He described what he envisioned they were made of, *peeshtah*, rather than what they did, and used *bad(eem)* to describe the mystical costume of angels. This is

ai. Ezek. 9:2, 3, 11; 10:6, 7

no different from the tortuous way in which he described the *cherubim*. Of course, he was using his "visions" to make a point. Lastly, Daniel too had visions and saw a man clothed in *badeem*.

∞∞

DERIVATION

What can be ascertained from the derivation of *bad*? BDB and Milgrom say the derivation is unknown.[35] HAL has a question mark after the word and points out that the Arabic *batt* is "rough garment" and *batta* is "cut."[36] Strong's says it is possibly from *bawdad*, translated "alone" in Leviticus, Numbers, and Deuteronomy.[aj]

Bad means "separation" when it is used with the preposition *l* (*lamed*), as in the curtains of the tent being "by themselves (*l'bad*)."[ak] It is used as such in Genesis, Exodus, Numbers, and Deuteronomy as well as many following books. "Beside" is the only use in Leviticus, and "alone, beside, only, staves" are the only uses anywhere in the Five Books. Other translations of *l'bad* are "apart, bar, branch, except, strength."[37] Whether speaking of *bad*, *bawdawd*, or even perhaps *bawdal*, "to separate," the letters *bd* convey the idea of "separate, apart."[al] All are said to derive from *bdd*, which HAL translates as "scatter, be lonely." In the Akkadian, it says *badadu* D is "squander" and in the Arabic *badda* means "separate."[38]

Amazingly, *bad* as "stave" or "pole" turns out to be a technical term only used in connection with the ark, the table of showbread, the altars of burnt offerings, and the incense altar, all of which were used in the tent of meeting.[am] Inserted into rings, the poles were used to carry these items, in effect *separating* the priests from direct contact with them. Stave is used this way in Exodus and Numbers, as well as 1 Kings 8:7, 8 and 2 Chronicles 5:8, 9, in reference to its use in the temple. Nowhere else. As to other etymological possibilities, there is a word *bd*, which Gardiner translates as a kind of "natron."[39] Natron is a compound of sodium carbonate and sodium bicarbonate that was used as a drying agent in the ancient Egyptian mummification process.[40] It is also the substance that was used in the purification process for the king as part of the temple ritual.[41] It was thought to have cleansing and purification powers.[42] It was also commonly used as soap.[43]

The determinative for natron is 〈. Thus, the word is 〈〈. Gardiner even says that 〈 is an abbreviation for natron. It is notable that the determinative is a combination of two symbols: 〈 is god, *ntr*, and ᴅ is "a bag of linen," *ssr*. Thus, for some reason, the concept of linen is pictured in the word along with the very definite meaning of a purifier, or, in my terms, a protector. Even as a drying agent, its purpose was to "protect" the body from decomposition.

The Sumerians, thought to be the originators of cuneiform writing, also had the word *bad*. The Sumerian Dictionary devotes some 16 pages to its various meanings. Under *bad* B, #3, the meaning is "to *separate*, to part," and under #4, "to remove, to make distant." The word was used from the Presargonic time (before 2300 BCE) through UrIII (2000 BCE) to Old Babylonian and post Old Babylonian. The quotes used as examples

aj. *bawdad*, 909

ak. *l'bad*, 905; Exod. 26:9

al. *bawdal*, 914

am. Exod. 25:14–15, 27, 27:6; Exod. 30:4

talk mostly of separating heaven from earth. Then under *bad* A the meanings are "wall, fortification." This, too, stretches from Presargonic to post Old Babylonian.

Some of the quotes are noteworthy:

"To build the wall of Uruku as protection ..."

"I (Enanedu) set up a spacious shrine over the resting places of the former *en*-priestesses, I surrounded its tumbledown spots with a great wall, I set up a strong guard, and I purified that place."

"(You instructed me) to build a wall in order to cut off their path."

"As symbol of divine or royal protection ..."

"Ninurta, [son of storm god En-lil of Sumerian mythology] you are the great wall for Sumer."

"I am the great (defensive) wall of the troops, the sunlight shining forth on his land."

(Hammurabi) "He blocked off the approaches to the country like a mighty wall."[44]

So the Egyptian word *bd* meant "protect," and the Sumerian, Old Babylonian, and post Old Babylonian *bad* meant "separate" and "protect." I'll set them aside for a moment and get back to the Hebrew word *bad* and its use as linen.

Applying the translation "separation" to *bad* suddenly makes the technical purpose of the *bad meech'nawss* (a unique costume) clear, as well as that of all other *bad* items: to separate for protection. Exodus 39:28 should read, "the breeches of separation, linen conditioner/ separators (*meech'nawss bad shaysh mawsh'zawr*)." They protected by separating the priests' genitals from radioactivity when they worked in the dangerous part of the tent.[45] Now Leviticus 16:4 fits into the context of the rest of the chapter. Almost desperately, "after the deaths of Aaron's sons," rules for preventing that catastrophe from recurring are cited: "A conditioning, separating (*bad*) coat he will put on, and separating (*bad*) breeches will be on his flesh, and with a separating (*bad*) girdle ... and a separating (*bad*) miter he will wrap [himself]; they are conditioning garments." Leviticus 16:23 underscores the *bad*/protective concept:

[23]"And Aaron will come into the tent of meeting and he will take off the *bad* garments, which he put on when he went into the super-conditioned place, and he will leave them there." (Lev. 16:23)

Also, the Exodus 40:13 instructions are now understandable, to make Aaron's garments to "condition him that he may be a priest to Me."

This closer look at *bad* shows that it was never intended to mean linen. The words from which *meech'nawss* and *bad* possibly derived were extremely old. When *bad* did enter the Hebrew, the separation and protection meanings were sustained. In following books such as Samuel and Chronicles, the few times it was used it was parroted as having to do with the *ephod*.

So *meech'nawss* and *bad* are two more words that appear to denote the protective nature of the priests' garments. Keep in mind that there were several layers of clothing including the robe of the *ephod*, which covered the priests from neck to foot. The meanings are there. They have to be excavated, dusted off, and held up to the light of day in order to take their part in the lexicon of technical terms.

Glory and Beauty

Two words in Exodus 28 seem to contradict the garments' purpose if translated traditionally. They are *kawbode* and *teeferet*, translated "glory and beauty" only in the following verses:[an]

an. *kawbode*, 3519; *teeferet*, 8597 (or *teefawraw*, only in Isa. 28:5 and Jer. 48:17)

> [2]"And you will make conditioning garments for Aaron your brother for glory and for beauty." (Exod. 28:2)

> [40]"And for the sons of Aaron you will make coats and … girdles, and head-tires … for glory and for beauty." (Exod. 28:40)

Why would the reason for making the garments be for glory and beauty if they were used as protections against danger and death? The answer is it isn't. Glory and beauty simply aren't the proper translations.

Glory

The following are some of the passages where glory (*kawbode*) is mentioned. In reference to the Lord being the instrument for action through His *kawbode* …

> [10]And all the congregation said to stone them with stones when the *kawbode* of the Lord appeared in the tent of meeting to all the Israelites. (Num. 14:10)

Regarding the presence of the glory with the dangerous cloud …

> [15]And Moses went up to the mountain and the cloud covered the mountain.

> [16]And the *kawbode* of the Lord dwelt on Mount Sinai … and He called to Moses on the seventh day out of the midst of the cloud. (Exod. 24:15–16)

ao. Exod. 40:9–10

After the original conditioning of the tabernacle …[ao]

> [34]Then the cloud covered the tent of meeting, and the *kawbode* of the Lord filled the tabernacle.

> [35]And Moses was not able to come into the tent of meeting because the cloud dwelt on it. (Exod. 40:34–35)

This was exactly the same reaction that was observed in Solomon's Temple.[ap] In the Korach revolt against Moses and Aaron, which resulted in the fire of the Lord consuming the 250 men …

ap. 1 Kgs. 8:10–11

> [19]Korach assembled all the congregation against them to the door of the tent of meeting, and the *kawbode* of the Lord appeared to all the congregation. (Num. 16:19)

After the rebels had been killed …[42] The congregation assembled against Moses and against Aaron that they turned toward the tent of meeting; and behold, the cloud covered it, and the *kawbode* of the Lord appeared. (Num. 16:42)

Just these few quotes are enough to indicate that "glory" needs careful scrutiny.[46]

To understand the meaning of *kawbode*, it is necessary to study the related verb *kawbade*.[aq] The common root *kbd* is translated "to be heavy" and "to be honoured."[47] *Kbd* is variously translated in the Five Books as "to be dim, glorified, glorious, grievous, harden, honor, promote, honorable, and rich." Strong's translates *kawbade* as an adjective meaning "great, grievous, hard, heavy, laden, much, slow, sore, thick."[ar] Strong's also gives the translation "liver" described as "heavy" or "thick."[as] HAL has other thoughts, but for the purpose of this discussion uses "thick."[48] In the following books, Strong's gives such translations as "abounding with, afflict, boast, be chargeable, glorify, be glorious, glory, great, be grievous, harden, be heavy, honor, be honorable, lade, prevail, promote, be rich, be sore, stop." With the multitude of definitions, it seems an overwhelming problem to get to the basic meaning of the word *kawbade* as used in the Five Books, but a close reading of each reference shows that, just as with its root, there are really only two different ideas evident: (1) to be heavy/dense/thick and (2) to honor.

aq. kawbade, 3513

ar. kawbade, 3515

as. kawbade, 3516

Heavy

Almost all the definitions for *kawbade* such as "great, grievous, rich, harden," etc., can also be translated as "heavy," and in various Bibles they are. For instance, it would be redundant to use "great" for *kawbade* in Genesis 50:10, which uses *gawdole* as "great" in the same verse, but "a very great and heavy mourning" works nicely.[at] Genesis 43:1 could read, "famine was *sore* (or *heavy*) in the land." In Exodus 4:10, Moses could be *slow* of speech and tongue or *heavy, thick* of the same. Pharoah's heart

at. gawdole, 1419

could be *hardened* or *heavy* in Exodus 8:28, 9:34, 10:1, etc. Strangely, heavy or heavy-related words are not used for *kawbade* in Leviticus or Deuteronomy.

Honor

Now, what about translating *kawbade* as honor? Its first mention is in Genesis 34:19, in the story of Shechem, a Hivite prince who raped Jacob's daughter Dinah. When Shechem made what he thought were arrangements to marry her, calling for the circumcision of all the males in his city, he was then "honored (*kawbade*) above all his father's house." Subsequently, Jacob's sons, Simeon and Levi, slaughtered him and all the rest in revenge. Mention number two is the story of Balak, king of Moab, who hired the prophet Balaam to curse the approaching Israelite army. Numbers 22:15, 17, 37, and 24:11 speak of Balak's forlorn desire to honor Balaam if only he would carry out the curse, which he didn't. (However, the Balaam-Balak story has historical/mythological problems that make it suspect.)

Finally, in Exodus 20:12 and Deuteronomy 5:16 are found the famous references in the Ten Commandments to "honor your father and mother in order that your days be long and in order that it may be well with you upon the land that the Lord your God gives you." These three uses of *kawbade* as "honor" are overwhelmed by the 20-some uses that could be translated as "heavy," which are all a part of the Abraham, Joseph, and Moses-exodus narratives, and which were presumably passed on from oral histories and written down verbatim.[49]

Now, what happens with *kawbade* in the rest of the books? The easiest way to summarize it would be to say that the idea of "honor" or "glorify" with its spiritual connotation becomes more prevalent. It is used as "heavy" in such books as 1 and 2 Samuel, 1 Kings, 2 Chronicles, Nehemiah, Job, Psalms, Proverbs, Isaiah, and Lamentations, and heavy is just what it means. In addition, "glorified, glorifieth, glorify, glorious" in Isaiah, Ezekiel, Haggai, Psalms, Jeremiah, and 2 Samuel have an "honoring" sense. Furthermore, when translated as "honor" in Judges, 1 and 2 Samuel, 1 Chronicles, Job, Psalms, and Proverbs, the meaning is definitely "honor." The supremely important point is that *kawbade* has made a radical transformation from almost always meaning "heavy" in Genesis, Exodus, Leviticus, and Numbers to its other meaning of "honored" or "glorified" in the books following.

With these thoughts in mind, let's look at *kawbode*. In all the Five Books, there are only four references where *kawbode* is generally translated "honor" or "wealth":

(1) In Genesis 31:1, the sons of Laban accused Jacob of taking away their father's "wealth," referring to his stolen flocks.

(2) In Genesis 45:13, Joseph ordered his brothers, "Tell my father all my honor."

(3) In Genesis 49:6, Jacob's predictions for his sons' futures included the exhortation that his "honor not be united" with Simeon and Levi because they "killed a man" and "lamed an ox."[50]

(4) Numbers 24:11 says, "I thought I would greatly honor you, but behold, the Lord kept you back from honor (*meekawbode*)." This is simply another reference to the honor withheld from Balaam in the Balak story. All other references to *kawbode* found in Exodus, Leviticus, Numbers, and even Deuteronomy refer to the "glory (*kawbode*) of the Lord," but I assert that used in this context they do not mean glory.

Glory of the Lord

Then what does "*kawbode* of the Lord" mean? Since the related word *kawbade* was overwhelmingly found to mean to be heavy/dense/thick rather than to honor, it makes sense to check whether the same applies to *kawbode*. The key lies in the garments, which, again, were not for glory and beauty but *for protection from the kawbode—the dangerous substance in the cloud.* (For a further discussion of *kawbade* and its relationship to *kawbode*, see Appendix D.) Look at these "*kawbode* of the Lord" references:

• When Moses and Aaron spoke to the Israelites regarding the provision of manna for food ...

> [7]'And in the morning you will *see the kawbode of the Lord*.' (Exod. 16:7)

• To announce that the manna would be supplied ...

> [10]And it came to pass as Aaron [was] speaking to the Israelites, that they turned toward the wilderness, and behold the *kawbode of the Lord* appeared *in the cloud*. (Exod. 16:10)

• To receive the Ten Commandments ...

> [15]And Moses went up to the mountain and the cloud covered the mountain.

> [16]And the *kawbode of the Lord* dwelt on Mount Sinai, and the cloud covered it six days; and He *called* to Moses on the seventh day *out of the midst of the cloud*.

[17]And the *appearance of the kawbode of the Lord* [was] *like consuming* fire on the top of the mountain before the eyes of the Israelites. (Exod. 24:15–17)

- In the rituals necessary to install the priest …

  [43]"And there I will meet with the Israelites, and it [the tent] will be conditioned by *My kawbode*." (Exod. 29:43)

- Here is where the covenant between Moses and the Lord was sealed, and Moses beseeched Him to accompany the Israelites through the wilderness. The Lord said He would through his messenger and his "presence," and at that point …[au]

  au. Exod. 32:34, 33:14

  [18]He [Moses] said [to the Lord], "Let me see *Your kawbode*." (Exod. 33:18)

- Then a strange thing happened. The Lord said,

  [19]"I will cause all My *goodness* to pass before your face. And I will call out the name of the Lord before you. And I will favor whom I will favor, and I will have mercy on whom I will have mercy."

  [20]And He said, "You are not able to see My face; for no man sees me *and lives*."

  [21]And God said, "Here is a place by me. And you will stand on a rock.

  [22]And as My *kawbode* is passing, it will be that I will put you in a cleft of the rock; and I will cover My palm over you during My passing.

  [23]And I will remove My palm and you will see My back, but My face cannot be seen." (Exod. 33:19–23, my emphasis)

In other words, contrary to Moses' request, God *refused* to let Moses be directly exposed to a full dose of His *kawbode* from close up. He explained, somewhat cryptically, that He would, instead, cause His "goodness" to pass. In doing so and not letting Moses see the *kawbode*, He would protect or show favor and mercy specifically to that person He chose to so favor, which in this case was Moses. Moses was to hide in the cleft of a rock on Mount Sinai and be *covered* with God's palm until the *kawbode* passed.

The word here for "cover" is *sawchach*, which is used relative to the *cherubim* to connote screening, and therefore, protection.[51] In fact, elsewhere in the Five Books, *sawchach* and the noun derived from it, *mawsawch*, are *only* used in relation to the screen covering the ark, the *cherubim* on the ark, and to the screens or gates of the tabernacle and court. It seems more than coincidental that a term used only in connection with screening-communication-protection devices was used relative to God's palm protecting, covering, or screening Moses during communication. On the other hand, when used in the following books, the same words were used for covering anything. For example, in 2 Samuel 17:19, *mawsawch* is a "covering over the well's mouth."[av] So, although it once had specific technical use, in following books its use is general. It appears, then, that this seemingly simple request by Moses to "see Your *kawbode*" reveals a set of circumstances perfectly compatible with the danger of the substance.

Here are three more "*kawbode* of the Lord" examples. The first demonstrates the extreme danger in the tabernacle when the cloud actually descended on it:

> [34]Then the cloud covered the tent of meeting, and the *kawbode* of the Lord filled the tabernacle.
>
> [35]And Moses was not able to come into the tent of meeting because the cloud dwelt on it, and *the kawbode of the Lord* filled the tabernacle. (Exod. 40:34–35)

The second example is in connection with the necessity to offer certain animals and a meal offering:

> [4]"For today *the Lord* will appear to you …
>
> [6]This thing you will do; then will appear to you the *kawbode of the Lord*." (Lev. 9:4, 6)

The third example occurs a little later:

> [23]Moses and Aaron went into the tent of meeting. Then they came out, and they blessed the people; and the *kawbode of the Lord* appeared to all the people. (Lev. 9:23)

av. See also Nah. 2:5; Job 3:23; Isa. 9:11, 19:2; Job 38:8

Fig. 63

Photo courtesy of Tim Ivanic.[52]

To this point, each example of *kawbode* shows that it was a visible substance. It was contained within the cloud. Its appearance was "like consuming fire."[aw] The fire-like *kawbode* made the cloud glow at night, but it was invisible in the daytime. These verses even suggest that it was part of the Lord.[53] Like ash in hot, glowing volcanic clouds or the suspected ice particles in the so-called noctilucent, glow-in-the-night clouds, the *kawbode* substance contributed to the cloud's density and appearance.

It is interesting that *kawbode's* relative *kawbade* was also used in the description of the cloud on Mount Sinai:

> [16]And it came to pass on the third day when it was morning that there were thunders and lightnings, and a heavy (*kawbade*) cloud on the mountain, and a very strong voice of a horn; and all the people in the camp trembled. (Exod. 19:16)[54]

Actually, the description of *kawbode* suggests exactly the words "radiant" and "radiance" as they are defined in physics. The

aw. Exod. 24:17; cf., Num. 9:15–16

Merriam-Webster On-Line Dictionary says, "radiant, adjective, 1a: radiating rays or reflecting beams of light ... 3a: emitted or transmitted by radiation." It calls radiance, the noun, "the flux density of radiant energy per unit solid angle and per unit projecting area of radiating surface." Radiant energy is defined by *Merriam-Webster* as "energy traveling as electromagnetic waves."[55] The *American Heritage Dictionary of the English Language* says that radiant means, "1. Emitting heat or light. 2. Consisting of or emitted as radiation" and that radiance is "the radiant energy emitted per unit time in a specified direction by a unit area of an emitting surface ... 'radiant flux.'" It defines flux as "The rate of flow of fluid, particles, or energy through a given surface."[56] Thus, *kawbode* can reasonably be translated as radiance when referring to the *kawbode* of the Lord, and I will do so from this point forward.

Since the cloud was dangerous and since radiance (*kawbode*) could indicate heavy/dense/thick, it is possible that clothing was used as protection against the radiation emanating from the heavy or thick or dense mass in the cloud. Remember, the clothing is a part of the discussion of how to condition Aaron and his sons as priests to safely receive communication from the Lord in the newly constructed tent ...

[42]"Where I will meet with you to speak to you.

[43]And I will meet there with the Israelites and it [the tent] will be conditioned against My radiance (*beech'vodee* [*kawbode*])." (Exod. 29:42–43)

Here I am making an important change from "*by* My radiance" to "*against* My radiance." "Against" is one of the translations of the letter *bet* and it is a very common one.[57] It is used as such in all of the Five Books as well as in many following ones, e.g., Joshua, Judges, 1 and 2 Samuel, 1 and 2 Chronicles, Job, Isaiah, Jeremiah, and Ezekiel. It would make no sense at all if, at the end of these long, detailed instructions about managing the danger of the *kawbode*, the Lord suddenly contradicted Himself by saying that His radiance conditioned the priests.[ax] The verses continue:

ax. Exod. 29:1–45

44"And I will condition the tent of meeting and the altar; and Aaron and his sons I will condition that they may be priests to Me.

45And I will dwell among the Israelites, and I will be to them for a God.

46And they will know that I am the Lord their God who brought them forth from the land of Egypt, that I might dwell in their midst; I am the Lord their God." (Exod. 29:44–46)

It should be noted that here and in many other verses when the Lord said, "*I* will condition," He says it in the context of the priests being in proper condition to work with the tent.[ay] By "*I* will" He meant that *through His instructions* the priests would carry out the conditioning process and be ensured safety. These references to the process are quite different from His reference to "My radiance," the dangerous substance *against* which they needed protection.

ay. Exod. 31:13; Lev. 20:7,8, 21:8,15, 23, 22:9, 15

Since it was quite specifically God's plan to "dwell among the Israelites" and to communicate with them through the dangerous cloud, it is clear why the rules of protection had to be followed so carefully. They ensured the safety of the people and the area when the Lord spoke to them through the radiance in the cloud.

OTHER LANGUAGES

I find relatives of *kawbade* and *kawbode* supportive of my theory regarding the physical makeup of the radiance of the cloud. The Ugaritic *kbd* reinforces the concepts of heaviness, denseness, thickness, and honor. It also means "liver, insides."[58] DLU translates the Ugaritic root /k-b-d-/ as "honor, render honors, to receive," *kbd* (I) as "liver, entrails."[59] DLU says that Von Soden translates *kbd* as "weight, heavy."[60] DLU continues with *kbd* (III), which is the "first element of a divine name" and finally *kbd* (IV) as "honor, render honors, receive."

Even more important is the verb *kabatu*. It means both "to become heavy" and "to become important, honored."[61] *Kabattu* means "inside (of the body)."[62] More interesting still is the adjective *kabtu*, related to *kab tu*.[63] *Kabtu* is so specifically related to all the attributes of *kawbode* that it makes one think the whole process might have related to it. Among its meanings are "heavy, dense, dangerous, grievous, severe, honored, and venerable." CDA adds, "grave, serious, of wound, illness ... of mist, cloud."[64] However, the quotes offered in CAD are most fascinating.[65] Under "heavy, dense" is "I have made a *garment* or two, *heavy* ones." (Old Assyrian) And, "I had the wide sky covered as with a *dense fog.*" Then of "dangerous," etc., "said of *wounds* and *diseases* ... a *serious illness*, an evil affliction, a *dangerous wound.*" And "said of guilt, punishment, etc. ... leprosy, the *grievous divine punishment.*" "May (Marduk) make him have (dropsy), his *severe punishment* ... The gods ... imposed a *grievous punishment* upon him."[66] And "Said of divine utterances and acts ... he heeded their (the gods') *venerable* utterance" (my emphasis).[67] The words "thick, heavy, dense" are used in connection with "garments, fog, illness, divine punishment (in the form of leprosy), and communication"—all the concepts connected with the cloud and *kawbode*!

Look at these last few mentions of *kawbode* to see the pattern of radiance and communication repeated. Numbers 31:21–33 tells the story of the men sent by Moses to "spy out the land of Canaan." They were to learn as much as they could about the defenses and condition of the area. The spies brought back frightening stories about the terrible strength of the inhabitants. The congregation was distraught and rebellious, and when two of the spies loyal to Moses (Caleb and Joshua) tried to reassure the people, they were threatened with stoning:

[10]And all the congregation said to stone them with stones, *when the radiance of the Lord appeared* in the tent of meeting to all the Israelites.

[11]*And the Lord said* to Moses, "How long will despise Me this people ...."

[12]I will smite them [him] with radiation sickness." (Num. 14:10–12, my emphasis)

The radiance of the Lord appeared and *then* He spoke. Two other references to radiance in Numbers 14:21–22 relate to the story of the spies. Both refer to radiance as I have been discussing it.

The next mention of radiance is in the story of Korach in Numbers 16:19–20. When Korach revolted, "the radiance of the Lord appeared to all the congregation. And the Lord spoke to Moses and Aaron." In the same story ...

[42]And it came to pass when the congregation assembled against Moses and Aaron that they turned toward the tent of meeting, and behold the cloud covered it, and the radiance of the Lord appeared.

[43]And Moses and Aaron came to the front of the tent of meeting.

[44]And the Lord spoke to Moses saying,

[45]"Remove from the midst of this congregation, and I will consume them in a moment," *and they fell upon their faces.* (Num. 16:42–45, my emphasis)

The act of falling on the face is traditionally thought of as an act of reverence. However, the new understanding of the ancient derivations suggests that falling on the face may have been a protective measure against the radioactive cloud.

The next mention of radiance is in Numbers 20:6–7, the "Waters of Meribah" story. The people were again rebellious, this time for lack of water,

> ⁶And Moses and Aaron came from before the assembly to the door of the tent of meeting; *and they fell upon their faces;* and the radiance of the Lord appeared to them.

> ⁷And the Lord spoke to Moses saying ...

The last mention is in the recap of the Mount Sinai story in Deuteronomy 5:24. When the Lord spoke to the people from the burning mountain, they responded, "The Lord has shown us His radiance."

So all the references to *kawbode* are perfectly consistent. When used technically, it refers to radiance, the dangerous substance in the cloud and nothing else.

Beauty

The second reason the priests were to wear their special garments was for *teeferet*, usually translated "beauty." BDB translates it "beauty, glory."[az] Other meanings given by Strong's are "bravery, comely, fair, glory(ious), honor."

Strong's derives *teeferet* from *paw'ar*, which he says is a primitive root meaning "to gleam, embellish, boast, explain oneself, boast self, go over the boughs, glorify (self), glory, vaunt self." HAL agrees.[68] *Teeferet*, which HAL translates "beauty, ornament, glory, splendour, radiance, fame, honour, pride," is derived from II *p'r*.[ba] HAL says II *p'r*, "to glorify, show one's glory, boast against," is a denominative from *p'ayr*, which is called a loanword from the Egyptian *pyr*.[69] *Pyr* means "band" in Egyptian, and "head wrap, turban" in Hebrew. The Egyptian *pyr* is a late use not found in the Middle Egyptian.

In the first four books, *paw'ar* is only found in Exodus 8:5 where it is traditionally translated "glory" or "honor."[70] This

az. *teeferet*, 8597 (or *teefawraw*, only in Isa. 28:5 and Jer. 48:17)

ba. *paw'ar*, 6286; Exod. 28:2, 40

translation needs rethinking. HAL translates it as "Explain yourself to me!" This passage describes the plague of frogs that swarmed Egypt:

> [8]And Pharaoh called for Moses and for Aaron, and he said, "Entreat to the Lord, that he remove the frogs from me and from my people; and I will send away the people that they may sacrifice to the Lord."

> [9]And Moses said to Pharaoh, "[Have you this] *glory* (*hitpawayr*) [*paw'ar*] over me; for when will I entreat for you, and for your servants, and for your people, to destroy the frogs from you and from your houses, [that] only in the river they will remain?"

> [10]And he said, "For tomorrow." And he said, "[Be it] according to your word in order that you may know that there is not like the Lord our God." (Exod. 8:8–10; Heb. 4–6)

Moses agreed with Pharaoh's request to get rid of the frogs "tomorrow" so that Pharaoh would know for certain that there was "none like our God." But why did Moses start the sentence with "Have you this *glory* (*hitpawayr*) over me?" Here is what some commentators say regarding Exodus 8:5:

> Have thou this glory over me, i. e., "assume the honour of deciding when the plague will cease" or, "have this glory over me, in fixing the time when the plague will cease at my entreaty" (Luzzatto). The words are a polite address to the king.[71]

> *Have thou this glory over me.* Moses promised to have Pharaoh's reputation enhanced by imploring God to make the plague cease on the day fixed by him (F.) [Abraham Ibn Ezra]. R [Rashi] construes the phrase as a challenge thrown out by Moses to Pharaoh to give him a task, which the king thinks to be beyond his powers and he would complete it by set time. R finds this alluded to in the use of the Hebrew *lemathai*, "against what time," instead of *mathai*, "when."

> *Against what time.* Moses deliberately asked Pharaoh to fix a date as in the ordinary course of nature the frogs would not all die at once but gradually disappear (Sh) [Rashbam].[72]

There doesn't seem to be a lot of agreement among these commentators, probably because they are using *paw'ar* in the later sense of "honor." If they had gone back to the earlier meaning as did Strong's and Fuerst, ("to explain"), Gesenius and HAL ("to explain, declare oneself"), Zondervan ("declare"), or even Owens ("be pleased to command me"), suddenly the verse would make sense.[73] "Declare yourself to me when you want the frogs to go," said Moses. Do other languages help to clarify the meaning of *paw'ar*? In the Middle

Egyptian, *proo n r* means "utterance." *Prt-hroo* literally means "going, or sending forth of the voice," and can signify "invocation offerings."[74] In Hittite, *para-a* is "from out of the mouth."[75] Old Babylonian's *parasu* means "interpretation, explanation."[76] In Ugaritic, *p'r* (the sign ' corresponds to the Hebrew letter *ayin*) means "proclaim, announce."[77]

In all of these languages, there are no alternative meanings like "beauty" or "glory." These words, which indicate communicating in one form or another, have one thing in common, namely the letters *pr*. In the "Par For the Course" chapter, I will show how almost every Hebrew or foreign word with the root *pr* (*pay resh*) or *par* (*pay aleph resh*) has to do with communication in the early stages of their use.

As *paw'ar* fits into the *pr*-communication category, so does *teeferet*. Alternatively, it is translated as "glory," "beauty," or similar words over and over in the following books where it makes perfect sense.[bb] However, in *all* of the Five Books, *teeferet*

bb. e.g., Ezek. 16:12, "beauty," and Ezek. 24:25, "glory"

is used only in Exodus 28:2 and 40.[78] This is the explanation of the communication devices and the priests' protective clothing. Here, "beauty" cannot be the correct translation because the stated reason for wearing the clothes was to keep Aaron and his sons from getting killed, just as were the bells, the water,

bc. Deut. 28:35; Exod. 30:20–21; Lev. 10:6, 9

the untorn garments, and head coverings, etc.[bc] So while there is general agreement that *teeferet* is derived from the "beauty" meaning of *paw'ar*, this doesn't seem to be the case in the two Exodus references. Once again, other languages may offer the technical word that describes the purpose of the priests' clothing, a purpose that was totally new to the Israelites.

Assuming a 400-year relationship between the Israelites and the Egyptians, the Egyptian would have had the most direct influence. *Tp-r*, the Egyptian word for "utterance," might fall into the *par*-related classification. It is a compound made up logically of *tp*, "head," and ⌒ r, "mouth."[79] There is no alternative translation here indicating "beautify" or "glory." Also, the commonly used word, *nfr*, means "beautiful, fair, fine, goodly," etc.[80] This provides a hint. Here are two totally separate *par*-related words with the two meanings found in *paw'ar* (communication and beauty). The communication-related word sounds surprisingly like *teeferet*.

In the Babylonian, the word *taparu* has several meanings, the most common indicating "to drive away, separate, break off, remove."[81] In the "Par for the Course" chapter, I will show that the idea of "separation" and "breaking" is intimately connected with communication.

Napardu, another *pr*-communication word, entered the Standard Babylonian and Neo-Assyrian languages roughly 800 years later (1000 BCE). In meaning #1 it is translated "to become bright, illuminated, to become cheerful, joyous, pleased." Under meaning #2 it becomes *shupardoo*, and is translated "to brighten, illuminate, to make cheerful, cheer up, to make clear, explicit, to elucidate."[82] At this very late time, there is somewhat of a split in meanings. Words like "bright, brilliant" could be equated with "beautiful" and "to make clear, explicit, elucidate" could be equated with "communicating." This would be quite similar to "utterance" and "beauty," the two meanings in the Middle Egyptian.

In the Hittite, according to Friedrich, the word *tapar(r)iia* is "decide, instruct (order, arrange)."[83] He gives the present singular of *tapar(r)iia* as *taparriiasi*. It is not much of a jump from the Egyptian "utterance" to the Hittite "order" or "instruct." They are communication functions. There is no "beauty, glory" meaning apparent here, and there is no *nfr* equivalent word listed.

The Ugaritic has no clear-cut parallels. It is possible that as *pr* words are communication words in the ancient languages, so are *tpr* words in the Middle Egyptian, the Hittite, and the Babylonian. As the Egyptians had another *par*-related word for "beauty," *nfr*, so did the late Babylonians have *napardu*. It is possible then that *paw'ar* derives from the *pr* words, and the original *teeferet* meaning derives from the *tp-r* words. As the *pr* and *tp-r* words seem related, the relation of *paw'ar* and *teeferet* seems logical. The meaning given to *paw'ar* in the following books may have mistakenly taken the unrelated meaning of *teeferet* with it. This may also prove to be the case because *paw'ar* is a word used nowhere else from Genesis to Leviticus and whose technical meaning may have been no longer understood. So later, puzzled scribes may have defined *teeferet* as "beauty" just as *paw'ar* went from "explain" to "glory" or "honor" in Exodus 8:5.[84]

If all of this is true, then the special garments made for Aaron and his sons (1) were for protection from the dangerous *kawbode* and (2) ensured safe communication with the Lord in the super-conditioned place. Exodus

28:39–43 specifies that the clothing be worn "that they carry not impurity and die" when they go into the tent. This is then perfectly consistent with the Exodus 28:2 passage that states that the garments are to be for protection from the danger related to the system of communication. This, then, could be the new translation:

> "And you will make the checkered coat of *shaysh* and ... a miter of *shaysh* and a girdle ... And for the sons of Aaron you will make coats ... and girdles and head-tires ... against radiance (*kawbode*) and for communication (*teef'awret*). And you will fill their hands and you will condition them that they may be priests to Me. And make for them protective (*bawd* [i.e. *bad*]) loin covers (*meechn'say*) to cover the flesh ... from the loins to the thighs they will be. And they will be on Aaron and on his sons, when they go into the tent of meeting, or when they come near to the altar to minister in the super-conditioned place that they carry not impurity and die." (Exod. 28:39–43)[85]

So much for the priests' clothing and devices. Replacing the traditionally translated "glory" and "beauty" with the earlier meanings of "radiance" and "communication" clarifies their purpose with a perfectly logical rationale.

Oil

Next, the priests and their garments had to be anointed with oil.[bd] Oil extracted from olives was a well-known substance at the time. It was used in the sacrificial process to provide fuel for lighting the lamps and to protect against the radiance in the cloud.

The first mentions of oil are in Genesis 28:18 and 35:14 when, after receiving communication from God on two different occasions, Jacob poured it over rocks he set up as pillars. The second mention is in the list of the things God commanded Moses and his artisans to manufacture in the assembling of the tabernacle, the place of communication.[be] The third is in the general summary of the conditioning of Aaron and his sons.[bf] Oil was listed along with other protective elements to "be upon Aaron and his sons ... that they carry not impurity and die" in

bd. Exod. 29:21

be. Exod. 25:6

bf. Exod. 28:41, 29:7, 21

the danger area.^{bg} Its purpose is revealed in the section where the bg. Exod. 28:41–43
directions for making incense is outlined:

> ²²And the Lord spoke to Moses saying,

> ²³"And you, take to you chief spices [of] flowing myrrh five
> hundred [shekel], and [of] spicy cinnamon its half two
> hundred and fifty, and [of] spicy calamus (cane?) two hundred
> and fifty.

> ²⁴And of cassia five hundred, by the shekel of the super-
> conditioned place, and of olive oil a hin.

> ²⁵And you will make it a conditioning, anointing oil, a
> compounded mixture [after] the art of the apothecary (mixer);
> a conditioning anointing oil will it be." (Exod. 30:22–25)⁸⁶

So anointing was not simply a ritual. Applying oil to the skin
protected the priests against falling radioactivity. It was equally
important to put oil on anything or anybody who came in
contact with the tent and its instruments. This was because they
could become saturated with fallout:

> ²⁶"And you will anoint with it the tent of meeting, and the ark
> of communication,

> ²⁷And the table and all its vessels, and the candlestick and
> its vessels, and the altar of incense,²⁸ And the altar of burnt
> offering and all its vessels, and the laver and base.

> ²⁹And you will condition them, and they will be thoroughly
> conditioned. And all touching them shall [i.e., must] become
> conditioned." (Exod. 30:26–29)⁸⁷

The amount of oiling that was going on just couldn't have been
a symbolic gesture. Think about Jacob oiling the stone that was
used as a memorial pillar after God communicated with him.
He may have been covering contaminated rocks with a sealing
coat of oil to protect passersby who might inadvertently touch
them.

In the very next verse of the passage, the reasons for oil are
hammered home: "Aaron and his sons you will anoint; and
you will condition them, that they may be priests to Me."^{bh} In bh. Exod. 30:30
Leviticus 8:10–12, Moses follows the commandment to anoint:

¹⁰And Moses took the anointing oil and he anointed the tabernacle and all that was in it and conditioned them.

¹¹And he sprinkled of it on the altar seven times and he anointed the altar and all its vessels, and the laver and its base, to condition them.

¹²And he poured of the anointing oil on Aaron's head, and he anointed him to condition him.

Leviticus 10 shows further use of oil as protection in the all-important story of the deaths of Aaron's sons when they offered the wrong incense. After Nadab and Abihu were carried out, Aaron and his remaining sons were still in the most dangerous area, the super-conditioned place:

⁶And Moses said to Aaron and to Eleazar and to Ithamar, his sons, "You will not uncover your heads and you will not tear your garments that you will not die [after being exposed] and that He will [not be] angry on all the congregation; but your brethren, all the house of Israel, may weep for the burning, which the Lord has kindled.

⁷And from the door of the tent of meeting you will not go out, lest you die; for the anointing oil of the Lord is on you." (Lev. 10:6–7)

This passage requires a careful reading because of the questions raised. Moses warns Aaron and his sons not to take off their protective headgear or tear their clothing (traditional mourning) lest they get such a dose of radiation in the exposed areas that they would be killed as were their brothers. Remember, the robe of the *ephod* had to have a heavy binding around the neck "that it be not torn."ᵇⁱ

bi. Exod. 28:32

The next phrase is strange: "And that He will [not] be angry on all the congregation." Why should the Lord be *angry* on *all* the congregation? The word for "angry" here is *kawtsaf*.ᵇʲ Strong's says it is a primitive root meaning, "to crack off, i.e., figuratively burst out in rage."⁸⁸ There is no fully agreed upon derivation of the word. The noun is *ketsef*, "a splinter (as chipped off)."ᵇᵏ The *Theological Dictionary of the Old Testament* wonders if this can be true and compares it to the Arabic *qasafa*, "to break."⁸⁹ HAL and

bj. *kawtsaf* with a *koph*, 7107

bk. *ketsef*, 7110

BDB say *ketsef* has two meanings: "anger" and "snapping off."[90] On the other hand, Fuerst says it is "to snort, snuffle, storm; hence [figuratively] to be angry or wroth."[91]

There is no question that *kawtsaf* can mean "angry" in the conventional sense of the word. Moses "was angry (*yeek'tsofe*)" with Aaron's remaining sons.[bl] "Pharaoh was angry (*kawtsaf*) with his servants."[bm] Moses was angry (*yeek'tsofe*) with some of the people for leaving manna until morning. He was angry (*yeek'tsofe*) with his officers for leaving the women and male children alive after a war with the Midianites.[bn]

bl. Lev. 10:16

bm. Gen. 40:2, 41:10

bn. Exod. 16:20; Num. 31:14

When *kawtsaf* is used in relation to the *Lord*, things are not so simple. For example, the conventional concept of being angry in Leviticus 10:6 makes no sense because the people had done nothing to incur the Lord's wrath!

Another example is after the appointment of the Levites over the tent and everything pertaining to it. God declared, "But the Levites will camp around the tabernacle of *edut* that there will be no anger (*ketsef*) on the Israelites."[bo] Later, the specific reason why the Levites were to serve at the tent of *edut* emerged: "That there will not be radiation [affliction related to the Lord's presence] when the Israelites come near to the super-conditioned place."[bp]

bo. Num. 1:53

bp. Num. 8:19

A third example is when the Israelites turned on Moses and Aaron after the Korach-Dathan-Abirim episode, the anger, *ketsef*, is also related directly to the plague.

> [11]"Take the firepan … lay the incense on it and carry it quickly to the congregation and cover on them, for the anger (*ketsef*) has gone forth from the Lord and plague (*negef*) has begun." (Num. 16:46; Heb. 17:11)

After that episode, the Lord told Aaron what items he, his sons, and the Levites were to handle in the tent. He told Aaron that he and his sons "will keep the charge of the super-conditioned place and … the altar, that there be no more anger (*ketsef*) on the Israelites."[bq]

bq. Num. 18:5

So while the Lord may or may not have meant to *punish* wrongdoers in these instances, the word *ketsef* could not have been used to express the conventional meaning of anger or wrath. Rather, *ketsef* described a natural, predictable event that took place with the coming of the cloud and the radiance. This event could lead to random fallout of radioactivity and cause radiation burn.

So why were Aaron, Eleazar, and Ithamar not to leave the tent? The rest of the passage answers this question: "You will not go out of the door of the tent of meeting lest you die, for the anointing oil of the Lord is upon you."[br] This has to mean that the deaths of Aaron's sons interrupted the consecration service. They had not finished protecting the area from the radiance of the Lord because they offered the wrong materials, which had no protective ability. Not only Aaron's remaining sons but the whole congregation was still in danger because the radiance appeared "to *all* the people."[bs] In essence, they were told, "Don't stop the process of protecting the area from exposure or you can expect the usual, fatal consequences."[bt] That is, the *ketsef* of the Lord would result in the continued indiscriminate spread of radiation. This thought is made clear by the instructions to continue with the conditioning process.[bu]

Three other points are worth noting relative to the anointing oil. One is that anointing was to be a perpetual process:

> [31]"And you will speak to the Israelites, saying, 'A conditioning, anointing oil will this be to Me *for your generations*.
>
> [32]Upon the flesh of a man it will not be poured, and in its proportion you will not make like it. It is a conditioner. Conditioning it will be to you.'" (Exod. 30:31–32, my emphasis)

Regarding the sacrifices, "And the priest that [will] be *anointed in his place from* [among] his sons will offer it" (Lev. 6:15, my emphasis). The second point is that, when ingested with other ingredients, oil seemed to act as a protective substance. The third point refers to a series of prohibitions that specifically applied to the priests and high priest. The prohibitions in Leviticus 21 might once have been puzzling, but in light of my theory, they now make sense:

br. Lev. 10:7

bs. Lev. 9:23

bt. cf., Lev. 21:12

bu. Lev. 10:12–18

¹⁰"And the priest who is highest of his brothers, on whose head has been poured the anointing oil and they have filled his hand to put on his garments, and his head will not be uncovered, and his garments he will not tear.

¹¹And to any dead person he will not go in. To his father and to his mother he will not make himself *tawmay*.

¹²And from the super-conditioned place he will not go out that he will not expose the super-conditioned place of his God, for the crown of the anointing oil of his God is on him. I am the Lord." (Lev. 21:10–12)

Several notes can be made regarding these verses. First, the prohibitions are a formalization of the rules that Moses hurriedly transmitted to Aaron and his sons just after the deaths of Nadab and Abihu.[bv] Their purpose was to protect the priests from death. The statement, "for the anointing oil of the Lord is upon you," was simply a way of saying, "continue with the protection process." Here the same sense is found in the statement, "for the crown of the anointing oil of his God is on him." In other words, "Do not go to the dead because you will become *tawmay* and have to re-*tawhor* yourself. Your job is to continue to protect the super-conditioned place from exposure to My radiance." bv. Lev. 10:6–7

Second, the word meaning "expose" is *chawlal*.[bw] The same concept is used implicitly in Leviticus 10:6–7. That is, in both instances the same rules applied: "*Don't expose your head and go out of the super-conditioned place because the oil is on you.*" This is most important because while *chawlal* is variously translated "pollute, profane, defile," it *does* mean "expose" or, literally, "to make unprotected." Thus, if the priest left the super-conditioned place and became *tawmay*, it would leave time for the super-conditioned place to become exposed to or unprotected from the radioactivity. bw. *chawlal*, 2490

Third, in Leviticus 21:12, the crown of the anointing oil is mentioned. Yes, this is our friend *nezer* again. Applying the new information about the plate, the concept of separation fits here perfectly. As the plate is a separator from radioactivity, so also is the oil![92]

Sacrifices

The sacrifices were probably the most important and at the same time the most complicated form of protection. They embodied the use of many different substances—animal, vegetable, and mineral. The use of these substances formed an extremely intricate system that protected different groups of people, from the individual to the entire congregation, depending on their vulnerability to the cloud. The entire next chapter, Congregation Covers, is devoted to the subject of sacrifice.

Meat

Meat for the sacrifices was obtained from cattle, sheep, goats, and birds. Depending on the type of sacrifice, the whole animal was burned on the altar or only the internal parts were burned and the meat eaten. Meat was rarely mentioned in the following books.

Blood

Blood was a protective substance whose covering functions are found throughout the Five Books. As early as the Cain and Abel story, when the active substance of a victim's blood was spilled on the ground, it made that ground polluted and unusable.[bx] Only the blood of the murderer could be used to cover the land.[by]

bx. Gen. 4:10–12

by. See also Gen. 9:4–6

> [33]"And you will not pollute the land wherein you are; for it is the blood that pollutes the land; and no covering can be made for the land for the blood that was shed therein but with the blood of him that has shed it.
>
> [34]And you will not make the land *tawmay*, which you inhabit in the midst of which I dwell, for I, the Lord, dwell in the midst of the Israelites." (Num. 35:33–34)[bz]

bz. See also Lev. 18:24–26[93]

Remember that *tawmayness* was a condition that could attract radiation. Could blood shed by a murderous act somehow attract the drifting radioactive cloud?

One purely physical purpose of blood was to make the land that was polluted by the blood of a murdered person *tawhor*, so God could dwell with the Israelites. Another was to cover:

animal blood was to be sprinkled or poured on both altars, at the veil of the super-conditioned place, on the ark cover, on the priests, on the people, and on a plagued house. Blood also covered the "soul." The verse following one of many warnings not to eat blood says,

> [11]"For the soul (*nefesh*) of the flesh is in the blood, and I have given it to you on the altar to cover on your souls; for it is the blood that covers in the soul." (Lev. 17:11)

In other words, the burning of animal blood on the altar was done to protect the substance in the human blood called *nefesh* (soul).

A comment here on this second purpose: Leviticus 17:11 has caused conniptions for scholars over the years because of the two uses of the word *bet*. The first is clear: "For the soul of the flesh is [located] *in* the blood (*banefesh*)." It's the second that has caused the problem. Most translations read, "for it is the blood that covers on the soul (*banefesh*)." Without going into burdensome detail, the prevailing theory seems to be that it should be translated "expiation is effected by means of blood."[94] There are other thoughts, but "by means of" is among them. But is this correct?

To review, the soul of an animal is located *in* the blood.[95] When animal blood is poured or sprinkled on the altar, it covers (chemically saturates or infiltrates) the soul substance of the blood in humans. In other words, the soul substance in the animal blood works into the soul substance of human blood. Thus, the last part of the sentence should read, "for it is the blood that covers *in* the soul." The prepositions used in this verse all seem quite content to be what they are.

> [11]"For the soul (*nefesh*) of the flesh is in the blood (*dawm*), and I have given it to you on (*al*) the altar to cover (*l'chapayr*) [*keeper*] on (*al*) your souls; for (*kee*) it is the blood that covers in the soul (*banefesh*)." (Lev. 17:11)

The first *ba* is clearly "*in* the blood." The first *al* is "*on* the altar," and the second *al* always refers to "*on*" when used with *keeper*. Then there is *kee*, which is clearly "*for*" or "*because* it is the blood." This leaves the last *ba*, which suddenly gets translated "for" or "by means of." It seems to me that with this absolutely physical description, there is no reason that the second *ba* shouldn't follow the normal usage in the verse and also mean "*in*!"

Where this logic does not work is in Leviticus 17:14. Here a totally different point is made in this veritable litany of warnings not to eat blood. This verse seems to be written only to strengthen the warnings, completely abandoning the chemical description for a metaphysical one. And here only one *bet* is with another of its meanings, "with":

> [14]"For the soul of all flesh *is* its blood, it is *with* its soul (*b'nafshoe*) and I say to the Israelites blood of all flesh you will not eat, for (*kee*) the soul of all flesh *is its blood*." (Lev. 17:14, my emphasis)

This statement was made to underline the importance of not eating blood. As a matter of fact, Leviticus 17:12 and 15 translates *nefesh* as "a person."

So there is no attempt to be consistent here, only to pound home a point.[ca]

Fat

Fat was a byproduct taken from various sacrificial animals and was burned on the altar. Like the blood, it was not to be eaten. Leviticus 3:17 warns against eating *any* fat. Leviticus 7:23 specifically prohibits eating the fat of the ox, sheep, or goat, and verse 24 does the same for an animal that dies by itself or is torn by beasts (though the fat could have been used "for all manner of work"). Verse 25 then says, "For whoever eats fat of a beast, of which one offers a fire offering to the Lord, that person will be cut off from his people." It is peculiar that all these prohibitions seem to finally focus on the animal that was sacrificed. That is, if verse 25 was just another category wherein fat-eating was taboo, then it would have started with the word "and" as did verse 24. However, verse 25 begins with "for," *kee*, meaning "because." So while this is not crystal clear, it would seem that the idea was not to eat an animal's fat from an offering, i.e., from a contaminated (radioactive) area, or from animals found dead because of spoilage caused by decay. If this is the reason for the prohibition, then it is quite different from the one for blood.

Fat was burned for sweet savor and covering. Several times it was specifically stipulated that the fat came from the intestines, kidneys, the lobe on the liver, the flanks, the fat tail, and once, "close by the backbone."[cb] Sometimes all the fat was used. Fat was specified for consecration of the priests, for a general burnt

cb. Lev. 3:9

offering, for the groups and people who contaminated through error, for the continual burnt offering, and for the yearly covering, *Yom Kippur.*

In the following books, the use of fat as a sacrificial material is found in 1 Samuel and 1 Kings as well as in 2 Chronicles in relation to Hezekiah, Isaiah, and Ezekiel.

Bread

Bread, leavened and unleavened, depending on its use, could be part of the sacrifices made by priests and people. Also, depending on the service, bread was eaten or burned. It was used in the consecration of the priests as well as for internal protection. It is used as an internal protection in Exodus 29:32–34, which says of Aaron and his sons during the consecration process that they will

> [32]"Eat ... the bread ... at the door of the tent of meeting.
>
> [33]And they will eat those [by] which covering is made, to consecrate, to *condition* them ...
>
> [34]And if any is left ... of the bread until the morning, you will burn what is left with fire ... *It is a conditioner.*" (my emphasis)

The exact chemical reason for eating the bread (along with meat) is unknown. However, it is interesting that moldy bread was used as an antibiotic in ancient Egypt. Thus, in his paper titled "Pharmacological Practices in Ancient Egypt," Michael D. Parkins of the University of Calgary says,

> Bread was common food stuff in ancient Egypt. The Egyptian *swnw* [physicians] recognized that "bread in rotten condition"—mouldy bread—was regarded as one of the best treatments for intestinal ailments, diseases of the bladder and purulent wounds. Thus, it appeared that the *swnw* recognized the benefits of antibiotics produced by the contaminating bread moulds without understanding their mechanism of action.[96]

Whether it had an equivalent effect from sickness caused by inhaling the cloud is, of course, just an interesting conjecture.

Alcohol

cc. *nesech* or *naysech*, 5262

From ancient times, alcohol was used to make the drink offering, *nesech* or *naysech*.[cc] In addition to "drink offering," *nesech* also means "cover." On the second occasion that the Lord appeared to Jacob, He promised that he would become a great nation: "And God went up from him in the place where He had spoken with him. And Jacob set up a pillar ... of stone; and he poured out upon it a drink offering (*nesech*) and he poured on it oil."[cd] The drink offering was alcoholic.[ce] It is notable that, while Jacob used oil both times he spoke with the Lord, he used the *nesech* only once. I don't know why, but it may be significant that the first encounter was in a dream, while the second where the drink was used seemed to be a live experience.[cf]

cd. Gen. 35:14
ce. e.g., Exod. 24:40
cf., Gen. 28:12, 18

Nesech is used in all Five Books and in many of the following ones. The drink offering was used along with other material for the holidays, for the Sabbath, for the nazirite, for people contaminated through error, and for the continual burnt offering. The formal laws concerning the drink offering specified using alcohol in conjunction with the meal offering and with the meat offering in specified amounts, depending on the animal with which it is offered. The Bible gives no indication of the chemical use of alcohol. It may have been used for its disinfectant quality, but that is only conjecture.

cg. *shechawr*, 7941
ch. Lev. 10:9, Num. 6:3 etc.
ci. Num. 28:7

Another drink offering, *shechawr*, is translated as "strong drink."[cg] This might have been a wine with a higher alcohol content or a beer as in the Akkadian *sikaru*.[97] Drinking it was prohibited under certain circumstances.[ch] *Shechawr* is only mentioned once as a sacrifice in connection with the continual burnt offering.[ci] While the Akkadian meaning is probably the correct explanation, it is interesting that the Egyptian word *shr* means "cover, coat, overlay."[98] If the words were related, it would mean that *shechawr* had a "covering" implication, as did *nesech*.

Meal

The substances used for the meal offering were wheat and, in at least one case, barley. In some instances meal was mixed with oil, frankincense, and salt. The meal offering was used to stimulate memory, for protection, in the consecration process, and with the drink offering. It was common in following books.

Rest

Rest was used to protect the soul substance in the blood. It was the central purpose for observing the Sabbath and the various festivals.

> [16]"And the Israelites will keep the Sabbath for their generations as a perpetual covenant.

> [17]Between Me and between the Israelites it is a sign forever; for [in] six days the Lord made the heaven and the earth, and on the seventh day He rested and was *refreshed*." (Exod. 31:16–17, my emphasis)

The Sabbath rest was a method of conditioning/protecting, specifically for the purpose of refreshing the soul substance. The word translated "refreshed" is *nawfash*.[cj] It is the word from which *nefesh* is derived and suggests recharging (re*nefeshing*) the *nefesh*. In several places it is explained that both man (including "sojourners") and animals are to rest.[ck]

Evidently this soul substance was also present in the Lord. Leviticus 26:11 says, "And I will set My dwelling in the midst of you; and My soul will not reject you.'"[cl] Therefore, when the Lord rested, perhaps it was for resting His soul like people and animals. Support for this notion is in Leviticus 11:44:

> [44]"For I am the Lord your God. You will therefore condition yourselves, and you will be conditioned for I am conditioned, and you will not make your *souls* unclean with any creeping thing that moves on the earth." (my emphasis)

In addition to the Sabbath, eventually the festivals of Passover (*Pesach*), the following Festival of Unleavened Bread (*Chag Hamatzot*), the Feast of Weeks (*Shavuot*), the Festival of Booths (*Succot*), *Rosh Hashana*, and *Yom Kippur* all emphasized rest. I believe that they were all for refreshing the *nefesh*. The one holiday description that does mention the soul is *Yom Kippur*,

cj. *nawfash*, 5314

ck. Exod. 23:12; Deut. 5:14

cl. cf., Lev. 26:30

cm. Lev. 16:29–34

but the mentions are very difficult to figure out.[cm] Consider Leviticus 16:29–34 or these Leviticus 23 verses:[27]

> "Also, on the tenth [day] of the seventh month this is the day of coverings; a conditioning convocation will it be to you, and you will *afflict your souls*, and you will offer a fire offering to the Lord. Any work you will not do on the same day, for it is a day of coverings to cover on you before the Lord your God …

> [32]A Sabbath of rest (*shabat shabatone*) it will be to you, and you will *afflict your souls*; on the ninth [day] of the month at evening, from evening to evening you will keep your Sabbath (rest your rest)." (Lev. 23:27, 32)

cn. *awnaw*, 6031

These verses call for "afflicting," *awnaw*, the soul.[cn] This has always been translated in connection with *Yom Kippur* as meaning "to fast," but there is disagreement on this. While it is possible that the soul was "afflicted" by fasting, there is no direct mention of anyone fasting in the Five Books. There are several mentions in the following books. Moses went without food when he was on Mount Sinai, but there is no evidence that he did so purposely.

It is quite unusual for such an important biblical command as fasting not to be spelled out clearly. If fasting was required, the order would be, "And you will *awnaw* your souls by eating no food." That is exactly what Psalm 35:13 says: "I afflicted my soul with fasting," which both specifies what is being done and demonstrates that fasting is but one way to "afflict." Isaiah seems to have included fasting as a way to afflict the soul, but there is

co. Isa. 58:3–5, 10; cf., Ezra 8:21

no indication that he is speaking of *Yom* Kippur.[co] *Awnaw* is generally translated "humbled" in this instance.

So, if *awnaw* doesn't mean "fast," what could it mean? Leviticus 23:27–28 says that "you will afflict (*eeneetam*) your souls (*nafshosaychem*) and you will offer a fire offering to the

cp. *eeneetam*, the piel perfect tense of *awnaw*

Lord.[cp] *Any work you will not do.*" Verse 32 says, "A Sabbath of rest it will be to you, and you will afflict your souls." A similar juxtaposition was seen in Leviticus 16:29, "You will afflict

cq. *t'anoo*, the piel imperfect of *awnaw*

(*t'anoo*) your souls, and all work you will not do."[cq] Then verse 31 says, "It is a Sabbath of rest to you, and you will afflict your souls." In the repeat of the law, Numbers 29:7 says of the tenth day of the seventh month, "A holy convocation it will be to you and you will afflict your souls; any work you will not do." In all these references there is the prohibition against doing any work coupled directly with "afflict your souls." Perhaps, then, *awnaw* indicated resting, which was done to the soul in order to refresh it.

Now *awnaw* has many translations including to "heed, sing, shout, testify, answer."[cr] Strong's translates another *awnaw* as cr. Exod. 19:19 "abase self, deal hardly with, humble, ravish," and the familiar "afflict." HAL says, "to be wretched, emaciated, to cringe [a lion], crouched, hunched up, suffering, to bend, submit to, be (become) bowed, weak, to oppress, humiliate, to castigate oneself [Leviticus 23:27–8, 32 and Numbers 29:7], to do violence, to become degraded ... to be troubled."[99] Common translations in the lexicons and literature are, e.g., "be humbled by fasting."[100] Under *eeneetam nafshosaychem* in the Leviticus and Numbers references are "humble oneself," "afflict yourselves," and "practice self denial ... literally you will afflict yourselves."[101]

However, combining "you must do no work whatsoever, rest completely" with "fast or humble or castigate oneself" makes little sense. How can you both rest and punish the body at the same time? Hardly would going without food contribute to total rest. In fact, it would have the opposite effect. (A common result of going without food for a day in the modern observance of *Yom Kippur* is a headache!) So, since *awnaw* has many translations, it would be logical to pick one that would make sense when coupled with the mandatory rest warning. Of course, it is possible that the recorders of the law hadn't the faintest idea what the whole process was about and used a common word that seemed to fit the case.

The Akkadian and Middle Assyrian provide logical concepts for rest. The exact cognate *enoo* in the Akkadian is translated, among other meanings, "to displace, to shift, to change."[102] Regarding "to shift, to change," one of the quotes attested to the Middle Assyrian is "like the dead, (lie still and) do not change the side (lit. 'kidney') (on which you sleep)."[103] If *awnaw* comes from the Akkadian, then changing the position of the body by resting so as to affect the soul would make some sense. That is something like, "you will *change* your soul and all work you will not do, a Sabbath of solemn rest it will be to you, and you will change your soul." This would be a direct statement that resting would lead to changing the soul substance to a calmed condition.

As noted, rest was also central to each of the festivals mentioned in the Five Books. That it was the important reason for the Sabbaths and festivals leads to another question. If the sacrifices and resting were for the purpose of protecting the area and the people from the cloud's effects and not for expiation and propitiation, then one must naturally wonder about another reason for offerings, "for a sweet savor to the Lord."

Rayach neechoach is mentioned approximately 39 times from Genesis through Numbers (no mention in Deuteronomy), from Noah through the carefully stated Levitical ordinances.[cs] It is translated "sweet savor," "pleasing odor," or "quieting, soothing, tranquilizing."[104] If this was "for a sweet savor to the Lord," then one must naturally conclude that the smell of the sacrifices was pleasing to the Lord, and therefore, He became partial to the requests of those who bribed Him in this manner. It is easy then to dismiss the sacrifices as a primitive rite (as in other groups where providing "sweet savor" for their gods was certainly common), and let it go at that. However, there is a problem with translating *neechoach* as "sweet, pleasing," etc. The word derives from our friend *nooach* and actually means "resting" or "rest." There is nothing new about this observation. In his book *Sacrifices in the Old Testament*, George Buchanan Gray says, "Etymologically [*rayach neechoach*] means 'a rest-giving smell.'"[105] More recently, Baruch A. Levine says the word "probably derives from the verb *nuah*, 'to rest, be at ease.'"[106] I have not found any scholar who follows through with this etymology. They either slip right into the "pleasing odor" definition and/or discuss the propitiatory or expiatory possibilities of the term. The reason for this seems to

cs. *rayach*, 7381; *neechoach*, 5207; Gen. 8:21

be that out of all the references to *rayach neechoach,* only Genesis 8:21 and Leviticus 26:31 have seemingly very anthropomorphic overtones.

Genesis 8:21 is the end of the Flood story. Noah, his family, and all the other living things had left the ark. He then built an altar and sacrificed to the Lord:

> ²¹And the Lord *smelled* the *rayach neechoach,* and the Lord said to his heart, "I will not again curse the ground because of man, because the purpose of his heart [is] evil from his youth, and I will not again strike every living [thing] as I have done." (Gen. 8:21)

According to the scholars this is anthropomorphic, but I think they are missing the point of what the writer is trying to convey. He is not interested in telling us this is God being soothed by the smell of sacrifice so He will not destroy life on earth again, nor is it about Noah giving thanks to Him for sparing his life. Rather, he is describing, almost in code, a law of nature. Look at what caused the flood:

> ¹¹And the earth was corrupt (*teeshachayt*) before God, and the earth was filled with violence.
>
> ¹²And God saw the earth and behold it was corrupted because all flesh had corrupted its way on the earth.
>
> ¹³And God said to Noah, "The end of all flesh has come before Me, because the earth is filled with violence because of them. And behold, I will destroy them (*mash'cheetawn*) [with] the earth." (Gen. 6:11–13)ᶜᵗ

ct. from *shawchat*, 7843

God makes a statement that He will rid the earth of its "corrupters." Since He did not destroy the earth, the wording "I will destroy them [with] the earth" makes no sense here.

These were similar conditions (albeit on a global scale) to the Leviticus 18 case in Canaan:

- There is a long description of behaviors (considered evil) and a warning to the Israelites to avoid them in Leviticus 18:1–23.
- Then the Lord warns that defiling the land would cause "vomiting out" of its inhabitants in Leviticus 18:25.
- The inhabitants engaged in the prohibited behaviors and had to be ejected in Leviticus 18:27. "For all these abominations

the men of the land have done that were before you, and the land became defiled."

Leviticus 26:31–39, the second seemingly anthropomorphic passage, wraps up the long list of do's and don'ts that begins with Leviticus 17–18. Scholars call this section of the Bible the "Holiness Code" or "H Code," and they ascribe it to the writing of some other group of priests at another time for another purpose. I think it was simply the addition of laws found necessary after the death of Aaron's sons. (I have put my full reasoning regarding the H Code in Appendix H.) It's a general warning of what will happen if the Israelites "will not listen to Me, but will walk contrary to Me."cu The reference says,

cu. Lev. 26:27

> 31"And I will make your cities a waste, and I will desolate your sanctuaries, and I will not smell your *rayach neechoachem* [plural].
>
> 32And I will desolate the land, that your enemies who live there will be astonished.
>
> 33… and your cities will be a desolation …
>
> 34Then the land will enjoy its Sabbaths all the days it lies desolate … then the land will *rest*, and it will enjoy its Sabbaths.
>
> 35All the days that it lies desolate it will have rest, the rest that it did not have when you dwelt upon it." (Lev. 26:31–35)

So the earth became "corrupted" during the Flood and "defiled" in the Leviticus 18 reference. In Leviticus 26 the land would be made "desolate." In each case the insult to the earth was caused by the misdeeds of the people, making it necessary to rid the earth of their polluting presence. Leviticus 26 gives the result of emptying the earth: it will then be able to "satisfy its Sabbaths;" "then will the land rest."cv This was a necessity detailed in the law of Leviticus 25:2–5, where every seventh year the land had to lay fallow, much like modern farming. Thus, we see natural laws unfolding: pollution of earth, destruction of the polluters, rest (rejuvenation) of the earth. What about Genesis? S*hawchat* was a sort of play on words indicating that the earth was corrupt (*shawchat*) and had to be destroyed (*shawchat*). Sarna points out

cv. Lev. 26:34

additional games with words in the Flood story that are quite fascinating, so much so that I believe it is worthwhile to quote the whole footnote about Genesis 5:29.[107]

Noah

The name as such is paralleled in biblical and extrabiblical sources. It would appear to derive from the stem *n-w-ḥ*, "to rest," and there are records of Akkadian and Amorite personal names compounded of this element. The explanation given in the narrative rests on similarity of sound, not on etymology, since Noah cannot derive from *n-ḥ-m*, "to comfort, give relief." The incongruity is noted in Genesis Rabba 25:2. In the Hurrian version of the Gilgamesh Epic, one hero of the flood is Naḥmasulel, and a dim recollection of this may have influenced the word play in our text. At any rate, the two stems, *n-w-ḥ* and *n-ḥ -m*, are subtly integrated into the language of the narrative. The first stem appears in 6:8 and 8:4, 9, 21; the second provides an ironic touch, for this same stem is used in 6:6, 7. As Rashbam observes, since Noah was the first to be born after the death of Adam, his arrival signified some easing of the curse laid on the soil through Adam's sin. The father looked to "relief" (*yenaḥamenu*) from "toil" ('*itsavon*), but instead came God's decision to wipe out civilization. God "regretted" (*va-yinnaḥem-niḥamti*) and was "saddened" (*va-yit'atsev*). (my emphasis)

The most notable point here is that the very name Noah (Hebrew, Noach) "would appear to derive from 'rest.'" Strong's takes this for granted.[108] The plays on the word *n- ḥ-m* (*nacham*) are interesting in that the concept of "relief" (rest) from "toil" is seen.

Regardless how the name was derived, the purpose of Noach, as far as his father Lemech was concerned, was to rest from work. "And he [Lemech] called his name Noach, saying this [one] will comfort us from our work and for the toil of our hands from the ground, which the Lord has cursed."[cw] The writer can't resist doing it again, so Sarna says in Genesis 8:4: "came to rest, Hebrew *va-tanah*, is another play on the name *noah*."[109] Regarding Genesis 6:8, "*Noah* found *favor*" Sarna says, "The two words in Hebrew constitute an anagram: *nh—hn*."[110] He might have mentioned Genesis 8:9, "But the dove did not find a resting

cw. Gen. 5:29

place, *mawnoach*." Sarna also points out the following regarding *shawcat*: "The key Hebrew stem *sh-h-t* occurs seven times in the narrative." "Go into" [the ark] is found exactly seven times in the chapter. There are seven pairs of animals and seven days, etc.[cx] Finally, he points to Genesis 8:21, that the Hebrew *neechoach* "is one more play on the name *noah*." Here he translates *neechoach* "pleasing."[111] I see no reason to do this. Everything in the Flood story points to an emphasis on the rest concept. The theory of a human-polluted land requiring rest is as strong in Genesis as in the Leviticus references.

Why all the word play in order to indicate this, I don't know. Was the idea of "sweet smelling" so inculcated in the general populace that the writer felt he had to code the true meaning to avoid personal vilification? Did he mask the true meaning so it would only be understood by those directly involved in the sacrificial process at a much later time? If people were aware of the other, older versions of the story, they may have "inherited" the idea that "sweet savor" was to please. In the Babylonian version of the Flood story, the gods did not sacrifice during the deluge, and they were hungry. So when they finally smelled the sweet odor, they "gathered like flies over the sacrificer."[112]

There is not the slightest hint that the sacrifice for *rayach neechoach* was for anything but providing a resting-protecting climate. It is also possible that the constant repetition of the sacrifice being for rest-smelling "to the Lord" was to make another point: just as it protected the people so there could be communication, the rest-smelling action could cause "rest" for the Lord's soul substance, which He had in common with man.

As to the actual word *neechoach*, it would seem to be a technical variation of *nooach* used specifically to describe the process. It is *only* used with *rayach* in the four books. It is not in Deuteronomy at all. As *rayach neechoaach*, it is only found in Ezekiel in the following books. Ezekiel used it pejoratively regarding idol worship.[cy] In Ezekiel 20:41, he used it in reference to the Lord, but perhaps without comprehension of its technical meaning. For example, he used *kawdash* in the traditional "sanctify"

cx. Gen. 7:2, 4

cy. Ezek. 6:13, 16:19, 20:28

sense rather than in a way that is related to a natural process: "I will be sanctified in you in the sight of the nations." As in so many instances, Ezekiel had the terminology but not the full understanding of the meanings.[113]

So *rayach neechoach* was a technical phrase that referred only to the sacrifices and related to the rest/protection/communication system. But how did the meaning form? To find out, it's necessary to take a closer look at its parent *nooach* and its relatives in other languages.

OTHER LANGUAGES

The word *nayhoo* basically means "rest" in Old Akkadian and Old Assyrian.[114] It means the same in the Ugaritic, *n'ch*.[115] It is common in other semitic languages. In the Ugaritic, Driver gives two interesting quotes. In the first, when King Danel learned that the god El (the senior god, the creator in the Ugaritic pantheon) was to give him a son, "He opened wide the passage of (his) throat and laughed, he put his foot on the stool, he lifted up his voice and cried: 'I myself will sit down and will *rest* (*wanhn*), and (my) *soul* (*nps*) will *rest* (*wtnh*)'" (my emphasis).[116]

The second quote is also found in an entirely different story using the exact words that are found in the first quote. In this quote, the soul (now the senior god El's rather than the King Danel's) "shall rest (*wtnh*)."[117]

Another related word is the Ugaritic *nht*. Gordon says it means "resting place, couch" and is probably derived from *nwh*.[118] Driver says, "rest, seat," and it derives from *nwh*.[119] DLU says it is "couch."[120] While *nht* is related to *n'ach*, the point of interest is a note in GORDON that the same word *nht* is found in the Pyramid Texts (5th–8th dynasties, ca. 2350–2160 BCE) "designating what the resurrected king is to stand upon."[121] It does not have the same meaning later.

Whether referring to *awnaw*ing, the soul, or providing *rayach neechoach*, all of this was done for protection and communication. Interestingly, the Egyptian word *nche* means "succor, protect."[122] Also, *nchoo* is "protector."[123] That *n'ach* is the essential part of the meaning is seen in the words *n'ach*, "escape death," *nht*, "shelter refuge," *nht* "magical protection," and *nhw*, "protection of king's arm."[124] Another Egyptian word is *nhi*, "pray for," and *n'ach*, *nht*, "prayer."[125] These words are more examples of the possible relationship between the protection/communication concepts in Hebrew and Egyptian.

Finally, turning to the Hittite, the word *na-ah-ha-an* means "reverence."[126] The quote used is, "Among the gods of my majesty, (of) his son, (and, of) his grandson, may there be reverence (*na-ah-ha-a-an*) to [the goddess]

Ishtar."[127] This is about as near to prayer to a god as you can get, and with a very similar word.

<hr>

It is no coincidence that *awnaw* and *rayach neechoach* strongly relate rest and communication with such a broad range of foreign word corroboration. What's possible for *nooach* is just as possible for *neechoach*. Because it derives from *nooach*, it has the same meaning, "rest," and it is only used in one type of situation—the sacrifices. It is only a technical variation of the parent word.

Veil

I have speculated that the veil, which divided the conditioned place from the super-conditioned place, played the dual roles of antennae and protection. To be exact, the *cherubim* woven into the veil were the antennae, and the material from which the veil was made served as a screen.

The veil could be used as a screen for the entrance of the super-conditioned place, so it was possibly of some use in screening the worst of the radiation that was in the super-conditioned place. It could also be used to wrap the ark when the congregation traveled, covering the dangerous ark while in transit.

Incense

Incense was another protective entity used against the radioactive emanations:

> [12]"And he will take a firepan full of coals of fire from off the altar before the Lord, and his hands full of incense, of spices (pounded) fine, and he will bring (it) within the curtain.
>
> [13]And he will put the incense on the fire before the Lord that the cloud of the incense may cover the covering, which is on the *edut*, and he will not die." (Lev. 16:12–13)

When the wrong ingredients were combined, the incense was ineffective to the detriment of everyone in the vicinity, as when Nadab and Abihu (Aaron's sons) brought the wrong ingredients to the altar and were "consumed."[cz]

cz. Lev. 10:1

The Numbers 16 story of Korach, Dathan, and Abiram also indicates the danger of using the wrong incense. (It is widely believed that these are two stories intertwined.) While in the wilderness, they assembled 250 "chiefs of the congregation" and tried to lead a revolt against Moses and Aaron. Moses was terribly upset when he heard the words of the revolutionaries:

> ³And they assembled against Moses and against Aaron and they said to them, "You [take] too much on you, for the whole congregation, all of them, are conditioned and the Lord is in their midst. And why do you lift yourselves above the assembly of the Lord?"

> ⁴When Moses heard, then he fell on his face,

> ⁵And he spoke to Korach and to all his congregation saying, "In the morning the Lord will make known who is His and who is conditioned, and the conditioned [people] He will bring near to Him, and whom He will choose He will bring near to Him.

> ⁶Do this: take firepans for yourselves, Korach, and all his company.

> ⁷And put them in fire and put on them incense before the Lord tomorrow, and it will be the man whom the Lord will choose, he is the conditioned [one]. You [take] too much on you sons of Levi!" (Num. 16:3–7)

Korach challenged Moses and Aaron by claiming the whole congregation was conditioned. Moses accepted the challenge. He instructed Aaron to put incense and fire in the firepan, and Moses, Korach, and his 250 men assembled at the door of the tent of meeting where the "radiance of the Lord" appeared. Then two separate phenomena occurred: (1) An earthquake split the earth "and swallowed them up, and their houses and all the men who were for Korach." (2) "A fire came forth from the Lord and consumed the 250 men that offered the incense."[da]

da. Num. 16:32, 35

It appears that Moses played a trick on his adversaries. He already knew from the tragic experience of Aaron's two sons that the exact material had to be used. Moses knew that only Aaron would have the proper incense when the Lord appeared and that what happened to Aaron's sons would happen to Korach's men. It did. Thus, Moses used what he knew would be a natural phenomenon under the right circumstances. Interestingly, God ordered Eleazar, the priest, to beat the incense pans into plates (the very incense pans used by the rebels) to cover the altar and as a reminder.

> ³⁹And Eleazar the priest took the ... firepans that those who [were] burned brought near [rebels], and they beat them [into] a cover for the altar,

> ⁴⁰A memorial to the Israelites, in order that (there) will not come near a strange man who is not of the seed of Aaron to burn incense before the Lord, that he will not be as Korach and as his company as the Lord spoke to him by the hand of Moses. (Num. 16:39–40)^{db}

db. Num. 17:4– 5

The writer of these verses mistakenly thought the memorial was for preventing people who were outside of Aaron's lineage from burning incense "before the Lord." In reality, the rebels died because they burned the wrong incense. Moses used his prior knowledge of the proper formulation of the incense to achieve his end, which was for the good of the people as a whole.

The People Complain

After the death of the rebels, the congregation complained to Moses and Aaron saying:

> ⁴¹"You have killed the people of the Lord."

> ⁴²And it came to pass, when the congregation assembled against Moses and against Aaron, that they turned toward the tent of meeting; and behold, the cloud covered it, and the radiance of the Lord appeared.

> ⁴³And Moses and Aaron came to the front of the tent of meeting.

> ⁴⁴And the Lord spoke to Moses saying,

> ⁴⁵"Rise up from the midst of this congregation, and I will consume them in a moment." And they fell on their faces.

> ⁴⁶And Moses said to Aaron, "Take the firepan, and put it on the fire from off the altar, and lay incense (thereon), and carry (it) quickly to the congregation, and cover on them for the anger has gone out from the Lord; the plague has begun."

> ⁴⁷And Aaron took [it] as Moses had spoken, and he ran into the midst of the assembly, and behold the plague had begun among the people, and he put on the incense and he covered on the people.

[48]And he stood between the dead and between the living, and the plague was stayed.

[49]And [there] were those that died in the plague fourteen thousand and seven hundred besides those that died about the matter of Korach.

[50]And Aaron returned to Moses to the door of the tent of meeting and the plague was stayed. (Num. 16:41–50; Heb. 17:6–15)

Again, the cloud caused the plague, and the incense protected against the harmful effects of the cloud, preventing further spread of the plague. Incidentally, the end of this story shows that while the people understood that the tabernacle was dangerous, they still didn't grasp exactly why it was so. This led to the terrible frustration shown in their cry:

[12]And the Israelites spoke to Moses saying, "Behold, we perish. We are undone ...

[13]Everyone who comes near to the tabernacle of the Lord dies. Will we totally be consumed with dying?" (Num. 17:12–13; Heb. 17:27–28)

A third example of the misuse of incense is found in the King Uzziah story.[dc] He defied his priests by brazenly entering the temple to burn incense and thereby contracted burning. [dc. 2 Chr. 26:16–21]

In any situation where a place was repeatedly exposed to doses of radioactive material, as when the cloud settled on the super-conditioned place, there must have been some residual danger. So the ark, situated in the super-conditioned place, continued to be dangerous. Therefore, one must ask if there wasn't some protective incense burning continuously to help take care of residue. There was. An incense altar was placed in front of the veil leading to the super-conditioned place, which housed the ark with the stones of communication.

[1]"And you will make an altar to burn incense on; (of) acacia wood you will make it.

[2]A cubit its length and a cubit its breadth; foursquare it will be; and two cubits its height; of the same piece, its horns.

³And you will overlay it (with) pure gold. Its top and its sides round about, and its horns, and you will make for it an edging of gold round about.

⁴And two rings of gold you will make for it under its edging on its two corners you will make [it], on its two sides; and they (it) will be for places for poles to carry it with them.

⁵And you will make the poles [of] acacia wood, and you will overlay them [with] gold.

⁶And you will put it *before the veil, which is by the stones of communication, before the covering, which is on the stones of communication,* where I will meet with you.

⁷And Aaron will burn on it incense of spices; every morning when he dresses the lamps, he will burn it.

⁸And when Aaron sets up the lamps toward evening, he will burn it, a *continual* incense before the Lord for your generations.

⁹You will not offer upon it *strange* fire nor burnt offering nor meal offering; and a drink offering you will not pour on it.

¹⁰And Aaron will cover on its horns once in the year; from the blood of the decontamination offering of covering, once in a year will he cover on it your generations; it is super-conditioned to the Lord." (Exod. 30:1–10, my emphasis)

The precise location of the incense altar in relation to the *edut* suggests very strongly that it was to be used continually in connection with the *edut*.

Many Altars

Incense was pervasive among the Israelites and other ancient peoples. Reference after reference shows that throughout history it was used before gods and kings as a propitiatory substance and as protection against demons and the like. In the following books, it was incorrectly used.[dd] There is disagreement among scholars as to whether incense was part of the original material used in the Hebrew sacrifices. This is nonsense, and I laboriously developed my reasoning. Since then Milgrom has neatly skewered the opposing scholars' thoughts pointing to many altars too small for animal offerings being found in

dd. e.g., Ezek. 8:11

Canaan dating to the Bronze Age. He said that "several of these altars were found in Israelite sanctuaries."[128]

Ezekiel omitted the incense altar from *his* temple.[129] Close reading shows that he took the presence of the two altars so much for granted that he merely mentions them incidentally, but mention them he does.[de] The fact is, the use of incense was always taken for granted, even though later mentions were mostly exhortations against using it with false gods.

de. Ezek. 40:47, 41:22

Whether incense was part of the earliest ritual isn't the issue. The real point is that the Israelites used the Lord's specified mixture in the early period for an entirely different reason— not to propitiate, not to make a nice smell, not to drive away demons, or please kings and pharaohs. They used it to protect the people from the effects of the cloud. This is chemical and in no way mystical or magical. As far as I know, no other group used it this way. Significantly, incense lost its purpose for the Israelites in later times. However, the little incense altars found in later periods all over biblical lands were probably simply for ritual purposes.

Othmar Keel points out, "Approximately 150 incense altars from the Persian period have been found at Lachish," the famous city inhabited by various peoples for hundreds of years.[130] Located at a site now known as Tell-ed-Duweir, "toward the lower W slopes of the Judean hill country ... The surrounding ridges have yielded finds of worked flints giving evidence of human habitation as early as Upper Paleolithic times."[131] Kurt Galling says, "These little limestone incense altars (sixth to fifth century [BCE]) are especially numerous in Lachish ... One of them has an Aramaic inscription beginning with the word 'incense offering.'"[132] Jacob Neufeld says, "From Iron Age [of Palestine] private houses various small stone altars were found ... as a rule having 'horns' in the four corners. In view of their small size these items can only be incense altars, which, because of the place where they were found, must have served as private censors."[133] The Iron Age in Palestine began around 1200 BCE.

The contribution from the other languages and the derivation in the Hebrew relate to the physical action of the incense. It was a material that had to be burned to become active and to smoke to become effective for protection. From the Hebrew instructions, a resinous material was formed from the mixture, and this was the desired result, not fragrance.

The Filling of Hands

[41]"And you will clothe [with] them Aaron your brother and his sons with him; and you will anoint them, and you will *consecrate* them, and you will condition them, that they will be priests to Me." (Exod. 28:41)

"Consecrate" is the traditional translation of the Hebrew phrase *oomeelaytaw et yawdawm*, but it literally means "fill the hands." The process of filling the hands was among the ordinances that the priests followed for protection against the effects of the cloud. This immediately raises the question, fill the hands with what?

According to *The Pentateuch and Haftorahs*, the priests filled their hands "with the first sacrifices." It calls consecration "the technical term for installing a priest into his office."[134] Soncino quotes Rashi's commentary, which also indicates installing the priests into office. Soncino continues: "The idiom means 'to complete' by investing them with authority to perform their sacred duties."[135]This interpretation is attributed to both Nachmanides and Sforno.[136] I think the priests filled their hands with incense. For example, after the death of Aaron's sons, the Lord commanded Moses to give Aaron the following orders:

[12]"And he will take a firepan full of coals of fire from off the altar before the Lord, *and his hands (oom'lai chawf'nawyv q'toret sawmaym) full of incense* of spices ...

[13]And he will put the incense on the fire before the Lord that the cloud of the incense may cover the covering that is on the *stones of communication*, and he will not die." (Lev. 16:12–13)

These verses indicate that consecration through filling the hands was not an initiation to install the priest. Rather, it was a specific description of how the protective incense was to be handled and its purpose.

Cyrus Gordon, in his fascinating book *Before Columbus*, has an interesting sidelight on this subject:

Stone pipes were used ritually in the ancient Near East. Such pipes consist of a bowl and stem carved out of one stone. Some have animal heads on the bowl, and some have a hand (with all five fingers) carved in relief on the bottom of the bowl. It is interesting to note that American Indian pipes sometimes have animal or human heads carved on the bowl, as well as hands with all five fingers carved beneath the bowl. The heads indicate that the bowls were personified, while the hands not only suggest that the fragrant smoke was being offered, but also that the whole cultic object was called a "hand" (*kaf* "hand" is the name of such an object in Hebrew).

Since such smoking bowls appear during Old Testament times in the Near East, it is possible that the American peace pipes are an adaptation of Near East *kaf* pipes. They could have been introduced by Canaanites like those who reached America in 531 B.C. or by later visitors … The substitution of tobacco for Near East incense is a common type of transformation; i.e., the employment of what is available locally instead of an ingredient too difficult to import from afar. The ritual use of copal in America seems to be a simple "translation" of frankincense and other fragrant smokes used to propitiate the gods in the Old World.[137] (my emphasis)

Actually *kaf* means "palm" of the hand and "bowl."[df] HAL says the *kaf* is a "metal bowl … in the shape of a hand."[138] Strong's translates *kaf* as "spoon" when related to the incense container. It is also used as "sole" of the foot in Genesis and Deuteronomy, "paws" in Leviticus, and "hollow" of Jacob's thigh in Genesis.

df. *kaf,* 3709

~~~~~~

OTHER LANGUAGES

Kaf is common in other ancient languages. In Ugaritic *kp* is "palm" and "*tray*" of scales, i.e., a *container* for stone weights used in the weighing process.[139] From Old Babylonian on *kappu* A means "wing, quill, plumage, frond, arm, *hand*, list, lobe of the lung, side part of horse bit, armrest." *Kappu* B is "bowl."[140] CAD notes that "this word has been separated from *kappu* A because it refers to a small serving container and need not have any etymological connection with *kappu* 'arm,' 'hand,' 'side,' etc."[141] However, one has to logically ask why it wouldn't have the same connection as the Hebrew or Ugaritic. While there is no direct equivalent for "hand" in the Egyptian, there are some correlations that would have to be called startling. These are found in the word *kap*. Depending on its spelling, the word means "burn incense, cense gods, fumigate patient, hut, hide of fowler, bandage, *cover*, roof over, hide oneself, take cover, royal nursery, child of the nursery."[142] Gardiner, too, says *kap* means "fumigate" and "harim, nursery."

He points out that ỏ in Dynasty XVIII, the sign for "censer for fumigation" that begins the word, "somewhat resembles a *wrist* and *hand*."[143]

~~~~~~

Was a *kaf* of incense originally a *portable protection* against the dangers of spreading radiation? Was the hand-shaped bowl a ritualistic portrayal of the filling of the hands of the priests? If so, it would explain this mysterious final rite in the preparation of the priests entering the danger area.

There is another category relating to the filling of the hands relative to the sacrifices. A meat offering, which was literally held in the hand, was called the ram of "consecration," literally "filling."[dg] Along with the ram, bread mixed with oil was offered.[dh] While this is explained as a command in Exodus 29:28, its presentation comes across more clearly in Leviticus 8:22–36. Here the fat of the ram of consecration was mixed with bread from the "basket of consecration," put on the palms of Aaron and his sons, and then burned as a "consecration offering."[di] The priests ate the unused meat (not fat) and bread. Yet another reference states, "And he offered the meal offering, and he filled his palms of it, and he burned [it] upon the altar, beside the burnt offering of the morning."[dj]

These references to hand filling provide a glimpse into how the process of conditioning was done. Exodus gives a good summary:

> [31]"And the ram of the filling you will take and you will boil its flesh in a conditioned place.
>
> [32]And Aaron and his sons will eat the flesh of the ram, and the bread, which is in the basket, [at] the door of the tent of meeting.
>
> [33]And they will eat those [things] by which covering was made, *to fill their hands, to condition them.*" (Exod. 29:31–33)

This passage puts the finishing touches on the explanation. The processes prepared the priests to safely enter the danger area. The preparation included *tawhor*ing or protecting the area from radiation by sacrificing animals. Then the priests ate the residue of the sacrificial material. I believe that eating at least some of

dg. e.g., Exod. 29:22–27

dh. Exod. 29:23

di. Lev. 8:31

dj. Lev. 9:17

the material was for internal protection. After cleansing, the priests went into the super-conditioned place, their filled hands with incense as an added protection. Only after taking some additional personal precautions, the high priest would be able to receive communication safely via the stones of communication.

Finally, Exodus 32 shows that the priests filled their hands for protection even before the tent was set up. Here is the well-known story of the Golden Calf. While Moses was on Mt. Sinai, some rebels demanded that Aaron make a god to lead them in place of Moses because the Israelites feared he had disappeared for good. When Moses saw the golden calf—the proof of their rebellion—he ordered the rebels killed and then begged the Lord to forgive the people. The verse says,

> [29]And Moses said: "*Fill your hands* today to the Lord, for every man [has been] against his son, and against his brother, and in order to give on you today a blessing." (Exod. 32:29)

The story ends in Exodus 32:35: "And the Lord plagued the people because they made the calf."

Knowing that, even if he implored the Lord not to bring destruction to the people, his proximity during this crisis would still be dangerous. Moses warned the people to "fill [your] hands today to the Lord." The act of filling the hands, whether with incense or sacrificial material, was of extreme importance in the protection process. This is underlined by the fact that it was done by both the priests and the people.

Special Fire

The word for "incense" is *k'toret*.[dk] It and its close relatives, e.g., *keetor* meaning "smoke, vapor," have been well studied in the literature.[dl] It is generally agreed that *keetar* derives from *kawtor*, meaning "burn," i.e., sacrificial burning.[dm] Words similar to *k'toret* are found in Akkadian, Ugaritic, etc.

dk. *k'toret*, 7004

dl. *keetor*, 7008

dm. *kawtor*, 6999

The instructions for making incense were quite precise:

> [34]And the Lord said to Moses, "Take to you spices, balm and onycha and galbanum, spices with pure frankincense; of each there will be an equal weight.

³⁵And you will make it incense, a mixture [after] the art of an apothecary with salt [sometimes translated "well-mingled," or in Septuagint, "tempered"], clean, conditioned.

³⁶And you will pound [some] of it very small, and you will put [some] of it before the stones of communication in the tent of meeting where I will meet with you. Super-conditioned it will be to you.

³⁷And the incense you will make. In its proportion, you will not make for yourselves. Conditioned it will be to you for the Lord.

³⁸A man who makes it to smell of it will be cut off from his people." (Exod. 30:34–38)

There were five ingredients that made up the incense. They were storax, galbanum, onycha, frankincense, and salt.

Storax

The first ingredient, "balm" or "stacte," *nawtawf*, is used only once in this Exodus 30:34 verse.ᵈⁿ Strong's says it is from *nawtaf*, "drop, prophecy."ᵈᵒ HAL says, "drip, secrete, cause to flow," but this is not found in the Five Books.[144] It is thought, among other possibilities, to be storax.

dn. *nawtawf,* 5198
do. *nawtaf,* 5197

The United States Dispensatory says, "Storax is a balsam obtained from the trunk of the *Liquidambar orientalis* Miller, known in commerce as Levant Storax, or of *Liquidambar Styraciflua* Linné, known in commerce as American Storax."[145] The Dispensatory says of the trees grown in Central America that "the exudate apparently was used by the aboriginal inhabitants of the continent; it was exported to Spain in large quantities in the 16th century for use both as a perfume and as a *vulnerary*" (my emphasis). Vulnerary denotes a substance used to promote the healing of wounds. The odor was balsamic. The taste, bitter. It is notable that the "residuary bark, after expression, is dried in the sun, and employed in various parts of Turkey for fumigation."[146] More importantly of the storax itself,

when heated it polymerizes to form transparent solids which have found extensive use in the manufacture of many molded articles and in the formulation of resinous protective coatings … Externally, mixed with two or three parts of olive oil, liquid storax was found by H. Schultze, of Magdeburg, to be very effective as a local remedy in scabies.[147]

It is

a stimulating expectorant and feeble antiseptic, which was at one time used in various catarrhs [inflammation of mucous membranes], but at present [1943] is very seldom used except as a constituent of the compound tincture of benzoin.[148]

Benzoin itself is used medically as an expectorant and antiseptic.[149] It is of some note that other suggestions such as oil from bitter almond and resin from *Pistacio Lentiscus* have more or less the same properties.[150]

As to foreign equivalents, the closest seems to be the Egyptian word *ntf,* which Faulkner says is "besprinkle."[151] Gardiner translates it as "irrigate, water."[152] This may relate to the "drop" (or "drip") that is found in following books.[153]

Galbanum

The second ingredient, galbanum, *chelb'naw*, is found only in Exodus 30:34.[dp] Strong's says it is derived from *cheleb* or *chayleb*, meaning "fat," the best or choicest part.[dq] However, the Dispensatory says the plant's reservoirs secrete a yellowish-white milky fluid.[154] Therefore, the word might come from *lawbawn* or *lawhayn.*[dr] They mean "white."[155]

dp. *chelb'naw,* 2464

dq. *chayleb,* 2459

dr. *lawbayn,* 3036

Of interest is the word *kalbaynu.*[156] It is a plant. CAD notes its relation to medical use. "You mix *k.*-plant together (with other plants)."[157] A note following says, "A connection with *kalbu* is doubtful; a foreign origin seems preferable."[158] Regardless of the origin, if *kalbaynu* and *chelb'naw* are related, they have medicinal use in other lands. The Dispensatory says,

This gum-resin was at one time official in both the U.S. and British Pharmacopoeias. It is mentioned by the earliest medical writers and was an ingredient of the incense used in the worship of ancient Israelites. At present rarely used in medicine … It is generally accepted that galbanum is derived from *Ferula galbaniflua* Boissier and Buhse.[159]

While there is some confusion as to the exact species, The Dispensatory says all *Ferula* species "are tall, umbelliferous herbs indigenous to Persia."[160] It says the odor is aromatic (while HAL says the odor is "foul-smelling") and the taste is "bitterish, warm and acrid."[161] Finally it says,

> Galbanum was, by the ancients, deemed stimulant, expectorant, and antispasmodic and was formerly used in chronic bronchitis, amenorrhea, and chronic rheumatism, but is now [1943] used only in the form of plasters as an external stimulant.[162]

Interestingly, both storax and galbanum are expectorants, "promoting the secretion of fluid from the respiratory tract."[163]

Onycha

The third ingredient, onycha, *sh'chelet*, like storax and galbanum, is only found in the Exodus 30:34 verse.[ds] Strong's relates *sh'chelet* to *shachal*, "lion," which is from an unused root probably meaning, "to roar."[dt] He says it is "apparently from the same as 7826 [*shachal*] through some obscure idea, perhaps that of *peeling* off by concussion of sound; a *scale* or shell, i.e., the aromatic *mussel*."[164] This is dubious. That it is a substance gotten from the closing flaps of a sea animal, "of certain mollusks, with pungent odour when burnt" is generally accepted, but this too seems rather strange in view of the fact that the animal itself would be in the unclean class.[165] The *Interpreter's Dictionary* points out that a "corresponding verbal root in Arabic is the basis for a noun denoting the husks of wheat and barley … A related post biblical Hebrew word [*sh'chalim*] is used for garden cress."[166] Gordon gives the Ugaritic word *shlt* as "a certain vegetable."[167] Interestingly, the Old Babylonian word *sahalu* means "to sift, or to filter."[168] CAD notes the word being treated as follows: "a) in medical and technical recipes … you place these eleven … plants together (in the liquid), you boil (it), filter (it), [*ta-sa-hal*] and bathe her with it."[169]

In addition, CAD guesses the Old Babylonian word *sahallu* may mean "a milling product" and may relate to *sahalu*.[170] Faulkner has *shns*. (The Egyptian sign for *n* can also be for *l*.) It means "make to stink."[171] Since the purpose for onycha was probably for fragrance, this obverse meaning may possibly relate.

ds. *sh'chelet*, 7827

dt. *shachal*, 7826

At any rate, onycha is not a substance found in the Dispensatory as a medicine. If the above words from other languages are indeed related to the Hebrew, the idea that a vegetable product was indicated, rather than the less logical *tawmay* sea animals, makes sense.

Frankincense

The fourth ingredient, frankincense, *l'bohnaw*, is derived by Strong's from *lawbawn* or *lawbayn*. It means "white."[du] Fuerst says the roots are the same.[172] Exodus, Leviticus, and Numbers use it in its sacrificial role. In following books, references show it accompanying offerings. It is also used in the following books as the familiar "frankincense and myrrh."[173]

du. *l'bohnaw*, 3828

The Dispensatory calls "the *frankincense* of the ancients" olibanum.[174] It is derived from the *Boswellia Carterii* and *Bosewellia Frereana.* "These are small trees of the Fam. *Burseraceae*, growing in Somaliland and Arabia."[175] The substance collected is a gum resin. "The odor is aromatic, balsamic; the taste slightly bitter ... Olibanum is *similar* to *turpentine* in its medicinal action, but is now very seldomly used. It is occasionally employed for *fumigation* and in unofficial plasters" (my emphasis).[176] The description of turpentine liniment is rather fascinating. In a quaint entry, the Dispensatory says:

> More than a century ago a Doctor Kentish proposed for the treatment of *burns* a mixture of resin cerate and oil of turpentine; this was known as *Kentish's ointment.* This was official in the first edition of the U.S.P. [United States Pharmacopoeia] and remained practically unchanged through the ninth revision and is now in the N.F. [National Formulary VII]. The original formula, for some inexplicable reason, was changed in the 1867 revision of the [British] by the substitution of soft soap for the cerate and an increase in the proportion of the oil of turpentine. This change produced a preparation of entirely different therapeutic properties, more fitted for a *counterirritant liniment* than for the treatment of inflammatory condition of the skin.[177]

Salt

Salt, *mawlach*, was used by all the ancients for one or more of three purposes:[dv]

dv. *mawlach*, 4417

dw. Job 6:6

1. with food as a seasoner and preservative[dw]
2. to seal treaties or covenants between man and man, and man and God[178]
3. as a protective substance

In the following books, only in Ezekiel's version of the temple is there any mention of salt used in the sacrificial process.

> "You will offer a young bullock ... and a ram ... and the priests will throw salt on them and they will offer them up for a burnt offering to the Lord." (Ezek. 43:23–24)

In these two quotes, salt falls into the protective function, but the verses themselves don't indicate protection as its purpose. However, Leviticus 2:13 says that the meal offering with its salt is for "the covenant of your God." A point could be made that the really early meaning of *b'rith* (covenant) regarding the Lord "cutting a covenant" with Noah and then with Abraham was an agreement that the Lord would protect them and their offspring.[dx]

dx. Gen. 9:13, 15:18

There are several possibilities for the use of salt in the manufacture of incense and in the sacrifices. Here is a clear statement of one possibility by T.H. Gaster:

> Every offering had to be accompanied by salt ... In the Levitical prescription, this is associated with the well-known custom of sealing covenants by sharing bread and salt (Numbers 18:19), being thus taken to symbolize the covenant thereby established between the god and his human "kinsman." In that case, the purpose of the salt would have been simply to prevent premature putrefaction of the covenantal fare. It is not improbable, however, that the real purpose—at least originally—was to avert demons, for the belief that salt, being an incorruptible substance, is immune to such corrosive influences and can impart this immunity to any who consume or hold it, is widespread in folklore, surviving even in the Catholic rite of baptism.[179]

Gaster also points out, "Salt, being incorruptible, averts demons and protects against black magic."[180] He notes that Ezekiel 16:4 talks of cleansing the newborn with salt and that the practice was done by the Greeks. Also,

> The Arabs protect their children from the evil eye by placing salt in their hands on the eve of the seventh day after birth … and a Palestinian proverb declares that "the skin which is not salted will suppurate."[181]

Further Gaster says,

> The apotropaic quality of salt underlies also the modern Egyptian custom of rubbing a bride with it to protect her against the evil eye, while in Morocco, Jewish women used to dip their hands in it before embarking on a journey.[182]

Of even more interest is Frazer's statement that Peruvian Indian women would burn salt to *disperse fog* from the area.[183]

These practices, while loaded with magic and superstition, still indicate that through the ages salt has been thought of as a protective substance. So it is possible that at one time, as is the case with so many other items that started in realty and ended in myth, salt was used to help accomplish actual missions as ordained in Exodus and Leviticus. As for its use in incense, there is no reason to doubt that it joined the other ingredients described above to protect against the cloud.

Combined Ingredients

So, a chart of these ingredients as utilized through the ages would look something like this:

Chart D—Incense Ingredients			
	ODOR	TASTE	USE
Storax	Balsamic	Bitter	Vulnerary, fumigation, protective coating (scabies), expectorant, anti-septic, perfume
Galbanum	Aromatic	Bitter	External stimulant, expectorant, antispasmodic
Onycha			Fragrance?
Frankincense	Aromatic	Bitter	Fumigation, burns, counterirritant
Salt			When used with the above chemicals in some unknown way helped disperse radioactivity.

While some ingredients gave it a pleasant odor making its constant utilization bearable, the incense was primarily used for protection. Its expectorant qualities would help expel dangerous materials inhaled. Its anti-burning, coating, and fumigating properties would counteract the effects of the cloud when it was in the vicinity and its residue when it was not.

Spice

Finally, let's look at the word "spice," *sam*, which was the generic term for all these chemicals.[dy] It has recently been discovered that certain spices can protect bacteria from radiation. An article in the May 25, 2000 *London Guardian* by David Bradley tells of findings by Indian researchers:

> The discovery that spices can protect bacteria from radiation might lead to a way of reducing the side effects of radiotherapy for cancer patients … The natural chemicals which give red chili powder, black pepper and turmeric their rich flavors and aroma, somehow shield bacteria like E. coli and Bacillus megatherium and its cousin pumilus from lethal gamma rays.[184]

The Indian researchers, whose article appeared in the *Journal of Agricultural and Food Chemistry*, conclude their article with this statement:

> These studies show the importance of spices in food as the dose-modifying factors during radiation processing. From another angle it may be interesting to further explore the radioprotective effects of chili. Radioprotective agents are of interest for their potential use in preventing injury not only during exposure to radiation but also during radiation therapy for protecting normal tissue.[185]

Sam is only used in the plural *sammim*, and is sometimes translated "sweet, fragrant," or "aromatic" when used with "incense" and sometimes "incense of spices." HAL translates the Hebrew as "spices, fragrant perfume, frankincense," but in this context "sweet" seems superfluous.[186] For example, Exodus 30:34 says, "Take for yourself *sammim*, stacte and onycha and galbanum, *sammim* and frankincense … and you will make it *k'toret*." Also in Exodus 37:29, "And he made holy anointing oil incense of the spices (*sammim*)."[187] Here are two examples where translating *sammim* as "sweet" or "fragrant" would not make sense. In addition, to use "sweet" directly before a listing of ingredients, some of which were bitter or foul smelling, makes little sense.

Whether translated as "sweet spices" (or perfume) or just "spices," *sammin* is only found in Exodus, Leviticus, and Numbers, with all references related to the incense. Incense is mentioned in 2 Chronicles 2:4 regarding Solomon's temple and in 2 Chronicles 13:11 regarding Judah following the word of the Lord under the reign of King Abijah. Since it isn't used in any other way, it seems to be a technical description of just this mixture.

OTHER LANGUAGES

Sammim is seen in other languages. In the Ugaritic, DLU translates *smm* simply "perfume," and relates it directly to the Hebrew *sm*.[188] However, this seems to be based on a misreading of Driver's translation, and in fact there doesn't seem to be a related word.[189] On the other hand, the Akkadian *shammu* is translated "[medicinal] herbs."[190] The later languages convey the ideas of "powder, medicament ... poison."[191] The Egyptian word *sm* is translated "herb, plant."[192] So without the doubtful Ugaritic "perfume" translation, the Hebrew word as used in all the other languages is exactly what I am indicating it is—an herb with medicinal, protective powers. Perhaps the last paragraph of Mankowski's treatment of *sammim* encapsulates the possibilities quite well:

> We return then, to the Akkadian loan conjecture. The meaning "plant" or "herb" would appear to be fundamental to Akkadian *shammu*, from which meanings such as "fodder" and "medicine" are derivative. It is significant that the specific meaning "poison" would seem to be limited to Neo-Assyrian, since this is one of the principal meanings of Aramaic *samm-*, and an Assyrian loan vector (shere) is indicated by both Aramaic and Hebrew. No specific instance of "incense" or "aromatic" is attested for *shammu*, although later citations include a number of uses in medicine and magical rituals for which its precise function is unclear. It may be as a medical ingredient or ritual component that *shammu* provided the basis for the Hebrew borrowing, but it must be admitted that this is the weakest part of the hypothesis.[193]

In fact, it may be very near the mark! Having discovered the true purpose of the incense, I can now clear up a mysterious concept: "consecrate," *mawlay*. It was used in relation to the preparation of the priests for service in the super-conditioned place.

Chapter 10

Congregation Covers

Discussing sacrifices without their religious connotations is a challenge. The writings of the classicist and anthropologist Sir James Frazer, among others, might lead the reader to the conclusion that at best, sacrifice was the superstitious response of primitives to problems of the unknown and at worst, in the case of human sacrifice, a horrible fraud perpetrated by the priest-ruler classes upon their subjects to keep them in line.[1] I believe that the later sacrificial practices were perverted descendants of what was originally a purely chemical phenomenon. I intend to pursue this theory as it relates to the laws described in Exodus through Numbers.

The first mention of sacrifices is in Genesis, long before the Israelites received formal rules regarding them. Abel sacrificed sheep; Cain gave a meal offering.[a] Next Noah, after the flood, "built an altar to the Lord, and he took from all [the] clean cattle and from all [the] clean fowl, and he offered burnt offerings on the altar."[b] Abraham, too, was perfectly familiar with sacrifice, as the story of almost offering his son Isaac demonstrates. Specifically he said, "God will provide for Himself the lamb for a burnt offering my son."[c] Later, Moses demanded that Pharaoh let his people and the animals go into the wilderness to sacrifice to the Lord. (This was a ruse to escape from the Egyptians.)

> [25]And Moses said, "You must also give into our hands sacrifices and burnt offerings that we may sacrifice to the Lord our God.
>
> [26]And also our cattle must go with us; [there] will not be left behind a hoof. For thereof we must take to serve the Lord our God: and we do not know [with] what we must serve the Lord, until we come there." (Exod. 10:25–26)

a. Gen. 4:3–7

b. Gen. 8:20

c. Gen. 22:8

Now why did people sacrifice? The stock answers are to propitiate and expiate. Propitiate means "to conciliate (an offended power); appease;" expiate means "to make atonement for; redress."[2] These two reasons for sacrificing have created a heavy burden of morality, leaving an absolutely indelible impact on religious attitudes, but no one seems to question the morality of, in effect, buying off God's anger with a sweet smelling burnt offering. Does the Bible even hint that God's and Moses' concern was a moral one? The answer is no. If moral principles were relevant, then how was it that only natural laws were involved?[3] If the Israelites wanted God to be in their midst, with the attendant danger inherent in His presence, they had to protect themselves via sacrifices. Leviticus 9:4–7, which follows the specific sacrifices to be made during the filling of the hands of Aaron and his sons, says that the sacrifices were to be made:

[4]*"For today the Lord will appear to you."*

[5]And they took that which Moses commanded in the front of the tent of meeting; and all the congregation came near, and they stood before the Lord.

[6]And Moses said, "This thing [making the sacrifices] that the Lord had commanded you will do; *then the radiance of the Lord will appear to you."*

[7]And Moses said to Aaron, "Come near to the altar and make your decontamination offering and your burnt offering and cover for yourself and for the people and make an offering of [brought by] the people, and cover [the altar] for them as the Lord commanded." (my emphasis)

Numbers 8:19 *only* says that sacrifices were to prevent the effects of radiation, "plague," among the people:

[19]"And I have given the Levites as a gift to Aaron and to his sons from the midst of the Israelites to serve the service of the Israelites in the tent of meeting, and to cover on the Israelites *that [there] will not be among the Israelites a plague (negah) when the Israelites come near to the super-conditioned place."* (my emphasis)

Notice two separate tasks: (1) "to serve the service" refers to the task of Aaron and his sons to communicate with the Lord; and (2) "to cover" refers to the Levites using sacrifices in order to protect the people from the danger inherent in communicating with God.

Cover

Covering (*kawfar/keeper*) was a function accomplished by sacrifice. Covering (*keeper*) was the action that led to cleaning (*tawhor*), resulting in conditioning (*kawdash*). "He ... will cleanse and condition from all the uncleanness ... And when he has finished covering the super-conditioned place ..."[d] The priest was responsible for covering in basically three ways: (1) sprinkling the blood of animals or birds on people and items in the tent; (2) covering the ark of communication with specially prepared incense; and (3) pouring oil on people and items in the tent. Understanding covering is the key to understanding sacrifices.

d. Lev. 16:19–20

In addition to meaning "cover," *kawfer* can also mean "to pitch," as in covering Noah's ark with pitch, *kofer*.[e]

e. *kofer*, 3724

> "Make for yourself an ark of *gopher* wood. You will make rooms in the ark and coat it inside and out with pitch." (Gen. 6:14)[4]

The related Hebrew and Old Babylonian words *kofer*, "pitch," and *kupru*, "bitumen" (an asphalt type material), describe a substance used to cover.[5] Early on, *kawfer* and *kofer* were synonymous, lending credence to the definition of *kawfer* as "to cover." *Kofer*, which is found twice in Exodus and twice in Numbers as well as in the following books, is translated "ransom," but was actually a tax used to subsidize the sacrifices.[6]

───

OTHER LANGUAGES

It has long been known that the *kawfar/keeper* words had equivalents in other languages. *Kupru* was used to caulk the ark in the very ancient versions of the Babylonian flood story.[7] *Kapayru* (definition A) can mean "to wipe off, to smear on (a paint or liquid)," and *kuppuru* is "to wipe off, to clean objects, to rub, to purify magically" from Old Babylonian on.[8] It is *kuppuru*, the third meaning of *kapayru* A, which describes purification of the king, temple, house, etc.[9] *Kupurtu* is "ointment" in Old Babylonian.[10]

The Ugaritic offers only one hint: *kpr*, meaning "henna." This plant was known throughout the ancient Near East and was used for its fragrance and dye (a covering). Henna is one of the meanings of *kofer*, albeit used only in the Song of Solomon. There doesn't appear to be a *kpr* word for the covering function in Ugaritic.

As for the Egyptian, a possibility is the word *kap*, which can mean "burn incense, cense gods," and "cover" among other things. This was connected with the use of incense. This leads me to wonder whether there might have been a connection between *kaf*, the instrument for covering, and *kawfar*, the operation of covering suggested originally by the Old Babylonian.

∞∞∞

Keeper is found 76 times in Exodus, Leviticus, and Numbers, and it is always used in its technical sense, i.e., for protection of the people, the dwellings, or the tent equipment. It is also found in Deuteronomy 21:8 twice, sometimes translated as "forgive," but "cover" works perfectly well. (Kohlenberger uses "atone.") These references refer to the purging of "innocent blood" of one who is murdered. Also, Deuteronomy 32:43 in the *Song of Moses* says, "He will avenge the blood of His servants and cover His land [and] His people." Both of these verses could be included with the technical references.

Now comes the important part. *Keeper* always means "cover" or "covering." The Hebrew almost always uses the phrasing *keeper al*, "cover on" a person or thing. However, *al* is usually translated as "for" when used with *keeper*, "atone for" with the connotation of "atone on behalf of."

The preposition *al* has many meanings: "on the ground of, according to, on account of, on behalf of, concerning, beside, in addition to, together with, beyond, above, over, by, on to, towards, to, against."[11] However, BDB makes a special case of using *al* as "for" saying that *al* is used "very often with [*keeper*] ... make atonement *for*. (Not very common with other verbs.)"[12]

> "And Aaron will cover on (*al*) its horns [the altar's] once in a year with the blood of the decontamination offering of *kipurim*; once in a year he will cover on (*al*) it for your generations; it is super-conditioned for the Lord." (Exod. 30:10)

Of the eight Bibles I checked, six used the traditional "for" here. Only Kohlenberger uses "with it," referring incorrectly to "blood." And JPS/Sarna did use "upon." Sarna also uses "on it" (the altar) in Exodus 29:36, but reverts to "for" (the altar) in the very next verse. With this discussion in mind, how does *al* hold up as "on" when combined with *keeper*, translated "cover"?

The first use of *keeper* is in Exodus 29:33 regarding the priests: "And they will eat those things by which *koopar* (*keeper*) was made *bawham* to fill their hand to condition them."[f] In the Hebrew, there is no "by" or "was made," and *bawham*, meaning "by/with them," traditionally goes untranslated, probably due to its difficulty fitting into the traditional translation. The verse actually reads, "And they [the priests] will eat them [the offerings] who [the priests] were covered (*keeper*) by them (*bawham*) [the offerings] to fill their hand to condition them." The purpose of the hand filling service was "to cover **on** you (*l'chayper alaycham*)," so the use of *al* is certainly implied here regarding the covering process.[g] Thus, the Hebrew rendering of "covered by them" is a more logical explanation of what happened than the English "atonement was made."

The fact that *keeper* appears suddenly and casually in this first reference means that it was well-known and that very probably some prior definition, now lost, was given to introduce this section. Some say this first reference followed the Leviticus explanation.

Next, cover appears in Exodus 29:36 in connection with cleansing the altar during the hand filling process:

> [36]"And a bullock of decontamination [offering] you will make daily on the coverings (*al hakipurim*) and you will cleanse *on* (*al*) the altar when you cover on it (*awlaw'v*), and you will anoint it to condition it."

A careful reading shows that despite always being translated singularly, the actual Hebrew is *al hakipurim*. (Translators also make *yom hakipurim* singular, "day of atonement.") The idea here is that a bullock was offered daily **on** the **coverings**.

Does this make sense? Yes. In the sacrifices leading up to this verse, the priests burned parts or all of one young bullock, two rams, unleavened bread, unleavened cakes with oil, and unleavened wafers with oil on the altar.[h] Exodus 29:33, the first *keeper* reference, distinguishes some of these items as material

f. *koopar* is the passive pual tense of *keeper*.

g. Lev. 8:33–4

h. Exod. 29:1–35

used in the covering process. (Others were used for rest-smelling.) In verse 36, it is perfectly natural to offer a whole bullock daily **on** parts of these burned items. Therefore, *al* holds up as **on** very logically.

In fact, proof positive can be found in the verses leading to Exodus 29:33. Aaron and his sons were to eat the offering items that came from parts of the ram of hand filling.[i] The rest was burned **on** the altar **on top of** the burnt offering, i.e., another ram that had been burned on the altar previously.[j] Thus, burning an offering **on** an offering was a clearly delineated and normal thing to do.[k]

The following are additional technical "on" references:

- Exodus 29:36–37 continue the covering process and follow the same logic. Verse 37 says, "Seven days you will cover on the altar and you will condition it, and the altar will be thoroughly conditioned."
- Exodus 30:10 is the first mention of cleansing the incense altar: "And Aaron will cover on its horns … he will cover on it."
- Exodus 30:12–16 is the law of the money used to "cover on your souls … as a memorial before the Lord to cover on your souls."
- Leviticus 1:4 begins the laws of sacrifice and outlined which animals were to be used for burnt offerings: "And he will lay his hand on the head of the burnt offering and it will be accepted for him to cover on him."
- Leviticus 4:20 says when the whole congregation errs, "the priest will cover on them with a young bullock."
- Leviticus 4:26 says when a chief errs, the priest will "cover on him" with a male goat.
- Leviticus 4:31 says when a person errs, the "priest will cover on him" with a female goat.
- Leviticus 4:35 says when a person errs, the priest could also use a female lamb "to cover on him."
- Leviticus 5:6, 10, and 13 speak of a person who contaminates through failing to come forward as a witness, who touches

i. Exod. 29:19–22

j. Exod. 29:18, 29:25

k. cf., Lev. 8:28

unclean things or people, or who forgets an oath he has sworn. "And the priest will cover on him [with a female lamb or goat or two turtle doves or pigeons or meal] for his contamination, which he has contaminated from one of these."

- Leviticus 5:16 says when a person commits a trespass, "the priest will cover on him with a ram."
- Leviticus 5:18 says when a person contaminates without knowing, "the priest will cover on him" with a ram.
- Leviticus 5:26 is for dealing falsely with a neighbor, robbery, etc. "The priest will cover on him" with a ram.
- Leviticus 7:7 is not an *al* verse but another clear demonstration that it is the *material* (the offering) that covers: "As is the decontamination offering, so is the trespass offering, one law for them: the priest that covers by it to him it will belong."
- Leviticus 8:34 is more on the hand filling process, using incense "to cover on you [Aaron and his sons]."
- In Leviticus 10:17, in the Nadab and Abihu episode, Moses questions Aaron's sons about not eating the sacrifice: "Why have you not eaten the decontamination offering … seeing it is super-conditioned and He has given it to you to … cover on them before the Lord?"
- Leviticus 12:7–8 explain the sacrifices used to finish cleansing a woman who has borne a child. She is to bring her sacrifice to the priest, and he is to "bring it before the Lord and cover on her and she will be cleansed."
- Leviticus 14:18–21, 29, 31 detail the various materials used to cleanse a burned person: "And the priest will cover on him who is to be cleansed before the Lord."
- Leviticus 14:53 discusses the process of the priest cleansing a house affected with radiation: "Cover on the house and it will be clean."
- Leviticus 15:15 and 30 detail the sacrifices for a man and a woman with discharges or who have had intercourse during menstruation. The priest would cover on them with two turtledoves or pigeons.
- Leviticus 16:10 is about a goat that was to be "set alive before the Lord to cover on him [the goat] to send him away to a solitary place, *Azawzel*, in the wilderness."[13]

- Leviticus 16:16 describes the process of covering on the super-conditioned place: "And he will cover on the super-conditioned place from the pollutions of the Israelites."
- Leviticus 16:18 continues the process of covering on the super-conditioned place by explaining that the priest "will go out to the altar … and cover on it."
- Leviticus 16:19 says, "And he will sprinkle from the blood *on* it."
- Leviticus 16:20 uses the Hebrew object word *et*: "And he will cover *et* the super-conditioned place."[14]
- Leviticus 16:27 is not an *al* verse, but significantly it reads, "And the bullock of the decontamination offering and the goat of the decontamination offering whose blood was brought in to cover *in* the most holy place." This verse describes a physical/chemical process.
- Leviticus 16:30 continues of the general cleansing process: "For on this day he will cover on you to cleanse you from all your contaminations," with the blood of the bullock and goats.
- Leviticus 16:32 is a continuation of *Yom Kippur* laws. Although it is not an *al* verse, it does issue a direct order: "And the priest, who will be anointed and who will have his hand filled in place of his father, will cover."
- Leviticus 16:33 continues the direct orders: "And he will cover the super-conditioned place and the tent of meeting and the altar he will cover, and on the priests and on all the people of the assembly he will cover."
- Leviticus 16:34: "And this will be to you for a statute forever to cover on the Israelites from all their contaminations once in a year." Both Leviticus 16:30 and 34 use the *mem* before "*all* your contaminations" and "*all* their contaminations." The *mem* in 16:30 is usually translated "*from* all your contaminations," but in 16:34 it is usually "*because of* all their contaminations." With the "cover" and "on" translations though, and thinking of the physical operation used to achieve covering, the word "from" works in 16:34 as it does in 16:30. In 16:30, use of the word cleanse ("to cleanse you from all your contaminations") makes it virtually impossible to translate this *mem* as "because of." This same mistranslation of *mem* as "because of" is seen in Leviticus 16:16.
- Leviticus 17:11 is the warning not to eat blood, "for the soul of the flesh is in the blood, and I have given it to you on the altar to cover on your souls for it is the blood that covers in the soul."

- Leviticus 19:22 instructs a man having intercourse with a pledged slave girl to bring a guilt offering to the priest: "And the priest will cover on him with the ram."
- Numbers 5:8 says when a man or woman sins against a person, "he [the priest] covers with it [a ram of coverings] on him."
- In Numbers 6:11, the priest is ordered to offer the contamination and burnt offerings for the nazirite who came in contact with a dead person: "And he will cover on him … and he will condition his head on that day."
- Numbers 8:12 shows that during the cleansing of the Levites, contamination and burnt offerings were sacrificed "to cover on the Levites."
- Numbers 8:21 is the continuation of the Levite's cleansing process: "And Aaron covered on them to cleanse them."
- Numbers 15:25 is about the sacrifices to be offered when the people erred: "And the priest will cover on all the congregation."
- Numbers 15:28 shows the sacrifice for a person who had erred: "And the priest will cover on the person … to cover on him."
- In Numbers 17:11, Aaron covered on the people with incense. To prevent plague (*nawgaf*) after the Korach revolt, Moses ordered Aaron to "lay on incense … hurry to the congregation and cover on them."
- In Numbers 17:12, Aaron ran among the assembly with the incense, "and he covered on the people."
- Numbers 25:13 is in the story of the heroism of Phinehas, son of Eleazar and grandson of Aaron. His actions helped stop a plague that resulted when the "anger of the Lord burned against Israel" (Numbers 25:3). They were worshiping Baal-peor and mingling with Moabite women. As a reward, Phinehas and his descendants were given the priesthood "because he was jealous for his God and he covered on the Israelites." For further discussion of this story see Appendix E.
- Numbers 28:22 prescribes the "he-goat for a decontamination offering to cover on you" for the first day of Passover.
- Numbers 28:30 prescribes "a kid for a decontamination offering to cover on you" for the Feast of Weeks.
- Numbers 29:5 prescribes "a kid for a decontamination offering to cover on you" for *Rosh Hashana*.
- Numbers 29:10 prescribes a "he-goat for a decontamination offering besides the decontamination offering of covering" for *Yom Kippur*.

• Numbers 31:50 describes the "Lord's oblation" of gold and other articles "to cover on our souls."[15]

These are the technical references to *al*. They do not vary. They make perfect sense as "on" rather than "for" in every case.

However, there *are* valid instances when "for" is used with "covering." Exodus 31:30, Leviticus 9:7, 16:6, 11, 17, and 24 all have "cover *for*." The word "for" in this case is *b'ad* and has the general meaning of "separation" or "distance from."[1] Milgrom, when discussing *'al* and *b'ad* in relation to *keeper*, says "they are not entirely synonymous. The difference is that *'al* can only refer to persons other than the subject, but when the subject wishes to refer to himself he must use *be'ad*."[16]

In addition, both HAL and BDB give many references, e.g., Exodus 32:30–32 and Numbers 21:7, indicating that *b'ad* had a protective significance, primarily by praying for someone or the people.[17] *B'ad* could also be used as protection in a general way. Thus, Job 1:10 says, "You have not made a hedge for him (*b'ado*)" and Lamentations 3:7 says, "He hedged for me (*b'adee*)." Zechariah 12:8 has the Lord putting a shield "around" (*b'ad*) the inhabitants of Jerusalem.

So while *b'ad* meant "for," it was a very special "for." It was a "for" with the distinct overtone of "for protection." Leviticus 16:6 uses *two* words for "for": the more usual *lamed*, *l'o*, "for himself," as well as *b'ad*. This indicates very strongly that *b'ad* is special and technical. It joins so many other words with unusual nuances.

I have doggedly and probably ad nauseam traced the words *keeper al*, "cover on," to show that they refer to a physical process. The people may or may not have done something ethically/morally wrong, but that was not the reason for the covering. It was a purely physical process for protection against the danger of the cloud, not a response to an ethical/moral situation.

From its extreme importance and always technical 76 mentions in Exodus, Leviticus and Numbers, *keeper's* usage almost totally changes in the mere 24 times it appears in the following books. Of these, only 11 can be considered technical.[m] Of the 11, only four use the phrase *keeper al*:

l. *b'ad*, 1157

m. 1 Sam. 3:14; 2 Sam. 21:3; Ezek. 43:20, 26; 45:15, 17, 20; 1 Chr. 6:34; 2 Chr. 29:24; 30:18; Neh. 10:34[18]

(1) 1 Chronicles 6:34 is an historical reference to Aaron and his sons offering "on the altar of burnt offering and on the altar of incense ... to cover on (*ool 'chapayr*) Israel."

(2) 2 Chronicles 29:23–24 refer to the sacrifices used to cleanse the temple and "to cover on all Israel" during King Hezekiah's reform (c. 715–687 BCE). 2 Chronicles 30:18, however, has Hezekiah using prayer to entreat the Lord to cover for, *chapayr b'ad*, (usually translated "*pardon* for") those people who had eaten the Passover lambs without cleansing themselves. Even with the protective nature of *b'ad, keepering* with prayer would have done no good. Prayer did not serve a protective function. When Moses prayed for the rebellious people in the golden calf episode of Exodus 32:30–35, it was of no use.[19]Either this was a total misunderstanding of the situation by the Chronicler, or the people received so little contamination that they quickly returned to normal. In any case there is no mention of "on" here.

(3) Nehemiah 10:33–34 uses "on" where he in 450 BCE he returned to Jerusalem as governor, at the command of the ruling Persian King Artaxerxes, to rebuild the sacked city's walls and to reestablish the temple service. He explained that a poll tax was charged yearly for all of the familiar sacrifices "and for the decontamination offerings to cover *on* Israel."

(4) Ezekiel 45:15 uses "cover on" for the sacrifices. However, Ezekiel was pretty lax in adhering to the rules in other references (as shown below).

Other references do not use the word "on," but still seem to fall into the *keeper*/physically cover category:

- 1 Samuel 3:14 (said to have lived ca. 1050 BCE) is about sacrifice but in a negative context: "And therefore I have sworn to the house of Eli that the impurity of Eli's house will not be covered with sacrifice or offering forever."
- 2 Samuel 21:1–9, the account of David and the Gibeonites, may seem at first to have only an ethical/moral meaning. However, the story confirms the technical nature of the matter, which is to be expected since David had access to the ark and *ephod*. A three-year famine had been caused by drought, "And David

sought the face of the Lord."[n] This is generally recognized as the wording for using the *ephod*. The Lord explained that the famine was because of "Saul and his house of bloodshed, because he put to death the Gibeonites."[o] "And David said to the Gibeonites, 'What will I do for you? And with what will I cover that you may bless the inheritance of the Lord?'"[p] The Gibeonites asked for seven men they could "hang ... up to the Lord."[q] Rather than "hang," though, *yawqah* really signifies "impale."[20] So this act provided redemption for spilled blood that polluted the land. Thus, the blood of those guilty was indeed to cover the blood of the murdered.[r] The threat of the Lord, that the land would have no rainfall if his laws weren't followed, was being carried out in this instance.[s] There is no explanation here as to why the sons were being punished for the guilt of their father. Perhaps, as Kimchi opines, Saul's sons were also involved in the slaughter of the Gibeonites.[21]

- Ezekiel 43:20 speaks of using blood to purify (decontaminate) and cover the altar. Verse 26 uses the untranslated object word *et* properly: "And they will cover *et* the altar." His understanding of *keeper's* technical use is fuzzy in 45:17, "cover for (*b'ad*) the house of Israel." 45:22 has preparation of sacrifice "for (*b'ad*) himself [the prince] and for (*b'ad*) all the people of the land" without mention of cover. Even farther off the mark is Ezekiel 16:63 where he uses *keeper* for "forgive": "'When I have forgiven (*b'chap'ree*) you all you have done,' says the Lord God."

Some following "on" references seem to have only an ethical-moral meaning.[t] They date from 742–500 BCE or 742–165 BCE (depending on the dating of Daniel), at least 300 years after Samuel was said to have lived. During that period one "on" was used in Psalm 79:9 and one in Jeremiah 18:23, but neither was used technically.

The technical use of *keeper* and its relatives, while it may have been known later on, was confused (purposely or not) with the general concept of good and evil. Eventually, this concept turned the body of law into a "religion." So Proverbs 16:6 says, "By *mercy* and *truth* iniquity is expiated (*y'koopar*); and by the

n. 2 Sam. 21:1

o. 2 Sam. 21:1

p. 2 Sam. 21:2

q. 2 Sam. 21:6;
yawqah, 3363

r. Num. 35:33–34

s. e.g., Lev. 26:19–20

t. Isa. 6:7, 22:14, 27:9,
28:18, 47:11 (from
the reigns of Uzziah
to Hezekiah); Prov.
16:6, 14; Ps. 65:4,
78:38, 79:9; Jer. 18:23;
Ezek. 6:63; Dan. 9:24

fear of the Lord [man] is turned from evil." It is also interesting that all the references from Isaiah on would seem to contradict the strict interpretation given to the law by Hezekiah, the last king in whose reign Isaiah was active. Even if Hezekiah didn't understand the technical nature of communicating with the Lord, he certainly grasped the fact that in some way there was a physical process involved and not a matter of good versus evil in the way Isaiah changed it. While there was much emphasis on sinning and then asking forgiveness or pardon, these concepts used different Hebrew words. The only conclusion one can come to is that the concept of *keeper* wasn't considered important enough to talk very much about later on, and consequently it was all but excluded from the daily lives of the Israelites almost as soon as they reached Canaan. Why? The answer is quite complex, so much so that I have put the complete explanation in Appendix F. At about the end of the reign of King David when the use of the ark ended, the cloud and the Lord withdrew from the people. Regardless of the *keeper* concept fading in later time, it was central and necessary to the activities of the early Israelites.

Who and What Was Covered

The Bible discusses six groups that needed to be covered and thus protected from the radioactive danger of the cloud. The covering prescriptions varied, depending on the situation:

(1) The people needing the most constant cover were the priests who came in contact with the danger area on a daily basis. Also, the items directly involved in that area had to be re-covered every day.

(2) Beyond the immediate area of the tent, certain individuals needed more cover than others. The person who had already received a dose of radiation and had suffered radiation burn needed the most attention.

(3) Next were those who might be in a position to receive radiation more easily than others. For example, a woman who had just borne a child was more vulnerable, "unclean," than usual (more so after bearing a daughter than a son).[u] What made her   u. Lev. 12:2–8

unclean was the "fountain of her blood." For a specified amount of time she could not touch any "conditioned thing or come into the tent area until the days of her cleansing are fulfilled."ᵛ In other words, she was not supposed to come into the danger area, and she had to sacrifice as well. Other examples would be those having intercourse during menstruation and a man having an "issue out of his flesh."ʷ

v. Lev. 12:4

w. Lev. 15:2

> ³¹"Thus, you will separate (*v'heezartam*, related to nazirite and crown of oil!) the Israelites from their uncleanness *that they do not die in their uncleanness* when they defile My tabernacle that is in the midst of them.
>
> ³²This is the law of him that has an issue, and of him from whom the flow seed goes out so that he is unclean thereby;
>
> ³³And of them that have an issue, whether it be a man or a woman; and of him that lies with her that is unclean." (Lev. 15:31–33)

For some reason, these "issues" made people unclean and therefore prone to becoming contaminated with radioactivity, the very material the priests were trying to remove from the tabernacle (their environment) every day of the year because it endangered lives. They had to be extremely careful, because if they actually became radioactive and went near the tabernacle they would again make it unclean.

The reality of the situation was not of one or two unclean individuals coming into the area of the tent and thus "defiling" it. The concern was that crowds of people with this or that condition threatened to re-contaminate the area where the priests lived and worked, and possibly a much wider area if the cloud drifted.

It is easy to confuse certain technical prohibitions with moral restraints, particularly when they addressed infractions that were both civil and natural, such as adultery, murder, or intercourse with a betrothed slave-girl. The key to look for is the "punishment." Was it stoning or covering?

Interestingly, these verses that speak to bodily issues are directly followed by the familiar warning to Aaron:

¹And the Lord spoke to Moses after the death of the two sons of Aaron when they drew near before the Lord and they died.

²And the Lord said to Moses, "Speak to Aaron your brother, that he come not at all times into the conditioned place within the veil before the covering that is on the ark, that he does not die. For in the cloud I will appear on the covering." (Lev. 16:1–2)

This is not a story interruption but a step by step detailing of the natural danger of the radioactive cloud. It is directly related to Numbers 45:35, "And you will not make the land *tawmay*, which you inhabit in the midst of which I dwell, for I the Lord dwell in the midst of the Israelites."

(4) The next group to be covered was the entire congregation when it contaminated through error. In each case, bullock blood was sprinkled in front of the veil of the super-conditioned place, on the horns of the incense altar, and at the foundation of the altar of burnt offering. Fat and some organs were burned on the altar and the rest was taken to a clean place outside the camp to be burned: "Thus, he will do with the bullock ... and the priest will cover on them and it will be forgiven them."ˣ There x. Lev. 4:20 is a subtle difference between when the entire congregation contaminated through error and when the priest contaminated through error, though the remedy was the same. The logic proves this out in a rather startling way. Leviticus 4:3 says, "If the anointed [oiled] priest contaminate ... the people [by offering an incorrect sacrifice], then he will offer ... a bullock." The priest's contaminating through error accidentally spread the danger to the people, but not to himself because he was already protected with oil! So, the reference here does not mention that the priest had to be covered. Rather, he had to do exactly the same things that he did when the entire congregation was contaminated through error, because in both cases they were not protected!

(5) Next was an ordinary person or a chief who contaminated through error.ʸ If an individual became radioactive, the extent y. Lev. 4:2, 22 of the exposure and therefore the danger would have been far less intense than if an entire congregation did. The prescribed

sacrifice for this person was similar to that used for the entire congregation, though not quite as thorough, e.g., the incense altar was not sprinkled with blood. The interesting point here is that breaking the commandment was not done on purpose. Why, when they finally learned they had broken the commandment, was it necessary to go through the covering procedure if not to protect against a physical danger?

(6) Finally, Leviticus 5:1–6 begins a strange grouping of people to be covered:

> ¹"And when a person contaminates and he hears the voice of swearing [requiring appearance as a witness], and he is a witness, or he has seen or known, if he does not tell it, then he will carry his impurity.
>
> ²Or a person who touches any unclean thing, or the carcass of an unclean animal or the carcass of unclean cattle or the carcass of an unclean creeping thing, and it is hidden from him, and he [is] unclean and is guilty
>
> ³Or when he touches [the] uncleanness [of] man, whatever his uncleanness [from] which he is unclean by it and it is hidden from him, and he knows and he is guilty
>
> ⁴Or a person when he swears, pronouncing with the lips to do evil or to do good, anything that a man pronounces with an oath and it is hidden from him,
>
> ⁵And he has known and he is guilty in one of these and it will be when he is guilty in one of these, and he will confess [that] which he has contaminated on that.
>
> ⁶And he will bring his guilt offering to the Lord on his contamination, which he has contaminated, a female of the flock, a lamb or a goat for a decontamination offering; and the priest will cover on him from his contamination."

Three types of individuals are combined in this passage: (1) the witness who didn't come forward, (2) the person who touched any unclean and/or dead thing, and (3) the one who broke an oath. Like the people with "issues," they became unclean based on their circumstance.

It is simple enough to explain the prohibition concerning the touching of any dead unclean things. Dead unclean things were attractors of the cloud and therefore dangerous. A person remained clean if he touched live unclean animals, such as horses and camels, and of course people; when he touched something dead and unclean, he became unclean. He had only to wash and was considered unclean until evening. The key difference in this passage is that the touching was hidden from the person. So, the fact that he was unaware that he had touched the unclean item meant that he had neglected to wash immediately and time had passed. Therefore, more than washing was needed; sacrifice became a necessary precaution. (Incidentally, this is quite different from the complete cleansing process for covering the burned person who was already contaminated by radioactivity and, after the lesions were healed, had to undergo the full cleansing operation—washing, shaving, scapebird, cedar wood, scarlet, hyssop, oil, blood, meal and meat sacrifices.)

On the other hand, why were the prohibitions against the witness or oath breaker necessary? Since both fell into the same category as the adulterous woman, the instructions for discerning the guilt or innocence of a woman suspected of committing adultery shed some light:

¹¹ And the Lord spoke to Moses saying,

¹²"If any man's wife go aside and commit a trespass against him,

¹³And a man lie with her carnally, and it is hidden from the eyes of her husband and is kept hidden, and she is unclean, and there is no witness against her, neither she is taken in the act,

¹⁴And the spirit of jealousy come upon him, and he is jealous of his wife, and she is unclean, or if the spirit of jealousy come upon him and he is jealous of his wife and she is not unclean,

¹⁵Then the man will bring his wife to the priest, and will bring her offering for her, the tenth part of an *ephah* of barley meal; he will pour no oil on it nor put frankincense on it because it is a meal offering of memorial bringing impurity to remembrance.

¹⁶And the priest will bring her near and set her before the Lord;

¹⁷And the priest will take conditioning water in an earthen vessel, and of the dust that is on the floor of the tabernacle the priest will take and put it into the water;

¹⁸And the priest will set the woman before the Lord, and shall uncover the woman's head, and put the meal offering of memorial in her hands, which is the meal offering of jealousy; and the priest will have in his hand the water of bitterness that causes the curse;

¹⁹And the priest will cause her to swear, and will say to the woman, 'If no man has lain with you, and if you have not gone aside to uncleanness, under your husband, be free from the bitter waters that cause the curse;

²⁰And you, when you have strayed, under your husband, and when you are unclean, and some man has lain with you beside your husband,'

²¹Then the priest will cause the woman to swear with an oath ... And the priest will say to the woman, 'The Lord make you a curse and an oath among

your people when the Lord makes your thigh to fall away and your belly to swell.

[22] And this water that causes the curse will go to your bowels and make your belly to swell and your thigh to fall away.' And the woman will say, 'Amen, Amen.'

[23] And the priest will write these curses in a book, and he will blot them out into the water of bitterness;

[24] And he will make the woman drink the water of bitterness that causes the curse; and the water that causes the curse will enter into her and become bitter.

[25] And the priest will take the meal offering of jealousy out of the woman's hand, and will wave the meal offering before the Lord and bring it to the altar;

[26] And the priest will take a handful of the meal offering as a memorial and burn it on the altar, and afterward will make the woman drink the water.

[27] And when he has made her drink the water, then it will come to pass if she is unclean and has committed a trespass against her husband, that the water that causes the curse will enter into her and become bitter, and her belly will swell and her thigh will fall away; and the woman will be a curse among her people.

[28] And if the woman is not unclean but is clean, then she will be free and will conceive seed.

[29] This is the law of jealousy, when a wife … is unclean …

[31] And the man will be free from impurity and the woman will bear her impurity." (Num. 5:11–31)

Now this operation was either pure magic or a pure chemical reaction. Since magic was strictly forbidden, that possibility can be ruled out.[z] Every element that follows naturally from the chemistry is here. Adultery, or hiding adultery, somehow made the woman unclean.

- To test if she had committed this offence, she had to uncover her head.[aa] This was exactly the opposite of what Aaron and his remaining sons had to do when they had been exposed to the cloud after the wrong incense was offered.[ab] Uncovering the head was possibly done to see if the hair would change color. This might be the case if the woman was unclean and

z. Lev. 19:26

aa. Num. 5:18

ab. Lev. 10:6

the minimal radioactivity would then affect her hair as well as the organs. Remember, the burned person's hair would turn white or yellow.

- In the next part of the test, she had to swear an oath. The word "swear" comes from the word "seven" and has the connotation of making a statement seven times, indelibly imprinting its truth or falsehood on the mind.

- Then the priest mixed what must have been slightly radioactive dust from the floor of the tabernacle with absolutely uncontaminated water. Possibly to enhance a dramatically emotional situation, he wrote the warnings to the woman on a scroll and blotted them in the water. She then drank the mixture.

- He then took the meal offering, which had no protective oil or frankincense in it, and burned its memorial (*azkawraw*) on the altar. (*Azkawraw* was a substance in flour that, when burned, could stimulate memory. Here it was used to bring "impurity to remembrance."[22] This was its purpose. In all other cases, the memorial that was burned with oil and/or frankincense was for rest-smelling.)

- Then she drank the water, possibly a second time.[23] If she was unclean because she broke an oath by lying, burning the *azkawraw* would make the radioactive mixture "remember," i.e., activate it. This resulted in impurity, mortal damage, in the woman's body. Breaking an oath may have caused a physical or chemical change in the body. It is possible that this test was a highly sophisticated lie detector that could spot that change. If this ordeal did not work and she was innocent, she would "conceive seed." This connects *awvone*, impurity, to the genetic connotation explained in the Radioactive Fallout chapter.

This whole process and the result of radiation contamination are made startlingly clear by correcting the translation of Numbers 5:21. The usual translation is that the Lord would "make your belly swell and your thigh to fall away." *Yawraych*, "thigh," also means "loins" or "the seat of procreative power."[ac]

ac. *yawraych*, 3409; e.g., Gen. 46:26, Exod. 1:5[24]

ad. *beten*, 990; Gen. 25:23, 24; 30:2; 38:27 Deut. 7:13

ae. *tsawbaw*, 6638, vb.; *tsawbeh*, 6639, adj.[25]

af. *nawaf*, 5003

ag. Num. 5:21–22

ah. Lev. 5:21–24

Then *beten*, "belly" in following books, also means "womb."[ad] *Tsawbaw/tsawbeh*, "swell," found only in Numbers 5:21, 22, 27, is said to be unknown in relation to other languages, but one possibility is the Egyptian word *dba* meaning "stop up, block."[ae] If one considers that the Egyptian *d* is equivalent to the Hebrew *t*, *tsaday*, then there is almost exactly the same pronunciation for both words.[26] If this is so, then the logical translation would be stopping up or blocking the womb, thus preventing conception. It is also interesting that the Hebrew word for "adultery," which is what this is all about, is *nawaf*.[af] The Egyptian word *nf* means "wrongdoing," and *nhp* is "copulate."[27] There is also an Akkadian word, *tsabatu*, which has many meanings, including "enclose, bind, set" and "block" as in "block road" and "grown together."[28] So the translation should be, "makes your womb to block up and your loins to fall away."[ag]

This scientific test is quite different from the river ordeal found in the famous Code of Hammurabi (1728–1686 BCE) where the man charged with sorcery

> … will throw himself into the river, and if the river has then overpowered him, his accuser will take over his estate; if the river has shown that seignior to be innocent and he has accordingly come forth safe, the one who brought the charge … against him will be put to death.[29]

The Code also addresses the alleged adulterous woman saying, "If a finger was pointed at the wife of a seignior because of another man, but she has not been caught while lying with another man, she will throw herself into the river for the sake of her husband."[30] Drowning is usually an unfortunate result of an inability to swim, not guilt; whereas, if a woman's womb became blocked, it had experienced a complicated physiological reaction. A little further on in this sequence of who needed covering, the robber and someone who lied (to or against his neighbor) were added in the witness/oath breaker group.[ah] They each kept something secret that should have been told. Whether a person forgot or purposely hid his infractions (?), he could experience a chemical change, making him prone to the cloud's effects, endangering him and, more importantly, the rest of the community.

In all these wrongdoings, if the perpetrator had sworn his innocence falsely, but recanted and then paid a fine, he could be covered. Anyone using material that resulted in both blood for the altar and meat for the burnt offering would be covered in the normal way, no matter how deeply the possible contamination was embedded. The fascinating thing about the witness, dead toucher, and oath breaker is that if they were too poor to bring an animal or bird for sacrifice, they had only to give a meal offering without the oil and frankincense and have a handful of meal burned on the altar:

> [11]"And if he cannot afford two turtle-doves or two young pigeons, then he who was contaminated will bring his offering ... fine flour for a decontamination offering; *he will not put oil on it and will not put frankincense on it because it is a decontamination offering.*
>
> [12]And he will bring it to the priest, and the priest will take from it his handful, *its memorial.* And he will burn it on the altar on the fire offerings of the Lord; it is a decontamination offering.
>
> [13]And the priest will cover on him on his contamination, which he has contaminated from one of these [things] and it will be forgiven to him; and it will be for the priest as a meal offering." (Lev. 5:11–13)

This type of offering was only used two times: here and in the test of the woman accused of adultery. Without oil and frankincense, the burned meal could do no more than its normal task of exposing the contamination. The continual fire offerings on which it was burned would do the covering. In other words, the poor person was allowed to share someone else's material for the fire offering and its protective powers. Working together, they would serve as a decontamination offering.

In Leviticus 5:11 above, the word for contamination is the familiar *chatawt.* In the case of the adulterous woman, there is a different concept for contamination and it was used along with the term *awvone,* meaning impurity.[ai] (See Appendix G.) There ai. Num. 5:15, 31 is an important technical reason for this. Adultery was a most serious crime punishable by death in common law as well as an act that could lead to horrible radiation sickness.[aj]

aj. e.g., Lev. 20:10

Yet, nowhere does it say that the action of an adulterous woman was a contamination (*chatawt*) or that she was contaminated (*chawtaw*) like the Leviticus 5 people where these words *are* used. She had done worse than *chawtaw*. She had "committed a trespass," *m'ohl ma'al*, against her husband.[ak] With this one exception, this phrase *m'ohl ma'al* is always used as "commit a trespass against the Lord," but even here, since adultery would have led to her becoming unclean, it was an action relative to the Lord.[al] It was not a "trespass" but a "super-contamination," a *ma'al*, a special phrase used to denote the greater harm done by the act of adultery. Thus, the general use of *avone* simply describes an impurity worse than *chatawt* resulting from *mawal ma'al*.

ak. Num. 5:12, 27

al. Num. 5:14

(7) Directly following the discussion of the test for the allegedly unfaithful wife is the description of the nazirite as "a man or woman when he will make a special vow of a nazirite to separate [himself] to the Lord."[am] Although there is no hint in the Five Books as to what the nazirite did during his separation period, some of the precautions he had to take were similar to those of the priests who went into the tent of meeting. The nazirite was to drink no wine or strong drink, and he was to stay away from dead bodies, even if they had been his close relatives. Strangely, like the allegedly adulterous woman, and unlike the priests, he was to keep his head uncovered; shaving his head was forbidden during the period of the vow. There may have been an important difference between the nazirite and the allegedly adulterous woman, though. The warning not to come near a dead person was,

am. Num. 6:2

> [7]"For his father or for his mother, for his sister or for his brother he will not make himself unclean for them when they die; for the separation (*nezer*) [to] his God is on his head.
>
> [8]All the days of his separation he will be [must be] conditioned (*kawdosh*) [be in a conditioned position to communicate] to the Lord." (Num. 6:7–8)

While the commentators define the separator as being his hair and likening it to the miter of the high priest, I believe this is only half correct.[31] The hair may have been like the miter in that, pursuing my theory, it was protective. Remember the warning of Leviticus 21:11–12 to the high priest not to leave the super-conditioned place "for a dead person for the *nezer of the anointing oil* is upon him." In addition to the protection of hair, it seems most likely that the nazirite, too, was protected by oil. If someone died suddenly beside him, he would become more susceptible to the effects of radioactivity and would have had to take additional, purely physical precautions:

> [9]"And when one will die beside him very suddenly, and he make *the head* of his separation unclean, then he will *shave his head* in the day of his cleansing; on the seventh day he will shave it.

> [10]And on the eighth day he will bring two turtle-doves or two young pigeons to the priest, to the door of the tent of meeting.

> [11]And the priest will offer one for a decontamination offering and one for a burnt offering, and he will cover on him from what he has contaminated *on the soul*, and he will condition [protect] *his head* on that day." (Num. 6:9–11, my emphasis)

These verses reveal that the act of covering the person, which is the main reason for the passage, fits with all the other covering situations. The phrase "on the soul" is generally translated "by [reason of the dead] person," meaning "contaminated by touching that person." Even the Talmud takes issue with this translation, saying that it refers to the nazirite himself, explaining (if tortuously) that he was ordered to "atone for his vow" to abstain from drinking wine. "Some rabbis held that man would be called to account for any unnecessary self-denial in regard to the innocent pleasures of life."[32] I think it means what it says: By becoming unclean, the person had made the soul substance in the blood (*nefesh*) and the exposed head (that had to be shaved) prone to contamination. Thus, Numbers 30:3 makes perfect sense: "When a man *vows a vow to the Lord* or swears an oath to *bind a bond on his soul*, he will not profane his word; according to all that proceeds from his mouth he will do" (my emphasis). Remember that it was a *vow* of separation that the nazirite took.

The special warnings in Leviticus 10:6–7 also related to a sudden death interrupting the priests' hand filling service. Sudden death could likewise interrupt the nazirite's period of separation, and in that event, it was necessary to cover him and start his time of separation again. The nazirite who had no such interruption could shave his head at the end of his separation period and

an. Num. 6:18

burn the hair "on the fire, which is under the sacrifice of the peace offering."[an] One could conjecture that even with the oil on the hair, it had soaked up some radiation during the separation period. Therefore, it would have been safer to shave and burn the hair than to endanger himself and others who might touch it.

ao. Lev. 13:33,
14:8–10

ap. Lev. 14:18, 29

The burned person who had radiation in his hair or beard, like any burned person, had to be shaved because the radiation made him unclean.[ao] (The reference in Leviticus 13:45 to the burned person who had to uncover his head refers to a bald person.) After shaving, the priest put oil on the man's head.[ap] During the cleansing and covering of the priestly tribe, the Levites in turn could "cover on the Israelites; that [there] will not be a plague when the Israelites come near the tent area."[aq] They, too, had to shave over "all of their flesh."[ar]

aq. Num. 8:19

ar. Num. 8:7

Chart E—Cloud Cover

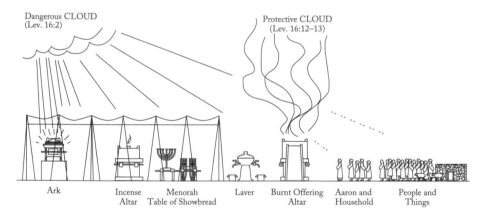

Ark   Incense Altar   Menorah Table of Showbread   Laver   Burnt Offering Altar   Aaron and Household   People and Things

(8) "Soul," *nefesh*, was used in two major ways in Exodus, Numbers, and Leviticus: One was as "person;" the other was as a substance found in the blood of animals and humans. There were different ways to cover/protect the *nefesh* in the blood. For instance, the human blood of a murderer had to be used to cover the blood of his victim in order to neutralize the danger of its attracting radiation. Animal blood was used to cover the *nefesh* of humans.[as]

as. Lev. 17:11

(9) Contaminated homes and the furnishing within were also treated with the covering process. Contaminated material was removed, the area re-plastered, and, if the radiation didn't spread, the house was then covered. (If the radiation did spread, the house was demolished.[at])

at. Lev. 14:43–45

> [49]"He will take … two birds, and cedar wood, and scarlet and hyssop.
>
> [50]And he will slaughter one of the birds in an earthen vessel over running (living) water.
>
> [51]And he will take the cedar wood and the hyssop, and the scarlet, and the living bird and he will dip them in the blood of the slaughtered bird, and in the running water, and he will sprinkle on the house seven times.
>
> [52]And he will decontaminate the house with the blood of the bird, and with the running water, and with the living bird, and with the cedar wood, and with the hyssop, and with the scarlet.
>
> [53]And he will let go the living bird outside the city into the open field; and cover on the house; and it will be clean." (Lev. 14:49–53)

(See Chart E.)

The use of hyssop to sprinkle blood goes back to Exodus 12:22. It was used to "strike the upper door post and the two side door posts with the blood." The plague struck the Egyptians, but the blood (of lambs) protected the Israelites.

> [23]"And the Lord will pass through to plague Egypt; and He will see the blood on the upper door post and on the two side door posts, and the Lord will pass over the door; and He will not allow the destroyer to come into your houses to plague you." (Exod. 12:23)[33]

Essentially, the same formula used to cleanse the house and the burned person—hyssop, scarlet, and cedar, along with the ashes of a red cow and "living" water for purifying—was also used for those who had touched a dead body.

Types of Sacrifices

Many of the substances used to protect people against the dangerous presence of the Lord were used in various types of sacrifices. The sacrifices included burnt, fire sacrifice (as a distinct type), peace, bread of presence, decontamination, guilt/trespass, vow, freewill, thanksgiving, wave, and heave offerings.

First, my approach to this subject. Sacrifice is an amazingly popular subject. Countless writers have explored the specific sacrifices of the Israelites, and the subject is fraught with questions and controversy. Many of these works didn't prove as helpful as I would have hoped, possibly because sacrifice is assumed to be a pagan rite. I found no study that questioned whether sacrifice existed for reasons other than superstition. Looking at past and present sacrifices among the peoples of this earth would hardly make anyone think differently.

To ascertain if sacrifices had chemical relevance, I launched my own study. I started with the long list of a myriad of details describing the kinds of sacrifices that are required for various "transgressions" in Leviticus. I looked at every mention of sacrifice in the Five Books to see whether the different types could shed any more light on the protection function.

First some general observations. According to my research, all the sacrifices, regardless of what they were called, were either for covering or rest-smelling or both, with the exception of the lie detecting function. All sacrifices are mentioned in the book of Leviticus. However, the guilt/trespass, thanksgiving, wave, and decontamination offerings are not mentioned in Deuteronomy, and the peace offering is only mentioned once.[au] Only the burnt offering and Cain's incorrect meal offering are mentioned in Genesis. The vow, guilt/trespass, and thanksgiving offerings are not mentioned in Exodus. Only the thanksgiving offering is excluded from Numbers. In fact, the thanksgiving offering is only mentioned in Leviticus, and then only in two places.[av]

The complete sacrificial system is presented in Leviticus and Exodus. It evolved from the burnt offerings and use of oil in early

au. Deut. 27:7

av. Lev. 7:11–15, 22:29

times to the interim arrangement of earthen and stone altars for burnt and peace offerings to the altar built for the tent.

Many important sacrifices were omitted from Deuteronomy either because they were forgotten or because Deuteronomy was compiled later when knowledge of them was taken for granted. Numbers, on the other hand, lists all the sacrifices except for the thanksgiving offering. Numbers is a natural continuation of the history of sacrifice observed, orally transmitted, and written in Genesis, Exodus, and Leviticus. While there are some variations in the sacrificial detail within these books (which the critics say are reflections of different writers in different times), there is no variation in the technical terms employed. Thus, while various scholars say there are different interpretations for the various sacrifices, and even that they do not understand the meanings of some of the terms, none of them denies this uniformity of technology. As Baruch Levine says in his Prolegomenon to Gray's *Sacrifice in The Old Testament*, "Despite all that has been written on biblical religion, we are still unable to define some of the basic terms."[34]

Burnt Offering

The burnt offering sacrifice, *olaw*, was used at the very beginning of the Bible, probably by Abel and specifically by Noah and Abram.[aw] It is in all Five Books and many following ones. Male cattle, sheep, goats, or fowl could be used. The whole animal, except the skin, was burned, and its blood was sprinkled on the side of the tabernacle's main altar. The purpose of the burnt offering was for covering and rest-smelling, setting up a protective condition similar to that achieved by rest.[ax]

aw. *olaw*, 5930

ax. Lev. 1:4, 9, 13, 5:10; Num. 29:36

OTHER LANGUAGES

The noun *olaw* is related to the verb *awlaw*, which has many meanings but generally denotes "to ascend, to go up" and more specifically, "offer."[ay] Thus, *olaw*, i.e., "that which goes up," refers to the rising smoke of the sacrifice.[35] There are many examples of them being paired to mean offer a burnt offering, *awlaw olaw*.[az]

Olaw is interesting because of the universality of the word in other languages. It is exactly the same in the Ugaritic. *'ly* means "went up, brought

ay. *awlaw*, 5927

az. e.g., Gen. 8:20, 22:2, 13; Exod. 24:5, 30:9, 32:6; Lev. 14:20, 17:8; Num. 23:2, 4, 14, 30; Deut. 12:13, 14

up, offered up," "to offer up [a sacrifice]."[36] Then there is the word *eloo*, which CAD says has 13 meanings in the verbal form, almost all generally indicating "to go up, to ascend."[37] Of special interest are the following CAD meanings: "to *cover* (said of animals), to make the water rise (referring to river ordeals)" and "to *offer* or dedicate (something) to a deity."[38]

As conjecture, there is an Egyptian word that means to "ascend, mount up, approach."[39] It looks like this: 𓏤𓂝𓈏 or 𓏤𓂝𓊪. Taking each letter separately, the 𓏤 is defined by Gardiner as "usually consonantal *y*." He says it corresponds to the Hebrew *yodh*, but he also says "at the beginning of words [it is] sometimes identical with 𓅡 ," which corresponds to the Hebrew *aleph*. Next is ʿ. It is a guttural sound that corresponds to the Hebrew *ayin*. Last there is ⟨r⟩, which is normally an *r* and corresponds to the Hebrew *resh* and rarely to the Hebrew *lamedh*. With the alternative letters, the Egyptian word would be *ayl*, rather close to all the other languages including Hebrew. The determinative in the first spelling is "stairs." In the variation it is 𓊪 , which is also seen in 𓊃, *s ʿr* meaning "make to ascend, *offer* up!"[40] Both Gardiner and Faulkner also say another variation is simply 𓂝𓊪, that is *ʿr* without the 𓏤.[41] Even without the Egyptian conjecture, it is a word of great antiquity for a process of great antiquity.

Fire Offering

ba. *eesheh*, 801; *aysh*, 784

Fire offering, *eesheh*, is most probably from *aysh*, "fire."[ba] Some researchers theorize that it may come from the Ugaritic *itt*, which is said to mean "gift."[42] The prevalent Ugaritic words for "gift" are *ushn*, *itnn*, *mnh*, and *th*.[43] Segert says *itht* questionably means "vow."[44] Driver translates the passage in Keret that Segert refers to using the word "vow" but spelling it *ett*.[45] To complicate things further, the usual Ugaritic for "vow" is *ndr*, the exact relative of the Hebrew *neder*, "vow."

The reason some call *eesheh* "gift" instead of fire offering is that it was used with wine, as food for the priests, and with

bb. Num. 15:10; Lev. 7:30–2; Lev. 24:7, 9[46]

the presence bread.[bb] It is not clear how the wine was used, but certain passages could be read as mixing the wine and oil with the meal offering.

> [3]"And you will make a fire offering to the Lord …
>
> [4]Then will bring … his offering to the Lord a meal offering of a tenth [of an *ephah*], of fine flour mingled with the fourth part of a *hin* of oil
>
> [5]And wine for a drink offering; a fourth of a hin you will prepare on the burnt offering or for the sacrifice for [each] one lamb …

⁷[For] rest-smelling for the Lord." (Num. 15:3–5, 7)

As to the possibility that the fire offering was food for the priests, Leviticus 7:31 explicitly orders them to burn the fat of the fire offerings but on the contrary says other parts may be eaten. While the bread of presence was eaten, the frankincense used with it was burned. In addition, the Hebrew word for gifts is *matawnaw*, which seems to be a separate category in the list of offerings.[bc] So the probability that *eesheh* does mean "fire offering" seems pretty high.

The fire offering was for rest-smelling. It was also used with the special vow and freewill offerings, the guilt/trespass offering, and may at times have been synonymous with the burnt offering.[bd] It was carried out with meal, wine, and oil as well as meat. All animals, goats, sheep, and cattle were used. Fire offerings were included in the festivals, where it again seems to have been synonymous with the burnt offerings.[be] The use of the fire offering for seven days at the feast of unleavened bread as a continual burnt offering and on *Yom Kippur* illustrates the importance of keeping the area clear of radiation even on Sabbaths.[bf] Fire offerings are not mentioned in Genesis and only once in Deuteronomy.[bg] Strikingly, unlike the burnt offering that is used throughout the Five Books and in many of the following ones, the term "fire offering" disappears after one use in Joshua and one in Isaiah.[bh] Both references are general. In fact, the reference in Joshua is the same as the one in Deuteronomy. While sometimes used with burnt offering, the fire offering differs in one important respect. With one exception in Numbers 18:9, the 58 mentions of fire offering in Exodus, Leviticus, and Numbers use wording that is related to the Lord:

- "to/for the Lord (*eeshay laYahweh*)"
- "from the fire offerings of the Lord (*mayeeshay Yaweh*)"
- "of rest-smelling to/for the Lord"
- "My fire offerings"

On the other hand, the burnt offering often uses the phrase "before the Lord."

bc. *matawnaw*, 4979, e.g., Lev. 23:37–8

bd. e.g., Num. 15:3; Lev. 7:5; e.g., Lev. 1:9, 13, 17; Num. 28:3

be. Lev. 23:1–14, esp. 7, 13; Num. 28:11–22, esp. 13, 19

bf. Lev. 23:8, 27

bg. Deut. 18:1

bh. Josh. 13:14; Isa. 2:28

bi. *liphne*, 6440

It seems that *eesheh* is a discrete, highly technical term. Its emphasis on "to/for the Lord" points to its very protective nature.

Sacrifice

Sacrifice, *zebach*, is the process of slaughtering an animal used for an offering.[bj] *Zebach* comes from the verb *zawbach* and is translated "to slaughter."[47] The general meaning is found in the Akkadian, Ugaritic, and Phoenician.[48] *Zebach* is related to altar, *meezbayach*.[bk] *Zebach* is found in all of the Five Books and is used widely in the following books. As a verb, it refers to the sacrificing of the usual animals.[bl] As a noun, it refers to the type of sacrifice, e.g., peace offering.[bm]

Zebach was the act of offering an animal to the Lord (or to idols). It differed from *shawchat* (ending with a *teth*, not to be confused with the same word ending with a *tav*) that actually meant to kill the animal for this purpose.[bn] While sacrifices were common from the very beginning, the words *zebach* and *zawbach* are used only twice in Genesis, both times relating to Jacob.[bo] In Exodus, the first mentions are in connection with the plea of Moses to Pharaoh to let the Israelites go into the desert to sacrifice. Later, Exodus 29:1–42 promulgates the first rules regarding sacrifice, which involve the hand filling of the priests. They also act as a preface for the full set of rules that follow in Leviticus. Leviticus 17:8 differentiates between a burnt offering and a sacrifice, while Leviticus 23:37–38 separates *zebach* from all the other offerings:

> [37]"These are the set feasts that you will proclaim to be conditioning convocations, to offer a fire offering to the Lord, burnt offering and meal offering, sacrifice (*zebach*), and drink offering, every thing on its day,

> [38]Beside the Sabbaths of the Lord, and beside your gifts and beside all your vows, and beside all your freewill offerings, which you give to the Lord." (Lev. 23:37–38)

There is also a distinction between the sacrifices and burnt offerings. Note where Moses said to Pharaoh,

bj. *zebach*, 2077

bk. *meezbayach*, 4196

bl. Lev. 9:2–4, esp. 4

bm. Lev. 7:11

bn. *shawchat*, 7819; *shawchat*, 7843, Lev. 1:5, 3:8, etc.

bo. Gen. 31:54, 46:1

[25]"You must also give into our hands sacrifices (*z'bawcheem*) and burnt offerings (*ohlot*) that we may sacrifice to the Lord our God." (Exod. 10:25)

God told Moses what to do when the Israelites came into the land of Canaan. He said,

[3]"You will prepare a fire offering (*eesheh*) to the Lord, a burnt offering (*olaw*) or a sacrifice (*zebach*) for a special vow or as a freewill offering, or in your set feasts to prepare a rest-smelling to the Lord, of the herd or of the flock." (Num. 15:3)

Leviticus 22:21 and Deuteronomy 15:21 admonish against sacrificing imperfect animals. Leviticus 7:29–34 speaks of the sacrifice of peace offering and the portion due Aaron and his sons, while Deuteronomy 18:3 delineates the priests' portion of the sacrifice in general. Joshua 22:26–29 also differentiates between the types of sacrifice, which is understandable historically considering it immediately follows the Five Books. That is, Joshua had just inherited Moses' mantle to lead the Israelites, so all the rules laid down by Moses still remained intact.

Attitudes toward sacrifice changed over time, but the original purpose was for rest-smelling as it pertained to the peace offering:

[1]"And if a sacrifice of peace offerings [is] his offering, if from the herd he offer[s] …

[2]He will lay his hand on the head … and slaughter it [at] the door of the tent of meeting, and [there] Aaron's sons, the priests will sprinkle the blood on the altar all around.

[3]And he will bring near from the sacrifice of the peace offering, a fire offering to the Lord, the fat that covers the inwards and all the fat that is on the inwards,

[4]And the two kidneys and the fat that is on them, which is on the flanks, and the lobe on the liver with the kidneys, which you will remove.

[5]And Aaron's sons will burn it on the altar on the burnt offering, which is on the wood that is on the fire, a fire offering of rest-smelling to the Lord." (Lev. 3:1–5)

Sacrifice was also for rest-smelling in relation to the vow and freewill offerings:

[3]"And you will make a fire offering to the Lord, a burnt offering, or a sacrifice for a special vow or as a freewill offering or in your set feasts to make a rest-smelling to the Lord from the herd or from the flock." (Num. 15:3)

There is no direct mention of the covering function of sacrifice, but covering was the other purpose. Notice how *zebach* relates to the peace offering:

> ⁵"In order that the Israelites may bring their sacrifices (*zaycham*), which they sacrifice on the open field, and that they may bring them to the Lord to the door of the tent of meeting … and sacrifice (*v'zawb'choo*) them, peace offerings"
>
> ⁶"… and he will burn the fat for rest-smelling to the Lord."
>
> ¹¹"For the soul of the flesh is in the blood, and I have given it to you on the altar to cover on your souls, for it is the blood [that] covers in the soul." (Lev. 17:5–6, 11)

In other words, the purpose of the peace offering sacrifice (*zebach*) was to use its fat for rest-smelling and its blood for covering.[bp] In following books, the peace offering sacrifice was taken for granted.[bq] Actually, a close reading of Exodus 29:27–28 indicates that "the ram of filling," parts of which were eaten by Aaron and his sons, were from the Israelites, from the sacrifices of their peace offerings. "And they will eat those [things] that he was covered by [or 'with'] to fill their hands to condition them [Aaron and his sons]."[br] Thus, it is even stated here that these parts of the peace offerings were used for covering.

Peace Offering

Peace offering sacrifice, *shelem*, is always, with the exception of Amos 5:22, in the plural, *sh'lawmim*.[bs] *Shelem* comes from the root *sh-l-m*, which HAL says in its qal verb form can mean "to be completed, ready, to remain healthy, unharmed, [i.e., safe], to keep peace, to make intact … make restitution, to recompense, reward, to restore, replace, to finish … to deliver up."[50]

The peace offering is not mentioned in Genesis and only once in Deuteronomy. It is in all the rest of the Five Books. In the following books, it is found in Joshua, Judges, 1 and 2 Samuel, 1 and 2 Kings, 1 and 2 Chronicles, Proverbs, Ezekiel, and once in Amos.

The peace offering is first mentioned in Exodus 20:21 in God's order for Moses to make "an altar of earth" and to "sacrifice on it your burnt offerings and your peace offerings." David built

---

bp. cf., Lev. 7:14, 33; 9:18⁴⁹

bq. E.g., Ezek. 45:15, 17

br. Exod. 29:33

bs. *shelem*, 8002

this early altar style to stay the plague in 2 Samuel 24:25. It was also used in 2 Chronicles 30:22 after the people were healed of radiation burn that they contracted, because they didn't cleanse themselves before celebrating Passover. The peace offering is mentioned in a group of sacrifices for atonement in Ezekiel 45:15, 17.

Regarding the animals to be sacrificed in the peace offering, Moses used *parim*, translated "oxen" or "bullocks" in Exodus 24:5–8, but in Leviticus 3:1,6,7,12, animals from the herd or flock, sheep or a goat, male or female could have been used.[bt] Words for the animals were quite interchangeable: *shore* for bullock or ox in Leviticus 9:4 and *bawkawr* in Numbers 7:17, 15:7, and 9 for the same.[bu] So much has been written about the actual meaning of *shelem* in relation to sacrifice that I will only mention some of the theories. In addition to "peace offering," *shelem* has been designated "a welfare offering," "fellowship offering," "well-being offering," "praise offering," and "safety offering."[51] Fuerst disagrees with this last.[52] However, the Septuagint uses *soteria*, which actually means "salvation, rescue."[bv] To these HAL adds "conclusion offering," "community offering," and "covenant offering."[53]

bt. *parim*, 6499

bu. *shore*, 7794; *bawkawr*, 1241

bv. Sept., e.g., Lev. 7:1, 3–5, 10, 11; Heb. 6:11, 13–15, 19, 21

<><><><><><><><><><><><><><><><><><><><><><><><><><><><><><><><><><><>

OTHER LANGUAGES

The roots *shlm* and *shlmm*, with more or less the same meanings as are found in Hebrew, are common throughout the ancient near east.[54] In the Ugaritic, both the singular *shlm* and plural *shlmm* are used for sacrifice.[55] DLU translates *shlm* (I) "bonanza," "peace, health, well-being, calm." He translates *shlm* (II) as "victim/sacrifice of communion, peaceable or peaceful."[56] HAL translates *shlm* as "salutation offering, gift."[57]

For the Akkadian, CAD devotes 22 pages to *salmu* with 14 meanings. Important to this subject is "to stay well ... to be completed ... to guard, to protect ... to carry out a ritual."[58] Under the translation "prayers" there is the quote, "Let me have life and good health so that I may walk well protected before your great majesty."[59] Under "other occurrences" there is, "The person who offers the sacrifice (niqê) will get well."[60] CAD also lists the following under "other occurrences": "It is in your power to safeguard offspring (?), to protect the weak," "Have a protective spirit and a personal god who keeps (me) safe ... stand by me."[61] Under the translation "to carry out a ritual in full," CAD uses the quotes "as soon as he has finished making the offerings of Ur" and "to make in a ritually pure manner the *taklīmu* offering."[62]

One more language should be examined for relevance to the discussion. By now one might wonder if Moses and Aaron would not be looking for an exact description of this sacrifice, which differed from the others in that anyone could eat the meat, even though the blood was for the usual purpose—to cover the area so communication could be safely effected— and the fat and some organs were for rest-smelling. Where did they often seem to turn when looking for technical terms? Over and over it was to their former home—Egypt. Here there is found a most interesting word. It is *snm*. Remembering that *n* can also be *l*, it is possible to have the pronunciation *slm*. Faulkner says *snm* spelled ⸺𓏏𓀁𓏤𓏜 meant "feed s'one [someone]; consume food; supply necessities." He says that *snmw* is "food-supply" and that *snm* spelled ⸺𓏏𓀁𓏤 means pray; with determinants 𓀀𓀀, it means prayer![63] It should be noted that the peace offering was nicknamed the "food of a fire offering to the Lord."[bw] In this connection, it is important that the parts of the peace offering used on the altar, like the meal offering, were burned on the fire offerings, in this case on the *olaw*.[bx] It was fuel or "food" for the fire offering. The remaining meat was eaten. So, maybe there was one word describing two aspects of the so-called peace offering, its burnable part and its edible part. If this were so, it once again points to the antiquity of the word.

bw. Lev. 3:11, 16

bx. Lev. 3:5, 6:5

∞∞

There are, I think, good reasons for referring to other languages when discussing the peace offerings. One is the fact that Ugaritic texts, written in the 14th and 13th centuries BCE, refer to sacrifices translated as "peace offerings," and they use the same word as the Hebrew.[64] The Akkadian, Ugaritic, and, peripherally, the Egyptian concepts of "stay well, become safe, completed, protect, carry out a ritual" fit perfectly into the reasons for using the peace offering. They remind us that the purposes for the peace offering were rest-smelling and covering. The protective nature of the offering (to ensure the continued health of the group) is made more evident by some of the other situations in which it is used. In the now familiar story of the hand filling, in addition to the decontamination, burnt, and meal offerings, Aaron and his sons were to use the ox and the ram for the peace offering on the eighth day, "for today the Lord will appear to you."[by] "And Moses said, 'This thing that the Lord had commanded you will do; then the radiance of the Lord will

by. Lev. 9:2-4

appear.'"[bz] All of the sacrifices were necessary to protect the   bz. Lev. 9:6
Israelites from the radiance.

Numbers 6:14–17 refers not only to the peace offering, but
to all the others. They were all used when the nazirite had
fulfilled the days of his vow. I wonder if the Akkadian concept
of completion is a description of this "offering of completion."

Interestingly, verse 18 of this story says that the nazirite should
shave his head and put his contaminated hair "on the fire, which
is under the sacrifice of the peace offering." The fact that it was
the peace offering on which it was burned shows, I think, that
the peace offering was capable of covering.

Numbers 7:88 summarizes verses 17–83, which include
the peace offering animals brought by the rulers of the tribes
of Israel for the dedication of the altar. Immediately after the
anointing of the altar, Moses went into the dangerous tent to
speak with the Lord about the next steps in the operation of
the service. Leviticus further explains that the peace offering
may have been used as a thanksgiving offering if combined
with cakes and oil, and in that event its meat must be eaten
the same day.[ca] Otherwise, it may have been used as a vow or   ca. Lev. 7:15–6
freewill offering and could be eaten in two days.[cb] How did the   cb. Lev. 7:11–21
requirement to eat the meat within different time periods relate
to the protective nature of the sacrifice? Let's look at the law:

> [11]"And this is the *law* of the sacrifice of the peace offering,
> which will be brought to the Lord.

> [12]If for a thanksgiving offering he will bring it, then he will
> bring it with the thanksgiving offering unleavened cakes
> mixed with oil and flour soaked (*rawbach* [usually translated
> "baked," but actually means "to soak or saturate"]) cakes
> mingled in oil.[cc]   cc. *rawbach*, 7246

> [13]With cakes of *leavened* bread he will offer his oblation with
> the sacrifices of his thanksgiving-peace offering.

> [14]And he will offer of it one of every oblation [for] a heave
> offering to the Lord; to the priest that sprinkles the blood of
> the peace offerings it will belong to him.

¹⁵And the flesh of the thanksgiving-peace offering on *the day* of his oblation it will be eaten; he [the person] will not leave of it till morning.

¹⁶But *if a vow or freewill offering* is the sacrifice of his oblation, *on the day* of his offering his sacrifice it will be eaten and *on the morrow* that which is left will be eaten.

¹⁷But what is left of the meat of the sacrifice *on the third day* it will be burned with fire.

¹⁸And if it is eaten of the meat of the sacrifice of his peace offering on the third day, it will not be accepted; he that offers it, to him it will not be accounted; it will be an abomination (*peegool*) and the person that eats of it will carry his impurity." (Lev. 7:11–18)[65]

The Bible says that the peace offering (i.e., the animal's blood, fat from various organs, kidneys, and lobe of liver) was to be offered on oil-soaked, unleavened material as well as leavened bread. One part of each of the unleavened and leavened items was for the priest who sprinkled the blood in the danger area. The meat from the sacrifice had to be eaten by the offerer(s) on the same day the sacrifice was made. Presumably, the residue was to be burned as were any leftovers after two days.

The answer to the question of why the one and two day periods must lie in the difference between the materials used in the sacrifice. Evidently, in addition to the blood, fat, oil, etc., the meal products formed a chemical substance that could attract radioactivity to the altar area where the peace offering would neutralize it. Therefore, the meat of the animals would naturally be more prone to contamination. So it was necessary to eat it quickly before it became too exposed and contaminated.

On the other hand, the vow and freewill offerings, working with the blood but without the additional chemicals, wouldn't be able to attract the dangerous material to the altar area as well. So, it would take longer for that meat to become contaminated and it could be eaten over a two-day period.[66] After that, it was too dangerous. If anyone ate it on the third day, he would carry his impurity. See the further discussion in the verses that follow:

¹⁹"And the meat that touches any unclean thing will not be eaten; it will be burned with fire; and the meat, every clean [person] will eat meat.

²⁰But the person (soul) that eats meat of the sacrifice of the peace offering, which is to the Lord, when his uncleanness is on him, then that person will be cut off from his people.

²¹And when a person touches any unclean [thing] of the uncleanness of man or an unclean animal or any unclean creature and he eats of the meat of the sacrifice of the peace offering of the Lord, that person will be cut off from his people." (Lev. 7:19–21)

The warning is this: The meat of the peace offering sacrifice was already somewhat contaminated, more so if the sacrifice was made with the oiled meal offering. If it then touched anything unclean, it became more prone to contamination and had to be burned. A clean person could eat the meat because he was less vulnerable to the meat's contamination than an unclean person. Finally, a clean person who ate the peace offering but touched something unclean, thereby making him unclean, would also be "cut off." "Will be cut off" could mean anything from temporarily quarantined to permanently exiled.ᶜᵈ

Completely apart from the eating of the residual meat, the officiating priest was to eat the portion of unleavened cakes, wafers, fine flour cakes mixed with oil, and leavened bread.⁶⁸ The meal offering was for internal protection, a conditioner and a super-conditioner.ᶜᵉ The only difference here was that it was eaten with leavened bread as well.

cd. *kawrat*, 3772; e.g., Lev. 17:10; e.g., Exod. 12:15⁶⁷

ce. e.g., Lev. 2:10

Leaven

Leaven was generally forbidden, and explicitly so as part of the meal offering. Evidently, the only real prohibition regarding leavened bread is that "you will not burn it [as] a fire offering to the Lord."ᶜᶠ There doesn't appear to be a prohibition against eating it in Leviticus 7:13–14 except on Passover.⁶⁹ But why the leavened bread here? There can be only one plausible explanation: the bread, with its ability to ferment or turn moldy (like penicillin), was another internal protection. This was also true of the showbread. So, quite contrary to later attitudes that leaven was equated with evil, it may have had a definite protective function.⁷⁰

cf. Lev. 2:11

There were two other uses of leavened bread. In both, it was eaten. The first was the bread offered on the festival of *Shawvuot*:

¹⁶ "Until the day after the seventh week you will count fifty days, and you will bring a new meal offering to the Lord.

¹⁷Out of your habitations you will bring two wave-loaves of two tenth parts of flour they will be, leavened they will be, baked first fruits to the Lord.

¹⁸And you will bring with the bread seven lambs ... and one young bullock and two rams. They will be a burnt offering to the Lord, with their meal offering and their drink offering, a fire offering of rest-smelling to the Lord.

¹⁹And you will bring one he-goat for a decontamination offering and two he-lambs ... for a sacrifice of peace offering.

²⁰And the priest will wave them with the bread of the first fruits, a wave offering before the Lord on two lambs, conditioners will be to (for) the Lord to (for) the priest." (Lev. 23:16–20)

Here the meal and the drink offerings were made, and two leavened loaves were offered "to (for) the Lord for the priest" to eat.^{cg} They were conditioners along with the two lambs that serve as a peace offering.

The second use is in the next chapter:

⁵"And you will take fine flour and you will bake [of] it twelve cakes.

⁷And you will put on the row ... frankincense that it may be with the bread, a memorial (*azkawraw*), a fire offering to (for) the Lord.

⁹And it will be for Aaron and for his sons and they will eat it in a conditioned place for it is a super-conditioner from the fire offerings of the Lord." (Lev. 24:5, 7, 9)

This bread was not specified as leavened, but in its highly important role here it would be most unusual not to carefully explain that it was *un*leavened if that were the case.[71] So here again, the bread for the Lord and for Aaron and his sons was an offering used as a conditioner when eaten. Comparing these references to the Leviticus 7 verses, portions of various unleavened materials, along with the leavened bread, were to be "a heave offering for the Lord, for the priest."^{ch} The fact that this was "the priest that sprinkles the blood of the peace offering" once

cg. Lev. 2:14

ch. Lev. 7:14

more shows that the peace offering was for covering/protection. It is implicit that the rest of the offering materials allotted to this priest were used for covering also. It was this priest who was in the danger area and had to do everything possible to protect himself, including, in this specific case, eating the leavened bread. The peace offering, i.e., the meat, could be eaten outside the altar area as long as the place was clean.^{ci}

ci. Lev. 10:4

Since the leavened bread couldn't be burned on the altar and was ingested for whatever chemical qualities leavening (fermentation) contained for internal protection, what was the purpose of *matzah*?[72] It probably only served as a quick, easily prepared deliverer of oil and possibly frankincense.^{cj} It was used internally with countless sacrifices. Thus, just as the bread delivered fermented material (but never oil), *matzah* delivered oil, and that may have been its primary role. So the chemical reactions were just as to be expected. The problem comes with trying to follow this rule forward from this point, because there is some flipping back and forth between the anointing day of Aaron and his sons, the general wilderness period, and what is to be done in the future. So no other reference is as clear as the law regarding the peace offering. From then on, mentions of the peace offering show up in bits and pieces:

cj. e.g., Lev. 6:7

- Leviticus 3 refers to peace offerings at the tent.
- Leviticus 7:29–36 continues a point made earlier in 7:11–21: In the case of the peace offering, any one of the Israelites who brought it could have shared it with the priest. Verse 36 ends by saying that this was the anointing portion given to Aaron and his sons in "the day when He anointed them."
- Leviticus 9:1–4 is a list of sacrifices, including the peace offering to be used on the eighth day of filling, so it is anointing-related.
- Leviticus 17:1–9 warns that sacrifices be brought to the tent door—not out in the field—to sacrifice them as peace offerings to the Lord. This really seems to be a warning against idolatry, but once again, I am talking of the wilderness and tent here with an extension that it is "perpetual for their generations."

This warning also admonishes against eating blood (e.g., verses 10–14).

- Leviticus 19:5–8 mentions the peace offering, generally repeating the rule about eating it on the second but not on the third day, as though it were a peace-vow or peace-freewill offering, although these are not specifically mentioned. This law pertains to the future. It is included with variations of the Decalogue: You will be conditioned because I am conditioned; every man will fear his father and mother; keep My Sabbaths; do not make molten gods; do not wholly reap the corners of your field when you harvest your land; do not glean your vineyard (leave the residue for the poor); do not steal, lie, etc.

- Leviticus 22:18–21 indicates rules that the people were to observe once they settled in their land. Interestingly, it draws the distinction between vow and freewill offerings as separate oblations and as subgroups of the peace offering. Leviticus 22:18 says, "Any man … who offers his oblation for any of their vows and for any of their freewill offerings, which they offer to the Lord for a burnt offering …" Leviticus 22:21 says, "And when a man offers a sacrifice of the peace offering to the Lord as a special vow or as a freewill offering …"

- Leviticus 23:19 is part of the list for *Shavout*, so it is future.

- Numbers 7:17–10:10 is history, which definitely pertains to the wilderness.

- Numbers 15:1–9 seems to contradict the law as given in Leviticus 7:11–21. Numbers 15:4 says that the vow and freewill offerings should be made with a meal offering with oil, and Numbers 15:8–9 says the same again for the vow, adding, "or a peace offering to the Lord." There are several possibilities here. The most probable is that the vow and freewill offerings referred to here were the separate ones stipulated in Leviticus 22:18. This seems most probable because of Numbers 15:8, which separates the two by saying the vow *or* peace offering. Another possibility is that if they were vow and freewill-peace offerings, then the rule changed to meet new conditions: "When you will come unto the land of your habitations …"[ck]

That is, the sacrifice was fine-tuned during the wilderness sojourn to prepare for permanent dwelling in the land of Canaan. If a person (and possibly his family) wanted to bring these voluntary offerings, from whatever distance he lived from the central place of sacrifice to be shared with the priests, he would probably want to eat his share as soon as possible and get back home. This would benefit the priests too, because of the additional decontaminating property of the oiled vow and freewill offerings. Still, a third possibility is that the critics' theory is correct. That is, competing priestly groups hundreds of years later formulated different rules and cast them back to the earlier period. I believe that the rules changed over time in the wilderness (remember the quick change of mind about who could accompany Moses up Mt. Sinai) than that the priests contradicted each other and then froze the contradictions in their cast-back "histories."

Surely the evolutionary pattern of *Yom Kippur* allowed for changes. What happened during Aaron and his sons' first hand filling was quite different from the somewhat later daily sacrifices in the tent in the wilderness, which was far different from the settlement period activities. It makes perfect sense that plans had to be made for each of these phases, and that they evolved to meet the changing needs.

Whether or not there is a contradiction in Numbers (and no matter how much the later references to the peace offerings flip back and forth with the evolutionary pattern), the chemical principles laid out in the original law remain logical and fit neatly with everything now known. To reiterate, the peace offering was for rest-smelling and covering and, therefore, was another of the protective sacrifices that maintained the health and safety of the users. When the sacrificial parts were used with a meal offering and oil, it absorbed more radiation and so the remaining meat had to be eaten quickly. When used without oil, they did not have the same soaking property; thus, the residual, edible meat was somewhat safer to eat over a slightly longer period. Beyond that period, it was just too dangerous to eat. The fact that this entire section speaks of protecting the meat of the sacrifice from *any* kind of uncleanness certainly indicates that it was subject to contamination and was therefore potentially dangerous to handle. One last point must be made regarding the so-called "thanksgiving-peace offering." The critics agree that the strange conflation of the two words popping up in the midst of the Leviticus 7:11–21 passage (especially verse 15) indicates that the thanksgiving part was probably a later historical development inserted by the priestly writers. Elsewhere, the thanksgiving sacrifice was separate from the peace offering. The example given is Leviticus 22:29: "And when you sacrifice a sacrifice of thanksgiving, you will sacrifice it for your acceptance. On the same day it will be eaten; you will not leave of it until morning." This is said to be in the so-called H Code, discussed in Appendix H.

I would go further than this. It is possible that there was *no* thanksgiving offering in the Five Books. In the first place, the only mentions of the word thanks or thanksgiving, *todaw*, as a sacrifice or anything else in the entire Five Books are in the Leviticus 7 law and the Leviticus 22:29 verse.[cl] Actually, there doesn't seem to be a concept of thanking the Lord or anyone else from Genesis to Deuteronomy. Second, the purported purpose, thanking the Lord for favors received, completely conflicts with the protective purposes of all the other sacrifices, i.e., covering and rest-smelling. On the other hand, the thanksgiving offering as such *was* known in 2 Chronicles, Psalms, probably Nehemiah, Amos, and Jeremiah. Third, the Septuagint *never* uses thanksgiving offering. In Leviticus 7 references, it uses *aineseos*, the word for "praise." In Leviticus 22:29, it doesn't even come close: "And you will offer a sacrifice, a wish (prayer) of *rejoicing* to the Lord." In the following books it uses "praise, confess, bring gifts" instead of "bring offerings of thanksgiving" as in the Hebrew.[cm]

Perhaps some editor stuck the thanksgiving offering to the peace offering in Leviticus 7 at the later date in order to fit it into the much later concept of thanking the Lord. The omission of thanksgiving would not change the reasoning surrounding the peace offerings having to be eaten in one day when combined with the meal and oil. The chemical reaction was the same.

Showbread

The showbread, *lechem pawneem*, is among the protective substances used as a part of a sacrifice. Literally the "bread of faces," it is called by many names:

- the bread of presence[cn]

cl. *todaw*, 8426

cm. Sept., Jer. 33:11

cn. *lechem pawneem*, 3899, 6440; Exod. 25:30, 35:13, 39:36; 1 Sam. 21:6; 1 Kgs. 7:48; 2 Chr. 4:19

- "arrangement [or row] of bread" (*erech lechem*) or simply "arrangement" or "row," *erech*[co]
- the "continual bread" or the "bread of continuity" (*lechem hatawmeed*)[cp]
- "row" or "line" (*ma'arechet*)[cq]
- "bread of arrangement" (*lechem hama'arechet*)[cr]
- "table of the arrangement"[cs]
- "row of bread" (*ma'arechet lechem*)[ct]
- "continual arrangement" (*ma'arechet tawmid*)[cu]
- "cakes" or "loaves" (*challa*).[cv]

co. *erech*, 6187;
Exod. 40:4

cp. *hatawmeed*, 8548;
Num. 4:7

cq. *ma'arechet*, 4635

cr. Lev. 24:6, 7;
1 Chr. 9:32, 23:29;
Neh. 10:34

cs. 1 Chr. 28:16, 29:18

ct. 2 Chr. 13:11

cu. 2 Chr. 2:4

cv. *challa*, 2471

The idea of bread as a sacrifice to the gods was known throughout the Middle East.[73] "Among the constituent parts of a Babylonian sacrifice was the laying of unleavened loaves before deity in sets of twelve or multiples of twelve. The Hebrew name [*lechem pawneem*] has its counterpart in the Assyrian *akal panu*."[74] However, in the case of *lechem pawneem* and its use, the passage is fraught with difficulties.

The following ia at the very beginning of the description of utensils to be used on the table with the bread:

> [29]"And you will make its dishes (*k'awraw*) and its bowls (*kaf*) and its pitchers (*kawshaw*) and its purifying tubes (*m'nakeet*) wherewith [the bread] is covered. [Of] pure gold you will make them." (Exod. 25:29)[cw]

cw. *k'awraw*, 7086;
kaf, 3709; *kawshaw*,
7184; *m'nakeet*, 4518

The translations of these four utensils can be practically any other words you want. For instance, in other verses, (1) *k'awraw* has been translated "molds for the loaves," (2) *kaf* has been translated "spoons" or "ladles," and (3) *kawshaw* as "supporters."[75] One explanation describes these three utensils as "'props' for the loaves of bread on display."[76] *Kawshaw* has been translated as "pitchers" or "jars" or "jugs," and it is often associated with "libation," i.e., "drink offering."[cx] Here in Exodus 25:29, instead of the words "wherewith [the bread] is covered (*yoosach*, the hophal imperfect form of *nawsach*)," the translation could be "with which to offer libations."[77] The libation translation has been refuted, though, by those who point out that Exodus 30:9 prohibits pouring a drink offering on the incense altar. I disagree with the

cx. Exod. 25:29,
37:16; Num. 4:7

libations translation because the law of the showbread does not mention an accompanying drink offering. Finally, 4) *m'nakeet* has been translated elsewhere as "cup" or "jug" for the drink offering.[78] Other explanations say the following:

> The literal meaning of the word should be "cleansers;" indeed, Bekhor Shor takes them to be utensils for clearing ashes from the oven and for cleaning the table. Menahot 97a takes them to be rods in the shape of hollow reeds broken in two that were placed on the table to permit free circulation of air between the cakes to keep them clean and fresh.[79]

The issues of how the utensils were used and whether or not alcohol was involved are of secondary concern in context. Protection is central in the law concerning the *lechem pawneem*:

> [5]"And you will take flour and you will bake it with twelve cakes [of] two tenths [of an *ephah*] will be one cake,
>
> [6]And you will set them [in] two rows six [in] a row, on the clean table before the Lord.
>
> [7]And you will put on [each] row pure (*zachaw*) frankincense, and it will be with the bread for a *memorial*, a *fire offering* to the Lord.
>
> [8]On *every Sabbath* he will arrange it before the Lord continually from the Israelites, a perpetual *covenant*.
>
> [9]And it will be for Aaron and for his sons and they will eat it in a conditioned place because it is a super-conditioner to him from the fire offering of the Lord, a perpetual *statute*." (Lev. 24:5–9, my emphasis)

According to these verses, the priests would bring the bread into the conditioned place where the incense altar, the *menorah*, and the golden table with all its utensils were. This was the second most contaminated part of the tent and its surrounding court. The bread would sit there for seven days, be eaten by the priests, and then replaced with new loaves. Theoretically, they would eat the bread for internal protection, but that bread could have been dosed with radiation from the cloud for up to a week. How could this be? Let's check the accuracy of the translations in this verse.

The first key term is "clean," *tawhor*, referring to the clean table. I defined *tawhor* as a condition wherein the danger of the cloud's radiation is either minimized because one is properly protected, or it has been removed by washing, sacrifice, etc. In this case, the table and everything else in the area was made super-conditioned by the conditioning, anointing oil. Also, Aaron and his sons were conditioned the same way before coming into the danger area. So, the table and those working with it were already protected.

The second term, translated "pure," is *zawch*.[cy] It is used only in terms of frankincense and oil. This remarkable word is used only four times in the Five Books, twice in Exodus and twice in Leviticus:

cy. *zawch*, 2134

- Exodus 27:20 discusses the olive oil for the continually burning lamp in the tent.
- Exodus 30:34 describes the *zawch* frankincense, which is used with the rest of the material to form the incense, which was put in front of the *edut*. This incense is *tawhor qodesh*, "clean conditioned," and a *qodesh qawdawsheem*, super-conditioner.[cz]

cz. Exod. 30:35–36

- Leviticus 24:2 repeats the command to take the *zawch* olive oil for the lamp.
- Leviticus 24:7 refers to the *zawch* frankincense used on the bread.

There is no other mention of frankincense (and oil) having to be *zawch*, even including the anointing oil. So, I jump to the conclusion that the oil for the continually burning lamp and the frankincense used with the bread had to be of a very special quality.

In following books of Psalms, Job, Micah, Proverbs, and Lamentations, *zawch* and its relatives *zawchaw* and *zawchach* are used in the moral terms of purity or righteousness of people, nobles, the heavens, stars, and moon.[da] It is never again used regarding chemical purity.

da. *zawchaw*, 2135; *zawchach*, 2141

The chemical purity sense of *zawch* agrees with the Assyrian and Babylonian *zakû*, which has the meanings of "clear, clean, cleansed, in good order, plain, refined (as in metals) pure, free of claims."[80] As a verb, *zaku* means "to become clean, clear, light, to become free from specific claims or obligations, to obtain a clearance through accounting."[81] *Zukku* means "to cleanse, clear of impurities, to winnow, to wash, to free, release, to make ready for departure, to use fine materials."[82] *Shuzkoo* means "to cleanse ritually."[83] Though the word is used in many different ways and throughout a long time period, the general idea of cleansing, freeing from impurities, or just freeing, is paramount. Never is there a hint of a moral overtone. Another possibly related word in Egyptian is *sk*. Faulkner says it means "wipe, wipe out, wipe away," and Gardiner says it means "wipe, sweep."[84] Gardiner defines the determinative as a "swab made from a hank of fibre."[85]

If *zawch* is related to the Assyrian, Babylonian, and Egyptian words, its use in Exodus and Leviticus was an attempt to illustrate the dual attributes of this particular frankincense: (1) it was highly refined and thus different from what was used otherwise; and (2) in its chemically pure state, its purpose was to cleanse the bread (possibly by fumigation when the frankincense was burned) of any cloud contamination it might have absorbed over the seven days so that it could be eaten by the priests. For ease of translation, simply stick to the accepted word "pure" for *zawch*. This is just half the story.

The next term is "memorial," *azkawraw*. I have described *azkawraw* as the substance in flour, which, when burned, could stimulate memory. Depending on its function, it could be used with or without oil and frankincense. In the bread verses, the frankincense "will be with the bread for a memorial, a fire offering to the Lord."[db] Remember, oil and frankincense were mixed with the meal offering for rest-smelling in all cases except those of the adulterous woman, the witness, and oath-breaker. Could rest-smelling be the purpose here? I believe so, and here's the logic: First, all fire offerings in Exodus, Leviticus, and Numbers are "to/for the Lord" with one exception and a couple of minor variations.[dc] Second, the vast majority of references indicate fire offerings were for rest-smelling (or strongly imply it as in Leviticus 2:16).[dd] Third, rest-smelling was not the purpose only when the fire offerings were stipulated as decontamination or trespass/guilt offerings. Rest-smelling resulted from peace, vow, freewill, burnt, sacrifice, and fire offerings. The materials used were meat, meal, wine, oil, and frankincense.[de]

db. Lev. 24:7

dc. Num. 18:9

dd. cf., Lev. 2:2, 9

de. Num. 15:7

So, what is the significance of all this? First, as with all fire offerings, the showbread is also "to/for the Lord."[df] Second, it df. Lev. 24:7 is for a memorial offering, not a decontamination offering or trespass/guilt offering. Evidently, the memory stimulating aspect of the offering was necessary to ensure that Aaron and his remaining sons followed each step of the sacrifice carefully so as not to experience the same tragedy as Nadab and Abihu. Third, frankincense was one of the chemicals that had to be used with meal to allow its memorial to be burned to produce rest-smelling. Thus, Leviticus 24:7 states, "you will put on [each] row pure frankincense and it will be with the bread for a memorial, a fire offering [of rest-smelling] to/for the Lord." I do think the above evidence is enough to make a strong case that rest-smelling is implied.

The next terms of importance are "conditioned place" and "super-conditioner." Aaron, his sons, and the priests who would follow them were to eat the loaves in a conditioned place (probably the court of the tent of meeting where the main altar was doing its work) *because* the bread itself was a super-conditioner.[dg] In dg. Lev. 6:9, 24:9 other words, everything about this decontamination process had to be in perfect order. It would do no good to eat the bread in a place that could re-contaminate it. So the process of a) cleansing and b) rest-smelling (the chemical equivalent of rest) produced a substance—the treated bread containing fermentation material that, when eaten, could condition internally. That is, this was the result after the frankincense had worked on the bread for seven days and then was burned above it. Then the priests who were protected externally (oil, garments, etc.) were safe to breathe in this very contaminated section of the tent. If not for a given, stated purpose, internal protection, why else eat stale bread once a week?

Sin Offering

It was sometime in the 1950s when I first wrote about the improbable translations of the noun *chatawt*. I objected to suggesting that a woman had "sin" due to childbirth or that a burned person needed to present a "sin offering" to be declared well. Instead of sin, I defined *chatawt* as "contamination, decontamination offering." More than "to do wrong," I said the corresponding verb *chawtaw* meant "to become contaminated with the dangerous materials in the cloud or to contaminate," that is, to trigger a situation on purpose or in error that could lead to contamination or at least to susceptibility to the cloud's effects.

Still later, when explaining the decontamination offering, my first drafts went into great detail about *chawtawt's* translation in other languages. When Hawley pointed out errors in my etymology, I realized that my original questioning of the translation "sin" (and "atone") was the important point here.[86] Hawley constantly admonished me to stick to the context of the Hebrew words, and put secondary emphasis on etymology. So, to properly supplant my originally drafted discussion of the decontamination offering, see Milgrom's explanation:

> To my knowledge, all versions and translations, old and new, render the *hattā't* sacrifice as "sin offering." This translation is inaccurate on all grounds: contextually, morphologically, and etymologically.
>
> The very range of the *hattā't* in the cult gainsays the notion of sin. For example, this offering is enjoined upon recovery from childbirth (chap. 12), the completion of the Nazirite vow (Num 6), and the dedication of the newly constructed altar (8:15; see Exod 29:36–37). In other words, the *hattā't* is prescribed for persons and objects who cannot have sinned.
>
> Grammatical considerations buttress these contextual observations. Morphologically, it appears as a *piel* derivative. More importantly, its corresponding verbal form is not the *qal* "to sin, do wrong" but always the *piel* (e.g., 8:15), which carries no other meaning than "to cleanse, expurgate, decontaminate" (e.g., Ezek 43:22, 26; Ps 51:9). Finally, the "waters of *hattā't*" (Num 8:7) serve exclusively a purifying function (Num 19:19; see Ezek 26:25). "Purification offering" is certainly the more accurate translation. Indeed, the terse comment of Rashi (on Num 19:19) is all that needs to be said: "*hattā't* is literally the language of purification."[87] The decontamination offering is not mentioned in Genesis or Deuteronomy, but it is found in Chronicles, Ezra, Nehemiah, and Ezekiel. In these books, the offering was used for covering, but its use

for rest-smelling is not mentioned. Strangely, rest-smelling is only mentioned once in the Five Books in connection with the decontamination offering. That mention refers to a person becoming contaminated through error:[dh]

dh. Lev. 4:27–35

[31]"And all its [the decontamination offering's] fat he will remove as fat is removed from off the sacrifice of peace offering: and the priest will burn [it] on the altar for a rest-smelling to the Lord; and the priest will cover on him, and it will be forgiven to him." (Lev. 4:31)

Rest-smelling is not mentioned in the Numbers repeat of the rule.[di] Numbers also varies from Leviticus in the verses discussing the congregation becoming contaminated through error.

di. Num. 15:27

Leviticus 4:13 says a bullock is to be used for the decontamination offering and does not mention meal and drink offerings. Numbers 15:24 says the bullock is for the burnt offering and for rest-smelling with meal and drink offerings, and a he-goat is for the decontamination offering for covering.[88] Here, I can only reiterate the possibility that the rules changed to meet the new conditions, "when you will come into the land of your habitations."[dj]

dj. Num. 15:2

The most important decontamination offerings were those connected with the decontamination of the tent of meeting area and the entire congregation. They involved the bullock for the priest, a ram for a burnt offering, and two goats for the people in the beginning stages of *Yom Kippur*. One goat was for the decontamination offering; one was to be sent into the wilderness. The blood was sprinkled right on the ark, on the incense altar, and the whole area.[dk]

dk. Lev. 16

[25]"This is the law of the decontamination offering: in the place where the burnt offering is slaughtered, the decontamination offering will be slaughtered *before the Lord*; it is a super-conditioner.

[26]The priest that offers it (*ham'chatay*) [actually decontaminates it] will eat it; in the conditioned place it will be eaten, in the court of the tent of meeting.

[27]Whoever touches its flesh will [must] be conditioned, and when [there] is sprinkled of its blood on a garment, what it is sprinkled on you will wash in a conditioned place.

²⁸But an earthen vessel wherein it is boiled will be broken; and if in a copper vessel it be boiled, then it will be scoured and rinsed with water.

³⁰Any decontamination offering, whereof any of the blood is brought into the tent of meeting to cover in the super-conditioned place, will not be eaten; it will be burned with fire." (Lev. 6:25–28, 30; Heb.18–23)

Actually, this meat, like that for the peace offering, had become fairly well contaminated. It had been slaughtered *before the Lord*, i.e., in a place of high radioactivity. It had to be eaten in a conditioned place, and the priests who ate it had to be conditioned first. The blood had done its job, soaking up the radiation. So, if it got on a garment, that garment had to be washed. Incidentally, this was analogous to the effects of plague caused by the cloud landing indiscriminately on houses and garments that required washing. If the flesh touched dishes or pots or pans, they had to be treated in exactly the same way as the vessels that came into contact with an unclean animal.[dl] If the blood was drained in the super-conditioned place where the radioactivity was most prevalent, then the meat from which it came was simply too contaminated to be eaten and had to be burned.

The primary byproduct of the decontamination offering was blood for protection against radiation. (Secondarily, the offering itself provided food for the priests.) In addition to its use on *Yom Kippur*, the decontamination offering corrected any errors committed by the anointed priests, congregation, chiefs/princes, and individuals as explained in Leviticus 4. It was not for purposeful wrongdoing, except in the case of the reluctant witness.[dm]

What happened was this: If the anointed priest committed an error that involved all the people (excluding himself because he was protected), he had to sacrifice a bullock, sprinkle its blood in front of the veil of the super-conditioned place and on the horns of the altar of incense, and pour the rest at the base of the altar of burnt offering. In other words, he worked from the very door (veil) of the ark room outward to the altar "which is at the door of the tent of meeting."[dn] The fat, kidneys, and liver were

dl. Lev. 11:32–33

dm. Lev. 5:1

dn. Lev. 4:3–12

burned on that altar, and the rest of the animal (the meat) was taken outside the camp "to a clean place" where the ashes were poured out. "And he will burn it on the wood with fire; where the ashes are poured out it will be burned."[do] The meat was too contaminated to be eaten, having been exposed to the radiation from whatever error the priest made that resulted in its spread.

When the entire congregation erred and so caused contamination, exactly the same operation was carried out.[dp] In other words, in both cases where everyone except the priest was threatened, it was necessary to use a large animal and to neutralize the whole area except for the ark itself. This degree of contamination is not as obvious as it looks at first glance.

> [13]"And if all the congregation of Israel will err (*y'shgoo*) and a thing be hidden from the eyes of the assembly, and they *do one of all the commandments* (*mitzvot*) *of the Lord* that ought not to be done, and they are guilty." (Lev. 4:13, my emphasis)[dq]

How could "all the congregation err" at the same time? And even if they did, what kind of error could they all commit out of ignorance? The answer seems to come out of two words that are used in the warnings in these passages. One is *sh'gawgaw*, the word for "error" or "ignorance."[dr] It is only used in connection with contamination through error in a few places where Strong's translates the word as "ignorance."[ds] It is used as "err, go astray" in other contexts elsewhere.[89] The other word is *mitzvot*, which only means "commandments."[dt]

Translators have hedged Leviticus 4:13 (see also verse 2) to read "do any of the things that the Lord has commanded not to be done," or "one of the prohibitions of the Lord." This seems to me to be quite a different meaning from what the Hebrew says. The Hebrew indicates that they did one of the things the Lord *commanded* them to *do* (*v'awsoo achat mechawl mitzvot Y'hovaw*), but they did it wrongly or maybe at the wrong time. What probably happened was that once again the high priest or one of the other priests made a mistake in dealing with the dangerous ark area and the congregation was ignorant of it.[90] When it was discovered, the same large sacrifice was used to

do. Lev. 4:12

dp. Lev. 4:13–14

dq. *shgoo*, from *sh'gawgaw*, 7684

dr. *sh'gawgaw*, 7684

ds. Lev. 4:2, 13, 22, 27; 5:13, 18; Num. 15:24–29

dt. *mitzvot*, 4687

protect them as in the first case. Thus, in this case *sh'gawgaw* is technical in meaning and its limited usage bears this out. The word "commandments," *mitzvot*, means just what it says.

When the chief or prince became contaminated through error, he had to pour the blood of a male goat onto the horns and the base of the burnt offering altar.[du] It was *not* offered on the incense altar. The same was done for any individual, except the sacrifice was a female goat or lamb, because the individual was not in a position to endanger as many people as the chief who presumably had a much larger household, servants, etc.[dv] It was not necessary to have as much blood for the chief or any other individual as it was for the group.

Now what had the chief or individual done wrong? The Bible is not specific. Leviticus 4:13 only says, "if the congregation err by doing one of the commandments that ought not be done, and is guilty." Here I must carry through my logic about the words contamination, commandments, and error. The error must have involved using faulty material for the sacrifice or interfering with the priests' work in some way. So, in a lesser way, they contributed to radiation spread and possibly contaminated themselves. Since they could not get near enough to the incense altar to contaminate it, there was no need to neutralize it. Evidently, it was only necessary to neutralize the burnt offering altar, and this would provide enough general protection.

In each of these instances of contamination through error, the words "and he is guilty (*awshame*)" are found.[dw] They are very, very important.

> [27]"And if any person becomes contaminated through error by doing one of the commandments of the Lord, which ought not be done, and he is guilty
>
> [28]Or it is made known to him his contamination that he has contaminated, then he will bring his oblation ..."
> (Lev. 4:27–28)

Margin notes:
du. Lev. 4:22–23

dv. Lev. 4:27–28

dw. *awshame*, 816

Guilty

At first it appears that guilt would automatically follow if the person, congregation, or chief did one of the commandments incorrectly. I believe the verses indicate that guilt may or *may not follow*. Whatever one did in these cases was *accidental* and might or might not affect that person. That is, the sentence does *not* read, "If he does this, he *will* be guilty." Since covering was the goal of sacrifice, one could assume that being guilty had the connotation of being contaminated or *susceptible* to contamination. The Hebrew word here is *awshame*, but rather than meaning "guilty," I believe the correct definition in these instances of contamination is "susceptible," and that in all cases being susceptible was accidental.

When used with *awshame*, there are three Hebrew words that can demonstrate that becoming susceptible was not an automatic phenomenon but rather an accidental byproduct of radiation spread that *might* affect a person. Those three words are (1) the Hebrew letter *vov* or *v'*, meaning "and, when, then"; (2) *eem*, with several meanings including "if"; and (3) *oh*, also with several meanings, but primarily "or, when, if."[dx]   dx. *eem*, 518; *oh*, 176

I'm going to put the next few verses in Leviticus 4 and 5 under a microscope to see if my definition of *awshame* holds up. I find them exceedingly complex in the subtlety of wordings.

> [1]And the Lord spoke to Moses, saying,

> [2]"Speak to the Israelites, saying, 'When a person contaminates through error against any of the commandments of the Lord that ought not to be done, and he does one of them,

> [3]If (*eem*) the anointed priest contaminates to the susceptibility (*ahsh'mot*) of the people, **then** (*v'*) he will bring on his contamination, which he has contaminated, a young bullock without blemish to the Lord for a decontamination offering …

> [13]And if (*v'eem*) all the congregation of Israel err, **and** (*v'*) a thing be hidden from the eyes of the assembly, **and** (*v'*) they do one of all the commandments of the Lord that ought not to be done, **and** (*v'*) they become [or are] susceptible,

[14]**When** (*v'*) it becomes known, the contamination they have contaminated on it (*awleyaw*), **then** (*v'*) the assembly will offer a young bullock for a decontamination offering, and they will bring it before the tent of meeting … [91]

[22]When (*asher*) a chief contaminates [is contaminated], and he does one of the commandments of the Lord his God that ought not to be done, through error, **and** (*v'*) he is susceptible (*awshame*)

[23]**Or** (*oh*) it be made known to him his contamination wherein he has contaminated, **then** (*v'*) he will bring his oblation a goat, a male, without blemish …

[27]**And if** (*v'eem*) any person contaminates through error of the people of the land by his doing one of the commandments of the Lord that ought not to be done, and he be susceptible (*awshame*)

[28]**Or** (*oh*) it be made known to him his contamination, [by] which he has contaminated, **then** (*v'*) he will bring his oblation a goat, a female, without blemish, for his contamination [by] which he has contaminated.'" (Lev. 4:1–3, 13, 14, 22, 23, 27, 28)

As seen by the use of the *vov* consecutive perfect (if/when-then) throughout these verses, the *awshame* conclusion of the matter is by definition conditional. This passage is a chain of possibilities, not probabilities: "If the anointed priest contaminates," "and if the whole congregation err," "*and* … be hidden," "*and* they do," "AND THEY BECOME SUSCEPTIBLE (*awshame*)," "when it becomes known," "the assembly will offer."[92] Stringing together possibilities and completing the thought logically is common with the *vov*-consecutive.

In Leviticus 5, there are more *oh*s used properly as "or," but here the "ands," "ifs," and "ors" come into sharper perspective:

[1]"And a person, when (*chee*) he contaminates in that he hears the voice of swearing and he is a witness or (*oh*) he has seen or (*oh*) known, if (*eem*) he does not tell [it], then (*v'*) he will carry his impurity.

[2]Or (*oh*) a person who touches any unclean thing or (*oh*) the carcass of an unclean beast or (*oh*) the carcass of unclean cattle or (*oh*) the carcass of an unclean creeping thing, and *(v')* it be hidden from him and (*v'*) he is unclean, then (*v'*) he will be susceptible (*awshame*).

[3]Or (*oh*) when (*chee*) he touches the uncleanness of man, whatsoever his uncleanness [is] wherewith he is unclean, and (*v'*) it is hidden from him, and (*v'*) he knows [of it], then (*v'*) he will be susceptible (*awshame*).

[4]Or a person, when (*chee*) [he] swears pronouncing with the lips to do evil or (*oh*) to do good, whatsoever [it is] that a man pronounces with an oath

and (*v'*) it is hidden from him and (*v'*) he knows [of it], then (*v'*) he will be susceptible (*awshame*) to (*l'*) one of these [things].

⁵And it will be when (*chee*) he is susceptible in one of these [things], then (*v'*) he will confess [that] wherein he has become contaminated." (Lev. 5:1–5)

Verse 1 is the only instance of contamination on the list that was done purposefully or knowingly. That is, the individual knows he has done something that can contaminate him, so he is very likely to carry impurity rather than simply be susceptible. Since it still is in the realm of possibility (maybe probability is a better word), the same *vov* consecutive perfect ("when–then") is used. (This is significantly different from the adulterous woman who will definitely carry her impurity, as evidenced by the use of the qal imperfect *teesaw*, "will carry."[dy])

dy. Num. 5:31

Verse 2 starts a group of possibilities beginning with *oh*, "or." Here the person is unaware of what he has done and he can only do something about it if he finds out somehow. These possibilities are in the uncertain rather than the likely category of verse 1. Nevertheless, they all depend on the thought begun there, namely, this is what will (or can) happen to the individual. So the sense should be,

> "*When* a person contaminates and does not tell it … *or* touches an unclean thing, etc. … *and* he is unclean *and* [therefore] he is susceptible *or when* he touches the uncleanness of man … *and* it is *hidden* from him *and* he knows *and* he will be susceptible *or* … *when* he swears … with an oath … *and* it be hidden … *and* he knows *and* he is susceptible *to* one of these *and* it will be *when* he is susceptible to one of these *then* he will confess that he has contaminated on it [the congregation]."

This "when–then" pattern completes the thought, that is, his acknowledgement of these formerly hidden contaminations.

Up to this point, anyone who triggered a contaminating situation (*chawtaw*) and thus became susceptible (*awshame*) had to bring a decontamination offering, *chatawt*. However, Leviticus 5:6 says that the offering for being susceptible

dz. *awshawm*, 817
(fem. *ash'maw*, 819)

(*awshame*) is an *awshawm*, traditionally translated as a guilt or trespass offering.[dz]

Guilt, Trespass Offering

The guilt or trespass offering, *awshawm*, which I call the anti-susceptibility offering, is used in Leviticus and Numbers.[93] Genesis 26:10, interestingly, mentions the possibility of susceptibility as the same word for anti-susceptibility offering, *awshawm*, being brought on the Philistine King Abimelech and his court if one of his people had committed adultery with Isaac's wife, Rebekah. In other words, adultery might have resulted in susceptibility among the whole group.[94] Either this is an amazing coincidence relating to the adulterous woman laws or, just possibly, this phenomenon was known and taken for granted in much earlier times and by other peoples. They had similar attitudes toward adultery, and some used ordeal as a test for it. Certainly, these same Philistines were aware of it during the time of the Samuel story. On the other hand, Genesis 42:21 uses *awshame* in the contemporary way.[ea] This is regarding Joseph's brothers' guilt toward him.[95] There is no mention of the *awshawm* at all in Exodus or Deuteronomy. The fact that there is no mention in Deuteronomy isn't too unusual. There are few mentions of any but the most common offerings there.

ea. *awshame* (adj.),
818

As to the following books, the writer(s) of 2 Kings 12:16 (during the time of Jehoash, king of Judah, 837–798 BCE) must have known about the concept of offering, because it mentions *awshawm* money. If it is correct that Deuteronomy was discovered during the reign of Josiah, almost two hundred years after Jehoash, then in that long span of time with little attention paid to observing regulations, it would have been easy to completely forget those rules not specifically mentioned in that book.[96] In 1 Samuel 6:3, *awshawm* is related to the ark and the Philistines. It is used in Ezekiel 6:6, which also uses *awshame*, but as "waste" or "desolate." Ezra 10:19 talks of an *awshawm* for intermarriage, unknown in the Five Books, and Isaiah 53:10 talks of the soul offering itself as an *awshawm*. However, Ezra in four other places, Jeremiah, 1 Chronicles, Psalms, Proverbs, and Amos all use *awshawm* as guilt or trespass without the offering connotation. It is also in 2 Samuel 14:13 regarding King David.

In Leviticus 5:6, for the first time the classification of decontamination offering (*chatawt*) suddenly becomes an anti-susceptibility offering (*awshawm*). Why? The answer is in the size of the animal offered.

> 6"And he will bring his anti-susceptibility offering (*awshawmo*) to the Lord on his contamination (*chatawto*) when he has contaminated (*chawtaw*), a female out of the flock, a lamb or a goat, for a decontamination offering (*chatawt*); and the priest will cover on him from his contamination.
>
> 7And if he cannot afford [literally, "hand reach not a lamb"], then he will bring for his anti-susceptibility offering when he has contaminated, two turtle-doves or two young pigeons to the Lord, one for a decontamination offering and one for a burnt offering.
>
> 8And he will bring them to the priest, and he will offer that which is first ...
>
> 9And he will sprinkle from the blood of the decontamination offering on the wall of the altar: and the rest of the blood will be pressed out at the base of the altar; it is a decontamination offering.
>
> 10And the second he will offer [as] a burnt offering according to the ordinance, and the priest will cover on him from contamination when he has become contaminated and it will be forgiven to him.
>
> 11And if he cannot afford two turtle-doves or two young pigeons, then he will bring his offering, he who contaminated, the tenth [part] of an *ephah* of fine flour for a decontamination offering;
>
> 12He will not put oil on it, nor will he put frankincense on it, for it is a decontamination offering. And he will bring it to the priest and the priest will take of it his handful its memorial, and he will burn [it] on the altar on the fire offerings of the Lord; it is a decontamination offering.
>
> 13And the priest will cover on him on his contamination, which he has [become] contaminated from one of these [things] and it will be forgiven to him, and it will belong to the priest as the meal offering." (Lev. 5:6–13)

eb. Lev. 5:7–10

If birds were all he could afford for his anti-susceptibility offering, the contaminator had to offer one for a decontamination offering and one for a burnt offering.[eb] It must be assumed that this was simply spelling out what was normally done with the decontamination offering, i.e., the blood was sprinkled on the altar and the flesh burned on it, both for the purpose of covering. Thus, when the lamb or goat was used in Leviticus 5:6, it served as both a decontamination and a burnt offering.

What of the meal offering in verses 11 through 13? When the memorial of the meal offering was all that was affordable, burning it could only result in bringing up or exposing the contamination, *chatawt*. Then the fire offerings, on which it was burned, could do the actual covering.

Regardless of which material was used, the fact remained: The greater the contamination, the greater the need for larger offerings. It was not until the amount of contamination, and susceptibility to it, became greatest that the offering became a 100 percent *awshawm*. So, these offerings might be thought of as transitional between the 100 percent *chatawt* and the 100 percent *awshawm*. The *chatawt* was only used for the smallest chance of susceptibility of becoming a contaminant.

Leviticus 5:15–19 continues the laws relating to contaminating through error, specifically when a person committed a "trespass" and contaminated someone. In this instance, the person who became contaminated didn't know it until he actually noted the impurity on him:

> [15]"A person when he commits a trespass (*m'ohl ma'al*) and he contaminates through error *in* the conditioning [things] (*mee qawd'shay'hvaw*) of the Lord, then he will bring his anti-susceptibility offering to the Lord, a ram without blemish from the flock according to your estimation [in] *shekels* of silver, in the *shekel* of the super-conditioned place for an anti-susceptibility offering.

> [16]And that which he contaminated from [not "in"] the conditioning [things] he will pay, and the fifth [part] he will add to it, and he will give it to the priest, and the priest will cover on him with the ram of the anti-susceptibility offering and it will be forgiven to him.

¹⁷And if a person contaminates and does any of the commandments of the Lord that ought not to be done, and not know and he is susceptible and carry his impurity,

¹⁸Then he will bring a ram without blemish from the flock according to your estimation for an anti-susceptibility offering to the priest and the priest will cover on him for which he erred and did not know, and it will be forgiven to him.

¹⁹It is an anti-susceptibility offering; he has certainly become susceptible to the Lord."

These verses pose some questions. First, what does *ma'al* mean? Second, why is "in" or sometimes "against" used with the conditioning things when the letter *m* in *mee* (the *mem*) is the shortened version of the word *min*, meaning "from"? Third, why was the ram required for these contaminations rather than the female lamb, goat, birds, or meal offering of anti-susceptibility in the previous verses?

To the *ma'al* question, much has been written on the word. It is usually translated "trespass," but in Appendix G, relative to the possibly adulterous wife, I called it a "super-contamination." It is used only in Leviticus, Numbers, and Deuteronomy in the Five Books. The only Deuteronomy reference is to Moses *ma'al*ing against the Lord in the matter of Meribah: "because you *ma'al*ed against Me."ᵉᶜ It is a relentlessly technical term used "against the Lord" in Leviticus, Numbers, Deuteronomy, and the following books where it is also translated "transgression." It is used "against a man" only once in the Five Books, in the case of that possibly adulterous wife.ᵉᵈ However, lying or oath-breaking, as the wife may have done, was really an act leading to uncleanness, and so it created a danger directly related to the Lord.

While in no way do I argue with the various scholars' translations as generalizations, I think the concept of "cover" is what *ma'al* intends to convey, only exactly the opposite of *keeper*. Instead of covering to protect the super-conditioned area, it signifies covering the area with a contaminant. Repetition (*m'ohl ma'al*) emphasizes the action. So, instead of "a person when he commits a trespass (*kee tee m'ohl ma'al*)," Leviticus 5:15 might read, "a person when he *covers* with a [heavy] cover," thus, my

ec. Deut. 32:51

ed. Num. 5:12, 27

definition of *ma'al* as a "super-contamination." Granted, I am dealing with much conjecture here, but with all the words in this section being so technical, it would not be unusual to see *ma'al* join them. Regarding the *mem* question, I believe it is incorrect to translate the verse, "*in* the conditioning [things]." The very next verse uses the whole word *min*, "from," but is again translated "*in* the conditioning [things]" in almost all versions. I think the word "from" is correct here. In this passage, somehow an unprotected person entered the danger area where exposure to the cloud was highest, and he came into contact with contaminated articles there or where the animals for sacrifice were kept. In the case, of the animals, either he has taken one and eaten it, or one has wandered onto his property from the danger area and he has eaten or even just touched it. In any case his action was an error. Unprotected, he is now susceptible to contamination *from* the conditioning things. In other words, "from the conditioning [things]" is a parenthetical explanation here.[ee] The only thing he could do, besides replacing the value of the animal "in *shekels* of silver" plus a fifth, was to bring another and have the priest to cover him with it.

ee. e.g., Lev. 2:3
minhamin-chaw and
mayeeshay; Lev. 4:26
maychatawto

Now to the third most difficult question of all. Why use a ram to protect persons who have contaminated or become contaminated?[ef] These were individuals. They were not (1) the priest "to the susceptibility of the people" (bullock), or (2) the "whole congregation" (bullock), or (3) the ruler who could endanger larger numbers of people (male goat).

ef. Lev. 5:15–18

I believe that the rules designating the size of the animal relate to the level of danger in each susceptibility-causing occurrence. In other words, blood and fire offerings (the antidotes for each instance of contamination) varied in quantity depending on what the person did to make himself more or less attractive to, susceptible to, or actually contaminated with radioactivity. There was no controllable, discernible rationale for whether what he did would attract more or less material. It was just a natural phenomenon. Therefore, the people had to be directed in detail how to protect themselves. I think that detail for the individual, while it is logical, is most subtle and most difficult to comprehend. In order to get that detail into sharper focus, I am going to put Leviticus 4 and 5 back under the microscope.

Leviticus 4 explains what must be done in the case of individual human error:

> [27]"And if a person contaminates through error ... by doing one of the commandments of the Lord that ought not to be done and he is susceptible ... or it is made known to him, then he will bring his oblation, a goat, a female." (Lev. 4:27)

The individual could also have brought a lamb, but the requirement was the same: blood and fire offering. The point is, the person made a mistake. Apparently, the type of contamination this precipitated didn't cause too much harm, but he had nevertheless become susceptible. So to protect himself, the priest had to cover him with a small amount of animal's blood and fat.

In Leviticus 5, the first example of an individual's error is not coming forward as a witness. This person ran a good chance of getting impurity on himself as a result.

This type of contamination is lumped with that of a person who touched unclean things and didn't know it. If he did know it, he only had to bathe at sundown to become clean. Since he was unaware, the chances of susceptibility turning into contamination were somewhat greater.

In the same group was the oath-swearer who did not really know he had sworn an oath. (If anything proves that this is an automatic physical trigger for susceptibility and not wrongdoing, this certainly does. He could have sworn to do something good or evil. It did not make any difference! It was the *act* of swearing that triggered the susceptibility.) When somehow he discovered his problem, he had to get covered, but the smaller offering sizes, i.e., the female goat or lamb down to the birds or meal, suggest that, in these cases too, the chances of his susceptibility turning to contamination were not as great as for others.

The second example of individual error is the Leviticus 5:15 person with his super-contamination who contaminated through error. The probable cause of the increased contamination was that he had touched or eaten something from the danger area. This must have made him more susceptible. Thus, the ram—a larger animal.

The anti-susceptibility offering would protect against triggering contamination that would cause susceptibility under heavily contaminated circumstances. This was not true for the decontamination offering as found in Leviticus 4:3 and 5:6, 7. Was the larger offering just protective enough to reduce the risk from contamination to susceptibility?

The second ram offering in Leviticus 5:17–19 gives a hint. While these verses are a part of the Leviticus 5:15–16 thought, they are directly related to Leviticus 4:27 (with definite, significant differences).[97] Compare verse 5:17 with 4:27:

> [17]"And if a person contaminates and does any of the commandments of the Lord that ought not to be done, but he does not know that he is susceptible and carry his impurity …
>
> [19]He has most certainly become susceptible *to* the Lord (*awshowm awsham l'yhovaw*)." (Lev. 5:17 … 19, my emphasis)
>
> [27]"And if a person contaminates through error … by doing one of the commandments of the Lord that ought not to be done and he is susceptible … or it is made known to him, then he will bring his oblation, a goat, a female." (Lev. 4:27)

An individual has triggered the mechanism for contamination in both verses. As with the congregation and the chief, he made a mistake in carrying out one of the Lord's commandments.[eg] Now the significant difference: Whatever he did in Leviticus 5:17 not only made him susceptible, it *caused awvone*, translated "impurity," to fall on him. Evidently, the act of getting *awvone* on one's body took it out of the 4:27 category where the individual was merely susceptible, and it put him into the more dangerous, super-contaminating situation. He needed to offer a larger animal, the ram, with its greater quantity of blood so that, while he was contaminated and susceptible to danger, the covering was enough to neutralize the contamination. Because it was in the super-contaminating category, it could be called an anti-susceptibility offering.[99] Now the added emphasis in Leviticus 5:19 becomes very clear. Since he had *awvone* on him, "he has most certainly become susceptible *to* the Lord,"

eg. Lev. 4:13, 22[98]

meaning the cloud. The usual translations read, "he has trespassed *against* or *before* the Lord."[100]

For more on how not following certain commandments correctly could actually cause impurity to fall on someone, look at Leviticus 22:1–9. This passage discusses coming into contact with unclean things. It expands on Leviticus 5:14–17 by warning certain groups of people not to eat the conditioning things when unclean because it would lead to death by contamination. Then Leviticus 22:14 explains what Leviticus 5:16 indicates: "And a man, when he eats the conditioning thing through error, then he will add a fifth part to it and he will give to the priest the conditioning thing," not give *it* to the priest *with* the conditioning thing as is normally translated. The passage continues:

> [15]"And they will not expose the conditioning [things] of the Israelites, which they offer to the Lord,
>
> [16]And *load on themselves* the impurity of the anti-susceptibility offering *when* they eat their conditioning things, for I am the Lord who conditions them." (Lev. 22:15–16)

In other words, do not further expose the animals and make them more susceptible to contamination and so load more impurity on yourselves!

A third category of situations in Leviticus 6:2–7 necessitated a ram offering: lying, robbery, oppression of a neighbor, dealing falsely about a lost thing, etc. Here, once again, super-contamination is mentioned specifically.

> [2]"When a person contaminates and super-contaminates (*mawl aw ma'al*) against the Lord, and deals falsely with his neighbor in a matter of deposit or of bargain or in a robbery, or he has oppressed his neighbor,
>
> [3]Or he has found a lost thing and he has dealt falsely therein, and he has *sworn* to a *lie* in any of all [these things] that a man may do to contaminate thereby,
>
> [4]And it will be, when he contaminates and is susceptible, then he will return the robbery that he has robbed, or the thing that he has gotten by oppression, or the deposit that was deposited with him, or the lost thing that he has found,
>
> [5]Or anything about which he has sworn falsely; and he will pay it in full, and the fifth [part] thereof he will add to it; to whom it belongs he will give it *in* the day of his anti-susceptibility offering.
>
> [6]And his anti-susceptibility offering he will bring to the Lord a ram without blemish out of the flock according to your estimation for an anti-susceptibility offering to the priest.

> [7]And the priest will cover on him before the Lord; and it will
> be forgiven him concerning any of all [these things] that he
> has done to become susceptible."

The reasons for using the ram are all here. The person has gone against the Lord, he has triggered a super-contamination, and if it turns out that he is susceptible, he must make some restitution to the person who has been wronged *and* bring the ram for covering. On the other hand, contaminating knowingly put him in a separate category. In this case, the laws begin with "And the Lord said," which is a first among susceptibility laws. For some reason, maybe a scribal error, Leviticus 6:7 (5:26) uses *ashawmaw*, anti-susceptibility offering, rather than *awshame*, "susceptible." (I would add here that Numbers 5:6–10 repeats, with some expansion, the Leviticus 5:21–26 law: the restitution of the principal plus the fifth and the ram of covering for a "man or a woman, when he or she commits any of the contaminating acts of man to super-contaminate against the Lord, and that person is susceptible."[eh]) All of these contaminations or commandments have one thing in common: They relate only to the Lord, i.e., "against the Lord." That is, while they may or may not be civil crimes, that's not why they're listed here. There was no punishment involved (unless adding a fifth is considered punishment). A person could be a robber, an "oppressor," a cheat, etc., but as it related to the Lord, only a sacrifice was necessary and this for the purpose of covering. Thus, the idea of susceptibility must refer to physical-chemical change. Surely, robbers and false dealers were punished by civil law, but that is completely beside the point. *Awshawm* and *awshame* never related to punishing the "guilty." These terms indicated a susceptibility to the Lord's danger and the ability of the individual and the community to withstand it. It is absolutely astonishing that the exact conditions apply to the case of the man who "lies carnally with a woman and she is a slave-girl betrothed to a man but is actually not redeemed nor freedom given to her."[ei] In this case, civil law is totally lenient. The verse continues with, "There will be an inquiry (*beekoret*); they will not be put to death because she

eh. Num. 5:6

ei. Lev. 19:20

was not free."[101] Physiologically, there is little difference between him and the adulterous woman:

> [21]"*And* he will bring his anti-susceptibility offering to the Lord to the door of the tent of meeting, a *ram*, an anti-susceptibility offering,

> [22]And the priest will cover on him with the ram of susceptibility before the Lord on his contamination, which he has contaminated, and he will be forgiven from his contamination that he has contaminated." (Lev. 19:21–22)

Physiologically, this was not a minor infraction even though it involved a slave-girl and was evidently considered so in the civil law. Rather, it was like all of the above situations, and the physical-chemical change made the perpetrators so susceptible that a *ram* was needed to cover.

One might wonder why there was no mention of a super-contamination "against the Lord" in this slave girl prohibition. A very careful look at Leviticus 19 reveals a notable peculiarity. In all but verses 21–22, the direction is to the people. "You will do this or not do this." The commandments tend to be quite general in nature. The only verses that suddenly become very specific, written in the third person, relate to the slave-girl. "And when a man…" "She is a slave girl…" "They shall not be put to death."

Leviticus 19 relates to the "H code" that contained the 16 repetitions of "I am the Lord." There is no such mention of "I am the Lord" other than in these verses (with the possible exception of Leviticus 19:5–8). Thus, I deduce that Leviticus 19:21–22 are out of place. Actually, if they are removed, the verses beginning with 19 and ending with "I am the Lord" in 25 deal mostly with agricultural topics and so make sense as a unit. So verses 21–22 may belong in chapter 20, which speaks in detail and in the third person of sexual crimes (perhaps after verse 10). While not explicitly stated, the Leviticus 20 crimes are "against the Lord." This is implied by verse 23 that says, "And you will not walk in the customs of the nations, which I cast out before you, because they did all these things and therefore I abhorred them."[ej] Or, they might belong in the adulterous woman section where super-contamination has been used against the husband, but relative to the Lord. Whatever the answer, these crimes are

ej. Lev. 19:23

different from the other infractions in the chapter. Someone, sometime, knowingly or unknowingly, made a clear distinction between the mild civil attitude toward this "crime" and the necessity to cover and protect against the physiological problem. The only reason to use the larger animal would be because these actions made the individual more susceptible to contamination than those not in the super-contamination category. To repeat, the super-contaminations are (1) coming in contact with "the conditioning things of the Lord" through error, (2) doing any of the commandments of the Lord that are not to be done, not knowing it, and becoming contaminated/carrying impurity, and 3) lying, robbing, or oppressing neighbors, etc.

In discussing the anti-susceptibility offerings, it is important to consider them relative to two specific individuals. First is the *healed* burned person. Leviticus 14 describes his treatment, which was pretty much the same as for a contaminated house and the person who had touched a dead body. The treatment included the scapebird and sacrificed bird just as Aaron used the scapegoat and sacrificed goat in the decontamination of the entire congregation. However, there was one difference. The burned person also needed an anti-susceptibility offering.[ek] Why?

Compare the burned person to the contaminated house. Remember that the infected area of the house was to be scraped. If the plague did not return, the decontaminating operation was put into effect. If the plague did return, the house was destroyed and removed. Things had gone too far. The house could not be covered. It was doomed.

Now contrast the burned person to the person who touched a dead body. The use of the purifying water was evidently enough to guarantee decontamination of the latter. A carcass was apparently not a powerful attractor of radioactivity, so a decontamination offering, burnt offering, and oil were not necessary. This was contrary to the case with the burned person.

The burned person had been heavily contaminated. That's why he was in such a fix. You could not scrape him, and if he got re-infected you could not do away with him. So an anti-susceptibility offering had to be added to the decontamination operation to prevent the return of contamination. Blood of the anti-susceptibility offering (and oil) was applied directly to the victim, possibly to soak up any leftover radiation.

The other person who needed an anti-susceptibility offering was the nazirite, "when one will die beside him very suddenly."[el] el. Num. 6:9 This seems to be in contradiction with the person touching a dead body who did not need the anti-susceptibility offering, but there was a marked difference. The nazirite was, for all intents and purposes, like the priest. He could not drink alcohol nor come near a dead person, including his father or mother. For the "days of his separation he is conditioned for the Lord."[em] Remember this means he had to be in a condition to em. Num. 6:8 communicate safely with the Lord, because he was in a highly exposed situation. If yet another contaminant was added to his already volatile mix, it was certainly necessary to protect against the possible results. He had to use one turtle-dove or pigeon for a decontamination offering and another for a burnt offering (1) to get covered from what he had accumulated, and (2) because he was going to start his days of separation again. In addition, he had to bring a he-lamb for an anti-susceptibility offering! It is perfectly logical that, like the burned person, he was now so susceptible to contamination that it was necessary to add the anti-susceptibility offering. When his separation time was completed, he then had to use every kind of offering: decontamination (ewe-lamb), burnt (he-lamb), peace (ram), cakes with oil, meal, unleavened wafers with oil, and drink. The decontamination and burnt offerings were for the nazirite because he had to come right to the altar to burn his newly shaven hair. The peace offering was for its rest-smelling attribute—to cover—and part of it was to protect the priest who was working with the nazirite.[en] Why, with these super-contaminated en. Num. 6:19–20 situations, was only a he-lamb used as an anti-susceptibility offering for both the burned person and the nazirite rather than the ram previously described in the super-conditioning, *ma'al* cases? Remember, the greater the contamination, the larger the animal. In both cases, *additional* material was required—a lot more in the burned person's case. In the nazirite's case, birds were used. So, evidently, the additional material equaled or surpassed the ram and thus made its use unnecessary.

Vow Offering

Vow offering in the Hebrew is *neder*. It is mentioned in Genesis, Leviticus, Numbers, and Deuteronomy as well as in many following books.^{eo}

eo. *neder*, 5088

In Genesis 28:20–22, Jacob made a covenant with God to accept Him as his God if He would give Jacob clothing, food, and safe passage. For this, Jacob would give God a pillar to be "God's House" and a tenth of "all that you will give to me." The idea of the vow as a tithe continues to Leviticus 27, which lists actual values for men, women, wealth, and age for the "special vow."

Numbers 15:1–5 seems to alter the vow offering sacrifice, but it does not. Neither does it alter the original peace offering rules in Leviticus and Numbers. Rather, it gives additional rules for special vow or freewill offerings. It also gives additional rules for fire offerings, burnt offerings, and sacrifices made during the set feasts.^{ep} Verse 3 clarifies the purpose of the vow offering when

ep. Num. 15:3

used as a sacrifice: "to make a rest-smelling to the Lord." So, while a vow could be viewed as an oath (promise) or a tithe (resulting from a promise to make that tithe), when it was a vow to sacrifice, that sacrifice joined all the others as part of the protective mechanism. In other words, the vow offering was simply another opportunity to protect the area from impurity. It possibly had the specific purpose of protecting the person who brought the offering from the effects of making vows and forgetting or accidentally breaking them, the result being suffering through the conscience-psychological syndrome. (See 1 Samuel 1:21 where Elkanah went up to the Lord to sacrifice and vow his vow.)

Freewill Offering

The freewill offering, *n'dawbaw*, carries the connotation of giving something as an offering willingly. It is first mentioned in Exodus.^{eq} However, these verses refer to when the Israelites

eq. *n'dwbaw*, 5071; Exod. 25:2, 35:21, 22, 27–29 (first time as *nadawbaw*) 35:5, 36:3

voluntarily gave materials toward the construction of the Tabernacle. Leviticus, Numbers, and Deuteronomy mention the freewill offering in connection with actual sacrifice. *N'dawbaw* is also used as a sacrifice in Chronicles, Ezra, and Ezekiel.[er]

er. 2 Chr. 31:14, Ezra. 3:5, Ezek. 46:12

Numbers 15:3 says that the freewill offering, along with other sacrifices, is to be used for rest-smelling protection. Like the vow, it had to be eaten in a prescribed time.

The concept of voluntarily giving the materials for this sacrifice was the accepted one from the beginning. One could surmise that when used for rest-smelling it was offered when the person felt there had been the possibility of contamination.

Thanksgiving Offering

I have postulated that thanksgiving offerings did not exist in the Five Books. There doesn't seem to be a concept of thanking the Lord from Genesis to Deuteronomy. However, thanksgiving offerings, *towday*, are made in the following books.[es]

es. *towdaw*, 8426

Wave Offering

The wave offering, *t'noofaw,* is only used in Exodus, Leviticus, and Numbers in the Five Books and not in the following.[et] The word *t'noofaw* doesn't really mean "wave." *Noof,* from which it derives, can mean "elevate," e.g., "lift up your sword."[eu] The Ugaritic word *np* means "height: or elevation."[102]

et. *t'noofaw,* 8573, from the vb. *noof,* 5130

eu. Exod. 20:25; Deut. 27:5

The materials used in the wave offering were the fat, breast, and right thigh of the ram, a loaf of bread, a cake of oiled bread, a wafer, and a basket of unleavened bread. It had many uses:

- Along with the hand filling of the priests (Aaron and his sons), the wave offering was used for rest-smelling.[ev]

ev. Lev. 7:35, 9:21, 10:14–15; Num. 18:18

- It was also used as part of the heave offering, which was taken from the peace offerings.[ew]

ew. Exod. 29:22–28; Lev. 8:25–29

- It was also done with the freewill offering of gold and copper, articles that were used in the construction of the tabernacle.[ex]

ex. Exod. 35:22, 38:29, 34

- As a peace offering, anyone could bring the fat and the breast to the priest for waving, the fat to be burned on the altar, and the breast for Aaron and his sons to eat.[ey]

ey. Lev. 7:29–34

- The wave offering was also used to decontaminate someone exposed to radioactivity, a burned person. "The priest will take one of the he-lambs and he will offer him for an anti-susceptibility offering and the log of oil, and he will wave them [for] a wave offering before the Lord."[ez] The purpose of the decontamination process was to cover the exposed person.[fa] This person was to offer one lamb and two turtle-doves or pigeons. "Then he will take one he-lamb [for] an anti-susceptibility offering to be waved to cover on him."[fb]

- The next waving is found "when you come into the land that I give to you."[fc] The priest was to wave an *omer* (a specific measure) of the first fruit of the harvest. It, along with other materials, was used for a rest-smelling.

- On the festival of *Shavout*, seven lambs, a bullock, and two rams with meal and drink offerings were burned for rest-smelling. One he-goat was for a *chatawt* offering, and two he-lambs were for a peace offering.[fd] "And the priest will wave them with the bread of the first fruits a wave offering before the Lord with the two lambs: conditioning they will be to [for] the Lord to [for] the priest."[fe]

- The "meal offering of jealousy" was taken from the hand of the woman suspected of adultery by the priest. He waved it before the Lord and brought it to the altar where the memorial part was burned.[ff]

- At the end of the nazirite's period of separation, he was to make various sacrifices: decontamination, burnt offering, and a peace offering.[fg]

  "'And the priest will take the boiled shoulder of the ram, and one unleavened cake … and one unleavened wafer. And he will put [them] on the palms of the nazirite … and the priest will wave them a wave offering before the Lord; it is a conditioner to [for] the priest, with the breast of the wave offering.'" (Num. 6:19–20)

- Numbers 8:11, 13, and 15 are among those verses, which speak of "waving the Levites" for a wave offering. I've read several standard explanations for this strange practice and several conclusions that there is no explanation. Actually, this

ez. Lev. 14:12

fa. Lev. 14:18

fb. Lev. 14:21

fc. Lev. 23:10

fd. Lev. 23:16–19

fe. Lev. 23:20

ff. Num. 5:25–26

fg. Num. 6:13–17

was part of the whole decontamination process of the Levites
so that they could serve safely in the tent of meeting.[fh] This is
the section that charged the Levites with the duty of covering
the Israelites so they would not become contaminated when
they came near the super-conditioned place.[fi] The Levites
themselves had to be covered during this process.[fj]

fh. Num. 8:6–26

fi. esp. Num. 8:19

fj. Num. 8:12

Heave Offering

The heave offering, *t'rumaw*, is in Exodus, Leviticus, Numbers,
and Deuteronomy as well as Isaiah, Ezekiel, Nehemiah,
Malachi, and 2 Chronicles.[fk] It was used in conjunction with
other offerings. Milgrom points out that *t'rumaw* is always "to
the Lord" and *t'noofaw* (wave offering) is always "before the
Lord."[103]

fk. *t'rumaw*, 8641,
from the vb. *room*,
7311

Milgrom takes issue with the commonly held assumption that
the heave offering is done with a vertical motion.[104] He quotes
Leviticus 48:10, 31, 35 and Numbers 16:21, 17:10 to show
that *t'ruma* is synonymous with words meaning "removing" or
"setting apart":

> Consequently, the noun *t'rûmâ* can refer only to that which is
> set apart or dedicated, and hence must be rendered 'dedication,
> contribution.' ... The function of the *t'rûmâ* is to transfer the
> object from the owner to the deity.[105]

He points to the Targums, the Septuagint, and the Akkadian
for confirmation of these definitions.[106] However, many other
references indicate that *t'ruma*, in its verb form, also means
"lift up."

- "And it [the ark] was lifted (*vatawrawm*) from the earth."[fl]
- "I have lifted up (*hareem'see*) my hand to the Lord."[fm]
- "and set it up (*vay'reemehaw*) as a monument."[fn]
- "No man will lift up (*yawreem*) his hand."[fo]
- "And he lifted up (*vayawrem*) (with) his staff."[fp]
- "Moses held up (*yawreem*) his hand."[fq]

fl. Gen 7:17

fm. Gen. 14:22

fn. Gen. 41:44

fo. Exod. 7:20

fp. Exod. 17:11

fq. Exod. 17:11

Even the references given by Milgrom, while synonymous with
"removing," have the physical action of "lifting off" and "get you
up."[107]

The heave offering was comprised of materials the Israelites gave to make and operate within the tabernacle.

- Gold, silver, and copper were used. The silver was to pay "for covering on your souls."[fr]

fr. Exod. 30:12–16, 15:2–7, 35:5–9, 21, 24, 36:3, 6

- All of the cakes, oil, and unleavened bread of the thanksgiving peace offering were for a heave offering "to the Lord."[fs]

fs. Lev. 7:11–14

- The right shoulder was "for a heave offering [with the wave offering, breast] to the priest."[ft]

ft. Lev. 7:32, 34, 10:14–15; Num. 6:20

- A daughter of a priest, when she is married to a non-priest, may not eat of the heave offerings of the conditioning [things].[fu]

fu. Lev. 22:12

- The conditioning things served as restitution for *awshawm* when a man or woman wrongs one another.[fv]

fv. Num. 5:5–7

- The first of their dough was used as a heave offering to the Lord "when you come into the land where I bring you."[fw]

fw. Num. 15:18–21

- They were for the anointing portion to Aaron and his sons.[fx]

fx. Num. 18:8

- "And this will be yours: the heave offering from their gifts, even all the wave offerings of the Israelites ... the tithe ... the captives, oxen, asses and sheep and gold taken in war."[fy]

fy. Num. 18:11, 19, 24, 26–32, 31:25–30, 41, 52

- Actually, the gold was used in a census context, where the Hebrew soldiers covered their souls with the captured gold articles in the same way silver was used in the total census of the Israelites.[ga]

ga. Deut. 12:6, 11, 17

- Then there was a repeat of previous rules with caution as to where offerings should be eaten.[gb]

gb. Num. 31:25–54

- The verses in Numbers 31 support Milgrom's *t'rumaw* as "setting apart" point. The captives, animals, and gold were divided, not elevated, between the army and the congregation with the part of the army's portion going to the priests.[gc]

gc. Num. 31:50

The important point is that these offerings were part of the general protection process.[gd]

gd. Exod. 29:27–28

These, then, are the sacrifices. Some are easy, some difficult to fathom, but all had the one purpose of protection in common. It made no difference whether that protection was covering or rest-smelling. All had to be carried out so that all was in perfect order for safe communication.

Chapter 11

Par for the Course

From the beginning of this exercise I have said that all of the tent's machinery and all of the sacrifices were used to facilitate communication between God and man. Word after word either falls easily or comes kicking and screaming into the communication lexicon. However, I believe there is one word, or really a combination of letters, that is so important in this regard that it must have a chapter of its own. Specifically, it appears to me that so many words containing the Hebrew letters *pay-resh* (*pr*) are in some way related to communication and the communication device that it is far beyond the bounds of coincidence. In addition, the same combination relates directly to the sacrifices and to the reason for sacrifices, namely to cover, *keeper*:

> ¹⁵"Then he will slaughter the goat of the decontamination offering, which is for the people, and he will bring its blood within the veil (*pawrochet*) and he will do with its blood as he did with the blood of the bullock (*par*) and he will sprinkle it upon the covering (*caporet*) and before the covering (*caporet*).

> ¹⁶And he will cover (*keeper*) on the conditioned place from the uncleanness of the Israelites." (Lev. 16:15–16)

At first glance this remarkable interrelationship seems quite improbable, but after comparing various Hebrew *pr* words, as well as those in other languages preceding, concurrent with, and following Hebrew, it becomes practically undeniable that they follow a path that leads inexorably to the concept of communication. First to the meaning of the basic two letters—*pay-resh*.

Pr

a. *par/pawr*, 6499

Pr is pronounced *par* or *pawr* depending on the Hebrew vowel sign under the *pay*. Strong's says that *par* is a "bullock, calf, ox."[a] It is especially thought of as a young animal, *par ben bawkawr*, to be used for sacrifice, particularly for the decontamination offering.[b] The ashes from burning a red cow, *pawraw*, were used in the water of purification.[c]

b. Lev. 4:3–5

c. *pawraw*, 6510, f. of *par*

In Ugaritic, *pr* means "bull" and *prt* means "cow." In Egyptian, one of the meanings of *pree* with a determinant ⟨determinant⟩ is "champion bull."[1] Strong's suggests that the Hebrew *pawr* meaning "bull" connotes "breaking forth in wild strength" or "dividing the hoof."[2] DLU states that the Ugaritic *pr* is derived from "separate."[3] In this chapter, I will show that this important notion of breaking forth can be traced through many *par* words. It eventually develops into words depicting both (1) the communication and (2) the sacrifice concepts.

From breaking forth to communicating

- *pawrach* – budding, blossoming
- *pawratz* – breaking up/out/forth, spreading/ separating/dividing, and in the following books scattering
  - *pawrash* – declaring, and in the following books separating
    - *sawfar* – speaking (i.e., spreading or scattering words), declaring

From broken up materials that can scatter to covering

d. *awfawr*, 6083

e. *ayfer*, 665; Lev. 17:13

- *awfawr* – dust[d]
- *ayfer* – ashes[e]
- *pawrochet* – veil
- *caporet* – ark cover
- *kippur* (Yom Kippur)
- *keeper* – cover

Breaking Forth ◄─────────► Communicating

The communication words, along with the covering words, all relate directly or indirectly to communication with God. Look for these concepts in my following study of *par* words.

Pawraw

Found in Genesis, Exodus, and Leviticus, *pawraw* denotes the idea of "be fruitful and multiply and fill the earth," in other words, "grown and *spread*."[f] It is interesting that *pawraw*, ending in an *aleph* rather than *hey*, means the same.[g] However, it is only used once in Hosea 13:15.[4]

<aside>f. *pawraw*, 6509</aside>
<aside>g. *pawraw*, 6500</aside>

Pawrach

As used in Genesis, Exodus, Leviticus, and Numbers, the range of meaning shows the relationships of *pawrach* to the other *par* words.[h] In Genesis 40:10, it is the budding of grapevines in the cupbearer's dream to be interpreted by Joseph. In Exodus 9:10, it is the "breaking forth" with boils caused by the soot thrown at the Egyptians by Moses and Aaron. In Leviticus 13:12, it is a burning that has broken out in the skin. In Leviticus 13:57, it is the plague spreading in a garment. In Leviticus 13:39, it is "bright spots" broken out in the skin or "growing" according to Strong's. Leviticus 14:43 has "break out" relating to plague in the house. Numbers 17:23 has Aaron's staff blossoming or budding buds, *perach* (derived from *pawrach*).[i] *Perach* is found in Exodus and Numbers only relative to the flowers fashioned on the tent's candlestick. Interestingly, *perach* in Late Egyptian is "to unfold, to bloom, to open up." The late Egyptian period was during the reign of Rameses II (1301–1234 BCE) because the word is found in Leyden Papyrus I 350.[5] That would make it just prior to or at the same time as the Exodus (anywhere from 1280 to 1230 BCE depending on the source).[6] Note that the *par* word *parsdu* in Hittite is "bud, shoot."[7] Also, one meaning of *parkiia* is "grow."[8]

<aside>h. *pawrach*, 6524</aside>
<aside>i. *perach*, 6525</aside>

Peer'chach

j. *peer'chach,* 6526

I am including *peer'chach* to show how words evolve.[j] It is only found in Job 30:12, which states, "Upon my right hand rise the brood (*peerchach*). They send away my feet and they cast up again against me their ways of destruction."[9] Here, "brood" is used as a metaphor for a "wretched crowd."[10] This *par* word is isolated to Job, a very late book, and means the same as the other *par* words.

Pri

k. *pri,* 6529

Pri is directly related to *pawraw,* "fruitful."[k] It is found in all Five Books and Psalms.

Pri is common in the other languages. Gordon says one of the meanings of the Ugaritic *pr:pree* is "fruit."[11] Driver gives a quote for "*pr[pree]*" as "fruit of the trees."[12] He also gives a word *pr'ee,* "fruit or first fruits," and the quotes he uses indicate that they are normally thought of as sacrifices. BDB, under "bear fruit, be fruitful," says the Assyrian word *pir'u* means "posterity."[13] Von Soden gives many examples of *per'u(m), perhu* as "shoot, sprout," and "offspring," with quotes from Old Akkadian, Old Assyrian, and New Babylonian, and compares *pri* to "*he.perah.*"[14] He relates it to the Hebrew *pawrach,* but I am including it here because of the probable pronunciation of *per'u* being fairly close. Its pronunciation as *perhu* would be closer to *pawrach.* This thought is strengthened by the fact that another meaning for *per'u* in the Old Assyrian and Old Babylonian according to Von Soden is "destroy, lasting."[15] BDB may have gotten the idea of "posterity" from Von Soden quotes in the Late Babylonian, the idea of "duration, lasting."[16] Faulkner translates the Egyptian *prt* as "fruit" ⬚◦⩓ with the determinative ⩓, a plough (an earth breaker) and "seed" ⬚◦ with the determinative *** for grain.[17] Then, "in the sense of offspring, posterity," there is ⩓ꕯ, ⬚◦⬚, and ⩓ from three different references. Gardiner simply translates it as "seed" and gives ⬚⩓ꕯ or abbreviated as ◦ꕯ.[18] There are different hieroglyphic spellings depending on the reference, but the pronunciation is the same, and the full range of meanings from "seed" to "fruit" to "offspring" is the same as the Hebrew. The Hittite word *para,* which can mean "from out of the mouth," can also mean, "forth, forward."[19] This relates to the idea of offspring coming forth.

Pere(h)

Pere(h), "wild ass," is used only once in the Five Books.[1] This is the prediction that Ishmael, Abram's son by Hagar the concubine, would also be progenitor of multitudes. "And he will be a wild ass (*pere*) of a man, his hand against everyone and the hand of everyone against him; and before all his brothers he will dwell." Job, Psalms, Isaiah, Jeremiah, and Hosea describe similar situations with a free-running, wild animal. That is, the word has to do with being "a swift runner, a fleeting one ... a figure of roughness, wildness, irrationality."[20]

The Akkadian word *parû(m)* means "mule" and possibly relates to the Hebrew.[21] There does not seem to be a corresponding word in Ugaritic or Egyptian.

l. *pere(h),* 6501 ending with *aleph* or later *hey;* Gen. 16:12

Pawrad

Pawrad is found in eight Genesis references. It basically refers to (1) a river going out of Eden and dividing into four branches, and (2) the separation or division of peoples into nations (after the Flood).[m] It is used once in Deuteronomy also referencing the peoples of the world being separated into nations.[n] Its exclusive use in Genesis until its repeat in Deuteronomy might hint at when these stories were transferred from their oral transmission to the written text—at the time of Deuteronomy.

m. *pawrad,* 6504; Gen. 2:10, 10:5

n. Deut. 32:8

Ezekiel 1:11 uses *pawrad* as "stretch" in stretching of wings of the four creatures that were drawing the chariot. Job 41:9 uses it as "sunder" regarding the scales of the leviathan (crocodile?). Psalms 22:15 uses it as "out of joint," relating to one's bones. 2 Kings 2:11 uses it in the separating sense when Elijah and Elisha are parted. The same holds true with Proverbs 18:18 where the "contentious" are parted by lot. Job and Psalms use it also as "scattered": "Lions' whelps are scattered abroad"; and "Workers of iniquity shall be scattered."[o] As "severed, broke away, left," it is used in Judges 4:11: "Had severed (broken away) himself from

o. Job 4:11; Ps. 92:9

the Kenites." As "dispersed," *pawrad* is used in Esther 3:8, "There are people scattered abroad and dispersed among the people."

Pawrochet

Pawrochet is a technical word meaning "veil" or curtain that

p. *pawrochet*, 6532

screened the super-conditioned place.ᴾ It possibly also served as an antenna.

I could not find an Egyptian word to cover this concept, but there are derivations in another language.[22] Most references point to the Akkadian *parayku*, "bar," as in the purpose of the veil, and *parakku*, "shrine," as possible derivations.[23] BDB says Assyrian *parayku* relates to the Hebrew letters *pay resh khahf* (*prach*) and means "bar, shut off." BDB also says Assyrian *parakku* means "shrine."[24] Von Soden says Assyrian *parakku* means "holy place," but of *parayku(m)* he offers many meanings, including the New Babylonian "interfere, intervene, come into action" in the military sense.[25] He gives references from Old Babylonian on. Of the many meanings Von Soden gives, they all come down to "blocking" or "interfering," the idea of lying across something. Labat says *parayku* means, among other things, "to bar, to fence up, to obstruct."[26] Even the word sounding most like *pawrochet*, namely *parkish*, means "across" and "transversely."[27] Derivatives in the early and later words have the same idea. The Middle/ New Babylonian *parriku(m)* is "lie across itself, oneself" and the verbal adjective of *parayku* in the Old Babylonian is *parku(m)*, "lie across."[28] One of the meanings of *parayku* is "plowing across" in the Old Babylonian. It has the significance of *breaking* the ground in the same sense that the Egyptian determinative of the plough is/was used in the words for "seed" and "fruit." So, there is the idea of "blocking (*parāku*) off" the "holy place," *parakku*. Two borrowed words signifying "holy place" and "block off" may have been used to develop a technical term relating to the purpose of the veil, *pawrochet*. It is rather fascinating that another word, *pâru(m)*, means "seek," a "seeker"—in the wider sense, being "one who seeks God, truth."[29] However, Langenscheidt says that in the wider sense, one of its meanings is to seek "advice."[30] The idea that the *pawrochet* separates the outer area from that which houses the communication device is what makes this concept so fascinating.

Perech

Perech ends with a *kaph*.[q] It refers only to ruling harshly and is found in Exodus, Leviticus, and once in Ezekiel.

q. *perech*, 6531

Strong's says *perech* means "cruelty, rigour" and is "from an unused root meaning 'to break apart; fracture.'" Von Soden gives it many meanings. In this case "fight, meet" is late, but he also gives the meaning "impede, interfere" as Old Babylonian. Another meaning is "stop someone" in Old Akkadian.[31] BDB translates it "harshness, severity" and says there is an Assyrian word, *parâku*, that means "display violence."[32]

Pawram

Pawram relates to God's warning to Aaron and his remaining two sons not to uncover their heads or tear their garments. This was after the deaths of Nadab and Abihu when they offered the wrong materials before the Lord.[r] The same words are used with reference to the burned person and again with the priests.[s] This is a perfect example of a *pr* word having another sound (not *par, puraw, pawrach, pawrad*, etc.) but still having the same general meaning. It is interesting that this *pr* word is found only in these Leviticus references. In all three cases, *pawram* refers to not rending garments in a radioactively dangerous area.

r. *pawram*, 6533; Lev. 10:6
s. Lev. 13:45, 21:10

Pawrah

Pawrah has early and late meanings. Important here is its use in Exodus as "broken loose" or "go loose": "And when Moses saw the people that it was broken loose (*pawrooah*) for Aaron had let it loose (*p'rawch*)."[t] Other references relate to the priests, the burned person, and the adulterous woman letting the hair go loose (uncovering their heads).[u] The fact that the general meaning of *pawrah* regarding hair is "uncover," the opposite of *keeper*, further proves the argument that *keeper* means "cover." A closely related word, *perah*, is translated "hair" or "locks"

t. *pawrah*, 6544; Exod. 32:24, cf., Prov. 29:18
u. Lev. 10:6, 21:10; Lev. 13:45; Num. 5:18

regarding the nazirite: "All the days of the vow of his separation shall no razor pass over his head; … he shall let grow the locks (*perah*) of the hair of his head."[v] It could just as easily mean "let grow *loose* the hair of his head."[33]

As to derivation, Von Soden says one of the meanings of the Akkadian word *parayru(m)* is "loosen."[34] The word *paray'u(m)* is Old and New Babylonian for "cut through" and "cut off, away, shear off, slice, crop" (hair).[35] Interestingly, the second meaning for the word in Old Assyrian is "come up" or "shoot up." It is also notable that *payrtu* means "hair of the head" in Old Akkadian and Old Assyrian.[36]

Pawratz

Pawratz basically means "break forth." In Exodus 19:22 and 24, the priests were first warned to condition themselves at Mount Sinai, "lest the Lord break forth among them."[w] Then, to be even safer, they were simply told to stay away altogether, along with all the people, "lest He [the Lord] break forth among them." *Pawratz* can also mean "spread," "increase," "broke," and "breach."[x] Strong's translates it as "grew." In the following books, *pawratz* is translated as "abroad, breach, burst out, compelled, dispersed, urged, open," but in all cases the words "broken out" or other variations of "break" would probably suffice. Depending on the Bible, the word is used rather doggedly.[37] So, all of the usual variations of a *pr* word are found here. Without belaboring the point, the related nouns *peretz* and *meph'rawtz*, also meaning "breach" and "breaking forth," are derived from *pawratz*.[y]

Pawratz's relation to Ugaritic is interesting though not surprising. Gordon directly relates it to *prtz*, which he says means "to open."[38] DLU also relates it to the Hebrew noun "breach, opening."[39] Driver says *prtz* means "chink, gap."[40] Thus, in the tablet that contains the text of a poem to the gods, Schachar and Shalim ii 36, the lines are "watchman, open; and he himself does open a chink (*prs*) behind them."[41]

There are no equivalent Middle Egyptian words in Faulkner or Gardiner that mean "break through" or "break open," but there is a Late Egyptian word *prt,* meaning "to break."[42] This is in the Papyrus Anastasi written in the 19th Dynasty at the end of the 13th century BCE.

Most importantly, Von Soden translates the word *paraytzu(m)* as "break through, in two."[43] BDB also says it is "break through."[44] So, a Hebrew word that can mean "break through" finds striking similarities in older and contemporary words.

Pawrock

Pawrock follows the now familiar pattern of starting with the meaning "break off."[z] Isaac blessed Esau by saying, "You shall break off (*oophawroktaw*) his yoke from on your neck."[aa] This is also translated "tear off, tear away." Aaron told the people to break or tear off their golden rings, *pawr'koo* and "the people broke off (*pawr'koo*) the golden rings" to make the molten calf.[ab] The nuance here is more of tearing something away from something or, later, someone.[ac] In Psalm 136:24, the meaning is more of "freeing, delivering, rescuing" as in "breaking the yoke." In Psalm 7:3, it is "tearing, rending" David's soul. Ezekiel 19:12 uses it in the familiar mode of breaking off rods or branches.

A related word, *pereck,* is used in Obadiah 14 as "crossway," "fork," or "separation in the road."[ad] It is also seen as "robbery" or "plunder" in Nahum 3:1, as in "snatched away." The related word *pawrawk* is translated "broth" in Isaiah 65:4, with the understanding of crumbled, broken up, meat.[ae]

In the Ugaritic, there is the word *prq,* "to break."[45] Gordon compares it directly to *pawrock* and says it is used "sometimes in the sense of 'to liberate, save'" The idea of "to break" is used idiomatically in the sense of opening the mouth. This appears in several stories in *Canaanite Myths,* always as *yprq.lsb wyshq*: "He [El] opened wide the passage of his throat and laughed."[46] Segert also uses the word "sever" as an alternative to "open" in the same quotes. He compares it to the Akkadian *parayqu,* "to sever."[47] However, Von Soden says the word *parāqu* is New Babylonian, so that at best it is contemporary with the Ugaritic.[48]

z. *pawrock,* 6561

aa. Gen. 27:40

ab. Exod. 32:2–3, 24

ac. Lam. 5:8

ad. *pereck,* 6563

ae. *pawrawk,* 6564

Pawrar

af. *pawrar*, 6565

Pawrar means "break."[af] It is found in Genesis, Leviticus, Numbers, and Deuteronomy as breaking a covenant or commandment. In following books, it is used with covenant as

ag. Job 5:12; Isa. 24:5, 33:8; 1, Kgs. 15:2; 2 Chr. 16:3

well as other subjects.[ag] *Pawrar* is also translated "make void." This is regarding making null and void, *hawphayr yawphayr*

ah. Num. 30:9, 13, 14, 15, 16

(*pawrar*), thus a daughter or wife *breaking* the oath.[ah] In the following books, Strong's also gives the meanings "cast off, cause to cease, defeat, disannul, disappoint, dissolve, divide, fail, frustrate, bring to naught," but the idea of "breaking up" runs through all of the uses.[49]

Prr in Ugaritic also means "to break." The quote given by Driver is "Consider, pray: does Keret then break [*t.pr*], or does [the king] altar [his] vow? Shall I break [*t.pr*] [my] promise?"[50] (Note here, the words in brackets are Driver's guesses.) Another quote uses "shatter": "With the jubilation of jubilant men … [missing text because of broken tablet] is shattered (*npr*)."[51] Gordon too says *prr* means "I shall break (an agreement)." He likens it to the Hebrew *hawphayr*, "to annul."[52]

Even more important is the Babylonian. For this I will come back to *parayru(m)* (mentioned in connection with *pawrah*), which means "loosen," but like other *pr* words it has additional familiar meanings. Von Soden says *paru(m)* means "break apart" in the Old Babylonian. He sites a quote relating to a demon breaking apart like a pot.[53] In the New Babylonian, there is also "break through." This simply demonstrates that the Babylonians actively used the word in its "breaking" meaning for a long time. BDB says the Assyrian word means "destroy, shatter."[54]

Pawrahs

Pawrahs, ending with the letter *samekh*, is related to "breaking," or in Leviticus and Deuteronomy, "divide" regarding the law of eating those animals that chew the cud and have a divided

ai. *pawrahs*, 6536; e.g., Lev. 11:4, 7

hoof.[ai] It is used as "tear" in Jeremiah 16:7 and once to actually mean "hoof" in Psalms 69:31, but this indicates a clean animal (bullock). Otherwise, the word for hoof is *parsaw*, which seems to be derived from *pawrahs*.[aj] Isaiah 58:7 actually uses *pawrahs* as "break" in "to break bread to the hungry." It is related to the Akkadian *paraysu(m)*.[55] Von Soden says it means "separate, sever, divide" and "decide, determine."[56] Also, BDB calls *paraysu* "divide, hinder," and Labat gives us *paraysu* as "separate, sever," "cut off, decide," "interdict, prohibit," and "decide, determine."[57]

aj. *parsaw*, 6541

Pawrahs

Pawrahs ends with a *sin*, which differs from *pawrahs*, which ends with a *samekh*.[ak] It is overwhelmingly used as "spread," another extension of the basic *pr* meaning; when something breaks, it scatters or spreads. *Pawrahs* is found as "spread" in Exodus, Numbers, Deuteronomy, and commonly in the following books. It is not used in Leviticus. Lamentations uses it twice as "spread" and once as "break."[al] Anything can be spread—hands, wings (of *cherubim*), tent, cloth—so it should not be thought of as a technical word.

ak. *pawrahs*, 6566

al. Lam. 1:10,13, 4:4

Pawrahs is translated as "chop up" or "break in pieces" in Micah 3:3 and nowhere else. It is translated "lays open," "exposes," or "spreads out" in Proverbs 13:16: "a fool lays open his folly." It is translated "scatter" in Ezekiel 17:21 and 34:12, but "spread" would also make sense in this context. *Pawrahs* is translated "stretch" ("forth" or "out") in reference to hands or wings in Exodus 15:20, for example. *Meep'raws*, the noun form of *pawrahs*, is used as "something spread" once in Ezekiel 27:7 (a sail) and once in Job 36:29 (clouds).[am]

am. *meep'raws*, 4666

In Ugaritic, the word *prsh* means "was spread, covered," as in "A footstool for a god which is [*prsh*] covered (?) with leather."[58] The footnote after "covered" says that *prsh* literally means, "spread."[59]

There is no Middle Egyptian word equivalent to *pawrahs*. However, again Leonard H. Lesko, in *A Dictionary of Late Egyptian*, translates the Late Egyptian word *prsh* as "to rend, to tear, to break open."[60]

Interestingly, the Hittite word *parsh* is translated by Friedrich as "break (to pieces), crack, crumble, split, divide, divide by boundaries, limit"; *parsha* is "breadcrumb."[61] Other related words are *parshiia, parshiul, archa parshula* ("broken in pieces") and *parshulli, parshur* (?).[62] It is also of note that the same Hittite word, *parsh*, means "flee."[63] *Partauar* is "wing."[64]

Turning again to Ugaritic, one of the meanings of *pr* is "flee," referring to fleeing and flying away of Hirgab, the father of eagles whose wings Baal broke.[65] Both Klein and BDB say Akkadian *parashu* means "fly" or literally "*spread* wings."[66] (BDB calls it Assyrian.) Labat says *parayshu* iv is "flight."[67] The Egyptian word *pr(i)* is "escape."[68]

Transition Words

Pawrash

Pawrash has the same spelling as *pawrahs* except it ends with a *shin*.[an] Keep in mind, the Masoretes applied vowels and sibilant symbols to the original Hebrew Bible, but this occurred much later in 6th–9th centuries CE. Thus, pronunciations are guesses. As in the case of *pawrash*, when two words have the same meaning but different ending letters, our educated guess was that the sounds of the ending letters were the same. The only way one can know whether a word ends with a *sin* or a *shin* (which look the same) is to compare it with a word that (1) has the same meaning, and (2) ends with a *samekh* (same *s* sound), i.e., the word can be spelled both ways. As a matter of fact, BDB says that *pawrahs* (*sin* ending) is interchangeable with *pawras* (*samekh* ending). He calls the use of *pawrahs* (*sin* ending) erroneous.[69] Klein calls *pawrahs* (*sin* ending) "a secondary form of *pawrahs* (*samekh* ending)."[70]

From my point of view, *pawrash* is the most important of all the words discussed so far in this series, because it represents a transition to *pr* words that only relate to communication. In the Five Books, *pawrash* is found twice. (1) Leviticus 24:12 refers to the young man who, while fighting, blasphemed the name of the Lord: "And they put him under guard to be declared (*leep'rosh*) on the mouth of God," meaning they put him under guard until it should be declared by the decision of God. (2) Numbers 15:34

an. *pawrash*, 6567

pertains to the man caught carrying sticks on the Sabbath who was put under guard "because it has not been declared (*porash*) what should be done to him."

In the following books, *pawrash* takes on the meaning of communicating "distinctly." Nehemiah 8:8 (in the Aramaic) refers to reading the law of the Lord "distinctly," *m'pohrawsh*. Ezra 4:18 refers to "plainly" reading a letter to the Persian King Artaxerxes (465–425 BCE). In Esther 4:7, *pawrawshat ha keseph* is translated as "the exact sum of the silver." Esther does not use *pawrash* here as "declare," but the very next verse uses the words *ool'hagid* as "and to declare." Nevertheless, in 10:2, *oophawrawshat* is used as "and a declaration." (Both 4:7 and 10:2 actually use the word *pawrawshaw*, which is derived from *pawrash* and is only used in these verses.[ao]) *Pawrash* is the "sting" of a snake in Proverbs 23:32, probably a late part of the book. This is the only use of "sting" either in the Five Books or following ones, and here it seems to mean "to cut into," thus "to separate" or "pierce."[71] Von Soden says that *parush'shu* is "sharp stick" in Old Assyrian and New Babylonian, and quotes one use as "pierce or stab me."[72] Finally, Ezekiel 34:12 also uses it as "separated," relative to sheep being separated. Many references either compare this to *pawrahs* or say it should probably be read using that word.

It is notable that *pawrash* is rarely used in these contexts. While there is no question that its use as "separate" relates it to the words meaning "break," the books that treat it as "separate" are late writings. The significant point is that Leviticus and Numbers used *pawrash* in its communication sense, and the communication meaning carried over into the much later post-exilic books, i.e., Nehemiah, Ezra, and Esther.

The following *pawrash* derivatives, *pawrawsh* and *peresh*, hint that *pawrash* was understood to mean "break" in Genesis to Numbers as well as the following books:

ao. *pawrawshaw*, 6575

Pawrawsh

ap. *pawrawsh*, 6571

Pawrawsh is derived from *pawrash*, meaning "horsemen" or "steed."[ap] It is used in Genesis and Exodus and most probably means "horsemen" rather than "steed" from the contexts. The common word for horse is *soos*, and in following books, when *pawrawsh* is thought to mean "steed," it is differentiated as "war horse."[aq] Whether it is "horseman" or "horse," it must be derived from the idea of "breaking through" as either a war horse or a Calvaryman would do. Its use in Genesis and Exodus and almost everywhere else is with "chariot," so the military context is obvious. Interestingly, the Hittite word *parh* means "course, chase, drive, hunt" and "(horse)-ride fast, gallop."[73]

aq. *soos*, 5483

Peresh

Another derivative of *pawrash* is *peresh*, used in Exodus, Leviticus, Numbers, and Malachi 2:3. It means "dung," suggesting material "breaking forth" or being "separated" from the body.[ar] Von Soden translates the old/new Babylonian word *parshu* as "fecal matter" or "dung." Thus, *pawrash* and its derivatives had the communication *and* breaking meanings. And so, since *pawrash* has both attributes, it is the word that makes the transition to the wholly "communication" type *pr* words.

~~~~~~

OTHER LANGUAGES

Keeping all of these nuances in mind, what else do the surrounding peoples have to say about them? First, regarding the "declare" connotation, in Ugaritic there is the *basic* word *p'r*, pronounced *p'ar*, which is translated "proclaim, announce."[74] All the authors compare *p'ar* to the Hebrew *paw'ar* (with an *ayin*), "open (the mouth)," but it more likely compares to *paw'ar* (with an *aleph*), which means "declare, explain."[as] *Paw'ar* is not in the Five Books.

as. *paw'ar*, 6473

In Egyptian, *proo n r* means "utterance" and *prt-hroo* means "invocation offerings," literally "going or sending forth of voice." The word *hrw* means "cry, voice, sound." I should mention per Faulkner and Gardiner that all of the *prt*, *pri*, etc., words relate to the word *pr*, which simply means "house." Gardiner says, "hence phon. *pr* in *pri*... 'go forth.'" Thus, the idea of "going out," etc., originally meant "going out of the house." The religious significance came from words like *pr-nsw*, "temple," and *pr-a*, which originally meant "great house" or "palace," and eventually turned into the familiar "pharaoh."

In Hittite, *par-na-ash* means "house." Another meaning of *parā* is "from out of the mouth."[75] Once again, Akkadian wins the award for being the most interesting. *Parāsu*, which means "separate, sever, divide," has other important meanings. The first is the Old Babylonian, translated by Von Soden as "interpretation, explanation!" He quotes a sentence: "The outcome is contradictory, not *clear*." So there are the obvious meanings of both "communication" and "distinct." The second, also Old Babylonian, is "decide."[76] Remember, both the Leviticus and Numbers references had the culprits put under guard until the Lord decided their fates. Both declarations were of the type that demanded decisions as to what that fate should be! Klein translates *parash*[I] as "to make distinct" and *parash*[II], "to keep off."[77] Von Soden says the word means "flatter" and Labat translates it as "flight."[78] Thus, *paw'ar* had an early meaning of "to declare" and is most closely related to *pawrash*. Not surprisingly, the Hittite *tapar(r)iia* and the Old Babylonian *paraysu* have as one of their meanings, "decide."

∞∞∞

P'rat

Finally, the word *p'rat*, "Euphrates," is found in the Five Books.[at] at. *p'rat*, 6578 Strong's says it is "from an unused root meaning: 'to break forth; rushing.'" Fuerst says "a bursting or rapid stream."[79] Klein says,

- to be divided into
- divide
- branch off ... probably a blend of the base [*pawrad*] (– to divide)
- the name of the river [*p'rat*] ('Euphrates') [literally] meaning 'to be divided' (into branches) like the Euphrates.[80]

BDB says it's from the Assyrian *purattu*.[81]

These *pr* words from other languages relate to "break" as it is seen in the beginning of this discussion with the word *pawrach*. They make the transition to the idea of "explaining," i.e., communicating as shown finally in the word *pawrash*. I have shown that this double meaning of *pr* words is also found in other languages. Now I'm going to take this reasoning to the next step, namely those other *pr* words, which specifically have to do with communication.

Communication Words

Sawfar

Sawfar is variously translated in its verbal form as "count, declare, number, reckon, speak, talk, tell."[au] As a noun, it is translated "scribe, writer," and "enumerator, muster officer, secretary."[82]

au. *sawfar*, 5608

Sawfar means "tell" in Genesis and Exodus, "told" in Genesis, Exodus, and Numbers, "declared" in Exodus, and "number" or "count" in Genesis and Leviticus. *Sawfar's* communication sense is found very early:

- Genesis 24:66 says, "And the servant told (*vahy'safayr*) to Isaac all the things that he had done."[av]

av. Gen. 29:13, 37:9, 10, 40:9, 41:8, 12

- In Exodus 9:16, the Lord orders Moses to quote him to Pharaoh, saying, "And for this reason I have preserved you in order to cause you to see My power and in order to declare (*safayr*) My name in all the land."
- Exodus 10:2 on the same subject says, "And in order that you may tell (*t'sapayr*) in the ears of your son ... what I have wrought in Egypt."
- Further along on the exodus itself, Exodus 18:8 says, "And Moses told (*va'y'sapayr*) his father-in-law all that the Lord had done to Pharaoh and the Egyptians."

The ideas "scribe" and "writer," which evolve naturally from these words, are not found until following books.[83]

The relationship to contemporary and older languages is close, though no longer unexpected. In Ugaritic there is *spr*, which Driver translates as "counted, reckoned, wrote down ... was recited ... number."[84] Segert divides the letters into four words: *tspr*, to count (related to Hebrew *sayper* and *yispore*); *spr*, scribe (related to Hebrew *soper*, Aramaic, *saypar*, and Akkadian *shaypiru*); *spr*, written text, document, list, treatise (related to Hebrew *saypaer*, Akkadian *sipru*); and *sprt*, recitation (?).[85]

To expand on the Akkadian-Assyrian-Babylonian, CAD spends some 18 pages discussing the word *sapayru*.[86] The various meanings are as follow:

1) to send a person, to convey goods [or] animals, to send against;

2) to send word, to send a report [or] a message, to write;

3) to order, give orders, to command, to administer, to control, to govern, rule. ("Rule" is possibly related to the Hittite *tapar(r)iia*, "arrange, order, instruct" mentioned as being related to *teeferet*, as well as the word *tapar*, meaning "lead, manage, rule.")[87]

4), 5) and 6) are all variations of the same. CAD says all are from Old Akkadian on, and suggests comparisons with other *pr* words, e.g., *nashpartu* A and B. *Nashpartu* A is (1) "letter, message, instructions, written order," (2) "proxy, agency," and (3) "service, business," from Old Assyrian and Old Babylonian on. *Nashpartu* B in Old Babylonian is "messenger." Then there is *nashparu* A, "envoy, delegate, messenger, representative" in Old Babylonian, Mari, and Standard Babylonian.[88] *Nipru* (a word beginning with "n") also means "offspring."

Another comparable word is *shaypiru* in Old Akkadian, which means "overseer, ruler, king." *Saypirutu* means "position, command, sovereignty" in Old Babylonian and Mari. *Shapru* B is "envoy, messenger," and *tashpartu* is the same as *shapru*.[89] The Akkadian word *shipru* means "message, announcement, report" (probably Segert's *sipru* above). It serves as the ideogram in Hittite texts for *hatressar*, also meaning "message, announcement, report."[90]

Interestingly, a perfectly natural evolution of the *spr* meaning arises in the words (1) *sepayru* (Neo-Babylonian, Aramaic loanword) meaning "to write alphabetic script (on skin)" and (2) the related *sepiru* (Neo to Late Babylonian, Aramaic loanword) meaning "scribe writing alphabetic script (mostly on skin)."[91]

Finally, I will turn to Middle Egyptian to find the word *spr*. In its form 🔤 it means "appeal to, petition."[92] *Sprw* and *sprty* mean "a petitioner." A petitioner communicates his needs to someone else. While it may be stretching, the word *sphr* is "copy, write down."[93]

There seems little doubt, then, that the Hebrew *sawfar* had ancestors and contemporary relatives with similar meanings. In many cases, the relatives themselves consisted of interrelated words with essentially the same meanings.

Sayfer

aw. *sayfer*, 5612

Sayfer basically means "book," and is derived from *sawfar*.[aw] It is used as "book" in Genesis, Exodus, Numbers, Deuteronomy, and throughout the following books. In Deuteronomy, Isaiah, and Jeremiah, *sayfer* is used as "bill, or certificate of divorcement." As "letters," it is found in 1 and 2 Kings, 2 Chronicles, Esther, Isaiah, and Jeremiah. It appears as "evidence" or "sign" in Jeremiah only, "learning" or "writing" in Daniel only, "register" in Nehemiah only, and "scroll" in Isaiah only. The purpose of the *sayfer* was to communicate.

ax. *meespar*, 4557

Meespar, which also derives from *sawfar*, overwhelmingly means "number" in the Five Books and most others.[ax] However, it is most interesting that in Judges 7:15 it means "telling" and in 1 Chronicles 27:24 it means "account" in the sense of "telling" (preceded by *meespar* meaning "number!"). In Ugaritic, *mspr* means "narration, passage of text."[94] Gordon translates it "story, narration" under *spr*.[95] There is no alternative meaning of "number."

Shofawr

ay. *shofawr*, 7782

Since the *shofawr* is for communication, it is probably natural to include it in this grouping.[ay] It means "cornet, trumpet" according to Strong's, and elsewhere "ram's horn." *Shofawr* is found in Exodus, Leviticus, and the following books. BDB compares it to Assyrian *shappar(u)*, "a species of wild goat."[96] This is *sappayru* according to CAD.[97] In the later Standard Babylonian, *sappartu* means "tip of an animal's horn."[98] Once again, *sappartu* demonstrates *pr* interrelationships in the Hittite: *paray* means "blow"; *pariparay* means "music instrument."[99] There does not appear to be a corresponding Ugaritic word, although another word for "horn," *grn*, is the equivalent of the

Hebrew *qeren*, commonly found in the Five Books (excluding Numbers) and following books.

Awfawr

Awfawr, "dust," is found in the Five Books and commonly elsewhere.[az] *Awfawr* is translated as "ashes" in Numbers 19:17 and 2 Kings 23:4. It is "earth" or "dirt" in Genesis, Job, and Isaiah (although far more seldomly than the Hebrew word *eretz*, "earth."[ba]) As "mortar" or "clay," it is in Leviticus 14:42 and 45 only. As "ground," it is found once in Job; as "ore," it is in Job 28:26. As "powder," it is in 2 Kings 23:6 and 15 only, and as "rubbish," in Nehemiah 4:2 and 10 only.

az. *awfawr*, 6083

ba. *eretz*, 776

Awfawr is included among the *pr* communication words for three reasons. First, "dust from the ground," *adawmaw*, is material the Lord used to form man, says Genesis 2:7. Whether the passage is analogous to the potter molding an image out of clay and investing it with life as is seen in the mythology of other nations, or is an acute observation by early man of the process of evolutionary development, I don't know. Genesis 1:24 indicates that *all* of the beasts of the earth (*eretz*) were created therefrom. "And God said let the earth bring forth living soul after its kind, cattle and creepers and beasts of the earth after its kind."[100]

Thus, it could be said that the verses are indicating that living things are formed from the very matter of the universe, *awfawr*, and so create a universal bond (material communication) between them and their Creator. On that subject, the following excerpts are of interest. (Also, on this topic, see my last chapter, "What Is God?")

Physicists Discover Inorganic Dust With Lifelike Qualities

Life on earth is organic. It is composed of organic molecules, which are simply the compounds of carbon, excluding carbonates and carbon dioxide. The idea that particles of inorganic dust may take on a life of their own is nothing short of alien, going beyond the silicon-based life forms favoured by some science fiction stories.

Now, an international team has discovered that under the right conditions, particles of inorganic dust can become organised into helical structures. These structures can then interact with each other in ways that are usually associated with organic compounds and life itself.[101]

Amino Acids from Interstellar Space

A team of scientists including SETI Institute and NASA researchers today announced the successful creation of amino acids, chemicals essential to life, in a laboratory simulation of conditions found in deep space.

At NASA's Ames Research Center, Moffett Field, CA, the team reproduced the freezing conditions that exist in the gigantic interstellar clouds of dust, gas, and ice that are the birthplaces of new stars and planetary systems ...

Previously, members of this team had demonstrated that irradiation of interstellar ice analogs results in the production of other compounds that are also of potential biological interest. These include a class of compounds called amphiphiles that can self-organize to form membranes and a class of compounds called quinones, aromatic ketones that play important roles in the metabolisms of living organisms on the modern Earth. "Taken in combination, these results suggest that interstellar chemistry may have played a significant part in supplying the Earth with some of the organic materials needed to get life started," Sandford concluded.[102]

Amino Acids From Ultraviolet Irradiation of Interstellar Ice Analogues

Amino acids are the essential molecular components of living organisms on Earth, but the proposed mechanisms for their spontaneous generation have been unable to account for their presence in Earth's early history. The delivery of extraterrestrial organic compounds has been proposed as an alternative to generation on Earth, and some amino acids have been found in several meteorites. Here we report the detection of amino acids in the room-temperature residue of an interstellar ice analogue that was ultraviolet-irradiated in a high vacuum at 12 K. We identified 16 amino acids; the chiral ones showed enantiomeric separation. Some of the identified amino acids are also found in meteorites. Our results demonstrate that the spontaneous generation of amino acids in the interstellar medium is possible, supporting the suggestion that prebiotic molecules could have been delivered to the early Earth by cometary dust, meteorites or interplanetary dust particles.[103]

The second reason *awfawr* is included in the communication words is that it was used in the test of the possibly adulterous woman.[bb] As such, it was part of the technical, sacrificial process used to determine an unclean situation and it resulted in what might be called a *physiological communication.*

bb. Num. 5:11–31

The third reason is the most direct and the most curious. Numbers 19:1–9 describes the use of the red cow's ashes along with cedar, hyssop, and scarlet (here, probably referring to scarlet cloth or thread) to form the water of separation for decontamination. Verse 9 says, "And a clean man shall gather up the *ashes* of the cow and lay them up outside the camp." Verse 17 says, "And they shall take from the unclean person from the *ashes* of the burning of the decontamination offering and shall put on it living water." This is the cleansing process for the person who has touched a dead body. The curious thing here is that the Hebrew word for the first two "*ashes*" in verses 9 and 10 is *ayfer*, and the word for the very same "*ashes*" in verse 17 is *awfawr*, dust.[bc] They are identical in letters except the *aleph* begins the first word and *ayin* the next.

bc. *ayfer*, 665

Why is *awfawr* used here instead of *ayfer*?[104] Before I give a possible solution, it is instructive to look at other languages: *'pr* is "dust" and "ground" in Ugaritic.[105] From Old Babylonian forward, the word *eperu* means all that *awfawr* means: "dust, earth, loose earth, debris, scales, ore, mortar, territory, soil, area, volume (as math term)."[106] From *eperu* one can find derivatives having all the familiar relationships.

- *Apayru* B in Babylonian is a West Semitic gloss from the Tel El Amarna letters (14th century BCE).[107] It means "dust."
- Then there is *chaparu*, also a West Semitic gloss from the El Amarna Letters meaning "dust."[108]
- *Apayru* is from Old Babylonian and means (1) "to provide with a headdress [cf., I Kgs. 20:38, 41], to put a covering on someone's head"; (2) "to be covered, coated"; (3) about the same as 1); and (4) "to be crowned, covered."[109] The "covered, coated" meaning gives two interesting quotes: "the oil sinks, rises to the surface, and is still coated with water," and "if

sheep's tongue has a coating ... ([Old Babylonian] behavior of a sacrificial lamb)."[110]

- Then there is *appayru*, a Sumerian loanword from Old Assyrian and Old Babylonian on, "reed marsh, reed bed, lagoon."[111] There are many later variations, all with the *pr* consonants, but the point is made—all of these words interrelate, too. Later Hebrew words relate to these words, showing the natural evolution seen before.[112]

Notice another point: None of these uses ever mentions the word "ash," that is, the result of burning. They either mean "dust" or "earth" or what dust does, i.e. coating, covering, but never the result of burning. Thus, while *ayfer* later means other related things (even related to *awfawr* and its later meanings), the early meaning is only "ash" and doesn't seem to come from anywhere else. Ash is probably related to the breaking, scattering idea of *pr*. Yet, it is definitely distinct from *awfawr*. Genesis 18:27 shows Abraham negotiating with the Lord about trying to save Sodom: "Behold, now, I have taken it on myself to speak to my Lord, [though] I [am but] dust (*awfawr*) and ashes (*ayfer*)."[bd] So if *awfawr* means dust, etc. only and *ayfer* means ashes only, how is it that this one time in all of the Five Books *awfawr* means ashes too?

bd. cf., Job 30:19, 42:6

The only explanation that makes sense is a chemical one. What has actually happened is that the red cow has been burned with the familiar cedar, hyssop, and scarlet. This has produced an inert substance, ashes, but when it is to be mixed with the "living" water it takes on a totally different character. It becomes active and can be used for decontamination.[be] In other words, it turns from the inert ash, *ayfer*, to a "living" material, *awfawr*, with all of the attributes and possibilities that word contains. It did not have to be a particularly powerful chemical agent because the chance of becoming contaminated was remote when the person lived far from the super-conditioned place. No covering was mentioned, and there was no actual declaration that the person who touched the dead body or body part had to leave the camp.[113] This was quite different from the nazirites

be. e.g., Num. 19:12, 13, 19

who were exposed to a dead person during their separation and who probably lived in close proximity to the tent, as did the priests. Certainly, they had many of the same constrictions as the high priest and had to be conditioned the whole time.[bf] So their protection had to be extensive.

bf. Num. 6:5

Still, in Numbers 19, the body or parts *were* unclean and *did* convey that condition to the toucher. So, it was necessary to be sure he was made clean. The process of making the toucher clean in turn made the sprinkler of the chemical unclean. The fact is the ashes were unclean, and anyone who actually touched them became so.[bg] So, too, was the water/ash combination.[bh] This was probably because the whole animal with its certainly unclean dung was burned. This is no different from the wholly burned (except the blood) goat and bullock in the *Azawzel* story:

bg. Num. 19:10

bh. Num. 19:21

> [27]"And the bullock of the decontamination offering and the goat of the decontamination offering whose blood was brought in to cover in the super-conditioned place he shall bring out outside the camp; and they shall burn their skins and their flesh and their dung.
>
> [28]And he that burns them shall wash his clothes, and he shall bathe his flesh in water, and afterward he shall come into the camp." (Lev. 16:27–28)

In the decontamination of the person who touched the dead body, the person who sprinkled him could not just leave the burned animal that made him unclean "outside the camp." He had to use its ashes again and again. This would be similar to the x-ray technician needing extensive protection from the cumulative dangers of roentgen rays while the patient does not, or the worker in drug manufacturing handling very powerful ingredients to make medicines that are relatively safe in small doses. At the end of the day, that worker also will be most likely to wash his/her hands. The select few who decontaminated the many people who needed it would be constantly exposed, while the contaminated people only received a few necessary sprinkles.

All of the above clarifies the point that before the ashes were mixed with the water they were just that—ashes. So using *ayfer* would be correct. However, when the living water was added, the purpose dictated using a word that denoted a mixture becoming a living, active substance. Thus, the word *awfawr* was used.[114]

This, then, is the interrelation/development of the *pr* words as they aim like an arrow toward the tent of meeting: *par, pawraw, pawrochet, perach, shophar, sayfer, pawrah, caporet, keeper*. The general meanings were the same among the surrounding peoples before, during, and after their use in Hebrew, and the same meanings continue throughout the world down to the present day. Thus, in Indo-European, to which the Hittite belonged, the root is *per*. In Greek it is *pro*. In Latin it is *par* as are, e.g., Afro-Asiatic and Drawidian.[115] And in a straight line it comes down to us in English, French, German, etc. There is, e.g., part(ed), depart, separate in the "to go forth" category; part(s), particle, particulate, the results of "breaking up;" impart, repartee, parley, parlance, as communication; prepare, Latin *parare*, becoming in Italian *parare* with the idea of "to prevent, to ward off," the *protection* achieved through the *preparation* of sacrifices resulting in *keeper*.[116]

This is an oversimplification of the etymology of *pr*. There are more examples I have not taken the space to mention.[117] The point is that the more one examines *pr*, the more the interconnections seem beyond coincidence. They are indeed stunning in describing the communication apparatus and its related operations. It is fascinating that the once puzzling laws governing the communication process seem to spring from one universal and very ancient root, *pr*.[118]

To believe that a much later priest group would have manufactured these *pr* words in order to cast back myths seems impossible. There is no way they could have known the technical purposes for words like *pawrochet, caporet*, etc., at a time when the ark was long out of use. The system and its terminology had to have been described by contemporary observers, and the technical words, no longer understood, had to have been passed down through the centuries.

Chapter 12

What is God?

If you have had the patience and fortitude to get through all of this, then you have been well exposed (over-exposed?) to all the evidence I can muster for my thesis. Does it prove that the observations of the people living during the exodus-wilderness period and later recorded by others were accurate portrayals of what happened? We cannot know. What the evidence does indicate is that something happened and was duly reported. That is, it didn't *not* happen. To reject this notion is to reject the etymology, the archeology of words, that tells this story. Of the words used to recount what happened, I believe the Hebrew ones are too technical and the related words too ancient to have been "made up" hundreds of years after the occurrences they describe, especially when the operations they depict were long abandoned and mostly forgotten. In addition, so many of the related words in other languages are either contemporary with or predate the Hebrew, giving a strong indication of the true age of Hebrew words. The fact that so many Hebrew words changed their meanings to non-technical applications in the following books seems to indicate a lack of the writers' knowledge of their primary significance. On the other hand, the technical meanings never varied when used in the early context.

As to the occurrences and operations that these words describe, I hope I've shown that they followed a logical progression (e.g., the evolution of *Yom Kippur*), which continued inexorably as long as applicable, despite doubts and debates as to strands, sources, or centuries. The occurrences and operations as described, and as they impact on the heart of this whole work, i.e., communication between God and man, adhered strictly to natural laws.

At the very outset I said that the only purpose for the *arone ha edut* was to convert a beam of transmitted energy into sound waves. [See Chart F below.] Up to this point I have not discussed the nature of this energy. So, it is time to make some observations and ask some questions.

The wilderness observers described the cloud that led the Israelites through the 40-year trek and that descended on Mount Sinai, then onto the tent, and over the ark. There were times when the *kawbode* of the cloud glowed a dull red at night, dull because the glow was not visible during the day. Also, there were times when the Lord came down in the cloud and His "anger" glowed. This could erupt into "fire of the Lord." The Lord's *kawbode* was in the cloud. It could cause plague and it was the substance through which He communicated.[a] Relative to this point, *kawbode* even appeared to be a part of or extension of the Lord, comparing Leviticus 9:4 and 6.

a. Exod. 13:21–22, 19:9

Chart F—Electromagnetic Spectrum of Wavelengths		
FREQUENCY	NAME OF WAVE	MEANS OF DETECTION
High ↑	*Kawbode*	Visible Affect on humans and animals (implicitly)
	Gamma rays	Gamma ray telescopes
	X-rays	Photographic plate or fluoroscope screen
	Ultraviolet rays	UV telescopes, UV camera spectrograph Affect on humans
	Violet	Visible
	Blue	Visible
	Green	Visible
	Yellow	Visible
	Orange	Visible
	Red	Visible
	Infrared rays	Thermometric apparatus
	Kawbode	*Edut*
Low ↓	Microwaves	Antenna, microwave telescope
	TV, radio	Radio instruments

These wavelengths are arranged according to size starting with the smallest, which have the greatest energy, and descending in the list to the larger forms having less energy. The addition of energy places the wavelength higher in the list, and giving off of energy places it lower. Loss of energy may be accompanied by various manifestations such as heat, fire, smoke, cloud formation, luminosity, electrical discharges, radioactivity, lightning, or other phenomena.

To explain the material nature of the *kawbode*, I will turn to some elementary physics such as Gerald Schroeder's explanation of energy and radiation in *Genesis and the Big Bang*. It is important to note that radiation is a constant fact of life. It is not confined to extreme cases like nuclear radiation.

> The microwaves in the kitchen microwave oven, the light by which we read, the X-rays that let a doctor see a broken bone, and the gamma rays released in a nuclear explosion are all composed of electromagnetic radiation. The only difference among them is their wavelength and the frequency of the wave. The higher the energy of the radiation, the shorter its wavelength and the higher its frequency. Aside from this they are identical.[1]

Schroeder expands on this:

> Radiation is often discussed with reference to the temperature to which an opaque, colorless (or black) object must be heated to emit the identical radiant energy that is coming from the place or object being studied. It is remarkable that this radiation is independent of the material from which the object is made. It depends only on the temperature of the "black body." In fact, an ideal black body is not really an object at all. It is the radiation measured in the cavity of a box having opaque walls.

> Although at absolute zero all thermal motion ceases, at all temperatures above absolute zero, thermal radiation is constantly being emitted. Humans and most higher animals are quite sensitive to radiations associated with black body temperatures of several thousand degrees Kelvin. We call this radiation *light*, and we measure its wavelength or frequency with our eyes as the different colors of the spectrum. Nerves in our skin are receptors of radiation associated with temperatures of hundreds of degrees Kelvin. This we feel as *infrared heat*. *Radio waves* are examples of radiation from very low temperature bodies. So are *microwaves*. At radiant temperatures much higher than those seen as light, the radiation enters the region of *X-rays* and *gamma rays*. This radiation is so powerful that it can penetrate our bodies. The general relationship among the different energies of radiation is that as the energy gets higher, the frequency also gets higher and the wavelength gets shorter. The higher the radiation energy, the higher the temperature of the black body that will emit this radiation. *Regardless of the particular energy, all radiation is carried by photons.* (my emphasis)[2]

As to light itself, I will turn to the physicist James Trefil's *Reading the Mind of God* for an explanation of what is known in the world of physics as quantum mechanics. Giants in the field laboriously evolved findings in this science. Names such as Newton, Foucalt, Faraday, Maxwell, Hertz, Planck, Einstein, Bohr, Compton, Pauli, De Broglie, Heisenberg, Dirac, Schröedinger, Oppenheimer, Gamow, Condon, the Curies, Urey, Bethe, Feynman, Gell-

Mann, and on to Hawking (and I've left out many more than I've listed) are a few notable examples. Through their failures and successes, they have brought us to a better understanding of the nature of light. Trefil says of quantum mechanics,

> One of the principle tenets of this science is that at the atomic level nothing is continuous. Everything, even light, comes in bundles of matter and energy called *quanta* (singular: *quantum*, the Latin for "so much").
>
> The quantum of light—the bundle in which it comes—is called a *photon* …
>
> The bundle of energy we call the photon moves through space, losing no energy as it goes. The rules of quantum mechanics tell us that the energy it carries is related simply to the wavelength of the light—the shorter the wavelength, the higher the energy. Since red light has a wavelength almost twice as long as blue, a photon of red light will have half as much energy as a photon of blue light.
>
> There is a rough kind of confirmation of this notion in everyday experience. If you put a piece of metal into a fire, it will start to glow as it heats up. The first color you will see is red, corresponding to the lower energy photons of visible light. When the metal is white hot, it is emitting light of all wavelengths. It has to be at a very high temperature before it emits photons at wavelengths corresponding to blue light and becomes blue hot.[3]

When the cloud functioned as a guide, its *kawbode* provided just enough energy to generate the red glow at night. This lower dosage must also have been present when Moses went up Mount Sinai into the cloud for a prolonged period since he survived the encounter and only came down with a glowing face. Moses' experience fits the expected consequences of coming near low levels of radiation unprotected. When it settled over the tent to enable communication, the cloud's fire-like (red glow) appearance suggests low, yet still dangerous radioactivity levels.[b] (An actual fire would have burned up the tent.) When the "anger" of the Lord glowed, the frequency seemed to have increased to highly radioactive levels capable of intense damage.[c]

b. Num. 9:15–16; Exod. 24:17–18

c. e.g., Lev. 9:34; Num. 11:1

Cloud, *kawbode*, now photons. An interesting grouping. What more can be said of the photon for my purposes? Returning to Schroeder, he says,

> When the universe was very young it was also very small. All the energy that today is spread over the reaches of space was concentrated into that confined, primordial volume. The *substance* of the early universe *consisted mainly of high energy photons* and neutrinos plus, relatively speaking, a tiny amount of matter in the form of individual protons, neutrons, and electrons. (my emphasis)[4]

He also points out that photons are "the dominant entity of this early period."[5] I do not intend to get into a detailed discussion of the big bang theory of the creation of the universe. That's been done over and over by professionals. The important point here is seen in Schroeder's statement that the first "light" would not have been visible. Thus, he says, "We have learned from science that the 'light' of that early period was in the energy range of *gamma rays*" (my emphasis).[6] Paul Davies in *Superforce* explains that during the big bang there was matter and its opposite antimatter. There was a tiny bit more matter than antimatter:

> When the universe eventually cools, the antimatter annihilates, and in so doing it destroys nearly all the matter. But not quite all, as there is ... one part in a thousand million excess of matter over antimatter that remains left over. It is from this minute residue ... that all the objects in the universe, including us, are made ...

> If this analysis is to be believed, the overwhelming majority of matter that emerged from the big bang disappeared before the first few seconds had elapsed, along with all the cosmic antimatter. Now we know why there is so little antimatter left in the universe. But this vanished material has left an echo of its erstwhile existence in the form of energy. The matter-antimatter annihilation produced about a thousand million *gamma ray photons* for each electron and each proton that remained unscathed. Today this radiation has been cooled by the cosmic expansion, and forms the *background heat radiation that fills the universe*. Apart from the energy locked up in matter, this background heat accounts for the greater part of energy of the universe. (my emphasis)[7]

Schroeder continues with the evolution of the universe: "Several hundred thousand years passed. Temperatures and photon energies had continued to fall in proportion with the universe's expansion. When the temperature fell below 3000°K, a critical event occurred: Light separated from matter and emerged from the darkness of the universe."[8] Schroeder presents a nice comparison between the creation of the universe and the creation of light as described by physics and Genesis.[9] Gamma rays, heat, and light. All three are photons. All are central to the development of the universe.

Now we come to an attribute of particles known as entanglement, which is possibly the underpinning of the communication mechanism, the ark. In the *New Scientist* journal, Mark Buchanan explains entanglement as "a quantum effect in which particles become linked, so that even if they are separated, a disturbance to one immediately affects the others."[10] This phenomenon has been known for some time, but an Austrian team has been able to produce two pairs of entangled photons by firing a laser through a crystal.

> Then, by sending the four photons through mirrors and beam splitters, they redistributed the entanglement, exchanging the two entangled pairs for one entangled trio and one independent photon. In the trio, two of the photons had horizontal polarisations, while the third had vertical polarisation. But in this entangled state, which particle has the vertical polarisation remains indefinite until the particles are measured. If a measurement of one photon shows it has vertical polarisation, the other two immediately take on horizontal polarisations ... The team plans to use the entangled trios to help confirm that the quantum world is "nonlocal" and permits a strange linking of distant points in space.[11]

Buchanan concludes by saying that physicists have used entangled pairs since the early 1980s, "but this requires millions of pairs and complex statistical analyses. In principle, a simpler and more convincing proof could be achieved with a single entangled trio."[12]

The long-distance communication between particles is surprising enough, but there have been opinions about the nature of the quantum world by physicists that boggle the mind. In the *Dancing Wu Li Masters*, author Gary Zukov, writing more than 20 years ago and referring to an earlier double-slit experiment, quotes theoretical physicist Henry Stapp:

> "The central mystery of quantum theory," wrote Henry Stapp, is "How does information get around so quick?" How does the particle know that there are two slits? How does the information about what is happening everywhere else get collected to determine what is likely to happen here?[13]

Zukov then says, "There is no definitive answer to this question. Some physicists, like E. H. Walker, speculate that photons may be *conscious!*"[14] Then he quotes Walker:

> "Consciousness may be associated with all quantum mechanical processes ... since everything that occurs is ultimately the result of one or more quantum mechanical events, the universe is 'inhabited' by an almost unlimited number

of rather discrete conscious, usually nonthinking entities that are responsible for the detailed working of the universe."[15]

Zukov continues:

> Whether Walker is correct or not, it appears that if there really are photons (and the photoelectric effect proves that there are), then it also appears that the photons in the double-slit experiment somehow 'know' whether or not both slits are open and that they act accordingly.*
>
> *An explanation other than "knowing" might be synchronicity, Jung's acausal connecting principle.
>
> This brings us back to where we started: Something is "organic" if it has the ability to process information and to act accordingly. We have little choice but to acknowledge that *photons*, which are energy, *do appear to process information* and to act accordingly, and that therefore, strange as it may sound, they *seem to be organic*. Since we are also organic, there is a possibility that by studying photons (and other energy quanta) we may learn something about us. (my emphasis)[16]

Back to 1998, in another article entitled "Beyond Reality," Mark Buchanan says,

> A growing band of physicists believe that information is a superweird new substance, more ethereal than matter or energy, but every bit as real and perhaps even more fundamental. For them, information is a kind of subtle substance that lies behind and beneath physical stuff. "Information is deeper than reality," says Anton Seilinger, a physicist at the University of Innsbruck.
>
> Zeilinger's shattering insight comes after years of studying information in the quantum world—one of the great challenges for frontier physicists. In the everyday world, information stays the same no matter how you choose to convey it. When driven into quantum terrain, however, it behaves oddly. Attach it to a quantum particle and suddenly it's everywhere and nowhere, on the edge of collapse and tricky beyond belief. In the past few years, this freakish behavior has conjured up all sorts of exotic possibilities from *Star Trek*-style teleportation to quantum computing.[17]

Buchanan continues:

> It may seem, then, as if information takes its quantum colours from the inhabitants of the quantum world on which it resides. But Zeilinger and others aren't so sure. Could it be the other way around? Quantum particles might be catching their behavior from the information they contain. "By thinking this way," says Zeilinger, "we get a deeper grasp of quantum physics. And we begin to see that quantum theory is more than a theory of physics— it's a theory of information."[18]

Buchanan then discusses electron pair entanglement "even when separated by a huge distance," and the theoretical "teleportation" of quantum information such as sending a cup of coffee from London to New York. He quotes Charles Bennett of IBM's Research Division, Yorktown Heights, New York:

> "In an entangled state ... distant particles are linked in a way that they classically couldn't be unless they were in the same place." ... In 1993 Bennett used the equations of quantum theory to show that entanglement, in principle, provides a way to make such a teleportation device. Even though quantum information cannot be copied or read, there is still a way to send it from one place to another—you just can't know what it is you're sending. Zeilinger and his colleagues at Innsbruck have now put Bennett's ideas into practice, and are routinely teleporting single photons around their lab ... In Bennett's scheme, the working channel for teleporting a photon is an entangled pair of subsidiary photons: A at the sending station and B at the receiving station. The "message" photon to be teleported, C, is also located at the sending station ... The goal is to copy the quantum state of photon C into that of photon B, effectively moving photon C across the gap and into B's spot, even though C never really moves physically.[19]

This is a fascinating article, and I have only touched on a small portion of what it has to say and the implications of these and other physicists' theories. If you can get it, I suggest you read all of it. However, for our purposes, the following by Buchanan is most significant:

> Why is the quantum world as weird as it is? This may seem like an unanswerable question. Or perhaps the quantum landscape is the way it is because it must conform to the laws of some deeper level where information is supreme. If so, information would truly be the most fundamental level of reality. This possibility becomes quite plausible when you start to think about the smallest possible pieces of quantum information, one of which is the qubit. Does entanglement also have a smallest unit? Bennett thinks so. In 1996, he and other researchers introduced the idea of "the amount of entanglement in a maximally entangled pair." They called it an ebit—a single "particle" of entanglement. Thinking of qubits and ebits as "particles" of information shows just how much quantum information is beginning to look like real matter.[20]

He concludes: "So in the context of quantum theory, information and physical stuff are beginning to blur into a kind of supersubstance that goes beyond the properties of either."[21]

These conjectures seem to have taken a quantum leap in the work of physicist Roy Frieden at the Optical Sciences Center, University of Arizona. In a *New Scientist* article by Robert Matthews, Frieden points out that quantum theory has passed every single test with flying colours, with some predictions vindicated to 10 places of decimals. Not surprisingly, physicists claim quantum theory as one of their greatest triumphs.

But behind their boasts lies a guilty secret: they haven't the slightest idea why the laws work, or where they come from. All their vaunted equations are just mathematical lash-ups, made out of bits and pieces from other parts of physics whose main justification is that they seem to work.

Now one physicist thinks he knows where the laws of quantum theory came from. More amazingly still, Roy Frieden thinks he can account for all the laws of physics, governing everything from schoolroom solenoids to space and time. Sounds incredible? You haven't heard the first of it. For Frieden believes he has found the Law of Laws, the principle underpinning physics itself.

The laws of electricity, magnetism, gases, fluids, even Newton's laws of motion—all of these, Frieden believes, arise directly from the same basic source: the information gap between what nature knows and what nature is prepared to let us find out. Using sophisticated mathematics, Frieden has shown that this notion of physics as a "quest for information" is no empty philosophical pose. It can be made solid, and leads to a way of deriving all the major laws of fundamental physics—along with some new ones.[22]

The article goes on to explain just how Frieden and his colleagues have gone about getting at the basis for all the laws of physics, and again makes for fascinating reading, but his last quote sums up Frieden's work: "What I and my co-workers have done so far is by no means the final word, but it does offer a systematic way to finding laws for new phenomena. And it seems that *information* is what physics is all about" (my emphasis).[23] Paul Davies, commenting on Matthews' article in the same issue of "The New Scientist," says the following:

This increasing application of the information concept to nature has prompted a curious conjecture. Normally we think of the world as composed of simple, clod-like, material particles, and information as derived phenomenon attached to special, organized states of matter. But maybe it is the other way around: perhaps the Universe is really a frolic of primal information, and material objects a complex secondary manifestation.[24]

He concludes:

If information is indeed poised to replace matter as the primary "stuff" of the world, then an even bigger prize may lie in store. One of the oldest problems of existence is duality between mind and matter. In modern parlance, brains (matter) create thoughts (mental information). Nobody knows how. But if matter turns out to be a form of organized information, then consciousness may not be so mysterious after all.[25]

It's almost impossible to pick up a science journal today without reading of some new discovery in this field. Let's keep in mind, though, that the rules of physics, chemistry, etc., were *always* in effect. We just did not know them. Our discoveries are just now bringing us to an understanding of a system that was developed billions of years ago. We tend to confuse our ever more sophisticated understanding of the universe, through the discoveries of science, with *when* it all came into being. So, by the time you read this, there is no telling what advancements will have focused a brighter light on the puzzles of quantum mechanics. Even at this point, however, there seems to be enough evidence to say that at an almost infinitesimal level there is interconnection and information exchange throughout the universe. With this and the rest of the discussion in mind, would it be possible to conclude that the *kawbode* substance in the cloud was composed of photons or some such subatomic particles? And since we have posited that *kawbode* is actually an *extension* or manifestation of God, would this be the reason that the otherwise strange use of the plural *Elohim* is employed when referring to that name? Here it makes no difference whether there's a J, E, or P. When speaking of God in the El terminology, overwhelmingly the plural is used. This would certainly explain the use of *Elohim* in Genesis 1:26, the Creation story, and specifically of "us" and "our" in "Let's make man in our image."[26]

Is it then possible that instead of YWH *Elohim* "the Lord God," we have YWH *of Elohim*, "Lord *of* Gods," *Elohim* being the interconnected *extensions* of Him throughout the universe?[d] There is a clear statement of this in Numbers 14:21: "And as I live, *all the earth* shall be filled with the glory of the Lord," regarding the punishment of the people after the report of the spies, etc. While the tense is niphal imperfect 3rd masculine singular, "shall be," the idea here is that this is a natural phenomenon that is always in force. Thus, it is often translated "is filled, and he fills, and fills," etc.[27] The addition of the word "of" in the phrase "Lord of Gods" would put the phrase in the construct state, perfectly acceptable grammar.[28]

d. Gen. 3:22

Thus, could this be the underlying system for the phenomena I have discussed, ranging from communication to plague? If so, was the concept of a pantheon of gods, rife in other nations, a perversion of the original meaning? Was there once a more enlightened, ancient civilization that grasped this idea to some degree? There are hints that this may on some level have been the case in Egypt.

Long before Akhenaton developed his monotheistic ideas, the sun-god Ra was considered "the universe, the 'sole god who made himself for eternity.' He is invoked in *The Litany* under his *seventy-five names which are his bodies, and these bodies are the gods*" (my emphasis).[29] The venerable E. A. Wallis Budge believed that the Egyptian concept of monotheism even predated dynastic times.[30] As to Akhenaton, 100 years before the exodus, the Hymn to Aten says, "Thou madest millions of forms of thyself alone."[31] Of all of the above, we can only conjecture and question and question some more.

If there is anything at all to my theory, why was *this* system of communication chosen with its inherent danger? Why was it constructed in such a way that it had to completely stop after Solomon at the latest? What role, constructively or obstructively, did the priests actually play vis-à-vis the eventually useless temple and in relation to the later prophets?

Finally, skipping 100 other questions, why this study? Here I must make a leap of logic. Either I have offered a description of a system that is accurate and actually operated or inaccurate and just another myth. If accurate, then at the least the interrelated, institutionalized religions as practiced today (Judaism, Christianity, Islam) become quite untenable. If inaccurate, then each is left to continue to float about aimlessly, bumping up against evermore enlightening new knowledge of our universe and against the other competitive religions, each with its firm belief in its own veracity and rejection of *any* others.

Even if my description is historically accurate and the mechanism did work, how does that affect us today? There is no easy answer to this question. Perhaps there is the feeling that one should always be ready to reestablish communication with God, to be in a position to receive through the prescribed wave-lengths, and by observing the instructions for becoming clean one would be in the most ideal condition to hear Him. Perhaps someday through medical advances we will be able to completely understand the physiological changes brought about by shifting from an unclean to a clean condition, and be able to bring them about in a simpler, more controlled fashion than was necessary at the time of the tent. Perhaps a team of scientists in a multimillion-dollar facility owned by a giant, high-tech conglomerate, or someone working all alone in a makeshift basement lab will be able to recreate an *arone ha edut*. And we might then remember the words in Joshua 3:8–9:

> [8]"You shall command the priests that bear the ark of communication, saying, 'When you are come to the brink of the waters of the Jordan, you shall stand still in the Jordan.'
>
> [9]And Joshua said to the Israelites, 'Come here, and hear the words of the Lord your God.'"

Appendix A

Edut in the Following Books

The *edut* used in relation to the ark is only found in Exodus, Leviticus, and Numbers with two exceptions. My explanation for these anomalies is below:

Exception 1

Joshua 4:16 says, "And the Lord spoke to Joshua saying, 'Command the priests that bear the ark of the *edut*, that they come from the Jordan.'" Every other reference in Joshua is to the "ark of the covenant (*b'rith*)," the "ark of the Lord (*Ywh*)," the "ark of your God (*Elohim*)," or the "ark of the covenant of the Lord (your God)." The Septuagint uses both words in the *edut* reference in Joshua 4:16 "the ark of the covenant (testament) of testimony (witness)." Joshua has some 23 references that fall into one or another of these categories, excluding references simply to the ark. Why?

Later editors of Joshua included some phenomena they could understand, but also some with which they were unfamiliar. One such unfamiliar concept was the technical use of the ark of the *edut*—its communicative purpose and its danger. However, the ark was too important, at least at the beginning, to leave out of the book. So they separated the word *edut* from ark and changed "ark of the *edut*" to "ark of the covenant (*b'rith*)." *B'rith* was a word and concept they understood.

That would explain some of the seeming contradictions. The one-time use of *edut* in Joshua could simply have been left in inadvertently from an earlier version of the story where originally all the references were to *edut* instead of *b'rith*. Several points are in favor of this possibility. First, the Lord used only the word *edut*, never covenant in Exodus, Leviticus, and Numbers in His orders to Moses. The fact that all but this one reference changed to "ark of the *b'rith*" or simply "the ark" in Joshua 6:4 hints that here, too, His orders to Joshua originally only used *edut*, and an editor just missed the one exception when making the changes to *b'rith*, etc.

Second, all references to the ark are in the early part of Joshua

a. Josh. 3:3–8:33

and completely disappear after that.[a] Thus, the only mention of this all-important device is in that part of the story that could reasonably have been a continuation of Numbers—the history of the journey that extended into the first months in Canaan. It would have been natural to continue calling it *edut* in this early part, and very strange to change it to *b'rith*, unless these were later editors who had lost the meaning. A couple of additional leftovers might lend even more validity to the thought that edut was inadvertently left in and made it into the final edition of Joshua. Two telling events, both still at the beginning of Joshua when the Israelites were just entering Canaan, seem to indicate that the original use of the ark as a direct medium of communication was also, knowingly or unknowingly, left in from the earlier story by later editors.

Crossing Jordan

The first is in Joshua 3:5–9 when the Israelites crossed the Jordan. Here, Joshua is setting the stage for communication with God. He ordered the people: "Condition yourselves for tomorrow the Lord will do wonders [split the Jordan] among

b. Josh. 3:5
c. Josh. 3:6

you."[b] Then he ordered the priests to "take up the ark."[c] Then "the Lord said to Joshua, 'This day I will begin to make you great,'" and "Joshua said to the Israelites, 'Come here and hear

d. Josh. 3:7, 9

the words of the Lord your God.'"[d] This does indicate a cause-effect situation inadvertently left in by some editor(s). While the ark would have been wrapped for travel with the priest bearers and therefore useless at that time, it might have been specifically unwrapped for this one occasion.

It is rather interesting that this one little communication

e. Josh. 3:6, 8

section of the story calls the ark *arone hab'rith*, *ha* meaning "the."[e] This is the same pattern used with *edut*, i.e., *arone haedut*. When the ark is simply carried by the priests and its communication function isn't stated, the story calls it *arone b'rith* with the *ha* omitted. Note the following versions:

f. Josh. 3:11

- *arone hab'rith adone* (not *Ywh*)[f]

- *arone Ywh*[g]
- *haarone hab'rith*[h]
- *hawarone*[i]
- *hawarone b'rith Ywh*[j]

g. Josh. 3:13

h. Josh. 3:14

i. Josh. 3:15

j. Josh. 3:17

Perhaps one editor copied the verses with the communication suggestion but used the specific arone hab'rith appellation, whereas others used the different terms and simply reported that the ark was carried by the priests, with no comment or understanding regarding its use.

Battle at Ai

The second ark of communication reference in Joshua 7:10–13 follows the crossing of the Jordan and the capture of Jericho. Joshua planned to attack the city of Ai. He sent spies who came back with the report that only 2–3,000 men would be necessary to do the job.[k] However, the army of Ai beat back the Israelites and killed 36 of them. "And Joshua tore his clothes and fell to earth on his face *before the ark of Ywh* until the evening, he and the elders of Israel, and they put dust on their heads."[l]

k. Josh. 7:2

l. Josh. 7:6

Joshua pled—communicated—with the Lord to help the people. Then the Lord gave a most peculiar reason for the people's plight, their defeat at Ai. He said,

[10]"Get up! Why are you fallen on your face?

[11]*Israel has contaminated* and also has taken the devoted thing and also stolen ... and put it among their things.

[12]Therefore the Israelites cannot stand before their enemies ... because they were [near] to a devoted thing. [The usual translation is "because they have become accursed" or "have become a thing for destruction." "A devoted thing" is the more logical translation given the events, and is grammatically acceptable.] I will not be with you any more if you do not destroy the thing from among you.

[13]Up! *Condition* the people and *condition* yourselves ... against tomorrow ... [There is] a devoted thing among you." (Josh. 7:10–13)

It turned out that a young man, Achan, had stolen some of the material captured at Ai and had hidden it in his tent. No one was supposed to touch the "devoted thing," but the "silver and gold and vessels of brass and iron" were "conditioned for the Lord; they will come into the treasury of the Lord."[m] So Achan and his entire family were stoned to death. After that "the Lord turned from the fierceness of His anger."[n]

m. Josh. 6:18–19

n. Josh. 7:26

Joshua 8 begins with the Lord telling Joshua not to fear, and that he should take *all* the people and attack Ai. Joshua then took 30,000 men, 10 times as many as at first, and with famously brilliant strategy captured and burned the city. This time the Lord said, "And you will do to Ai … as you did to Jericho … *only* its *spoil* and its cattle will you take for *yourselves*."[o](!)

o. Josh. 8:2

The Achan story is referred to again in Joshua 22:20 and 1 Chronicles 2:7, so it was well known. The details of the battle have been much studied. It has been difficult to verify archaeologically when and if the attack on Ai actually occurred. Some think the whole thing is a folk legend, but that is not my concern here. I am looking for a pattern and an explanation for what right now is a senseless story. And a pattern there is.

Joshua appeared before the ark definitely using it as a communication device to converse with the Lord. Then the Lord said, "*Condition* the people … against tomorrow."[p] Now, instead of reading the last half of that verse, "For thus says the Lord the God of Israel, 'There is a devoted thing in the midst of you,'" I think the story should pause here at "against tomorrow." If I were the editor, I would have cut the Achan story from the chapter.

p. Josh. 7:13

The Achan story is ridiculous because it sacrificed 36 men for one man's "sin," plus all of Achan's own family. The punishment was completely contradicted in the next attack on Ai when it was alright to keep the very things for which Achan and Company were stoned. This is not the work of "the Lord of all the earth."[q] If the Achan story were cut, it would pick up again at Joshua 8:1. So it would read,

q. Josh. 3:11, 13

[13]"Up! Condition yourselves against tomorrow."

> ¹And the Lord said to Joshua, "Do not fear nor be dismayed. Take with you all the people of war and arise. Go up to Ai. See I have given into your hand the King of Ai and his people and his city and his land." (Josh. 7:13a, 8:1)

Actually, the section could even start with Joshua 7:10 which says, "And the Lord said to Joshua, 'Get yourself up. Why now are you fallen on your face [before the ark]?'" Then it could continue with 7:13a, "Up! Condition yourselves…" This skips the Lord's comment on the devoted thing in Joshua 7:11–12 and flows directly to Joshua 8. The reasoning now is much more logical, i.e., the spies had miscalculated the strength of Ai. The *Lord* says "all" the people are needed to do the job. Joshua used an army 10 times larger than the first and the battle was successful. Even more important, the spoils were *now* to go to the people as a simple command, obviously differing from the command at Jericho but without a contradictory punishment story stuck in the middle. I must also add that if you look at the section carefully, you'll see that the beginning of the story starts strangely. Instead of beginning at Joshua 7:2, "And Joshua sent men from Jericho to Ai … saying, 'Go up and spy out the land,'" it starts with 7:1, which tells the Achan story before it begins!

> ¹And the Israelites [*all* of them!] committed a trespass concerning the devoted thing; for Achan, the son of Carmi, the son of Sabdi of the tribe of Judah, took from the devoted thing, and the anger of the Lord glowed against the Israelites.

Then the spy story starts, and 11 verses later the "devoted thing" story begins. In other words, to make the "devoted thing" story work, someone has stuck in a little piece at the very beginning, which gives the whole thing away. Not very logical if one is to believe that this was once a continuous story.

Finally, when the original Ai attack story starts, the terminology for the ark is only *arone Ywh.*ʳ Thus, the same term is used here ᵣ.Josh. 7:6 for the communication device as was sometimes used for the ark when carried by the priests across the Jordan in the Joshua 3–4 story and almost entirely in the Jericho battle story in Joshua 6 as some sort of an instrument of war.

Regardless of terminology, the fact is that the proper ingredients were present—conditioning and the presence of the Lord—to affect the original purpose of the ark, i.e., direct communication with Him. Logically, later writers would have simply recorded events and phenomena as they were passed down from the early time of entry into Canaan when the ark was still used for this purpose. One could expect, though, some confusion in their writing when they had little or no understanding about this purpose, and when they had long before adopted new terminology to convey entirely different concepts. Thus, it seems likely that a later writer simply left in the original word, *edut*, because he was not thorough. It was part of the early story just as the early communication use of the ark. An editor could change the words, but if he were simply recording events, he could not change the facts. The subject matter was key, not the words.

Exception 2

2 Chronicles 24:6 is the second and final use of *edut* as testimony in the following books:

> [6]And the king [Joash of Judah, 800 BCE] called for Jehoiada the chief and said, "Why have you not required of the Levites to bring in out of Judah and out of Jerusalem the tax of Moses, the servant of the Lord, and of the congregation of Israel for the tent of the testimony (*ohel edut*)?"

Its use here is one of the many mysteries of the Bible. There is speculation as to when the Chronicles were written. Some say around 350 BCE.[1] Others around 250 BCE.[2] Certainly it was post-exilic, and most agree that the writer(s) had a definte point of view. He championed the Levites and praised only those kings who followed God's laws. He certainly had the earlier books to research for his writing. Herein lies the mystery.

In telling the story of King Joash asking Jehoiada (the regent who ruled while Joash was too young) about the taxes, the writer used the term *ohel edut*.[s] It is only used in Numbers.[t] This is not true of the Septuagint, which differs from the Hebrew. The Septuagint mostly uses *ohel edut*. The Greek word for *edut*

s. *ohel*, 168

t. Num. 9:15, 17:22, 23, 18:12

is *martirioi*, translated "witness" in this exception verse, but it is also translated "testimony" when used with "ark."[u] Since u. Exod. 26:34, etc. the chronicler had Numbers to work from, why would he use *ohel edut* here, particularly since the Exodus law from which it comes uses the common *ohel moed*, "tent of meeting"?[v] Again, v. *moed*, 4150; Exod. 30:11–16 the Septuagint uses *ohel edut*, but there is no real explanation as to why the Numbers references use the rare term *edut*— unless the Septuagint translations were the correct ones, and the Chronicles writer simply used the common form found originally throughout Numbers.

Elsewhere in 2 Chronicles, *edut* as testimony is not used. Instead, the following are used: "the ark," "ark of the covenant, (*b'rith*) of the Lord," "ark wherein is the covenant (*b'rith*) of the Lord," "ark of the Lord (*Ywh*)," "the ark of God (*Elohim*)," "ark of your strength," and "the holy ark."

Appendix B

Does *B'rith* Really Belong in Numbers?

In Exodus, Leviticus, and Numbers, the term *arone haedut* is used when referring to the ark of communication. There are two exceptions in Numbers 10:33 and 14:44 where *arone hab'rith*, ark of [the] covenant, is used. This is the terminology of Deuteronomy and the following books. *B'rith* doesn't belong in Numbers, and I give my reasoning below.

Exception 1

Numbers 10:33 recounts the Israelites' journey from Mt. Sinai, and it details a most peculiar assignment for the ark. Instead of being an instrument in the hands of a specified person, e.g., the priest(s), and basically being his (their) charge, it suddenly becomes a decision-making object unto itself. Thus, the wording is as follows:

> ³³And they journeyed from the Lord's mount, a three days' journey: and the ark of the covenant (*b'rith*) of the Lord journeyed before them a three days' journey to *seek for them a resting place* [or just 'rest']. (Num. 10:33)

This is immediately followed with, "And the cloud of the Lord was over them by day when they journeyed from the camp."ᵃ _{a. Num. 10:34}

The two verses are most important in their placement one right after the other. Together they show that it was the *cloud's* job to lead the Israelites, not the ark's. Nowhere else is the ark an independent operator acting as a guide. Some have said that in Joshua 3:6 and 3:11 the ark was used as a guide, but there is no mention of that function there.[1] Actually, it was Joshua and the Lord who were giving orders to the priests as to when and where the ark was to be carried.ᵇ _{b. Josh. 3:6–8}

Further, earlier in Numbers it is made very clear that the ark was completely covered while journeying. Therefore, it would theoretically have been rendered inert at this time:

> ⁵"Aaron and his sons will go in when the camp is to journey, and they will take down the veil of the screen, and they will cover with it the ark of the *edut*.

> ⁶And they will put on it a covering of *tachash* skins and they will spread a cloth entirely of blue from above."^c (Num. 4:5–6)[2]

c. *tachash*, 8476

The cloud as a guide is first mentioned just as the Israelites were leaving Egypt way back in Exodus 13:21: "And the Lord went before them by day in a pillar of cloud to lead the way and by night in a pillar of fire to give light to them." There are several other references including the following:^d

d. Exod. 40:36–38; Num. 9:15–23, 14:14; Deut. 1:33

> ¹¹And it came to pass in the second year on the twentieth day of the month, the cloud rose from over the tabernacle of the *edut*.

> ¹²And the Israelites journeyed…from the wilderness of Sinai, and the cloud dwelt in the wilderness of Paran. (Num. 10:11–12)

Two more verses seem to clinch the argument of the ark not being the guide: "Then the tabernacle was taken down and [there] journeyed the sons of Gershon and the sons of Merari."^e They were the caretakers of the tabernacle.^f "Then journeyed the Kehathites, the carriers of the super-conditioned place, and [the sons of Gershon and Merari] set up the tabernacle against their coming," meaning "before they arrived."^g In other words, the tabernacle went first, was set up, and was then *followed* by the ark. At that point the ark was installed in the tabernacle.

e. Num. 10:17

f. Num. 3:25, 36

g. Num. 10:21

Then a peculiar break in this sequence appears in Numbers 10:29–32. Suddenly Moses is begging his father-in-law, Hobab, to stay with him and guide the Israelites. Hobab simply replies, "I will not go [with you], but to my land and to my kindred I will go." His reply, incidentally, is out of order in the verses, coming in the middle of Moses' plea. Hobab is called Reuel in Exodus 2 and Jethro in Exodus 18. As Jethro he visits the wilderness (Exodus 18 reports), to bring Moses' wife and son from Midian to join Moses. The chapter ends with, "And Moses sent away his father-in-law and he went his way to his land."[h] The story takes h. Exod. 18:27 place at the beginning of the exodus from Egypt, not the "the second year, in the second month" when Hobab was his name.[i] i. Num. 10:11

Much has been written about the three different names, the different circumstances, etc., and theories abound.[3] Whatever the explanation, the fact is that the Hobab event seems unfinished or fragmentary, and its inclusion here seems out of place. In the same way, Numbers 10:33 regarding the ark seems to have been pasted there out of context. It immediately follows the Hobab story and just precedes what seems to be the continuation from Numbers 10:11 about the cloud's role. This is made more evident by the fact that just following the cloud verse, reference is made once again to the ark.[j] This time it is what is thought to be a j. Num. 10:34 fragment of an old war song, added here by another editor.

> [35]And it came to pass when the ark journeyed that Moses said, "Rise up, Lord, and let your enemies be scattered and let your haters flee before your face."

> [36]And when it rested he said, "Return Lord, [to] the myriads of the thousands of Israel." (Num. 10:35–36)

However these verses got there, they don't seem to belong. It could be said that the concept of the ark was not originally part of the sequence at all. Thus, it would follow that the terminology "ark of the covenant (*b'rith*)" might have been added at a later date.

Exception 2

Numbers 14:44 is the second reference to "ark of the covenant (*b'rith*)." Here is the presumptuous, ill-fated attack by the Israelites on the Canaanites and Amalekites without "the ark of the covenant of the Lord" to help them. Similar to the Numbers 10:33 passage, mention of the "ark of the covenant (*b'rith*) of the Lord" in Numbers 14:44 comes at the end of a chapter that has long been recognized as having a lot of problems. Its combination of stories has some contradictions regarding the same event.[4] The preceding chapter, Numbers 13, tells of the revolt of the Israelites against Moses and Aaron after Israelite spies had reported that the land they were entering would be too difficult to conquer. Then Numbers 14 seems to have the two stories about what happened.

In both stories the Israelites were warned, after they were punished for their rebellion, not to go through the territories of the Amalekite and the Canaanite who "dwell in the valley" in the first story and the same groups "that dwell in that mountain" in the second story.[k] It's almost impossible to separate the stories because of the all-important "punishment" dealt to the people by the Lord, which is essentially the same in both.

The verses at the end quote Moses:

> [42]"Do not go up, for the Lord is not in your midst, that you may not be smitten down before your enemies.

> [43]For the Amalekite and the Canaanite are there before you, and you will fall by the sword because you have turned back from following the Lord. Therefore the Lord will not be with you." (Num. 14:42–43)

Then follow verses that say,

> [44]Yet they presumed [or persisted] to go up to the top of the mountain, but [literally, "and"] the ark of *b'rith* of the Lord and Moses did not move from the midst of the camp.

> [45]Then came down the Amalekite and the Canaanite that dwell in the mountain … and beat they them down to Hormah. (Num. 14:44–45)

All this time, only the Lord had been the instrument for the action. In this case, He worked through His "glory" causing the spies to die of "plague" and He withdrew from the midst of the people, leaving them vulnerable to attack by their enemies.[l] However, suddenly, in order for the people to be protected when they go to war, they need the ark of *b'rith* in their midst.

The use of the ark as an instrument of war is totally unheard of at this time, but it is common in later times, e.g., in the capture of Jericho and in the battle with the Philistines.[m] There has never been a hint that the ark of the *edut* was anything but

k. Num. 14:25, 45

l. Num. 14:10, 37

m. Josh. 6:6–7, 1 Sam. 4

a communication device up to this time. And here, as in Numbers 10:33, the reference wasn't to the ark of the *edut* but the ark of *b'rith*.

It is conceivable that the editor(s) of this chapter used the word *b'rith* to insert another concept of the ark into an early event. Thus, it is possible that the original book of Numbers never contained the word *b'rith* as it pertained to the ark. Therefore, the original communication purpose would have been all that was ever intended.

Documentary Hypothesis ABCs

Critics say that the phrase "ark of the *edut*" was used only by a group of priests who lived, worked, and wrote any time from the eighth to the fifth century BCE. They say the priest(s), designated P, took earlier writings, recast them, and made up the story of Moses and the exodus (the patriarchs, etc.) to give a history to a disparate group of people (according to some, this was during and after the Babylonian exile) and to give credence to the laws and points of view they wished to promulgate. Thus, *edut* is said to be only a priestly (P) word as used with the ark. The idea, say the critics, was a late development inserted into the history of the Israelites.

On the other hand, "ark of the *b'rith*" is said to be used by a writer or a school of writers called the Deuteronomists, designated D.[1] They supposedly contributed to Deuteronomy as well as Joshua, Judges, Samuel, and Kings, and probably compiled the works in the 700s–600s BCE. Some think the book of Deuteronomy is that which was found in the temple at Jerusalem during the reign of Josiah, king of the Southern Kingdom of Judah, 641–609 BCE, which prompted his reforms.[2]

Now "ark of the Lord (*Ywh*)" is said to be used by a writer or writers living in Judah anywhere from the 10th to the sixth century BCE. They are designated J for Yahwist. (J is pronounced Y in German.)

"Ark of God (*Elohim*)" is said to have been written by the Elohist(s), designated E, in the Northern Kingdom of Israel anywhere from the ninth to the sixth century BCE. He/they used the words *El*, *Elohai*, and *Elohim* for God. "Ark of *Elohim*" appeared once in 2 Chronicles 1:4.

The fact is that the dating of these "sources" has become totally chaotic. The eminent scholar Jacob Milgrom says that P should be dated no later than 750 BCE.[3] On the other hand, Robert Pfeiffer says it was written by a priest in Jerusalem in 450 BCE.[4] B.A. Levine claims P is dependent on D and earlier writing.[5] "Essential D," he says, is lately thought to have been written "in the late eighth century B.C. ... [a] north Israelite creation, transmitted to Judea during the reign of Hezekiah, sometime before 686 B.C." But, he says, certain sections of P can be shown to date from the Persian period with a term in Leviticus found in Aramaic papyri from Elephantine "dated to the fifth century B.C."[6] At the same time Walter Brueggemann says of J, "Although older critics dated J somewhat later, it is now generally ascribed to the tenth century B.C., either in the time of Solomon (962–922) or just after, in response to the crisis of culture and faith evoked by Solomon."[7] But John Van Seters dates Yahwist to "the sixth century B.C."[8] He says that the Yahwist uses "the historiographical techniques and formulas" of Deuteronomist history, which he terms DtrH.[9] He says J is a work "produced by one or more Dtr [D] redactors…that extends from Joshua to 2 Kings and includes Deuteronomy with chapters 1–4 as its prologue."[10] To continue the controversy, Van Seters states that P cannot "be viewed as independent from J."[11] Remember, he says J came *after* DtrH, but Weinfeld says P and D are "two literary schools representing two ideological currents, the provenance of one being the temple (P), and the provenance of the second the royal court (D)."[12]

This debate has been going on at least a couple of hundred years, mostly generated by Julius Wellhausen and other 19th century German scholars. And it rages today. Whatever side one takes, whatever theory one holds, source criticism pervades all thinking as to the historicity and reliability of the Hebrew Bible.

For the purpose of this discussion I will use the prevalent theory that J and E came first, followed by D and P. "Ark of *edut*" is said to be P. "Ark of *b'rith*" is said to be a Deuteronomic phrase. Well almost, but not quite. As used in Numbers 10:33 and 14:44 (see Appendix B), "ark of *b'rith*" is said to be J or Redactor JE.[13] So, used in this context and even related ones, *b'rith* is said to be the *early* word because it is J and/or E or a redaction by D. (The prevalent thought is that *b'rith* is a redaction by D in following books.) And *edut*, as used in connection with the ark and stones, is called the *later* word because it is P.

Logically, however, if *edut* is the late word, why does it almost completely disappear as such in the following books? And if *b'rith* is the early word, why is it not used in connection with the ark until later where it replaces *edut* in that context? And even more puzzling, why does *edut* completely lose its equivalency with the "stones" in the following books and instead take on the contemporary meaning of "testimony" or "witness"?

In other words, why wouldn't P have inserted the late word *edut* with its meaning of "stones" in all the books he was supposed to have redacted and done away with the early word meaning "covenant"? Could it be that *edut* really was early and had another meaning, and *b'rith* was a word that was always understood as "covenant" and simply continued to be used as such later? The fact that *edut* had a different meaning in the following books lends some credence to the thought that possibly an early meaning had been forgotten, misunderstood, or suppressed, and that "covenant" was being used instead to try to clarify the new or different meaning.

It's interesting that Nahum Sarna says that "*edut* and *berit* [*b'rith*] are synonymous; *edut* is a very ancient Semitic term that fell into disuse in Hebrew and was displaced by *berit*."[14] This is use of simple logic, uncluttered by the Documentary Hypothesis!

On the other hand, Cross, who says P is sixth century BCE "late in the exile," says, "The 'covenant' or covenant document proper in P ... consists of the tablets of the law, that is, the decalogue that he designated the 'covenant,' *edut*, which ... is another instance of P taking up an archaic word and using it as a technical term."[15] However, P would have a problem if he followed Cross' theory. How could he have taken an archaic word, *edut*, and designated it "covenant" for use as a technical term when clearly "covenant" was a late meaning encompassed by *b'rith* and the later utilization of *edut*? If P was looking for the archaic, he would have taken the much older communication meaning and forced it into every mention of the *edut*. If there ever was a P redactor representing priests of the exilic/post-exilic period, he would have had no idea what the early *edut* word meant.

Appendix D

Kawbade

The traditional translation of *kawbade*, "glorified" or "honored," is used in Leviticus 10:3, one of the most obscure passages in the first four books. It is situated immediately after the tragic deaths of Aaron's sons, Nadab and Abihu.

> ³And Moses said to Aaron, "This is what the Lord spoke, saying, 'By those that are near Me I will be conditioned, and before all the people I will be glorified [or honored] (*ekawbade*).'" And Aaron kept silent. (Lev. 10:3)

This statement is either horrifying arrogance or sheer nonsense. I believe the latter. For God to speak of being conditioned, glorified, and/or honored before all the people while Aaron's sons lay dead at the altar simply does not follow. In fact, nowhere else in the Five Books is it even suggested that a phenomenon such as the deaths of priests occurred. These simply do not reflect the actions of God.

This is quite different from the erratic, sometimes quite childish behavior of the gods in Mesopotamian and Greek mythology. On the other hand, if this were simply an observation of an event being described as accurately as possible, then it would make sense. The original observers knew that *kawbode* was in the cloud and that it was dangerous. One need only refer again to Leviticus 16:2 to see the relationship clearly:

> ²And the Lord spoke to Moses after the death of the two sons of Aaron when they came *near* before the Lord and they died. And the Lord said to Moses, "Speak to Aaron your brother, that he come not at all times into the super-conditioned place within the veil, before the covering, which is on the ark, *that he die not*; for in the cloud I will appear on the covering."

In fact, Leviticus 16:1–16 should again be noted to see the purpose of the clothing and other protections.

In order to understand Leviticus 10:3 clearly, it is necessary to look at it in context. Leviticus 9 describes the culmination of the preparations for the Lord appearing to the Israelites. Moses ordered the people to bring the material for the sacrifice:

[5]And all the congregation came *near*, and they stood before the Lord.

[6]And Moses said, "This thing that the Lord had commanded, you will do; then will appear to you the *kawbode* of the Lord." (Lev. 9:5–6, my emphasis)

They sacrificed:

[23]And Moses and Aaron went into the tent of meeting. Then they came out and they blessed the people; and the *kawbode* of the Lord appeared to all the people,

[24]And fire came forth from before the Lord, and it consumed their burnt offering on the altar … and *all* the people saw [it] and they shouted and they fell on their faces. (Lev. 9:23–24, my emphasis)[1]

So the people were near to the area, in the general vicinity of the altar, where the burnt offerings were made. They saw the sudden appearance of the fire "from before the Lord" and they fell in panic on their faces. Believing they had to prepare the area quickly to protect the nearby people, Nadab and Abihu each took …

[1]His firepan, and they put in them fire, and they put upon it incense, and they offered before the Lord strange fire …

[2]And [there] came forth fire from before the Lord and it consumed them … and they died before the Lord. (Lev. 10:1–2)

They did the right thing, but with the wrong materials, so it didn't do any good. The materials they used did not abate the radioactive danger that was present in close proximity to the Lord, so Nadab and Abihu were "consumed." They were not burned up. Rather, they were removed "in their coats," indicating they had been irradiated, not incinerated.

Aaron's sons were unfamiliar with the procedure, so they panicked and acted hastily. They and the people had been terrified by the fire of the Lord once before at Mt. Sinai. They made human errors. Their actions were not purposeful wrongdoings any more than was the action of Uzzah when he put out his hand to grab the ark "and the anger of the Lord was kindled against (Uzzah) … and he died there by the ark of God" (2 Sam. 6:6–7).

Taking another look at the strange passage and applying the translation "heavy" rather than "glory," suddenly there is a perfectly logical meaning.

[3]And Moses said to Aaron, "This is what the Lord spoke, saying, 'By those [the priests] that are near Me I will be conditioned [for safety] when on the face of the people I [meaning His glory (*kawbode*)] will be heavy [or thick] (*ekawbade*).'" And Aaron kept silent. (Lev. 10:3)[2]

(I have retranslated the *vov* from "and" to "when" and *al p'nay* from "before" to "on the face of."[3])

In other words, the priests protected everyone in the area against the danger of the cloud by using the precise material. Then, if the cloud settled on the people during the process of converting *kawbade* to sound waves, no harm would come to them. If the priests failed to follow the rules exactly, they would endanger themselves and the community as Aaron's sons did.

So *kawbade* in Leviticus 10:3 should be translated "heavy." One might ask why the translators used "glorified" or "honored."[4] They made the same word choice in Exodus 14:4, 17–18 where Pharaoh and his army pursued the escaping Israelites:

> [4]"And I will harden (*v'cheezahktee*) [really strengthen] Pharaoh's heart, and he will pursue after them, and I will be *honored* (*v'eekawv'daw*) through Pharaoh and through all his army." (Exod. 14:4)

Exodus 14:17 and 18 say essentially the same thing, except they add that He "will be honored ... through his (Pharaoh's) *chariots* and through his horsemen." (Some Bibles translate the *bet* as "upon" rather than "through," but the concept is the same.) I suppose one could say that by defeating Pharaoh, his army, and his horsemen, the Lord would "be honored." However, aside from the fact that this is a human need, not one necessary for the Lord of the universe, how would He "be honored ... through (Pharaoh's) chariots?" It does not make much sense, but that is the traditional translation and so goes hand in hand with its counterpart in Leviticus 10:3.

Well, what if I retranslate *kawbade* in these passages the same way I translated it in Leviticus 10:3? And what if I translated the *bet* not as "through" but as "against," which is another common meaning for *bet*.[a] Then I would get the following:

a. e.g., 2 Sam. 6:7

> [17]"And I, behold, I will strengthen the heart of the Egyptians, and they will follow them; and I will be *made heavy against* Pharaoh, and *against* all his army, and *against* his chariots and *against* his horsemen." (Exod.14:17)[5]

"Heavy" can also be used for Exodus 14:4 and 18.

So, the Lord did not command that He was to be "honored" through pharaoh's horsemen (animate) and chariots (inanimate), but rather that the dangerous cloud would fall "heavily" on the Egyptians. Why is this translation logical? Because that is exactly what happened immediately after He gave that order. The very next verses, Exodus 14:19–23, speak of the cloud in its role as a protector.

> [19]And the messenger of God, which went before the camp of Israel, removed and went behind them. And the pillar of the cloud went from before their face, and stood behind them.
>
> [20]And it came between the camp of the Egyptians and the camp of Israel. And it was a cloud and darkness to them, but it gave light by night to these: so that the one came not near the other all the night.
>
> [21]And Moses stretched out his hand over the sea and the Lord caused the sea to go back by a strong east wind that night, and made the sea dry land and all the waters were divided.
>
> [22]And the Israelites went into the midst of the sea upon the dry ground, and the waters were a wall unto them on their right hand, and on their left.
>
> [23]And the Egyptians pursued, and went in after them to the midst of the sea, even all Pharaoh's horses, his chariots, and his horsemen.

The critics notwithstanding, this is a perfectly flowing continuation of the prior verses.[6] It speaks of the cloud moving from in front of the Israelites to a position between them and the Egyptians. Then a "strong east wind" blew *all* night. In addition to drying up the Sea of Reeds, the wind must have been blowing parts of that dangerous cloud all over the Egyptians who were to the west during that time.

> [24] And it was in the morning watch [that] the Lord looked at the camp of the Egyptians, through the pillar of fire and cloud, and confused the camp of the Egyptians,
>
> [25]And took off [or bound or jammed] the wheels of their chariots, and they drove them with difficulty (*beechabadoot*) [or heavily, another use of *kawbade*]. And the Egyptians said, "Let's flee … for the Lord is fighting … against (*b'*) the Egyptians." (Exod. 14:24–25)*

*There is no question that the *bet* (*b'*) here means "against."

Two other words clarify the cohesiveness of the entire passage. They are "looked" and "confused." The terminology is specific and limited to this and similar situations.

Looked

Hertz's *Pentateuch and Haftorahs* says, "The text does not allude to the means whereby the panic ... was produced."[7] Is that really true? Let's see.

The word for "looked" used here is *shawkaph*.[b] Rashi says, "The verb generally signifies 'looking with the intention of doing evil.' God looked to destroy the camp of the Egyptians."[8] Not bad.

b. *shawkaph*, 8259

Of the dozens of times the Five Books refer to the act of looking, the following are the only other ones that use the Hebrew *shawkaph*:

- When messengers of the Lord visited Abraham, they had two missions: (1) to tell him that his wife, Sarah, was going to have a child, Isaac, in her old age, and (2) to tell him that they were on their way to the sinning cities of Sodom and Gomorrah to totally obliterate them from the face of the earth.

  [16]And the men rose up from there, and looked (*vyash'keeyfool*) on the face of Sodom. (Gen. 18:16)

  Next, Abraham surveyed God's destruction:

  [28]And he looked (*vayash'kaphe*) on the face of Sodom and Gomorrah and on all the face of the land of the circuit; and he saw, and, behold the smoke of the land went up like the smoke of a furnace. (Gen. 19:28)

- Genesis 26:8 describes looking through a window.
- Numbers 21:20 and 23:28 refer to high places that "look down" on lower areas.
- Deuteronomy 26:15 exhorts God to "look down from [His] conditioned habitation."

With the exception of the Genesis 26:8 reference, they each speak of destruction and/or looking down from a great distance. So I think the text is clear that the Lord looked at the Egyptians to destroy them.

Confused

In Exodus 14:24, the word for *confused* is *hawmam*.[c] It is the same word used in connection with the Lord sending the "hornet" in Exodus 23:

c. *hawmam*, 2000

[27]"My terror I will send before you, and I will *confuse* all the people among whom you will come, and I will make all your enemies [turn] to you [their] back.

[28]And I will send the *hornet* before you, and it will drive out the Hivite, the Canaanite, and the Hittite from before you." (Exod. 23:27–28)

Even in Deuteronomy, in Moses' summary of the Israelites' 40 years in the wilderness, *hawmam* is used in the sense of discomfit. "And also the hand of the Lord was against them, to discomfit them [the "men of war"] from the midst of the camp, until they were consumed."[d]

d. Deut. 2:15

Thus, the Exodus uses of *kawbade* do not mean "honor." The only reason translators could have rendered it as "honored" or "glorified" rather than "heavy" in both the Exodus verses and in Leviticus 10:3 is that they were unsure of what *kawbade* really meant. Someone knew at one time and used the proper terminology to tell these stories.

For instance, the person who told the 1 Samuel story of the Philistines' experience with the ark also used the *kawbade* terminology. The Philistines captured the ark and chaos ensued when they brought it to Ashdod:

[6]And the hand of the Lord was heavy (*vateechabad*) on the people of Ashdod, and He destroyed them, and He smote them with *t'chorim* (or *afoleem*), Ashdod and the borders thereof. (1 Sam. 5:6)[e]

e. See also
1 Sam. 5:11

This is such a clear example of the hand of the Lord (synonym for the cloud) causing plague that the translators were forced to render it with its original meaning.[f]

f. 1 Sam 6:4

The logic for translating *kawbade* as "heavy" in Leviticus 10:3 then is very strong, and the various pieces of the puzzle fall nicely into place.[9] This view does have its critics, however.

From the critics' points of view, the "heavy" translation is part of one of the most persuasive arguments for the Documentary Hypothesis. To simplify a rather complex bit of reasoning, go back to Exodus 7, the story of the plagues and Moses' attempts to persuade Pharaoh to free the Israelites. Critics have observed that certain verses explain that after a plague ended, Pharaoh's heart was hardened or made heavy and he refused to let the people go. Two words are used for "harden" or "make heavy." They are our friend *kawbade* and the verb *chawzaq*.

The critics say that all uses of *kawbade* as "harden" or "make heavy" are J and *chawzaq* as "harden" or "strengthen" are P.[g] They say that two plague stories wind their ways through Exodus: one by the older Yahwist writers (J) and the Elohist (E) and the other, for his own purposes, by the later priestly writer (P). They say each writer used terminology peculiar to his style. The problem here is that, as I have just argued, Leviticus 10:3 and Exodus 14:4, 17, and 18 use *kawbade* as "harden" or "make heavy," which would put these verses in the J category. However, the critics ascribe them to P, just as they ascribe *chawzaq* verses to P. Well, Exodus 14:4 and 17 use *chawzaq* **and** *kawbade*. Maybe this awkward meeting of these two words in the same verses caused the translators to traditionally use "harden" for *chawzaq* and shift to "honor" or "glory" for *kawbade* in these verses that the critics call P. The critics say P always uses *chawzaq*, never *kawbade*, to denote the idea of "harden" or "make heavy." Something must be wrong.

I will get right to the crux of the problem. The real point is not whether P used *kawbade* as "harden" or "make heavy," but that, with the exception of these four uses, P *did not use kawbade in any way at all!* So why, regardless of whether he meant it as "honor," "glory," *or* "make heavy," did P suddenly use the word *kawbade* in these verses only? Exodus 14:4 and 17 were both J and E using *chawzaq* and *kawbade* or P using the technical "make heavy" meaning of *kawbade*. These verses use *kawbade* relative to the Lord.

Consider these "P verses" in Exodus 14. Note the use of *chawzaq* and *kawbade*:

¹And the Lord spoke to Moses, saying,

²"Speak to the Israelites that they return and encamp before Pi Hahiroth, between Migdol and between the sea before Baal Zephon. Opposite it you will encamp by the sea.

g. *kawbade:* Exod. 7:14, 8:11, 28, 9:7, 34, 10:1; *chawzaq:* Exod. 7:13, 22, 8:15, 9:12, 35, 10:20, 27, 11:10, 14:8

³And Pharaoh will say of the Israelites, 'They are entangled in the land. The wilderness has shut them in.'

⁴And I will strengthen (*chawzaq*) Pharaoh's heart, and he will pursue after them, and I will be made heavy (*kawbade*) against Pharaoh and against all his army; and the Egyptians will know that I [am] the Lord." And they did so. (Exod. 14:1–4)

¹⁰And Pharaoh came near and the Israelites raised their eyes. And behold, the Egyptians were marching after them. And they feared exceedingly. And the Israelites cried to the Lord. (Exod. 14:10)

¹⁵And the Lord said to Moses, "Why do you cry to Me? Speak to the Israelites that they move forward.

¹⁶And you lift up your staff, and **stretch out your hand** over the sea, and divide it; and the Israelites will go into the midst of the sea on the dry ground.

¹⁷And I, behold, I will strengthen the heart of the Egyptians, and they will follow them; and I will be *made heavy against* Pharaoh, and *against* all his army, and *against* his chariots and *against* his horsemen.

¹⁸And the Egyptians will know that I [am] the Lord when I will be made heavy (*kawbade*) against Pharaoh, against his chariots, and against his horsemen." (Exod. 14:15–18)

²¹And Moses stretched out his hand over the sea; and the Lord caused the sea to go [back] by a strong east wind all the night, and he made the sea dry land, and the waters were divided.

²²And the Israelites came into the midst of the sea on the dry ground; and the waters [were] a wall to them from their right hand and from their left hand.

²³And the Egyptians pursued, and they came after them, [even] all Pharaoh's horse[s], his chariot[s], and his horsemen, into the midst of the sea. (Exod. 14:21–23)

²⁶And the Lord said to Moses, "Stretch out your hand over the sea, and the waters will return on the Egyptians, on their chariot[s], and on their horsemen."

²⁷And Moses stretched out his hand over the sea, and the sea returned at the turning of morning to its strength, while the Egyptians [were] fleeing against it.

²⁸And the waters returned, and they covered the chariot[s], and the horsemen, together with all the army of Pharaoh, that came after them into the sea. [There] did not remain even one.

²⁹But the Israelites walked on dry ground in the midst of the sea; and the waters [were] a wall to them from their right hand and from their left hand. (Exod. 14:26–29)

Now for the critics' rules: In the *P* version, the Lord is said to speak to both Moses and Aaron. (Please read all of Exodus 14 to see how I cut it.) In the J and E or JE versions, He speaks only to Moses. In the P version, it is Aaron who does the stretching of the hand. When Moses does it, it's J or E depending on the critic.

The interesting point here is that verse 1 says, "And the Lord spoke to Moses." It is a P verse. Verses 15–16 say, "And the Lord spoke to Moses … lift up your staff and **stretch out your hand**." Nevertheless, Friedman and Harper call verses 15–18 all P.[10] Interpreter's, however, sees the pitfall. It calls 15a E to get rid of the problem of the Lord speaking to Moses alone in a P verse; it also calls 16a E and defuses the debate about who is being told to stretch out his hand.[11] However, if you start with 15b you have no transition from verse 4 where Interpreter's says P first ended. So I would go along with Friedman. Lastly, verses 21 and 26 have Moses stretching out his hand. By this time both Friedman and Interpreter's have given up and call these verses P, and so does Harper's. The fact is, Aaron isn't mentioned at all in Exodus 14.

Now I'd like to discuss problems with the Documentary Hypothesis as I see them. From Witter to Wellhausen to Friedman and Bloom-Rosenberg, scholars have been building a case for it. This has led to some pretty strong conclusions that must be confronted by biblical students, including the idea that each of the strands was written by a person or persons who had his/her own axe to grind. (Friedman does an admirable job of explaining this in his book, *Who Wrote the Bible?*) They say that the Five Books were written long after the events occurred and that each source, J, E, P, and D, wrote at a different time and place. Furthermore, they say a redactor, R, compiled everything much later.

Stories of the patriarchs, the tabernacle in the wilderness, and the exodus itself are considered "castbacks"—stories created to give a "history" to this group of people in their exilic and post-exilic periods. In fact, scholars such as Donald B. Redford say, "any modern interpretation which depends heavily on the details of this [OT] Exodus tradition is at once both naive and gratuitous, if not downright dishonest."[12] Manfred Beitak puts Exodus in quotes in his article, "Comments on the 'Exodus.'"[13] In a paper titled "Is There Any Archeological Evidence for the Exodus?" William G. Dever said,

> The driving force behind the Israelite ethnic movement may indeed have been Yahwism, as the later biblical sources maintain, or the revolutionary social

reforms of a peasant revolt, as Norman K. Gottwald and many other biblical scholars have argued. But however clearly the social and economic changes accompanying this ethnic movement may be seen in material culture remains, I would suggest that the ideology of our proto-Israelites will be reflected only indirectly in the archeological record. Some, of course, would question whether we can even identify the archeological assemblage as Israelite, but I am not so skeptical. In any case, all we can say thus far is that between the late 13th century BCE, and sometime in the mid-11th century BCE there occurred such far-reaching socioeconomic, technological, and cultural changes in central Palestine that the millennia-old Bronze Age may be said to have given way to a new order, the Iron Age, dominated soon by the emergent Israelite state. Yet all of these developments appear to be part of indigenous sociocultural changes at the end of the Late Bronze Age and the beginning of the Iron Age. They are natural and even predictable oscillations in the long settlement history of Palestine, not unique episodes that the archaeologist or historian is forced to explain by positing marauding hordes from the desert, wholesale destructions, and abrupt changes in material culture (much less divine intervention).

The implication of the new picture of indigenous Late Bronze Age Cannanite origins for the majority of the early Israelite population is clear. Not only is there no archaeological evidence for an exodus, there is no need to posit such an event. We can account for Israelite origins, historically and archaeologically, without presuming any Egyptian background. As a Syro-Palestinian archaeologist, I regard the historicity of the Exodus as a dead issue, despite this symposium's raising it again.[14]

Certainly there is much to commend about the scholarship that has gone into the Documentary Hypothesis. (When I say "the Documentary Hypothesis," understand that scholars do not agree on any specific theory, and attitudes change over the years.)[15] However, theories must hold up in all cases, not just when it is convenient. I use the classic JEDP theory with some variations. Others disagree to such an extent that they do away with the theory altogether or digress into the previously accepted sub-sub divisions of the strands.[16]

Ahlström says the following:

The theory of an invasion of Israelites from Egypt ... would be hard to maintain. One possibility is that some Semites who left Egypt at the end of the Bronze Age also settled in the *hills of Palestine*.[17]

While Ahlström is not speaking of the Hapiru, he is agreeing with Tubb and Chapman about the settlement of wanderers in the hill country.[18] Tubb and Chapman call them "dispossessed or homeless peoples." Along comes the "archeozoological" approach, though, and you get the following view quoted from *Biblical Archaeologist*:

> Paula Wapnish of the University of Alabama at Birmingham discussed integrating scientific methods of research with concerns of the biblical archaeologist in a paper titled "Archaeozoology: The Integration of Faunal Data with Biblical Archaeology." Wapnish used faunal data from Tell Jemmeh, Tel Dan, and Tel Miqne to demonstrate how ecological reconstruction may aid archaeologists in understanding the development of a tell. For example, she said, *faunal data from Tel Dan do not support a scenario in which disenfranchised peasants from the lowlands reestablished themselves in highland settlements.* Rather, she said, a more complex process is evidenced, the results of which will have important consequences for understanding, among other things, the emergence of the Israelites in the Iron Age.[19] (my emphasis)

I'm including all this to show that the only constant among biblical scholars is disagreement. Yet the general trend has been to emphasize those theories, which tend to denigrate the accuracy of observers who first noted the happenings in ancient times.[20] Friedman points out that "P was written as an alternative to JE. The JE stories regularly said: 'And said to Moses...' But the author of P often made it: 'And Yahweh said unto Moses and unto Aaron.'"[21] J. L. Mikelic and G. E. Wright say the following:

> In separating the P source certain characteristics are observed: In JE Moses is the chief actor on God's behalf while Aaron, if he appears at all, is only the silent partner ([Leviticus] 8:8–9, 12—H 8:4–5, 8; 8:25–26—H 8:21–22; 9:27–29; 10:8–9); in P Aaron is the chief actor. P's typical literary formula is, "Then Yahweh said to Moses, 'Say to Aaron, Stretch out your rod.' Aaron stretched out his hand."[22]

For the most part, scholars agree that the writer of the P strand, fighting for domination of his group over rival faction(s), has included and emphasized Aaron in activities with Moses as much as possible. Friedman also says P went out of his way to denigrate Moses.[23] To understand how he accomplished this, go to the beginning of the story, not the middle.

Exodus 4:21 is the first problem:

> [21]And the Lord said to Moses, "When you go to return to Egypt, see all the wonders that I have put in your hand, and do them before Pharaoh; but I will harden (*chawzaq*) his heart and he will not send away the people."

The Lord speaking to Moses alone should make the verse J or E, but here *chawzaq* is "harden" in reference to Pharaoh's heart, and that's P. Interpreter's calls it J. Friedman says the first part of the sentence is J all right, but the redactor (R) added the last part. *No one calls it P.*

Next, a few verses later in Exodus 4:27, the Lord spoke directly to Aaron alone telling him to "go to meet Moses in the wilderness," a perfect P opportunity. However, the classicists call it E. Friedman says R stuck it in here.

Afterwards, Exodus 4:29–30 reads,

> [29]And Moses and Aaron went, and they assembled all the elders of the Israelites.

> [30]And Aaron spoke all the words that the Lord had spoken to Moses; and he did the signs before the eyes of the people.

Another P natural, but Interpreter's says it's J. Friedman says R. Then Exodus 5:1 says,

> [1]And afterwards Moses and Aaron came, and they said to Pharaoh, "This the Lord has said … 'Send away My people, that they may hold a feast to Me.'"

Surely, according to the logic of the critics, this must be P. No. Interpreter's says it's E, and Friedman thinks it's J! The same disagreement holds true for the mention of both Moses and Aaron in Exodus 5:4, but they both think Exodus 5:20 is J.

Exodus 6:1 follows:

> [1]And the Lord said to Moses, "Now you will see what I will do to Pharaoh, for with a strong (*chawzawqaw*) hand he will send them away, and with a strong (*chawzawqaw*) hand he will drive them out of his land."

The fact that God was speaking to Moses alone suggests that this should be a J or E verse, but the adjective *chawzawq* is used. Not *chawzaq*, but *chawzawq*. Yet, *chawzawq* refers to Pharaoh's hand just as the verb *chawzaq* refers to Pharaoh's heart. We are not supposed to see *chawzaq* in relation to Pharaoh in anything but P, except we already have. Interpreter's and Friedman say it is J. Nowhere else is *chawzawq* used as "strong" relating to Pharaoh, and in all other cases where it is used relating to someone or something else it is J or E.

Perhaps these are isolated problems, so I'll go on to the first "Lord spoke to Moses and Aaron" verse, Exodus 6:13. This is a pretty important one:

> [13]And the Lord spoke to Moses and to Aaron, and He commanded them concerning the Israelites and Pharaoh, the king of Egypt, to bring the Israelites out of the land.

This verse is a P argument because where Aaron was included, P strove to keep him prominently in the act. While Interpreter's agrees, Friedman says a redactor was responsible for this, too! Harper's simply says it is "secondary material."[24]

Before coming to the next "And the Lord spoke to Moses and Aaron," look at Exodus 7:1–3:

> [1]And the Lord said to Moses, "See, I have made you a god to Pharaoh; and Aaron your brother will be your prophet.
>
> [2]You will speak all that I command you, and Aaron your brother will speak to Pharaoh …
>
> [3]… and I will multiply My signs and My wonders in the land of Egypt."

Surely this beginning must be J or E. The Lord was speaking to Moses alone about a subservient Aaron, but everyone calls it P! Well then, since these verses are P, they should use "harden," *chawzaq*, when referring to Pharaoh's heart, only they use *qawshaw*.[h] *Qawshaw* is seldom used this way.[25]

If ever there were verses that should be J or E or even D, the first five in Exodus 7 are the ones. P should pick up with the next "Moses and Aaron" in verse 6, but it wouldn't make sense to start the P story with "and Moses and Aaron did so." So you are forced to relate it to a patently non-P formula, which definitely ties the whole thought together in a logical flow! Exodus 7:1–14 reads as follows:

> [1]And the Lord said to Moses, "See, I have made you a god to Pharaoh; and Aaron your brother will be your prophet.
>
> [2]You will speak all that I will command you, and Aaron your brother will speak to Pharaoh, that he will send away the Israelites out of his land.
>
> [3]And I will harden (*kashaw*) the heart of Pharaoh, and I will multiply My signs and My wonders in the land of Egypt,
>
> [4]But Pharaoh will not listen to you. And I will lay My hand on Egypt, and I will bring out My hosts, My people, the Israelites, out of the land of Egypt with great judgments.

⁵And the Egyptians will know that I [am] the Lord when I stretch out My hand over Egypt, and I bring out the Israelites from their midst."

⁶And Moses and Aaron did as the Lord had commanded them. So they did.

⁷And Moses [was] eighty year[s] old, and Aaron [was] three and eighty year[s] old, when they spoke to Pharaoh.

⁸And the Lord said to Moses and to Aaron, saying,

⁹"When Pharaoh will speak to you, saying, 'Give a wonder for yourselves,' then you will say to Aaron, 'Take your staff and cast it before Pharaoh.' It will become a serpent."

¹⁰And Moses and Aaron came to Pharaoh and they did so as the Lord had commanded; and Aaron cast his staff before Pharaoh and before his servants, and it became a serpent.

¹¹Then Pharaoh also called for the wise men and for the magicians; and also the magicians of Egypt did so by their secret arts.

¹²And they cast every man his staff, and they became serpents; but Aaron's staff swallowed up their staffs.

¹³And the heart of Pharaoh was strengthened and he did not listen to them as the Lord said.

¹⁴And the Lord said to Moses, "The heart of Pharaoh is heavy and he refuses to send away the people."

Verse 8 is the next "Lord said to Moses and Aaron." It begins the plague series and fits the critics' formula. P runs through verse 13 and talks of Pharaoh's strengthened (*chawzaq*) heart. Then verse 14 has the Lord speaking only to Moses, mentions Pharaoh's heavy (*kawbade*) heart and is called J.²⁶ From this point, there are the divisions of *chawzaq* and *kawbade* and Aaron stretching out his hand with his staff (not casting it down), but there is a "but." The whole idea here is to show how P emphasizes Aaron's importance by including him in the action. Yet J does the same thing. For example, Exodus 8:8 (Heb. 8:4) says, "And Pharaoh called for Moses and Aaron, and he said, 'Pray to the Lord that He remove the frogs from me and my people.'" Exodus 8:12 (Heb. 8:8) says, "And Moses and Aaron went out from Pharaoh." The two are mentioned again in Exodus 8:21 as being called by Pharaoh, yet in verse 26 it says, "And Moses went out from Pharaoh." The entire section though is called J. On the other hand, Exodus 9:11 says, "And the magicians were not able to stand before Moses because of the inflammation" and that is called P! Again Moses and Aaron were called to Pharaoh in Exodus 9:27 and that is J. Again in Exodus 10:8 and 16 the two were called, but in 10:24 only Moses was called to Pharaoh—still all J. On the other hand, Exodus 10:20, the locust plague, says, "But the Lord hardened (*chawzaq*) Pharaoh's heart." Interpreter's and Harpers say it is E. Friedman resorts to R! Finally in Exodus 13, still very much a part of the Exodus story, verse 1 says, "And the Lord said to Moses." This is P according to Interpreter's and Harpers and E to Friedman. Verse 9 says, "With a strong (*chawzaq*) hand has the Lord brought you up out of the land of Egypt." Interpreter's says R and Friedman says E, and no one says P! Note again that chapter 14 never mentions Aaron.

You can see that this passage is brutally chopped to pieces by the disagreeing critics. The fact remains that according to their rules, it should be J or E or JE, not P because the Lord spoke to Moses alone. If P's goal was to emphasize Aaron in the story as a whole, he doesn't do it any more or less than does J or E. You can't just pick out a few verses to make your point. You have to look at the whole story to build your case. This in no way was done. Aaron is present or absent, on-again-off-again, in no fixed way by either P or E or J. If you read it, you'll see that Moses comes off as the undisputed leader with Aaron in a secondary role.

What about the overriding theme, which says that all this is to build Aaron at the expense of Moses (Aaronide priests vs. Mushites)?
- In Exodus (not counting "And the Lord commanded"), the Lord spoke to Moses and Aaron five times and to Moses alone 56 times.
- In Leviticus, where P should really have had the chance to glorify Aaron, the Lord spoke to Aaron and Moses four times and to Moses 30 times.
- In Numbers, the Lord spoke to Moses and Aaron six times and to Moses 59!

So it's Moses and Aaron 15 to Moses alone 145. However, Friedman says,

> P was written as an alternative to JE. The JE stories regularly said, "And Yahweh said to Moses" but the author of P often made it "And Yahweh said to Moses *and* unto Aaron."

What of the denigration of Moses that Friedman asserts? He cites two examples of P putting Moses down for his own purposes.

The first is the story of Moses striking the rock at Meribah. The first time Moses struck the rock, water came out and everything was fine.[i] The second time, enigmatically the Lord said, "Because you did not trust Me ... you will not bring this community to the land that I have set for them."[j] (Friedman's translation) The first story is said to be JE; Moses did well. The second is said to be P; Moses made a grievous error into which poor Aaron was pulled. However, a simple reading of the passages shows that it was not that way at all. Moses and Aaron were involved together from beginning to end.

Below is Friedman's own translation of Numbers 20:2–13 with the priestly text in boldface capitals:

2. AND THERE WAS NOT WATER FOR THE CONGREGATION, AND THEY ASSEMBLED *against Moses and Aaron.*

3. AND THE PEOPLE QUARRELED WITH MOSES, AND THEY SAID, "AND WOULD THAT HE HAD EXPIRED WHEN OUR BROTHERS EXPIRED BEFORE YAHWEH.

4. AND WHY DID YOU BRING YAHWEH'S COMMUNITY TO THIS WILDERNESS TO DIE THERE, WE AND OUR CATTLE?

5. AND WHY DID YOU BRING US FROM EGYPT TO BRING US TO THIS BAD PLACE? IT IS NOT A PLACE OF SEED AND FIG AND VINE AND POMEGRANATE, AND THERE IS NO WATER TO DRINK."

6. AND *Moses and Aaron* CAME BEFORE THE COMMUNITY TO THE ENTRANCE OF THE TENT OF MEETING, AND THEY FELL ON THEIR FACES. AND THE GLORY OF YAHWEH APPEARED TO THEM.

7. AND YAHWEH SPOKE TO MOSES, SAYING,

8. "TAKE THE STAFF AND ASSEMBLE THE CONGREGATION, *you and Aaron your brother* AND YOU SHALL SPEAK TO THE ROCK IN THEIR SIGHT, AND IT WILL GIVE ITS WATER, AND YOU SHALL BRING WATER OUT OF THE ROCK FOR THEM AND YOU SHALL GIVE DRINK TO THE CONGREGATION AND THEIR CATTLE."

9. AND MOSES TOOK THE STAFF FROM BEFORE YAHWEH AS HE COMMANDED HIM.

i. Exod. 17:2–7

j. Num. 20:2–13

10. AND *Moses and Aaron* ASSEMBLED THE COMMUNITY OPPOSITE THE ROCK. AND HE SAID TO THEM, "LISTEN, REBELS, SHALL WE BRING WATER OUT OF THIS ROCK FOR YOU!"

11. AND MOSES LIFTED HIS HAND, AND HE STRUCK THE ROCK WITH HIS STAFF TWICE, AND MUCH WATER WENT OUT. AND THE CONGREGATION AND THEIR CATTLE DRANK.

12. AND YAHWEH SAID TO *Moses and Aaron*, "BECAUSE YOU DID NOT TRUST IN ME TO MAKE ME HOLY IN THE CHILDREN OF ISRAEL'S SIGHT, THEREFORE YOU SHALL NOT BRING THIS COMMUNITY TO THE LAND I HAVE SET FOR THEM."

13. THEY ARE THE WATERS OF MERIBAH, OVER WHICH THE CHILDREN OF ISRAEL QUARRELED WITH YAHWEH, AND HE WAS MADE HOLY AMONG THEM. (my emphasis)[27]

The fact that Moses did the actual striking in no way exonerates Aaron. Whatever happened, the brothers were in it together.

Friedman says,

> Theological interpreters have pondered this passage for centuries, trying to understand just what the nature of Moses' offense was. Was it that he struck the rock instead of talking to it? Was it that he called the people "rebels"? Was it that he said, "Will *we* bring out water from this rock?" instead of "Will God …"? But whatever the offense was, the important point for our present purposes is: it was not in the earlier version of the story. The P author has gone out of his way to introduce it into the story. (And he refers to it again later on in his narrative.) And he has portrayed Aaron as innocent and suffering for Moses' sin."[28]

In the context of this story and the Documentary Hypothesis, the Lord would not say "to Moses *and* Aaron, because you did not believe in Me" if both weren't equally guilty of something. P's supposed penchant for mentioning Moses and Aaron together surely does Aaron no good here.

The second story Friedman sites is when Moses wore his veil upon descending from Mount Sinai:

The Veil of Moses

> The author of P also told a version of the story of the revelation at Mount Sinai. In many ways it was similar to the JE version. The mountain is fiery. Moses goes up alone. But the Priestly writer added a detail concerning Moses at the end of the story. He wrote that there is something unusual about Moses' face when he comes down from the mountain. *When the people see him they are afraid* to come near him. Moses therefore wears a veil from then on whenever

he speaks to the people. That is, according to the P source, whenever we think of Moses during the last forty years of his life, we are supposed to imagine him with a veil over his face.

What is it about Moses' face in the Priestly source? The meaning of the Hebrew term in the text is uncertain. For a long time people understood it to mean that Moses has horns. This gave rise to hundreds of depictions of a horned Moses in art, the most famous of which is the Moses of Michelangelo. Then the term was understood to mean that Moses' skin somehow beams light. Recently an American biblical scholar, William Propp, has assembled evidence that the term probably means that Moses' face is disfigured. This makes sense in the P context because Moses has just stepped out of the cloud surrounding the "glory of Yahweh." The last P narrative before this in the text informs us that the appearance of this "glory of Yahweh" is "like a consuming fire." Moses has been in a fiery zone that is otherwise forbidden to humans. The result is some frightening effect on his skin that people cannot bear to see. In P, Moses is perhaps too ugly to be seen. At minimum, he is not to be pictured. That is not exactly a denigration of Moses. But it is not exactly attractive either.[29] (my emphasis)

It is interesting how Friedman comes close to the cause-effect reason for the veil. He seems doubtful of his own theory of denigration, but that's not why I'm quoting him. Friedman says, "When the people see him [Moses] they are afraid to come near him." He leaves out an important word here: Aaron.

[30]And *Aaron* and all the Israelites saw Moses, and behold, it shone the skin of his face; and they feared to come near to him.

[31]But when Moses called to them, and there returned to him *Aaron* and all the chiefs in the congregation, and Moses spoke to them. (Exod. 34:30–31)

This is a put-down all right, but of Aaron, not Moses. Aaron was so afraid of his brother that he ran away from him. From then on, he was permanently established as second to Moses.

To be accurate, Friedman uses a third example, but it is even weaker. And while I'm on the subject, the verse that started this discussion, Leviticus 10:3, is a complete put-down of Aaron. It emphasizes Moses as God's intermediary, and quotes God as speaking to Moses. Moses is in charge. Moses tells Aaron and his nephews what to do. This relationship continues throughout the section.

My purpose here is not to put down Friedman and his scholarship, but simply to point out that his is a continuation of the selective process used by so many of the critics to make this theory hold water. Actually, things get much more complex if you look at the various explanations of why Moses and Aaron begin to disappear in the following books. The critics have wonderful, if conflicting reasons.[30] If you choose to look them up, keep one thing in mind: there are more references to Moses than to Aaron in the books following the Pentateuch.

Neither statistically, factually, or by selective exposition did Aaron surpass Moses in importance in any of this writing, whether it is J, E, or P. When it's necessary for the critics to force an issue, they must depend on a redactor. This is the case even when a verse, which has been chopped up, actually flows with perfect logic as a whole.

Appendix E

The Phinehas Story

Numbers 25:3–19 tells of the straying of the Israelites and of Phinehas' intervention. The story begins at Shittim when the people "began to commit whoredom with the daughters of Moab" and to worship their god, Baal-peor. The "anger of the Lord glowed against Israel" and a plague ensued, the natural result of the Lord's anger (*af*). According to the story, Phinehas stopped the plague by killing an Israelite man. He had brought a Midianite woman into the tent of meeting and was having intercourse with her there, evidently as a symbol of rebellion. Phinehas drove a spear through both of them.

This horrendously complex story has been labored over by scholars with much disagreement. Some say it is a compilation of the unfinished fragments of three stories. Others say it is one story and that the seeming incompleteness is really the rapid changing of events.

God told Moses to impale the chiefs, now changed to "judges," and to slay anyone who had followed Baal-peor. Both orders were suddenly made unnecessary by Phinehas' action in spearing the Israelite man and the Midianite woman. There is also no real explanation as to why the problem was originally with the "daughters of Moab" but suddenly it was a Midianite woman who came into the tent.[1]

From my point of view, the major misunderstanding is that "covering" was caused by Phinehas' killing of the couple, rather than the normal use of protective materials to stay the plague. Strangely, plague is casually mentioned for the first time here in Numbers 25:8. Even more puzzling is God's acquiescence to the process. Actually, nothing here makes much sense.

The normal processes for protection were not followed. Moses' order to slay the guilty was not accompanied by the order to "fill the hands" as he did in the golden calf episode, and God's original order to impale the chiefs would have no effect on staying the plague because without fail, incense or blood in its proper places, etc., were used for that purpose.[2]

The fact that the Baal-peor story is the only one that varies from the normal processes of protection makes it suspect, all the more because it involves Baalam, the man who refused to curse the Israelites for Balak, king of Moab. In the ensuing war with the Midianites (not the Moabites!) to avenge the Baal-peor incident, Moses said to his officers,

[15]"Have you saved all the females alive?

[16]Behold they were [the cause] to the Israelites *through the word of Balaam* to commit trespass against the Lord regarding the matter of Peor, and the plague was among the congregation." (Num. 31:15–16)

The prevailing theory is that the original Baalam-Balak story, complete with a talking ass, was a combination of ancient folktales and maybe some fact. Certainly, it is strangely placed in Numbers and fraught with contradictions. For example, while Baalam is sometimes portrayed as good and God-fearing and sometimes as evil, in the Baalam-Balak story he is both good and evil, or at least disobedient to the Lord. He was well known to the ancients, and is even found in a non-Israelite story of the eighth century BCE.[3] In this Baal-peor story he is in his evil mode.

After he complained to his officers about saving the women, Moses then told them to kill all the male children and married women, and then to stay outside the camp seven days:

[19]"Decontaminate yourselves … and your captives …

[20]And every garment and every vessel of skin and every work of goats [hair] and every vessel of wood you will decontaminate."

[21]And Eleazar the priest said to the men of war, "This is the statute of the law, which the Lord has commanded Moses.

[22]Nevertheless the gold and silver, the copper, the iron, the tin, and the lead,

[23]Everything that can come into the fire, you will make pass through the fire, and it will be clean. Only with the water of impurity it will be decontaminated and all that cannot come into the fire you will make pass through water.

[24]And you will wash your clothes on the seventh day, and you will be clean; and afterward you will come into the camp." (Num. 31:19–24)

Now this is the normal, great detail that follows the process for becoming clean after killing, in this case following the Baal-peor incident. There is no mention of Balaam in the narrative. I must assume that a large section of that story is missing since out of nowhere Balaam is described in his evil mode. The story takes for granted that the reader knows much more about Moses' activity in relation to Baal-peor than only his query to his officers about sparing the women. What is here has the elements of the Balaam-Balak folktale in it. The complete Baal-peor story would have contained the proper methods of protection: Phinehas would have covered the Israelites with animal blood, incense, etc.; the Lord's order to Moses to impale the chiefs would have been followed by the appropriation of one of the protective materials; and Moses' order for the judges to slay the guilty would have included the requisite protections. Phinehas' killing the couple certainly would not have done the job of staying the plague, not when every other reference in the story is to the familiar chemical protection system.

The fact is Moses knew exactly what to do in the circumstance. He had been through it before. He would have given the order:

> [11]"Take the firepan and put it on the fire from on the altar and carry [it] quickly to the congregation to cover on them; for the anger has gone forth from the Lord; the radiation has begun." (Num. 17:11)

One possibility is that Phinehas, the son of Eleazar, the high priest, did do the proper things to stay the plague, but by killing the errant couple he would then have had to decontaminate himself. This detail could have been omitted as was the whole story of Balaam's involvement. (Lest one wonders why Eleazar didn't do all this, he was the high priest and he certainly couldn't have killed anyone.)

Another possibility is that Phinehas killed the couple and was wrongly credited with staying the plague through the author's misunderstanding of the events. If this were the case, then the radiation would have simply abated with the passage of time.

A hint in Joshua might solve the mystery. During the initial settlement period, the tribes of Reuben, Gad, and the half-tribe of Manasseh built an altar in their appointed territory. The other Israelite tribes misinterpreted this as rebellion and demand,

> [16]"What treachery is this ... in that you have built an altar to rebel this day against the Lord?
>
> [17]*Is the iniquity of Peor* too little for us, *from which we have not cleansed ourselves to this day*, though there came the *radiation* on the congregation of the Lord?" (Josh. 22:16–17)

The radiation from the Baal-peor incident might have abated by itself, but its effects would have lingered at least until the time of the settlement period.

Appendix F

Yom Kippur

A look at *Yom Kippur* might explain why the related *keeper* (cover) concept faded in importance in later times. *Keeper* is only found a few times in a few of the following books, and *Yom Kippur*, the most important day in the Jewish calendar, is found in none, not even Deuteronomy.

The scholarly view is that *Yom Kippur* is a very late development. There are reams of rationale for this thinking. The general argument says that there are references to fasts or fast days in following books, i.e., Zechariah (ca. 520 BCE), Ezra (ca. 458 or 397 BCE), and Nehemiah (ca. 450 BCE), but none of them is on the tenth day of the seventh month, (*Tishri*) as is *Yom Kippur*. For example, Ezekiel 45:19–20 mentions two days for purifying his newly envisioned temple, the first and seventh days of the first month, to "cover the house." Also, during the reign of Hezekiah (ca. 8 BCE), Isaiah 58:3–7 speaks of fasting to afflict the soul in a negative manner, but not specifically on a given day.

J.C. Rylaarsdam says, "Apparently even at this late date the Day was not yet generally recognized, but only by the temple priesthood."[1] He believes it began "as a priestly rite of propitiation," and gradually came to be used as a general atonement day for the people. He also points out that the scapegoat idea was joined to the sacrifice even later.

On the other hand Milgrom, as usual, does a masterful job of refuting these arguments. He feels that *Yom Kippur* was observed in pre-exilic times at Solomon's temple as an annual event for its purgation.[2] *Yom Kippur* would certainly have been observed but not necessarily mentioned, he says, because it fell during the dedication of the temple, and so coincided with the daily purgation rites lasting 14 days. Also, he feels that fasting was not a part of the original rites. He feels that during the era of Solomon's temple it was an occasion for joy, but when it became a time of penitence is unknown. As to the use of the scapegoat for *Azawzel*, he says the system was very ancient and was practiced by many peoples beside the Israelites, albeit for different reasons.

Having investigated the various permutations of *Yom Kippur* in the first four books, I can now address the non-use of *Yom Kippur* in following books and the fading use of *keeper* as a technical word. They both disappear for the same reason.

Yom Kippur

The general laws of *Yom Kippur* are laid out in Leviticus 16. The chapter begins after the untimely death of Aaron's sons. In verse 2, God warns Aaron to protect himself so that he can work "within the veil ... that he die not, for in the cloud I will appear." Verses 3–4 detail the sacrifices and garments needed for that protection. From that point, things get confusing.

Scholars say Leviticus 16 was written by different people stressing their special interests at different times, and only gradually did all the various parts come together as *Yom Kippur*. They point out which disparate verses fit together and they prove their points with the repetitions in Leviticus 16:6, 11, 29a, and 34a.[3] What I've seen is a chaotic situation caused by a terrible, traumatic tragedy—the death of Aaron's sons. The writing itself highlights the confusion that followed their deaths, and from beginning to end Leviticus 16 explains the solution to managing this deadly problem caused by the cloud.

- In Leviticus 16:5, after God's warning for Aaron to protect himself, God suddenly orders Aaron to take two he-goats for a decontamination offering and one ram for a burnt offering from the congregation of the Israelites. This seems strange because as protective elements these offerings were used for the people's protection, not for Aaron's.
- That idea is then dropped, and in verse 6 He tells Aaron to "bring the bullock, which was for himself and [now still another thought] his household."
- Verse 7 veers back to the congregation's two goats, which were set before the Lord at the door of the tent of meeting.
- Lots were then put on the goats in verse 8.
- The one goat chosen "for the Lord" in verse 9 was for a decontamination offering, and the other in verse 10 was to be "set alive before the Lord to cover on him [the goat], and then [to be sent] to *Azawzel* in the wilderness." Never again is the use of a scapegoat mentioned. This makes me think that this was meant to be a one-time event to protect the people from the saturation caused by Aaron's sons' error when the radiance of the Lord appeared. In this sense it was no different from Moses' staff, which was used for various

purposes but never heard of after his death, or the copper serpent that healed the people's snake bites in the wilderness but was never again used in that way.[a] *Azawzel* was discussed in Rabbinic times, and evidently the process was even carried out then, but nothing like it is mentioned elsewhere in the entire Bible.

a. Num. 21:6–9; 2Kgs. 18:4

- Then back to Aaron's bullock, verse 11 repeats verse 6, except now there is the direct order to slaughter it. So maybe that was not a repeat as the scholars argue, but rather just an expansion of that step in that operation.
- Now the next verses, 12–13, go all the way back to verse 2, to the personal protection of Aaron. He was to take fire from the main altar and incense into the super-conditioned place and burn the incense so that its cloud "may cover the covering that is on the *edut* that he die not."
- In verse 14 he was to take his bullock's blood and sprinkle it before the *edut* cover.
- In verse 15 he was to take the goat's blood and sprinkle it on the covering and before it.
- Then, for the first time, verse 16 explains why Aaron was to sacrifice for the people: the blood on the ark cover ...

> [16]"Will cover on the super-conditioned place from the uncleanness of the Israelites and from all their transgressions with all their contaminations, and so will he do for the tent of meeting that dwells with them in the midst of their uncleanness."

The people who had become contaminated were both endangered by the presence of the cloud and were *themselves* a danger to the area that needed to be cleansed. Thus, that area (super-conditioned place, altars, tent, etc.) needed to be protected from them!

- Verse 17 says that no one was to be in the super-conditioned place when Aaron performed the sacrifices.
- It is at this point in verses 18–19 that God orders Aaron to go out to the incense altar just outside the veil and cover it with the blood of the bullock and the goat. He had to put the blood

on the horns of the altar to "cleanse it and condition it from the uncleanness of the Israelites."

- Verses 20–22 detail how the goat was to be sent with the Israelites' impurities into the wilderness, highlighting the need to remove additional impurity.
- Verses 23–28 explain the very logical precautions taken by those who handled the goat and the bullock. They had to wash their clothes and themselves.
- The tragedy that befell Aaron's sons could happen again, so it was necessary to formalize the directions for covering the area to protect the people from the danger caused by the cloud. Verses 29–34 begin the first of the explicit orders regarding what actions to take on the 10th day of the seventh month:

> 29"And it will be to you for a perpetual statute: in the seventh month, on the tenth [day] of the month, you will afflict your souls, and any work you will not do, the native or the stranger that sojourns in the midst of you.
>
> 30For on this day he will cover on you to cleanse you; from all your contamination before the Lord will you be clean.
>
> 31It is a Sabbath of solemn rest to you, and you will afflict your souls [as] a perpetual statute.
>
> 32And [there] will cover the priest who will be anointed and whose hand will be filled to be priest in his father's stead, and he will put on the linen garments, the conditioning garments.
>
> 33And he will cover the super-conditioned place and the tent of meeting and he will cover the altar; and on the priests and on all the people of the assembly he will cover.
>
> 34And this will be to you for a perpetual statute, to cover on the Israelites, because of all their contamination once in the year." And he did as the Lord had commanded Moses.

While these orders are explicit, they are nevertheless summarized. There is no detail as to sacrifices. There is no mention of the actual day, *Yom Kippur*. There are, though, new instructions regarding "afflicting the soul," resting, and performing this process in the future.

Rather than a hodge podge by various writers, I think that Leviticus 16 may be a verbal evolution of the protective process, incrementally adding detail and purpose. That is, first God handled the immediate problem verbally: *Aaron, this is what you have to do to protect yourself and those immediately nearby from a repeat of the radiation of your sons.* Then, at some point a scribe wrote down those verbal instructions exactly, including whatever repetitions were made either for emphasis or inadvertently. Finally, at an even later point, these instructions were formalized into a systematic operation for *future* priests in the event of repeated visitations of the cloud.

This is also what happened earlier at Mount Sinai. Out of the uncertainty, chaos, and dire necessity came the first codified rules for protection. From those instructions given as far back as Mount Sinai to Leviticus 16 and beyond emerged three protective factors that eventually merged into *Yom Kippur*: (1) the laws of Sabbath, (2) the sacrifice for rest smelling, and 3) the peace offering.

The Laws of Sabbath

The purpose of the Sabbath day was to rest, and rest was for protection. The concept goes all the way back to the Creation story. Genesis 2:3 says, "And God blessed the seventh day and conditioned it [meaning, He made it a conditioning day] because in it He rested from all His work, which God had created to make." Observing the Sabbath became law in Exodus.

At the very beginning of the Israelites' journey in Exodus 16:23–30, the Lord gave them the law regarding when to gather manna. It was to be collected for six days, but not on the seventh day, which was a rest day, a conditioning Sabbath, *kawdash shabawtone*.[b] Exodus 20:8–11 shows the Lord giving the law of the Sabbath day from the mountain directly to the people, again with the conditioning note: "Remember the Sabbath day to condition it [make it a conditioning day]." In Exodus 23:12, the Lord gives part of the Sabbath law to Moses in the thick cloud on Mount Sinai. Sabbath is mentioned in Exodus 34:21, but it is probably a repeat of Exodus 23:12. Amazingly, in Exodus 31:13–17, at the end of the instructions for conditioning Aaron and his sons, there is suddenly another long warning to keep the Sabbath day.

b. *shabawtone*, 7677; Exod. 16.23

> [13]"My Sabbaths you will keep ... to know that I am the Lord who conditions you ...
>
> [14]You will keep the Sabbath for it is a conditioner for you ...
>
> [15]Six days may work be done, but on the seventh day is a Sabbath of solemn rest (*shabat shabawtone*) conditioner for

the Lord. Everyone doing work on the Sabbath day will surely be put to death."

¹⁶And the Israelites will keep the Sabbath to observe the Sabbath for their generations, a perpetual covenant.

¹⁷It is a sign forever between Me and the Israelites, for in six days the Lord made the heavens and the earth and on the seventh day He rested and was refreshed.

Just before the Lord explained how to build the tabernacle and furnishings, seemingly out of nowhere He repeated the Sabbath law: the seventh day is to be a "conditioner for you, a Sabbath of solemn rest for the Lord."[c] This time He added the admonition not to kindle a fire on the Sabbath day!

c. Exod. 35:2–3

So, in a relatively short space and time, 14 mentions of the word Sabbath occur in five scenarios (six counting the possible repetition). In all these references, the Sabbath is a conditioning day. It was resting that did the conditioning and thus protecting.

Rest-Smelling

The second factor relating to *Yom Kippur* was the sacrifice for rest-smelling, *rayach neechoach*. *Neechoach* means "restful," and along with the Sabbath, it was part of the protective system of resting. The rest-smelling sacrifice was used to condition Aaron and his sons in Exodus 29:18, 25, and 41. The Lord gave the orders for conditioning to Moses when he was on the mountain the first time receiving the laws concerning the tabernacle and the priests.

Peace Offerings

Peace offerings, the third *Yom Kippur* factor, were used for both rest-smelling and covering. They are included in the pre-tent altar of earth/stone sacrificing laws in Exodus 20:24. They are also found in Exodus 24:5, in the sacrifices that the young men performed before Moses went up to get the tabernacle laws. In addition, they are in Exodus 29:28 as part of the heave offerings, which are in the same section of the chapter as the rest-smelling sacrifices.

Keeper ... Kippur

Following this last peace offering reference is the first reference to cover (*keeper*). It is found in Exodus 29:33 relative to the hand filling of Aaron and his sons. Exodus 29:36 and 37 are the second and third references to covering the main altar. The fourth is Exodus 30:10 relative to the incense altar. This one is very important because it has long been considered the first reference to *Yom Kippur*. I doubt it. I think verse 10 is part of this verbal evolution toward *Yom Kippur*. Notice that Exodus 30:1–6 is the order to manufacture the incense altar. The verses that immediately follow, including verse 10, indicate what Aaron had to do at the time the altar was completed:

> [7]And Aaron will burn upon it incense of spices; every morning, when he dresses the lamps, he will burn it.
>
> [8]And when Aaron sets up the lamps toward evening, he will burn it, a *perpetual* incense before the Lord for your generations.
>
> [9]You will not offer upon it strange incense, nor burnt offering, nor meal offering; and a drink offering you will not pour upon it.
>
> [10]And Aaron will cover on its horns once in the year; with the blood of the decontamination offering of covering, once in a year will he cover on it for your generations; it is super conditioned for the Lord."

Continual vs. Perpetual

What timeframe is the Bible referring to here? The answer is given in verse 8 and the question is settled in verse 10. *At the time of the manufacture of the incense altar*, Aaron was to burn the incense daily and apply the blood once within that year. This is different from the day of *Yom Kippur*, which would be observed annually.

An error in interpretation makes this difficult to understand. The key word is *tawmeed*, traditionally translated in Exodus 30:8 as "perpetual."[d] Green, Hertz, Soncino, Owens, and Strong's agree. JPS says it's "regular" and Kohlenberger translates it

d. *tawmeed*, 8548

"regularly." However, the idea of *tawmeed* is actually "continual."
The word that is translated "perpetual" or "forever" is *olawm*.[e]

e. *olawm*, 5769

There are basic differences between *tawmeed* and *olawm*, but this is the point: *Tawmeed* ("continual") refers to something occurring continually *at the time* (unless the writer clearly indicates that it is also to occur in the future.)[4] *Olawm* ("perpetual") refers to something occurring continually at the time *as well as* in the future. The words are never interchangeable!

A phrase that can go with both *olawm* and *tawmeed* is "for your generations," *l'dorotaychem*. It is used in both Exodus 30:8 and 10.

L'dorotaychem is used with *olawm* over 30 times in Genesis, Exodus, Leviticus, and Numbers, and almost always with "statute" (*choke*).[f] For example, Exodus 30:21 says, "And they will wash their hands and their feet [so] that they will not die, and it will be to them a perpetual statute (*chawk olawm*), to him and to his seed for their generations (*l'dorotawm*)." Another example is Exodus 40:14–15, which summarizes the rules for anointing the priests. While "statute" (*choke*) isn't specifically mentioned, there is no doubt that the future is meant:

f. *choke*, 2706

> [14]"And his [Aaron's] sons you will bring near, and you will clothe them with coats.
>
> [15]And you will anoint them as you have anointed their father that they may be priests to Me; and [this] will be ... for a perpetual (*olawm*) priesthood for their generations."[g]

g. cf., Exod. 28:43, 29:9, 28–30

Where *tawmeed* is used within a future context, it is disconnected from "statute" (*choke*). The future idea is clarified using *chawk olawm* at the end of such verses.

> [20]"And you will command the Israelites that they take to you olive oil ... for the light to set up a lamp continually (*tawmeed*).[21] In the tent of meeting ... Aaron and his sons will arrange it [the lamp] from evening to morning [referring just to them at that time, but then ends with...], a perpetual statute (*chookat olawm*) for their generations among the Israelites."[h] (Exod. 27:20–21)

h. cf., Lev. 24:3–4, 8

Over and over this formula is used, from the first order to observe the exodus, through all the conditioning days, to the warning for the Israelites not to come near the tent again (thus assigning the Levites to the task).[i] Wherever *tawmeed* means to do something in future generations, it explicitly says so.

i. Exod. 12:14; e.g., Lev. 23:14, 21, 31, 41; Num. 18:22–23

The only possible exception is Exodus 29:42, which calls the items for conditioning the main altar "a continual (*tawmeed*) burnt offering for your generations" as one thought.[5] All other references to burnt offerings are separate from the phrase "for your generations." When statute is mentioned, the burnt offerings are to be done when ordered and in future generations. For example, all instructions to perform burnt offerings in Leviticus 1–3 are a perpetual statute, *olawm chock*, per Leviticus 3:17.[j] Likewise, all the sacrifices in Numbers 28 are to be done in the future, the passage beginning, "When you will come into the land … that I will give you."[k]

j. See also Lev. 6:11, 15; Heb. 6:18, 22

k. Num. 15:2

So, why isn't Exodus 29:42 speaking of something to be done by future generations even though it plainly says "for your generations?"

(1) It does not mention "perpetual statute" (*olawm chock*) in this or following verses. Instead, it says the burnt offerings are to be "continual" (*tawmeed*).

(2) In context, Exodus 29:28–30 is the "perpetual statute" of the heave offering and it indicates the conditioning garments for Aaron and "the son who takes his [Aaron's] place as priest."

(3) Exodus 29:31–41 describes the conditioning process Aaron and his sons were to follow right then.

(4) Exodus 29:42 then labels the conditioning sacrifices as occurring continually at the time for the protection of future generations from the present danger! What danger? The very next verse, 43, says the Lord will meet with the Israelites there at the tent "and it will be conditioned against My *kawbode* [radioactivity with genetic effects]." Thus, the absence of the perpetual statute clause in Exodus 29:42 underscores that the verse is speaking of what must be done in the present to protect future generations. Likewise, the timeframe of Exodus 30:8 and 10 was the present. The criteria are all there: (1) In verse 8 *tawmeed* does not mean "perpetual," but "continual" as it always does. (2) There is no

mention of the perpetual statute, *olawm chawk*. (3) Only Aaron was to burn the incense on the altar every morning. There was no mention of his sons. (4) Most importantly, only Aaron was to cover the incense altar with the blood "once in a year" per verse 10. So the conclusion is inescapable. Just as Moses alone was to cover the main altar during the hand filling service to protect future generations from the effects of the cloud, Aaron alone was to cover the incense altar.[1]

l. Exod. 29:36

Genetics

Now as part of the *Yom Kippur* evolution discussion, let me briefly elaborate on the genetic implications of the radioactivity in the cloud. The breeches worn by the priests protected their genitals from radiation when they were working in the dangerous part of the tent, "that they don't carry the impurity and die."[m]

m. Exod. 28:42–43

This genetic concern was stated earlier in the Sinai episode. Exodus 19:24 is the warning to keep everyone away from the mountain lest the Lord "break forth among them." The next verses, Exodus 20:1–14, begin the first version of the Ten Commandments, and the very first issue dealt with is the warning against manufacturing false gods. The reason for this is that when one is in a danger area and he sacrifices uselessly to idols instead of correctly to the Lord, he is still vulnerable to the danger. That happened almost immediately after the warning during the golden calf episode. However, the warning goes much further. Exodus 20:3 and 4 are the exhortations against having other gods and making graven images. Then verse 5 says,

> [5]"You will not prostrate yourself to them for I the Lord your God am a jealous God visiting the impurity of fathers on children on the third [generation] and on the fourth [generation] of haters of Me."

Although the meaning of this verse and its repeats have always been discussed and explained in philosophical, ethical terms, there is much disagreement as to exactly what it means.[n] However, it seems perfectly logical that this is about a physical phenomenon in light of a) its juxtaposition to danger warnings,

n. cf., Deut. 5:9, 6:14–15; Exod. 34:7; Num. 14:186

b) the nature of impurity, c) the generational effect of radiation, and d) the protective precautions later taken by the priests.[7]

In addition, this verse leads directly to the Sabbath laws, to warnings against some contaminations that can cause susceptibility to impurity, then to the danger itself, to the order to sacrifice, and (full circle!) to the genetic danger that accompanies sacrificing: "And you will not go up by steps on My altar with your nakedness uncovered on it."[o] This, too, evolves into the breeches law when there was need for protection in the tent area. There probably were steps or a ramp up to the main altar. More changes with necessity! Also, most striking is the famous fact that if one did not break the laws, the Lord would show "kindness to thousands [i.e., the thousandth generation] to those who love Me and keep My commandments."[p]

Just after the golden calf episode with its radiation causing danger, when Moses went back up the mountain with the new tablets and again exposed himself to the cloud, the verse revisiting the impurity of the fathers on the third and fourth generations is repeated.[q] Again there is a warning against false gods, but this time specifically. The Israelites were to destroy other people's places of worship when they occupied their lands to formalize the rest days—Passover, Sabbath, and the other festivals. There was no mention of *Yom Kippur* here because, so far, it was not a rest day, only a nameless, altar-cleansing, covering process. Later, in Numbers 14:18, the idea of visiting impurity on following generations is repeated when the people rebelled after hearing frightening news from the spies Moses had sent to Canaan. The Lord became angry with them for their lack of faith. When His radiance appeared, Moses referred to His cloud and quoted His own words about being slow to anger and visiting impurity, etc., in defense of the people. In other words, once again danger was present. Deuteronomy 5:9 is only a much later repeat by Moses of events that had happened in the wilderness in his farewell address to the people. All of this again highlights the fact that impurity, when visited by the Lord, was not only dangerous at the time but also had a future, generational, genetic effect.

o. Exod. 20:8–10, 13, 18–21, 24, 26

p. Exod. 20:6, Deut. 5:10

q. Exod. 34:7

Now what does all this mean? Remember the problems leading to vast changes in the protection laws at Mount Sinai? The original laws included a few sacrifices that produced a resting condition. Then problems with the cloud, its radiance, and the impurity it generated led to the evolution of these sacrifices into the sophisticated process that became the life work of the priests. The expanded laws included instructions for building the tabernacle and an apparatus for funneling most of the cloud to a central place so that communication with the Lord would be reasonably safe then and for future generations. At exactly the time everything should have finally worked perfectly, it did not. Aaron's sons died, and Leviticus 16 was the next response.

So in Leviticus 10, after Nadab and Abihu were burned, Moses becomes angry with Aaron because he did not eat the proper sacrifices right after his sons' deaths.[r] Then Leviticus 11 elaborates on what the Israelites were to eat, i.e., which animals were considered clean versus unclean. Leviticus12 explains what the pregnant woman had to do to come near the tent. The two long chapters that follow (13, 14) discuss how to care for the radiated person, house, and things. Chapter 15 describes what made men and women clean or unclean, affecting the safety level of communication with God. And chapter 16 continues to list the new laws that were established "after the death of the two sons of Aaron." In other words, chapters 10 through 16 are not an interruption but an explanation and logical expansion or evolution of operating rules in light of what had happened.

Now I have suggested that Exodus 30:10 is not a description of *Yom Kippur* per se but rather a temporary system for protecting (1) the priests from the high doses of radiation released during the hand filling operation, and (2) their offspring from genetic problems: "He will cover on it [the incense altar] for your generations."[8] The annual bullock blood offering of Exodus 30:10 is not consistent with that of Leviticus 16:18 where the bullock's blood was mixed with the goat's blood and sprinkled on the altar. The purposes for the two sacrifices were different: Exodus 30:10 was to protect the priests from the cloud; Leviticus 16:18 was to

r. Lev. 10:16–17

protect the altar and area from any people with impurities who could contaminate it. Leviticus 16:19 says, "And he will cleanse it and condition it from the uncleanness of the Israelites." The Exodus 30 discussion moves from a general rule about the newly built altar to a specific rule to use a heavier decontaminant because the people with impurities could contaminate the altar. This rule became an element in the formalization of the *Yom Kippur* rules. The most important new rule among those formalized is in Leviticus 16:31. Rest was added:

> [29]"And it will be a perpetual statute; in the seventh month in the 10th day of the month ... you will do no work ...

> [30]For on this day he will cover you ...

> [31]It is a Sabbath of rest." (Lev. 16:29–31)

Rest, too, was a perfectly logical part of the evolution, right at the post-Nadab/Abihu episode. Rest was emphasized from the very beginning in the simple laws of Sabbath, rest-smelling, and peace sacrifices. They each resulted in resting and covering. Adding the strict admonition of rest to the protective sacrificial laws in the face of the foregoing problems seems not only logical but absolutely necessary.

The first reference to *Yom Kippur* using its name is in Leviticus 23:27. It immediately follows the laws pertaining to the other holidays called "set feasts."[s] It was natural that Leviticus 23:27 s. Lev. 23:1–26 came after the Leviticus 16:18 reference, which commands Aaron to cover (*keeper*) the altar though it doesn't mention *Yom Kippur* (*keeper*) specifically.

Scholars tell us that *Yom Kippur* is in the "Holiness Code" or "H Code," which they say runs from Leviticus 17 to 26. They say these chapters were written by priests differing from the P group at another time for another purpose. In another work on the priests, I intend to discuss this Code in detail. For now I will only make a few points as it pertains to the *Yom Kippur* discussion. My conclusion is this: It is not a separate section; it is all part of the general flow of the laws throughout Leviticus. This flow has natural divisions of rules and regulations:

- Chapters 1–3 speak of the Israelites' voluntary "oblations" and warn them against eating blood.
- Chapters 4–5 are offerings for various contaminations.
- Chapter 6 begins with "the law of the burnt offering."
- Chapter 7 begins with "the trespass offering."
- Chapter 8 begins with the anointing of Aaron and his sons.
- Chapters 9–10 begin with elders, Aaron, and his sons performing sacrifices for the appearance of the Lord; they end with the deaths of Aaron's sons.
- Chapter 11 speaks of the dietary laws.
- Chapters 12–15 are laws pertaining to unclean people, including the burned person.
- Chapter 16 details the protection for coming into the super-conditioned place and ends with the "Sabbath of rest," which became *Yom Kippur*.
- Chapter 17, which is said to be the beginning of the so-called H Code, establishes the rule to bring sacrifices to the tent of meeting. It also repeats the prohibition against eating blood.
- Chapter 18 prohibits intercourse with certain people because it makes the land unclean and has genetic ramifications.
- Chapter 19 addresses many different concerns including idolatry, civil laws, the Ten Commandments, the corner of one's fields (they are for the poor and stranger), familiar spirits and wizards, Sabbaths (said *twice*), etc. It also repeats that all the Israelites were to be conditioned because the Lord is.
- Chapter 20 repeats the spirits and wizards law and the intercourse law, adding punishments.
- Chapters 21–22 are rules for the priests.
- Chapter 23 tells of the "set feasts," repeats the laws of Sabbaths and the corners of fields, and formally introduces the law of "*Yom Kippur*."
- Chapter 24 tells of the menorah, the 12 cakes, punishing the man who blasphemed the Name, and it introduces the talion concept (law of retaliation, "eye for an eye").
- Chapter 25 tells of the Sabbath year in the seventh year, the jubilee Sabbath in the 50th year in the seventh month at *Yom Kippur* (where there will be trumpet blowing), and civil rules.
- Chapter 26 (the last of the H Code) repeats the warning against idols and the Sabbaths statement. It also tells how the Lord will walk in their midst if

rules are kept and repeats how the Lord will bring a multitude of disasters on the people if rules are broken.

• Chapter 27 talks of the vow that results in donations to the priests. Actually, the flow of laws runs from the latter part of Exodus into Numbers. There are bumps in the road, and the critics have sliced and diced the chapters to show by language, style, repetition, ideas, and seeming contradictions that many hands were at work with different motives in mind. Maybe so, but I think that the entire work, including the H Code, holds together. (See Appendix H for detail on the H Code.)

"Set Feasts"

Leviticus 23, in the discussion of the set feasts, was included in what had been termed H. It, too, was part of the expansion process and not necessarily written by a different hand. In addition to the first mention of *Yom Kippur*, the rest day that is incorrectly called the New Year (*Rosh hashana*) was first mentioned in Leviticus 23:24. It is really the first day of the *seventh* month. Only Ezekiel 40:1 used the term *Rosh hashana*, and he referred to a jubilee year, not a new year.

Now, in Deuteronomy 16:10 and 13, the "set feasts" are eventually called the Feast of Unleavened Bread (*Chag haMatzot*), Feast of Weeks (*Chag Shawvuot*), and Feast of Booths (*Succot*). However, until they get to Deuteronomy, as far as names go, the road is very bumpy, and *Chag haMatzot* remains so. For the record, Exodus 23:15 begins with *Chag haMatzot* along with Feast of Harvest (*Chag hawKawtzeer*), and verse 16 lists the Feast of Ingathering (*Chag haAwseef*). The next laws call the feasts *Chag hamatzot* in Exodus 34:18 and in Exodus 34:22, *Chag Shawvuot* and *Chag haAwseef*. In Leviticus 23:6, it is *Chag haMatzot* followed by a general description in verse 10 of what to do when you come into the land and reap its harvest (*k'tseeraw*). (You wave a sheaf and sacrifice on the day after the Sabbath—which Sabbath is not specified.) Then, in seven weeks, i.e., without specifically mentioning the term, on *Shawvuot* you make additional offerings, have a conditioning convocation, and rest. This is followed by *Chag haSuccot* in verse 34. The next law is in Numbers 28 where there is the usual *Chag haMatzot* in verse 17 (actually "*a chag* in which *matzot* will be eaten") and in verse 26, the "day of first fruits … in your weeks (*shawvuotaychem*)." *Shawvuotaychem* means *Chag Shawvuot*, but there is no specific mention of the word *Shawvuot* (though the date and sacrifices are described). All these variations lead finally to their aforementioned appellations in Deuteronomy 16. In addition, the exact time of these events varies from general statements, e.g., the end of the year, to specific days, e.g., "15th day of the seventh month." These variations are again explained as being the result of the different strands written at different times, including post-exilic, depending on the scholar. The arguments are compelling and possibly irrefutable, except there still isn't much agreement. And several words are interesting regarding timing. Take the term "set feasts." *Moahday* is primarily translated "appointed times" or "seasons."[t] Thus, a *chag* was held at an "appointed time," e.g., "*Chag hamatzot* you will keep … at the appointed time (*l'moade*) of the month of *awviv*."[u] Going all the way back to Genesis 1:14, "And the Lord said, 'Let there be lights in the expanse of the heaven to divide between the day and the night, and let them be for signs and for seasons (*ool'moadeem*) and for days and for years.'" Also in Genesis are the two stories of the Lord's promise to Abraham that Sarah would bear a son (Isaac) in her old age. The first says, "And My covenant I will establish with Isaac whom Sarah will bear to you at this set time (*l'moade*) in the next year."[v] The second says, "Is anything too hard for the Lord? At the set time (*la-moade*) I will return to you … and to Sarah [will be] a son."[w] The significance of these two references is that, according to the critics, the first is P and the second J. So, regardless of the age (and J is considered the older), the word was in general use from early times.

In Leviticus 23:2, 4, 37, 44 and Numbers 15:31 *moaday* is used as "feasts." Leviticus 23:4 uses it in both contexts. "These are the set feasts (*moaday*) of the Lord, the conditioning convocations, which you will proclaim in their appointed seasons (*b'moadawm*)."

As to "tent of meeting" (*ohel moade*), its other meaning of an "appointed place" is expressed. Aside from Exodus, Leviticus, Numbers, and Deuteronomy, the tent is mentioned in Joshua, 1 Samuel, and 1 Kings. I'll leave aside the discussion of when Joshua was written and mention that Szikzai calls the 1 Samuel 2:22 J.[9] So *moade* was not a late word used in exilic or post-exilic

t. *moahday* (pl.) from *moade*, 4150

u. Exod. 23:15; cf., Exod. 34:18

v. Gen. 17:21

w. Gen. 18:14

time and then "cast back" by groups living then. Rather, it was an old word used throughout for a specific purpose.

Finally, other languages were familiar with *moade*. It was common in the Ugaritic as *m'd*. Driver translates *m'd* as "convocation" in the Baal epic, but in a footnote says, "Literally 'the assembly' or 'totality of the appointed meeting.'"[10] There is no mention of "feasts" in the translations.

There are other Hebrew words closely related to *moade*, which basically mean "appoint, meet, congregation" or "time." *Yawadh* is a verb meaning "appoint, meet."[x] *Aydaw* means "congregation."[y] *Ahd* has the primary meaning of "time," among many others, including "to, until."[z] Note that none of them is related to "feasts."[11]

x. *yawadh*, 3259; e.g., Exod. 29:42, 30:6

y. *aydaw*, 5712; e.g., Exod. 12:3, 6

z. *ahd*, 5703

With these words in mind, CAD shows the word *adannu*, which in Old Babylonian and the Middle Assyrian era forward means, "1. A moment in time at the end of a specified period, 2. A period of time of predetermined length or characterized by a sequence of specific events." CAD shows an Old Babylonian quote that says, "PN did not bring the lady on the day appointed to him," as well as other quotes specifically referring to seasons.[12]

Sticking to the idea of "events happening in a fixed time" seems to agree nicely with *moade*'s contemporaries, relatives, and ancestors. It was not only an old word, but possibly borrowed. *Chag* means "feasts" and was always connected with the three "appointed times."[aa] In this combination, *chag* certainly indicated celebrations, often called "pilgrimage festivals." (Arabic *hajj* is "pilgrimage.") The word *chag* itself is found as early as Exodus 10:9 when Moses told Pharaoh that the Israelites had to leave Egypt: "For we [must hold] a *chag* to the Lord." In the golden calf episode, Aaron called out "a *chag* to the Lord tomorrow!"[ab]

aa. *chag*, 2282

ab. Exod. 32:5

In its verb form, *chagag* is found in exactly the same connection even earlier in Exodus 5:1.[ac] The connotation is "to hold or keep a feast." *Chag* and *chagag* are used together in the very first reference about what would become of the three feasts. This is the *Chag hamatzot* law following the Passover (*Pesach*) described in Exodus 12:14: "and you will keep (*chagoetam*) a *chag* to the

ac. *chagag*, 2287

Lord." Exodus 23 is linked for the very first time with the other two feasts where it is finally called by its formal name, *Chag hamatzot*.[ad] There is no question, though, that Exodus 12:17 means the same thing: "And you will observe the unleavened bread (*hamazot*)."[ae]

ad. Exod. 23:15

ae. cf., Exod. 13:6

Chag and *chagag* are also found in Leviticus, Numbers, Deuteronomy, and a number of the following books as early as 1 Samuel 30:16. These terms signify sacrifice in Exodus 23:18 where it is "fat of My feast" (*chayleb chagi*).[af] In Psalm 107:27, *chag* means to "reel" like a drunken man.

af. cf., Mal. 2:3

Of great interest are the middle Egyptian words *h3g*, "be glad," and *h3g3g*, "rejoice."[13] These could be forerunners of *chag* and *chagag* to signify the emotions that accompanied the feasts. Perhaps Pharaoh became intransigent and angry because Moses used *chagag* in connection with his request for the Israelites to leave and sacrifice in the wilderness.

So, as with *moade*, *chag* is a very old, possibly borrowed word. The critics note that many of the references that include it are called J.

Finally, again, there is the concept of rest. The *chag*s in Exodus 23 did not mention rest, but from the earlier Exodus 12:14–20, there were already rest days: "And the first day a conditioning convocation, and on the seventh day a conditioning convocation will be to you; all work will not be done in them." So it must have been taken for granted that at least one of the three *chag*s in Exodus 23 included rest. The three references in Exodus 34 do not mention rest either. However, since the general idea of *Chag hamatzot* is that "which I commanded you at the appointed time (*l'moade*) of the month of *aviv*," the rules for rest in Exodus 12:14–20 are implied.[ag] In Leviticus 23, all the *chag*s have rest days.

ag. Exod. 34:18

One day is included here that has not been added—the Sabbath. It starts off the list. It has been called an appendage to the chapter, but it is also included at the beginning of the Exodus 23 and 34 references in just the same manner.[14] It could be said that just as the first *Chag hamatzot* reference included rest and then became part of the three-*chag* process, the inclusion of the Sabbath at the beginning of the law of *chags* from Exodus 23 on emphasizes rest, even though the Sabbath was not a *chag* and certainly not a pilgrimage. As the environment became ever more dangerous, rest was described as a key part of the other two *chags'* protective processes. Then the first day of the seventh month and *Yom Kippur*, the epitome of rest days, were added to the list.

One more protective measure began to appear here— sacrifices, but only some of them. The sacrifices for the first day of the seventh month, *Rosh hashana*, as well as those for *Yom Kippur* at this stage of the development of the law are only called fire offerings.[ah] It's true that Leviticus 16 mentioned the goats and bullock, but this was directly related to protection from the problems caused by the deaths of Aaron's sons. When the law for the future was given, it only said that future priests should cover the super-conditioned place, tent, priests, and people, but not how.[ai]

ah. Lev. 23:27

ai. Lev. 16:29–32

For the 14th day of the first month, assume that *Pesach* here means the older offerings of the lamb.[aj] On the 15th day, *Chag hamatzot*, a fire offering, was ordered.[ak] One *omer* (measure) of the first harvest was offered "on the morrow after the rest day," as well as a he-lamb for a burnt offering, a meal offering for rest-smelling, and a drink offering.[al] *Shawvuot* recounts a full-complement of sacrifices.[am] However, for *Succot* there is again only a mention of fire offerings.[an]

aj. Lev. 23:5

ak. Lev. 23:8

al. Lev. 23:11–13

am. Lev. 23:16–19

an Lev. 23:34–36

I have noted considerable and logical expansion of the rest-sacrifice process. As for *Yom Kippur* and the sacrifices, the mention of fire offerings in Leviticus 23:5–36 represents only a slight expansion of detail. The next mention of *Yom Kippur* is just that, a mention in relation to the jubilee. In the 50th year, possessions and people were returned to original owners and to freedom: "You will let resound a *shofar* blowing in the seventh month on the tenth day of the month, on *yom hakeepureem*."[ao] That brief mention ends the references to *Yom Kippur* in Leviticus.

ao. Lev. 25:9

The next time *Yom Kippur* appears is in the context of the fully expanded rest-sacrifice process. Numbers 28–29 list all the occasions and purposes for the sacrifices. They were performed at the beginning of the months (added here), on the Sabbath, *Pesach*, *Chag hamatzot*, *Shawvuot*, the first day of the seventh month, *Yom Kippur*, and *Succot*. Two clues lead me to believe that these chapters were known to be a repeat of every familiar occasion, albeit with much more detail. (1) With the exception of *Pesach*, none of the holidays is mentioned by name, "though it is obvious they are being referred to."[15] (2) Living in booths for *Succot* is not mentioned in Numbers 29:12–38 among all the other detail for the 15th day of the seventh month.[16]

Expansion in Numbers

Why the repeat? Why the detail? Why the expansion? Friedman and B. A. Levine assign these chapters to R; the Jewish Encyclopedia, with all the layers of P, concludes these chapters were compiled by a redactor; Milgrom says they are P.[17]

There is almost universal complaint about Numbers' lack of organization and its historical problems. Milgrom agrees there are problems, but also sees a general organizational pattern to the book. He says that its use of certain terms and institutions indicates great antiquity in parts of Numbers.[18] The fact remains, there are differences between the sacrifices here and those previously outlined, and these differences generally mean additions. Why? What has really happened here?

The book of Numbers gives a general outline of the wanderings of the Israelites. It's not perfect. As always, it represents human beings' observations of what happened and is dependent on their ability to pass that information along. From my point of view, though, there are some large-scale events that seem to add up to a general pattern. Keeping in mind the ever-growing danger from Sinai to Aaron's sons, Numbers continues to explore and expand on the problem. Here is a brief summary:

(1) Chapters 3, 8, and 18 assign the tent service to the Levites, basically "to cover on the Israelites that there will not be …

radiation when the Israelites come near to the super-conditioned place."[ap]

ap. Num. 8:19

(2) Chapter 9 tells of the constant presence of the cloud over the tabernacle once it had been set up.[aq] The cloud presented a danger that was not there before.

aq. Num. 9:15–22

(3) In chapter 11:4–44, the people want meat, not manna. The Lord commanded Moses to tell the people, "Condition yourselves for tomorrow, and you will eat flesh."[ar] Then, "the Lord came down in a cloud and took the spirit that was in him [Moses] and put it on seventy men."[as] Later, "a wind went forth from the Lord and it brought quails."[at] The people gathered the quails and "the flesh was yet between their teeth ... when the anger of the Lord glowed against the people, and the Lord smote the people with a very great *plague*."[au] Evidently the people did not condition themselves since there is no mention of either sacrifice or cleansing at this time. So a natural thing happened, which was interpreted by the writer(s) as punishment: a) the cloud came down, b) a wind blew in the quails *and* the cloud to the people, and c) the unprotected people got the "plague."[19]

ar. Num. 8:18

as. Num. 8:25

at. Num. 8:31

au. Num. 11:33

(4) In chapter 12 the cloud descended, causing Miriam to get radiated.

(5) Chapters 13–14 bring us once again to the story of the men Moses sent to "spy out the land of Canaan."[av] The radiance of the Lord appeared.[aw] Then Numbers 14:37 states, "Those men died who brought an evil report of the land by [the] *plague* before the Lord." Actually, this just scratches the surface of the story.

av. Num. 13:2

aw. Num. 14:10

(6) Chapters 16 and 17 detail the revolt of Korach, Dathan, and Abiram, which ended in the appearance of the cloud, the plague, and the consequent deaths of "fourteen thousand and seven hundred beside those that died about the matter of Korach."[ax] It has to be understood that the innocent died with the guilty. (This catastrophe was followed in chapter 18 by the third reference to the Levites serving at the tent so the Israelites wouldn't come near it and die.)

ax. Num. 17:42, 46–50; Heb. 17:7, 11–15

(7) Many people die from the radiation mentioned in chapter 17. So it seems natural that chapter 19 instructs how to combine the red cow's ashes with water to decontaminate a person who had touched a dead body.

(8) Chapter 25 is the story of the apostasy of the Israelites through their worship of Baal-peor. "And the anger of the Lord glowed against Israel."[ay] A plague began, "And those that died by the plague were four and twenty thousand."[az] Evidently the people did not condition themselves since there is no mention of sacrifice or cleansing at this time.

Each of the above events is new. Whenever the cloud appeared, more radiation accumulated, usually resulting in immediate, dire consequences. If this communication system was to continue, it was logical for chapters 28 and 29 to repeat and expand on the essential protections, especially considering the Sinai and Nadab-Abihu problems. One writer or 20, ulterior motives or not, these events override biases and flow together.

Zeroing in on *Yom Kippur*, the same logic holds true. It was equally essential to repeat the rest component in Leviticus 23 and then expand from the generality of the fire offering to the specifics of the sacrifices necessary to observe the day. After the book of Numbers, *Yom Kippur* is never mentioned again. There is not a word or even a hint of it in Deuteronomy. Only the Sabbath is mentioned in Deuteronomy's version of the Ten Commandments. As to rest, it is parroted in the *Pesach* law, but only on the seventh day, and there is no specific reference to *Chag hamatzot*. Theories as to when and why Deuteronomy was written have been often and clearly set out. Its emphasis is quite different from other books. It is not particularly interested in the idea of rest. It demands that activities such as participation in festivals and sacrifices be done at a central location. There are also strange historical references. For example, in Deuteronomy 27:4–6, Moses is said to have commanded the Israelites to build an altar of stones for sacrifice when they had finally passed over the Jordan. This was just what was done at Sinai forty years earlier before the tabernacle was built. There would have been

ay. Num. 25:3

az. Num 25:9

no reason to do this at a time when the entire tent apparatus was available.[ba]

Despite the Deuteronomy 27:4–6 example, 99 percent of Deuteronomy does not present active history. It is really a review of what happened in the wilderness and a warning of what will happen in the future if the law is not observed. The Lord only spoke briefly to Moses, and basically those were personal conversations.[bb] So, other than taking us to the end of the wilderness journey and Moses' death, there is little or no description of what actually happened during the time covered. That means the development in Exodus, Leviticus, and Numbers stops cold, and there is no further elucidation of laws I have been discussing. Thus, Deuteronomy may have been composed from older writings at a time when the technical meanings were forgotten or misunderstood. Some familiar words might have been used, but the reasons for them were unclear. These words were put together with a short history of the final days of Moses, which would have worked better at the end of Numbers. This is all conjecture, but certain is the fact that *Yom Kippur* was unknown or unaccepted when Deuteronomy was written.

bb. Deut. 31:14–21, 32:38

Disappearance of *Keeper*

Why did *Yom Kippur* disappear after Deuteronomy even though the three festivals (*Succot*, *Pesach*, and *Shawvuot*) were mentioned later? Why is cover (*keeper*) found so seldom in the following books? I think the answer can be found in the diminished use of the communication apparatus, which happened almost as soon as the Israelites came into Canaan.

After David's time, there is no story that specifically details the use of the *ephod* in a communication situation. While there are two hints of communication stories in Joshua 3 and 7–8, there is no mention of the ark after chapter 8.

At first glance Judges, too, mentions knowledge of communication by the ark. This is seen in the sad story of the Israelites turning on their brother tribe of Benjamin in revenge for the rape and murder of a Levite's concubine in their territory.

After the Israelites had been beaten twice by the Benjaminites, they …

> [27] Asked of the Lord—and the ark of the covenant of God was there [in Beth-el] in those days,
>
> [28] And Phinehas, the son of Eleazar, the son of Aaron, stood before it in those days—saying, "Will I yet again go out to battle against the sons of Benjamin or will I cease." And the Lord said, "Go up, for tomorrow I will deliver him into your hand." (Judg. 20:27–28)

However, in Judges 20:18, at the beginning of the story when the Israelites first went to Beth-el and "asked counsel of God" and queried, "Who will go up for us first to battle against the sons of Benjamin," the answer was "Judah first."[bc] Then, after being thoroughly beaten, they regrouped and "asked of the Lord, saying, 'Will I again draw near to battle with the sons of Benjamin my brother?' And the Lord said, 'Go up against him.'"[bd] These cryptic responses suggest that the *ephod*, with its *Urim* and *Thummin*, was used in the first two cases at Beth-el rather than the ark, which would have engendered a conversation.[be] Thus, there is no reason to assume that the *ephod* was not also used in the third case.[bf]

May I strengthen the argument against use of the ark here? Look at several possibilities:

(1) The tent was located at Gilgal after Joshua led the Israelites across the Jordan.[bg] It was then moved to Shiloh.[bh] There is no other mention (besides Judges 20:27–28) in all of Joshua, Judges, 1 and 2 Samuel, and 1 and 2 Kings of its being anywhere else until it was captured by the Philistines some 200 years later.

(2) The Levite whose concubine was killed had originally followed her to Bethlehem. When leaving Bethlehem to return home, he explained to an old man who had queried him, "We are passing from Bethlehem in Judah to the other side of Mt. Ephraim. From there [Ephraim] I went to Bethlehem … I am now going to *the house of the Lord*."[bi] Since Beth-el was south and Shiloh was north of it in Ephraim, this statement must have referred to Shiloh as containing "the house of the Lord," and

bc. cf., Judg. 1:1–2

bd. Judg. 20:23

be. e.g., Josh. 7:6–15

bf. Josh. 20:27–28

bg. Josh. 4:18–19, 5:10, 9:6,

bh. Josh. 18:1, 19:51

bi. Judg. 19:18; cf., 19:1

therefore, logically, the ark. Yet, this is the same story that says the ark was in Beth-el at the time.

(3) In the first two instances of seeking the Lord's counsel at Beth-el, no sacrifices were mentioned. However, in the third, where the ark was included, the people fasted and offered burnt and peace offerings.[bj] On what? If there was a super-conditioned place there to house the ark on a permanent basis, there should have been an altar.

bj. Judg. 20:26

(4) However, the same story in Judges 21:1–5 says that "the men of Israel," having finally beaten Benjamin, suddenly realized that they had practically wiped out the tribe. They were most repentant because they had earlier sworn not to "give his daughter to Benjamin to wife."[bk] With all the Benjaminite women killed, what to do? The people *came to Bethel* and wept,

bk. Judg. 21:1

> ³And they said, "Oh Lord, the God of Israel, why is this come to pass in Israel that there should be today one tribe lacking in Israel?"
>
> ⁴And it came to pass on the morrow that the *people* rose early, *and built there an altar* and offered burnt offerings and peace offerings. (Judges 21:3–4)

So either there were two altars, one for the sacrifices in Judges 20:26 and another for 21:1–5 (for what purpose?), or the 20:26 offering was done on the ground (highly unlikely), or something is confused in the writing.

While the first three encounters with the Lord ended with His brief words of counsel, the fourth, where there was sacrifice on the "new" altar, got no response. Further, the rest of the decisions in the story are made by the whole congregation or the elders immediately *after* they built the altar and sacrificed.[bl] Nowhere is this explained.

bl. e.g., Judg. 21:5, 10, 13, 16

Finally, look again at the wording of the first two references. Judges 20:18 says, "And the sons of Israel *arose* and *went up to Beth-el* and asked of God, and they said, 'Who will go up for us first to battle against the sons of Benjamin?' And the Lord said, 'Judah first.'" Judges 20:23 says, "And the sons of Israel *went up and wept* before the Lord until evening, and they asked of

the Lord, 'Will I again draw near to battle against the sons of Benjamin my brother?' And the Lord said, 'Go up against him.'"
However, the third reference, Judges 20:26–28, says,

> ²⁶Then ALL the sons of Israel AND ALL THE PEOPLE went up and came to Beth-el and wept AND SAT THERE BEFORE THE LORD, AND FASTED THAT DAY until evening, AND THEY OFFERED BURNT OFFERINGS AND PEACE OFFERINGS BEFORE THE LORD.

> ²⁷And the sons of Israel asked of the Lord—AND THE ARK OF THE COVENANT OF GOD WAS THERE IN THOSE DAYS,

> ²⁸AND PHINEHAS, THE SON OF ELEAZAR, THE SON OF AARON, STOOD BEFORE IT IN THOSE DAYS— saying, "Will I yet again go out to battle against the sons of Benjamin my brother or will I cease?" And the Lord said, "Go up, for tomorrow I will deliver him into your hand."

If you strip the capitalized words from the verses you are left with pretty much the same sense and wording as seen in the other two verses. That is, without them and their reference to the ark, you are back to the same words that indicate the *ephod* with its *Urim* and *Thummin*.

Judges has been run completely through the critics' wringer. Though there are various opinions as to just how the final book was compiled, all agree that it went through many revisions for the usual political reasons as evidently did Joshua.[20] In other words, there were many hands in the pot. One example is the reference to "and all the people" in addition to the Israelites.

bm. Judg. 20:26

^{bm} This phrase is nowhere else except when it reads "strangers" or "mixed multitude" or a similar appellation for non-Israelites. What purpose does it serve here? Another is the just demonstrated, extremely rare and clumsy break in the Judges 20:27 sentence inserting the part about "the ark of God."

It is tempting to include the rather rare shift to God (*Elohim*) from the much more common Lord (*YWH*) found before the break, but *Elohim* is also found in Judges 20:18 of the same

bn. e.g., 1 Sam. 4:4; 2 Sam. 6:12–13

story and several other places relative to the ark.^{bn} Yet 2 Samuel

15:24–25, a David story, refers only to the "ark of the covenant of God" and the "ark of God" twice, but ends with "find favor in the eyes of the Lord (*YWH*)." Is all this E and J combined into one piece by D?[21] I don't know, but the idea that 20:27 originally read without the ark like 20:18 and 20:23 seems pretty good.

Therefore, it is possible that the ark was not mentioned in Judges. I am not saying that Beth-el was not a well-known meeting place at various times. It even contained a golden calf under Jereboam.[bo] It was on Samuel's circuit with Gilgal and Mizpah where he judged the people, but even there it was interesting that he came back to his own town of Ramah to build an altar to the Lord.[bp] Again, there is never a mention of the ark being at any of these places and probably not in Judges at all, but the use of the *ephod* seems quite possible. So, though the story itself seems quite senseless, and certainly unnecessarily cruel if it purports to be action ordered by the Lord, it does show knowledge of communication using an instrument.[22]

Ark or no ark, Judges also had a prophet and a messenger of the Lord as intermediaries.[bq] The key verse that provoked the change was Judges 2:10. After the deaths of Joshua and his generation, "there arose another generation after them that knew not the Lord, nor the word that He had wrought for Israel." Thus began the behavior of the Israelites "which was evil in the sight of the Lord." In chapter 7, the Lord spoke directly to Gideon without a device. In chapter 10:11–14, the Lord spoke to the Israelites. The Soncino translation of the Bible confidently says this was by a prophet.[23] Chapter 11 again used a messenger. Samuel had mechanical and direct communication, albeit with the caveat that "the word of the Lord was rare in those days [just prior to founding of monarchy—1020 BCE]; there was no vision [*chawzone*—a word not in the Five Books] breaking through."[br] He heard the Lord speak to him when he was very young "in the temple of the Lord where the ark of God was."[bs] He also wore an *ephod*.[bt] Here, too, the systems vary and can be vague. Thus, in 1 Samuel 8:6–9, Samuel prayed to the Lord from his house at Ramah and was answered by the Lord. This was about the

bo. 1 Kgs. 12:26–33

bp. 1 Sam. 7:16–17

bq. Judg. 6:8,11

br. 1 Sam. 3:1; *chawzone*, 2377

bs. 1 Sam. 3:3–4

bt. 1 Sam. 2:18

Israelites' plea for a king. However, the tent was at Shiloh and

bu. 1 Sam. 4:3–4

so was the ark.[bu] There is no note of a device, although it is true he had built an altar there. Direct conversation was evidently held at a "high place" at Ramah regarding the Lord's choice of

bv. 1 Sam. 9:12–17

Saul as king, probably at the same altar.[bv] The *Urim* was possibly employed in 1 Samuel 10:22. There was much conversation between Samuel and the Lord, again without a device, e.g., in Chapter 16. Since Samuel had returned to Ramah, he possibly talked to God at his altar.

It is significant that there were only a few reports of this mechanical communication from Joshua's time through David's. Whether because of geographic dispersion, lack of leadership, political expediency, continued belief in magic and idolatry, or outright fear of it, the apparatus for communicating directly with the Lord fell into disuse.

When Solomon built his temple and moved the ark and equipment into it, and while the ark naturally attracted the cloud, there is absolutely no mention of it ever being used.

bw. 1 Kgs. 3:5, 6:11, 9:12; 2 Chr. 1:7, 7:12

Solomon himself received the Lord's word only in dreams and an enigmatic "word of the Lord."[bw] He spoke directly to the

bx. 1 Kgs. 8:22–53

Lord at the dedication of the temple.[bx] In the prayer, he showed little understanding of the ark's operation. For example, in 1 Kings 8:45 and 49, he implored the Lord to hear the people's prayers "in heaven." Most significantly, the Lord did not answer him. Stuck in the middle of a description of Solomon building his empire is the statement that he (meaning his priests) offered burnt and peace offerings three times a year at the major festivals.

by. 1 Kgs. 9:25

[by] This is such a minor mention as to almost be an afterthought. True, this is somewhat expanded in 2 Chronicles 8:12–13, but it is still only mentioned once. Of the few times the Lord spoke to Solomon, the last time was when He chastised the king for

bz. 1 Kgs. 11:11–13

turning to idolatry.[bz] Here the punishment is so improbable as to be unbelievable. The kingdom was to be lost, not in Solomon's time, but in that of his sons. For a high liver like Solomon, one would think he would heave a sigh of relief and say, "So what?" And why would the Lord punish the people?

One mechanical problem may have blocked reception during Solomon's time. The ark, when installed in Solomon's Temple, naturally attracted the cloud, but the *cherubim* he built didn't touch the ark. 1 Kings 6:23–27 says,

> [23]And in the super-conditioned place he made two *cherubim* of olive-wood, each ten cubits high ...

> [27]And he set the *cherubim* within the inner house: and the wings ... were stretched forth, so the wing of the one touched the one wall, and the wing of the other cherub touched the other wall; and their wings touched one another in the midst of the house.

Then 1 Kings 8:6 says,

> [6]And the priests brought the ark of the covenant of the Lord to its place to the super-conditioned place of the house, to the super-conditioned place *under* the wings of the cherubim. (my emphasis)

The fact that the wings of the *cherubim* did not touch the ark would have severely diminished their use as antennae. In addition, they were wood, not metal as the original *cherubim* were, and wood is not a conductor.

This leads me to ask the following: If these giant items were used, what happened to the original small ones on the ark cover? One possible answer is that someone disposed of the ark cover with its *cherubim*. Why? Apparently it was the most dangerous part of the mechanism. Aaron couldn't go "at all times ... before the covering" because the Lord would "appear in the cloud on the covering."[ca] The cloud of incense had to cover the ark cover on the *edut* "that he die not."[cb] The heightened danger was a strong motive to get rid of the ark cover somewhere along the line (or at least to isolate it). If this were true, then the apparatus' receiving capability would have been diminished, because Solomon's devices would have done little or no good.

A close reading of 1 Chronicles 28:10–11, the only place outside of Exodus, Leviticus, and Numbers where the ark cover is used, may give some credence to this idea. David was giving

ca. Lev. 16:2

cb. Lev. 16:13

his son, Solomon, the plans for the Temple, which he himself was not permitted to build.

> [10]"Take heed now for the Lord has chosen you to build a house for the super-conditioned place ..."

> [11]Then David gave to Solomon ... the pattern of the porch, and of the houses and the treasuries and the upper rooms and the inner chambers and of *the house of the ark cover.* (1 Chr. 28:10–11, my emphasis)

Why "the house of the ark cover?" 1 Chronicles has no problem saying "ark" when it means ark. For example, in 1 Chronicles 28:2, at the beginning of the same chapter on the same subject David said, "Hear me my brothers and my people. As for me it was in my heart to build a house of rest for the ark of the covenant of the Lord." So why, out of nowhere, refer to a house for the ark cover unless the cover was to be put in another place entirely? I think the house of verse 10 is the same as the house of verse 2. I believe the house of verse 11 is new and different.

Maybe the ark didn't work. Maybe Solomon gave orders not to use the device so that he could pursue the good life without interference from the priests. Maybe it was in constant use and later writers did not know it. Regardless, there is no record of the ark's use after Solomon's time. The rise of the intermediary prophets, almost unheard of in Genesis–Numbers, supplanted the ark and *ephod.* There is no mention of machinery to get their messages. It's just, "And the word of the Lord came to so and so." This could be through visions, dreams, or direct voice.

"The word of the Lord" is a study unto itself. It is mentioned at the beginning of Samuel, and with David's prophets, Nathan and Gad.[cc] Only later does it take on a life of its own and become *the* system for communication for prophets such as Elijah, Elisha, Jeremiah, and Ezekiel. This was essentially after the kingdom was split.

In addition, the prophets themselves did not agree, or they could have been false, or just plain wrong.[cd] Thus, even in the case of the reform king Josiah (c. 640–609 BCE), his high priest Hilkiah, who found the Book of the Law, could not

cc. 1 Sam. 15:10; 2 Sam. 7:4 (cf., 1Chr. 17:3), 24:11, but not 1 Chr. 21:9

cd. e.g., 1Kgs. 22:5–8

communicate. Josiah asked him to "inquire of the Lord."[ce] This ce. 2 Kgs. 22:13–14
was the standard order that should have meant using the ark or
ephod, but instead, Hilkiah had to go to Huldah the prophetess
who predicted a peaceful life and death for Josiah. Josiah was
killed in battle.

Jeremiah, who also prophesied during Josiah's reign and was
the son of a priest (if not the priest Hilkiah) even said,

> [16]"And it will come to pass when you are multiplied and
> increased in the land in those days," *says the Lord*, "they will
> say no more, the ark of the covenant of the Lord, *neither
> will it come to mind*; neither will they make mention of it;
> neither will they miss it; neither will it be *made* any more."
> (my emphasis)

The actual words of the Lord that "came to" the prophets could
be unbelievably nonsensical. See, for example, the indescribably
evil Ahab, king of Israel (876 BCE), as Elijah spoke to him and
the culmination of the episode as commanded by the Lord.[cf] cf. 1 Kgs. 21:27–29
See also 2 Kings 21:10–15 as being the words actually spoken
by the Lord through prophets. There are many other examples
of "prophets" trying to influence matters by supposedly quoting
the Lord, but their Lord is portrayed by these men as a ranting,
blow-hard, complainer, employed to predict the collapse of
kingdoms. He is not the Lord who led the Israelites out of
Egypt, who made a covenant with Abraham, Isaac, and Jacob,
and who established the law with Moses. The prophets received
no communication. They simply said they heard the voice of
God for either good or evil purposes. Some may even have truly
believed they heard His voice, but there is no way they could
have done so *safely* and there is no report of any of them either
protecting themselves or contracting radiation sickness. As to
the kings, there was little incentive for them to work with the ark
even in the later lives of David and Solomon, and virtually none
after the kingdom was split. Of the 39 kings who ruled Judah or
Israel, all but eight "did that which was evil in the sight of the
Lord." Of the eight, six allowed the "high places" to continue,
leaving only Hezekiah (715 BCE) and Josiah (640 BCE), kings
of the remaining Judah, as true followers of the Lord.

During this period, Israel was lost and the role of the prophets became one of predicting its downfall. Later, the same fate ensued for Judah. With friends like these, the last thing these kings needed was also to be faced with an operational ark or *ephod*.

When the last king, Zedekiah of Judah, fell to the Chaldean dynasty of Babylonia (587 BCE), only the priests and the prophets retained any influence. Depending on the scholar, P was *finalized* in the 500s or 400s BCE. Then, it is said, the priestly redactor sewed everything together and gave us the law as it is known today. He concocted the story of the wondrous instruments the priests had to work with, and then supposedly cast it back to the "mythical" time of Moses. Strangely, this story was said to have been written at a time when the ark was long gone and when the second temple was built. P was describing an important machine at the time when no machine existed. How did the priests of P's time handle the idea of the Lord speaking to so-and-so "from between the *cherubim* above the ark of the communication" when there wasn't one? Actually, this concept was never mentioned.

A new concept arose early. It was that the Lord sat or dwelt there, and evidently did nothing else. This extended from 1 Samuel 4:4, at the war with the Philistines, when the ark was captured to the time of Hezekiah.[cg] "Sit" and "dwell" are completely different concepts from those in Exodus and Numbers, which express the idea of the Lord "meeting" and/or "speaking" there, or actually hearing His voice from there.[ch]

cg. Isa. 37:16

ch. Exod. 24:22, 30:6, 36; Num. 7:89, 17:19

Whatever the concept and whether or not the ark could be used, observers concluded that, while it did exist, it predictably remained dangerous (radioactive) from the effects of the cloud. Anyone who was not properly protected still ran the risk of radiation burn. The last reported time the cloud covered the ark was at the completion of Solomon's temple (c. 950 BCE). So if Uzziah (Azariah) was affected by it, its danger extended ca. 160 years to his reign (c. 790 BCE), and if Hezekiah was affected, that added another 70 years (c. 720 BCE).

The last mention of the ark being actively handled (not referred to as past history) was during Josiah's reign (c. 640 BCE). There is no report of his having personal contact with it or in any way being affected by it, but it would seem that, although it was not used to communicate, Josiah took pains to have the priests adequately condition themselves.[ci] The best I can say, then, is that its danger seemed to last 230 years, and if it was still radioactive in Josiah's time, the total would have been about 310 years, after which there is no more record.

ci. 2 Chr. 35:6

One could write any sort of story from sensible to nonsensical about this long period, but the observations of the effects of the ark's danger seemed to remain absolutely consistent. This consistency, in the face of use, disuse, myth, and fact, strengthens the possibility that in the ark was a real, not fanciful article. While there may or may not have been a P, and he may or may not have been collating a history, what is read today is not a cast-back. It is a recognition of these observations.

The reality also is that the ark was not actually used for its communication purpose from the time of David forward. So, there would be absolutely no reason for *Yom Kippur* any time after David. You could go through the motions of cleansing the temple, sacrificing, even observing *Yom Kippur* in much later times, having been exposed to the early writings, but, if there was no communication there would be no cloud. If there was no cloud, there would be no reason to annually cover the super-conditioned place (*Yom Kippur*), nor to cover (*keeper*) the Israelites. The priests might or might not have known all this as the years went by, but for any or all reasons stated above they were not about to do anything that could activate the device.

In addition to the possibility that the ark did not work, there is another problem that could have prevented its use. Regicide and every other kind of murder made the land red with blood. The blood of the guilty was needed to cover the blood of the murdered or the land would be polluted: "No cover (*y'choopar*) can be made for the land for the blood that was shed therein but by the blood of him who shed it."[cj] Not only would defiling

cj. Num. 35:33

ck. Lev. 18:24–28;
Num. 35:34

cl. e.g., 1Chr. 22:8;
possibly Isa. 27:21;
Ezek. 24:6–8,
1Kgs. 2:31–35

the land cause vomiting out of the Israelites, the Lord would not continue to dwell "in the midst of the Israelites."[ck] While there seems to be recognition of the problem, there is no way that there could have been a formalized cleaning of the land from all its spilled blood.[cl] The possibility, from this perspective alone, that the ark could be used as a communicating device seems slim.

So perhaps the chaos that existed at Mount Sinai and later with Aaron's sons continued and expanded upon reaching Canaan and in the ensuing years. Again, following the logical extended flow of the overall story, the Lord would have withdrawn from the area leaving only a useless but residually "hot" ark in His wake. With all its twists and turns, myths and facts, the evolution of *Yom Kippur*, beginning to end, has a logic of its own. It follows a pattern from rules that were promulgated in very ancient times, through futile attempts to revive them from time to time, on to a clearly historical period when nothing was left to a conquered remnant but the original words and dim, confused memories.

Appendix G

Impurity

Avone is traditionally translated "iniquity, punishment," or "guilt, fault," but on close examination these translations do not hold up. I have defined *avone* as "impurity caused by radioactive contamination from exposure to the cloud." In each place where *avone* is used, I believe it should read "impurity."

DERIVATION

The traditional theory is that *avone* comes from the root *awvaw* (not used in the Five Books), meaning "commit iniquity."[a] Thus, *awvaw* is used as a. *awvaw*, 5753 "wrongdoing" along with equivalent words such as "(do) perverse(ly), (do) wicked(ly)." HAL says that the related Old Babylonian *ewoom* is translated "to burden with," possibly suggesting putting something on someone or something.[1]

Avone is first used almost immediately in Genesis 4:13. This was the well-known statement by Cain to the Lord traditionally translated, "My punishment (*avonee*) is greater than I can carry." This was said after the Lord condemned him to life as "a vagabond and a fugitive." The sentence actually reads, "Great [is] my *avonee* from carrying." At first glance this seems, indeed, to be a punishment for his killing Abel, but there could be another interpretation. What follows is Cain's plaint that because the Lord had driven him from the land,

> [14]"From your face I will be hidden ...and all who find me will kill me." ...

> [15]And the Lord said to him, "Anyone who kills Cain will be avenged seven fold." And the Lord set a sign on Cain that anyone who finds him should not smite him. (Gen. 4:14–15)

The word to watch here is "sign," *oht*.[b] *Oht* is always God-given in Genesis b. *oht*, 226 and Numbers and almost always in Deuteronomy; it is not used in Leviticus. *Oht* takes different forms, but here what may be unwittingly meant is the "sign" that appears after being "before the Lord." In other words, Cain's face may have been affected by proximity to the Lord as was Moses' on Mount Sinai. This was also the case when the Lord visited the unprotected Miriam (and Aaron and Moses) and she turned white. So Cain's statement may have meant, "I carry great impurity (*avone*) on me, so people who see me will want to kill me," as they were ordered to do if any of the Israelites came too close to Mount Sinai when at the time of the Lord's appearance. Or, it is possible that God was saying that people who saw Cain would be afraid of him because of his appearance, "sign," as they were of Moses'. *Avone* as punishment doesn't really exist in the Five Books, nor for that matter in the following books either (although in the following books punishment can result from becoming impure). An example of clear delineation between punishment and *avone* is in Psalms 39:11 (Heb. 39:12) where the word *y'sar* is used *with avone*: "With rebukes do You punish (*y'sar*) man for impurity (*avone*)."[c] *Y'sar* has several other translations, e.g., "chasten," "chastise," and "reprove." It is only found in Leviticus, Deuteronomy, and following books.

The next mention of *avone* occurs when the Lord made a promise to Abram regarding the Israelites' future:

> [15]"But you will go to your fathers in peace; you will be buried in a good old age.

> [16]And in the fourth generation they will return here; for the impurity of the Amorite is not complete until then." (Gen. 15:15–16)

The Lord was telling Abram that not until the fourth generation would the plague weaken the Amorites enough for the Israelites to attack and beat them.[d] Note that the Amorites also did things that caused impurity to fall on them and the radioactive consequences lasted at least four generations. The dangerous radioactive condition also persisted through four generations of the Israelites after the plague of the golden calf episode in the wilderness.

Genesis 19:15 is the story of the Lord's messenger urging Lot and his family to flee Sodom before it is destroyed, "lest you be consumed in the impurity of the city." Here again, there was the buildup of impurity due to contamination that ultimately destroyed the entire area. "And the Lord said, 'The cry [against] Sodom and Gomorrah is indeed great, and their contamination [is] very heavy.' "[e]

Genesis 44:16 is the only place where *avone* as a wrongdoing seems to be the correct translation. This is related to Joseph's errant brothers. "God has found the iniquity of your servants," seeming to refer to the brothers' former mistreatment of him.

c. *y'sar*, 3256

d. Lev. 18:24–25, 20:22–23

e. Gen. 18:20

Generational Effects

Exodus 20:5 is the first of the verses that speaks of "God visiting the impurity of the fathers on children, and on the third and the fourth [generation] to them that hate Me." This is actually part of the Ten Commandments, warning against idol worship with the admonition not to "prostrate yourself to them." Using my definition of *avone*, perhaps this was a warning not to expect protection from inanimate idols. The danger lay in exposing oneself to the impurity caused by the Lord's cloud. Remember, when suddenly in the presence of the Lord, the person would quickly "bow down," probably as a way to protect the face.

The next mention of *avone* took place as Moses met the Lord on Mount Sinai. This verse is particularly useful in showing the distinction between impurity, contamination, and transgression.

> 5And the Lord descended in the cloud and he stood with Him there, and he proclaimed the name of the Lord.
>
> 6And the Lord passed *before his face* and [Moses] proclaimed, "Lord, Lord …
>
> 7Keeping kindness *to the thousandth*, forgiving impureness and transgression and contamination, but who will surely not clear [the guilty] visiting the impurity of fathers on the children and on the children's children, on a third [generation] and on a fourth [generation]."
>
> 8And Moses hastened and bowed down to the earth, and he prostrated himself.
>
> 9And he said, "If now I have found favor in Your eyes, Lord, let the Lord, I pray You, go in our midst: for it is a stiff-necked people; and pardon our impureness and our contamination, and take us as Your possession." (Exod. 34:5–9, my emphasis)

All of the elements are here: the cloud and Moses' proximity to it, the warning of the impurity's effect on future generations, and Moses quickly bowing "to the earth" for protection.

Another verse that speaks of the Lord visiting impurity of the fathers on succeeding generations is Numbers 14:18. It gives the familiar phrasing,

> 18The Lord is slow of anger and great in kindness, forgiving impureness and transgression but who will surely not clear [the guilty], visiting the impurity of fathers upon children on a third [generation] and on a fourth [generation]. (Num. 14:18)

This verse follows Moses' spies' "evil report" that the peoples of Canaan were too strong to attack. This information brought revolt among the Israelites, which incited the anger of the Lord. Just as they were about to stone Moses and Aaron, the "*kawbode* of the Lord appeared in the tent of meeting to all the Israelites."[f] f. Num. 14:10

This should have meant danger for all the people and it did, as is borne out in the following verses:

> ¹¹And the Lord said to Moses, "How long will this people despise Me …
>
> ¹²I will smite him with radiation sickness and I will destroy him and I will make [of] you a greater and mightier nation than he is." (Num. 14:11–12)

Many assume that Moses persuaded God not to do this, theoretically appealing to God's pride by saying that if He destroyed this people, other nations would say, "Because the Lord was not able to bring this people into the land … therefore He has slaughtered them in the wilderness."ᵍ Actually, the Lord did not heed his appeal. In Numbers 14:17–18, Moses quoted God from Exodus 34:5–9, but used *sawlach* for "pardon" instead of *nosay* (*nawsaw*). The two words are used interchangeably in the Five Books. However, *nosay* means many things in addition to "pardon," including "lift up," "take away," or "carry" in the sense of "carrying impurity," which is its meaning in the Numbers passage.² Moses pled, "Pardon (*sawlach*) … the impurity of this people … as You have pardoned (*nosay*-God's word) this people from Egypt until now."ʰ

Now the next verses say,

> ¹⁹Forgive (*sawlach*) … the impurity of this people …
>
> ²⁰The Lord said, "I have pardoned (*sawlach*) [!] according to *your* word.
>
> ²¹But as I live and [as] *all the earth is filled* [*with*] the *kawbode* of the Lord,
>
> ²²That all the men who have seen My *kawbode* …
>
> ²³ … will not see the land." (Num. 14:19–23)

Then the Lord became specific. All the people over 20 "that have murmured against Me" will die in the wilderness.ⁱ He said that the children would carry (the other meaning of *nosay*) their parents' whoredoms and that they would carry (the other meaning of *nosay*) their impurity.ʲ Then Numbers 14:37 says,

g. Num. 14:16

h. Num. 14:18

i. Num. 14:29

j. Num. 14:33–4

"Those men died, [who] have brought up an evil report of the land, in the plague before the Lord." Here we have a totally predictable, but nevertheless, astounding series of events.

- When the *kawbode* appeared at the time Moses and Aaron were threatened, it appeared "to *all* the Israelites."
- When the Lord said, "I will smite them with radiation sickness," He had already done so by having His *kawbode* appear.
- When Moses quoted the Lord about His slowness to anger, he quoted the same seeming paradox we have seen before, i.e., clearing (*sawlach*) the guilty but not removing (*nosay*) the impurity. In other words, those who were contaminated were contaminated. There was nothing to be done about it. When Moses asked for "pardon" (*sawlach*), the Lord answered in effect, *All right, I will sawlach as you have asked, but I will not nosay. Everyone over 20 who was exposed to the cloud will die over the next 40 years. I will listen to you and not kill them outright, but they will never make it to Canaan.* The children would necessarily carry the effects of their parents' impurity. As would be expected, the *kawbode* resulted in plague and the immediate death of those who were most in the thick of things, except Joshua and Caleb who were presumably protected.

There is a natural relationship between Numbers 14:12, "I will smite them with radiation sickness," and Numbers 14:37, the resulting plague that did its ultimate damage. The fact that there seems to be a combination of stories in chapter 14 makes little difference. The result, contamination, is the same.

Deuteronomy 5:9 is the last verse regarding "visit." It is a repeat of the Ten Commandments in a section where Moses reviews all that had transpired in their 40 years in the wilderness. When one is subject to impurity, he could experience genetic or hereditary effects.

Exodus 28:38–43 describes the protective clothing Aaron and his sons were to wear when working with the radioactive conditioning things and the altar, "that they not carry the impurity (*avone*) and die." This was the first hint that *avone* meant more than a moral wrongdoing, but rather an actual physical condition caused by radioactivity.

Leviticus 5:1 begins the discussion of doing various things that could cause the attraction of radioactivity. The result would be impurity.

Leviticus 7:18 is the warning not to eat the flesh of the peace offering on the third day. "The person that eats of it will carry his impurity."

Leviticus 10:16–18 is the story of Moses searching for the missing decontamination offering after the deaths of Aaron's two sons when they used the wrong material for sacrifice. Here comes another of those possibilities that makes this study an adventure with clues turning up as they do in the best of detective stories. Verse 17 has Moses saying to Aaron,

> [17]"Why have you not eaten the decontamination offering in … the super-conditioned place, for it is super-conditioned, and He has given it to you to carry (*sayt*) the impurity of the congregation to cover on them before the Lord?"

Moses charged the priests to bring the contamination offering into the conditioned place so that its blood could be used to take away the impurity of the people. This is, again, a clear statement that impurity was a condition to be removed, and in this case it greatly disturbed Moses because the priests *failed* to do so.

In this verse, the infinitive construct form of *nawsaw*, *sayt*, is translated "to carry." A similar word, *sayt*, also derived from *nawsaw*, means "an elevation, a leprous scab … rising."[k] "When a man will have in the skin of his flesh a rising (*sayt*) or a scab or a bright spot, and it will become in the skin of his flesh the radiation burning."[l] Remember the "rising" on the burned person. The connection is immediate. Here is the possibility that the carrying away (*nawsaw*) of impurity from the people may have the connotation of "unscabbing" or "unrising," or, in other words, decontaminating them from their contamination!

Since the word *sayt* is used as "rising" only in Leviticus 13 and 14, and only in connection with the burned person, it may well have been just a common word with the general meaning of elevation used to describe a phenomenon new to these specific people at this specific time. This is true of the parent word *nawsaw*, which is used for carrying away generally, and specifically carrying away impurity when used with *avone*. Also, *sayt* does not seem to be remotely connected with the other words used for "rise, risen, rising" in the Hebrew Bible.

Leviticus 16 is a continuation of Leviticus 10. Here the deaths of Nadab and Abihu served as a stark warning not to come into the ark area unless properly protected, "because in the cloud I will appear on the covering."[m] This chapter deals with use of

k. *sayt*, 7613

l. Lev. 13:2

m. Lev. 16:2

various animals for protection and Aaron's choice by lot to send a goat to *Azawzel*. To accomplish this, he had to lay both his hands on the head of the living goat and confess on him,

> [21]"All the impurities of the Israelites, and all their transgressions with all their contaminations, and he will put them on the head of the goat, and he will send [him] away by the hand of an appointed man into the wilderness.

> [22]And the goat will carry upon him all their impurities into a solitary land; and he will let go the goat in the wilderness." (Lev. 16:21–22)[3]

Now this is notable. Even though Aaron confessed both impurities and transgressions with contaminations on the goat, verse 22 becomes specific and says that *only* the impurities were to be borne into the solitary land.[4] Nothing can give a stronger indication of the difference in the meanings of those words than this point. It is clearer than ever that *avone* is treated as the actual impurity resulting from the radioactivity that had to be removed. It was borne on the people, on things, and on the sacrificial animals, i.e., scapebirds and scapegoats.

There was no such thing as an impurity offering. On the other hand, there was a decontamination offering (*chawtawt*) for preventing the act of becoming contaminated (*chawtaw*). The act of becoming contaminated would not be borne "into a solitary land," only the resultant impurity itself. Reading further, the man who handled the contaminated goat had to do just what the man who handled the contaminated sacrifices did. He had to wash his clothes and bathe himself.[n]   n. Lev. 16:26

Chawtaw also has an opposite meaning: cleanse, or in my terminology, decontaminate—a far cry from the concept of wrongdoing.[o]   o. Lev. 14:49, 52

> "And a bullock of the decontamination offering you will make daily on the coverings and you will decontaminate (*cheetaytaw*) on the altar when you cover on it: and you will anoint it to condition it." (Exod. 29:36)

Actually, "decontaminate" is the most accurate translation for *chawtaw* when used in this way. *Chawtaw* is used for decontaminate only when mentioned in conjunction with the substance that is doing the decontamination. Thus, in addition to this Exodus 29:36 reference, Leviticus 8:15 uses blood to decontaminate the altar and Numbers 8:7 speaks of "the water of expiation" or purification, but the word is still *chawtaw*. Numbers 19:1–13 speaks of ashes of a red cow, which are used with water to make "water for separation (*needaw*)."[p] In these verses, the water is used to decontaminate a person who has touched a dead body.[q] Numbers 31:19–23 also uses the water for separation to decontaminate people and things after the attack on the Midianites. Leviticus 17:15–16 is a straightforward statement regarding the need for a person to wash himself and his clothes when either "a native or a stranger" eats anything "which dies of itself or that is torn of wild beasts." For some reason, this made these animals unclean. The person stayed unclean until evening, and if he did not wash, "then he will carry his impurity." The fact that a stranger could also be contaminated simply strengthens the concept that anyone in the vicinity could become affected.

Leviticus 18 is a long list of prohibitions including those regarding relatives with whom one could not have intercourse. The nations, whose territory the Israelites were entering, had violated these prohibitions and had thereby defiled themselves: "And their land was defiled, and I will visit the impurity thereof on it, and the land will vomit out her inhabitants."[r] The list is too long and varied to take the word *avone* literally as used here at the end of the list. It is used generally and not meant to be a technical term. However, in Leviticus 20 the specific punishments for each of the wrongdoings are listed. They are fascinating!

The following are examples of those put to death for wrongdoings: an adulterer, a man who had intercourse with his father's wife (not his mother) or his daughter-in-law, a man who has intercourse with both his wife and her mother, homosexuals, and anyone having sex with a beast. However, if a man has intercourse with his sister "he will carry his impurity."[s] The same was the case with his mother's or father's sister: "For he has made naked his near kin. They will carry their impurity."[t] However,

p. Num. 19:9; *needaw*, 5079

q. Num. 19:12, 17, 19, 20

r. Lev. 18:25

s. Lev. 20:17

t. Lev. 20:19

"if a man will lie with his uncle's wife ... they will carry their *contamination*; they will die childless. And if a man will take his brother's wife, it is separation ... they will die childless."[u] While *needaw* is normally translated "impurity" or "indecency," here it actually means "set apart." It can also refer to "separating from" a woman in her uncleanness." Childless, *areeree*, can mean simply that the resulting children, if any, wouldn't amount to anything.[v]

u. Lev. 20:20–21

v. *areeree*, 6185; Jer. 22:30

Carry Contamination

Only in those cases where there can be a genetically negative result (e.g., birth defects due to incest) is the Hebrew word *avone* used! The use of the phrase "carry *contamination*" in intercourse between a man and his non-related uncle's wife is either a throwback to the word's simple use as wrongdoing or part of the conscience group (false witness, lying, etc.) that might make a person prone to becoming contaminated. Another possibility here is that if the woman became contaminated, it would be of a similar nature to the adulterous woman and then would lead to barrenness.

While I am on the subject of "carrying contamination (*chatawt*)," I should discuss those few additional places where this phrase is used. Only Leviticus and Numbers mention it. Leviticus 19:17 is part of the wonderful, unique philosophy that ends with the admonition to "love your neighbor as yourself." The particular verse tells us not to "hate your brother in your heart; you will surely rebuke your neighbor, and not carry contamination because of him." This could either be a moral statement or part of the conscience group.

Leviticus 24:15 talks of carrying contamination because of cursing the name of the Lord. Since the punishment was death by stoning, and all that heard the culprit were to lay their hands on his head (touch him), we can infer either that this was considered a wrongdoing or that the person was contaminated, and that those who touched him were properly protected.

Numbers 9:13 is the law that orders all clean men to prepare the Passover lamb or his soul "will be cut off from his people because the oblation of the Lord he did not offer in its appointed season; his contamination that man will remove." This, again, is a direct cause and effect, warning the unclean person to sacrifice lest he be removed from the congregation. This verse follows the explanation of what to do about Passover for those who are unclean because they touched a dead body. They may make the offering in the second month on the fourteenth day. Since unclean persons are already contaminated, the protection of sacrifice will do them no good. It is to be presumed that they are to follow the laws in Numbers 5:2–3 and Numbers 19:11–17.

> [2]"Command the Israelites, that they send out of the camp every leper, and everyone that has an issue, and everyone that is unclean by a [dead] person.
>
> [3]Both male and female you will send out; outside the camp you will send them out that they defile not their camps, which I dwell in their midst." (Num. 5:2–3)

Numbers 19:11–17 explains in detail what that person who touched the dead body was to do. He was to be sprinkled with the water for separation made with the ashes of the red cow. If he did not decontaminate himself (*veeschataw*) he remained unclean. This had to be done on the third and seventh day during the seven days that the person touching the dead remained unclean. Also, the man doing the sprinkling had to wash his clothes in water, bathe himself, and then he would be clean by the evening. This is a chemical decontamination, not a protection.

Numbers 18:22 follows a tighter organization of the priests' duties vis-à-vis the tent of meeting.

> [22]"And the Israelites will no more come near to the tent of meeting, to carry contamination to die [thereby].
>
> [23]But the Levite[s] themselves will serve the service of the tent of meeting, and they will carry their impurity." (Num. 18:22–23)

Since it was simply too dangerous for anyone unprotected to approach the area lest he become contaminated, the priests were to take this duty exclusively and carry the impurity because they were adequately protected. The difference in the meanings of *chatawt* and *avone* is clearly drawn here.

The last mention of "carry *chatawt*" immediately follows these verses. The context is of giving the tithe of the heave offering to the priests because they will have no property inheritance. The best part of the offering is to be for the Levites:

> ³¹"And you may eat it in every place, you and your household: for it is a reward for you in exchange for your service in the tent of meeting.

> ³²And you will carry no contamination because of it, when you have lifted up the fat from it." (Num. 18:31–32)

In other words, eating the offering outside the tent area will not contaminate the priests and their families. This ends the references to "carry *chatawt*." The phrase is not used in place of "carry *avone*," but it has its own meaning.

Continuing the study of *avone*, Leviticus 18:25 states that "the land became defiled and I visited its *avone* on it, and the land vomited out its inhabitants." In other words, the peoples of the inhabiting nations had done things that caused impurity to come upon them and on the land itself. These offending groups may once have had a relationship with the same system now offered to the Israelites. The thought is strengthened further in Leviticus 18:27 that says, "For all these abominations have the men of the land done that [were] before you, and the land became defiled (*tawmay*)."

Leviticus 19:8 warns against eating the peace offering sacrifice on the third day. "And whoever eats it will carry his impurity; for the conditioning thing of the Lord he has profaned (exposed); and that soul will be cut off from his people." Once he has eaten contaminated material he must be isolated.

Leviticus 20:17 and 19 caution against having intercourse with close relatives to prevent carrying impurity.

Leviticus 22:16 relates to eating of the conditioning things discussed in relation to the anti-susceptibility offering.

Leviticus 26 recounts a part of the long conversation the Lord had with Moses on Mount Sinai regarding various laws, warnings, and consequences. Verse 39 is generally translated as follows:

> ³⁰"And they that are left of you will pine away (*mawcock*) in their impurity in the lands of their enemies, and also in the

w. *mawcock,* 4743

impurity of their fathers *with them* they will pine away." (my emphasis)ᵂ

Mawcock is only used in this one verse in the Five Books. The actual meaning is "decay, rot, fester."⁵ "Pine away," then, is a figurative usage, and *mawcock* was never understood that way. Thus, in following books it is used as "to consume away" in relation to the flesh because of plague; "to fester," as of wounds;

x. Zech. 14:12;
Ps. 38:6; Ezek. 4:17,
24:23, 33:10; Is. 34:4

as well as "to waste away in impurity;" and "dissolve."ˣ There is no reason to translate *mawcock* as "pine away" in the Leviticus verse. It was a physical, not a moral, consequence of impurity. It is interesting that the derivative word *mock* in Isaiah (only place

y. *mock,* 4716;
Isa. 3:24; 5:24

used) is translated *"decay," "rottenness."*ʸ In the Ugaritic, DLU says /m-k/ is "to fall, decay."⁶ And, of course, they will suffer from the impurity of their fathers. This would be most puzzling if we were talking about moral sins, but if the children were reacting to the parents' contamination, it would make perfect sense.

The verses following Leviticus 26:39 need some clarification:

⁴⁰"And they will confess their impurities and the impurities of their fathers in their trespass (*b'm'lawm* [*ma-al*]) that they trespassed (*mawaloo*) against Me and also because they walked *contrary* (*k'ree*) to Me,

⁴¹I also *walked contrary* to them, and I brought them in the land of their enemies; *if* their uncircumcised heart is then humbled, and they *accept* (*yeer'tsoo* [*rawtzaw*]) their impurity

⁴²Then I will remember My covenant [with] Jacob ... and the land I will remember.ᶻ

z. *ma'al,* 4604; *k'ree,*
7147; *rawtsaw,* 7521

⁴³For the land will be forsaken by them and it will enjoy its Sabbaths in the desolation without them; and they will accept their impurity because ... My ordinances they rejected, and My statutes their soul abhorred.

⁴⁴And yet for all that, when they are in the land of their enemies, I will not reject them, neither will I abhor them, to *destroy* them *utterly,* [and] to break My covenant with them; for I am the Lord their God." (Lev. 26:40–44; my emphasis)

The first phrase, "they will confess their impurity," probably refers to the same process as Aaron physically transferring the impurities, transgressions, and contaminations of the Israelites onto the head of a goat before sending it to *Azawzel*. If those that were not "utterly destroyed" became contaminated by not following the rules, they had to do the best they could to become decontaminated. This is emphasized by the necessity to confess "the impurity of their fathers in their trespass that they trespassed against Me." The word traditionally translated "trespass" is *ma'al*, which signifies a heavy cover of contamination, a "super-contamination." So in this context, "confess the impurity of their fathers" makes perfect sense. The errant people acknowledge (confess) the fact that the accumulated impurity was caused by their own and their fathers' super-contamination (*ma'al*). This resulted from disobeying "[the Lord's] commandments" and walking contrary to the Lord.[aa] The phrase "because they walked *contrary* to Me" is what needs clarification.   aa. Lev. 26:15

The word *q'ree* means "contrary." It comes from *qawraw*, a root meaning "to light upon (chiefly by accident)."[ab] The whole idea of the word is "to meet." *Q'ree* connotes a hostile encounter. HAL agrees and says it derives from I *qrh*, "to meet, encounter, happen to," which is a by-form of II *qra*, which can also mean "to meet someone, encounter, happen to someone" and "contrary to, opposite."[7] The Septuagint uses *playgios*, "oblique, side, indirect." Strong's says, "to encounter whether accidentally or in a hostile manner."[8]   ab. *qawraw*, 7136

Q'ree is *only* used in Leviticus 26 and only in relation to the people walking contrary to God and God walking contrary to the people.[9] It is first used in Leviticus 26:21–24 as part of the warning phrases. Verse 21 says, "And if you will walk contrary to Me ... then I will add on you *plague* seven fold according to your contaminations." The important point here is that this "punishment," plague, for "walking contrary" is singular and isolated. It is included with other things that will happen to the people. This is true because the rarely used word for "plague," *makaw*, in verse 21 is singular, although often translated plural. So, it *does not* introduce the disasters listed in verse 22 such as beasts eating the children, destruction of cattle, people becoming few, and the roads becoming desolate. These were not plagues. "Walking contrary" and "plaguing" are also threatened in verses 24 and 28. If the people purposely broke the laws, they would naturally "meet" God unprotected and get the "plague," radiation contamination.[10] This is strengthened by the just preceding warning to do the commandments or else: "I also will do this to you: I will visit on you terror, the consumption and the fever that consume [the] eyes ... and I will set My face against you and you will be smitten (*neegafteem* [*nawgaph*]) before your enemies."[ac] If this is taken literally rather than figuratively, then "facing God" (that is, by my definition, being contaminated with radiation because they had not followed the rules) would cause "consumption" and "fever" that eats the eyes, the first and most vulnerable part of the body to be harmed by radiation.[11]

The next uses of the word *q'ree* are in Leviticus 26:27–28: "And if by this you will not listen to Me, but you will walk contrary (*q'ree*) to Me, then I will walk contrary (*q'ree*) to you in wrath." The word for "wrath" is *chaymaw*.[ad] It derives from *heat*.[12] The literal heat (radiation) of the Lord would affect the people when exposed to Him.

What happens next? God says that when the Israelites come to their enemies' land, *if* their uncircumcised hearts are humbled (a figure of speech for not keeping the covenant, just as not being circumcised would break the basic covenant) and they "*accept* (*rawtzaw*) their impurity (*avone*)," the Lord will "remember" *not the people*, but "the *land*."[ae] Strangely, the word used here for "if" is the Hebrew "*oh*." Overwhelmingly, the Hebrew word for "if" is *eem*. Just as overwhelmingly, the word for "or" is *oh*. The word *oh* is *only* used here as "if" with "then, *awz*." I do not know why. (Nowhere in their treatment of conditional clauses do Waltke and O'Conner, in *An Introduction to Biblical Hebrew Syntax*, discuss *oh* as sometimes translated "if.")

The next word I'd like to explain is *rawtzaw*.[af] It has many meanings throughout the scriptures but is only used as "accept" and "enjoy" or "satisfy" in the Five Books.[13] The same word is used earlier in this section relative to the land. If the people

ac. Lev. 26:16–17, cf., Deut. 28:22–25

ad. *chaymaw*, 2534

ae. Lev. 26:41–42

af. *rawtzaw*, 7521

wouldn't listen to the Lord, He would not smell their rest smelling odors, their land would become desolate, their cities a waste, and "then will the land enjoy (or 'satisfy') its Sabbaths all the days it lays desolate."[ag] It is as though it was *natural* for the land to be unused, unnatural, even harmful for it to be tilled.[ah] (In normal times, every seven years the land had to lay fallow.) Even though many of the people wouldn't survive, the now desolate land would survive.[ai] The fact is that these descriptions are physical phenomena, so that even if the words are obscure, they hew to the line followed so far.

One question regarding the land is why it would both "enjoy" or "satisfy" its rest and become *desolate*.[aj] Here I can only conclude that the land, too, will naturally become so irradiated that it will be useless for a time. There is some evidence to back this up. First, the word "desolate" (*shawmame*) has a second meaning of "to destroy" in such a way as to cause "astonishment" and "wonder."[ak] Second, the cities will be a *waste*.[al] *Chawrbaw* comes from *choreb*.[am] *Choreb* means "drought, dry, heat, waste."[14] Third, the long reprise of warnings in Deuteronomy addresses the tragedies that will result from spurning the covenant with the Lord:

> [20]"The Lord will not pardon him, but then the anger of the Lord will *smoke* and His jealousy against that man ...
>
> [22]And the latest generation will say, your children that will rise up after you, and the foreigner that will come from a far off land, when they see the *plagues* of that *land* and *its* sickness by which the Lord made it sick,
>
> [23]*Brimstone* and *salt*, a burning is the whole land; it is not sown, and *does not sprout nor grows* therein *any grass*, like the overthrow of *Sodom* and *Gomorrah*, *Admah* and *Zenoiyim*, which the Lord overthrew in His *anger* and in His *wrath*.
>
> [24]Then all nations will say, 'Why has the Lord done this to this land? What means the *heat* of this great anger?'
>
> [25]Then men will say, 'Because they have forsaken the covenant of the Lord, the God of their fathers, which He made with them ...
>
> [26]And they went and served other gods, and they prostrated themselves to them ...

ag. Lev. 26:31

ah. Lev. 26:35

ai. Lev. 26:44

aj. Lev. 26:32–35, 43

ak. Lev. 26:32
al. Lev. 26:31, 33
am. *chawrbaw*, f., 2723; *choreb*, 2721

^{27}Therefore the anger of the Lord *glowed* against that *land*, to bring on it all the curse that is written in this book.'" (Deut. 29:20, 22–27, my emphasis)

Here the land would suddenly be rendered useless due to "heat" that "glowed against that land." A by-product would be plagues and radiation sickness. The same relationships to *avone* are present. They are physical phenomena. And the fact that Deuteronomy was a late book does not mean that these observations were not age-old writings. Numbers 5:15 explains the law regarding an adulterous woman. The end of this section is rather interesting.

^{29}"This is the law of jealousy, when a wife, being under her husband, goes aside, and is defiled,

^{30}Or when the spirit of jealousy comes on a man … then will he set the woman before the Lord, and the priest will execute on her all this law.

^{31}And the *man* will be *free* from impurity." (Num. 5:29–31, my emphasis)

The last sentence has had quite a few interpretations, some pretty awful.[15] I think it is a straightforward statement: no matter how contaminated the wife becomes, it won't affect the husband.

Numbers 14:18 warns that while the Lord will forgive impurity and transgressions, He will not clear the guilty. He will "visit the impurity of the fathers on the children," on the third and fourth generations.

In Numbers 14:34, the Lord says that as a consequence of their transgressions, the Israelites over the age of 20 will "carry your impurity forty years."

Numbers 15:27–29 reiterates what had to be done if a person contaminated or was contaminated through error.[an] He was to bring his sacrifice to the priest, and the priest covered on him. However, verses 30–31 explain that if a person broke a commandment on purpose, "that person will be utterly cut off; his impurity is on him." In other words, the presumptuous person, in not receiving the protection of that sacrifice, would become contaminated. It must be assumed that the wrongdoings meant

an. Lev. 4:27–29

here were so bad that *avone* was assured and nothing could be done about it. This is different from the man who refused to tell what he had witnessed, because an anti-susceptibility offering was all that was needed to protect him.

Interestingly, an example of a person willfully breaking the Sabbath law is given in the very next verses following this warning. Numbers 15:32–36 tells about the man who gathered wood on the rest day. His punishment was predictable. He was to be stoned to death "outside of the camp." (One must assume his impurity was "on him.") Remember the "punishment" for man or beast that got too close to Mt. Sinai when the cloud was there? It was necessary to get them away from the camp.

In Numbers 18:1–3, Aaron and his sons "carry the impurity of the super-conditioned place" and the "impurity of your priesthood." Only they could work with the articles in the super-conditioned place while the tribe of Levi was assigned to the area outside the super-conditioned place. All this was to protect the rest of the people from the radiation that the preceding story of Korach and his revolt so graphically illustrated. Once more I will point out that this radiation was indiscriminate and that the assignment of Aaron's sons was to prevent its spread. To repeat: "And you will keep the charge of the super-conditioned place, and the charge of the altar; that there be no more anger on the Israelites."[ao] Only they were trained to "carry the impurity" on the super-conditioned place and on themselves.

ao. Num. 18:5

Numbers 18:23 repeats the orders in Numbers 3:7–8, charging the Levites "to serve the service of the tent of meeting, and they will carry their [the people's] impurity."

Numbers 30:16 refers to the laws of vows and oaths first seen in Leviticus 5:4, 24. It tells of the responsibility of the husband if he makes his wife's vows null and void. He will then carry her impurity. This is expanded in the discussion of the vow offering in Types of Sacrifices.

Deuteronomy 5:9 is in Deuteronomy's repeat of the Ten Commandments regarding God visiting the impurity of the fathers on the third and fourth generations "of them that hate [Him]."

Deuteronomy 19:15 is a simple statement that it must take two or more witnesses to accuse a person of any impurity or any willful contamination. Once again impurity and contamination are used, so we must assume that there was some understanding of the distinction in Deuteronomy.

Avone in the following books is found twice in Joshua. The first is the reference to Baal-peor: "Is the impurity of Peor too little for us, from which we have not cleansed to this day, even though there came a plague on the congregation of the Lord?"[ap] The second refers to the questionable Achan incident: "Did not Achan ... commit a *ma'al* concerning the devoted thing, and was there not anger *on all* the congregation of Israel? And the man perished not alone in his *impurity*?"[aq] The first reference seems to be an exact interpretation of the word and the process, but the second confuses the killing of 36 men in battle with being the result of the Lord's anger.[ar] Then it calls impurity the instrument for their deaths. Even if this story made sense, this couldn't have been the case because there was no mention of a resultant plague, only that "the Lord turned away from the fierceness of his anger."[as]

In the books following Joshua, there seems to be no pattern regarding the technical use of *avone*. Some seem to equate *avone* with wrongdoing.[at] There are, however, references that at least parrot the use in the Five Books, e.g., possibly 1 Samuel 3:13–14 is "curse God" instead of "bring a curse on themselves." Both tradition and the Septuagint so translate it.[16] Jeremiah 2:22, while it was probably intended as an analogy, may preserve a dim memory of *avone* as an impurity. "'For though you wash yourself with nitre, potash, and take for yourself much soap, your *avone* is stained before Me,' declares the Lord."

There is overwhelming support for *avone* being the impurity by reason of becoming contaminated from the radioactivity in the cloud. Since impurity was to be scrupulously avoided, it is easy to see how *avone* took on the connotation of something evil in later years when its true meaning was forgotten.

ap. Josh. 22:17

aq. Josh. 22:20

ar. Josh. 7:5

as. Josh. 7:26

at. e.g., 1 Sam. 20:1; 2 Sam 19:20; Isa. 1:13; Jer. 33:8; Ezek. 7:19; Hos. 12:8

Appendix H

Holiness (H) Code

The Holiness Code or H Code is said to run from Leviticus 17 – 26. Some critics suppose it was written by a group of priests with their own interests in mind who either preceded or followed P. Every time H's style and bias are found anywhere else in Leviticus (and it is), it is an insertion in those verses by the hand of H. I will consider the so-called H chapters in light of both the traditional translation of *qodesh*, "holy," and my translation, "conditioned."

H's "dominant theme is holiness."[1] Scholars say that the H Code differs from the rest of Leviticus because it emphasizes what is called the "divine first person," "I." Davies says it is "more sermonic" and gives Leviticus 17:10 as an example.[2] "I will set my face against the person that eats the blood and I will cut him off from the midst of his people." He points to statements such as "I am the Lord," "I am the Lord their/your God," and "You will be holy for holy am I the Lord your God."[a] If H is credited with verses where the Lord refers to Himself as "I," then H should also be credited with His references to Moses, Aaron, Aaron's sons, and the Israelites as "you." Such references should be primarily found in Leviticus 17–26. However, the fact is that first person references to the Lord are found in the pre-H chapters 6, 7, 8, 10, 11, 14, 15 ("*My* tabernacle"), and 16. The Lord saying "you" is in all chapters but 4 and 12. Chapter 4 connects non-stop to chapter 5, which does contain "you" relative to "your estimation."[b] In other words, the Lord spoke directly in all but two chapters. Now to the phrases "I [am] the Lord (YWH)" or "I [am] the Lord (YWH) your God (*Elohim*)."[c] They are found in Genesis, Exodus, Leviticus (outside the H Code), Numbers, and the reprise in Deuteronomy.[d] There is no

a. e.g., Lev. 19:2, 20:7, 26, 21:8

b. Lev. 5:15,18, 25
c. YWH, 3068; *Elohim*, 430
d. Gen. 15:7, 17:1, 26:24, 28:13, 31:13, 35:11, 46:3; Exod. 3:6, 4:11, 6:2, 6, 7, 8, 29, 7:5, 17, 10:2, 12:12, 14:4, 18, 15:26, 16:12, 20:2, 5, 29:46, 31:3; Lev. 11:44, 45; Num. 3:13, 41, 45, 10:10, 14:35, 15:41; Deut. 5:6, 9

reference in the opening chapter 17 of the H Code itself. On the other hand, the *Jewish Encyclopedia* explains exactly what "interpolations" *P* put into the H code.[3] Friedman says,

> The P stories certainly seem to be by one person ... The P *laws*, on the other hand, may well have come from a variety of collections of laws. The Holiness Code ... might originally have been a separate Aaronid document. This writer added laws of his own day and gathered all of the legal material together to form the definitive law code. He embedded the law code in the P stories. This gave it historical *authority*. No one had to ask from where these laws came. The text was explicit: they came from God through Moses—and Aaron. (my emphasis)[4]

There is general agreement with that statement. Of all the different possibilities suggested, skeptical scholars could not accept that the story was true. Many think it would be childish, naïve, and ridiculous to assume that there was actually a mountain and a tent where God communicated with the Israelites. The scholars with their fine exegeses have shown that the peculiar nature of H along with all of the interpolation, repetition, and contradictions in Leviticus make strong cases for what they posit.

Scholars say that holiness is emphasized in H above all, but look at the raw numbers. "Holy," "hallow," "hallowed," "sanctify," "sanctified" appear 47 times prior to H in Leviticus 2, 5, 6, 7, 8, 10, 11, 12, 14, 16. In the H chapters, from Leviticus 17 to 26, they appear 57 times (though not in chapters 17, 18, or 26). After the H chapters, they number 17 in chapter 27, which critics call an appendix to the H chapters.

One argument is that H is different because it emphasizes that "the people of Israel bears the collective responsibility to seek to achieve holiness."[5] Again, "You will be holy for holy am I." The argument continues that in H, all of the Israelites are addressed with this collective responsibility in mind as opposed to the rest of Leviticus, which addresses the Israelites "exclusively" in matters of ritual practice.[6] JPS says, "Virtually all sections of the Holiness Code open with the injunction to speak to the Israelite people; chapters 17, 18, 19, 20 and 22 begin in this way."[7] In contrast, JPS says Leviticus 1:2, 4:1, and 7:28 refer to proper modes of sacrifice.

However,
- chapter 17 also is specifically on sacrifice;
- chapter 19, after the "I-You" in verse 2, goes into a discussion of sacrifice;
- chapter 21 is not addressed to the Israelites at all, but to the priests;

- chapter 22 starts as an address to the priests, but verses 17–29 are to Aaron, his sons, and "to all of Israelites" on the subject of sacrificial rules;
- chapter 23 is to the Israelites on the subject of the feasts and their sacrifices;
- chapter 24 is to the Israelites on the oil they were to bring for the lamps, and the rule of the fire offering of incense with the loaves of bread; and
- chapter 26 does not contain the injunction to speak to the Israelites anywhere.

Given these H references to sacrifice, the rest of Leviticus is hardly alone in its emphasis on sacrifice. On the other hand, the pre-H chapters 1, 4, 7, 9, 11, 12, and 15 are specifically addressed to *all the people*. Chapters 1 and 4 do cover sacrifice. Chapter 7 covers sacrifice up to verse 23 where "Speak to the Israelites" appears, and from there to 27 has to do with the people not eating fat or blood. (The critics say this is H's hand.) Chapter 9, while it does discuss sacrifices, is specifically for the appearance of the radiance of the Lord in the wilderness. All of chapter 11 is on dietary rules, and verses 44–45 are in the "I-You" pattern: "For I am the Lord your God, and you have 'sanctified' (*qawdash*) yourselves, and you have become *qodesh*, for [I] am *qodesh*." (The critics say much of this is H because it has the necessary attributes.) Chapter 12 is indeed about the sacrifices for the unclean woman. Chapter 15, again on unclean men and women, primarily prescribes washing and additionally sacrifices.

Now, in addition to these examples of straying from the H/non-H rules, I must discuss pre-H chapters 2, 6, and 11 to emphasize the point that *qodesh* should be used as "a conditioner," not "holy."

- Leviticus 2 is a continuation of chapter 1, which is addressed to all the people. The chapters together tell what is to be done when anyone brings an oblation for the various types of sacrifices. Verses 2:3 and 10 say, "And what is left of the meal offering [will be] for Aaron and his sons; [it is] a super-conditioner (*qodesh qawdawsheem*) of the fire offerings of the

Lord." In other words, it is the responsibility, or at least the fervent desire, of one of the Israelites to bring material that ends up *qodesh*, a conditioner.

- Leviticus 6:7(14)–11(18) tells what has to be done with the meal offering that was brought by one of the Israelites who "contaminated."[e] In the traditional translation, after burning some of it, Aaron and each of his sons had to eat the rest "in a holy (*qodesh*) place in the court of the tent of meeting." The offering itself was "most holy (*qodesh qodesheem*)."[f] This law was to be observed "for your generations from the fire offerings of the Lord: all who touch them *must be* holy (*qodesh*)."[g] Holy? Holy like what? Like the people who had the "collective responsibility **to seek to achieve** holiness?"[8] A different responsibility? A different holiness? Of course not. The meal offering was a super-conditioner to be eaten in a conditioned place by conditioned people. Just as *qodesh* is found in H, so it is in the pre-H chapters.[9]

- Leviticus 11:44–45 falls into this category with it's "I-You" pattern and mention of becoming *qodesh*. The fact that the priests were involved and sacrifice was mentioned cannot be separated from the "holiness" of the rest of the people. All the Israelites were responsible for delivering the material that was used to condition the area, priests, and eventually the people in the wilderness. This led to collective conditioning—enough conditioning to adequately protect them all. This was the sole purpose of *qodesh*, conditioning/protection (until the word took on its meaning as understood today). Exodus 19:5–6, part of the Sinai covenant, promised that the Israelites would be "a kingdom of priests, a conditioned nation" if they listened to the Lord. Exodus 22:30 says, "Conditioned men you will be to me." (Mercifully, no one seems to think these verses are H.) The employment of the technical terms, *qodesh*/conditioner, is exactly the same in Exodus as they are in Leviticus in the rules for the manufacture of the original tent with its concomitant danger, as well as the description of its machinery. The same terminology exists in Numbers, e.g., regarding (1) the Nazirite

e. Lev. 5:11–13

f. Lev. 6:10, Heb. 6:17

g. Lev. 6:11, Heb. 6:18; cf., Lev. 6:18–20, Heb. 6:25–27; Lev. 7:1, 6, 10:10–11; (esp. 12–13), 14:13

and (2) the entire congregation in the misstatement of Korach and company.[h] So, the idea of *qodesh* in its technical sense flows continuously through Leviticus, Exodus, and Numbers when translated as "condition" as I think it should be.

h. Num. 6:8, 16:3

Whether or not there was an H or Hs, P or $P_{1,2,3,4,}$ etc., does not change the purpose one bit, but what about the repetition of words and concepts? They are so pervasive in H itself that one would wonder, if redactors were at work, why didn't they do a better job of editing? The pat answer is that it was not their job. They didn't want to touch anything already written, so they just added to what was already there for their own purposes. That brings us full circle. If nothing changed in the technical purpose for sacrifice—conditioning—what could have been the purpose of the redactors?

The traditional answer is that each redactor had his own religio-political ax to grind in whatever much later period he lived. I don't think that's a good answer. A possible alternative is found in what was reported, i.e., what the books say was going on at the time. According to Exodus, Leviticus, and Numbers, the Israelites were getting their instructions at various times during the wilderness period from either Mount Sinai or the tent. For the most part, these were verbal instructions. There was no shorthand, and recorders weren't available. Therefore, these rules had to be remembered, passed on verbally, and eventually written down at some unknown later time. How did you make sure the rules were understood? You repeated, clarified, and sometimes expanded them. You gave them in logical sequence sometimes and sometimes out of sync when, for some long-forgotten reason, it was necessary. You hoped they were passed on correctly.

As to word variations, regardless of whether or not synonyms were used to later write down what was once verbal, the real thing to watch for is the persistent use of ancient words in the technical discussions. I hope that by the time I finish this work I will have shown they never varied.

So, what about the changes? What changes am I really talking about? Looking at Exodus, Leviticus, and Numbers historically and literally, I am not talking of rules that changed in the years following the arrival in Canaan. I am talking of changes made during the 40 years of wandering in the wilderness, some of which were aimed at what to do when the Israelites reached Canaan. Again, there is one reason for the changes at this period: a growing realization of the necessity to protect against the danger of persistent radioactivity caused by the Lord's cloud being "in your midst." Thus, additions or even corrections to the laws of sacrifice, which are found in Leviticus and Numbers, are logical.

Finally, there is no question that in the later chapters of Leviticus there is a larger concentration of certain words and phrases. However, I think all that means is that in those chapters it was the *time* to talk about the subjects to which they referred, just as in the earlier chapters it was propitious to talk about rules and regulations pertaining to developments at that time. For example, "burnt offering" is mentioned 74 times in all but two chapters between Leviticus 1–16. From 17–26, it is mentioned five times in only three chapters (17, 22, 23). Yet, its use in so-called H is in the same sense as in the earlier chapters. It was just that for the time being, in the context of subjects under discussion, there was no reason to cover it in the later chapters including 27.

Also, it is true as the critics claim that there was a difference in style in some of the later chapters, but now there was what I think was a fundamental, traumatic change. The style change followed the deaths of Aaron's sons. Everything had changed. All rules had to be focused on danger. The overwhelming need was to protect against uncleanness and to remain conditioned. Not to do so would have been all too lethal. This is what the constant repetition of "I am the Lord" means. Implicit is a phrase ending *I am the Lord whose presence is dangerous. Protect yourselves!* All of the preceding has built up to these chapters and finally exploded in chapter 19 with its 16 repetitions of "I am the Lord" and then is repeated less frequently in the following chapters as a reminder.

While the technical language did not vary the whole time, it remained theoretical until the deaths of Aaron's sons. When they died, reality set in and nothing was ever the same again. The fact that there was a "style change" under these circumstances seems perfectly natural. So I am claiming that H was in reality only a part of the general expository development of a set of rules, which evolved and expanded out of necessity in a relatively short time in the wilderness period.

Glossary

(including New Nomenclature and Definitions)

English	Hebrew	Significance
TRADITIONAL TRANSLATION: anger [of the Lord], angry ISAACS TRANSLATION: **a radioactive event**	*ketsef, kawtsaf, af*	A natural event that took place with the descent of the cloud and its dangerous radiance. "The anger of the Lord burned...."
TRADITIONAL TRANSLATION: ark	*arone*	A chest was made to contain the stones (*edut*) from Mount Sinai. It was used in the communications process. See "Communication Station."
TRADITIONAL TRANSLATION: testimony ISAACS TRANSLATION: **stones**	*edut*	The two stones Moses brought down from Mount Sinai were put into the ark to form the "ark of communication" (*arone ha edut*), the transmitting/receiving device used to communicate with the Lord. See "Tables of Stone."
TRADITIONAL TRANSLATION: mercy seat ISAACS TRANSLATION: **ark cover**	*caporet*	The ark cover was made of "pure gold" and was attached to the top of the ark. See "Communication Station."
TRADITIONAL TRANSLATION: cherub(im)	*cherub(im)*	The fixtures attached to the top of the ark cover were made with the dual purpose of antennae for the ark and screen for the ark cover. See "Communication Station."
TRADITIONAL TRANSLATION: ephod	*ephod*	A portable device worn by the high priest that, with the breastplate, was used as a walkie talkie to communicate with the Lord. See "Walkie Talkie."
TRADITIONAL TRANSLATION: breastpiece of judgment	*chosen ha meeshpawt*	The breastpiece was a device that held the 12 stones of communication and the on/off switches, *Urim* and *Thummim*. It was wired to the walkie talkie (*ephod*). See "Walkie Talkie."
TRADITIONAL TRANSLATION: stones of memorial ISAACS TRANSLATION: **stones of communication**	*abnay zeekawrone*	There were two stones in the shoulderpiece of the walkie talkie and 12 in its breastplate. Their light was used in a system for receiving communication from the Lord. See "Walkie Talkie."

English	Hebrew	Significance
TRADITIONAL TRANSLATION: lights ISAACS TRANSLATION: **on switch**	*urim*	The mechanism activated the lights in the stones of communication in the breastpiece. See "Walkie Talkie."
TRADITIONAL TRANSLATION: perfections ISAACS TRANSLATION: **off switch**	*thummim*	The mechanism that deactivated the lights in the stones of communication in the breastpiece. See "Walkie Talkie."
TRADITIONAL TRANSLATION: plate	*tzitz*	Item was worn on Aaron's forehead while in the super-conditioned place to protect that part of the body from impurity (*awvone*). See "Priestly Protections."
TRADITIONAL TRANSLATION: sanctuary ISAACS TRANSLATION: **super-conditioned place**	*kodesh hakawdawsheem*	The super-conditioned place, the inner-most area of the tent, housed the ark. See "Communication Station."
TRADITIONAL TRANSLATION: veil	*pawrochet*	A curtain with *cherubim* woven into it screened the super-conditioned place. It may also have served as antennae. See "Communication Station."
TRADITIONAL TRANSLATION: plague ISAACS TRANSLATION: **radiation**	*negah*	Radiation resulted from sudden appearance of the Lord's cloud. See "Danger, Danger!"
TRADITIONAL TRANSLATION: leprosy ISAACS TRANSLATION: **burn**	*tsawra-at*	Burn of people and/or things was caused by radioactivity that emanated from the cloud. See "Danger, Danger!"
TRADITIONAL TRANSLATION: plague of leprosy ISAACS TRANSLATION: **radiation burn**	*negah tsawra-at*	Radiation burn was an affliction that resulted from unprotected proximity to the radioactive cloud. See "Danger, Danger!"
TRADITIONAL TRANSLATION: pestilence ISAACS TRANSLATION: **radiation sickness**	*deber*	Radiation sickness caused by radiation burn. See "Danger, Danger!"

English	Hebrew	Significance
TRADITIONAL TRANSLATION: clean	*tawhor*	Clean was a technical term for the condition wherein the danger of the cloud's radiation was a) minimized because people and things were properly protected, or b) removed by washing, sacrifice, etc. One could also be clean simply because there was no radiation present. To be clean was to be in a state or condition free of radiation and not a radiation attractor. This state allowed for the Lord to safely dwell in the midst of the people. See "Puzzling Laws."
TRADITIONAL TRANSLATION: unclean	*tawmay*	Unclean was a technical term for the condition wherein the danger of the cloud's radiation was maximized because people and things were not properly protected. A person or thing could also be unclean because radiation was present. In this state it was unsafe for the Lord to dwell in the midst of the people. A person or thing could also actively spread material or create a condition that could attract radiation from the cloud, preventing the Lord from dwelling in the midst of the people because of the danger. See "Puzzling Laws."
TRADITIONAL TRANSLATION: guilty ISAACS TRANSLATION: **susceptibility**	*awshame*	A person or thing could be susceptible to contamination from the cloud's radiation. See "Congregation Covers."
TRADITIONAL TRANSLATION: holy ISAACS TRANSLATION: **condition (n.)**	*kodesh*	Proper condition of people and things was achieved through various processes for safe communication with the Lord through the ark or the *ephod*. See "Holy Isn't Holy."
TRADITIONAL TRANSLATION: sanctify ISAACS TRANSLATION: **condition (v.)**	*kawdash*	The conditioning or processing of people or things by the priests to put them in a clean and safe condition for communication with the Lord through the ark or the *ephod*. See "Holy isn't Holy."

English	Hebrew	Significance
TRADITIONAL TRANSLATION: sin (v.) ISAACS TRANSLATION: **contaminate**	*chawtaw* (vb.)	To contaminate or to become contaminated by the dangerous material (*kawbode*) in the cloud, thereby triggering susceptibility to radiation burn. See "Danger, Danger!"
TRADITIONAL TRANSLATION: sin (n.) ISAACS TRANSLATION: **contamination** TRADITIONAL TRANSLATION: sin offering (n.) ISAACS TRANSLATION: **decontamination offering**	*chayt* (n.m.) *chatawaw* (n.f.) *chatawt* (n.f.)	Contamination was the state that rendered people and things susceptible to radiation burn. It could result from certain actions, conditions, or contact with the dangerous material (*kawbode*) in the cloud. *Chatawaw* and *chatawt* are also used as decontamination offering. See "Danger, Danger!"
TRADITIONAL TRANSLATION: iniquity ISAACS TRANSLATION: **impurity**	*avone*	Impurity was caused by contamination from the cloud's radiation. See "Radioactive Fallout."
TRADITIONAL TRANSLATION: atone ISAACS TRANSLATION: **cover**	*keeper*	Covering people and things with the various materials (incense, sacrifices, etc.) protected them against radiation. See "Congregation Covers."
TRADITIONAL TRANSLATION: trespass ISAACS TRANSLATION: **cover**	*ma'al*	Covering people and things with contamination endangered them at the appearance of the cloud. *M'ohl ma'al* meant super-contamination.
TRADITIONAL TRANSLATION: soul ISAACS TRANSLATION: **soul substance**	*nefesh*	A substance in the blood of humans and animals was evidently also present in the Lord. It was necessary to refresh this substance by resting. The Hebrew term was also synonymous with "person." See "Priestly Protections."
TRADITIONAL TRANSLATION: cloud	*awnawn*	The radioactive cloud settled over the ark for communication between the Lord and Moses. The cloud also led them on their journey through the wilderness. See "Radiation Fallout."
TRADITIONAL TRANSLATION: glory ISAACS TRANSLATION: **radiance**	*kawbode*	Radiance was the dangerous substance in the cloud through which the Lord's voice was transmitted. It glowed at night and was radioactive. See "Priestly Protections."

Bibliography

Achtemeier, Paul J., ed. *Harper's Bible Dictionary*. San Francisco: Harper, 1985.

Albright, William Foxwell. *Yahweh and the Gods of Canaan*. Winona Lake, IN: Eisenbrauns, 1994.

Aldred, Cyril. *Akhenaten Pharaoh of Egypt*. London: Sphere Books, 1972.

Avigad, Nahman and Yegael Yadin. *A Genesis Apocryphon: A Scroll from the Wilderness of Judea*. Jerusalem: Magnes Press of the Hebrew University, 1956.

Avinoam, Reuben, compiler, M. H. Segal, ed. *Hebrew English Dictionary*. Israel: Dvir, Ltd., 1957.

Benno, Jacob. *The Jewish Encyclopedia*. New York: Funk and Wagnalls, 1903.

"The Biblical Archaeologist." *Journal of the History of Medicine and Allied Sciences*. Vol. 34, May 1971.

Bietak, Manfred. "Comments on the 'Exodus.'" *The Journal of Near Eastern Studies* 49, no. 4.

Black, Jeremy, Andrew George, and Nicholas Postgate, eds. *A Concise Dictionary of Akkadian*. Wiesbaden: Harrassowitz Verlag, 2000.

Bloom, Harold. *The Book of J*. Translated by David Rosenberg. New York: Grove Weidenfeld, 1990.

Blumberg, Harry and Mordecai H. Lewittes. *Modern Hebrew*. New York City: Hebrew Publishing Company, 1968.

Botterweck, G. Johannes and Helmer Ringgren, eds. *Theological Dictionary of the Old Testament*. Grand Rapids, MI: Eerdmans, 1990–2001.

Bradley, David. "The Spice of Life." *The Guardian*. London: Guardian House, May 25, 2000.

Brenton, C. L. *The Septuagint with Apocrypha: Greek and English*. Peabody, MA: Hendrickson Publishers, 1992.

Brown, Francis. *The New Brown-Driver-Briggs Gesenius Hebrew and English Lexicon*. Peabody, MA: Hendrickson, 1979.

Brueggemann, Walter. "Yahwist." *Interpreter's Dictionary of the Bible*. Nashville: Abingdon, 1962.

Buchanan, Mark. "Spooky Trio to Explore the Quantum Universe." *New Scientist*. 5 December 1998.

———. "Beyond Reality." *New Scientist*. 14 March 1998.

Budge, E. A. Wallis. *The Egyptian Book of the Dead*. New York: Dover, 1967.

———. *The Gods of the Egyptians*. New York: Dover Publications, 1969.

Chicago Assyrian Dictionary. Chicago: The Oriental Institute.

Cohen, Rev. Dr. A., ed., *Soncino Chumash*. Hindhead, Surrey: The Soncino Press, 1947.

Cronkite, E. P., V. P. Bond, and C. L. Dunham, eds. "Some Effects of Ionizing Radiation on Human Beings: A Report on the Marshallese and Americans Accidentally Exposed to Radiation from Fallout and a Discussion of Radiation Injury in the Human Being." Washington, D.C.: United States Atomic Energy Commission, July, 1956.

Cross, Frank Moore. *Canaanite Myth and Hebrew Epic*. Cambridge, MA: Harvard University Press, 1975.

Dahood, Mitchell. Afterword to *The Archives of Ebla*. Garden City, NY: Doubleday, 1981.

Dalley, Stephanie. "The god Salmu and the Winged Disc." *Iraq*. London: British School of Archaeology, 1986.

Davies, G. Henton. "Ark of the Covenant." *Interpreter's Dictionary of the Bible*. Nashville: Abingdon, 1962.

Davies, Paul. *Superforce: The Search for a Grand Unified Theory of Nature*. New York: Simon & Schuster, 1985.

Del Olmo Lete, Sanmartin J. *Diccionario de la Lengua Ugarítica*. Barcelona: Editorial AUSA, 1996.

Dentan, R. C. "Book of Numbers." *Interpreter's Dictionary of the Bible*. Nashville: Abingdon, 1962.

Dever, William G. "Is There Any Archeological Evidence for the Exodus?" *Exodus: The Egyptian Evidence*. Edited by Ernest S. Frerichs and Leonard H. Lesko. Winona Lakes, IN: Eisenbrauns, 1997.

Driver, G. R. *Canaanite Myths and Legends*. Edinburgh: T. & T. Clark, 1971.

Eissfeldt, Otto. "Genesis." *The Interpreter's Dictionary of the Bible*. Nashville: Abingdon, 1962.

Englund, Gertie. *Middle Egyptian: An Introduction*. Uppsala, Sweden: Uppsala University, 1988.

Faulkner, Raymond O. *A Concise Dictionary of Middle Egyptian*. Gateshead, England: Paradign Press, 1986.

Fohrer, George, ed. *Hebrew and Aramaic Dictionary of the Old Testament*. Translated by W. Johnstone. Berlin: Walter de Gruyter, 1973.

Frazer, James G. *The Golden Bough: A Study in Magic and Religion*. New York: Macmillan Company, 1935.

Friedman, Richard Elliott. *Who Wrote the Bible?* New York: Summit Books, 1987.

Friedrich, Johannes. *Hethitisches Wörterbuch*. Heidelberg: Carl Winter Universitätsverlag, 1952.

Fuerst, Julius. *The Hebrew & Chaldee Lexicon to the Old Testament*. Translated by Samuel Davidson. Leipzig: Bernhard Tauchnitz, 1871.

Gardiner, Alan. *Egyptian Grammar*. Oxford: Griffith Institute (Ashmolean Museum), 1982.

———. "Late Egyptian Miscellanies" 6, 8. *Bibliotheca Aegyptiaca*. Bruxelles: Fondation Égyptologique, 1937.

Gaster, Theodore H. *Myth, Legend, and Custom in the Old Testament*. New York: Harper & Row, 1969.

———. "Sacrifices and Offerings, OT." *The Interpreter's Dictionary of The Bible*. Nashville: Abingdon, 1962.

A General Introductory Guide to the Egyptian Collections in the British Museum. London: British Museum Publications, 1975.

Gilbert, Katharine Stoddart with Joan K. Holt and Sarah Hudson. *Treasures of Tutankhamun*. New York: Metropolitan Museum of Art, 1976.

Ginzberg, Louis. *The Legends of the Jews*. Philadelphia: The Jewish Publication Society of America, 1947.

Glatt, David A. and Jeffrey H. Tigay. *Harper's Biblical Dictionary*. San Francisco: Harper, 1985.

Good, E. M. "Book of Joshua." *The Interpreter's Dictionary of the Bible*. Nashville: Abingdon, 1962.

Gordon, Cyrus H. *Ugaritic Textbook Glossary*. Rome: Pontificium Institutum Biblicum, 1967.

———. *Before Columbus*. New York: Crown, 1971.

Gray, George Buchanan. *Sacrifices in the Old Testament*. New York: KTAV, 1971.

Gray, John. *The Canaanites*. New York: Frederick A. Praeger, 1965.

Green, Jay P., ed. and trans. *The Interlinear Hebrew-Aramaic Old Testament*. Peabody, MA: Hendrickson, 1985.

Griffith, F. Ll., ed. *Hieratic Papyri from Kahun and Gurob*. London: Bernard Quaritch, 1898.

Gurney, O. R. *The Hittites*. London: Penguin Books, 1990.

Haran, Menaham. *Temples and Temple Service in Ancient Israel*. Winona Lake, IN: Eisenbrauns, 1985.

Hastings, James, ed. *A Dictionary of the Bible*. New York: Charles Scribner's Sons, 1909.

Hatch, Edwin and Henry A. Redpath. *A Concordance to the Septuagint: And the Other Greek Versions of the Old Testament (Including the Apocryphal Books)*. Grand Rapids, MI: Baker Books, 1998.

Heidel, Alexander. *The Gilgamesh Epic and Old Testament Parallels*. Chicago: The University of Chicago Press, 1963.

Held, Warren H., Jr., Williams R. Schmalstieg, and Janet E. Gertz. *Beginning Hittite*. Ohio: Slavica, 1988.

Hertz, Joseph Herman, ed. *The Pentateuch and Haftorahs*. New York: Oxford University Press, 1936.

Howie, C. G. "Ezekiel." *The Interpreter's Dictionary of the Bible*. Nashville: Abingdon, 1962.

The Interpreter's Dictionary of the Bible. Nashville: Abingdon, 1962.

The Interpreter's Dictionary of the Bible Supplementary Volume. Nashville: Abingdon, 1962.

The Jewish Encyclopedia. New York: Funk and Wagnalls, 1901.

Johnson, George. "Linguists Debating Deepest Roots of Language." *New York Times*. New York: New York Times Company, 27 June 1995.

Kalisch, Marcus Moritz. *A Historical and Critical Commentary on the Old Testament: Leviticus*. Pt. 1. London: Longmans, Green, Reader, and Dyer. 1867.

Keel, Othmar. *The Symbolism of the Biblical World*. New York: Crossroad, 1985.

Klein, Ernest. *A Comprehensive Etymological Dictionary of the Hebrew Language for Readers of English*. New York: Macmillan, 1987.

Knapp, A. Bernard. *The History and Culture of Ancient Western Asia and Egypt*. Belmont, CA: Wadsworth, 1988.

Koehler, Ludwig and Walter Baumgartner, et. al. *The Hebrew and Aramaic Lexicon of The Old Testament*. Leiden: Brill, 1999.

Kohlenberger, John R., III, ed. *The NIV Interlinear Hebrew-English Old Testament*. Grand Rapids, MI: Zondervan, 1985.

Kramer, Samuel N. "Sumer." *The Interpreter's Dictionary of the Bible*. Nashville: Abingdon, 1962.

Labat, Réne. *Manuel D'Épigraphie Akkadien*. Paris: Librairie Orientaliste Paul Geuthner, S. A., 1976.

Lambdin, Thomas. "Egyptian Loan Words in the Old Testament." *Journal of the American Oriental Society*, 1953.

Langenscheidt's New College German Dictionary. New York: Langenscheidt, 1990.

Lesko, Leonard H. *A Dictionary of Late Egyptian*. Berkley: Scribe, 1989.

Levine, Baruch A. "Priestly Writers." *Interpreter's Dictionary of the Bible*. Nashville: Abingdon, 1962.

———. *The JPS Torah Commentary: Leviticus*. Philadelphia: The Jewish Publication Society, 1989.

Lurker, Manfred. *The Gods and Symbols of Ancient Egypt*. London: Thames & Hudson, 1980.

Magil, Joseph. *Magil's Linear School Bible*. New York: Hebrew, 1905.

Mankowski, Paul V. *Akkadian Loanwords in Biblical Hebrew*. Winona Lake, IN: Eisenbrauns, 2000.

Matthews, Robert. "I is the Law." *New Scientist*. 30 January 1999.

Mendehall, George E. *The Tenth Generation*. Baltimore: The Johns Hopkins University Press, 1974.

Mercer, Samuel A. and Frank Hudson Hallock, eds., *The Tel El-Amarna Tablets*. Toronto: Macmillan Co. of Canada, Ltd., 1939.

Meyers, Eric M., ed. *Biblical Archeologist*. Durham, NC: Sept. 1990.

Mikelic, J. L. and G. E. Wright. "Plagues in Exodus." *Interpreter's Dictionary of the Bible*. Nashville: Abingdon, 1962.

Milgrom, Jacob. *The JPS Torah Commentary: Numbers*. Philadelphia: The Jewish Publication Society, 1990.

Milgrom, Jacob. "Leviticus 1–16." *The Anchor Bible*. New York: Doubleday, 1991.

———. "A Prolegomemnon to Leviticus 17:11." *Journal of Biblical Literature*. 1971.

———. *Cult and Conscience*. Leiden: Brill, 1976.

Miller, Madeleine S. and J. Lane Miller. *The New Harper's Bible Dictionary*. New York, Harper & Row Publishers: 1973.

Millgram, Abraham E. *Sabbath: The Day of Delight*. Philadelphia: The Jewish Publication Society of America, 1944.

Morris, William, ed. *The American Heritage Dictionary of the English Language*. Boston: American Heritage Publishing Co., Inc. and Houghton Mifflin Company, 1969.

Moscati, Sabatino. *Ancient Semitic Civilizations*. New York: G. F. Putnam's Sons, 1957.

Muilenberg, James, "Holiness." *The Interpreter's Dictionary of the Bible*. Nashville: Abingdon, 1962.

Muraoka, Takamitsu. *Hebrew/Aramaic Index to the Septuagint: Keyed to the Hatch-Redpath Concordance*. Grand Rapids, MI: Baker Books, 1998.

Nussbaum, Rudi, PhD and Wolfgang Köhnlein, PhD. "Health Consequences of Exposures to Ionizing Radiation from External and Internal Sources: Challenges to Radiation Protection Standards and Biomedical Research." *Medicine and Global Survival*, vol. 2, no. 4. Cambridge: International Physicians for the Prevention of Nuclear War, December 1995.

Oates, Joan. *Babylon, Ancient Peoples and Places*. London: Thames & Hudson, 1970.

Owens, John Joseph. *Analytical Key to the Old Testament*. Grand Rapids, MI: Baker Book House, 1990.

Pace, Mildred Mastin. *Wrapped for Eternity*. New York: McGraw Hill, 1974.

Pardee, Dennis. "Ugaritic Bibliography." *Archiv für Orientforschung*. Austria: Ferdinand Berger & Son, Horn, 1987.

Partridge, Eric. *Origins, A Short Etymological Dictionary of Modern English*. New York: Macmillan, 1963.

The Pentateuch with Haftaroth and Five Megiloth. Translated by Alexander Harkavy. New York: Hebrew, 1933.

Pettinato, Giovanni. *The Archives of Ebla*. Garden City, NY: Doubleday, 1981.

Pfeiffer, Robert. "Sources." *Harper's Bible Dictionary*. New York: Harper & Row Publishers, 1973.

Porter, J. R. "Ark." *Harper's Bible Dictionary*. San Francisco: Harper, 1985.

Pritchard, James B. *Ancient Near Eastern Texts*. Princeton, NJ: Princeton University Press, 1969.

Rainey, Anson F., ed. *Egypt, Israel, Sinai: Archeological and Historical Relationships in the Biblical Period*. Tel Aviv: Tel Aviv University Press, 1987.

Romer, John. *Ancient Lives: The Story of the Pharaohs' Tombmakers*. London: Weidenfeld & Nicolson, 1984.

Sarna, Nahum M. *The JPS Torah Commentary: Exodus*. Philadelphia: The Jewish Publication Society, 1991.

Sarna, Nahum M. *The JPS Torah Commentary: Genesis*. Philadelphia: The Jewish Publication Society, 1989.

———. *Exploring Exodus*. New York: Schoken, 1986.

Segert, Stanislov. *A Basic Grammar of the Ugaritic Language*. Berkley: University of California Press, 1984.

Sharma, Arun, S. Gautum and S. S. Jadhave. "Spice Extracts ad Dose-Modifying Factors in Radiation Inactivation of Bacteria," *Journal of Agricultural and Food Chemistry*. Mumbai, India: Food Technology Division, Bhabha Atomic Research Center, 2000.

Sjöberg, Ake W., ed. *The Sumerian Dictionary of the University Museum of the University of Pennsylvania*. Philadelphia: The Babylonian Section of the University of Pennsylvania Museum, 1984.

Strong, James, S.T.D., LL.D. *The New Strong's Exhaustive Concordance of the Bible* and *A Concise Dictionary of the Words in The Hebrew Bible: with their Renderings in the Authorized English Version*. Nashville: Thomas Nelson Publishers, 1984.

———. *A Concise Dictionary of the Words in The Hebrew Bible: with their Renderings in the Authorized English Version*. Madison, NJ: Thomas Nelson Publishers, 1890.

Sturtevant, Edgar Howard. "Hittite Glossary." *Language Monographs*. Baltimore: Waverly Press, Inc., 1931.

Tigay, Jeffrey H. *The JPS Torah Commentary: Deuteronomy*. Philadelphia: The Jewish Publication Society, 1996.

Tov, Emanuel. *The Text-Critical Use of the Septuagint in Biblical Research*. Jerusalem: Simor, 1981.

Trefil, James. *Reading the Mind of God*. New York: Charles Scribner's Sons, 1989.

Tubb, Jonathan N. and Rupert L. Chapman. *Archeology and The Bible*. London: British Museum Publications, 1990.

Ungnad, Arthur. *Akkadian Grammar*. Revised by Lubor Matous. Translated by Harry A. Hoffner, Jr. Atlanta, GA: Scholars Press, 1992.

Van Seters, John. *The Life of Moses: The Yahwist as Historian in Exodus-Numbers*. Louisville: Westminster/ John Knox, 1994.

Von Soden, Wolfram. *Akkadisches Handwörterbuch*. Wiesbaden: Otto Harrassowitz, 1981.

Waltke, Bruce K. and M. O'Connor. *An Introduction to Biblical Hebrew Syntax*. Winona Lake, IN: Eisenbrauns, 1990.

Webster's Encyclopedic Unabridged Dictionary of the English Language. New York: Portland House, 1989.

Webster's New International Dictionary. 2nd edition. Springfield, MA: G and C Merriam Co., 1948.

Weinfeld, Moshe. *Deuteronomy and the Deuteronomic School*. Winona Lake, IN: Eisenbrauns, 1992.

Weingreen, *A Practical Grammar for Classical Hebrew*. New York: Clarendon Press and Oxford University Press, 1959.

Wellhausen, Julius. *Prolegomena to the History of Israel*. Atlanta: Scholar's Press, 1994.

Whitelaw, Dr. W. A. ed. The Proceedings of the 10th Annual History of Medicine Days. Faculty of Medicine, The University of Calgary. March 2001.

Wilford, John Noble. "Greek Myths: Not Necessarily Mythical." *New York Times*. New York: The New York Times Company, 4 July 2000.

Wise, Michael O., Norman Golb, John J. Collins, and Dennis G. Pardee. *Methods of Investigation of the Dead Sea Scrolls and the Khirbet Qumran Site*. New York: The Anals of the New York Academy of Sciences, 1994.

Wood, Horatio C., Jr. and Arthur Osol. *The Dispensatory of the United States of America*. Philadelphia: Lippincott, 1943.

The Works of Flavius Josephus. Translated by William Whiston. Philadelphia: Claxton, Remsen, & Haffelfinger.

Wright, G. E. "Book of Exodus." *The Interpreter's Dictionary of the Bible*. Nashville: Abingdon, 1962.

Zukav, Gary. *The Dancing Wu Li Masters: An Overview of the New Physics*. New York: Bantam, 1989.

Notes

Introduction. Read This First!

1. *Webster's New International Dictionary*, 1458.

2. I distinguish between the Five Books and the "following books" rather than the traditional "later books" at the suggestion of my personal linguistics coach, Robert Hawley. He correctly points out that no one knows exactly when any of the books were actually written down.

3. From 600–1000 CE groups of Jewish scholars known as Mas(s)oretes wrote the Bible in what is known as the Masoretic Text. They introduced vowel signs into the alphabet to make the formerly only consonantal text clearer. The vowel signing under the letters is called "pointing."

Chapter 1. Learning to Communicate

1. I have no intention of getting into the well-known history of ancient mid-Eastern laws in this work. It has been thoroughly covered by others, and the relation or lack of relation of the Babylonian and other codes to the Hebrew has been theorized for years. My interest here is to convey the conditions under which this body of laws was communicated.

2. If I'm correct in saying that no tabernacle was contemplated until this time, a question arises as to what is meant by the reference to "house of the Lord" in Exodus 23:19. The answer is that "house of the Lord," as it was used then, didn't necessarily mean an actual structure. Thus, we see Jacob, the progenitor of the 12 tribes and the man from whom the Israelites got their name, meeting the Lord in a dream, waking and saying, "How fearful is this place! This is none other than the house of God … and [he] took the stone that he had put under his head and set it up as a pillar … and he called the name of that place Bet El (house of God) … and this stone that I have set up, a pillar, shall be God's house." (Genesis 28:17–22) It is interesting that Moses built one of these simple altars and 12 memorial pillars at the base of Mount Sinai, and out of the blue it was emphasized that they were for the 12 tribes of Israel. (Exodus 24:4) Then, when Jacob returned to the same place, "he built there an altar and called the place El Bet El because God revealed himself to him." (Genesis 35:7) So a stone or an altar could be called God's house.

   On this point one is forced to ask why the verse is repeated in Exodus 34:26. This is the order to bring first fruits to the house of the Lord and not to boil a kid in its mother's milk. (The kid-milk law is also in Deuteronomy 14:21, but in a different context and with no house of the Lord.) My feeling is that all of the material from Exodus 34:18–26, essentially a repeat of Exodus 23:12–19, was stuck in there for no good reason except perhaps to reemphasize the warning previously given. That is, verse 17 regarding the molten gods should end the first part of chapter 34, because all the other points are covered in the Exodus 23 references. Also, Exodus 34:24 represents the fact that the Lord will "drive out" the people now living in Canaan. So it logically skips from verse 17 to verse 27, omitting the repetition of verses 18–26. Consequently, there is no need for a post-calf mention of "house of the Lord."

Chapter 2. Puzzling Laws

1.   Morris, *American Heritage Dictionary*, 249.

Chapter 3. Holy Isn't Holy

1.   It should be noted that Deuteronomy 5:12–15 gives a different reason for the Sabbath, "because you have been a servant in Egypt." The original idea had not, evidently, gotten into this book. For a discussion of the two reasons for the Sabbath, see Weinfield, *Deuteronomy and the Deuteronomic School*, 222. Weinfel believes "the law of P, and the theological conception underlying it, are much older that those of D." Ibid., 180.

2.   Milgrom, *Leviticus 1–17*, 346.

3.   Waltke and O'Connor, *An Introduction to Biblical Hebrew Syntax*, 388–91.

4.   Whether there was one or a dozen Isaiahs responsible for the book of Isaiah is not pertinent here, but I intend to develop his/their influence on the rest of Jewish history in another work in the future.

5.   Reiner and Biggs, eds., *Chicago Assyrian Dictionary*, vol. 13, 46 in the Old Akkadian, Old Babylonian, Alalakh (a city-state in West Syria), Old and Middle Babylonian, see Oppenheim, ed., *Chicago Assyrian Dictionary*, vol. 6, vi.), Ras Shamra, and Standard Babylonian (Knapp, *The History and Culture of Ancient Western Asia and Egypt*, 146–7). This is similar to the use of cedar, hyssop, etc., in Exodus, Leviticus, and Numbers regarding the conditioning of the nazirite and a house.

6.   Black, George, and Postgate, eds., *A Concise Dictionary of Akkadian*, 286, 292 and Koehler and Baumgartner, et al., *Hebrew and Aramaic Lexicon*, 1073.

7.   Reinner and Biggs, eds., *Chicago Assyrian Dictionary*, vol. 13, 294.

8.   Del Olmo Lete, *Diccionario de la Lengua Ugarítica*, 363.

9.   Ibid., 364. The noun is "sanctuary." Also see Koehler and Baumgartner, et al., *Hebrew and Aramaic Lexicon*, 1076 and Akkadian *qasdu(m)* in Black, George, and Postgate, eds., *A Concise Dictionary of Akkadian*, 286.

10.   Koehler and Baumgartner, et al., *Hebrew and Aramaic Lexicon*, 1072.

11.   Klein, *A Comprehensive Etymological Dictionary of the Hebrew Language for Readers of English*, 563.

12.   Milgrom, "Leviticus 1–16," *The Anchor Bible*, 730–1.

13.   Muilenberg, *The Interpreter's Dictionary of the Bible*, vol. 2, 617.

14.   Brown, *The New Brown-Driver-Briggs Gesenius Hebrew and English Lexicon*, 869.

15.   *Strong's Hebrew Dictionary*, 102.

16.   There are words dating from the Old Akkadian on, which mean the same thing. *Qadaydu* means "1. to bow, to bend down … to incline, 2. to bow … 3. *quddudu* to bend, to prostrate … Old Akkadian, Old Babylonian, Tel El Amarna tablets, Standard Babylonian, Neo-Assyrian." Reiner and Biggs, eds., *Chicago Assyrian Dictionary*, vol. 13, 44. *Qaddish* is "bowed, hunched" in Old Babylonian and Standard Babylonian. Ibid., 47. None of these quotes refers to bowing before a deity, so even if it's used as such elsewhere, there was no special meaning for which the words were designed. Strangely, there seem to be no equivalent words in the Ugaritic. The words for "bow down, to" are *hbr*, *hwy*, and *kr*. Gordon, *Ugaritic Textbook Glossary*, 531. Driver, *Canaanite Myth*, 137, 139, 145. Whether the Hittite adverb *kat-ta* meaning "down, with" is equivalent is a guess. Held, Schmalstieg, and Getz, *Beginning Hittite*, 153. Its use is seen as "down" in this quote: "But when my brother Muwattallis … marched *down* (*kat-ta*) into the Lower Country … my brother took along the gods … of Hatti, and brought them *down* (*kat-ta*) into the Lower Country." Ibid., 111. Similarly, the word *kat-ta-an* means "down." Ibid., 153. For exmple: "And while my father was *down* (*kat-ta-an*) in the land of Carchemish …" Ibid., 141. The words certainly describe the direction downward.

Chapter 4. Tables of Stone

1.   Koehler and Baumgartner, et al., *The Hebrew and Aramaic Lexicon of The Old Testament*, 790–1. Strong, *A Concise Dictionary of the Words in The Hebrew Bible*, 85.

2.   Koehler and Baumgartner, et al., *Hebrew and Aramaic Lexicon*, 795.

3.   Technically, the first mention of the word *edut*, pertaining specifically to the stones in the ark, is found in Exodus 16:34. This was relative to the commandment to store a sample of manna before it. However, commentators have noted for centuries that this detail is out of chronological order since there was no tent, ark, or *edut* as yet. See Sarna, *The JPS Torah Commentary: Exodus*, 91.

4.   Compare, e.g., Psalm 78:5.

Chapter 5. Communication Station

1.   Gilbert, *Treasures of Tutankhamun*, plate 8.

2.   Ibid., plate 9.

3.   Oppenheim and Reiner, eds., *Chicago Assyrian Dictionary*, vol. 1, pt. 2, 231.

4.   Gordon, *Ugaritic Textbook Glossary*, 366.

5. All references to the ark cover are called P, and so *sakaku* is considered a late word. See, e.g., Brown, *The New Brown-Driver-Briggs Gesenius Hebrew and English Lexicon*, 498. This seems rather strange since "ark," as in "ark of the covenant," is supposed to have been known by the older writers. Also, while *cherubim* are called P when making the ark, the word itself is known to J in relation to the Garden of Eden. (Gen. 3:24) So the lid, *caporet*, of which the *cherubim* that cover the ark are a part, would certainly be integral to and of equal antiquity with these items.

6. C. G. Howie says it is from the "first half of the sixth century [BCE]" in *The Interpreter's Dictionary of the Bible*, vol. 2, 207.

7. Richard Friedman calls Genesis 3:24 J. Friedman, *Who Wrote the Bible?* 246.

8. Sarna, *The JPS Torah Commentary: Exodus*, 161.

9. Ibid.

10. Oppenheim, Reiner, and Biggs, eds., *Chicago Assyrian Dictionary*, vol. 8, 559.

11. Koehler and Baumgartner, et al., *Hebrew and Aramaic Lexicon*, 497.

12. From Old Assyrian and Middle Babylonian on. Oppenheim, Reiner, and Biggs, eds., *Chicago Assyrian Dictionary*, vol. 8, 192.

13. Ibid., 197. Compare Von Soden, *Akkadisches Handwörterbuch*, 445.

14. Roth, ed., *Chicago Assyrian Dictionary*, vol. 8, 197.

15. For an extensive discussion see Koehler and Baumgartner, et al., *Hebrew and Aramaic Lexicon*, 1132–7.

16. Gordon, *Ugaritic Textbook Glossary*, 480. Compare Driver, *Canaanite Myth and Legends*, 143.

17. Faulkner, *Dictionary of Middle Egyptian*, 174. Compare Gardiner, *Egyptian Grammar*, 582.

18. See Weingreen, *A Practical Grammar for Classical Hebrew*, 3.

19. Keel, *The Symbolism of the Biblical World*, 27–8.

20. Ibid., 28.

21. Lurker, *The Gods and Symbols of Ancient Egypt*, 130. Also see Dalley, "The God Salmu and the Winged Disk," *Iraq*, vol. 48, 95.

22. Pritchard, *The Ancient Near East*, vol.2, fig. 40. (Wikipedia - LMLK seal.)

23. Ibid., vol. 2, fig. 87.

24. Ibid., vol. 2, fig. 46. http://en.wikipedia.org/wiki/Tudhaliya

25. Ibid., vol. 1, fig. 99.

26. Ibid., vol. 1, fig. 130.

27. Ibid., vol. 1, fig. 130.

28. Keel, *The Symbolism of the Biblical World*, fig. 22, 28.

29. Ibid., fig. 33, 38.

30. Ibid.

31. Ibid., fig.187, 141.

32. Ibid., fig. 221, 160.

33. Ibid., fig. 222, 162.

34. Ibid., fig. 283, 213.

35. Ibid., fig. 290, 213.

36. Ibid., fig. 321, 235.

37. Chapman, *Archaeology and the Bible*, fig. 36, 83.

38. Ibid., 41.

39. Ibid., 55.

40. Ibid.

41. Ibid., fig. 9, 42.

42. Ibid., fig. 10, 45.

43. Ibid., fig. 14, 49.

44. Ibid., fig. 19.

45. Ibid., fig. 20, 52.

46. Courtesy of the Oriental Institute of the University of Chicago.

47. Keel, *The Symbolism of the Biblical World*, fig. 24, 29.

48. Ibid., fig. 23, 29.

49. Ibid., fig. 186, 140.

50. Mendenhall, *The Tenth Generaion*, fig. 7, 41.

51. Ibid., fig. 6, 40.

52. Ibid., fig. 5, 40.

53. Dalley, *The God Salmu and the Winged Disk*, 92.

54. Black, George, and Postgate, eds., *A Concise Dictionary of Akkadian*, 312.

Chapter 6. Walkie Talkie

1. There were other types of *ephods*, but they were iconic in nature. (No related languages use words related to *ephod* in an iconic manner.) One such is Gideon's golden *ephod*, which first appears in Judges 8:27. This is the story of Gideon, the hero who rescued his farmer Israelite brothers from a raid of the Midianites. (For discussion of Gideon and Source detail, see C. F. Kraft, *The Interpreter's Dictionary of the Bible*, vol. 2, 393–5, 1019–20 and bibliographies of these articles.) After his mighty victory, Gideon asked his adoring men for golden earrings from the spoils of battle.

²⁵And they did cast there every man the earrings of his spoil.

²⁶And the weight of the golden earrings that he requested was a thousand and seven hundred shekels of gold; besides the crescents, and the pendants, and the purple garments … and besides the chain that was about the camels' necks.

²⁷And Gideon made an ephod thereof, and put it in his city, in Ophrah; and all Israel went astray after it there; and it became a snare to Gideon, and to his house. (Judg. 8:25–27)

Whatever this thing was, it must have been huge, primarily gold, and eventually worshipped as some sort of idol. It is very doubtful that it was similar to the first *ephod* mentioned in Exodus and Leviticus. See *The Jewish Encyclopedia*, vol. 5, 185–6.

An Ephraimite named Micah had another, possibly third type of *ephod*. Judges 17:1 begins his story. His mother had a graven image and a molten image made for him. He created a "house of God" in his home, and in it he set up a shrine using these two objects along with an *ephod* and *teraphim* (8655). *Teraphim* are family idols or household gods. He then hired a Levite to be his private priest. Ultimately a group of Danites came along and removed all the paraphernalia, as well as the Levite, and then set up the graven image as an idol in the city of Dan: "And these men went into Micah's house, and fetched the graven image the *ephod*, and the *teraphim*, and the molten image." (Judges 18:18) Most Bibles insert "of" in this verse, "graven image [of] the *ephod*," indicating that the *ephod* was a graven image (an idol), but it seems more logical to assume that the Hebrew is missing an "and." It should have read, "the graven image [and] the *ephod*" as stated in Judges 18:14, 17, and 20. The Septuagint does supply the "and." Inserting "and" leaves its appearance and its type a total mystery.

For now, it only remains to mention the last reference to *ephod* where Hosea makes this prophecy: "The Israelites will sit solitary many days without king, and without prince, and without sacrifice, and without pillar [an item used in pagan worship], and without *ephod* and *teraphim*." (Hosea 3:4) Once again, since the pillar and *teraphim* were forbidden idols, this *ephod* was probably meant as an iconic figure.

There is one strange occurrence in Isaiah where *ayfoodaw* (642), the feminine of *ephod*, is used: "And you will defile your graven images overlaid with silver and your molten images covered (*ahfoodat*) with gold." (Isaiah 30:22) The word *ayfoodaw* is variously translated. Green uses both "case" and "covering" as does *tzeepoo*. Green, ed. and trans., *The Interlinear Hebrew-Aramaic Old Testament*, vol. 3, 1666. Koehler and Baumgartner, et al, *Hebrew and Aramaic Lexicon*, 77, say "covering." Kohlenberger, *The NIV Interlinear Hebrew-English Old Testament*, vol. 4, 60 says "covered." *Strong's Hebrew Dictionary*, 15, says "ornament." Brown, *The New Brown-Driver-Briggs Gesenius Hebrew and English Lexicon*, 65–6 says "sheathing." Fuerst, *The Hebrew & Chaldee Lexicon to the Old Testament*, 133 says "covering" but that others "understand it of the idol itself." Whatever the exact meaning was, in this verse it was associated with idols and had no relation to the *ephod* of Exodus and Leviticus. The important fact is that, with the exception of the word *ayfoodaw*, there are no other words in Hebrew to relate to it.

2. At this point one can get engulfed in a morass of questions, such as whether it was or wasn't necessary to have the *ephod* in order to communicate with God, or whether, when the ark is mentioned as the instrument in 1 Samuel 14:18, it is the *ephod* that is really meant. (The Septuagint *does* use "*ephod*.") It is certainly true that there are times when there is communication and no instrument is specifically mentioned, e.g., 1 Samuel 23:2 in the David at Ziklag story and before Abiathar meets David with the *ephod*: "And David inquired of the Lord saying, 'Shall I go and smite these Philistines?' And the Lord said to David, 'Go, and smite the Philistines and save Keilah.'" Verse 4 has David inquiring of the Lord again. So does 2 Samuel 2:1, etc. However, I think it is pointless to try to draw a distinction. The *ephod* was used as a communication device to talk with God in the same manner as the less portable ark. Also, from the casual way it is mentioned, its purpose was taken for granted and it was part of the everyday life of the people of the time. However, by the time these stories were set down in writing, there were variations in their telling (cf., Chronicles and Samuel). There is much more discussion of the total machine as a communication device than of the ability to communicate without it at the time in question.

3. Driver, *Canaanite Myths and Legends*, 103, 136. See also Koehler and Baumgartner, et al., *Hebrew and Aramaic Lexicon*, 77.

4. Gordon, *Ugaritic Textbook Glossary*, 364.

5. Del Olmo Lete, *Diccionario de la Lengua Ugarítica*, 43–4.

6. Faulkner, *Dictionary of Middle Egyptian*, 17.

7. Fisch, *Soncino Books of the Bible: Ezekiel*, 86. See note on verse 10. The Targums were probably written from the 2nd century CE.

8. Another translation for *shaysh* or *shayeesh* (7893) is "alabaster" or "marble," as in 1 Chronicles 29:2, in Esther 1:6 twice, and in Song of Solomon 5:15.

9. Koehler and Baumgartner, et al., *Hebrew and Aramaic Lexicon*, 1663.

10. Sarna, *The JPS Torah Commentary: Exodus*, 157.

11. Koehler and Baumgartner, et al., *Hebrew and Aramaic Lexicon*, 1456.

12. Klein, *A Comprehensive Etymological Dictionary of the Hebrew Language for Readers of English*, 648. Also see Brown, *The New Brown-Driver-Briggs Gesenius Hebrew and English Lexicon*, 1004.

13. *Strong's Hebrew Dictionary*, 114.

14. Fuerst, *Hebrew & Chaldee Lexicon*, 1366.

15. Since the Egyptian writing system like that of Hebrew in the biblical period, did not record vowels, one can only guess at actual sounds. What one looks for in comparing words is consonant similarity. As for *d*, Gardiner says the approximate sound value in addition to *dj* was "also a dull emphatic *s* (Hebrew)," that is the letter *tsaday*. Gardiner, *Egyptian Grammar*, 27.

16. Faulkner, *Dictionary of Middle Egyptian*, 324.

17. Gardiner, *Egyptian Grammar*, 27. Both the ▬ and the ⎮ eventually came to stand for *s*, but, according to Gardiner, the ▬ was originally "much like our *z*."

18. Gardiner, *Egyptian Grammar*, 604.

19. Faulkner, *Dictionary of Middle Egyptian*, 324.

20. Ibid., 325. In mentioning "Holy of Holies," Faulkner is referring to the temple of Der el-Bahri. Unfortunately, he doesn't say which temple, but the latest king whose temple is there is Thutmoses III, 1504–1450 BCE.

21. Ibid.

22. Budge, *The Egyptian Book of the Dead*, 463. Hieroglyphic vocabulary.

23. Lesko, *A Dictionary of Late Egyptian*, 166. 19th–21st Dynasties, ca. 1300–1070 BCE.

24. "Being" is the actual translation because *shawzar* is *always* preceded by a *mem*, *mawsh'zawr*, which means it is in the *hophal* verb pattern. This is a passive causative, "to cause to be," and the use of *mem* means it is participial. So, "being holy" is the way one would translate it.

25. The Septuagint is the Greek translation of the Bible from the mid third century BCE. It is the oldest known version.

26. There are complex explanations as to exactly what the two words *toela'at shawnee* meant, but perhaps the clearest is in Sarna's *The JPS Torah Commentary: Exodus*, 157: "Hebrew *tola'at shani*. The first word means 'a worm'; the second signifies the color. The combination designates the brilliant red dye produced from the eggs of scale insects of the Coccidae family that feeds on oak trees." Sarna translates the words together as "crimson." See also Koehler and Baumgartner, et al., *Hebrew and Aramaic Lexicon*, 1603, 1702, especially, for the cognate languages and the explanation "literally glow-worm, used to designate crimson red material." For simplicity I will use "scarlet." Wickwire, *The Interpreter's Dictionary of the Bible*, vol. 1, 450 ("blue") and vol. 3, 969 ("purple").

27. It's also interesting that there is an Egyptian word that means "faience, glass": *thnt* or, in its Old Kingdom form, *thnt*, the *t* being pronounced *tsh*. Gardiner, *Egytian Grammar*, 505, 600–1. Faulkner, *Dictionary of Middle Egyptian*, 306. At first there would seem to be no connection, but three points make the word a possible relative: First, the *n* in Egyptian can also be an *l* and the *h* is pronounced as an emphatic *h*. Gardiner, *Egyptian Grammar*, 27. Second, faience made by the Egyptians "consists of a core made of small grains of quartz sand or quartz pebbles or rock crystal ground into a fine powder." This material was bound together chemically, glazed, and used for small objects, "beads, pendants, rings, ... amulets, *shabti* figures, *pectorals*." (my emphasis) *Introductory Guide to the Egyptian Collections in the British Museum*, 198. Of particular note is that the "most common colour of the glaze is blue, green, or greenish-blue ... A particular vivid blue is characteristic of the New Kingdom." (c. 1567–1085 BCE) Third, the use of faience items on pectorals (i.e., breastplates) commonly found in Egypt almost forces one to make a connection. There is a stunning necklace/pectoral found in the tomb of Tutankhamun, which has all the colors of the *ephod* and "ten bead tassels each ending in a [blue] faience corrolla ... attached to a gold bar." See plate 19 in *Treasures of Tutankhamun*, Metropolitan Museum of Art, 142. Understanding that the material for the manufacture of items pertaining to the

tent most probably came from despoiling the Egyptians, here is still another word relating to the *ephod* that might have been Egyptian.

28. Brown, *The New Brown-Driver-Briggs Gesenius Hebrew and English Lexicon*, 107. Koehler and Baumgartner, et al., *Hebrew and Aramaic Lexicon*, 123.

29. Koehler and Baumgartner, et al., *Hebrew and Aramaic Lexicon*, 1697–8. Gordon, *Ugaritic Textbook Glossary*, 497.

30. Koehler and Baumgartner, et al., *Hebrew and Aramaic Lexicon*, 358–60.

31. *Strong's Hebrew Dictionary*, 49.

32. Koehler and Baumgartner, et al., *Hebrew and Aramaic Lexicon*, 360.

33. Del Olmo Lete, *Diccionario de la Lengua Ugaritíca*, 184–5.

34. According to Gardiner, the Middle Egyptian period runs from 2240–1314 BCE. Gardiner, *Egyptian Grammar*, 1. Though other scholars vary the range somewhat, e.g., Oriental Institute says 2213–1293 BCE, it is hundreds of years before the time scholars say the various strands were written and 300 years before Saul became the first king. The Exodus is said to have occurred some time in the 1200s, varying with the individual scholar.

35. Faulkner, *Dictionary of Middle Egyptian*, 197. Faulkner gives the same reference as Gardiner—Beni Hasan ii, 4.

36. Englund, *Middle Egyptian: An Introduction*, 1.

37. In Lesko, *A Dictionary of Late Egyptian*, 140, see Kitchen, *Rammeside Inscription*, in "Sethos I, Kamais, Great Inscription, Year 9" 1. 69. 10. In "Sethos I, Abydos, Great Dedicatory Stela for Ramesses I" 1. 114. 12. Sethos I (or Seti) was the son of Ramesses I and reigned from 1318–1304 BCE or 1290–1268 BCE.

38. "Hieratic Papyri" from KAHUN is correctly ILLAHUN according to Gardiner, *Egyptian Grammar*, 22. In Faulkner, *Dictionary of Middle Egyptian*, 178, see Griffith, *Hieratic Papyri from Kahun and Gurob*, The Petrie Papyri P1. 31. 4.25 of the Letters.

39. See explanation of how "*n*" can also be an "*l*" in Walkie Talkie endnote 28. Also see Lambdin, "Egyptian Loan Words in the Old Testament." *Journal of the American Oriental Society*, vol. 73, 147.

40. Gardiner, *Middle Egyptian Grammar*, 585. Faulkner, *Dictionary of Middle Egyptian*, 193.

41. See explanation of how "*n*" can also be an "*l*" in Walkie Talkie endnote 28.

42. "Green feldspar" is from Faulkner, *Dictionary of Middle Egyptian*, 140. "White-blue feldspar" is from Lambdin, *Journal of the American Oriental Society*, vol. 73, 152. "Orange colored zircon" is from Garber and Funk, *The Interpreter's Dictionary of the Bible*, vol. 2, 901. (Not covered by Gardiner.)

43. Lambdin, "Egyptian Loan Words in the Old Testament." *Journal of the American Oriental Society*, vol. 73, 152. Lambdin uses notes from Albright, *Yahweh and the Gods of Canaan* to trace *nofek* and it says is the Egyptian Old Kingdom *mefkat*. Gardiner

and Faulkner call it the same. Gardiner, *Egyptian Grammar*, 568. Faulkner, *Dictionary of Middle Egyptian*, 106 uses one reference, which is 18th Dynasty.

44. Faulkner, *Dictionary of Middle Egyptian*, 264. (Not covered by Gardiner.)

45. Ginzberg, *Legends of the Jews*, vol. 3, 172. Actually, this function seems to have been taken for granted in legend, e.g., Ginzberg's vol. 3, 455 and vol. 4, 8.

46. Josephus, *Antiquities of the Jews*, book 3, chapter 8, section 9.

47. For the source fans, *zawchar* (2142), is E, J, P, R, whereas *zecher* (2143) in Exodus 3:15 and 17:14, is said to be E. *Zeekawrone*, 2146, is E and P depending on the verse.

48. See Brown, *The New Brown-Driver-Briggs Gesenius Hebrew and English Lexicon*, 269–271. *Strong's Hebrew Dictionary*, 35 and Koehler and Baumgartner, et al., *Hebrew and Aramaic Lexicon*, 269–71.

49. Compare Genesis 41:9, Koehler and Baumgartner, et al., *Hebrew and Aramaic Lexicon*, 270.

50. Gelb, Landsberger, and Oppenheim, eds., *Chicago Assyrian Dictionary*, vol. 21, 16–22, from Old Akkadian, Old Babylonian on.

51. Tel el-Amarna was the site of the city of Akhenaton, the Pharaoh who exclusively worshipped Aton the sun-god. In 1887, a cache of tablets was found there dating from the second half of the second millennium BCE.

52. Gordon, *Ugaritic Textbook Glossary*, 403, 393. Driver, *Canaanite Myths and Legends*, 149.

53. Gelb, Landsberger, and Oppenheim, eds., *Chicago Assyrian Dictionary*, vol. 21, 17–8.

54. Faulkner, *Dictionary of Middle Egyptian*, 240.

55. Budge, *The Egyptian Book of the Dead*, 172.

56. Ibid., 87.

57. Ibid., 182.

58. Faulkner, *Dictionary of Middle Egyptian*, 240. Gardiner, *Egyptian Grammar*, 591.

59. Koehler and Baumgartner, et al., *Hebrew and Aramaic Lexicon*, 271.

60. Interestingly, Koehler and Baumgartner, et al., *Hebrew and Aramaic Lexicon*, 271 uses this verse to translate *zaycher* as "mention," rather than "remembrance."

61. Koehler and Baumgartner, et al., *Hebrew and Aramaic Lexicon*, 1791 says regarding Leviticus 23:24, "But see Elliger p. 318: the sense of [*zeekawrone*] is *not really a commemoration, but an announcement.*" (my emphasis)

62. Owens, *Analytical Key to the Old Testament*, vol. 2, 735.

63. Kohlenberger, *The NIV Interlinear Hebrew-English Old Testament*, vol. 3, 45.

64. Green, ed. and trans., *The Interlinear Hebrew-Aramaic Old Testament*, vol. 2, 1099.

65. Slotki, ed., *Soncino Books of the Bible: First Chronicles*, 90.

66.   Koehler and Baumgartner, et al., *Hebrew and Aramaic Lexicon*, 270.

67.   *Strong's Concordance*, 863.

68.   Brenton, *Septuagint*, 550.

69.   Brown, *The New Brown-Driver-Briggs Gesenius Hebrew and English Lexicon*, 271.

70.   Driver, *Canaanite Myths and Legends*, 12, 52–3, 75, 91, 138. Koehler and Baumgartner, et al., *Hebrew and Aramaic Lexicon*, 358, also points to the Akkadian *ershu*. Del Olmo Lete, *Diccionario de la Lengua Ugarítica*, 181. Weidner, Hunger, and Hirsch, *Archiv für Orientforschung*, 397.

71.   Segert, *A Basic Grammar of the Ugaritic Language*, 189, directly compares it to the Hebrew word *charawsh*.

72.   *Jewish Encyclopedia*, vol. 12, 385.

73.   Ugaritic: Driver, *Canaanite Myths and Legends*, 153. Egyptian: Faulkner, *Dictionary of Middle Egyptian*, 298. Also see Koehler and Baumgartner, et al., *Hebrew and Aramaic Lexicon*, 1742–50.

74.   See Koehler and Baumgartner, et al., *Hebrew and Aramaic Lexicon*, 1750 for discussion of 1 Samuel 14:41 with both opinions, and 1750–1 for *Thummim* specifically. In all cases Koehler and Baumgartner, et al., *Hebrew and Aramaic Lexicon* is uncertain. Tov, *The Text-Critical Use of the Septuagint in Biblical Research*, 187–8, says, "This section must have been omitted accidentally." However, he believes that *Urim* and *Thummim* were meant.

75.   Lampe, ed., *A Patristic Greek Lexicon*, 340.

76.   Hastings, ed., *A Dictionary of the Bible*, 839.

77.   That it was the *ephod* is also taken for granted by Rashi and Kimchi. See the note about 1 Samuel 14·18 in Goldman, ed., *Soncino Books of the Bible: Samuel*, 78.

78.   The possibilities in Koehler and Baumgartner, et al., *Hebrew and Aramaic Lexicon*, 362 all have question marks.

Chapter 7. Danger, Danger!

1.   In this work I do not intend to get into the possible relationships between the Hebrew for cloud, *awnawn*, and similar sounding words in other languages for two reasons: (1) That discussion is a work in itself. Similar words range from names of gods, e.g., the Sumerian moon-god Nanna, sky-god An and its Semitic counterpart Anu, the also Semitic Ugaritic sister of Baal, Anat, who was also an Egyptian goddess, to the exact word *an'n* in the Ugaritic. To work out these possibilities would be compelling but not pertinent to what we are discussing. For a classic study of *awnawn*, see George Mendenhall, *The Tenth Generation*, 209–13. (2) It would not be necessary because, unlike many of the other words we have been and will be discussing, there is no question that *awnawn* means "cloud." Thus, looking for its roots would not make the meaning any clearer. It is used as such in all Five Books, and it is the only word used. It is also seen in following books: 1 Kings, 2 Chronicles, Nehemiah, Job, Psalms,

Isaiah, Lamentations, Ezekiel, Hosea. In the plural, it is also in Jeremiah, Daniel, Joel, Nahum, and Zephaniah.

2.   The reference to "priest" in Exodus 19:24 raises a question. There were no Israelite priests then. They were named as such in Exodus 28:1. Theories are that this represents a different strand as it relates to the origins of priesthood (Sarna, *The JPS Torah Commentary: Exodus*, 107) or that they were the firstborn (Rashi, Ibn Ezra; Hertz, ed., *The Pentateuch and Haftorahs: Exodus*, 208), because in Exodus 13:2 they were all sanctified to the Lord. My own feeling is that since the first official priests were Aaron and his sons (Exodus 28:1), and it was Aaron and his sons, Nadab and Abihu, who went up the mountain on several occasions with Moses and the elders at this time, it is they who are (even though prematurely) being referred to as "priests."

3.   Milgrom, "Leviticus 1–16," *The Anchor Bible*, 830–1.

4.   Cohen, ed., *Soncino Books of the Bible: The Five Books of Moses with Haphtaroth*, 492, 1033.

5.   Reider, *The JPS Torah Commentary: Deuteronomy*, 86–7.

6.   Sarna, *The JPS Torah Commentary: Exodus*, 149.

7.   *Strong's Hebrew Dictionary*, 101.

8.   Fuerst, *Hebrew & Chaldee Lexicon*, 1211.

9.   Brown, *The New Brown-Driver-Briggs Gesenius Hebrew and English Lexicon*, 864. Koehler and Baumgartner, et al., *Hebrew and Aramaic Lexicon*, 1057.

10.   Oppenheim and Reiner, eds., *Chicago Assyrian Dictionary*, vol. 16, 98–9.

11.   Gelb, Landsberger, and Oppenheim, eds., *Chicago Assyrian Dictionary*, vol. 16, 100.

12.   Ibid., 102–4.

13.   Von Soden, *Akkadisches Handwörterbuch*, 1083.

14.   Koehler and Baumgartner, et al., *Hebrew and Aramaic Lexicon*, 1057.

15.   Gelb, Jacobsen, Landsberger, and Oppenheim, eds., *Chicago Assyrian Dictionary*, vol. 16, 106.

16.   Ibid., 110.

17.   Ibid., 110.

18.   Ibid., 113.

19.   Ibid., 114.

20.   Ibid., 207.

21.   Ibid., 207.

22.   Ibid., 209.

23.   Ibid., 209.

24.   Ibid., 256.

25. Ibid., 257. Nuzi is a North Mesopotamian city. History dates from 4000 BCE, tablets written in Old Babylonian cuneiform, 15th century BCE.

26. Ibid., 260.

27. Gordon, *Ugaritic Textbook Glossary*, 113.

28. Del Olmo Lete, *Diccionario de la Lengua Ugarítica*, 421.

29. Roth, ed., *Chicago Assyrian Dictionary*, vol. 4, 184, 46. See also vol. 4, 246 regarding *epqu* (Nuzi, Standard Babylonian), another word for "leprosy," and vol. 5, 46, regarding *garaybu* (Old Babylonian, Standard Babylonian), "leprosy, scab," all equating with the Sumerian.

30. Ibid., vol. 15, 36–7.

31. Koehler and Baumgartner, et al., *Hebrew and Aramaic Lexicon*, 669.

32. Brown, *The New Brown-Driver-Briggs Gesenius Hebrew and English Lexicon*, 620.

33. Koehler and Baumgartner, et al., *Hebrew and Aramaic Lexicon*, 546.

34. Ibid., 209.

35. Ibid., 209–10.

36. Ibid., 211.

37. See Brown, *The New Brown-Driver-Briggs Gesenius Hebrew and English Lexicon*, 181 about "destroy," 2 Chronicles 22:10. See 2 Kings 11:1. See Psalm 41:8 (9) for "disease," as in Green, ed. and trans., *The Interlinear Hebrew-Aramaic Old Testament*, 1423; Cohen, *The Soncino Books of the Bible: Psalms*, 128.

38. Brown, *The New Brown-Driver-Briggs Gesenius Hebrew and English Lexicon*, 182.

39. Von Soden, *Akkadisches Handwörterbuch*, 168.

40. Roth, ed., *Chicago Assyrian Dictionary*, vol. 3, 135.

41. Driver, *Canaanite Myths and Legends*, 106–11, 154.

42. Del Olmo Lete, *Diccionario de la Lengua Ugarítica*, 128–9.

43. There are only two possible exceptions to words describing a single "plague," but which are plural in the early books. They are Genesis 12:17 regarding *negah, n'gaweem* and Exodus 9:14 regarding *magayfaw, magayfotai.*

    In the Genesis reference, there is no indication what the "great plagues" were that afflicted Pharaoh "and his house." Nor is there actually any explanation as to why there would be more than one "plague." It's possible that the plural referred to a single plague inflicted on multiple individuals in the household. There might be a hint of this and, generally, what the plague *was* if we equate the Pharoah story with a similar story in Genesis 20. That is, in the Genesis 12 story we see Abram and Sarai leaving Haran and going into Egypt. It was here that Sarai was kidnapped by Pharaoh's princes and brought to his house. At that point, the plague ("plagues" in the Hebrew) was brought on all of them by the Lord, and Pharaoh was forced to release her. In chapter 20, the same occurrence took place with Abimelech, king of Gerar. He, too, kidnapped Sarah (her name now), but this time the punishment by the Lord was revealed. When Abimelech was warned by the Lord to release Sarah he did so:

> [17]And Abraham (his name now) prayed to God and God healed Abimelech and his wife and his maid-servants and they bore [children],

> [18]For the Lord had fast closed up every womb of the house of Abimelech because of Sarah, Abraham's wife. (Gen. 20:17, 18)

However, since *both* Abimelech and his women needed healing, we can assume the same thing affected all of them. One possible culprit might have been a mild dose of radiation, "plague," enough to cause temporary sterility. Observers at the time would have had no idea what was going on, so they could have only described the circumstances.

As to the second exception, Exodus 9:14, it is a verse that precedes hail, locusts, darkness, and death of firstborn, the last four plagues against the Egyptians. The Lord instructed Moses to tell the Pharaoh, "I [am] about to send all my plagues (*magayfotai*) to your heart and against your servants and against your people in order that you may know there is none like Me in all the earth." It would seem that in this one place the Lord, through Moses, was not using the meaning technically, but in a way Pharaoh could understand. Nevertheless, it is most interesting that to hammer the point home, in the very next verse, Exodus 9:15, He referred to *deber*, a very technical word and yet one Pharaoh could have understood: "For by now I could have stretched out my hand and smitten you and your people with *pestilence* [*badawber*] and you would have been *destroyed from the earth*." When talking to Moses and Aaron, though, He reverted to the singular relative of *magayfaw*, *negeph*. He used *negeph* when discussing the actual protection from the "plague," which caused the death of the firstborn in Egypt. Of course, when referring to any of these words as spoken to *Pharaoh*, it would have to have been equivalent in meaning in the Egyptian. (Either that or Pharaoh understood Hebrew.)

Coming to grips with the various words used for "plague," it would be easy to say that they were the work of the different sources. However, the different sources seemed to know and use the different words, and so did the same ones. Thus, *magayfaw* is J in Exodus 9:14, but P in Numbers. *Nawgaph* in Exodus 12:23 is J, JE, (or even P secondary in *Harper's Bible Dictionary*) and Exodus 32:33 is E. On the other hand, its noun, *negeph*, is P in Exodus 12:13, 30:21, Numbers 8:19, etc. The important *negah* is J in Genesis 12:17, J or E in Exodus 11:1, and of course P in Leviticus. (Critics say Leviticus is essentially all P.) *Makaw* is P in Leviticus 26:21 and J in Numbers 11:33. In Leviticus, where one would expect the same word to be used every time, we find *nawgaph* used as "smitten" in Leviticus 26:17, and in the same story *nachaw* is "smite" in Leviticus 26:24, where, as noted, *makaw* is used for "plague" in 26:21. Both are obviously P. We see the same case in Exodus 7:25 where *nachaw* is "smitten," but in verse 27 of the same story, *nawgaph* is "smite," yet both are J. Later, in Numbers 17:11–12, *negeph* is used as "plague," but in the same story, in the following verses 13–14, its derivative *magayfaw* is used. Yet, these verses are all called P. So, it would seem possible that writers were simply using different, related words for literary variation, rather than as representatives of different "schools" or interests. See also Appendix C.

44. E and J sources are represented according to the critics.

45. Gordon, *Ugaritic Textbook Glossary,* 489. Driver, *Canaanite Myths and Legends,* 147. Roth, ed., *Chicago Assyrian Dictionary,* vol. 17, pt. 2, 78. Old Babylonian, Middle Babylonian, Tel El Amarna tablets, Standard Babylonian, Neo-Assyrian, Neo-Babylonian.

46. Faulkner, *Dictionary of Middle Egyptian,* 241. For similar translations in Ugaritic, see Del Olmo Lete, *Diccionario de la Lengua Ugarítica,* 435, and in relation to Akkadian and Arabic see Pardee, *Archiv für Orientforschung,* 34, note by Charles Virolleaud.

47. Pfeiffer, "Sources," *Harper's Bible Dictionary,* 550.

48. Of the individuals who got the highest doses of radiation following the detonation of the nuclear device, "about two-thirds ... were nauseated ... and one-tenth vomited and had diarrhea." Cronkite, Bond, and Dunham, "Some Effects of Ionizing Radiation on Human Beings. A Report on the Marshallese and Americans Accidentally Exposed to Radiation from Fallout and a Discussion of Radiation Injury in the Human Beings," 16.

49. Tigay, *The JPS Torah Commentary: Deuteronomy,* 263–4. Koehler and Baumgartner, et al., *Hebrew and Aramaic Lexicon,* 861.

50. The *k'ri* or *qere* word is the interpretation or oral tradition of the Masoretic scribes (particularly 6th–9th century) in marginal notes in the Masoretic text of the Bible. This differed from the *k'tib* (*kethibh*) word, which was the authoritative one. The *k'ri* word had to be said instead of the *k'tib* word. Koehler and Baumgartner, et al., *Hebrew and Aramaic Lexicon,* 374.

51. The Vulgate is the Latin version of the Bible prepared by Jerome in the fourth century.

52. Tigay, *The JPS Torah Commentary: Deuteronomy,* 264.

53. Cohen, ed., *The Soncino Books of the Bible: First Samuel,* 30, note 4.

54. Green, ed. and trans., *The Interlinear Hebrew-Aramaic Old Testament,* 721. Koehler and Baumgartner, et al., *Hebrew and Aramaic Lexicon,* 1308.

55. *Josephus,* book 6, chapter 1, section 4. Also see Goldman, ed., *The Soncino Books of the Bible: First Samuel,* 34 for a rabbinic comment on the subject.

56. For discussion of *shal* see Koehler and Baumgartner, et al., *Hebrew and Aramaic Lexicon,* 1502.

57. For similar stories in classical literature, see Gaster, *Myth, Legend and Custom in the Old Testament,* 476, #138.

Chapter 8. Radioactive Fallout: From Moses to the Marshall Islands

1.   A sidelight is the use of *tawmay* in the famous *A Genesis Apocryphon*, the scroll found at the site of Qumran. It was written in Aramaic at ca. 73 BCE–AD 14. Wise, Golb, Collins, Pardee, *Methods of Investigation of the Dead Sea Scrolls and the Khirbet Qumran Site*, 443. It is a retelling of some of the Genesis stories. The one of interest here is a fanciful retelling of the story of Abraham in Genesis 12. Here Abram (his name at the time) tells his wife Sarai (Sarah's name at the time) to say she is his sister when they go down to Egypt so that the servants of Pharoah wouldn't kill him. Genesis 12 tells the story in a straightforward manner, but the *Genesis Apocryphon* has Abram and his nephew Lot weeping when Sarai is forcefully taken from him to be a concubine of the Egyptian king. Column 20, line 15 has Abram beseeching the Lord "to descend upon him [the king] and all his household and may he not this night defile (*tawmay*) my wife." Avigad and Yadin, *A Genesis Apocryphon, A Scroll from the Wilderness of Judea*, 43.

2.   Koehler and Baumgartner, et al., *Hebrew and Aramaic Lexicon*, 375. See also Botterweck and Ringgren, eds., *Theological Dictionary of the Old Testament*, vol 5, 330.

3.   Gordon, *Ugaritic Textbook*, 406.

4.   Driver, *Canaanite Myths and Legends*, 150.

5.   Faulkner, *Dictionary of Middle Egyptian*, 295. The exact Hebrew word, *toor* (2905), means "row" as used in Exodus 28:17–20 and 39:10–13. It refers only to the rows of jewels on the high priest's breastpiece. In following books, it is used as rows of building material in the temple.

6.   Gardiner, *Egyptian Grammar*, 514.

7.   Faulkner, *Dictionary of Middle Egyptian*, 295.

8.   Ibid., 300. Gardiner, *Egyptian Grammar*, 445.

9.   Cronkite, Bond, and Dunham, "Some Effects of Ionizing Radiation on Human Beings. A Report on the Marshallese and Americans Accidentally Exposed to Radiation from Fallout and a Discussion of Radiation Injury in the Human Beings," III.

10. Ibid., 16.

11. Ibid., 27.

12. Ibid.

13. Ibid., 28.

14. Ibid.

15. Ibid.

16. Ibid., 33.

17. Ibid.

18. Ibid.

19. Faulkner, *Dictionary of Middle Egyptian*, 225.

20. Reiner and Biggs, eds., *Chicago Assyrian Dictionary*, vol. 15, 151–3. From Old Assyrian, Old Babylonian on.

21. Scall, *netek* (5424), is derived from the word *nawtock* (5423), meaning "pull, draw, tear away, apart, off," e.g., Leviticus 22:24. Brown, *The New Brown-Driver-Briggs Gesenius Hebrew and English Lexicon*, 683, says that *netek* is literally "a tearing off, i.e., what one is inclined to scratch or tear away." The word *nasayhu* from Old Akkadian on has as one of its meanings "to tear out parts of the body … to pull out hair … to pull, tear out objects." (Roth, ed., *Chicago Assyrian Dictionary*, vol. 11, pt. 2, 1). Even though the meaning is the same, the *s* and *h* are not directly etymologically cognate with the *t* and *k* of *netek*. More to the point is *nataku(m)*, Black, George, and Postgate, *Concise Dictionary of Akkadian*, 246. It is translated "to drip … trickle, ooze from the mouth, trickle repeatedly."

22. Koehler and Baumgartner, et al., *Hebrew and Aramaic Lexicon*, 1007.

23. Milgrom, "Leviticus 1–16," *The Anchor Bible*, 792.

24. Brown, *The New Brown-Driver-Briggs Gesenius Hebrew and English Lexicon*, 843.

25. Nussbaum and Köhnlein, "Health Consequences of Exposures to Ionizing Radiation from External and Internal Sources: Challenges to Radiation Protection Standards and Biomedical Research," *Medicine and Global Survival*, 11–2.

26. http://edition.cnn.com/2007/WORLD/asiapcf/08/30/btsc.chance.nukes/index.html#cnnSTCVideo

27. In September of 1970, I had a piece of unbleached, woven wool exposed to gamma rays. Exposure turned the wool to a uniform reddish-beige color. Exposure time was 141.5 hours at 500,000 rad/hr = roentgens/hr, total 7×70 rad = 70 million rad. (I do not consider that experiment at all conclusive.)

Chapter 9. Priestly Protections

1. *Wisdom of Sirach*, 45– 9. Green, ed. and trans., *The Interlinear Hebrew-Aramaic Old Testament*, 1864–5.

2. Koehler and Baumgartner, et al., *Hebrew and Aramaic Lexicon*, 1023 for II *tsitz*. The Jeremiah reference is in the New International Version translation.

3. Takamitsu Muraoka, *Hebrew/Aramaic Index to the Septuagint: Keyed to the Hatch-Redpath Concordance*, 93. Hatch and Redpath, *A Concordance to the Septuagint*, 182–3.

4. Oppenheim and Reiner, eds., *Chicago Assyrian Dictionary*, vol. 16, 214.

5. Black, George, and Postage, eds., *A Concise Dictionary of Akkadian*, 339. Tel Mishrifreh is a city founded in third millennium BCE, located 180 km. north of Damascus, central Syria.

6. Milgrom, "Leviticus 1–16," *The Anchor Bible*, 511–2.

7. Koehler and Baumgartner, et al., *Hebrew and Aramaic Lexicon*, 1023.

8.   Driver, *Canaanite Myths and Legends*, 150.

9.   Pritchard, *Ancient Near Eastern Texts*, 137.

10.   Driver, *Canaanite Myths and Legends*, 150.

11.   Gordon, *Ugaritic Textbook Glossary*, 535. Del Olmo Lete, *Diccionario de la Lengua Ugarítica*, 422. Note translation of *tsitz* in Koehler and Baumgartner, et al., *Hebrew and Aramaic Lexicon*, 1023.

12.   Driver, *Canaanite Myths and Legends*, 87. Baal V iii 60–iv 4.

13.   Howies, *The Interpreter's Dictionary of the Bible*, vol. 2, 208.

14.   Interestingly, the blue wire was used to fasten the plate, *tsitz*, to the miter and was used with the fringe, *tsitzit*.

15.   Sarna, *The JPS Torah Commentary: Exodus*, 183.

16.   Hertz, ed., *The Pentateuch and Haftorahs*, 342. Koehler and Baumgartner, et al., *Hebrew and Aramaic Lexicon*, 684.

17.   Faulkner, *A Concise Dictionary of Middle Egyptian*, 140. The spelling for "anoint" is *nsr*. The figure s is actually pronounced as "z" according to both Gardiner, *Egyptian Grammar*, 27 and Faulkner, *Dictionary of Middle Egyptian*, 140.

18.   Oppenheim, Reiner, and Biggs, eds., *Chicago Assyrian Dictionary*, vol. 11, pt. 2, 33, 39. The *s* in the Akkadian *nasayru* is equivalent to the Hebrew *tsaday* found in *nezer*, but of the *s*, Akkadian Grammar says, "In older periods of Akkadian writing many sounds could not be represented unambiguously in writing. For instance, the emphatic sounds, for which there were no syllabic signs in the Sumerian, were represented by the signs for similar sounding voiced and voiceless phonemes: … *s* by *z* … *t* by *td*; even *s/sh/z* and *'h* could not be precisely distinguished from one another." Regarding the translation of the word, while "dedication" and "consecration" are the usually accepted ideas, it is interesting that Koehler and Baumgartner, et al., *Hebrew and Aramaic Lexicon*, 684, says, under *nzr*, that the Arabic *nadira* is "to be on one's guard." Ungnad, *Akkadian Grammar*, 14.

19.   That the use of the plural here cannot support the argument that later there were multiple sanctuaries, Wellhausen, et al., is clear from the mention of the veil and the general context of Leviticus 21:22, 24. Also see Milgrom, "Leviticus 1–16," *The Anchor Bible*, 754.

20.   For the grammatical rules see Weingreen, *A Practical Grammar for Classical Hebrew*, 26–31. Exodus 30:37 says of the incense, "Conditioning it will be to you for (*la*) the Lord," according to Strong's, Hendrickson, Magil's, Oxford, Soncino, JPS, and just plain logic. Leviticus 23:20 shows the interchangeability in one verse: "Conditioned they are to (*la*) the Lord for (*la*) the priest." Clearer meanings surface by interchanging to's and for's, as in Exodus 30:10 where the blood offered once a year to cover the horns of the altar is better described as "super-conditioned for" instead of "super-conditioned to" the Lord. It is absolutely fascinating that *la* as "for" shows up again in the conditioning/ protection of the nazirite's head:

⁵"All the days of the vow of his separation (*nezer*) no razor will pass over his head; until the days be full, which he separated for the Lord (*yazeer laY'h'vaw*), he will be conditioned [with oil]. He will let the hair of his head grow.

⁶All the days of his separation for the Lord (*hazeero laYaw'y*) he will not come to a dead person." (Num. 6:5–6)

Verse 7 strengthens the point that lamed may be used as "for." Five times lamed is used as "for" regarding the people affected. However, when it comes to "separation" at the end of the verse regarding God, it is considered unnecessary to repeat the *lamed*:

⁷"For his father and for his mother, for his brother and for his sister (*l'awveev oo'l'eemo l'awcheev oo'lchoto*), he will not make himself unclean for them (*lawhem*) when they die because the separation (*nezer*) [for] his God is on his head." (Num. 6:7)

Verse 8 uses the same words that are on the plate! "All the days of his separation he is conditioned for the Lord (*kadosh laY'h'vaw*)." Finally, verse 12 commands the nazirite to "separate himself for (*la*) the Lord" and to bring a he-lamb "for a trespass offering (*l'awshawm*)." Thus, the perfectly acceptable shift of *la* from "to" to "for" shows the protective attribute of the plate.

21.   Fuerst, *Hebrew & Chaldee Lexicon*, 808.

22.   Brown, *The New Brown-Driver-Briggs Gesenius Hebrew and English Lexicon*, 488.

23.   Faulkner, *A Concise Dictionary of Middle Egyptian*, 286. Faulkner has a ? at the meaning.

24.   Gardiner, *Egyptian Grammar*, 467, 507, 597,

25.   Josephus, *Antiquities of the Jews*, book 3, chapter 7, section 1.

26.   Milgrom, "Leviticus 1–16," *The Anchor Bible*, 385,

27.   There are many references to linen as *bootz*, but it is not used in the Five Books at all. Koehler and Baumgartner, et al., *Hebrew and Aramaic Lexicon*, 1663, says, "*Shaysh* occurs with and has the same meaning as *bootz*, but occurrences show that the word *shaysh* existed already in the older stages of the language, while *bootz* belongs to a rather later period." Sarna, in *The JPS Torah Commentary: Exodus*, 157, says, "In late biblical Hebrew *shesh* was replaced by *buts*, from which Greek *byssos*, Latin *byssus*, and English 'byssus' are all derived."

28.   Gordon, *Ugaritic Textbook Glossary*, 472. Del Olmo Lete, *Diccionario de la Lengua Ugarítica*, 359.

29.   Koehler and Baumgartner, et al., *Hebrew and Aramaic Lexicon*, 983. Brown, *The New Brown-Driver-Briggs Gesenius Hebrew and English Lexicon*, 833.

30.   Since *tawhor* suggests protected in my terms, the "clean (*tawhor*) place" in Leviticus 6:10–11 (H 6:3–4) had been made safe for depositing the animal burnings. There are other references to burnings being deposited in "a clean place," e.g., Leviticus 4:12 and Numbers 19:9, where the area would have had to be protected. On the other hand, it can be assumed that the highly contaminated, "plagued" stones that had to

be removed from a house would be thrown "outside the city" (Lev. 14:40–41) into a dump that held so much other dangerous material that no *tawhor*ing would have been possible. (Reminds me of the different degrees of difficulty faced in storing radioactive waste of different strengths.)

31. If the Documentary Hypothesis is given any credence, both the Exodus and the Leviticus references are said to be P. So, if *bad* means linen, then some P writer (remember the actual word for linen in Leviticus is *peeshteh*) whimsically changed it from *shaysh* to *bad* just this time. Even the critics would say this was unlikely.

32. It is interesting that in the 1 Samuel 2:18–19 reference Samuel was wearing the *bad ephod* and the robe (*m'eel*) at the time he was ministering in the super-conditioned place. The word *m'eel* is only used as "robe of the *ephod*" in Exodus and Leviticus. It is used as an ordinary robe in following books. But here, Samuel was in the danger area, and one can only guess whether by this time the garment, called *ephod*, was used as a protection, because the breeches were no longer known. The same might be said of David wearing the *bad ephod* while dancing before the dangerous ark. Certainly, the *ephod* itself was still known at this time.

33. None of this explains the "Doeg the Edomite" story in 1 Samuel 22:18, because nowhere else is a group wearing *ephods*. I can only guess that there was great confusion because of the rare times **the** *ephod* was properly identified, as opposed to **an** *ephod*.

34. Fisch, *Soncino Books of the Bible: Ezekiel*, 47.

35. Brown, *The New Brown-Driver-Briggs Gesenius Hebrew and English Lexicon*, 94. Milgrom, "Leviticus 1–16," *The Anchor Bible*, 1016.

36. Koehler and Baumgartner, et al., *Hebrew and Aramaic Lexicon*, 109.

37. Strong, *Strong's Hebrew Dictionary*, 19. Strong's wrongly uses "staff" instead of "staves."

38. Koehler and Baumgartner, et al., *Hebrew and Aramaic Lexicon*, 109. It also details other *bad* words coming from other roots.

39. Gardiner, *Egyptian Grammar*, 502, 564. Faulkner, *A Concise Dictionary of Middle Egyptian*, 86.

40. *A General Introductory Guide to the Egyptian Collections in the British Museum*, 145.

41. Ibid., 125.

42. Pace, *Wrapped for Eternity*, 48.

43. Romer, *Ancient Lives*, 52.

44. Sjöberg, ed., *The Sumerian Dictionary*, vol. 2, "B," 33, 36, 39, 40, 42.

45. It's probably worth noting that the strange one-time use of *bad b'vad* in Exodus 30:34 might also have had the secondary meaning of "separation": "And the Lord said to Moses, 'Take you spices, balm, and onycha and galbanum, spices with pure frankincense; of each there will be an equal weight (*bad b'vad*).'" There are more specific translations of the two words. Thus, "a part shall be for a part," or "amount

for amount." Green, ed., *The Interlinear Hebrew-Aramaic Old Testament*, vol. 1, 226. Kohlenberger, *The NIV Interlinear Hebrew-English Old Testament*, 234. Koehler and Baumgartner, et al., *Hebrew and Aramaic Lexicon*, 109, says "in equal portions, separated (?)." Perhaps Fuerst comes closest when he translates bad as "1. dismembered, singled out, separated, hence Ex. 30:34 [bad b'vad] separated upon separated, i.e., each apart, part by part." Fuerst, *Hebrew & Chaldee Lexicon*, 179. The original meaning, then, may have been both the idea of the ingredients being of equal measure and for protection by separation, chemically. This was the whole purpose for the incense. Or perhaps only the latter concept was meant. I wonder about this for two reasons: (1) For something as important as the incense, why weren't the exact weights and the word "weight," *meesh'kawlcr*, used as in the case of the manufacture of the anointing oil just a few verses back in Exodus 30:22–25? *Meesh'kawl* is commonly found in Genesis, Leviticus, and Numbers. Surely it would have been clearer to list the weights of the ingredients as was done with the oil, or, at the very least, explain that they "will be of the same weight, *meesh'kawl*." As to sources, this variation can't be blamed on different ones because everyone calls both references P. (2) Where dual words are meant to express equality, the inseparable preposition *kaf*, meaning "as" or "like" was used. Thus, while much later, in Deuteronomy 18:8, again the only place found, it is *chaylek k chaylek* and is translated "like portions" or "portion like portion they will eat." So it just might be possible that *bad b'vad* was used in this one place only to make clear the purpose for the incense. This is made more plausible because the next verse, Exodus 30:35, explains that the incense should be pure (*tawhor*), holy (*kodesh*), and verse 36 says, "holy of holies (*k'desh kawdawsheem*) will it be to you."

46.   There are many words used for "glory," but astoundingly *only three* in the Five Books, *all* found in Exodus, and one of these, *paw'ar* in Exodus 8:5, is importantly *not* "glory" here. (It will be discussed in my explanation of "beauty.") The other two are in Exodus 15:2, 6, 11, 21, a song attributed to Moses and Miriam and obviously inserted in this part of the Exodus story.

As to the rest of the books, the vast majority of the uses are in the "honor" vein. Where there is use in relation to the Lord, a close reading reveals either a poetic depiction, e.g., "the whole earth is filled with his glory" used as the ending for some of the Psalms and Isaiah 6:3, or a vision such as Ezekiel's in 31:18 who also used it as "honor." As with so much of his writing, Ezekiel seemed to know all the words (*cherubim*, etc.), but by that time had only a mythical, mystical grasp of them. When one thinks early Isaiah might have a notion, immediately there are many "honor" meaning uses that jump up. In verses such as Isaiah 35:2, the word is used in connection with *both* Lebanon *and* the Lord! In later Isaiah, there is no doubt at all that "honor" is the overriding use.

The glaring exceptions are 1 Kings 8:11, 2 Chronicles 5:14 and 7:1–3. These all pertain to the completion of the Temple and the installation of the equipment in the super-conditioned place, which predictably caused the *kawbode* of the Lord to appear and the atmosphere to be dangerous.

The references in 1 Samuel 4:21–22 must be noted. They refer to Phinehas' dying wife, naming her newborn Ichabod (literally, "woe," "glory"): "glory is departed from Israel because there was taken the ark of God." This, in relation to the rest of the story may have some significance.

47.   Koehler and Baumgartner, et al., *Hebrew and Aramaic Lexicon*, 455.

48.   Ibid., 456.

49.   Brown, *The New Brown-Driver-Briggs Gesenius Hebrew and English Lexicon*, 458.

50.   If one turns to the Documentary Hypothesis, it helps little. Genesis 31:1 is said to be from E, Friedman, *Who Wrote the Bible?* 248; Holzinger, et al., *The Jewish Encyclopedia*, vol. 5, 607. Genesis 45:13 is J and 49:6 is J, however, the song "was probably not composed by the author of J, but was rather a *source* that this author used and then wove into the narrative." (my emphasis) Friedman, *Who Wrote the Bible?* 258. The fact is that it is a piece or pieces written when the events they predicted happened, and so is an insertion here of much later date in the historical flow being described. Compare Genesis 25 and 26 with Deuteronomy 33:13–16.

51.   *Sawchach* is always spelled with a *samekh*, except in the above Exodus 33:22 where it is with a *sin*. Koehler and Baumgartner, et al., *Hebrew and Aramaic Lexicon*, 754, calls it a byform of the root *schch* with the *samekh*. That word is related to the Akkadian *sakayku*, "to block." Black, George, and Postage, eds., *A Concise Dictionary of Akkadian*, 312.

52.   A substance in the clouds forms a noctilucent glow.

53.   It is quite interesting that the Septuagint refers to the appearance of Moses' face on descending from Mt. Sinai as being "glorified" and "glorious" ("glory," *doxa*) rather than "shone" or "put forth rays." (Exodus 34:29, 30). The word *qawran*, "to shine," is the denominative verb from *qeren* translated "horn, corner, tip, ray, strength, etc." Koehler and Baumgartner, et al., *Hebrew and Aramaic Lexicon*, 1144. Wittingly or unwittingly, the Septuagint was using a word that described the exact phenomenon.

54.   Actually, there is something of a mystery in the full quote. In Exodus 19:9 the word translated "thick" (i.e., "heavy") before "cloud," *awnawn*, is *not kawbade* but *awv* (5645) which also means "thicket" *and* "cloud" but *not* in the Five Books. As "thicket" it is found once in Jeremiah. As "cloud" it is in 1 Kings, Job, (where in 37:11 *both awnawn and awv* are used), Proverbs, Isaiah (where *also*, in 44:22, both words are used), Judges, 2 Samuel, Psalms, and Ecclesiastes. However, in Exodus this is the only place the word *awv* is found. The only other place *awv* is used as "thick" is in Ezekiel 41:25, and this refers not to a thick cloud, *awnan*, but to "thick wood." However, with that one exception in Ezekiel, it is always used as *cloud* later on and even interchangeably so. The mystery: how did it get into Exodus as "thick" when in the very same chapter, Exodus 19:16 uses the common *kawbode awnawn*? This would be a handy place to turn to the Documentary Hypothesis to show that *awv* in Exodus 19:9 was one strand and *kawbade* in 19:16 was another. Let's see:

Exodus 19:9 awv	*Exodus 19:16 kawbade*
E. Interp.	E. Interp.
E. Friedman	J. Friedman
E. Cross	E. Cross
E. J. Encyc. ("chiefly")	E. J. Encyc. ("chiefly")
J. Van Seters	J. Van Seters

Only Friedman calls them two strands, and while Van Seters disagrees with the E idea, he called both J. So the Documentary Hypothesis is not much help. Koehler and Baumgartner, et al., *Hebrew and Aramaic Lexicon*, 773, says Ugaritic *gb/gbm* is "cloud … also *gb* darkness" and refers to the Akkadian West Semitic loanword *eboobatu* forest and the Syrian *aba* forest. However, it seems much more likely that the word is related to the Akkadian (Old Babylonian, New Babylonian, New Assyrian) *eboo(m)* translated "thick" and "dense" from which *ebubatu* called New Babylonian, not a loanword, possibly derived later. Black, George, and Postage, eds., *A Concise Dictionary of Akkadian*, 65. It may have been that some early scribe, *knowing that it was a synonym for kawbade*, dropped in *awv* because he liked the sounds within the verse, i.e., "in a thick cloud in order (that the people may hear)." This is conjecture, pure and simple. In any case, it in no way changes the thoughts on *kawbode* and *kawbade*.

55. http://www.merriam-webster.com/dictionary/radiant energy.

56. http://www.bartleby.com/61/1/F0210100.html. *American Heritage Dictionary of the English Language*, 507.

57. See Waltke and O'Connor, *Biblical Hebrew Syntax*, 197.

58. Gordon, *Ugaritic Textbook Glossary*, 417.

59. Del Olmo Lete, *Diccionario de la Lengua Ugarítica*, 207–8.

60. Ibid., 208.

61. Oppenheim, Reiner, and Biggs, eds., *Chicago Assyrian Dictionary*, vol. 8, 14–8. From Old Assyrian and Old Babylonian on.

62. Ibid., 12. From Old Babylonian on.

63. Ibid., 24. From Old Assyrian, Old Babylonian on.

64. Black, George, and Postage, eds., *A Concise Dictionary of Akkadian*, 140.

65. Oppenheim, Reiner, and Biggs, eds., *Chicago Assyrian Dictionary* vol. 8, 25.

66. Ibid., 26.

67. Ibid., 27.

68. Koehler and Baumgartner, et al., *Hebrew and Aramaic Lexicon*, 1772.

69. Ibid., 908.

70. In Deuteronomy 24:20 only, *paw'ar* is "the boughs."

71. Hertz, ed., *The Pentateuch and Haftorahs: Exodus*, 86.

72.   Cohen, *The Soncino Books of the Bible: Exodus*, 362.

73.   Fuerst, *Hebrew & Chaldee Lexicon*, 1112. Davidson, *Analytic Hebrew and Chaldee Lexicon*, 620. Kohlenberger, *The NIV Interlinear Hebrew-English Old Testament*, vol. 1, 164. Owens, *Analytical Key to the Old Testament*, vol. 1, 268.

74.   Faulkner, *Dictionary of Middle Egyptian*, 91. Gardiner, *Egyptian Grammar*, 565, 172, 493, O_3.

75.   Friedrich, *Hethitisches Wörterbuch*, 159. While Hittite is an Indo-European language, its texts contained Sumerian, Akkadian, and Luwian words, and it loaned words to Biblical Hebrew. Held, Schmalstieg, and Gertz, *Beginning Hittite*, 3. Mankowski shows relevant examples of Hittite loanwords in *Akkadian Loanwords in Biblical Hebrew*, 21–2, 38, 66.

76.   Von Soden, *Akkadisches Handwörterbuch*, 831.

77.   Driver, *Canaanite Myths and Legends*, 70–1, 74–7; 80–1, 162. Segert, *A Basic Grammar of the Ugaritic Language*, 198. Del Olmo Lete, *Diccionario de la Lengua Ugarítica*, 342–3.

78.   Deuteronomy uses *teeferet* once in verse 26:19 as the later "honor" or "glory," depending on the translation, but elsewhere it uses *yafah* (3303), the generally accepted word for "beauty, goodly" or "fair," e. g., Deuteronomy 21:11. Also, see Genesis 12:11, 14: 29:17, 39:6.

79.   Gardiner, *Egyptian Grammar*, 577. Faulkner, *Dictionary of Middle Egyptian*, 298. Faulkner also says *tpr* means "breathe."

80.   Faulkner, *Dictionary of Middle Egyptian*, 131–2. Gardiner, *Egyptian Grammar*, 574.

81.   The *t* (with the point beneath) is called a "dental." It is pronounced with the tongue against the upper front teeth. Ungnad, *Akkadian Grammar*, 14 says that in older periods of Akkadian *t* was represented by *t/d*. Von Soden, *Akkadisches Handwörterbuch*, 1380.

82.   Oppenheim and Reiner, eds., *Chicago Assyrian Dictionary*, vol. 11, pt. 1, 278.

83.   Friedrich, *Hethitisches Wörterbuch*, 211.

84.   The critics say Exodus 28:2 and 40 are P. If this is so and "glory" and "beauty" are *correct* translations, then P *contradicts* himself as to the reason for the garments.

85.   The Hebrew in Exodus 28:40 is *l'kawbode*, which could be translated "against (*l*) radiance." See Koehler and Baumgartner, et al., *Hebrew and Aramaic Lexicon*, 509 about Zacharias 13:1, and specifically, 689 where it translates the words *meetnachay l'chaw* in Genesis 27:42 as "plot revenge against." Also, Numbers 22:22 is "as an adversary *against* him." Green, ed. and trans., *The Interlinear Hebrew-Aramaic Old Testament*, 413. Brown, *The New Brown-Driver-Briggs Gesenius Hebrew and English Lexicon*, 510 notes Exodus 11:7 that is translated as "*against* the children of Israel ... *against* man." Without changing the concept of the purpose of the clothes, the *lamed*, *l*, could also be translated "because of." Koehler and Baumgartner, et al., *Hebrew and Aramaic Lexicon*, 510 points out that when *l* is used as "because of," it "introduces

cause or motive," referring to Genesis 4:23, "I have slain a man because of the blood (*l'dom*) that was shed there."

86. What the actual calamus plant is can only be guessed, but *qawneh* (7070) means "branch, reed, stalk" among other things. *Qn(m)* are "reeds" in Ugaritic. Gordon, *Ugaritic Textbook* Glossary, 479. *Kni* is "sheaf" or "bundle" in the Egyptian. Faulkner, *Dictionary of Middle Egyptian*, 279.

87. In the 29th verse, the translation of "will be conditioned" as "must become conditioned" has always led to controversy. This is because the word *yeek'dawsh*, "will be conditioned," is in the future tense called *qal* imperfect. In addition, the word *cawl*, meaning "all," is thought to mean "*what*ever" (touches them) rather than "*who*ever" (touches them). This puts a totally different cast on the meaning, indicating whatever *objects* came in contact with the consecrated altar received the passive *transfer* of the *property* of "holiness."

Aside from the fact that I am positing that "conditioned" is a state, not a property, the translation "must *become* conditioned" is proper and grammatically correct. In order to understand this, it is important to remember that this whole section has to do with "consecrating" Aaron and his sons to "make [them] conditioned:"

> [21]"And you will take from the blood which is on the altar, and of the anointing oil, and you will sprinkle [it] on Aaron and on his garments, and on his sons, and on the garments of his sons with him." (Exod. 29:21)

The sacrifices follow to "consecrate" the altar in Exodus 29:22–28, which is thereby finally "cleansed," *v'cheetaysaw*, in Exodus 29:36, "And you will cleanse." Then comes the verse that has caused the trouble:

> [37]"Seven days you will cover on the altar; and you will condition it, and the altar *will be* thoroughly conditioned, and *all* who touch the altar *will be conditioned.*" (Exod. 29:37)

The "will be conditioned" of the altar is termed a *qal* perfect *vov* consecutive that in the Hebrew is reversed to mean the same as the imperfect, that is, the future. The "will be conditioned" referring to "all" is a straight *qal* imperfect, meaning the two are exactly the same tense.

What is being ordered here is that Aaron and his sons and their garments should become conditioned by the blood and oil so they can minister before the altar. The altar in turn is to become conditioned by sacrifice and anointed with oil, and thus, the warning to be sure to become properly conditioned *before* working with the altar. The conditioning requirement is made even more explicit by Exodus 30:26–29, which includes anointing and thus conditioning *everything* from the tent to the table. *All* of the items become "most," or "better," "thoroughly" conditioned, commonly translated "holy of holies." These verses do not suggest transference of a property from any of these items to those who touch them, but being conditioned to touch them.

Cawl, "all," refers to Aaron and his sons who are central to all this activity. This is further emphasized by the same two warnings (or orders), "*every male* will eat of it" and "*all* will be conditioned," regarding Aaron, his sons, and the meal offering. (Leviticus 6:11)

It's interesting that the following is found in the post-exilic Haggai:

> [10]In the four and twentieth day of the ninth month, in the second year of Darius, came the word of the Lord by Haggai the prophet, saying,
>
> [11]"Thus says the Lord of hosts: 'Ask now the priests for instruction, saying,
>
> [12]"If one bear hallowed flesh in the skirt of his garment, and with his skirt do touch bread, or pottage, or wine, or oil, or any food, will it <u>become</u> holy?"'" [*qal* imperfect] And the priests answered and said, "No."
>
> [13]Then said Haggai, "If one that is unclean by a dead body touch any of these, will it be unclean?" And the priests answered and said, "It will become [*qal* imperfect] unclean." (Hag. 2:10–13)

Whether this was a "test" or was to be used as analogy or whatever, it would seem that even after the destruction of the First Temple there was an ability to parrot what once had meaning. Thus, inert, clean, sacrificial material transmitted nothing, while unclean material did in the memory of the remnant of priests dwelling amidst the ruins of the Temple in 520 BCE.

88.   Strong, *Strong's Hebrew Dictionary*, 104.

89.   Botterweck and Ringgren, eds., *Theological Dictionary of the Old Testament*, vol. 1, 353.

90.   Koehler and Baumgartner, et al., *Hebrew and Aramaic Lexicon*, 1124–5. Brown, *The New Brown-Driver-Briggs Gesenius Hebrew and English Lexicon*, 893.

91.   Fuerst, *Hebrew & Chaldee Lexicon*, 1250.

92.   Fourth note. There is no mention of oil as an anointer for priests in either Deuteronomy or the following books. It seems strange that if there was a late P writer of Leviticus he would "cast back" and thoroughly discuss a function so important early on but one completely ignored in his own time.

93.   "Pollute," *chawnafe* (2610), also translated "profane," is only found in the Five Books. As "polluted with blood," it is in Psalm 106:38, which is an historical review. It actually makes the point that the shedding of the Israelite sons' and daughters' blood by sacrifice to Canaanite idols polluted (*tekenaf*) the land. This made them *tawmay* (verse 39), "And [therefore] the anger of the Lord was kindled against his people." (verse 40) Isaiah 24:5 mentioned pollution of the land, but not specifically with blood. Jeremiah 3:9 also did, but by idolatry. These, of course, as well as Daniel 11:33, etc., were prophecies and basically analogies rather than statements of fact. The word is also translated as "ungodly," and "hypocritical" in the following books. It is possible that the Egyptian *ch'np*, "rob, despoil" is the source. Gardiner, *Egyptian Grammar*, 585. Brown, *The New Brown-Driver-Briggs Gesenius Hebrew and English Lexicon*, 338 says Assyrian *hanpu* is "ruthlessness." Oppenheim, ed., *Chicago Assyrian Dictionary*, vol. 6, says *hanaypu* means "villainy" (p. 81), *hannipu* is "vileness" (p. 80),

and *hanaypu* A is "to commit villainy" (p. 76), all in the Amarna texts. *Chenep* is in the Ugaritic as "perhaps" equivalent to *chawnafe* and *hanaypu*. Gordon, *Ugaritic Textbook*, 403. Driver, *Canaanite Myths and Legends*, 139 says it is "rank growth," but translated in the text as "teeming," 56–7.

94.   Levine, *The JPS Torah Commentary: Leviticus*, 116.

95.   Though his conclusion is different, "Ibn Ezra [Abraham Ibn Ezra, 1098–1164, Spanish scholar and poet—no encyclopedia agrees on these exact dates] understands it as follows: 'By means of the "life" that is in it, (meaning "the blood") effects expiation.'" Ibid.

96.   Whitelaw, ed., "Pharmacological Practices of Ancient Egypt," *The Proceedings of the 10th Annual History of Medicine Days*, 10.

97.   Reiner, Biggs, and Roth, eds., *Chicago Assyrian Dictionary*, vol. 17, pt. 2, 420–8. From Old Akkadian on.

98.   Gardiner, *Egyptian Grammar*, 591. Faulkner, *Dictionary of Middle Egyptian*, 244.

99.   Koehler and Baumgartner, et al., *The Hebrew and Aramaic Lexicon of the Old Testament*, 852–4.

100.   Brown, *The New Brown-Driver-Briggs Gesenius Hebrew and English Lexicon*, 776.

101.   Botterweck, G. Johannes, and Helmer Ringgren, eds. *Theological Dictionary of the Old Testament*, 238. *The Interpreter's Dictionary of the Bible*, 313. Milgrom, *The JPS Torah Commentary: Numbers*, 246.

102.   *The Chicago Assyrian Dictionary of the Oriental Institute*, vol. 4, 173.

103.   Ibid., 176.

104.   Brown, *The New Brown-Driver-Briggs Gesenius Hebrew and English Lexicon*, 629.

105.   George Buchanan Gray, *Sacrifices in the Old Testament*, 77.

106.   Levine, *The JPS Torah Commentary: Leviticus*, 8.

107.   Sarna, *The JPS Torah Commentary: Genesis*, 44.

108.   Strongs, *Strong's Hebrew Dictionary*, 77.

109.   Sarna, *The JPS Torah Commentary: Genesis*, 57.

110.   Ibid., 47.

111.   Ibid., 51.

112.   Heidel, *The Gilgamesh Epic and Old Testament Parallels*, 256.

113.   This was the case even though Ezekiel had access to the earlier (so-called) P works.

114.   Koehler and Baumgartner, et al., *The Hebrew and Aramaic Lexicon of the Old Testament*, 679. Black, George, and Postgate, *A Concise Dictionary of Akkadian*, 232.

115.   Del Olmo Lete, *Diccionario de la Lengua Ugarítica*, 323; Koehler and Baumgartner, et al., *The Hebrew and Aramaic Lexicon of the Old Testament*, 679. Driver, *Canaanite Myths and Legends*, 156. Gordon, *Ugaritic Textbook Glossary*, 442.

116. AQHAT II ii 10–14

117. Baal III iii 15–19

118. Gordon, *Ugaritic Textbook Glossary*, 443.

119. Driver, *Canaanite Myths and Legends*, 156.

120. Del Olmo Lete, *Diccionario de la Lengua Ugarítica*, 324.

121. Gordon, *Ugaritic Textbook Glossary*, 443.

122. Faulkner, *Dictionary of Middle Egyptian*, 137. Gardiner, *Egyptian Grammar*, 575.

123. Gardiner, *Egyptian Grammar*, 575.

124. Faulkner, *Dictionary of Middle Egyptian*, 135.

125. Gardiner, *Egyptian Grammar*, 575. Faulkner, *Dictionary of Middle Egyptian*, 136.

126. Held, Schmalstieg, and Gertz, *Beginning Hittite*, 157.

127. Ibid., 83.

128. Milgrom, "Leviticus 1–16," *The Anchor Bible*, 236.

129. Galling, *The Interpreter's Dictionary of the Bible*, vol. 2, 699.

130. Keel, *The Symbolism of the Biblical World*, 147.

131. Hamilton, *The Interpreter's Dictionary of the Bible*, vol. 3, 53.

132. Galling, *The Interpreter's Dictionary of the Bible*, vol. 2, 699.

133. *The Biblical Archaeologist*, vol. 34, 60.

134. Hertz, ed., *The Pentateuch and Haftorahs: Exodus*, 339.

135. Cohen, *The Soncino Chumash*, 526.

136. That this was an ancient idiom and concept is seen in the quote dating from the time of the famous first dynasty Babylonian ruler and code-maker Hammurabi (1792–1759 BCE), which used *qaytu*, "hand," and *mulloo* (Hebrew *mawlay*), "fill," i.e., "when Enlil … handed their rule (i.e., over the people) over to him *serrasina ana qātišu ú-ma-al-li-ù*.") Oppenheim, Reiner, and Biggs, eds., *Chicago Assyrian Dictionary* vol. 10, pt. 2, 187, and see for other quotes. Koehler and Baumgartner, et al., *Hebrew and Aramaic Lexicon*, 694.

137. Gordon, *Before Columbus*, 142.

138. Koehler and Baumgartner, et al., *Hebrew and Aramaic Lexicon*, 492.

139. Driver, *Canaanite Myths and Legends*, 127, 146.

140. *Kappu* B is noted as "usually of metal" from Mari, Tel El Amarna tablets, Nuzi, Middle Assyrian, Standard Babylonian, Neo-Assyrian, Akkadogram in Boghazköy. Oppenheim, Reiner, and Biggs, eds., *Chicago Assyrian Dictionary*, vol. 8, 185–9.

141. Ibid., 189.

142. Faulkner, *A Concise Dictionary of Middle Egyptian*, 284.

143. Gardiner, *Egyptian Grammar*, 501.

144. Koehler and Baumgartner, et al., *Hebrew and Aramaic Lexicon*, 694.

145. Wood and Osol, *Dispensatory of the United States of America*, 1039–41.

146. Ibid., 1040.

147. Ibid., 1041.

148. Ibid.

149. *Webster's Encyclopedia Unabridged Dictionary of the English Language*.

150. Koehler and Baumgartner, et al., *Hebrew and Aramaic Lexicon*, 695.

151. Faulkner, *Dictionary of Middle Egyptian*, 142.

152. Gardiner, *Egyptian Grammar*, 576.

153. Koehler and Baumgartner, et al., *Hebrew and Aramaic Lexicon*, 694. Brown, *The New Brown-Driver-Briggs Gesenius Hebrew and English Lexicon*, 642–3.

154. Wood and Osol, *Dispensatory of the United States of America*, 1373.

155. *Strong's Hebrew Dictionary*, 58.

156. *Kalbaynu* is found in Standard Babylonian and Neo-Assyrian. Oppenheim, Reiner, and Biggs, eds., *Chicago Assyrian Dictionary* vol. 8, 67.

157. Ibid.

158. Wood and Osol, *Dispensatory of the United States of America*, 1373.

159. Ibid.

160. Ibid. Koehler and Baumgartner, et al., *Hebrew and Aramaic Lexicon*, 316.

161. Wood and Osol, *Dispensatory of the United States of America*, 1373.

162. Ibid.

163. *Webster's Encyclopedic Unabridged Dictionary of the English Language*, 501.

164. Strong, *Strong's Hebrew Dictionary*, 114.

165. Brown, *The New Brown-Driver-Briggs Gesenius Hebrew and English Lexicon*, 1006.

166. Rylaarsdam, *The Interpreter's Dictionary of the Bible*, vol. 3, 605.

167. Gordon, *Ugaritic Textbook Glossary*, 488.

168. Roth, ed., *Chicago Assyrian Dictionary*, vol. 17, pt. 1, 77. Also Middle Assyrian, Standard Babylonian, Neo-Assyrian, and Neo-Babylonian.

169. Ibid.

170. Ibid.

171. Faulkner, *Dictionary of Middle Egyptian*, 242.

172. Fuerst, *Hebrew & Chaldee Lexicon*, 726.

173. See Koehler and Baumgartner, et al., *Hebrew and Aramaic Lexicon*, 518 for further discussion of frankincense.

174. Wood and Osol, *Dispensatory of the United States of America*, 1461.

175. Ibid.

176. Ibid., 1462.

177. Ibid., 600.

178. Milgrom, *The JPS Torah Commentary: Numbers*, 154. See note on verse 19 about "covenant of salt," *b'rith melach,* Leviticus 2:13, Numbers 18:19, 2 Chronicles 13:5.

179. Gaster, *The Interpreter's Dictionary of the Bible*, vol. 4, 157.

180. Gaster, *Myth, Legend, and Custom in the Old Testament*, 618–9.

181. Ibid.

182. Ibid.

183. Frazer, *The Golden Bough: The Magic Art and The Evolution of Kings*, 314.

184. Bradley, "The Spice of Life," *The Guardian*, May 25, 2000.

185. Sharma, Gautam, and Jadhav, "Spice Extracts as Dose-Modifying Factors in Radiation Inactivation of Bacteria," *Journal of Agricultural and Food Chemistry*, vol. 48, no. 4, 1344.

186. Koehler and Baumgartner, et al., *Hebrew and Aramaic Lexicon*, 759.

187. Also see Exodus 31:11, 35:8, 15, 28.

188. Del Olmo Lete, *Diccionario de la Lengua Ugarítica*, 404.

189. Driver, *Canaanite Myths and Legends*, 42, translates verses 6–10 of Keret II iii as follows (my emphasis):

	MISLABELED LINE NUMBER	PROPER LINE NUMBER
...And the Most High's rain on the fields,	5	6
(for) the grace of Baal's rain on the earth	6	7
and (of) the Most High's rain on the fields,	7	8
(for his) grace on the wheat in the furrows	8	9
(and) the *spelt* on the plough-land,	9	10
as the scent (?) is fresh (?) on the ridge(s).	10	11

However, Driver's line 5 is mislabeled. It should be line 6. Therefore, the Ugaritic verse 10 (verse 9 of the above translation) is actually the one that Driver translates "(and) the *spelt* on the plough land." The Ugaritic word for spelt (a type of wheat) is *ksm*. Del Olmo Lete, *Diccionario de la Lengua Ugarítica*, 226. The Hebrew is *koosemet*. Koehler and Baumgartner, et al., *Hebrew and Aramaic Lexicon*, 490. Thus, in the Ugaritic line 10 reads *bm nrt ksmm*, literally, "In the ploughed land the spelt." Pritchard in *Ancient Near Eastern Texts*, 148, agrees calling *ksm* "emmer," also a word for a type of wheat. Gordon, *Ugaritic Textbook Glossary*, 422, says *ksm* is usually in plural, *ksmm*, which would agree with Driver's spelling, *ksmm*. It would seem, however, that Del Olmo Lete confused the word *ksm*, spelt, with *smm*, perfume. Therefore, instead of being translated as above, Del Olmo Lete translates it "(the rain) in the plowing is as a perfume," with *ksmm* then being translated *k* ("like" or "as") *smm* ("perfume"). Incidentally, where there might have been some confusion is in Driver's translation of the last line above: "As the scent (?) is fresh (?) on the ridge(s)." So the idea of perfume could have slipped in incorrectly. This, too, is a mistranslation, this time by Driver because of a misreading of the Ugaritic. Instead of reading "*'l tl k'tr trm*," it should probably read "*'l tl k 'trtrt*," which Del Olmo Lete, *Diccionario de la Lengua Ugaritíca*, 94, translates, "(the rain) on the knoll is like a diadem," with the word "diadem" questioned. Here he also quotes another translation of the word as "fragrant herbs." Noting from Driver's question marks, he questions the translations, too. At any rate, I can't see where there is a specific Ugaritic word, *smm*, meaning "perfume."

190. Koehler and Baumgartner, et al., *Hebrew and Aramaic Lexicon*, 759. See also Black, George, and Postage, eds., *A Concise Dictionary of Akkadian*, 353 and Mankowski, *Akkadian Loanwords in Biblical Hebrew*, 118–20.

191. Koehler and Baumgartner, et al., *Hebrew and Aramaic Lexicon*, 759.

192. Gardiner, *Egyptian Grammar*, 590 and 482 M21 for an explanation of the word.

193. Mankowski, *Akkadian Loanwords in Biblical Hebrew*, 120. I recommend a reading of the whole section, 118–20.

Chapter 10. Congregation Covers

1. See, for example, Frazer, "Taboo," in *The Golden Bough*, pt. 2, 210–19.

2. Morris, *American Heritage Dictionary*, 1049, 462.

3. In the case of Abel's sacrifice of sheep, it was accepted by God; Cain's meal offering of the produce of the ground was not. The charge that Cain's offering was in some way wrong or not good cannot be substantiated because meal was an important offering among the list of sacrifices. Strengthening the argument that good versus evil are not involved in Hebrew sacrifice, Cain went on to become a powerful man after he killed Abel. He established a city and his descendants were pioneers in various arts and crafts. Surely, if there were moral overtones here, one would have expected some form of serious punishment. On the other hand, the theoretically "good" Abel lost his life. This apparently unfair outcome of the story may be hard to take, but it's perfectly compatible with the "whys" of all biblical rules pertaining to communication with God. They follow natural laws, not moral ones.

4. However, Genesis 6:14 is attributed by the critics to the later P story of The Flood. There are two separate ones, J and P, they say. For a clear delineation of the two, see Friedman, *Who Wrote the Bible*, 54–60. If this is the case, then it was P who recognized the ancient meaning could be transposed to a techincal term, and did so for his own unfathomable purposes. Or, the word never meant anything else, even though, as we shall see, it fell into almost total disuse later on, and subsequent writers only faithfully recorded *well-known* facts. This latter point of view is strengthened by the fact that Genesis 32:21 says "I will cover his face (*achap'raw pawnawyv*)," in the Jacob meeting Esau story, and there is general agreement that the source of this is E! For complete

disagreement with the J/P theory of the Flood story, see Heidel, *The Gilgamesh Epic and Old Testament Parallels*, 245–8.

5.   Oppenheim, Reiner, and Biggs, eds., *Chicago Assyrian Dictionary*, vol. 8, 553.

6.   The significant quote is Exodus 30:12: "When you take the sum [literally, "raise the head"] of the Israelites, of their numbered, then every man will give a ransom (*kofer*) for his soul … that there be no plague among them when numbering them." Then the reason for using the cover-related word becomes apparent: each man over 20 was to give a half shekel "to make cover (*l'chaper/keeper*) on your souls. And you will take the silver of the coverings (*hakipurim*) from the Israelites and you will give it on the service of the tent of meeting; and it will be to the Israelites as a memorial before the Lord to cover (*l'chaper*) on your souls." (Exodus 30:16) Silver was used for "sockets" for the super-conditioned place, veil, and for hooks for the pillars (Exodus 38:25–28). Cover is the purpose, so words denoting cover are used. Two asides here: First, that the silver for covering on the souls are *kipurim*, coverings related to the sacrifices for the altar. (Exodus 29:36) This is because of the numbers of the material to be used. Second, the explanation for the silver being a memorial may be that, being used in the actual super-conditioned place, it would serve as an automatic "reminder" to institute the covering process.

7.   Heidel, *The Gilgamesh Epic and Old Testament Parallels*, 265.

8.   Civil, Gelb, Oppenheim, and Reiner, eds., *Chicago Assyrian Dictionary*, vol. 8, 178–9.

9.   Ibid., 179. It must be noted that *kuppuru* was in use in the Standard Babylonian (c. 930–612 BCE), Neo-Assyrian (700–600 BCE), and Neo-Babylonian (600–486 BCE) periods. This would mean that as a technical word the Hebrew priests *could* have adopted a contemporary word. However, its use can be seen in the Hebrew way back in Genesis 32:21. If the chronology of Genesis does not seem feasible, then turn to the critics. They say it was used by E (9th–8th centuries BCE). It was also used by E in Exodus 32:30. In relation to the golden calf story, Moses said to the Israelites, "Now I will go up to the Lord. Perhaps I shall atone (*achap'raw b'ad*) for your sin." Either way the word was known long before the Neo-Assyrian, Neo-Babylonian periods. If this were the case, is it possible that *some* of the late Babylonian and Assyrian rituals might have been adaptations *from* Israel during the captivity/exile, rather than the other way around? For still another possibility, see Milgrom's wonderful introduction to *The JPS Torah Commentary: Numbers*, pp. xxxii–xxxv in which he shows that "eleven priestly terms and fifteen priestly institutions mentioned in Numbers *disappear from usage* in the postexilic age. In addition, thirteen priestly terms and ten priestly institutions, although they may have continued in use in later times, originate in the *earliest period* of (or prior to) Israel's national existence. In sum, we have twenty-six strong reasons and twenty-three supportive ones for affirming the antiquity of the priestly material in the Book of Numbers." (my emphasis)

10. Ibid., 556. Elam and Old Babylonian economic texts from Babylonia.

11. Kohlenberger, *The NIV Interlinear Hebrew-English Old Testament*, vol. 1, 230. In Kohlenberger's literal translation, he agrees. However, in his English-only verses he

reverts to "by which." Also regarding Exodus 29:33, see Owens, *Analytical Key to the Old Testament*, 371.

12.   Others say it was simply another example of cast-back.

13.   There are three traditional explanations for the word *Azawzel*. (1) It is fashioned from two words *az azel* meaning "goat that departs" or "escapes"; (2) it signifies the place where the goat was sent *jubl 'azaz* meaning a "rugged cliff"; or (3) it is the name of a demon who dwells in the wilderness. In much later literature, there is an evil angel by that name. *The Interpreter's Dictionary of the Bible*, vol. 1, 325–6. Regardless of when or how the word, whatever it means, got into the story, there is no question that the destination of the goat was "a solitary [or cut off] (*g'zayraw*, 1509) land ... in the wilderness." (Leviticus 16:22) Compare with Leviticus 16:10, 21.

14.   "*Et* is placed before the direct object of a verb if the object is definite ... (There is no equivalent for the word *et* in English.)" Blumberg and Lewittes, *Modern Hebrew*, 17.

15.   The use of these materials could either be because it pertained to the counting of "men of war" or because these people had just come out of war and this was part of the sacrifice. In this case, material was used to pay for sacrifice, to redeem the blood spilled.

16.   Milgrom, "Leviticus 1–16," *The Anchor Bible*, 255.

17.   Koehler and Baumgartner, et al., *Hebrew and Aramaic Lexicon*, 141 and Brown, *The New Brown–Driver–Briggs Gesenius Hebrew and English Lexicon*, 126.

18.   They run chronologically from c. 1050–450 BCE. When they were written depends on the critic.

19.   In Numbers 21:7–9, the serpent story, Moses' prayer itself didn't remove the serpents, but the Lord's instructions to make a copper serpent became the vehicle for removal.

20.   *Strong's Hebrew Dictionary*, 51. Goldman, *The Soncino Books of the Bible: 2 Samuel*, 321, note 6.

21.   Goldman, *The Soncino Books of the Bible: 2 Samuel*, 322, note 9.

22.   Here I will bring to rememberance the Assyrian word *zakaru*. In addition to its meanings of "mention" and "speak," it also meant "to declare under oath" and as *auzkuru*, "to take an oath." It is conjecture, but certainly an interesting possibility that there may be a conceptual relationship between the Hebrew meal offering of remembering, *minchas hazeekawrone* (Numbers 5:18) from which the *azkawraw* was taken and the very ancient Assyrian *zakaru* "to declare an oath."

23.   A careful reading of these verses shows that either two versions were stuck together or the strange repetitions were for some sort of emphasis (cf., e.g., verses 16 and 18, 24, and 26). *The Jewish Encyclopedia*, vol. 9, 345 says, "The law in its present form combines two older laws, according to one of which the proof of the woman's guilt is presupposed, while the other regards it as indeterminate and provided an ordeal to

ascertain the truth." In its multiple divisions of P, it assigns the section to "a possibly older writer whom Carpenter and Harford-Battersby call *Pt*, *t* being for 'teacher.'" Friedman makes no distinction, calling everything from Numbers 3:2–9:14 P. See also Milgrom, *The JPS Torah Commentary: Numbers*, Excursus 8, 9, 10.

24. Brown, *The New Brown-Driver-Briggs Gesenius Hebrew and English Lexicon*, 347–8.

25. Gardiner, *Egyptian Grammar*, 604. Faulkner, *A Concise Dictionary of Middle Egyptian*, 321.

26. Gardiner, *Egyptian Grammar*, 27.

27. Faulkner, *A Concise Dictionary of Middle Egyptian*, 135, 131.

28. Black, George, and Postgate, *Concise Dictionary of Akkadian*, 330–1.

29. Pritchard, *Ancient Near East Texts*, 166, no. 2.

30. Ibid., 171, no. 132.

31. Hertz, ed., *The Pentateuch and Haftorahs: Numbers*, 59.

32. Ibid., 60 refers to mishna, order moéd, tractate Taanith 11a. The mishna is the recording of oral law in 63 tractates by Rabbi Judah the Prince L. 200 CE.

33. The word for "destroy" in this verse is *shawchat* (7843). It is used as something done by the Lord several times in the Five Books, once in this passage as well as in Genesis 13:10 and 19:29 in relation to His destruction of Sodom and Gomorrah. It is also used in the ordinary sense as in Exodus 21:26 where the destruction of a handmaid's eye is discussed. It is seen in the word "corrupt" in Genesis 6:12 where the earth was corrupted by violence and the Lord decided to destroy (Genesis 6:13) all the people. However, nowhere is the popular notion that the destroyer was an avenging angel. It was quite simply that some*thing* would destroy. The idea of an angel is in the translation of the word *malawch* (4397) in 2 Samuel 24:16 as "angel." This word, also used in the Five Books, means simply "messenger." It is significant that the passage in Samuel refers to destruction (again *shawchat*) by pestilence!

34. Gray, *Sacrifice in The Old Testament*, x.

35. Brown, *The New Brown-Driver-Briggs Gesenius Hebrew and English Lexicon*, 750. While there is some disagreement as to sources, all agree that J, E, P, and D, are represented.

36. Driver, *Canaanite Myths and Legends*, 64–65, 142. Gordon, *Ugaritic Textbook Glossary*, 456.

37. Roth, ed., *Chicago Assyrian Dictionary*, vol. 4, 114–5. From Old Akkadian on.

38. Ibid., 128, 130.

39. Gardiner, *Egytpain Grammar*, 497, 551.

40. Ibid., 551.

41. Ibid. Faulkner, *A Concise Dictionary of Middle Egyptian*, 45.

42. Koehler and Baumgartner, et al., *Hebrew and Aramaic Lexicon*, 93. Milgrom, *The JPS Torah Commentary: Numbers*, 312.

43. Gordon, *Ugaritic Textbook Glossary*, 533, 368.

44. Segert, *A Basic Grammar of the Ugaritic Language*, 180.

45. Driver, *Canaanite Myths and Legends*, 32–3.

46. Milgrom, *The JPS Torah Commentary: Numbers*, 124.

47. Koehler and Baumgartner, et al., *Hebrew and Aramaic Lexicon*, 261–2.

48. See Levine, *The JPS Torah Commentary: Leviticus*, 15 where it is explained that in the Akkadian cognate *zibu* it "may designate any offering of food," and "both Ugaritic and Phoenician texts indicate that other foodstuffs, aside from meat, could be termed *z-b-ḥ/d-b-ḥ*."

49. For a contrary view, see Milgrom, "A Prolegomenon to Leviticus 17:11," *Journal of Biblical Literature*, vol. 90, part 2, 149–156.

50. Koehler and Baumgartner, et al., *Hebrew and Aramaic Lexicon*, 1533–5.

51. Brown, T*he New Brown-Driver-Briggs Gesenius Hebrew and English Lexicon*, 1023. Kohlenberger, *The NIV Interlinear Hebrew-English Old Testament*, 283. Milgrom, in "Leviticus 1–16," *The Anchor Bible*, 220, also says it "is but one of many suggested translations." Kalisch, *A Historical and Critical Commentary on the Old Testament Book of Leviticus*, 241–9.

52. Fuerst, *Hebrew & Chaldee Lexicon*, 1398.

53. Koehler and Baumgartner, et al., *Hebrew and Aramaic Lexicon*, 1537.

54. Ibid., 1532–3.

55. Milgrom, "Leviticus 1–16," *The Anchor Bible*, 220. Driver, *Canaanite Myths and Legends*, 84–5, 86–7, 88–99.

56. Del Olmo Lete, *Diccionario de la Lengua Ugarítica*, 438–9.

57. Koehler and Baumgartner, et al., *Hebrew and Aramaic Lexicon*, 1536.

58. Reiner, Biggs, and Roth, eds., *Chicago Assyrian Dictionary*, vol. 17, part 1, 208–9.

59. Ibid., 210.

60. Ibid., 211.

61. Ibid., 219–20.

62. Ibid., 224. See also Black, George, and Postage, eds., *A Concise Dictionary of Akkadian*, 350–1. For other interesting thoughts on the peace offering see Levine, *The JPS Torah Commentary: Leviticus*, 14–5. Tigay, *The JPS Torah Commentary: Deuteronomy*, 250.

63. Faulkner, *A Concise Dictionary of Middle Egyptian*, 232.

64. Hawley has written in his critique of this book, "The really intriguing aspect of the Ugaritic usages, in my opinion, is the very fact that in 1200 B.C.E. these people had a sacrifice called *šlmm* (cf., Heb. [*shlmm*]), which was opposed in some sense

to another type of sacrifice, called *šrp*, and most likely referred to the whole burnt offering (Hebrew [*olaw*]). This pairing is more or less equivalent of that found in the description of the [*olaw*] versus the [*shlmm*] sacrifices in the Hebrew Bible; and I'm inclined to view that as an indication of the antiquity of these Hebrew sacrifices called [*olaw*] and shlmm, even if the narrative into which they've been incorporated is quite late. This is quite a departure from Wellhausen's classic position that everything 'priestly' is late; what comparative materials from the ancient Near Eastern cultures have shown us again and again is that, even if the P-material, as it stands now, represents a post-exilic composition (and I don't see any way of getting around that), the authors/compilers incorporated a good deal of material of great antiquity. Among these features of great antiquity in the Five Books are these two old Canaanite sacrificial traditions: a 'communal offering' (Ugaritic *šlmm*, Hebrew [*shlmm*]) and a 'whole burnt offering' (Ugaritic *šrp*, Hebrew [*olaw*])."

65.   If the meat of the sacrifice is not eaten in the prescribed time, then it becomes an "abomination" *peegool* (6292) (Leviticus 7:18). This is a very rare word used only in the sense of "unclean." It is found only three times more in *all* the scriptures: Leviticus 19:7, Isaiah 65:4, and Ezekiel 4:14. The much more prevalent word *sheqetz* (8263) is also used in this context, e.g., in verse 21 (see below), but the difference seems to be that the person who eats contaminated meat (that is *peegool*) will "bear his *awvone*." It is quite fascinating that it is said to be directly related to the Ugaritic word *pglt* which is translated "foul offering" or "foul food" or "foul meat." Del Olmo Lete, *Diccionario de la Lengua Ugaritíca*, 345. Driver, *Canaanite Myths and Legends*, 95, 163.

66.   The exception to the one-day/two-day rules was when the entire area was completely saturated by the cloud. This was the case in Exodus 12 when the Lord came down to plague and so kill the Egyptian first-born. Then the meat (lambs) eaten by the Israelites would have been so in danger of contamination that it would have had to be eaten quickly and the residue burned as it was in Leviticus 7. This was also done during the consecration of priests. (Leviticus 8:32) In this connection, it is interesting that blood on the doorposts has always been termed the protector or "sign" against the Lord's coming, but actually the familiar meat product protection was used here, too. So the reason for haste wasn't only that the Egyptians, in fear, hurried them out (Exodus 12:33), but it was also to eat the meat before it became too contaminated. Also, the bread did have to be unleavened in this one case because of the need to hurry.

Specifically, the verses say the following:

> [8]"And they will eat the meat in that night roasted with fire, and unleavened bread; on bitter [herbs] they will eat it.

> [9]Do not eat of it raw, or in any way cooked in water, but roasted with fire with its legs, and with its entrails. [Evidently, because of the hurry, the burning of the protective part (entrails) had to be done at the same time as the roasting of the meat.]

> [10]And you will not leave of it until morning, and that which remains of it until morning you will burn with fire.

¹¹And thus will you eat it: your loins girded, your shoes on your feet, and your staff in your hand: and you will eat it in haste; it is a passover to the Lord.

¹²And I will pass through the land of Egypt in this night, and I will smite every firstborn in the Land of Egypt." (Exod. 12:8–12)

So, here was the same process used as always to protect against the radioactivity at the very beginning of the wilderness journey. Later, the purpose during Passover seems only symbolic.

67. The word *kawrat* (3772) is an imprecise, non-technical term, one of the few used in Leviticus. It does basically mean "to cut off," but can have a broad spectrum of meanings within that category. At its strongest, it can mean the offender should die and be gotten rid of, e.g., Exodus 31:14. In the case of the Molech worshipper, the people were to stone him to death, or if they did not, the Lord would cut him and his family off. (Leviticus 20:1–7). Also, in addition to its weaker meaning of quarantine, it can simply mean "cut down," as in Leviticus 26:30, "And I will cut down (*v'heechratee*) your sun-images." It probably comes from the Egyptian *krs*, which means "bury." Faulkner, *Dictionary of Middle Egyptian*, 281. The same idea is found in the Ugaritic *chert* meaning "hole," referring to burying in the hole of the earth gods. Driver, *Canaanite Myth and Legends*, 63, 107, 139.

68. Leavened bread, *chawmets* (2557), may be related to the Ugaritic /h-m-s/. Del Olmo Lete, *Diccionario de la Lengua Ugarítica*, 178, says it is to make sour, which becomes to deteriorate, spoil, along with the noun *hms*, vinegar. Akkadian has *emetsu*, "sour, fermented," which is related to beer, dough, and vinegar. Sarna, *The JPS Torah Commentary: Exodus*, 59. Koehler, Baumgartner, et al., *The Hebrew and Aramaic Lexicon*, 329 also relates it to the Egyptian *hemat* "salt." Falkner, *A Concise Dictionary of Middle Egyptian*, 170.

69. Exodus 23:18 and 34:25 both have admonitions against sacrificing "the blood of my sacrifice **on** (*al*) leavened bread." Actually, Exodus 23:18 says you shall not offer, *z'bach*, and 34:25 says *sh'chat*, "slaughter," but the idea is the same. There are references to Passover, with 23:18 simply saying "my feast," *chagi*, and 34:25 saying specifically "Feast of the Passover," *chag hapawsach*. However, while this is traditionally interpreted as reinforcing the prohibition of leaven at this time, what may be meant is simply that you should not eat bread that was mixed with blood. For discussion, see Haran, *Temples and Temple Service*, 326.

70. Milgrom, "Leviticus 1–16," *The Anchor Bible*, 188–9. Sarna, *The JPS Torah Commentary: Exodus*, 58.

71. Levine, *The JPS Torah Commentary: Leviticus*, 43. See note on verse 13. 1 Chronicles 23:29 appears to make the distinction. It says, "For the showbread and for fine flour for the meal offering for the unleavened wafers, or (and) of that which is baked on the griddle or (and) that which is soaked..." Incidentally, the "fine flour," *solet* (5560), or in more contemporary terms "semolina" could be used leavened or unleavened depending on the situation. Thus, the *shavout leavened bread* was made with *solet*.

72. *Matzah* (4682), when referred to relative to the festival, is called *chag ha-matzot*. The Egyptian has the word *msyt*, meaning "supper, festival" depending on the determinatives. Faulkner, *Dictionary of Middle Egyptian*, 117. The symbol Σ used in one variation is a "t" and stands for bread. The symbol $\int$ is used in another and means "roll of bread" or "loaf." Gardiner, *Egyptian Grammar*, 532. See also 527, 547 for determinatives relating to "feast" and "festival." For general discussion, see Koehler and Baumgartner, et al., *Hebrew and Aramaic Lexicon*, 621.

73. For example, Gurney, *The Hittites*, 133. Pritchard, *Ancient Near Eastern Texts*, 396–400.

74. Beck, *The Interpreter's Dictionary of the Bible*, vol. 1, 464.

75. Sarna, *The JPS Torah Commentary: Exodus*, 163. Magil, *Magil's Linear School Bible*, 65.

76. Sarna, *The JPS Torah Commentary: Exodus*, 163.

77. For example, Haran, *Temples and Temple Service in Ancient Israel*, 216. Sarna, *The JPS Torah Commentary: Exodus*, 163.

78. Magil, *Magil's Linear School Bible*, 65.

79. Sarna, *JPS Torah Commentary*, 163.

80. Gelb, Landsberger, and Oppenheim, eds., *Chicago Assyrian Dictionary*, vol. 21, 23–5. From Old Babylonian, Old Assyrian only.

81. Ibid., 25, 28–32. Old Assyrian only.

82. Ibid., 25–32. Tel El Amarna tablets only. From Old Assyrian, Old Babylonian on.

83. Ibid. Mari only. From Old Assyrian, Old Babylonian on.

84. Faulkner, *A Concise Dictionary of Middle Egyptian*, 250. Gardiner, *Egyptian Grammar*, 525, 592.

85. Gardiner, *Egyptian Grammar*, 525.

86. For the etymology and various uses of the *chawtawt*, read Koehler and Baumgartner, et al., *Hebrew and Aramaic Lexicon*, vol. 1, 305–6, with particular attention to the *pi'el* form of *chatawt*. While these etymologies agree with the idea of sin/error, more important to this discussion is the definition of the Babylonian word *chatu(m)* meaning "to strike down" and "of illness." Black, George, and Postgate, *A Concise Dictionary of Akkadian*, 112.

87. Milgrom, "Leviticus 1–16," *The Anchor Bible*, 253.

88. Ibid., 264–9.

89. Brown, *The New Brown-Driver-Briggs Gesenius Hebrew and English Lexicon*, 992–3.

90. Hertz, ed., *The Pentateuch and Haftorahs: Leviticus*, 26. For agreement, see verse 13.

91. I have translated the word *awleyaw* (Leviticus 4:14, 6:5) as "on it" rather than "against it." Omitting it entirely is also common, because translators had no notion of the process. However, "on it" is what the word means, and using "on it" strikingly strengthens the idea of *chatawt* meaning "contamination." *Awleyaw* is the feminine singular of *ahl*, "on", and it relates to "congregation" in verse 13, which is also feminine singular. So we have the idea of the congregation being *susceptible* to *contamination*

[falling] *on it.* See also Leviticus 4:3, which has the command to the oiled priest who has caused contamination to "offer on (*al*) his *chatawtawto,* which he has *chawtaw*[ed], a young bullock ... *for* (*l*) a *chatawt-*offering."

92. Milgrom translates the phrase "and he feels guilt." Milgrom, "Leviticus 1–16," *The Anchor Bible,* 227. Hertz gives an alternative, "Or, 'and he become guilty.'" Hertz, ed., *The Pentateuch and Haftorahs: Leviticus,* 28.

93. The meanings of the words *awshame, awshawm,* etc., have been very thoroughly covered: e.g., Milgrom, "Leviticus 1–16," *The Anchor Bible,* 339–45; Botterweck and Ringgren, eds., *Theological Dictionary of the Old Testament,* vol. I, 429–37, written by D. Kellerman views are widely quoted by others: Koehler and Baumgartner, et al., *Hebrew and Aramaic Lexicon,* 95–6; Levine, *The JPS Torah Commentary: Leviticus,* 22–3. Kellerman particularly points out that there are many opinions from which to choose. There was also general agreement that looking to other languages for help isn't fruitful. There had been suggestions that the Ugaritic *athm* was related, but always with a question mark. Koehler and Baumgartner, et al., *Hebrew and Aramaic Lexicon,* 95–6. Gordon, *Ugaritic Textbook Glossary,* 369 directly related it to *awshawm,* "guilt-offering"? However, now Del Olmo Lete, *Diccionario de la Lengua Ugarítica,* vol. I, 61 quite positively lists the word, without questioning, as meaning "remain in debt" or "to owe," and refers to the Hebrew *awshawm* as quoted in Koehler, Baumgartner, et al., *The Hebrew and Aramaic Lexicon,* 96. Thus, the reparation idea (of the guilt-offering) is indicated, but the word *athm* actually gives no idea that sacrifice is involved, much less even a hint as to its purpose.

94. Genesis 26:10 is J according to Friedman, *Who Wrote the Bible?* 248; Brown, *The New Brown-Driver-Briggs Gesenius Hebrew and English Lexicon,* 79; *The Jewish Encyclopedia,* 608. Eissfeldt doubts J in *The Interpreter's Dictionary of the Bible,* 369.

95. Friedman, *Who Wrote the Bible?* 249. Brown, *The New Brown-Driver-Briggs Gesenius Hebrew and English Lexicon,* vol. 2, 79. *The Jewish Encyclopedia,* vol. 5, 608. All these call Genesis 42:21 E. Eissfeldt in *The Interpreter's Dictionary of the Bible,* 371 says it's JE. It would be nice to fully accept the source theory and say that since E was written after J, the word held the contemporary meaning when it got to E's time and place. However, there is too much doubt regarding the source idea to fall back on it just to make things easy. I have no explanation for its contemporary usage in Genesis 42:21 unless, again, I say this is one of those words that always had the meaning of "guilty" and also had the technical meaning when speaking of it relative to "sins." This, too, is an easy out. The fact that it had largely lost that meaning in *following books* leaves, I think, an unsolved mystery. The source people are quick to say that the "guilt" offering itself is known only to P, but that doesn't work because of the Rebekah and Samuel stories. It is the source folk who put Samuel somewhere around 1020–1000 BCE and P at 550–500 BCE, and no one would argue that, if Rebekah was by J, then this long predated P. Even Bloom says 500 years. So the Genesis 42:21 mystery remains. It is interesting to note that the actual quote is, "Truly we are guilty concerning our brother [Joseph] because we saw the *distress* (*tsawrar,* 6869) of his soul." This word, *tsawraw,* feminine of *tsawr,* 6862, is only used here and Genesis 35:3, the story of

Jacob, and nowhere else from Genesis to Numbers. It is used in Deuteronomy and following books. Whether the writer decided to use a word contemporary with his time in relating this story I don't know, but it just might be a hint as to why the contemporary use of "guilt" was also in the verse.

96.   Another mystery is how Ezekiel knew *most* of the details in *Leviticus*, even though he mixed them thoroughly with his visions, and yet he lived *after* Josiah, during the Babylonian exile, 598 BCE. The answer is, most probably, that the Zadokite priests of that time (one of whom was Ezekiel's father, Buzi), who were empowered by Josiah during his reform, knew much more of the laws than were set out in Deuteronomy, but they were unable to put them into effect because of the political climate of the time. Ezekiel railed at the wickedness of the Levites and praised the steadfastness of the Zadokites regularly (e.g., Ezekiel 44:15, 48:11). They will be the ones to perform the service in the super-conditioned part of the temple envisioned by Ezekiel.

97.   For discussion of the debate on this subject see Milgrom, *Cult and Conscience*, especially 74–83 and footnote 169. The reasoning is clearly delineated as far as it could go before my introduction of the *awvohn* theory. The theory totally changes previous ideas and maintains its logic throughout.

98.   Leviticus 4:2 also mentions the individual contaminating through error, but it is so completely out of place, being the same as 4:27, that it probably shouldn't be here at all.

99.   An added bit of reasoning to strengthen the fact that Leviticus 5:17–18 is part of the Leviticus 5:15–16 thought is the use of the words "and if" to start the verse. In this section, *new* thoughts are begun with "And the Lord spoke" (e.g., Leviticus 4:1) or "When" using *asher* (e.g., Leviticus 4:22), because the thought has switched from the bullock and the priest's sins regarding the whole congregation to the goat and the ruler's sins. This in turn connects with "and if" to the person's sins (Leviticus 4:27) because both *are* merely individuals or with a *vov* used as "when" (Leviticus 5:1–13) or with the beginning word alone (Leviticus 5:15). If you check Leviticus 1, you will see that the use of if/then, etc., according to *this rule fall neatly in place*. Also, using the rule, Leviticus 5:21 is a totally new grouping and this starts with "And the Lord said."

100.   See Milgrom, "Leviticus 1–16," *The Anchor Bible*, 334–5, for agreement with using the translation "to" here. He translates the sentence, "He surely has incurred liability to the Lord." His reasoning is that "… even if a person merely suspects that he has desecrated a sanctum, he should take no chances but promptly bring a reparation offering to avert the wrath of the Lord in case he actually committed sacrilege." (Ibid., 335).

101.   *Beekoret* (1244) is *not* "punishment" or "scourge" as sometimes translated, but clearly from *bawker* (1239) meaning, according to Strong's, et al., "inquire," "search," "seek out." *Septuagint episkopi* means "inspection, survey."

102. Driver, *Canaanite Myths and Legends*, 90–1, 157. See also Koehler and Baumgartner, et al., *Hebrew and Aramaic Lexicon*, 1762. Del Olmo Lete, *Diccionario de la Lengua Ugarítica*, 447.

103. Milgrom, *The Interpreter's Dictionary Of The Bible Supplementary Volume*, 391. See Milgrom, "Leviticus 1–16," *The Anchor Bible*, 415. In Milgrom's extended discussion, he also says the Ugaritic *trmt* is the exact cognate.

104. Milgrom, *The Interpreter's Dictionary Of The Bible Supplementary Volume*, 391–2.

105. Ibid.

106. Also Von Soden, *Akkadisches Handwörterbuch*, vol. 2, 987 says *reemootu* is "present," and is m/nA, m/spB. In Von Soden, *Akkadisches Handwörterbuch*, vol. 3, 1329 he says *tareemtu(m)* m/spB is the same idea. Both of these words are said to come from *raymu* III, "to present to, endow," in Middle/Neo-Babylonian, Black, George, and Postgate, *A Concise Dictionary of Middle Egyptian*, 298. Koehler and Baumgartner, et al., *Hebrew and Aramaic Lexicon*, 1788.

107. For the various ideas on the translation in Ugaritic, see Koehler and Baumgartner, et al., *Hebrew and Aramaic Lexicon*, 1788–90.

Chapter 11. *Par* for the Course

1. Gardiner, *Egyptian Grammar*, 565. Faulkner, *Dictionary of Middle Egyptian*, 91.

2. Strong, *Strong's Hebrew Dictionary*, 96.

3. Del Olmo Lete, *Diccionario de la Lengua Ugarítica*, 353.

4. Cohen, ed., *The Soncino Books of the Bible: The Twelve Prophets*, 51–2.

5. Pritchard, *Ancient Near Eastern Texts*, 8. Lesko, *A Dictionary of Late Egyptian*, 177.

6. Hertz, ed., *The Pentateuch and Haftorahs: Exodus*, xvi. Bloom, *Book of J*, 7. *The Interpreter's Dictionary of the Bible*, vol. 1, 584.

7. Friedrich, *Hethitisches Wörterbuch*, 164.

8. Ibid., 161.

9. Cohen, *The Soncino Books of the Bible: Job*, 152–3. See note to verse 12.

10. Brown, *The New Brown-Driver-Briggs Gesenius Hebrew and English Lexicon*, 827.

11. Gordon, *Ugaritic Textbook Glossary*, 470.

12. Driver, *Canaanite Myths and Legends*, 163.

13. Brown, *The New Brown-Driver-Briggs Gesenius Hebrew and English Lexicon*, 826.

14. Von Soden, *Akkadisches Handwörterbuch*, 856. Compare *nipru*, "offspring." Oppenheim and Reiner, eds., *Chicago Assyrian Dictionary*, vol. 11, pt. 2, 247.

15. Von Soden, *Akkadisches Handwörterbuch*, 856.

16. Ibid., 856.

17. Faulkner, *Dictionary of Middle Egyptian*, 91. Pritchard, *Ancient Near Eastern Texts*, 443, ix, 4.

18. Gardiner, *Egyptian Grammar*, 565.

19. Friedrich, *Hethitisches Wörterbuch*, 159. Sturtevant, "Hittite Glossary," *Language Monographs*, 51.

20. Fuerst, *Hebrew & Chaldee Lexicon*, 1159.

21. Von Soden, *Akkadisches Handwörterbuch*, 837.

22. For a dissenting view see Milgrom, *The JPS Torah Commentary: Numbers*, 59, 305. Note "cover" on page 59 and see note 23 on page 305.

23. "Veil of the Temple," *The Interpreter's Dictionary of the Bible*, vol. 4, 748.

24. Brown, *The New Brown-Driver-Briggs Gesenius Hebrew and English Lexicon*, 827.

25. Von Soden, *Akkadisches Handwörterbuch*, 828–9. *Langenscheidt's New College German Dictionary*.

26. Labat, *Manuel D'Épigraphie Akkadien*, 318.

27. Von Soden, *Akkadisches Handwörterbuch*, 834. Labat, *Manuel D'Épigraphie Akkadien*, 318.

28. Von Soden, *Akkadisches Handwörterbuch*, 834.

29. Ibid., 836.

30. *Langenscheidt's New College German Dictionary*, 520.

31. Von Soden, *Akkadisches Handwörterbuch*, 829.

32. Brown, *The New Brown-Driver-Briggs Gesenius Hebrew and English Lexicon*, 827.

33. Magil's, "Numbers," *Magil's Linear School Bible*, 19.

34. Von Soden, *Akkadisches Handwörterbuch*, 830.

35. Ibid., 832. *Langenscheidt's New College German Dictionary*, 29.

36. Ibid., 856.

37. For example, Green, ed. and trans., *The Interlinear Hebrew-Aramaic Old Testament*, 2 Samuel 13:25 uses "broke" instead of "urged."

38. Gordon, *Ugaritic Textbook Glossary*, 471.

39. Del Olmo Lete, *Diccionario de la Lengua Ugarítica*, 356.

40. Driver, *Canaanite Myths and Legends*, 163.

41. Ibid., 124–5. *The American Heritage Dictionary* defines "chink" as "a narrow *opening*."

42. Lesko, *A Dictionary of Late Egyptian*, 177.

43. Von Soden, *Akkadisches Handwörterbuch*, 832 translated from *Langenscheidt Dictionary*.

44. Brown, *The New Brown-Driver-Briggs Gesenius Hebrew and English Lexicon*, 829.

45. Gordon, *Ugaritic Textbook Glossary,* 471.

46. Driver, *Canaanite Myths and Legends,* 96–7. Baal II iv, line 28.

47. Segert, *A Basic Grammar of the Ugaritic Language,* 198.

48. Von Soden, *Akkadisches Handwörterbuch,* 829.

49. See e.g., Ecclesiastes 12:5 where translations are "fail" or "unstirred," etc., but in Green, ed. and trans., *The Interlinear Hebrew-Aramaic Old Testament* vol. III, 1602–3, Green sticks to "and *breaks* desire." See especially Isaiah 24:19, p. 1654. See also *poor* as related and used in following books, p. 1631.

50. Driver, *Canaanite Myths and Legends,* 38–9, Keret III iii 30.

51. Ibid., Baal III * B 10.

52. Gordon, *Ugaritic Textbook Glossary,* 471.

53. Von Soden, *Akkadisches Handwörterbuch,* 830.

54. Brown, *The New Brown-Driver-Briggs Gesenius Hebrew and English Lexicon,* 830.

55. Milgrom quite convincingly says this is not so. He claims that the words *mahp'rees parsaw* actually mean "that *grows* a *hoof.*" Milgrom, "Leviticus 1–16," *The Anchor Bible,* 646–7. If this is true, then it throws *pawrahs* back into the *growing* meaning, which was one of the alternatives in *pawrach.* As with so many other words that are technical in nature, both meanings may have been intended when used in context of this specific law.

56. Von Soden, *Akkadisches Handwörterbuch,* 830. *Langenscheidt's New College German Dictionary.*

57. Brown, *The New Brown-Driver-Briggs Gesenius Hebrew and English Lexicon,* 828. Labat, *Manuel D'Épigraphie Akkadien,* 318.

58. Driver, *Canaanite Myths and Legends,* 163. Baal II i 33, 92–3.

59. Ibid., 163. The question mark after *prsh* is because he notes *prsh* could mean "box-wood."

60. Lesko, *A Dictionary of Late Egyptian,* 177. One of his references is the Papyrus Sallier I from Gardiner, "Late-Egyptian Miscellanies," *Bibliotheca Aegyptiaca,* 5, 9, 6. This probably goes to the reign of Mer-ne-Ptah, which is given variously as ca. 1234–1222 BCE, Pritchard, *Ancient Near Eastern Texts,* 378, and ca. 1212–1202 BCE in "Chronology of Ancient Egypt," University of Chicago Oriental Institute, 2. This would very roughly coincide with Israel's conquest of Canaan, 1250–1200 BCE in Bloom, *The Book of J,* 7, 1240 or 1250 BCE in Friedman, "Chronology," *The Interpreter's Dictionary of the Bible,* 584, or even the Exodus 1230 BCE in Hertz, ed., *The Pentateuch and Haftorahs: Exodus,* xvi. This would be some 250–300 years before J was said to have been composed, 350–400 years before E, and 550–600 years before D, and some 700 years before P!

61. Friedrich, *Hethitisches Wörterbuch,* 163.

62. Ibid., 164.

63.   Ibid., 163.

64.   Ibid., 164.

65.   Driver, *Canaanite Myths and Legends*, 62–3, 163, Aqht A I iii 14, 28. See also Gordon, *Ugaritic Textbook Glossary*, 470–1.

66.   Brown, *The New Brown-Driver-Briggs Gesenius Hebrew and English Lexicon*, 831. Klein, *A Comprehensive Etymological Dictionary of the Hebrew Language for Readers of English*, 533.

67.   Labat, *Manuel D'Épigraphie Akkadien*, 318.

68.   Faulkner, *A Concise Dictionary of Middle Egyptian*, 90.

69.   Brown, *The New Brown-Driver-Briggs Gesenius Hebrew and English Lexicon*, 828.

70.   Klein, *A Comprehensive Etymological Dictionary of the Hebrew Language for Readers of English*, 533.

71.   Fuerst, *Hebrew & Chaldee Lexicon*, 1158. Brown, *The New Brown-Driver-Briggs Gesenius Hebrew and English Lexicon*, 831, which is compared to the Assyrian *parush'shu* "staff."

72.   Von Soden, *Akkadisches Handwörterbuch*, 837.

73.   Friedrich, *Hethitisches Wörterbuch*, 159.

74.   Driver, *Canaanite Myths and Legends*, 70–1, 74–5, 76, 77, 80–1, 162. Also see Segert, *A Basic Grammar of the Ugaritic Language*, 198. Del Olmo Lete, *Diccionario de la Lengua Ugarítica*, 342–3.

75.   Held, Schmalstieg, and Gertz, *Beginning Hittite*, 159. Friedrich, *Hethitisches Wörterbuch*, 159.

76.   Von Soden, *Akkadisches Handwörterbuch*, 831.

77.   Klein, *A Comprehensive Etymological Dictionary of the Hebrew Language for Readers of English*, 533. Klein shows a distinct development as well as relationship of all the *parash* (*shin* ending), *pawrahs* (*sin* ending), and *pawrahs* (*samekh* ending) words as follows:

> [1] *prsh* [the *p* in the following words is often the letter *fey* without a dot in the middle. If it had a dot in the middle it would be called a *pay*, but in ancient Hebrew, before the diacritical markings were used, there was no distinction between the letters, and they looked identical. For simplification I am using the *pay* pronunciation here.] to make distinct, express clearly, to declare, explain. Aram-Syr. *p'rash* (= he distinguished: he explained). *Akka, parashu*, [line over second *a*] *parasu* [line over *a*] (= to explain, decide as a judge). Possibly related to base *prsh* cp. *prsh*[II]. cp. also *prs* [with a *samekh*][1]. *Qal pawrash* tr. v. he made distinct, expressed clearly, clarified, declared, specified, explained, interpreted.—Niph. *neepawrash* MH was clarified, was explained, was interpreted.—Pi. *payraysh* PBH I he expressed clearly: 2 he clarified, explained.—Pu. *porash*1 was made distinct, was clarified, was

declared: 2 MH was explained; was interpreted.—Hith. *heet'pawraysh* PBH 1 was made distinct: 2 was clarified, was explained, was interpreted. Derivatives: *pawreeshawn, payroosh, peer'shone, heetpawr'shoot, m'pawraysh, m'porawsh.*

^{II} *PRSH* To keep off, keep aloof, *separate*, abstain; to retire. (Aram. *p'rash* (= he kept off, kept aloof, abstained). *ap'raysh* (= he separated, divided). Syr. *p'rash* (= he separated, set apart, divided; he distinguished, he kept off, kept aloof, abstained). Akka. *parashu, parasu* [lines over *a's*] (= to separate). According to several scholars *prsh*^I represents a special meaning of *prsh*^{II}. Accordingly the sense development base of *prsh* might be as follows: 'to divide, *separate*, make *distinct*, express clearly, clarify, *declare, explain*, interpret.'—Qal *pawrash* intr. v. 1 PBH he kept off, kept aloof, separated, abstained; 2 NH he retired; 3 NH he set out to sea, sailed.—Niph. *neep'rash* 1 was scattered; 2 PBH was separated; 3 PBH he departed, withdrew,—Pi. *payrash* tr. and intr. v. PBH 1 he withdrew, retired; 2 he set out to sea, sailed.—Pu. *poraysh* was separated.— Hith. *heet'pawraysh* PBH 1 he was separated; 2 he separated himself.—Hiph. *heep'reesh* tr. and intr. v. 1 it (the viper) secreted (poison); 2 he separated, set aside, dedicated; 3 NH he removed; 4 PBH he set out to sea, sailed.—Hoph. *hoop'rash* PBH 1 was separated; 2 was dedicated. Derivatives: *pawrawshaw, pawroosh, p'reeshaw, hep'raysh, hap'rawshaw, moop'rawsh, m'pawraysh*^{II}, prob. also *peresh.*

78. Von Soden, *Akkadisches Handwörterbuch*, 832. Labat, *Manuel D'Épigraphie Akkadien*, 318.

79. Fuerst, *Hebrew & Chaldee Lexicon*, 1160.

80. Klein, *A Comprehensive Etymological Dictionary of the Hebrew Language for Readers of English*, 534.

81. Brown, *The New Brown-Driver-Briggs Gesenius Hebrew and English Lexicon*, 832.

82. Ibid., 708.

83. There is the usual absolute agreement among the scholars that one or another of these references is either J, E, JE, or P₂.

84. Driver, *Canaanite Myths and Legends*, 147.

85. Segert, *A Basic Grammar of the Ugaritic Language*, 195. The same is found in Gordon, *Ugaritic Textbook*, 451. See also Del Olmo Lete, *Diccionario de la Lengua Ugarítica*, 406–8.

86. Reiner, Biggs, and Roth, eds., *Chicago Assyrian Dictionary*, vol. 17, pt. 1, 430–48.

87. Friedrich, *Hethitisches Wörterbuch*, 210.

88. Oppenheim and Reiner, eds., *Chicago Assyrian Dictionary*, vol. 11, pt. 2, 77.

89. A fascinating combination of familiar sounding *parash* and relatives, and the meanings seen above are found in the Mittanian words *par-ush*, "to send" and *par-ushi-hi*, "embassy, messenger." These were used in the letter written by the king of Mitanni, ca. 1400 BCE, to the king of Egypt and were found among the tablets at

Tel-el-Amarna. Mercer, The Tel-el-Amarna Tablets, vol. II, 880. See also Gurney, The Hittites, 103. Mittani was an "important kingdom in N Mesopotamia during the Amarna Age (fifteenth–fourteenth centuries B.C.). While the main stratum of its population was Hurrian ... and its monarchs occasionally used Hurrian as a language for royal correspondence, the Mitannian aristocracy were Indo-Iranian warlords in control of horse-drawn chariotry." The Interpreter's Dictionary of the Bible, vol. 3, 406. In the case of the king's letter, it was written in Hurrian with the exception of a few Mittanian words such as the above. Hurrian "is thought to be related to the East Caucasian group of languages." Gurney, The Hittites, 103. The Interpreter's Dictionary of the Bible, vol. 2, 664 says it is not related "to any of the linguistic stocks ... such as Semitic, Sumerian and Indo-European—Hurrian has generic affinities only with Urartian (the language of ancient Armenia); its only likely modern relatives would have to be sought among the Caucasic family, with which Hurrian shares certain structural features."

90.   Sturtevant, "Hittite Glossary," Language Monographs, 140. See also Klein, A Comprehensive Etymological Dictionary of the Hebrew Language for Readers of English, 455 regarding the Hebrew sayfer, which will be discussed later, and Reiner, Biggs, and Roth, eds., Chicago Assyrian Dictionary, vol. 17, 444 regarding shapayru, where the word in its meaning "to write" is used as Akkadogram in Hittite.

91.   Reiner and Biggs, eds., Chicago Assyrian Dictionary, vol. 15, 225.

92.   Faulkner, Dictionary of Middle Egyptian, 223. Gardiner, Egyptian Grammar, 589.

93.   Gardiner, Egyptian Grammar, 586. See Faulkner, Dictionary of Middle Egyptian, 223. For its possibility and the attendant problems as a loanword, see Mankowski, Akkadian Loanwords in Biblical Hebrew, 121–3.

94.   Driver, Canaanite Myths and Legends, 66–7, 98–9, 160.

95.   Gordon, Ugaritic Textbook Glossary, 451.

96.   Brown, The New Brown-Driver-Briggs Gesenius Hebrew and English Lexicon, 1051.

97.   Reiner and Biggs, eds., Chicago Assyrian Dictionary, vol. 15, 166. Old Babylonian, Middle Assyrian, and Standard Babylonian.

98.   Ibid., 165.

99.   Friedrich, Hethitisches Wörterbuch, 159–60.

100. These two references, Genesis 1:24 and 2:7, use two different words for the place from which living things are said to come. In Genesis 1:24, eretz (776) is called "country, earth, field, ground, land, way, word." Words similar to eretz are found in Akkadian and Ugaritic. Botterweck and Ringgren, eds., Theological Dictionary of the Old Testament, vol. 1, 390–2. Adamaw (127) is used in Genesis 2:7. It is translated "country, earth, ground, husband [-man] (-ry), land."

Since the critics have long called Genesis 1–2:3 the P version of the Creation story and 2:4–24 the J version, the use of the two different words for the same purpose and the lack of the word awfawr in Genesis 1 might seem to reinforce that idea.

However, actually in Genesis 1 *eretz* and *adawmaw* are both found, *eretz* 20 times, *adawmaw* once. In Genesis 1:25 *adawmaw* is translated "ground." It refers here to "every creeping (*remes*, 7431) thing of the ground (*adawmaw*)." In verses 24, 26, 28, and 30 the same phrase is used, "every creeping (*rawmas*, 7430) thing," but *eretz* is the word for what they creep or move on. Thus, it would be logical to say that here the words are used interchangeably, unless verse 25 is suddenly considered a J insert into the P version. To my knowledge no one has claimed that. The same holds true for Leviticus 11:41, 43, 44, and 46 talk of creeping or moving (*sheretz* (8317)) things on the *eretz*, while Leviticus 20:25 speaks of them creeping on the *adawmaw*. It is true that Leviticus 20 is called H, but even if you accept that, H is a priestly source, not J.

In Genesis, *eretz* is used eight times, five referring to "earth" and three to "land," as in "land of Havilah" and "land of Cush." As to *adawmaw*, it is there five times. It is difficult to say why the word is used in place of *eretz*, unless it might connote "soil" instead of the more general concept of "earth." However, even here they seem to be interchangeable. A look at each Genesis 2 reference shows the following: "And thus were finished the heaven and *eretz*." (verse 1) "These are the generations of heaven and *eretz* … The Lord God made *eretz* and heaven." (verse 4) "And every plant of the field was not yet in the *eretz*, and every herb of the field had not yet sprung up for the Lord God had not caused to rain on the earth and there was not a man (*awdawm*) to till the ground (*haadawmaw*)." (verse 5) Here, the first "in the earth," *eretz*, could just as well be *adawmaw*, and the last *adawmaw* could easily be *eretz*. "And a mist used to go up from the earth (*eretz*) and watered the whole face of the ground (*adawmaw*)." (verse 6) Here again, the words could be switched. "And the Lord God formed the man [of] dust, *awfawr*, from the *adawmaw*." (verse 7) "And the Lord God made to grow from the *adawmaw* every tree." (verse 9) Verses 11, 12 and 13 refer to *eretz* as "land." "And the Lord God formed out of the *adawmaw* every beast of the field and every fowl of heaven." (verse 19) In other words, animals and birds were also formed from the *adawmaw*, but here *awfawr* is not specifically mentioned. (Compare verse 9.) The fact that the phenomenon can be described in Genesis 2 without specifically mentioning "dust," and that *eretz* and *adawmaw* seem to be interchangeable, relates it to the bringing forth vegetation and animals from the *eretz* in Genesis 1. The fact that "dust" is the material from which living things are formed is specifically restated in the famous verse 19 of Genesis 3: "In the sweat of your face you shall eat bread until you return to the *adawmaw* for out of it you were taken for *awfawr* [are] you and to *awfawr* you will return."

As to the endless argument about Genesis 1 and 2 being two versions, P and J, of the creation story, a careful reading makes it quite clear that Genesis 1 is about the creation of the universe, including the earth, while Genesis 2 focuses only on the earth. Thus, there is no surprise that different terms were used to describe what was happening.

For a nice early piece on this side of the argument, see *The Jewish Encyclopedia*, vol. 5, 602. For the other side, see Eissfeldt, "Genesis," *The Interpreter's Dictionary of the Bible*, vol. 2, 368–80; Claus, Westerman, Rainer, Albertz, "Genesis Supplement," *The Interpreter's Dictionary of the Bible*, vol. 2, 356–61.

101. Institute of Physics, "Physicists Discover Inorganic Dust With Lifelike Qualities." Science Daily, 15 August 2007. http://www.sciencedaily.com/releases/2007/08/070814150630. htm.

102. SETI Institute, "Amino Acids from Interstellar Space." SpaceRef.com, 27 March 2002. http://www.spaceref.com/news/viewpr.html?pid=7865 .

103. Caro, Meierhenrich, et al., "Amino Acids from Ultraviolet Irradiation of Interstellar Ice," *Letters to Nature*, 28 March 2002. http://www.nature.com/nature/journal/v416/n6879/full/ 416403a.html.

104. From the critical point of view, this is all P. *The Jewish Encyclopedia* calls verses 1–13 Pˢ "a priestly expander" and 14–22 Pᵗ an older priestly writer. They say Carpenter and Harford-Battersby designate them Pᵗ because "he writes as a teacher." *The Jewish Encyclopedia*, vol. 9, 345. BDB is uncharacteristically silent on the subject, but at least no one argues that the verses are E or J. Friedman calls them P with no mention of the Redactor. Friedman, *Who Wrote the Bible?* 253.

105. Driver, *Canaanite Myths and Legends*, 48–9, 50–1, 70–1, 80–1, 86–7, 88–9, 142; Gordon, *Ugaritic Textbook Glossary*, 459 equates it with *awfawr*.

106. Oppenheim, ed., *Chicago Assyrian Dictionary*, vol. 4, 184–9.

107. Ibid., vol. 1, pt. 2, 168.

108. Ibid., vol. 6, 84.

109. Ibid., vol. 1, pt. 2, 166–8.

110. Ibid., 167.

111. Ibid., 179–81.

112. See Klein, *A Comprehensive Etymological Dictionary of the Hebrew Language for Readers of English*, 48–9 where these words are with the aleph, e.g. "aphar PBH [post-biblical Hebrew]" for "pasture, saturated with water."

113. This is an unsolved question. Numbers 5:1–3 says:

> ¹And the Lord spoke to Moses saying,
>
> ²"Command the Israelites that they put out of the camp every burned person, and everyone that has an issue, and all who are unclean by the [dead] person
>
> ³... that I dwell in their midst."

This would seem to contradict the idea that the dead toucher did not have to leave camp in the Numbers 19 story. There are four possible answers. The first is the rabbinic one explaining three classes of unclean. The leper was excluded from the whole camp, those with issues could not go near the super-conditioned place or camp of the Levites, and the dead toucher was only kept from the super-conditioned place. The second possibility is that, since the priest and the ash-remover had to remain outside the camp until washed, it is *implicit* that the dead toucher was also excluded. The third is Milgrom's that this was simply an old P tradition. Milgrom, "Leviticus 1–16," *The Anchor Bible*, 724. The fourth is that while it is certainly true that *nefesh* (soul) can sometimes stand for dead body as it is expected to here, it could also be translated "unclean person," and therefore not include the dead toucher among those who had to leave camp. For example, see Leviticus 22:4, Green, ed. and trans., *The Interlinear Hebrew-Aramaic Old Testament*, 318.

114. It should be noted that Numbers 19 has presented problems to scholars. *The Jewish Encyclopedia*, vol. 9, 346 says that Numbers 19:1–13 and 14–22 are two parallel stories on the same subject. Milgrom's analysis says that the "ashes of the red cow are the only vestige of a pre-Israelite exorcism for corpse contamination." Milgrom, *The JPS Torah Commentary: Numbers*, Excursus 48, 443. This is a vast oversimplification of his brilliant work, which should be read in its entirety. Since I feel my approach solves former problems, my own question is in regard to verses 6–7, which say that the priest who throws the cedar wood, hyssop, and *toela'at shawnee* into the midst of the burning cow must wash his clothes, bathe, and be *tawmay* until evening. This is the only place in the Five Books where a *priest* is called *tawmay*. One must ask why the priest wasn't adequately protected before he worked with a *tawmay*-producing item. There is only one explanation and it reinforces the whole theory. In all other cases of danger to the priests while carrying out their duties at the tent, their protection had to be from *awvohn* itself, not something that could *attract awvohn*. Thus, in Numbers 18:22 in the previous chapter, for example, the Israelites were warned not to come to the tent lest they become *chawtawt*[ed], contaminated, and die. However, verse 23 says the priests [in their stead] would bear the actual *awvohn* because, implicitly, *they* were protected. However, there was *no protection* against *tawmay* things except to wash them off as did everyone else! Since this was the only place where it was stated a priest *had* to work with this type of item (he didn't with the bullock and goat, only a layman was involved), this was the only place where it likely would be *stipulated* he should wash. Of course we must assume if he accidentally touched a *tawmay* item he would also have to wash just as anyone else would. The need to wash after working with the ashes was simply part of the detailed instructions given for the whole operation.

With this problem solved, I believe Numbers 19 does hang together as an entity, and without dwelling on detail, the past paradoxes are dissolved.

Where in all this does the *par* idea enter? Remember that all decontamination was to ensure safe communication. Now note the law requiring making the dead toucher *tawhor* as stated in Numbers 19:13:

> [13]Everyone that touches the dead, and he does not decontaminate (*yeetchataw*) himself, *has defiled* (*teemay*) *the tabernacle of the Lord*, because the water of separation he has not sprinkled on him. He shall be *tawmay*; his *tawmay*[ness] is on him.

Verse 20 of the same section says,

> [20]But the man that is unclean, and he does not decontaminate himself, that soul shall be cut off from the midst of the assembly because the *super-conditioned place* (*meek'dash*) of the Lord *he has defiled*: the water for separation (*needaw*) he has not sprinkled on him; he is *tawmay*.

The sole purpose, as with all other similar operations, is to protect the super-conditioned place. The relation to communication is direct. Whether the strange choice of the animal, *adome* ("red"), with its connection to "earth," *adawmaw*, and "heifer," *pawraw* was to make this clear is conjecture, but it is a distinct possibility given all we now know of *par*.

115. Johnson, "Linguists Debating Deepest Roots of Language," *New York Times*, June 27, 1995.

116. Partridge, *Origins: A Short Etymological Dictionary of Modern English*, 470.

117. Ibid., 470–3. *American Heritage Dictionary*, 1533–4. See per-[2], "wing." See per[3] "young cow." See also perd, "dung."

118. Now regarding this whole discussion, I am well aware that linguists would not agree with this theory. They would say I have overridden evidence of exact cognates, e.g., I have said *parΩsu* is related to √*p°r*, whereas the exact root equivalent is √*prs*. However, I'm interested in the astonishing "coincidences" of the *pr*'s in the words of the different languages all meaning the same thing, not the precise root similarities. It would seem to me that when words were borrowed or common in many languages, it was the similar *sounds* that were important, not the exact spellings. These, I would guess, came later and may or may not have appeared in the same roots.

That this study is far from an exact science may be seen in the discussion of the *hapex ab°raych*, Genesis 41:43 in Mankowski, *Akkadian Loanwords in Biblical Hebrew*, 16–20. This is the word called out before the chariot of Joseph. The traditional translation is, "And he [Pharaoh] made him to ride in the second chariot ... and they called before him 'bow the knee (*ab°raych*)!'" (Compare Genesis 24:11). Mankowski points out the word is variously thought to come from the Akkadian *abarakku*, "steward," *abriqqu*, "purification priest," and the Egyptian *ab-r.k*, "attention!" The Septuagint translates the verse, "And a *herald* (*kayroox*) made *proclamation*, *ekayrooxen* before him." What is interesting here is that Mankowski in note 9 on page 17 says, "It is also possible that [*kayroox*] was suggested to the translator by *phonetic* association with [??] arq," the word normally translated "called." However, Mankowski prefers the Egyptian explanation citing on page 18 how W. Spiegelberg proposed a noun phrase *b-r.k* in 1903 meaning "attention!" He cites a text from 1100–1000 BCE, and James Breasted quotes a text involving Ramses III 1198–1166 BCE, both using the expression. On page 20, Mankowski says, "The Speigelberg theory is the least unsatisfactory in that the proposed forebear of [*ab'raych*] is not a reconstruction but has been attested in Egyptian texts of the appropriate date and can be shown to have been used, in the plural form at least, in a context of specifically royal solemnity that is suited to the Genesis passage in question. While the singular inflection remains a difficulty, *it is not necessary to assume the Hebrew author would have understood Egyptian grammar well enough to reproduce the correct desinence, only that he was aware of the general appropriateness of its (commonest?) form.*" (my emphasis) J. Breasted says that "the second person singular suffix -k is strictly speaking inappropriate to the native context." (Ibid., 18.) So with one word there are (1) various etymological possibilities, (2) the suggestion of a *phonetic* association, not necessarily a correct one, of a Greek and Hebrew word, and (3) the idea that a Hebrew author might have generally, not specifically, from a grammatical point of view, reproduced a borrowed word. The whole point demonstrated here is that, right or wrong, the various ideas remain perfectly plausible ideas not strictly bound to set rules.

Chapter 12. What is God?

1.   Schroeder, *Genesis and the Big Bang*, 36.

2.   Ibid., 74–5.

3.   Trefil, *Reading the Mind of God*, 73–5.

4.   Schoeder, *Genesis and the Big Bang*, 87.

5.   Ibid.

6.   Ibid., 89.

7.   Davies, *Superforce*, 181–2.

8.   Schroeder, *Genesis and the Big Bang*, 88.

9.   See especially 87–90.

10. Buchanan, "Spooky Trio to Explore the Quantum Universe," *New Scientist*, 14, 5 December 1998, 14.

11. Ibid., 14.

12. Ibid., 14.

13. Zukov, *Dancing Wu Li Masters*, 63–4. From "Are Superluminal Connections Necessary?" *Nuovo Cimento*, 40B, 1977, 191.

14. Ibid., 63.

15. Ibid., 63. Walker, "The Nature of Consciousness," *Mathematical Biosciences*, 175–6.

16. Ibid., 63.

17. Mark Buchanan, "Beyond Reality," *The New Scientist*, March 14, 1998, 27.

18. Ibid., 27.

19. Ibid., 28.

20. Ibid., 30.

21. Ibid., 30.

22. Matthews, *New Scientist*, January 30, 1999, 24.

23. Ibid., 28.

24. Davies, *New Scientist*, 3.

25. Ibid.

26. *The Interpreter's Dictionary of the Bible*, vol. 2, 413 explains that Elohim "is often called the 'plural of majesty' … i.e., Elohim includes all gods: the fullness of deity is

comprehended in him." It then continues, "The 'plural of majesty' did not arise first in Israelite tradition as a result of the identification of Elohim with Yahweh or the gradual development from polytheism to monotheism. On the contrary, this is an ancient pre-Israelite expression which was employed in Babylonia and Canaan even with a singular verb. Thus, in Akkadian the plural word *ilanu* ('gods') could be used in homage to a particular god, like the moon-god Sin, to express the worshiper's view that he is the highest God, in whom the whole pantheon is represented. In the Amarna Letters, Canaanite vassals addressed the deified pharaoh as *ilania* ("my gods"), thus saying that the fullness of deity is concentrated in him." For another thought on this subject see Cross, *Canaanite Myth and Hebrew Epic*, 187, note 176.

27. Kohlenberger, *The NIV Interlinear Hebrew-English Old Testament*, 408. Magil, *Magil's Linear School Bible*, 44. Milgrom, *The JPS Torah Commentary: Numbers*, 112.

28. See Weingreen, *A Practical Grammar for Classical Hebrew*, 43–4.

29. Aldred, *Akhenaton Pharaoh of Egypt*, 125–6.

30. Budge, *The Gods of the Egyptians*, 132–155, especially 155.

31. Pritchard, *Ancient Near Eastern Texts*, 371. This is the hymn that has long been noted as having parallels in the 104th Psalm.

Appendix A. *Edut* in the Following Books

1. *The Interpreter's Dictionary of the Bible Supplementary Volume*, 157.

2. *The Interpreter's Dictionary of the Bible*, vol. 1, 580.

Appendix B. Does *B'rith* Really Belong in Numbers?

1. Milgrom, *The JPS Torah Commentary: Numbers*, 80. Cohen, ed. *Soncino Chumash* "Joshua and Judges," 13, note on verse 3.

2. No one knows what *tachash* means. It is variously translated "badger" and "dolphin," but these are highly unlikely substances for a covering of the tent. HAL says there is an Egyptian word *ths* meaning "to stretch a skin, stretch leather." However, it suggests that because the meaning of *tachash* is "difficult to define properly, the question arises of how best to translate the word [so] it is sometimes felt best to keep the [Hebrew] word untranslated." Koehler and Baumgartner, et al., *Hebrew and Aramaic Lexicon*, 1720–1. Black, George, and Postgate, eds., *A Concise Dictionary of Akkadian*, 395 has a *takkassu* which means "(small) block of stone" in the Babylonian and New Assyrian and "usually a semiprecious stone" as derived from the Sumerian with a question mark. Thus, if there is a relationship to the Hebrew, one might say it might indicate a jeweled covering, but both of these ideas are conjectural.

3. Sarna, *The JPS Torah Commentary: Exodus*, 12, note 18, 240 notes 29, 30, 31. Milgrom, *The JPS Torah Commentary: Numbers*, 78.

4. Milgrom, *The JPS Torah Commentary: Numbers*, Excursus 29, 389–90.

Appendix C. Documentary Hypothesis ABCs

1. Achtemeier, *Harper's Bible Dictionary*, 63. Davies, *The Interpreter's Dictionary of the Bible*, vol. 1, 222.

2. 2 Kings 22:8–20; 2 Chronicles 34:18–28. Friedman, *Who Wrote the Bible?* 146, says it was written by the prophet Jeremiah who lived during Josiah's reign. Weinfeld, *Deuteronomy and the Deuteronomic School*, 7 says the book of Deuteronomy was composed in the latter half of the seventh century BCE; the deuteronomic edition of Joshua–Kings in fixed form in the first half of the sixth century; and the deuteronomic prose sermons during the second half of the sixth century.

3. Milgrom, *The JPS Torah Commentary: Numbers*, 5.

4. *Harper's Bible Dictionary*, 700.

5. Levine, *The Interpreter's Dictionary of the Bible Supplement*, 684–5.

6. Ibid., 685.

7. Bruggemann, *The Interpreter's Dictionary of the Bible Supplement*, 972.

8. Van Seters, *The Life of Moses*, 2.

9. Ibid., 33.

10. Ibid., ix.

11. Ibid., 112.

12. Weinfield, *Deuteronomy and the Deuteronomic School*, 184.

13. **J:** Friedman, *Who Wrote the Bible?* 252–3. Brown, *The New Brown-Driver-Briggs Gesenius Hebrew and English Lexicon*, 75. *The Jewish Encyclopedia*, vol. 2, 107. ("Judean" and "Ephraimitic" sources) Van Seters, *The Life of Moses*, 156. Bloom, *Book of J*, 161–2; Haran, *Temples and Temple Service in Ancient Israel*, 260 (10:33 E, 14:44, J) Pfeiffer, *Harper's Bible Dictionary*, 701 (10:33 E, 14:44 D). **Redactor JE:** Denton, *The Interpreter's Dictionary of the Bible*, vol. 3, 568. Cross, *Canaanite Myth and Hebrew Epic*, 315, (Num. 10:29–33). Cross says Numbers 13 and 14 are "reworked and supplemented by the Priestly editor."

14. Sarna, *The JPS Torah Commentary: Exodus*, 160.

15. Cross, *Canaanite Myth and Hebrew Epic*, 300, 325.

Appendix D. *Kawbade*

1. The verb *v'yawr'noo*, "and they shouted," is the qal imperfect of the root *rawnan*, and generally is equated with a shout for joy. Koehler and Baumgartner, et al., *Hebrew and Aramaic Lexicon*, 1247, says the root is a by-form of *rnh*, which can be both a "cry of jubilation, rejoicing" and a "cry of lament, wailing." Jeremiah 14:12, Psalms 88:3, 106:44, 119:169, 142:7, 1 Kings 8:28, Jeremiah 7:16, 11:14 Psalms 17:1, 61, 2 Chronicles 6:19.

2.   The word for "near," *karobe* (7138), is derived from karov (7126), which means both "to draw near" and "to offer" pertaining to sacrifices. It is possible that the early meaning of *karobe* was literally, "near for the purpose of sacrificing," or in my terms, "neutralizing."

It is generally agreed today that the niphal tense of ekawdaysh is translated "I will show myself holy," (Owens, *Analytical Key to the Old Testament*, vol. 1, 466. Koehler and Baumgartner, et al., *Hebrew and Aramaic Lexicon*, 1073; Levine, *The JPS Torah Commentary: Leviticus*, 59) or "I shall be treated as holy," (Milgrom, "Leviticus 1–16," *The Anchor Bible*, 601). The logic says that since the qal of the root kdsh is intransitive, "to be holy," the niphal of kdsh cannot be passsive. However, Waltke and O'Connor point out that "verbs showing Piel:Niphal forms with no Qal or only marginal usage include ... *kbd* (Niphal passive) ... *qdš* (Niphal reflexive and passive)." Waltke and O'Connor, *An Introduction to Biblical Hebrew Syntax*, 393. Thus, translating *ekawdaysh* in the passive voice, "*qdš*."

3.   First the *vov*: There is, of course, no doubt whatsoever that this sixth letter of the Hebrew alphabet has the primary meaning of "and" or "but." However, it is also true that it is used to mean "when" and "if" many times in the Five Books. In its discussion of *vov*, Brown, The New Brown-Driver-Briggs Gesenius Hebrew and English Lexicon, 253 says, "in circumstantial clauses [*vov*] introduces a statement of the concomitant conditions under which the action denoted by the principal verb takes place: in such cases, the relation expressed by [*vov*] must often in [English] be stated explicitly by a [conjunction], as when, since, seeing, though, etc., as occasion may require."

Thus, Genesis 7:6 says, "And (*vov*) Noah [was] six hundred year[s] old when (*vov*) the flood of waters was on the earth." Genesis 19:23 says, "The sun had risen on the earth when (*vov*) Lot came into Zoar." Leviticus 26:17, 36, and 37 say, "They shall flee," or "They shall stumble, when (*vov*) none pursues." Numbers 14:10 says, "And all the congregation said to stone them with stones, when (*vov*) the glory of the Lord appeared in the tent of meeting."

The *vov* is used as "if" in Leviticus 10:19 in the very same story whose verse we are discussing:

And Aaron spoke to Moses: "Behold today they (his sons) have offered their decontamination-offering and their burnt-offering before the Lord; and there have befallen me things like these; 'if' (or 'and if') (*vov*) I had eaten the decontamination-offering today, would it be pleasing in the eyes of the Lord?"

Leviticus 13:3 says, "And the priest shall see the plague in the skin of the flesh; if (or "and if") (*vov*) the skin be turned white ... it is the plague of leprosy." There is no question that *vov* is used here as "if." To use it as "and" would be meaningless. To translate it "and if" would be possible. However, the very next verse begins with "and if" and uses the two words that actually mean them. They are v (*vov*) ("and") and *eem* ("if"). These two words are used through the rest of this section. (e.g., Leviticus 13:7, 12, 21, 22, 23, etc.) So the chance that "if" alone is meant here is very strong.

Incidentally, the same reasoning holds true with "when." For example, Leviticus 11:37, 38 and 39 use *v'chee* (*vov kaf yood*) the word for "and when." *Kee* is used all through Leviticus 13 as "when." *Bet* is also used for "when," e.g., Leviticus 19:9; 20:7, *vov bet* "and when." So one could assume that when "and when" or "and if" is meant as written out, *v'chee*, *v'eem*, and when only "when" or "if" is meant, they are at least generally written with the *vov* attached directly to the next word without a *kee* or a *bet* between. There are dozens of examples of *vov* used as "when" in conjunction with "then" throughout the Five Books and in all strands. For example, Leviticus 16:20: "When (*vov*) he has finished atoning the super-conditioned place ... then (*vov*) he shall bring the living goat."

However, these are what are called the *vov* consecutive, a strange grammatical twist found only in the Bible, where the use of the *vov* in front of a verb in the perfect tense changes it to an imperfect tense and vice versa. Since the *vov* in Leviticus 10:3 is not attached to a verb and is not part of a "when-then" phrase, which are all *vov* consecutives so attached, I can't include it among the many examples of stand-alone "whens" (and "ifs").

Finally, another example is Numbers 12:14, "If (*vov*) her [Miriam's] father had but spit in her face, would she not be ashamed seven days?" The use of "if" alone seems most plausible here also.

Second to *al p'nay*: With this discussion of the *vov* as at least possibly meaning "when" or "if," let's turn to the words to which it is attached—*al* ("on") *p'nay* ("face"). They are translated in different ways. For example, *al p'nay* is used as "open" only in relation to "field" in Leviticus, Numbers, 2 Samuel, Jeremiah, and Ezekiel; it is "open valley" in Ezekiel 37:2. Here we are concerned with their translation as "before." It is important to get the feel of the use of *al p'nay* as "before" as opposed to *leef'nay* as "before." In Genesis, *al p'nay* could be said to actually mean "before" six times, whereas *leef'nay* is used 51 times. In Exodus, the ratio is 73 to one. In Leviticus, there are 84 *leef'nays* to the one in question here. Numbers has some 90 to two, and, if you believe the critics, these two are in verses added by the so-called Redactor. Friedman, *Who Wrote the Bible?* 253–4. On the other hand, Genesis, Exodus, and Numbers freely use *al p'nay* to mean "on the face," e.g., Genesis 1:2. Therefore, there is no good reason to assume that *al p'nay* suddenly means "before" in Leviticus 10:3 rather than the literal meaning. In fact, from the beginning of the fire story in Leviticus 9:24 through the deaths of Aaron's sons in Leviticus 10:3, four verses, *leef'nay* is used as "before" four times and *al p'nay* as "on (their) faces" twice (Lev. 9:24 and 10:3).

I think we can feel perfectly confident that *v'alp'nay* means "when (or "if") on the face of," thereby removing the only time it is used as "before" in place of *leef'nay* in Leviticus.

4.   As to "glorified," it is absolutely fascinating to see *kawbade* used in the following books and to realize the prophets seem to have had no understanding of the word. Isaiah (eighth century), Ezekiel (sixth century), and Haggai (late sixth century) were prophets who used the word so translated. Isaiah 26:15 simply says of the Lord, "You have glorified yourself (*neechbawd'taw*)." Yet, e.g., Isaiah 49:3 has the Lord saying,

"You are my servant Israel in whom I will be glorified (*etpawawr*). Isaiah 49:5 says, "I am honored (*ekawbade*) in the eyes of the Lord." Isaiah 66:5 says, "Let the Lord be glorified (*yeech'bad*)." And regarding kawbode, "glory," and kawbade, "honor," Isaiah 60:13 says, "The glory (*kawbode*) of Lebanon shall come to you, the juniper, the box tree, and the cypress together to beautify (*pawayr*) the place of my super-conditioned place, and the place of my feet I will glorify (*akabade*)." In other words, there is a free interchange of different words now given the same meaning. Ezekiel 28:22 uses "glorified" and "conditioned" in what has now become a rote phrase à la Leviticus 10:3 with the meaning of "honor" in the former and no understanding or sense at all to the latter: "Thus says the Lord God: behold, I am against you Zion, and I will be glorified (*neechabad'tee*) in the midst of you; and they shall know that I am the Lord when I shall have executed judgments in her, and shall be conditioned (*v'neek'dashtee*) in the sight of the nations." This laudatory meaning given to the words is so wildly different from the technical, restricted meaning in Exodus 29:45 and Leviticus 10:3 that it is astonishing. Nowhere in the Five Books does the Lord seek to "glorify" Himself as is done on a regular basis later on. Ezekiel 39:13 is in the same vein: "The people of the land shall bury [them] ... in that day I will be glorified (*neekawv'dee*) says the Lord God." The same is the case with Haggai 1:8: "Go up to the mountain, and bring the wood, and build the house; and I will take pleasure in it, and I will be glorified (*v'ekawb'daw*, the *he* at the end of the word is unaccountably missing) says the Lord." The idea of "honor" and "pleasure" relative to the Lord is completely missing in the Five Books. In the following books of Isaiah, Ezekiel, and Haggai, the traditional translation of kawbade as "glorified" is satisfactory.

Very importantly, the word hawdar, 1921, which is recognized as meaning "honor," is used a little further on from Leviticus 10:3 in Leviticus 19:15 and 32 in sentences where this could be the only meaning.

5.   Brown, *The New Brown-Driver-Briggs Gesenius Hebrew and English Lexicon*, 457 regarding Proverbs 8:24. Green, The Interlinear Hebrew-Aramaic Old Testament, vol. 3, 1545.

6.   They have 19 as P, 20a as E, 20b as J, 25a as E, etc.

7.   Hertz, *The Pentateuch and Haftorahs*, note 24, 159.

8.   Cohen, *Soncino Chumash*, note 24, 413.

9.   It is interesting that this section causes problems and strange explanations. G. Henton Davies gives the following comments in Davies, "Ark of the Covenant," *Interpreter's Dictionary of the Bible*, vol. 3, 120. But perhaps his last sentence is most significant.

It is remarkable that following upon Aaron's consecration and his first ministry for his people, there is in the legislative narrative of ch. 10 the story of the first priestly transgression and the punishment that accrued. It is not clear wherein lay the fault of Nadab and Abihu, the sons of Aaron, and commentators seek to relate the story to various parts of the ordination or to the regulation concerning intoxicants which appears in the same context (10:8–9). The detailed connection of the story may not be certain, though it is, of course, in some way connected with priestly access to God; but the Heilsgesetz implication of the story is clear. The priestly fault so soon after the ordination must be seen in the light of similar stories. There is the Garden, but then the sin in the Garden; there is the release of Noah and all his family from the ark and the accompanying sacrifice, and then comes the story of his drunkenness. Similarly, at Sinai there is first the theophany and the covenant, but then the golden calf. So priestly trespass emerges immediately upon priestly ordination. Even priests can go wrong, and they can go wrong in the very aftermath of ordination. The story, then, is designed to warn and thus to save the ministry in Israel, and no doubt rests upon some historical reminiscence, even if from another context.

And J.C. Swaim in Interpreter's Dictionary of the Bible, vol. 3, 496 says of this son of Aaron:

> Afterward he became a priest (Exod. 28:1). Later tradition repudiated both Nadab and Abihu because they "offered unholy fire before the Lord: (Lev. 10:1; Num. 3:4). As a result they were consumed by fire (Lev. 10:1–7; Num. 26:61). The expression "offered unholy fire" occurs only in connection with this event, and probably means that Nadab and Abihu offered what was contrary to the express command of God. The nature of the actual offense, however, remains obscure. An old tradition explains the story on the ground that they offered unholy fire while under the influence of wine, but such an explanation is very unlikely. The source of this tradition is almost certainly the command in Lev. 10:9 forbidding Aaron and his sons to drink wine or strong drink when they went into the tent of meeting. Both brothers died without offspring. (Num. 3:4; I Chr. 24:2)

10. Friedman, *Who Wrote the Bible?* 251. *Harper's Bible Dictionary*, 701.

11. Wright, *Interpreter's Dictionary of the Bible*, vol. 2, 193.

12. Ahlström, "Egypt, Israel, Sinai: Archaeological and Historical Relationships in the Biblical Period," *Journal of Near Eastern Studies*, 369.

13. Beitak, "Comments on the 'Exodus,'" *Journal of Near Eastern Studies*, 163–71.

14. Dever, "Is There Any Archeological Evidence for the Exodus," *Exodus: The Egyptian Evidence* (Eisenbrauns), 80–1.

15. Gordon, "Documents," *Interpreter's Dictionary of the Bible*, vol. 1, 861. Wright, "Exodus," *Interpreter's Dictionary of the Bible*, vol. 2, 192.

16. Referring to Pedersen's study, Wright, *Interpreter's Dictionary of the Bible*, vol. 2, 194. Benno, *The Jewish Encyclopedia*, vol. 5, 303–5. For a totally "unstranded" way of looking at the section under discussion, this is what Sarna says in *Exploring Exodus*, 64:

> "The motif of the hardening of the pharaoh's heart occurs precisely twenty times in one form or another within the scope of the Exodus story between Chapters 4 and 14. Intriguingly, the distribution of the motif is exactly equally divided between the pharaoh and God as the direct cause of the hardening.

Ten times it is said that the pharaoh hardened his own heart, and ten times the hardening is attributed to God. Furthermore, it is not until the advent of the sixth plague that divine intervention begins. For the first five plagues the pharaoh's obduracy is the product of his own volition." (Lord: Exod. 4:21, Exod. 7:3; 9:12; 10:1, 20, 27; 11:10; 14:4, 8, 17. Pharaoh: Exod. 7:13, 14, 22; 8:11, 15, 28; 9:7, 34, 35; 13:15. Notes 2, 3, 10, 11 p. 228)

17.   Ahlström, "Review of Egypt, Israel, Sinai: Archeological and Historical Relationships in the Biblical Period," *Journal of Near Eastern Studies*, vol. 49, no. 4, 369.

18.   While there is still no agreement on just who and what the Hapiru or the Habiru were, the following is representative of one view:

> It is in the Amarna correspondence that we also encounter references to lawless groups of bandits, criminals and social misfits who are termed Hapiru. Sometimes it seems they were engaged as mercenaries employed by the ruler of one city state in order to menace and terrorise another. More often, however, they are represented as roaming bands, bound in independent communal or semi-tribal organisations, and living on the fringes of civilised society, to which they posed a constant threat. It would be tempting, perhaps, to equate these Hapiru with the biblical Hebrews, but additional textual sources (Babylonian, Ugaritic and Hittite) which also refer to the Hapiru, not only demonstrate that their sphere of activity was not confined solely to Canaan, but more significantly, make it clear that they had no single identity. In other words, Hapiru cannot be seen as an ethnolinguistic term, specifying a particular people, but rather it should be seen as a more general term for dispossessed or homeless people of varying ethnic backgrounds. In these terms people could become Hapiru by virtue of unfortunate circumstances. In all probability, therefore, there was a direct connection between the Hapiru and the Hebrews in as far as the Hebrews were undoubtedly Hapiru: not all Hapiru, on the other hand, were Hebrews …

It is important to note that despite the reservation regarding the Hapiru/Hebrew equation given above, the Egyptian Papyrus Leiden 348 records that Hapiru, together with soldiers, were employed in dragging stones for the construction of the gateway pylons of one of Ramesses II monumental buildings, the Hapiru having been presumably rounded up and taken prisoner during the Amarna period or during the campaigns of Seti 1. Certainly this apparent coincidence of Hebrews and Hapiru in large-scale building programmes of Ramesses II cannot be dismissed, and it may well be that the Hebrews of the exodus were indeed drawn from the Hapiru. Furthermore, it would seem reasonable to conclude under these circumstances, that Ramesses II was the unnamed pharaoh of the exodus and oppressor of the Israelite people.

The changed aspect of the Egyptian empire at the end of the Late Bronze Age had a profound and far-reaching effect within Canaan itself. For the selectivity of the reorganisation, in which only certain sites were allowed to prosper, meant effectively the demise of others. There must have been, therefore, a very great increase in the numbers of dispossessed or homeless peoples. It is likely that many of these people moved to the hill country, where a sharp increase in small village settlements can be observed at this time. The demographic dimorphism that ensued was to prove instrumental in the formation of early Israel. Indeed, the reference to 'Israel' as a socio-political entity on the victory stele of the pharaoh Merneptah (1235–1223 BCE) should be interpreted as a recognition of this population split—the urban Egypto-Canaanite policies on the one hand, and a coalition of dispossessed Canaanites now occupying the hill country, on the other: in the eyes of the Egyptians the latter would certainly have been seen as Hapiru." Tubb and Chapman, *Archeology and the Bible*, 71–2, 75.

19. *Biblical Archaeologist*, Sept. 1990

20. Wilford, in his article entitled, "Greek Myths: Not Necessarily Mythical," *New York Times*, July 4, 2000, referred to Adrienne Mayor's book, *The First Fossil Hunters, Paleontology in Greek and Roman Times*, it is theorized that there are "literary and artistic clues—and not a few huge fossils—that seem to explain the inspiration for many of the giants, monsters and other strange creatures in the mythology of antiquity." Ms. Mayor says, "I have discovered that if you take all the places of Greek myths, those specific locales turn out to be abundant fossil sites … But there is also a lot of knowledge embedded in those myths, showing that Greek perceptions about fossils were pretty amazing for a prescientific people." Thus, "in the earliest known illustration of the Heracles legend, painted on a Corinthian vase, the monster's skull [i.e., the monster of Troy slain by Heracles to rescue Hesion] closely matched that of an extinct giraffe." The point here is the "prescientific" people made observations of natural phenomena and reported those phenomena in the best way they could. It is perfectly possible that biblical observers did the same thing using only words to illustrate their points because depicting likenesses was forbidden.

21. Friedman, *Who Wrote the Bible?* 190.

22. Mikelic and Wright, "Plagues in Exodus," *Interpreter's Dictionary of the Bible*, vol. 3 822–4. (For a general discussion of the priestly problems, see the classic: Cross, *Canaanite Myth and Hebrew Epic*, 293–325.

23. Friedman, *Who Wrote the Bible?* 197–8.

24. Miller and Miller, eds., *The New Harper's Bible Dictionary*, 700–1.

25. See Exodus 13:14 where it is E. Friedman, *Who Wrote the Bible?* 258, and redactor, Wright, *Interpreter's Dictionary of the Bible*, vol. 2, 193.

26. "Heavy:" Magil, *Magil's Linear School Bible*, 19. Green, *The Interlinear Hebrew-Aramaic Old Testament*, 157. "Unyielding:" Kohlenberger, ed., *The NIV Interlinear Hebrew-English Old Testament*, 162. "Stubborn:" Hertz, *The Pentateuch and Haftorahs*, 81. Cohen, *Soncino Chumash: Exodus*, 358.

27. Friedman, *Who Wrote the Bible?* 199–200.

28. Ibid., 201.

29. Ibid., 201–2.

30. Just for starters, see "Aaron" by Ellis Rivkin in *Interpreter's* and *Interpreter's Supplementary Volume*, 1–3 and follow the disagreements cited in the texts. Also, see Haran's *Temples and Temple Service in Ancient Israel* where he discusses the view of the authors of the various sources. And for a fast, simple explanation, see *Harper's Bible Dictionaries*, 1973 and 1985.

Appendix E. The Phinehas Story

1. For two possible explanations, see Milgrom, *The JPS Torah Commentary: Numbers*, 218 and *Soncino Books of the Bible: Numbers*, 932–3.

2. Examples of healing from the radioactivity through the simple passage of time were Moses' hand in Exodus 4:6 and Miriam's skin in Numbers 12:10 and 14–15. Other possible examples of those healed over time are seen in the golden calf episode regarding all of the people in Exodus 32:35, the quail eating story in Numbers 11:33, and the spy story in Numbers 14:12, 22, and 37. It is also possible that the radioactivity resulting from the Lord's presence, from which the people seemed to be unprotected, was cumulative and so overwhelming that it eventually led to the total eradication of the wandering generation—those over twenty. See Numbers 32:13. The uses of incense or blood during the wandering period would have served as only partial protection against the danger all the way from the time of the exodus with the blood on the doorposts (Exodus 12:13), to the golden calf episode with the filling of hands (Exodus 32:29), to Aaron's own covering with incense (Leviticus 16:13), to the incense put on the discontented populace in the Korach incident (Numbers 17:11).

3. Milgrom, *The JPS Torah Commentary: Numbers*, Excursus 60, 473–6.

Appendix F. *Yom Kippur*

1. *The Interpreter's Dictionary of the Bible*, vol. 1, 314.

2. Milgrom, "Leviticus 1–16," *The Anchor Bible*, 1070–1.

3. *The Jewish Encyclopedia*, vol. 2, 288–9.

4. Koehler, Baumgartner, et al., *The Hebrew and Aramaic Lexicon*, 799.

5. It would not be logical to count Exodus 6:32–33 as an exception. The order to keep some manna "for your generations" is to serve as an historical artifact for the future, and there is no need to fit it into the sacrificial formula.

6. Cohen, *The Soncino Chumash*, 459. Sarna, *The JPS Torah Commentary: Exodus*, 110. Hertz, *The Pentateuch and Haftorahs: Exodus*, 214.

7. The word "jealous" would seem at first to be the reason for the Lord visiting the *awvone*, thus putting an anthropomorphic face on the verse and so apparently contradicting the purely physical argument. It is true that "jealousy," *keen'aw* (7068) and "jealous(y)," *kawnaw* (7065) unquestionably mean just that when referring to people in the Five Books. For example, Genesis 30:1 shows Rachel's envy (*kawnaw*) of her sister Leah; Genesis 37:11 shows the fact that Joseph's brothers envied (*y'kan'oo*)

him; Numbers 5:14 shows how the spirit of jealousy, *keen°aw*, made a husband jealous, *kawnaw*, of his wife. There is also no question that jealousy is the meaning in the following books. Tigay says "the root 'k-n-' apparently means 'become dark red.'" Tigay, *The JPS Torah Commentary: Deuteronomy*, 65–6. Sarna, *The JPS Torah Commentary: Exodus*, 110. Derived from the West Semitic, the word *qannay'u* is translated "jealous." Black, Jeremy, Andrew George, and Nicholas Postgate, eds., *A Concise Dictionary of Akkadian*, 284. See also Koehler, Baumgartner, et al., *The Hebrew and Aramaic Lexicon*, 1110 regarding *qna* where it derives *qannay'u* from the Canaanite *qannay'*. Driver, *Canaanite Myths and Legends*, 144 translates it as "was jealous, zealous for." Gordon also equates it with the Hebrew and quotes, "I am zealous." Gordon, *Ugaritic Textbook Glossary*, 479. However, bear in mind that any of these Hebrew words, when translated into English, are always approximations of the original meanings. Thus, the translation of "jealousy," "envy," "resentment" or the like is but one sense of the word in English. Another is "possessively watchful; vigilant … protective; solicitous." *The American Heritage Dictionary*, 702. It is "solicitous or vigilant in maintaining or guarding something" in *Webster's Encyclopedic Unabridged Dictionary of the English Language*, 765. So when referring to the Lord, and in context of what I am hypothesizing, this definition of "jealous" fits perfectly. That is, *kanaw* (7067, the adj.) in Exodus 20:5 could be translated "watchful, vigilant" in the guarding or protective sense: "I am a watchful God," *warning* the people. As Tigay says in *The JPS Torah Commentary: Deuteronomy*, 66, "God's *kin'ah* not only explains why He forbids worship of other gods. References to His *kin'ah* are usually accompanied by a description of His punitive action or power … The very mention of God's jealousy is therefore a warning against provoking it." Also, Koehler, Ludwig and Walter Baumgartner, et. al., *The Hebrew and Aramaic Lexicon of the Old Testament*, 1111, says of *keenaw*, which is derived from *qna*, that one of the senses is "God striving to achieve his goal," and refers to 2 Kings 19:3, Isaiah 37:32, Isaiah 9:6, 26:11, etc.

8.   I think this also may answer the oft-asked question of why the order for the incense altar manufacture is not mentioned until this point. Since the order is in the very next chapter and only a few verses beyond the *keepering* of the main altar, the two thoughts tie together here perfectly.

9.   Szikzai, *Interpreter's Dictionary of the Bible*, vol. 4, 206 calls the Samuel reference J.

10.   Driver, *Canaanite Myths and Legends*, 78–81, 159. See also Cross, *Canaanite Myths and Hebrew Epic*, 37 regarding the council of El, "toward the gathered council," "*impuḫri mô 'idi.*" Gordon, *Ugaritic Textbook Glossary*, 435 says that perhaps *m'd* equates with the Hebrew *moade* in *phr m'd*, "the group of the assembly (of gods)." Del Olmo Lete, *Diccionario de la Lengua Ugarítica*, vol. 2, 257, says "reunion."

11.   For *yawadh*, see Koehler and Baumgartner, et al., *Hebrew and Aramaic Lexicon*, 419, 557. For *ahd*, see Brown, *The New Brown-Driver-Briggs Gesenius Hebrew and English Lexicon*, 723–4.

12.   *Chicago Assyrian Dictionary*, vol. 1, pt. 1, 97–8, 101.

13.   Faulkner, *A Concise Dictionary of Middle Egyptian*, 163.

14. See Levine, *The JPS Torah Commentary: Leviticus*, 154; Milgrom, "Leviticus 1–16," *The Anchor Bible*, 19–28.

15. I cannot agree with Milgrom: "However it is significant that the festival is not called *hag* in the priestly texts (see Lev. 23:16–21), implying that pilgrimage to the sanctuary was not necessary (nor could it be expected in the midst of the grain harvest) ... in any case, the omission of the sanctuary requirements indicates the realistic, rather than the allegedly utopian, character of the priestly texts ..." (JPS "Nu." p. 245). The fact is Israelites were to bring the sacrificial material "out of your habitations ..." (Lev. 23:16). "And the priest shall wave them ..." (vs.20). Thus, the sacrifices had to be taken to the tent/temple, wherever that was at the time. (The law in Leviticus 23:10 was given for "when you come into the land."). As to the Numbers reference, it is worded exactly as Leviticus 23:17–20 regarding the *chag* on which unleavened bread should be eaten, as well as the *chag* of the here unnamed 15th day of the seventh month. So there is no reason to assume there was a P group who excused the people from pilgrimage.

16. Of all the descriptions of the major events in the Five Books, the combining of the Feast of Ingathering with the name and concept of the *Succot*, booths festival, is the most suspect. The critics call it everything from a borrowed Canaanite festival to an ancient Israelite tent festival. The fact that people had to live in booths or huts during the harvest or during the pilgrimages to Jerusalem gives an authentic reason for it. Later, there are references to the celebration in Ezra, Zechariah, and Nehemiah. 2 Chronicles 8:13 mentions it in reference to Solomon, but the same story in 1 Kings 9:25 only says "three times a year." The word as a "hut" is found many times, including in Genesis. However, there are no other references in the Five Books except Deuteronomy 16:13, 16 and 31:10, and those only mention the name and are theoretically late. So the *reason* to memorialize the living quarters of the Israelites in the wilderness is only given once in Leviticus 23:43: "In order that your generations may know that in booths I caused the Israelites to dwell when I brought them out from the land of Egypt." But they dwelt in tents! This is repeated over and over (Exodus 16:16; 18:7; 33:8, 10; Leviticus 14:8; Numbers 11:10; 19:14, 18). So unless they dwelt in booths some time in the first six weeks after leaving Egypt (Exodus 16:1, 16:16), there was no reason for the Leviticus 23 law. It seems highly unlikely that this would have been the case, i.e., that they would have wandered from place to place in those first weeks carrying the necessary wood and setting up and taking down structures rather than pitching and dismantling the tents they had all the rest of the time. Thus, the possibility that *Succot* was added to the ancient ingathering at a later date seems rather great.

17. Friedman, *Who Wrote the Bible?* 254. Levine, *Interpreter's Dictionary of the Bible Supplementary Volume*, 634. *The Jewish Encyclopedia*, vol. 9, 346. Milgrom, "Leviticus 1–16," *The Anchor Bible*, 20.

18. Milgrom, *The JPS Torah Commentary: Numbers*, xiii–xv, xxxiv.

19. It is interesting that in all four of the Numbers stories of revolt that brought on plague there is either no mention of conditioning and cleansing or, as in this case,

it is ordered but there is no report of its being performed. Thus, Miriam was not conditioned when the Lord appeared and she got burned. The spies weren't either. Korach and company were ordered to appear before the Lord but not to sacrifice or wash. This is in sharp contrast to Leviticus 8:5, 6, and 10 where Moses explained the Lord's command that he wash Aaron and his sons and then condition them, or Numbers 8:6–7 where he was commanded to cleanse the Levites "and they will wash their clothes and they will wash themselves." Then Numbers 8:21 says, "And the Levites decontaminated themselves and they washed their clothes." At Sinai "the Lord said to Moses, go to the people and condition them … and let them wash their clothes," (Exod. 19:10) followed by, "and he conditioned the people, and they washed their clothes." (Exod. 19:14; cf., Exod. 40:12–13 and then 40:31)

20.   Rogers, "Book of Judges," *The Interpreter's Dictionary of the Bible Supplementary Volume*, 514.

21.   Haran, *Temples and Temple Service in Israel*, 199, says, "Thus it appears that the whole parenthetical clause in Judges 20:27–28a (to 'in those days') is a Deuteronomistic rather than a priestly expansion, or (if the mention of Phinehas the son of Eleazar the son of Aaron is an indication of P) a conflation of both Deuteronomisitic and priestly additions."

22.   Cohen, *Soncino Books of the Bible: Joshua and Judges*, 308, note 21 explains the strange punishment of the Israelites for trying to right a wrong as being "for their failure to suppress the idolatry in the shrine of Micah." However, there is no mention of this at all in connection with this story.

23.   Cohen, *Soncino Books of the Bible: Joshua and Judges*, 248.

Appendix G. Impurity

1.   In the Arabic, the same spelling with a different root in the Arabic, *awah*, means "to bend." The other root *gwy* does mean "to err." Koehler and Baumgartner, et al., *Hebrew and Aramaic Lexicon*, 796.

2.   *Nsa* as "removed, pulled up" is found in the Ugaritic. Driver, *Canaanite Myths and Legends*, 157. Del Olmo Lete, *Diccionario de la Lengua Ugarítica*, 332.

3.   The word translated "appointed" is *iti*, 6261, a hapax. *Strong's Concordance Dictionary*, 93 translates it "fit." Brown, *The New Brown-Driver-Briggs Gesenius Hebrew and English Lexicon*, 774 says it is "timely, ready" i.e., "a man who is in readiness." Koehler and Baumgartner, et al., *Hebrew and Aramaic Lexicon*, 903 also translates it "timely," as do Levine, *The JPS Torah Commentary: Leviticus*, 106 and Fuerst, *Hebrew & Chaldee Lexicon*, 1108. They all say it is from *ayt*, a word whose general meaning is "time," but one wonders if the Old Akkadian and Old Babylonian word *itti* translated "with, be, stand, go, send with someone" might not be related. Black, George, and Postage, eds., *A Concise Dictionary of Akkadian*, 136. That is, it might simply be trying to say, "He shall send [him] away by the hand of a man *with* [who is with] him."

4.   The noun "transgression," *pesha* (6588), is found in the Five Books in Genesis 31:36, 50:17; Exodus 22:8, 23:21, 34:7; Leviticus 16:16, 21; Numbers 14:18. In later books,

it and the verb "transgress," *pawsha* (6586), are used frequently. The same word *pa* is found in Ugaritic. Driver, *Canaanite Myths and Legends*, 163, and Del Olmo Lete, *Diccionario de la Lengua Ugarítica*, 358 translate it "transgression" or "rebellion." Gordon, *Ugaritic Textbook Glossary*, 471 says it is "sin." The meaning in Hebrew seems to be a wrongdoing of which the perpetrator is aware or has even done on purpose. We get a pretty good hint of this in Exodus 23:21, which says of the Lord's messenger, "Beware of Him and hearken to His voice; do not be *rebellious* against Him for He will not forgive your transgression (*l'feesh'achem* from *pesha*)." The word used here for rebellion is *mawrar* (4843) meaning "bitter," but it is generally said that in this case it is the equivalent of *mawraw* (4784) which does mean "rebellious," e.g., Numbers 17:24. In fact, many but not all words beginning with *mem, resh* indicate violence of one sort or another. Here, the point is that the unforgiven transgression is knowingly caused. The word *mararu* is found in Old Babylonian, Standard Babylonian, Neo-Babylonian, and as *mararu* A, means "1. to be bitter, 2. (with *kakku*) to prevail; (said of military force), 3. *murruru* to make bitter, 4. *shumruru* (with *kakku*) to make prevail." Oppenheim, Reiner, and Biggs, *Chicago Assyrian Dictionary*, vol. 10, pt. 1, 267–8. Such quotes are noted: "Just as (this) gall is bitter, so may you, your wives, sons and daughters be bitter toward one another." "You made (people's) mouths bitter toward me." "The onslaught of my weapons which I made prevail over Urartu in a (violent) battle." Expanding on the "violence" theme, *mararu* C, which is Tel El Amarna tablets and Ras Shamra and is called a West Semitic word, is in "2. *shumruru* to expel" and in this quote: "the king, the Sun, ought to expel the enemies from his land." Ibid., 269. The word is *mr* in the Ugaritic. Driver, *Canaanite Myths and Legends*, 161; Gordon, *Ugaritic Textbook Glossary*, 437. There are other places beside Leviticus 16:21 where *pesha* is used with two or three of the above-mentioned words. Genesis 31:36 says, "What is my transgression (*peeshee*)? What is my sin (*chatawtee*)?" Genesis 50:17 says, "Forgive now the *pesha* of your brothers and their *chatawtawm*." Exodus 34:7 says, "Keeping kindness for thousands, forgiving *awvohn* and *pesha* and *chatawaw*." (See also Leviticus 16:16; Numbers 14:18.) So, one might assume that *pesha* refers very generally to any purposeful wrong-doing including those which cause danger vis-à-vis radioactivity. Therefore, it is not a synonym, but certainly a separate word from either *awvohn* or *chatawt*, which are different from each other.

5.   Brown, *The New Brown-Driver-Briggs Gesenius Hebrew and English Lexicon*, 596. Koehler and Baumgartner, et al., *Hebrew and Aramaic Lexicon*, 628–9, translates, it "rot; festering wounds" and for Leviticus 26:39, etc. "to melt, dissolve." See also Levine, *The JPS Torah Commentary: Leviticus*, note to verse 39, 190.

6.   Del Olmo Lete, *Diccionario de la Lengua Ugarítica*, 271.

7.   Koehler and Baumgartner, et al., *Hebrew and Aramaic Lexicon*, 1141, 1137–8, 1131. For Targums see Levine, *The JPS Torah Commentary: Leviticus*, note to verse 21, 186, but in light of the Ugaritic, they seem unlikely.

8.   *Strong's Hebrew Dictionary*, 104.

9.   In Ugaritic the word *qry* is variously translated "met, opposed" and "contrariety," said to be the equivalent of the Hebrew. Driver, *Canaanite Myths and Legends*, 144. In

Gordon, *Ugaritic Textbook Glossary*, 480, *qry* I is "to meet ... a sacrifice to the gods; offer up an offering." Del Olmo Lete, *Diccionario de la Lengua Ugaritíca*, 374–5, translates Hebrew *qrh*, "meet accidentally, to meet with, to depart to the passage, to present, to offer." In the Middle Egyptian, one spelling of *krí* gives us "draw near, attend." Faulkner, *Dictionary of Middle Egyptian*, 280.

10.   It's interesting that the same idea is covered in Exodus 5:3 using *kawraw*, 7122. The verse says:

> [3]And they (Moses and Aaron) said, "The God of the Hebrews has met with us. Let us go ... a journey of three days into the wilderness, and let us sacrifice to the Lord our God lest he strike us with pestilence or with sword."

What had actually happened was that the Lord had "visited" the Israelites (Exod. 4:31), they predictably "bowed down, and they prostrated themselves." "And afterwards Moses and Aaron came and said to Pharaoh, 'send away my people.'" (Exod. 5:1) Then when Pharaoh refused (Exod. 5:2), they explained their fear that since God had "met" the people they *had* to sacrifice (to protect themselves). Pharaoh could not possibly have understood what they were trying to do, so Moses added "sword" to make a more familiar and threatening situation. So, while Moses may have been trying to pull a fast one on Pharaoh by simply talking about a "three day journey," he still really must have felt it was necessary to get out and sacrifice.

11.   *Shachefet* (7829) is "emaciation, consumption." Koehler and Baumgartner, et al., *Hebrew and Aramaic Lexicon*, 1463. It *may* be of note that *shachefet* is the inversion (*metathesis*) of *saphachat* our old friend *scab*. It is said that it derives from *shachaf* (7828) meaning "to peel off." *Strong's Hebrew Dictionary*, 114; conjectured in Brown, *The New Brown-Driver-Briggs Gesenius Hebrew and English Lexicon*, 1006. Koehler and Baumgartner, et al., *Hebrew and Aramaic Lexicon*, 1067, says *kadachat*'s root is *kadach*, "to catch fire," and points to the Ugaritic substitution *qdhm*, "fire lighter or tow." See also Del Olmo Lete, *Diccionario de la Lengua Ugaritíca*, 362. Koehler and Baumgartner, et al., *Hebrew and Aramaic Lexicon*, 1463, says the underlying root for *shachefet* is probably *shp* "to be weakened ... to suffer from consumption." Del Olmo Lete, *Diccionario de la Lengua Ugaritíca*, 435 says the Ugaritic *shp* is "tissue, tender skin, weak." "Fever," *kadachat* (6920), = "burning," Koehler and Baumgartner, et al., *Hebrew and Aramaic Lexicon*, 1067, is "inflammation, fever."

12.   Several Hebrew words beginning with *chm* have the idea of "heat" in them. *Chome* (2527) means just that and appears twice in Genesis (both called J). There is an Egyptian word *chem* with determinate $\hat{1}$, which is a flaming brazier. It means "warm." Faulkner, *Dictionary of Middle Egyptian*, 190.

13.   Gordon, *Ugaritic Textbook Glossary*, 485 says it "occurs in *wyrs* ... if the meaning is 'and he will agree to everything,'" and compares it to the Hebrew "to accept" and the old South Arabic "to satisfy." Driver, *Canaanite Myths and Legends*, 155 says *rs* [√*rsy*] means "consented" and gives the same reference as does Gordon: K II i 45, 40–41. However, see Koehler and Baumgartner, et al., *Hebrew and Aramaic Lexicon*, 1281–2 for the possibility of two words translated I, "take pleasure in, be favorable to someone, be well disposed ... to accept with pleasure ... to become friends with," etc.,

and II, "to pay, redeem (re Lev. 26:41) to be carried off, away ... to replace, restore ... to bring for payment, have restored."

14.   *Strong's Hebrew Dictionary*, 43.

15.   Cohen, ed., *Soncino Chumas: Numbers*, 822.

16.   Cohen, ed., *Soncino Books of the Bible: 1 Samuel*, 18, note 13.

Appendix H. Holiness (H) Code

1.   Levine, *The JPS Torah Commentary: Leviticus*, 110

2.   Davies, *Interpreter's Dictionary of the Bible*, vol. 3, 121.

3.   *The Jewish Encyclopedia*, vol. 8, 54.

4.   Friedman, *Who Wrote the Bible?* 214–5.

5.   Levine, *The JPS Torah Commentary: Leviticus*, 111.

6.   Ibid.

7.   Ibid.

8.   Ibid.

9.   Compare Leviticus 6:25–27 (18–20); 7:1, 6; 10:10–13 (esp. 12–13); 14:13; and especially 16:16.

Language Index

(Sumerian, Assyrian, Babylonian, Egyptian, Ugaritic, Eblaite, Hittite, and Greek)

Canaanite

Egyptian

Greek

Hebrew

Hittite

archa parshula   286
hatressar   291
kat-ta   425
kat-ta-an   425
na-ah-ha-an   183
par-na-ash   289
para-a   162
paray   282, 292
parh   288
pariparay   292
parkiia   277
parsh   286
parsha   286
parsdu   277
parshiia   286
parshiul   286
parshulli   286
parshur   286
partau ar   286
tapar   163, 289, 291
tapar(r)iia   163, 291, 293

Indo-European/Hittite

per   157, 278, 288, 298, 361–362, 364

Italian

parare   298

Latin

par   7, 162–163, 275–278, 280–281, 284,
      289, 298, 463, 472
parare   298
quanta   302, 305
quantum   301–302, 304–308, 415, 473

Mittanian

par-ush   287, 466, 468

Nuzi

epqu   435

Phoenician

'dt(?)   51
adē   22, 51, 70, 95, 145, 212–214, 222, 283,
      370, 400, 420, 438, 454
z-b-h/d-b-h   457

Sumerian

appayru   296
bad   8, 145–149, 164, 333, 344, 403,
      442–443, 478
sachar.sub.ba   93
sahar   93

Syrian

aba forest   445
p'rash   467

Ugaritic

'ly   229, 387
/m-k/   399
ahl   32, 461
an'n   434
ar   77, 99, 151, 160–163, 226, 288–289, 373,
      404, 443, 446
argmn   65
arn   34
athm   461
aysht   137
bm nrt ksmm   453
bqrb   37
chenep   449
chert   459
ches's   73
emmer   453
epd   61
ett   230
grn   292
h-m-s   459

Index